BYRON

LIFE AND LEGEND

Fiona MacCarthy

ff

faber and faber

By the same author

ERIC GILL

WILLIAM MORRIS

First published in 2002
by John Murray (Publishers) Ltd

First published by Faber and Faber Ltd in 2003

Printed in England by Mackays

A catalogue record for this book is available from the British Library

ISBN 0-571-17997-5

2 4 6 8 10 9 7 5 3 1

BYRON
LIFE AND LEGEND

With her widely acclaimed book *Eric Gill*, published in 1989, Fiona MacCarthy established herself as one of the leading writers of biography in Britain. This was followed by *William Morris*, winner of several literary awards including the Wolfson History Prize for 1995. She writes regularly for the *Guardian* and lives in Derbyshire and southern Tuscany.

Byron
from an engraving by H. Meyer
of a portrait by George Sanders

Contents

Introduction   vii

CHILDHOOD AND THE EAST

1   Aberdeen 1788–1798   3
2   Newstead 1798–1799   13
3   Nottingham 1799–1800   21
4   Harrow 1801–1805   29
5   Southwell 1803–1805   45
6   Cambridge 1805–1807   56
7   London and Brighton 1808–1809   71
8   Mediterranean Travels 1809   89
9   Greece and Constantinople 1809–1810   109
10   Athens 1810–1811   125

THE MAKING OF A LEGEND

11   St James's 1811–1812   139
12   Melbourne House 1812   159
13   Cheltenham and Eywood 1812–1813   182
14   Six Mile Bottom 1813–1814   200
15   Seaham 1814–1815   224
16   Piccadilly Terrace 1815–1816   245
17   Piccadilly Terrace 1816   263

CONTENTS

CELEBRITY IN EXILE

18	Geneva 1816	283
19	The Swiss Alps 1816	304
20	Venice: Frezzeria and La Mira 1816–1817	316
21	Venice: Palazzo Mocenigo 1818	336
22	Venice and Ravenna 1819	353
23	Ravenna 1820–1821	374
24	Pisa 1821–1822	405
25	Genoa 1822–1823	435
26	Cephalonia 1823	464
27	Missolonghi 1824	487

THE BYRON CULT

28	The Return of the Remains	525
29	The European Byronists	544
30	The Byronic Englishman	555

Major Published Works of Lord Byron	575
Sources and Reference Notes	576
Acknowledgements	638
List of Illustrations	641
Index	645

Introduction

One of the sights of Europe in 1816 was the lurching progress of the self-exiled Lord Byron as he travelled from Brussels to Geneva and on to Italy in his monumental black Napoleonic carriage. This purpose-built coach, a de luxe version of the Emperor Napoleon's own celebrated carriage captured at Genappe, included not only Byron's *lit de repos* but his travelling library, his plate-chest and facilities for dining. Drawn by four or six horses, it was nothing less than a small palatial residence on wheels. The bill from Baxter the coach-maker amounted to £500. Poor Baxter was still pressing for payment in 1823, a claim dismissed airily by Byron with the words, 'Baxter must wait – at least a year.' Presumably the bill was still unsettled when Byron died in Greece in April 1824.

The long shadow of Napoleon loomed over Byron's life, an inspiration and an irritant. Byron, born in 1788, the year before the outbreak of the French Revolution, was conscious of living at an unprecedented period: as he put it, 'we live in gigantic and exaggerated times, which make all under Gog and Magog appear pigwean.' The apparition of Napoleon, almost twenty years his senior, was the spur to Byron's own ambition, his dissidence, the glamour of his arrogance, the sense of sweeping history that permeates his writing. Napoleon's flamboyance, his stamina, his dress, his stance, the assiduity with which he preened his image, nurtured Byron's own creative strain of mockery. As he told his friend Lady Blessington, 'with me there is, as Napoleon said, but one step between the sublime and the ridiculous.'

Byron was bound to Napoleon by ties as strong, or even stronger, than those of any of his sexual liaisons. He found fault with Napoleon, so the sharp-eyed Lady Blessington observed, only 'as a lover does with the trifling faults of his mistress'. His emotional involvement was already strong at Harrow in 1803 when the fierce schoolboy defended his bust of Napoleon, by then the official enemy of England, against the 'rascally time-servers' among his contemporaries. A few years later he had acquired a fine impression of Morghen's engraved portrait of Napoleon, which he sent to be framed resplendently in gilt.

His personal identification with the Emperor was such that Napoleon's defeats brought on a physical reaction. After Leipzig in 1813 Byron was prostrate with despair and indigestion, groaning in his journal: 'Oh my head! – how it aches! – the horrors of digestion! I wonder how Buonaparte's dinner agrees with him?' In the following year, after Napoleon's abdication and exile to Elba, Byron recorded: 'To-day I have boxed one hour – written an ode to Napoleon Buonaparte – copied it – eaten six biscuits – drunk four bottles of soda water – redde away the rest of my time.' That ode was both lament and reproach, for Byron could not approve the abject self-surrender of the hero who should rightly have died on his own sword like a defeated Roman or expired as defiantly as Shakespeare's Macbeth or Richard III. But Napoleon still dazzled him, in spite of the anguish of his disillusionment. For Byron, Napoleon was a kind of second nature, part of his thought processes, peculiarly embedded in the detail of his life.

After Napoleon's final demise Byron accumulated keepsakes: a lock of his hair, snuffboxes with his portrait, gold coins with the depiction of the Emperor that was. There was also the Napoleon cameo pin Byron gave to Lady Blessington in Genoa, removing it with a flourish from his breast, but reclaiming it the next day with the dubious excuse that 'memorials with a *point*' would bring bad luck. Before he left England in 1816, at the time of the separation scandal, Byron had reserved Napoleon's coronation robes, by then in the hands of a Piccadilly dealer, but never actually claimed them. He did, however, write a fond farewell letter to Margaret Mercer Elphinstone, shortly before he sailed, on writing paper pillaged from the imperial bureau at Malmaison and stamped with the Napoleonic eagle: he enclosed a few spare sheets as a parting present. Byron was apparently ecstatic when the death of his mother-in-law Lady Noel allowed him to sign himself NB 'because' (he told Leigh Hunt, admittedly a malicious witness) 'Bonaparte and I are the only public persons whose initials are the same'.

Byron's wanderings through Italy, from 1816 to 1823, were permeated with memories of Napoleon. He noted, near Milan, the remains of an unfinished triumphal arch, intended for Napoleon, 'so beautiful as to make one regret its non-completion', and on Isola Bella he discovered the large laurel tree on which Napoleon had carved out with his knife the word 'Battaglia' shortly before the battle of Marengo. Byron, himself no mean defacer of trees, had scrutinised the letters closely, by this time 'half worn out and partly erased'.

In the context of Italy, Napoleon seemed to Byron more than ever a Vesuvius, a powerful eruptive force whose final overthrow had let in the political light-weights throughout Europe: 'Since that period, we have been the slaves of fools.' There is no doubt that he saw his own incursions into European politics, first as a partisan of the Italian Risorgimento and then in the Greek War of Independence, with whatever undertones of irony, in quasi-Napoleonic terms.

In 1823 he was describing his personal subsidy of two hundred thousand piastres for a squadron of Greek ships to fight against the Turks as 'not very large – but it is double that which Napoleon the Emperor of Emperors – began his campaign in Italy'. He loved and understood the trappings of the military: the helmets, the uniforms, the grand theatricality of salutes and parades. There is an overt homage to Napoleon in Byron's carefully staged arrival at Missolonghi, as described by contemporary onlookers and mythologised in Theodoros Vryzakis's epic painting, now in the National Gallery of Greece, showing Byron in the guise of military hero and king-saviour of the nation. Byron's Napoleonism, his active involvement in political events of his own day and age, is the key to what distinguishes him most sharply from his contemporary English Romantic poets.

Well before Byron's death he and the Emperor Napoleon were yoked together as objects of derision by English newspapers. Byron mentioned the phenomenon in 1821 in a letter to his publisher John Murray: 'I perceive that the "two greatest examples of human vanity – in the present age" – are firstly "the Ex-Emperor Napoleon" – and secondly – "his Lordship the noble poet & c." – meaning your humble Servant – "poor guiltless I". Poor Napoleon! he little dreamed to what "vile comparisons" the turn of the Wheel would reduce him.' There is an obvious smirk in this report. The perspective of history would link them still more firmly. By 1831 Macaulay was recording their glittering precocity:

'Two men have died within our recollection, who, at a time of life at which few people have completed their education, had raised themselves, each in his own department, to the height of glory. One of them died at Longwood, the other at Missolonghi.'

Two years later, Carlyle set them together in a passage in *Sartor Resartus*, which emphasises wonderfully their shared theatricality:

'Your Byron publishes his *Sorrows of Lord George*, in verse and prose, and copiously otherwise: your Bonaparte represents his *Sorrows of Napoleon* Opera, in an all-too-stupendous style; with music of cannon-volleys, and murder-shrieks of a world; his stage-lights are the fires of Conflagration; his rhyme and recitative are the tramp of embattled Hosts and the sound of falling Cities.'

In the collective visual imagination they stood fixed in alliance, stocky powerful Napoleon, exquisitely handsome Byron, the superlative odd couple of their time. The ageing dandy George 'Beau' Brummell whiled away his days in exile in Calais working on a decorative screen, a collage of prints and drawings, intended for the Duchess of York. The sixth and final fold of the screen represents Napoleon and Byron, the latter well remembered by Brummell from his halcyon days in London. The figure of Byron is embowered in flowers, but a wasp is at his throat.

How exactly did it happen? How did this obscure, impecunious English aristocrat hoist himself to a world-historical position on a par with Napoleon's? How did the early writer of wishy-washy love poems transform himself into the European emperor of words? How indeed did the 'fat bashful boy' from Southwell, 'with his hair combed straight over his forehead', an object of some pity even in provincial England, become the international heartthrob whose subversive '*under* look' gave the most sophisticated society women palpitations? 'That beautiful pale face is my fate': when Lady Caroline Lamb made this histrionic entry in her diary after meeting Lord Byron she voiced the female fandom of the age.

Byron's transformation into the first European cultural celebrity of the modern age has often been described in terms of startling overnight success following publication of the first two cantos of *Childe Harold* in March 1812. Byron's own account is nicely judged: 'I awoke one morning and found myself famous.' But of course there was more to it than that, and during my five years of research for this biography of Byron – which has taken me to Venice, Rome, Ravenna, Pisa, Genoa, Athens and Missolonghi, as well as the city of his childhood, Aberdeen – it has been interesting to see what impulses chiefly drove him. As it seemed to Lady Blessington, when she first met him in 1823, 'Byron had so unquenchable a thirst for celebrity, that no means were left untried that might attain it: this frequently led to his expressing opinions totally at variance with his actions and real sentiments . . . there was no sort of celebrity he did not, at some period or other, condescend to seek, and he was not over nice in the means, provided he obtained the end.'

This book is about the nature of his fame: the ambition Byron felt as 'the most powerful of all excitements'; the degree to which he created and then manipulated his visual image, attempting to control the reproduction of his portraits; the complex and fascinating intertwining of his personal celebrity and literary reputation; his bitterness when fame turned to notoriety, and its consequences for the future generations of his family and entourage. Byron's influence lasted, and in many ways strengthened, after his early death at the age of thirty-six, and my book is necessarily not simply a life but the story of his posthumous reputation too.

Chief colluder in Byron's fame was, of course, his publisher the second John Murray, whose successor John Murray VII commissioned this new biography. I have enjoyed the sense of continuity. All my journeys in pursuit of Byron have begun and ended at 50 Albemarle Street, off Piccadilly, the dignified town house purchased by John Murray II in the wave of prosperity following the success of *Childe Harold*. Teasing contemporaries defined this as the moment at which the one-time tradesman-bookseller became a gentleman, and certainly John Murray's literary and social status advanced in relation to his author's meteoric rise.

'Your room speaks of him in every part of it,' the besotted Lady Caroline Lamb told John Murray. The Byronic reverberations are still there. In the drawing room at 50 Albemarle Street I sat directly beneath the famous Phillips portrait of Lord Byron, exposed to my subject's quizzical gaze as I worked through the extraordinary riches of the largest Byron archive in the world. Because of the many personal connections between the Murrays, Byron's half-sister Augusta Leigh and his friend and executor John Cam Hobhouse (later Lord Broughton), the archive does not consist simply of manuscripts and letters but includes also objects: portraits and miniatures, clothes and medals, accumulated memorabilia; a collection of adoring letters from women of all classes, many quite unknown to Byron, who wrote in desperation, seeking contact, assignations; a macabre assortment of hair, donated by his varied mistresses and kept in little packages carefully labelled by the late Lord Byron, who had his magpie side; a little slipper thought to have belonged to Allegra, Byron's daughter by Claire Clairmont, who died aged five in a convent at Bagnacavallo. Such small objects can bring a sharp frisson of immediacy, fixing the moment, the scene, the personality. The resources of the Murray archive can only be described as a burial hoard awaiting the biographer's careful excavation, a means to the retrieval of the past.

The last biography of Byron to be published by John Murray was Leslie Marchand's pioneering three-volume life, published in 1957, starting point for all subsequent Byron scholars. Since that time a great deal of new material has emerged relating, for example, to Byron's intimacy with the powerful 'autumnal' Lady Oxford (she was only forty); his disastrous marriage to Annabella

Milbanke; his final Italian liaison with Countess Teresa Guiccioli. A new cache of biographical evidence, altering former views of his male relationships, emerged with the dramatic discovery in 1976, in a vault in Barclays Bank, of the trunk of manuscripts and letters abandoned by Byron's friend Scrope Davies when he left London hurriedly in January 1820 to escape his creditors. Assiduous research has been devoted to previously neglected areas of his life, such as Byron's ill-disciplined but devoted servants; his yapping, screeching, clawing menagerie; the details of his household economy (or lack of it); his lameness, anorexia and depressiveness.

Most important of all has been the general change in attitudes towards biography in the last few decades. Marchand, writing at a time when homosexuality was still a criminal offence under British law, was compelled to temper his account not only of Byron's incestuous relations with his half-sister Augusta but also, and more crucially, of his recurring loves for adolescent boys. Marchand recalled in 1995 how Sir John Murray, then head of the firm, 'would not allow any plain statements drawn from the evidence in those matters'. He was allowed more leeway in *Byron: A Portrait*, the shortened biography published by Murray in 1971, after the death of Sir John Murray and a change in British law governing homosexual relations. But Marchand remained conscious that his treatment of these areas of Byron's life had been inadequate, through no fault of his own.

At a period in which sexual behaviour is considered an essential component of the biographical picture of person, time and place, I have been working under no such restrictions. Our understanding of Byron's bisexuality, an open secret within his own close circle, throws important light on the pattern of his life. In an essay in her book *Lord Byron: Accounts Rendered* Doris Langley Moore has argued that Byron's love affairs with women were his main emotional focus, his relations with boys being no more than diversions. I believe the opposite is true. Byron liked the chase, the reassurance of heterosexual conquest. But in general, Byron's female attachments dwindled quickly in intensity. Byron himself, half-jokingly, gave them a limit of three months – an estimate that proved fairly accurate in practice, with the exceptions of his half-sister Augusta and his last Italian mistress Teresa Guiccioli, though even with the amorous Teresa his interest eventually ebbed.

Byron's attraction to women could easily turn to physical revulsion. His dislike of seeing women eating became one of the recurring comic motifs of his life. Meanwhile, even in long absence, Byron's male loves seem to have deepened and flourished with the years. His erotic imagination brought him back inevitably to the idealised image of the boy. Witness the agonising tendresse of his later meetings with his by-now-ageing Harrow favourite Lord Clare, and the turmoil of his unrequited yearning for his page Lukas Chalandritsanos in his final months in Greece.

In public, he was careful in his censoring of references to things which, by his own reckoning, ought not to be revealed for the next three hundred years. He laughed about the danger, when writing his own journals with a view to probable publication, of 'letting out some secret or other – to paralyze posterity'. But in private, in letters to his confidential friends, Byron was much more open in describing the 'really *consequential & important* parts' of his own extraordinary double life.

Byron's innate sexual orientation towards boys explains many of the lingering puzzles of his history. His secretly acknowledged history of sodomy, a crime then punishable by execution, provides the only convincing reason for his exile in 1816, as rumours surrounding Byron's separation from his wife, at first concentrated on suspicions of incest, broadened to include accusations of sodomy as well.

The long habit of concealment of his sexual predilections had its impact on the dazzling obfuscations of his writing. The Lord so often vanishes. Byron's own 'hair-breadth existence', as he called it, encourages the author to be equally evasive. His multiple insecurities give Byron his reckless brilliance as a critic on the edges of society. He is everywhere and nowhere: English peer and European vagrant; the landowner turned landless; the disaffected orator from the House of Lords; the man 'of no Country', having given up England, who feels himself a floating global citizen, camping it up in Venice in his Mrs Radcliffe cloak, planning an improbable new life as a planter in South America. Byron was an internationalist before the term was thought of, and it is his paradoxical nature, his mobility of thinking, the multiplicity of voices in his writing, that connects him to the dislocated attitudes of the present age.

This book is deliberately packed full with quotation. The early nineteenth century was an energetically verbal period. Byron's reputation was formed by the praises and caresses of society, as it was eventually savaged by the circulating rumours and malicious innuendoes of the chattering classes of the day. In the cacophony of sophisticated voices, the female as self-assured and brittle as the male, Byron's own laconic tones stand out as irresistibly self-mocking. Accused of carrying off a girl from a convent:

'I should like to know *who* has been carried off – except poor dear *me* – I have been more ravished myself than anybody since the Trojan war.'

Here is Byron as progenitor of a high camp English manner of expression that extends to Oscar Wilde, Ronald Firbank, Noël Coward.

In working on this reassessment of Lord Byron I have been fortunate in having access to new material from the Murray archive. This is the complete run of correspondence from John Murray to Byron, recently transcribed by the leading Byron scholar Andrew Nicholson. Only isolated letters have been made available before. The complete correspondence, dating from 1811 to the end of 1822, throws much light upon the growing rift between publisher and author as Byron's poetry became, in Murray's conservative view, dangerously controversial. John Murray published the first five cantos of *Don Juan*, the poem generally considered Byron's masterpiece, but subsequent cantos and most of Byron's later works were published by John Hunt.

For Byron himself the severance from Murray was a matter of principle, an aspect of his strong love of liberty and a necessary stand against what we would now regard as the thought police: 'all the bullies on earth shall not prevent me from writing what I like – & publishing what I write – "coute qui coute".' It is possible to see Byron's stand for freedom of expression as an act of heroism on a par with his support for Greek independence. But for John Murray, whose investment in his author had gone far beyond mere commerce into the more vulnerable realms of loyalty and friendship, the loss of Byron amounted to a personal tragedy.

Does Byron matter these days? After what amounts to a five-year pilgrimage of my own, I would argue that he does. His poetry may sometimes be grossly uneven in quality, his thought processes slipshod. But if not a consistently great thinker he is always a great voicer, a conduit of feeling. He has a quality of empathy, a flow of human sympathy extending through the generations and the centuries. His visionary poem of catastrophe 'Darkness', written in Geneva in 1816, prefigures with an extraordinary bleakness the scenes of desolation and carnage we have known in our own times. Byron's importance is perhaps above all that of the survivor, the man of experience who has seen the world at its worst, lived a life of strange and often terrible excesses at a time of extreme revolutionary violence, but refused to be defeated. There is always a proviso: 'Build me a little bark of hope'.

During the years I was working on this biography a close friend died unexpectedly of cancer. I was asked to give a reading at her funeral. The lines chosen by her husband were 'So, we'll go no more a roving' which I read on that early summer day in a small grey church on a hillside in Northumberland. Byron still speaks the language of the heart.

CHILDHOOD AND THE EAST

1

Aberdeen
1788–1798

There was nothing exceptional about Byron's birth. It took place in London on 22 January 1788 in a rented apartment at 16 (later renumbered 24) Holles Street, between what is now Oxford Street and Cavendish Square. He was born in the back drawing room on the first floor, where his mother, new to the city, was attended through a long-drawn-out labour by a doctor, a nurse and a male midwife, or *accoucheur*, recommended by the wife of the lawyer John Hanson, to whom Mrs Byron had only very recently been introduced.

The baby was born with the caul, the inner membrane enclosing the foetus, still over his head. There was an ancient superstition that a caul had magic powers as a preventative against drowning. Mrs Mills the nurse sold off Byron's caul to Hanson the lawyer's brother, Captain James Hanson of the Royal Navy: the first but by no means the last sale of Byron relics to the gullible. Twelve years later Captain Hanson's ship, HMS *Brazen*, was wrecked off Newhaven, and Hanson was drowned with all but one of his crew.

It emerged within a few days of his birth that the baby had a deformed foot and lower leg. The eminent surgeon John Hunter, founder of the museum at the Royal College of Surgeons, was called in to give his view. The precise nature of this deformity has divided medical opinion ever since. In contemporary descriptions, it is generally referred to as a 'club-foot'. This is how his father, Captain John Byron, refers to it in a letter to his sister: 'for my son, I am happy to hear he is well, but for his walking, 'tis impossible, as he is club-footed.' However it is now generally agreed that the term 'club-foot' is a misnomer. Byron's disability was not a club-foot in the normal understanding of the term as a 'moulding deformity' which causes the foot to contract and turn upwards into a rounded club-like lump.

Some modern medical experts maintain that Byron's disability was due to the wasting of the calf muscles of the leg after an attack of infantile paralysis

3

(poliomyelitis). Others, on the evidence of the two thickly padded leather boots now in the Murray archive, argue more persuasively that the deformity was a 'dysplasia', a failure of the region to form properly. These inner boots, worn under ordinary boots or shoes, were purpose-made with padding on the inside leg to disguise Byron's grotesquely thin calf. The outer side of the sole was built up to counteract his abnormally small and inward-turning foot. A dysplasia would explain the sliding gait noted by several of his contemporaries, a trait that added to his image of the sinister and predatory.

Which *was* Byron's lame leg? So much mystery has shrouded the subject, some of it created by Byron himself in his attempts to draw attention away from his deformity, that Thomas Moore, collecting information for his biography of Byron only a few years after Byron's death, could not arrive at a consensus of opinion. Elizabeth Pigot, Byron's old friend from Southwell, Augusta Leigh, his half-sister and lover, and the old Nottinghamshire cobbler who made young Byron's special shoes for him, all said it was the right leg. Leigh Hunt and Mary Shelley maintained it was the left leg, as did Jackson the pugilist, drawing on his memories of Byron's stance when sparring, and Millingen the surgeon who attended Byron in his final illness. The notoriously inaccurate Edward Trelawny, in a high-flown description of his visit to 'the embalmed body of the Pilgrim', claimed to have discovered that *both* Byron's feet were clubbed. However, we can safely take his mother's word for it. As she told her sister-in-law, Mrs Frances Leigh, 'George's foot turns inward, and it is the right foot; he walks quite on the side of his foot.'

There is no doubt that Byron's lame leg was a torment to him, both in the degree of physical pain and in the mental anguish it caused. It became a weapon in the intermittent war that raged between the temperamental Mrs Byron and her son, she reproaching him with his disability, he blaming her for the 'false delicacy' at his birth 'that was the cause of that deformity', presumably referring to tight lacing or narrow corseting which could have injured the foetus in the womb. He was always to be conscious that his lameness marked him out as a freak and an object of derision, discounting the degree to which his deformed leg contributed to his image of perverse attractiveness. There is the ring of truth in his estranged wife's recollection that 'it was vain to seek to turn his thoughts for long from that *idée fixe*, with which he connected his physical peculiarity as a stamp. Instead of being made happier by any apparent good, he felt convinced that every blessing would be "turned into a curse" to him.'

Later in his life Byron liked to speculate on the chances of human reproduction:

'What a strange thing is the propagation of life – A bubble of Seed which may be spilt in a whore's lap – or in the Orgasm of a voluptuous dream – might (for aught we know) have formed a Caesar or a Buonaparte – there is nothing remarkable recorded of their Sires.'

George Gordon Byron was the only child of the hasty and, from her point of view, unwise union of Catherine Gordon, a young Scottish heiress worth £25,000 a year in land, shares and salmon fishing, 13th Laird of Gight in her own right, and the handsome, reckless Captain John Byron, eldest son of Admiral John Byron. The Captain, recently of the Coldstream Guards, had previously been married to the beautiful and wealthy Amelia, divorced wife of Lord Carmarthen and herself Baroness Conyers, after a highly scandalous elopement, and Byron's half-sister Augusta was their child.

Byron's father, known as 'Mad Jack' by his military cronies, has his own role in the Byron legend where he figures as a dashing but wholly reprehensible confidence trickster who, having run through all his first wife's money, set out after she died to find a second fortune to squander. This image has some truth in it. But John Byron was also a figure of some pathos, a social inadequate terrified of loneliness, with the dangerous lust for liaison, however unsuitable, that descended to his son.

He met the plain but eager Catherine Gordon at Bath, a spa town then at the height of its fashion, and they were married there in May 1785. John Byron took on the Gordon surname, in addition to his own, in accordance with a clause in his wife's parents' marriage settlement. Byron was known as George Byron Gordon as a child and his mother as Mrs Byron Gordon. Soon after the marriage John Byron had recovered the freehold of his wife's inherited Castle of Gight and sold it to the Earl of Aberdeen for the then substantial sum of £18,690. But before long his financial affairs were again in disarray. He and Catherine were forced to move to France to escape his creditors. She had returned alone to London late in her pregnancy. John Byron came back too, shortly before the birth, but from then on his appearances were fitful, concentrated on extracting money from his by now more realistic but still adoring wife.

It is unlikely that Byron's father was present at the baptism on 29 February 1788 at St Marylebone Parish Church where Mrs Byron's nominees as godparents – her kinsmen the Duke of Gordon and Colonel Duff of Fetteresso – took responsibility, almost certainly *in absentia*, for the religious upbringing of the infant who would cause enormous ructions within the Church of England in the following century.

*

5

Sometime in the summer of 1789 Mrs Byron and her son travelled north to Aberdeen. This was the summer of the French Revolution, 14 July being the date of the storming of the Bastille, an event of considerable interest to Catherine Byron whose political views were surprisingly progressive for a woman of her class. She told her sister-in-law Frances Leigh that she was 'very much interested about the French, but I fancy you and I are on different sides for I am quite a Democrat'. The political tensions of the time, as much as domestic instabilities, made the atmosphere *énervé* in a way that may well have rebounded on the child.

Catherine Byron took rooms first (probably) in Virginia Street, moving on to Queen Street, into lodgings rented from a perfumer, James Anderson. Of her former fortune, only £150 a year remained, the interest on a £3,000 life settlement. Living with Mrs Byron and her infant was a nursemaid, Agnes Gray. It was an anxious and claustrophobic life, made more so by the sudden arrival in Scotland of John Byron. He stayed with his family at first, then moved to his own lodgings at the other end of Queen Street where the fractious child once went to spend the night with his father, an experiment disastrous enough not to be repeated.

Byron claimed years later that his vivid memories of acrimonious quarrels between his parents gave him 'very early a horror of matrimony'. How true could this have been? Byron was only two and a half when he last saw his father, who soon made a rackety and impecunious return to France. But for a child as impressionable as Byron, exceptional in the intensity of his recall, it is not impossible that his later years were haunted by the image of an incompatible man and woman quarrelling in the confined quarters of the home.

In August 1791 John Byron died at Valenciennes, perhaps from tuberculosis, perhaps by taking poison, having claimed with his usual sense of drama to have reached the point of being without a sou or shirt. He appointed his small son, George Gordon, as heir to his non-existent estate, charged to pay his debts, legacies and funeral expenses. Later Byron, when it suited him, played up his father's dark side, giving him a leading role in the history of his violent, erratic forebears. A friend visiting Newstead when he was a young man remembered how, 'while washing his hands, and singing a gay Neapolitan air', Byron had suddenly turned round, announcing that there had always been madness in the family and that his father had cut his throat.

But there is no doubt that Byron loved and glamorised his father, seeking out the parallels between them, not least their shared conviction that Byrons were by nature irresistible. They were linked by their good looks, their charm, their instability and emotional evasiveness. They were linked too by their tendency to incest, which clusters within families, as is now well known. Captain Byron's incestuous relations with his sister Frances Leigh, with whom he lived in France, are documented in a series of letters between them. It is most unlikely that Byron would have seen these family letters or have known of the liaison before he embarked on his own sexual adventures with his half-sister Augusta, by then married to Colonel George Leigh, Frances Leigh's son. But the shared love of the profligate father was a factor in their intimacy: 'Augusta and I have always loved the memory of our father as much as we loved each other.' The sense of destiny and dynasty was strong in both of them.

Soon after her husband's death, Catherine Byron moved to 64 Broad Street, Aberdeen. She was only twenty-six, uncontrolled in her mourning for her husband, the 'dear Jonnie' she insisted she had 'ever sincerely loved'. All her hopes for the future were now invested in her son. The new lodgings, although more spacious than the last, still fell far below the expectations of a woman 'as haughty as Lucifer', obsessed with the finer points of her descent from the 2nd Earl of Huntly and his wife, Princess Annabella Stewart, daughter of King James I of Scotland. Aberdeen itself, then a developing city, already an important shipbuilding centre with an energetic cultural and intellectual life, seemed depressingly provincial to Catherine Byron, who lamented in her letters that bonnets 'are out of fashion in London before they come here'. In Aberdeen, the 'romping, comely, good humoured girl of sixteen, inclined to corpulence', as a relative remembered her, had become disappointed, overwrought and unhealthily obese.

In laying the blame for his own vicissitudes firmly on his mother and her devastating mood swings, complaining that her daily rages, explosions of verbal and physical abuse, had 'cankered a heart that I believe was naturally affectionate, and destroyed a temper always disposed to be violent', Byron in retrospect showed little understanding of his mother's true position, left stranded as she was, and financially anxious, removed from her class and her expectations. But although his later demonisation of his mother is palpably unjust, day-to-day existence at close quarters with the domineering Mrs Byron must have put enormous strain upon the growing boy. This may partly explain the debilitating headaches that assailed him through his childhood. He also had the nervous habit of gnawing at his nails.

Catherine Byron and her son's situation was more galling because of the proximity of relations living in the privilege of huge ancestral houses: the Gordons of Fyvie; the Aberdeens of Haddo, cultured aristocrats painted resplendently in ceremonial kilts by Pompeo Batoni in the course of their European grand tours. The Castle of Gight, where Catherine as 13th Laird had lived briefly with her husband in the months after their marriage, was now part of the Aberdeen estate. When the 3rd Earl of Aberdeen had purchased the neighbouring Gight Castle and its lands, he had intended it for his son Lord Haddo. The castle was abandoned when the young Lord Haddo died after a fall from his horse in 1791. We do not know if Byron ever visited the site. But numerous ghostly variations on Gight, tenantless ruined castles tormented by fierce winds, loom in Byron's poetry. Indeed he was so haunted by his mother's lost inheritance that in 1821 he proposed to buy Gight Castle back, 'even at a reduction of income'. In 2001 it was still standing deserted in a large hollow beside the River Ythan, invaded by ivy and cow parsley, a real Byronic ruin.

The small boy was managing to walk, but with a struggle. His mother, despairing of having a special shoe made locally, had had to send away for a shoe from London, reinforced to counteract his foot's inward-turning tendency. Byron was mortified at being identified with other disabled children, joking bitterly about another lame boy in the neighbourhood: 'Come and see the twa laddies with the twa club feet going up the Broad-Street.' (The quotation also reminds us of how strong his Scots accent would have been.) It is not surprising that his pain and frustration erupted into rages, though the multiple accounts of the appalling misdemeanours of the 'ill-deedie laddie', wrecking the miller's wheel, striking Lady Abercromby in the face, getting out his little whip to chastise a kindly person sympathising with his lameness, often read like tales concocted with the benefit of hindsight.

But one story that rings true is of Byron sitting with his mother in a pew in St Paul's Episcopal Chapel, entertaining himself at intervals by getting out a little pin and pricking her fat arms, encased in their kid gloves.

The earliest extant portrait of Byron, William Kay's watercolour of the boy aged seven, carrying his then fashionable miniature bow and arrows, marks a change of mood. In 1794 George Gordon became heir to the Byron title and estates following the sudden death of William Byron, grandson of the 5th Lord Byron, killed by a cannon ball at the siege of Calvi in Corsica, in one of those random events of history to which Byron himself became so sensitive. The portrait commemorates his altered status and, as in almost all future depictions, he stands very much alone. Not for Byron the convivial family groupings of contemporary Scottish aristocratic portraits by, for instance, David Allan, depicting proud fathers, sportive heirs, sisters and brothers, serene mothers with dimpled babies on their laps. This child, in open-necked white shirt, tight pantaloons and neat blue jacket, his lame leg diplomatically concealed by a clump of grass, seems already poised for his 'curled darling' years in London. From now on we become more aware of the early influences that made Byron what he was.

He was already a rapid if wilfully indiscriminate reader, quick on the uptake and exceptionally retentive, developing the trait that became an intrinsic part of his creative process, by which almost any passage in his reading triggered off a complex emotional response. By the time he arrived at Aberdeen Grammar School in 1794, after a succession of small local schools and tutors, Byron claimed to have devoured the Old Testament 'through & through', while showing less enthusiasm for the New Testament. Even at this stage his great passion was for history and what he (quoting Napoleon) would refer to as 'the March of events'. He entered the Grammar School in the first or second class, the register referring to him as 'George BEYRON Gordon', and in the course of his not especially distinguished progress up a school where the emphasis was on 'Latin, Latin, Latin', Byron began to develop his precocious interest in ancient power struggles and his fascination with political cause and effect, the theme of so much of his writing and the stimulus for his later personal involvement in the maelstrom of European politics. He also started to discover his compelling powers of narrative. A vivid story of this period is of Byron seeking refuge from a snowstorm in the back kitchen of an Aberdeen draper's shop with a group of smaller schoolboys, keeping them entertained with a tale from the *Arabian Nights*.

He became more mobile, taking to riding as a more practical alternative to walking, clattering over the cobbled streets of Old Aberdeen on a small fat Shetland pony belonging to a schoolfellow, to the Brig o'Balgownie, an ancient stone bridge straddling what to Byron were the enticingly deep, dark waters of the River Don. It was now he learned to swim, overcoming the shame of disability by his prowess in the water. He became familiar with the sandy stretches of Aberdeen Bay and the commotion of the harbour where, besides the local fishing fleet, foreign trade vessels were regularly arriving and departing. It was perhaps here that his passion for the sea first began and Byron became conscious of the power of the ocean landscape with its eddies, storms and billows: early intimations of sublime effects.

The child's horizons widened. His mother sometimes took him to the elegant seaside town of Banff on the coast twenty miles north-west of Aberdeen, to stay with her grandmother, Margaret Duff Gordon, Lady Gight. In the late eighteenth century, the ancient county town of Banff, thriving centre of the fishing trade, was still at the height of its prosperity and was the summer holiday resort of the extended Gordon family. For Byron, Banff was an introduction to genteel society against which he appears to have reacted with rebellious asperity. Another of the local anecdotes in circulation on the subject of 'that little deevil Geordie Byron' describes how he dressed a pillow in his clothes and threw it out of an upper window to the garden where his relations were assembled – a foretaste of more vicious black comedies.

When Byron became seriously ill with scarlet fever, in 1795 or '96, his mother transported him to Ballater Wells on Deeside, in the Highlands west of Aberdeen, to drink the goat's milk advertised in the contemporary *Aberdeen Journal* as beneficial to convalescents. Here they stayed in a modest straw-thatched cottage built of roughly hewn stone, with two narrow beds that could be folded out of sight to turn the bedroom into a daytime sitting room. The cottage was so austere it shocked Byron's publisher, John Murray, when he discovered and sketched it, late in the 1820s, on a Highland tour to gather information for Moore's *Life*.

'My "heart warms to the Tartan" or to any thing of Scotland which reminds me of Aberdeen and other parts not so far from the Highlands as that town.' The spectacularly beautiful country around Ballater, Inverness and Braemar, and the Highland people he encountered, became fixed in Byron's later reveries of childhood, as he reran the memories of lochs and haggis, Highland mists and Highland Marys with the bold sentimentality which has been well described as his 'discourse of poetic tartanry'. The high mountains of Morven and Lochnagar were a *feeling* to the child, as to Childe Harold, and in his later travels he would use them as his yardstick, comparing Scottish mountains to the rocky crags of Cintra and the rugged mountain landscapes of Albania and Greece.

Foremost amongst his long-running memories of Scotland are those of his first love. Byron, by his own account, was transfixed with a passion at the age of seven for his distant cousin Mary Duff, a child with dark brown hair and hazel eyes who lived near the Plainstones in Aberdeen. Byron treasured the remembrance of his 'first of flames, before most people begin to burn', summoning up with almost suspicious exactitude 'all our caresses, her features, my restlessness, sleeplessness, my tormenting my mother's maid to write for me to her'. These journal entries for 1813, by which time Byron had become a romantic icon, show signs of him becoming entrapped by his own publicity, treating as a phenomenon what is surely more prosaically explained as the longing for attachment in an isolated child.

They also display his talent for concealing his early, less idyllic heterosexual experiences, and his later sexual feelings towards boys, behind a self-consciously charming narrative of childhood love. His close and candid friend John Cam Hobhouse was caustic about Byron's ingenuous account of awakening passion in Aberdeen: 'With respect to the early development of these propensities in Byron I am acquainted with a singular fact scarcely fit for narration but much *less* romantic and *more* satisfactory than the amour with Mary Duff.'

There is a softness about Byron's recollections of Scotland that tempts us to discount a real grimness in his life there. It was not just the violence in his family history – his 'line of cut-throat ancestors', the deaths by drowning of his Gordon grandfather and great-grandfather, successively suicidal Lairds of Gight. Violence and feuding were endemic in Scotland itself which, less than fifty years after Culloden, was still riven with memories of internecine warfare. Byron absorbed, and to some extent revelled in, this violence: 'I like a row – and always did from a boy,' he told Sir Walter Scott in 1822.

All through his childhood, he was exposed to what he recollected as a particularly virulent strain of Aberdonian Scottish Calvinism, being 'cudgelled to Church' for his first ten years, and being indoctrinated by his tutors and schoolmasters with a sense of his own innate transgressions. With its emphasis on predestination, Calvinism nurtured Byron's characteristic pessimism, the fatalistic dramas that attached to the no-hoper. Lady Byron, not unconvincingly, blamed his early absorption of 'the gloomiest Calvinistic tenets' for much of the misery of Byron's life, maintaining that she herself had been 'broken against the rock of Predestination', as indeed was everyone connected with him.

There was also the weather. Aberdeen, with its high latitude and long hours of winter darkness, can be a dismal city, encouraging depression. A 1999 survey of residents found a high prevalence of seasonal affective disorder, otherwise known as 'winter blues'. Did Aberdeen affect adversely a temperament innately prone to melancholy – or, as Byron liked to call it, 'lemancholy', associating the word with love's disorders? Did SAD assail him too? Byron's love of Scotland ebbed and flowed; one January in Ravenna he complained that the weather was all too familiar – 'mist, mizzle, the air replete with Scotticisms, which, though fine in the descriptions of Ossian, are somewhat tiresome in real prosaic perspective'. Should we attribute to Byron's nine-year residence in Scotland his lifelong craving for the sun?

In May 1798 the ten-year-old George Gordon inherited the title on the death of his great-uncle William, the 5th Lord Byron. The entry in the Aberdeen Grammar School register was hastily altered: 'Geo. B. Gordon' was crossed out and 'Geo. Dom. de Byron' written in instead. Next time the daily roll-call was taken in assembly the sound of his new title, 'Georgius Dominus de Byron', greeted with yells from his contemporaries, reduced the Lord to tears. This scene, first related in Tom Moore's biography, is quite believable of someone whose emotions were always near the surface. Even as a man Byron's tears came easily, and changes made him nervous. There was some consolation in his rather unctuous reception by the headmaster, who sent for him and gave him cake and wine. It was Byron's first important lesson in the fact that aristocracy would bring about a change in other people's attitude.

2

Newstead

1798–1799

Byron's earliest ancestors in England were probably Ernegis and Ralph de Burun, of Norman extraction and owners of large estates in the north of England in the reign of William the Conqueror. Ralph de Burun appears as a landowner in the Domesday Book. The Priory at Newstead in the Sherwood Forest, with its surrounding lands, was acquired by the then Sir John Byron at a bargain rate from his patron Henry VIII, in the division of spoils that followed the dissolution of the monasteries. The young George Gordon had succeeded to a peerage dating back to the Civil War, when Charles I rewarded a later Sir John Byron, a general in the Royalist army, by creating him the 1st Baron Byron of Rochdale.

Without being over-attentive to detail, Byron revelled in the ancientness of this history. Though he usually spelled his name 'Byron', he occasionally signed himself Biron 'with ye "i"', explaining: 'it is the old spelling – & I sometimes slip into it.' His pronunciation could also be erratic. At school at Harrow he was Biron (pronounced Birron) with a short i. During his years of London fame, he was calling himself Byron with a long y, the pronunciation which is normally used now, then reverted to Biron after 1816, in his European exile. However, he perversely trained certain Italian friends to use the long y when addressing him although, as his friend Tom Moore rightly pointed out, Biron would have come more easily to them.

The Byron family coat of arms, described in the cryptic language of *Burke's Peerage* as 'Arg., three bendlets enhanced gu. Crest', shows two wild-maned and energetic chestnut horses surmounted by a mermaid with her comb and mirror. Byron would later be gratified to find that Sir Walter Scott's arms also contained a mermaid, 'and with precisely the same curl of tail – There's concatenation for you!' The mermaid reappears in Byron's poem *Don Juan* in which Englishwomen are compared to

'virtuous mermaids, whose
Beginnings are fair faces, ends mere fishes'.

Fish-tailed women held a curious fascination.

The motto 'Crede Byron' – 'Trust in Byron' – has a swagger and a confidence to which Byron himself to some extent gave credence, defending it valiantly against a jeering schoolfellow in a playground scuffle. To Leigh Hunt's consternation, Byron's coat of arms was fixed to a panel surmounting his large bed in his various Italian houses and palazzi, where the exact significance of the message 'Crede Byron' mystified his Italian-speaking mistresses. 'Crede Byron' was emblazoned on the military helmets made for Byron's departure to fight in the Greek War of Independence. But of course this was a motto that could all too easily be reversed, and Caroline Lamb, once she was discarded, had a gold locket containing Byron's portrait engraved with the reproachful 'Ne Crede Byron'. She threatened to repeat the message on specially engraved buttons for her pages' livery.

The child Byron and his mother made the journey south from Aberdeen to claim his inheritance in August 1798. Before he left, with precocious munificence, Byron had presented a gold watch to his namesake, George Gordon Melvin, infant son of his former nanny Agnes Gray, who was now married. Agnes's sister May replaced her and accompanied the Byrons in the coach to Newstead Abbey in Nottinghamshire, travelling via Loch Leven, where Catherine Byron regaled them with stories of the exploits of her forebears – 'the *old Gordons, not the Seyton Gordons*, as she disdainfully termed the Ducal branch'. Byron, writing from Ravenna in 1820, claimed to remember the journey through Scotland and the crossing of the Firth of Forth as if it were only yesterday. Though he sometimes made plans for returning, neither he nor his mother saw the Highlands again.

As the coach neared Newstead, they stopped at the tollgate. Mrs Byron, showing some of the talent for mystification that descended to her son, asked whether there was a nobleman's estate near by, and if so, who was the owner.

'"It was Lord Byron, but he is dead."

'"And who is the heir now?"

'"They say a little boy that lives in Aberdeen."

'"This is him, God bless him," says May Gray, the nurse, on cue, turning to the child and kissing him.'

This famous exchange, recounted in Moore's *Life* of Byron, may have its dubious features. For example, Moore maintains that the boy was seated on his nurse's lap, a considerable burden since Byron was then ten. But the story has a real poignancy in reminding us of Byron's unpreparedness for his role, so young, in a new country, without the family traditions of succession that, under normal circumstances, cushioned a young heir. He had had no contact at all with his great-uncle, the now deceased 5th Lord.

At first sight Newstead Abbey was, and is, stupendous. 'Newstead is the very abbey,' marvelled Horace Walpole a few decades before Byron's arrival. Surviving thirteenth-century ecclesiastical buildings of the original priory of Augustinian Canons merge intriguingly and strangely with domestic buildings of later centuries. In effect it is a house grafted on a ruin, with the great east window of the church, the monastic hall, refectory and cloister still eerily intact. A carving of the seated Virgin Mary and her child remains stranded in its niche, exposed to the elements high above the ancient church's skeletal façade. What appealed to Walpole the protagonist of Gothick, as indeed it did to Byron, was the sense at Newstead of the layerings of history, the way these buildings offered an entry to the past.

Early in the eighteenth century, Byron's predecessor, William the 4th Lord, a connoisseur, composer and watercolour painter, had landscaped the gardens in the French style, creating a long canal which later became a lake, and forming magnificent terraces above the square-shaped Eagle Pond. The 5th Lord, also William, began dotting the landscape with his Gothic follies. On the edges of the Upper Lake he built two miniature forts equipped with real cannons. His own twenty-gun schooner floated on the water, with an assortment of other boats around it. Here the ex-naval officer staged his nostalgic mock-heroic battles. Byron inherited a building full of the frissons of his ancestry, a house which was by any standards grandiose. When his kinsman-by-marriage Wilfrid Blunt visited Newstead in 1909 he commented in his diary: 'one can well understand how the sudden inheritance of it by Byron and his mother turned their heads, and helped to give him that exaggerated pride of birth and position which was his weakness.' Certainly Newstead encouraged Byron in a taste for architectural expansiveness. From then on he would steer away from little houses, preferring the palazzo. Newstead's scale and glamour helped to form his expectations of the world and of himself.

The Byrons were greeted by the aged servant Joe Murray, a relic of the regime of the 5th Lord, and by the family solicitor John Hanson and his wife who had journeyed up from London to receive them. Hanson had a new responsibility as Byron's guardian. The boy, as inheritor of an 'unsettled' estate while still a minor, automatically became a ward of the Court of Chancery. Of Byron's three official guardians – the others being Byron's mother and his grandee cousin, Frederick 5th Earl of Carlisle – John Hanson had by far the strongest influence on his affairs, becoming the quasi father-figure of Byron's early life.

Byron was evidently on his best behaviour. Hanson was especially impressed by the boy's verbal precocity. Asked what he missed most since leaving Scotland he replied it was the scenery and the little girl he loved in Aberdeen; he then launched into an ingratiating little poem:

> 'and she looked so pretty in her Bonnet
> I longed to sip
> from off her lip
> the Honey on it.'

A less endearing side of Byron soon emerges in the tale Hanson told of Byron's Newstead pet, a giant hybrid dog called Woolly, whose mother was a wolf. The lonely child lavished affection on animals but, when relationships went wrong, his reaction was violent. One day, in the garden, the wolf-dog nipped Lord Byron and he rushed into the Abbey, seized a loaded pistol belonging to the gamekeeper, pushed the dog on to its back, threatening to shoot it, exclaiming melodramatically, 'Woolly, you shall *die*.'

John Hanson spent the next three weeks at Newstead. There was much to unravel and investigate. The Byron family estates were large, far-flung and complex. In Nottinghamshire, besides the Park and Newstead Abbey, with the adjacent forest and mill, Byron inherited the manor of Hucknall, Bulwell Wood with park and forge, and a network of small villages and hamlets, amounting to 3,200 acres. The ramifications of Newstead become clear from John Hanson's account books, now in the British Library, giving details of the rents paid by fifteen different tenants of the farm, the mill and quarry; rents from the local clergyman for house, garden and paddock; payments for estate maintenance to fencers, carpenters, blacksmiths and a vet for 'Curing Cart Horse'; records of tree-felling, threshing, cutting crops and draining, mowing and haymaking. Such estates had their own seasonal demands and rhythms. They were run as small specialist worlds within the world.

By the time Byron inherited, Newstead was in disorder. In his last two decades, the financially hard-pressed 5th Lord had allowed his lands to run down badly. Hanson assessed the estates as being 'in confusion' and the farms at Newstead 'in a most neglected state'. Gradually the 5th Lord had denuded the landscape, selling off the timber that had been so essential a component of it. Newstead was now a barren territory, and the Abbey itself with its gardens, lakes, cascades and battlements had become sadly dilapidated. The 5th Lord's creditors had forced the sale of paintings by Rubens, Titian, Holbein, Canaletto, acquired by this compulsive purchaser of pictures and *objets de vertu* in more optimistic days. The majority of the old Lord's furniture had been seized by the attorneys. The building at the back of the courtyard had no roof on it. The reception hall and refectory of the old Priory were storerooms holding hay for the cattle now installed in the entrance hall and parlour.

The atmosphere was ghostly. In his last few years the 5th Lord, known as 'the Wicked Lord' after the reputed murder of his kinsman William Chaworth in the Star and Garter Tavern in Pall Mall, lapsed into a state of paranoia and depression. The disappointed and malevolent old man lay dying in the Abbey attended only by Old Joe and his servant-cum-mistress Mrs Hardstaff, known in the neighbourhood as 'Lady Betty'. Macabre entertainment was provided by an army of crickets which he had fed and tamed, encouraging them to run races all over his body, attacking them with a straw whip when they became too familiar. The 5th Lord's demise suggests that Byron's own depressive tendencies descended as much through the Byron as through the Gordon line.

Besides Newstead, the Byron estates included property at Wymondham in Norfolk and Rochdale in Lancashire. The Rochdale estates were particularly problematic, since the leasehold giving colliery rights on the property had been sold illegally by 'the Wicked Lord'. Litigation to recover the rights to these potentially lucrative coal mines rumbled on until 1823, by which time Byron was en route for Missolonghi. The inheritance was less propitious than it seemed.

Over that first Newstead autumn of 1798, unaware of the extent of the underlying problems, the new Lord and his mother made optimistic plans. Byron planted a symbolic oak tree in the grounds, subject of a later poem titled grandly, if not completely accurately, 'To an Oak in the Garden of Newstead Abbey, planted by the Author in the 9th Year of his age'.

Catherine Byron had hoped to bring up her son at Newstead. But Hanson was now pressing her to move to a house or lodgings in London until a more realistic assessment of the family finances could be made. Though not positively 'encumbered by debt', as has often been reported, the Newstead estates had been yielding less and less, declining to a level of £800 a year in the last few years of the 5th Lord's life. There was little income to build the estate up again. Mrs Byron's small brown leather account book, in the archive at John Murray, has an anxious entry for 'money laid out from 1st September 1798 to 1st June 1799': £99 6s 1d for repairs to Newstead House. Hanson's immediate strategy was to appoint an agent to put the estate in order, manage it more strictly, and to lease out Newstead with its shooting rights until Byron came of age.

Mrs Byron resisted London, perhaps still haunted by the traumatic weeks of her son's birth. She preferred to take Byron to Nottingham, twelve miles away from Newstead, where she now had contacts with Byron relatives. Here they both stayed for a short time with the Hon. Mrs Frances Byron, widow of the 5th Lord Byron's brother George, and Mrs Ann Parkyns, Frances Byron's widowed sister, in Gridlesmith Gate (later renamed Pelham Street). Catherine Byron soon returned to Newstead, leaving her son in Nottingham with his nurse May Gray. She was at the Abbey on and off over the years 1799–1800, with Byron returning there for holidays. She took over the running of the house in Byron's absence on his European travels from 1809 to 1811. But she never lived at Newstead permanently.

Byron's own tenure of Newstead was to be very intermittent, his longest stretch of time there being the winter of 1811–12. As a practical landowner the 6th Lord Byron was an unrepentant absentee. Had he had the more dutiful temperament, and the aristocratic landowning habits of, for instance, his Harrow contemporary the Marquis of Hartington, son of the 5th Duke of Devonshire, no doubt he could have pulled the Newstead estate round. But there was something in his perverse nature that preferred the flawed inheritance, the ruined noble Abbey, a romantic liability outdoing his mother's own abandoned Castle of Gight.

Before long, too, the decayed Abbey was to take on a newly fictionalised fame. The mirage-like Newstead that the young Byron had first glimpsed and then been exiled from acquired a more powerful identity through his poetry than it could ever have had in real life. The process began in his first published book of poetry, *Hours of Idleness* of 1807, in which three poems, 'On Leaving Newstead Abbey', 'A Fragment' and 'Elegy on Newstead Abbey', all written three or four years earlier, are shot through with the melancholy of departure, long-drawn-out laments for what might have been.

> 'Thro' thy battlements, Newstead, the hollow winds whistle;
>   Thou, the hall of my fathers, art gone to decay.'

Byron's early Newstead poems glorify an old world of 'mail-coated Barons' and heroic deeds. His recapitulation, more romantic than exact, of the exploits of his ancestors who fought in the Crusades, fell at Crécy in the forces of Edward the Black Prince, perished defending Charles I at Marston Moor, is a tragic and a proud one. The sense of his valiant forebears was extremely strong in Byron, no less genuine because he knew he overdid it, and not to be disparaged as a motivating force.

In these laments for the now derelict halls of his lost ancestors, with all their gimcrack scenery of ransacked graves and ghostly choirs, dingy cells, mouldering turrets, bats and sinister cowled figures, we see Byron confronting both his personal chagrin at his own ruined inheritance and what he was already defining as an early nineteenth-century England in terminal decline.

In Byron's yearnings back to the better, simpler days of his 'plain forefathers', the house itself emerges as its own Romantic hero, a prototype Childe Harold:

> 'Proudly majestic frowns thy vaulted hall,
>   Scowling defiance on the blasts of fate.'

He did not leave it there. In his imagination Newstead Abbey burgeoned. It recurs as the 'vast and venerable pile' from which the young Harold departs on his pilgrimage in Canto I of Byron's *Childe Harold*. A sinister approximation of Newstead – with its family portraits, gloomy lattices, stone floors, rustling tapestries and creaking doors – can be seen in the Gothic castle to which the mysterious figure of Lara, Byron's dark-browed pirate chief, makes his unexpected and threatening return.

Newstead gets its most mature and irresistible treatment in *Don Juan*, in the final 'English' cantos written when Byron was in his mid-thirties and living in Genoa. He writes with a sense of last things, reviewing his own history with Newstead reincarnated as Norman Abbey, the rural mansion in which Don Juan, recently arrived in England, is indoctrinated into the moral treacheries of English aristocratic country life. Norman Abbey, like Newstead, was

> 'An old, old monastery once, and now
>   Still older mansion of a rich and rare
>   Mixed Gothic.'

As at Byron's Newstead:

> 'Before the mansion lay a lucid lake,
>   Broad as transparent, deep, and freshly fed
>   By a river.'

Byron has often been accused of having no aesthetic sensibility. But his delineation of the Abbey in *Don Juan* shows an intense architectural awareness of the building itself in its wooded, watery setting, and of the way in which its architectural elements of many different periods come together to create the fluid random beauty so characteristic of the English country house.

Before Byron's own time, Newstead Abbey was impressive. Mid-eighteenth-century engravings show the antique building soaring gently in its setting of park and woodland, lake and waterfalls, crenellated follies, the perfect poised example of the English picturesque. Its buried monastic past served as an inspiration for the English Gothic novel. Ann Radcliffe, with her family connections nearby in Chesterfield and Mansfield, seems likely to have drawn on it directly as a setting for her tale of terror, *The Romance of the Forest*, written during the days of the 5th Lord, whilst Thomas Love Peacock's *Nightmare Abbey* has conscious overtones of Newstead, with Byron making an appearance as the languid Mr Cypress. The later raven-haunted, lightning-blasted buildings of Edgar Allen Poe carry echoes of it, too.

Byron himself, much as he enjoyed the spooks, took the idea of Newstead way beyond its role as an epitome of Gothic creepiness. His vision of Newstead as ruined repository of a vanished culture transformed it into one of the central symbols of the Romantic movement as a whole. His view of it became entwined with his deeply ambivalent responses to the French Revolution: his radical desire to see old orders changing, but his horror at the violence entailed. In a devastating image in *Don Juan* Byron compares the country house shooting party of a mellow English autumn, beating out 'the poor partridge' huddling in the fields, to the Septembrists of the French Revolution, massacring more than a thousand prisoners at the beginning of the Reign of Terror in Paris in September 1792.

The English love their mansions. Byron invested Newstead with the melancholy sparkle of an English aristocracy being hustled into change. He invented a Newstead corrupt, beautiful and fated. In the mid-twentieth century Evelyn Waugh's fictional Brideshead had a comparable resonance.

3

Nottingham
1799–1800

Byron spent eight months in Nottingham, from November 1798 to July 1799. He was eleven in January of that year. His pattern of life again altered dramatically as he exchanged the draughty and solitary splendours of Newstead Abbey for the cosier containment of the house in Gridlesmith Gate shared by the two widows, Byron's great-aunt, the Hon. Mrs Frances Byron, and her sister Mrs Parkyns, whose two young daughters became devotees of Byron, writing him the earliest of the many female fan letters addressed to him in his years of fame.

The boy was ensconced within the upper echelons of county town society, minor nobility and gentry, bankers, merchants, sheriffs, aldermen who lived in the substantial brick houses with large gardens spread out around the Castle. Late eighteenth-century Nottingham was a salubrious and self-sufficient place with its Exchange building, its Assembly rooms, its theatre and racecourse. In 1782 the German traveller Carl Moritz had described it as 'of all the towns I have seen outside London the loveliest and neatest'. He praised its 'modern look'.

Byron had been introduced into this society while still at Newstead. In a local lady's diary we catch tantalising glimpses of Lord Byron and his mother in Nottingham drinking tea at friends' houses and, on one occasion, visiting a bowling alley. It appears the two Miss Parkyns were often of the party. Presumably such routines continued once the Byrons came to live at Gridlesmith Gate. Byron had been described by John Hanson at this period as 'a fine sharp Boy a little spoiled by indulgence', and some of this sharpness emerges in his mordant verse caricature of his great-aunt Frances Byron:

> 'In Nottingham county there lives at Swine Green,
> As curst an old lady as ever was seen;
> And when she does die, which I hope will be soon,
> She firmly believes she will go to the moon.'

Gridlesmith Gate ran into Swine Green. He was already developing the knack of attacking the people closest to him, repeating the rhyme over and over, tauntingly.

At Nottingham, too, in a letter written to his mother in 1799, there is evidence of Byron beginning to control his own destiny. Since leaving Aberdeen, Byron had not attended school. Mrs Byron, by then back at Newstead, was discouraging plans for Byron to take lessons from the tutor Jeremiah 'Dummer' Rogers, who was teaching the Parkyns daughters; she was perhaps afraid of the expense. With provocative self-confidence Byron challenged her judgement: 'I am astonished you do not acquiesce in this scheme which would keep me in mind of what I have almost entirely forgot.' He continued: 'I recommend this to you because if some plan of this kind is not adopted I shall be called or rather branded with the name of a dunce which you know I could never bear.' He was finally allowed to enrol with 'Dummer' Rogers, 'Teacher of French, English, Latin and Mathematics', and read parts of Virgil and Cicero with him.

Byron's lame leg still caused agony. He was now receiving treatment from the dubious Dr Lavender, a truss-maker at the general hospital in Nottingham, whose method was to rub the foot with oil before forcing it into a corrective wooden frame in which it was left for hours at a time. The foot was in this frame while Byron had his lessons. The sympathetic 'Dummer' Rogers said to him one day, 'It makes me uncomfortable, my Lord, to see you sitting there in such pain as I *know* you must be suffering.' 'Never mind,' Byron answered, 'you shall not see any signs of it in *me*.'

The boy had now moved with his nurse May Gray to lodgings in St James's Lane (later 76 St James's Street), a house close to the hospital, kept by a Mr Gill. On 13 March Byron had written, in a letter to his mother, 'May Desires her duty.' But with little supervision in Nottingham May Gray's behaviour had become far from dutiful. As it emerged later in the year, she had neglected Byron and treated him with cruelty. Ann Parkyns had reported her suspicions to John Hanson: May Gray's dissipation was the talk of Nottingham.

It was John Hanson who coaxed the truth out of Byron, and wrote to Byron's mother indignantly:

'He told me that she was perpetually beating him, and that his bones sometimes ached from it; that she brought all sorts of Company of the very lowest Description into his apartments; that she was out late at nights, and he was frequently left to put himself to bed; that she would take the Chaise-boys into the Chaise with her, and stopped at every little Ale-house to drink with them. But Madam this is not all; she has even traduced yourself.'

Hanson later elaborated on this story to Byron's friend John Cam Hobhouse, who recalled how 'When Byron was nine years old, at his mother's house, a free girl used to come to bed with him and play tricks with his person – Hanson found out and asked Lord B – who owned the fact – the girl was sent off.'

This was presumably the episode to which Byron was referring when he wrote in his journal, 'My passions were developed *very* early – so early – that few would believe me – if I were to state the period – and the facts which accompanied it.' He saw it as one of the reasons for his lifelong sense of premature ageing, of having been deprived of the years of normal juvenile experience. It was knowledge of May Gray's seduction of Byron that rendered Hobhouse so sceptical about the much-vaunted childhood *amour* with Mary Duff.

Byron came to dread May Gray. If John Hanson's account is accurate, her abuse of the boy had started while they were still in Scotland, and so would have been going on for at least two years. Byron's tale of it was only extracted from him once he was in London, away from her immediate influence. His horror of coming face to face with her again was then so great that Hanson told Mrs Byron that her son would not want to see her if a visit entailed meeting May Gray as well. Mrs Byron evidently hesitated to dismiss her, possibly unwilling to believe such lurid stories which reflected badly on her own judgement of the servant. In autumn 1799 Byron entreated Hanson to get rid of the nurse, who had now become a figure of horror to him: 'And now if you are going to Newstead I beg if you meet Gray send her packing as fast as possible.' He signed the letter 'your little friend'.

The May Gray episode had important repercussions. Byron's nurse was ostentatiously religious, and the coexistence of pious Bible study and lascivious behaviour sharpened his awareness of hypocrisy and cant, deepening his scorn of false religiosity and over-zealous Calvinism in particular. The strange and furtive memories of sex being forced upon him at this early age also influenced Byron's sexual development, to a point where he negated the physicality of sex even as he indulged it. There are echoes of May Gray in a journal entry for December 1813:

'a true voluptuary will never abandon his mind to the grossness of reality. It is by exalting the earthly, the material, the *physique* of our pleasures, by veiling these ideas, by forgetting them altogether, or, at least, never naming them hardly to one's self, that we alone can prevent them from disgusting.'

Even his last mistress, the Italian Countess Teresa Guiccioli, in the course of a customarily effusive reminiscence, was to describe Byron as having 'a cold temperament'. The memories of female dominance, the large nurse in the small bed, affected his later attitudes to sex with women. Byron found a mature woman a complicated structure, threateningly flabby. He preferred the physique of young teenage boys, or the girls dressed as boys that became a feature of his early days in London. Byron's preferred bodies would be youthful, lithe and firm.

The socially ambitious solicitor John Hanson was the first person to recognise Byron's innate potential, writing of his ward: 'He has Ability and a quickness of Conception, and a correct Discrimination that is seldom seen in a youth, and he is a fit associate of men, and Choice indeed must be the Company that is selected for him.' In July 1799 he took Byron south in his carriage to stay in his own family house in Earl's Court, recently purchased from the executors of John Hunter, the surgeon who had been brought in for consultation at the time of Byron's birth. This was a substantial building originally containing Hunter's anatomical museum and a menagerie of animals whose carcasses were destined for anatomical experiment. Four of the Hanson children – Hargreaves, who was Byron's age, two sisters and Newton, three years younger – were assembled, curious to see the little Lord about whom their parents had already told them much.

It was a well-staged entrance, as described later by Newton:

'I have a perfect recollection of the room and the way in which the little Dramatis Personæ stood at the first moment after my father brought Byron among us . . . My father brought Lord Byron into the room in his Hand . . . all eyes were upon him but, as my father remained with him, he was not abashed.'

His youngest sister, then a child of about seven, examined the boy from head to toe, turning round to remark solemnly, 'Well, he is a pretty Boy, however': not the last time Byron was to be exposed to such searching female scrutiny.

Over the next few years the Hansons' Earl's Court house became almost a home to him, visited at Christmas and school holidays, while the Hansons became an approximation of the family he had so far lacked. According to Newton, he spent much of his time reading, but would 'sometimes throw the Book down and be in high spirits and ready for a romp'. Out in the garden, playing with the Hanson boys, he forced himself to climb one of the imitation Pyramids created by Hunter, an antiquarian enthusiast. There were incidents in London which show Byron reverting to the wild child. He would tease the Hansons' cook, bringing her out of the kitchen to set about him with her rolling pin. After John Hanson's mentally retarded protégé Lord Portsmouth playfully boxed his ears Byron viciously hurled a large ornamental shell at him, saying he would teach a fool of an earl to pull another noble's ears. But, on the whole, his life at the Hansons' had a reassuring normality. His fondness for John Hanson, the deep-rooted attachment Byron felt to those he recognised as his supporters, lasted through many professional vicissitudes in the years to come.

It was Hanson who persuaded the Earl of Carlisle, a reluctant recruit, to become Byron's guardian. The 5th Earl of Carlisle, by then in his early fifties, one-time gambler and man of fashion, was now mainly involved in politics and connoisseurship. He himself wrote poetry and was a wealthy patron of the arts. His family ties with Byron were not particularly close: Carlisle's father, the 4th Earl, had been married to the Hon. Isabella Byron, daughter of the 4th Lord Byron, sister of Byron's grandfather. Although Hanson managed to persuade him to negotiate a £300 per annum Civil List pension for Mrs Byron, Carlisle's guardianship of Byron was always to be lukewarm.

Early in his stay in London Hanson, wanting to discuss the boy's future education, had taken Byron to meet Lord Carlisle. The meeting was not propitious. Hanson surmised that the sensitive boy was embarrassed by the presence at the interview of Dr Matthew Baillie, anatomist nephew of John Hunter; Baillie was the specialist now in charge of the treatment of his foot. It is likely that Byron was overawed by his guardian's ponderous humour and patrician hauteur. Though Carlisle apparently tried to greet his ward with kindness, his was not the personality to put an edgy and self-conscious boy at ease. After they had been there for only a few minutes Byron turned to Hanson and said, 'Let us go.' That first meeting engendered a dislike of Lord Carlisle that Byron was to take to notorious extremes.

In autumn 1799 Byron moved into a new environment, attending Dr Glennie's Academy, a small boys' boarding school in Dulwich. Hanson's choice of the school was influenced by his Scots connections. It had been recommended by his friend James Farquhar; the headmaster, Dr Glennie, was another Scot who had 'travelled a great deal', as Hanson wrote to Mrs Byron. He informed her soothingly that Byron's twenty schoolfellows were 'very fine youths and their Deportment does great credit to their Receptor. I succeeded in getting Lord Byron a separate room.'

Byron seems to have been reasonably happy at Glennie's Academy. We should not take too seriously his supercilious reference to 'this damned place', written in a letter to his young cousin (and heir) George Byron in 1801, shortly before he left the school to go to Harrow. He made little progress in his study of the classics, despite 'Dummer' Rogers' Nottingham tuition, but as always he read voraciously, finding his own way to the knowledge he wanted, and he made a friend called Lowes, a clever boy who died young, like so many of Byron's schoolfellows and Cambridge contemporaries. It was probably at Glennie's that he acquired the nickname 'the Old English Baron', after Clara Reeve's Gothick novel of that name, in tribute to his frequent boasts of the superiority of the old English peerage as against more recent and dubious creations. Byron later admitted to such outbursts of pride but excused his boasting as a form of self-defence.

There were two main drawbacks to Dulwich. The new treatment for his foot, supervised by Dr Baillie and his colleague Dr Maurice Laurie, involved a corrective leg-brace constructed by a surgical appliance maker, Mr Sheldrake of the Strand, who used to come out to the school to fit the leg-iron. This iron, jointed at the ankle, was fitted down the outside of his leg and fastened to the sole of his shoe. As with Lavender's previous wooden instrument of torture, Byron disguised the pain it caused to such an extent that Dr and Mrs Glennie claimed to be unaware that he was suffering at all. But there are signs of his frustration in a letter to John Hanson: 'my foot goes but indifferently. I cannot perceive any alteration.' And Hobhouse remembered: 'This instrument he wore with much impatience and one day threw it in the pond.'

Besides it was impossible for Byron to settle into a regular routine at Dr Glennie's. He was subject to endless demands and interventions from his mother who had now taken lodgings in Sloane Terrace, within easy reach of Dulwich. To Dr Glennie's disapproval she extracted him from school for weekends, which often extended into the following week, distracting him from his studies and surrounding him with unsuitable companions. Perhaps Hanson's cryptic comment that May Gray had 'traduced' her mistress referred to her consorting at this period with people judged unsuitable for a widow of her social class.

Her instability increased her son's own insecurity. She was reputed to be drinking. According to Hobhouse Mrs Byron now 'fell in love with a French dancing master at Brompton and laid plans for carrying B. to France. The Frenchman called at Dulwich to take him away but the Master would not let him go.' The seductive Frenchman was probably the 'Monsieur St Louis' mentioned in Hanson's notes on this intriguing episode. Prompted by Hanson, Lord Carlisle intervened. The threatened abduction was the more irresponsible since this was a deeply unsettled period of England's war with France; after this Mrs Byron was forbidden to take Byron home at weekends. Dr Glennie overheard a schoolfellow tell Byron, 'Your mother is a fool', to which he replied, 'I know it', the most shameful of admissions for a boy of twelve.

In the summer holiday of 1800 Byron was back in Nottingham with his mother, visiting Newstead as well. He fell in love again in Nottingham, another of the youthful idylls he described with extravagant nostalgia in later life and another of the smoke-screens he erects in journal entries intended for eventual publication in his memoirs, which make no direct mention of his love for boys. This new child-love was Margaret Parker, 'one of the most beautiful of Evanescent beings'. Byron later boasted that Margaret was daughter of one Admiral Parker and granddaughter of another. More pertinently her mother, Charlotte Augusta Parker, was Byron's father's sister. Like Mary Duff, Margaret was Byron's cousin and a further example of his susceptibility to those already tied to him by family connections, from whom he could be certain of an affectionate response. As he once confessed to Lady Melbourne, 'I could love anything on earth that appeared to wish it': his heart alighted automatically on the nearest perch.

Margaret Parker was thirteen or so, older than Mary Duff. She was dark eyed, long lashed and, as Byron remembered her in 1821 after his own immersion in Mediterranean classical art, of a 'completely Greek cast of face and figure'. It was she who inspired Byron's 'first dash into poetry', always to flow most easily under the pressure of strong emotion. This first poem has disappeared. But we still have the elegy he wrote in 1802 when both Margaret and her sister had just died of consumption:

> 'Hush'd are the winds, and still the evening gloom,
>   Not e'en a zephyr wanders through the grove,
> Whilst I return to view my Margaret's tomb,
>   And scatter flowers on the dust I love.'

Byron added a note of apology when the poem was published in *Fugitive Pieces*, and it is certainly a jejune composition. But it is a reminder of how intensely he responded, at such an early age, to the experience of loss.

Byron's contacts with Nottingham would be important to him both personally and politically. At the time when he first knew it Nottingham was in a phase of great expansion, brought about by local development of the hosiery trade. The influx of 'framework knitters', outworkers who produced stockings and gloves on frames in their own homes, resulted in new areas of artisan housing on the outer edges of the city. There were other levels of society besides the genteel tea drinkers with whom the Byrons mixed. The population had expanded from around 11,000 in 1750 to 28,861 at the time of the census in 1801, and Nottingham had become a highly radicalised city, disputing issues of parliamentary reform and revolutionary politics with rising anger – an anger that finally erupted into the Luddite riots with which Byron would later be concerned. Even as a boy, mixing with the articulate elite of town society, exposed to the strong views of his Whig-supporting mother, Byron must have been aware of the mounting tensions of the city he was soon to describe as 'that *political Pandemonium*, Nottingham'. His political education may well have started here.

Other political issues that troubled the end of the eighteenth century also began to impose themselves on him. Byron became absorbed by the rebellion in Ireland. His imagination was fired by the exploits of Lord Edward Fitzgerald, revolutionary son of the Duke of Leinster, who became the leading military strategist of the extremist Society of United Irishmen and planned the uprising against the occupying English forces in 1798. As originally envisaged this uprising would have been supported by a simultaneous invasion of Scotland by French forces. Fitzgerald's betrayal and arrest in Dublin was a contributory factor in the failure of the rebellion, and he died of wounds in prison in June 1798.

Sixteen years later, when Napoleon's defeat had so greatly depressed Byron and other young idealists of his generation, giving them the impression there were no great causes left, his old feelings revived for the hero of his childhood, the brave handsome aristocrat, wearing the green neckerchief of the Revolution. He regretted the fact that he had only been a boy at the time of the Irish rebellion: 'If I had been a man,' wrote Byron in his journal, 'I would have made an English Lord Edward Fitzgerald.'

4

Harrow

1801–1805

Byron entered Harrow School in April 1801, the year in which Napoleon became a Life Consul. Harrow saw the small beginnings of Byron's own aggrandisement:

'I will cut myself a path through the world or perish in the attempt. Others have begun life with nothing and ended Greatly. And shall I who have a competent if not a large fortune, remain idle, No, I will carve myself the passage to Grandeur, but never with Dishonour.'

Byron wrote this to his mother, probably in 1804, when he was sixteen. He wrote it in a rage, smarting from the repeated insults of three masters, including the headmaster, said to have called the boy 'a Blackguard'. Insults, real or imagined, were firing his ambitions, as they were soon to elicit the most brilliantly insolent of Byron's verse.

Harrow, a school dating back to the mid-sixteenth century, has drawn its special character from its commanding situation high on Harrow Hill, northwest of London, with vistas out over Windsor Castle towards Winchester and Oxford. Harrow pupils have the sense that a world is at their feet. Byron arrived at a school then in the full flowering of its popularity, with 250 pupils ranging in age from six to eighteen, rising to 350 by the time he left in 1805. Its status can be gauged by the fact that Mrs Byron, faced with Byron's frequent requests to leave the school, only considered Eton as a serious alternative; Westminster was beyond the pale.

Harrow had an especially high proportion of pupils from the nobility. In 1803, the school roll included one current and three prospective dukes, one of whom, the Duke of Dorset, became Lord Byron's fag. At that time the school also contained a future Marquess, two actual and five future Earls and Viscounts, four other Lords (presumably including Byron), twenty-one Hons.

and four Baronets. Aristocracy at Harrow was a commonplace. Rufus King, the American Minister to London, sent his two sons to Harrow as being the 'only school in England in which no special honour was attached to rank'. Of Harrow's total of seven British Prime Ministers, Lord Palmerston was almost and Robert Peel precisely of Byron's generation. He had suddenly arrived in an environment of the highest worldly expectations.

Byron began his somewhat erratic connection with Harrow in the boarding house of Henry Drury, recently promoted son of the headmaster. The young Henry Drury was also his tutor and so responsible for both his day-to-day welfare and his intellectual progress. Their relationship was to be tense. At this stage little about Byron seemed exceptional. The boys noticed that one of his grey-blue eyes was bigger than the other, the difference being that of a sixpenny piece in relation to a shilling, 'so they at once called him Eighteen pence'. Otherwise he seemed merely 'a rough, curly headed boy', veering between shyness and aggression.

Byron did not stand out as particularly clever: indeed he was still backward, and the headmaster, the Reverend Dr Joseph Drury, tactfully shielded him from the derision the boy dreaded by arranging special tuition until he caught up with his contemporaries. Nor did Byron appear conspicuously poorer than the other boys at Harrow. Though the family finances were known by the authorities to be precarious, this would not have been obvious to the boys. Mrs Byron was more generous with allowances to Byron than her straitened circumstances allowed. Her account books show not only circumspect repairings to greatcoats and refacings of sleeves but also extravagances such as 'A pair of fine Stripe Ticking Trousers', 'A Coat superfine Olive Cloth', 'A pair of Buckskin Breeches'. Byron could act self-confidence: 'I have as much money, as many Clothes, and in every respect of appearance am equal if not superior to most of my schoolfellows.' Nevertheless his early schooldays were a battle, and he would remember how acutely he had hated Harrow at first.

'There goes Birron, straggling up the Hill, like a ship in a storm without a rudder or compass.' So wrote the headmaster's wife, Mrs Drury, giving us a picture of the lame boy isolated in the mêlée of the overcrowded school. From Byron's point of view Harrow's hill was not an asset. In the early days at school his leg, under loose corduroy trousers, was still encased in its heavy iron cramp. But, instructed by Byron's doctors, Sheldrake, the surgical instrument maker, had evolved a special built-up boot for him, with a brace around the ankle for support. In May 1803, Byron wrote from Harrow to his mother: 'I wish you would write to Sheldrake to tell him to make haste with my Shoes.' By June nothing had happened. He complained to Mrs Byron, 'I have already wrote to you several *times* about writing to Sheldrake.' He had even written himself without result. 'I wish you would write to him or Mr Hanson to call on him, to tell him to make an instrument for my leg immediately, as I want one, rather.' The tone was becoming desperate.

Byron's disability made it impossible for him to reach Duckpuddle, the Harrow bathing pond, without hiring a pony. As at Dr Glennie's there was also the embarrassment of having the specialist call at the school to treat his foot. The boys inevitably taunted him. He would wake to find his lame leg dunked in a tub of water. Years later, under fire for his controversial 'Lines to a Lady Weeping', Byron commented: 'The M[orning] Post in particular has found out that I am a sort of R[ichar]d 3d – deformed in mind & *body* – the *last* piece of information is not very new to a man who passed five years at a public school.'

He neglected his treatment. On one of his visits Dr Laurie was dismayed to find him with 'the Shoe intirely wet through, & the brace round his ancle quite loose'. Such thoughtless bravado made Byron's foot noticeably worse, aggravating a condition which must have been partly responsible for what he described as his 'turbulent and riotous disposition' while at Harrow School. He was a fighter and a terrorist, in perpetual motion of flailing arms and whamming fists. His contemporary Peel, inventor of the Metropolitan police force, later described Byron's compulsive playground violence not simply as self-defence but as a homage to the grandfather who murdered William Chaworth. Duelling was something 'he accustomed himself to connect with the name of Byron'. Emulating his ancestors kept present pain at bay.

How did Byron emerge from his period of misery? How had Harrow transformed itself by 1807 into 'the *Blest Spot*' of Byron's nostalgic reverie? No other English public school has been memorialised with such ecstatic depictions of Arcadian boyhood as are found in Byron's early nineteenth-century Harrow poems. Underlying the alteration from resentment to affectionate involvement was, first, Byron's strong rapport with Harrow's headmaster and, second, the cluster of romantic friendships which from 1804 onwards gave him an emotional focus and through which he gradually discovered a male-oriented sexual identity.

Joseph Drury would have been a remarkable headmaster in any period. His incumbency at Harrow lasted twenty years, from 1785 to 1805, and he had been a master at the school for even longer, ever since he left university. Fifty-one when Byron joined the school, Drury viewed the youth at their first meeting as 'a wild mountain colt' but one who showed ability and might be led 'by a silken string to a point, rather than a cable'. Drury's educational aim was to get inside the mind of the individual child. His methods were pacific and persuasive. He did not beat the senior boys, subjecting them instead to verbal admonition – what Byron called Drury's 'Jobations'. Even allowing for his diplomatic skill in dealing with parents, and the schoolmaster's temptation, which Byron was to satirise in *Don Juan*, to flatter a well-born child, Drury seems to have had a genuine perception of Byron's potential. When he writes, 'I am much interested in Lord Byron's welfare', it is easy to believe this to be true.

Byron was a provoking pupil. Early in 1803, after bitter complaints from his son Henry of Byron's 'inattention to business and his propensity to make others laugh and disregard their employments as much as himself', Dr Drury agreed to Byron's transfer from Henry Drury's house to Mr Evans'. By the end of 1804, Byron's 'animal spirits, and want of Judgement' prompted the headmaster to suggest he should take a private tutor and not return for his final year at Harrow, a suggestion Byron then chose to ignore.

But Dr Drury did not lose his faith in Byron's great abilities. When Lord Carlisle paid a rare visit to the school to enquire about his ward's progress Drury, to Carlisle's surprise, was staunch in praise of him: 'He has talents, my Lord, which will add *lustre to his rank*.' Byron reciprocated by referring to Drury in 'Childish Recollections' as 'the dear preceptor of my early days'. In a rush of nostalgia for Harrow Byron claimed the Reverend Doctor, so mild and unpedantic, as the best and worthiest friend he ever had.

One of the trials that had been patiently endured by Dr Drury was Byron's nonappearance at Harrow for the autumn term of 1803. His mother, by then living at Burgage Manor, Southwell, sent a distraught letter to John Hanson on 30 October confessing, 'the truth is I cannot get him to return to School tho' I have done all in my power for six weeks past he has no indisposition that I know of but love desperate love the *worst* of *all maladies* in my opinion.' The object of this 'desperate love' was Mary Chaworth. His heart, again, had alighted on a nearby perch since Mary was a distant cousin, a daughter of the Chaworths of Annesley Hall, the estate adjoining Newstead, with whom the Byrons had been locked in protracted feuding, and a descendant of the William Chaworth so notoriously murdered by the 5th Lord Byron. When Byron first met Mary as a child at Newstead, soon after his arrival in 1798, he had replied pertly to Hanson's jocular suggestion that the two should marry: 'What, Mr Hanson, *the Capulets and Montagues intermarry*?' Now that Byron was fifteen, and Mary herself eighteen, the idea of intermarriage had developed a perverse attractiveness.

Newstead Abbey was now let to a sporting young bachelor, Henry Edward, Baron Grey de Ruthyn. Lord Grey, who was away travelling that summer, had invited Byron to ride over from Southwell whenever it suited him. From early August Byron was back at Newstead. 'Boards and Sleeps at my House and he talks of stopping a Month here,' grumbled Owen Mealey, the steward now in charge of the estate, to John Hanson. Byron soon gravitated to Annesley Hall, first on daytime visits, later sleeping there as well, paying court to slim, 'shy and singular', flirtatious Mary Chaworth with her light brown hair who, in the mythology perpetrated as much by Byron himself as by later commentators, occupies the place of his lost 'beau idéal'.

Mary Chaworth is portrayed in Byron's later memoirs as the first object of his adult sexual feelings. In a passage written in the early 1820s he describes an expedition made with Mary and some friends to the Peak Cavern at Castleton, a popular tourist attraction, classed by the guidebooks as 'amongst the Wonders of Derbyshire'. They entered the Cavern through Peak's Hole, a huge natural aperture in the rock, overlooked by the ruins of Peveril Castle high on the hill above. With candles to light their path they processed slowly through a geological wonderland of spars, fluors and stalactites and crystallised formations as the first Grand Chamber led into smaller chambers, past surprising little ledges and through even narrower passageways.

At one point a subterranean stream had to be crossed in a boat in which only two people could lie down. Byron gives a suggestive account of the moment in this wooden punt

'with the rock so close upon the water – as to admit the boat only to be pushed on by a ferry-man (a sort of Charon), who wades at the stern stooping all the time. – The Companion of my transit was M[ary] A. C[haworth] with whom I had been long in love and never told it – though *she* had discovered it without. I recollect my sensations – but cannot describe them – and it is as well.'

The party then travelled on to Matlock Bath, going to a ball at the Old Bath Hotel where, to Byron's indignation, Mary danced with an admiring stranger, leaving Byron standing by the wall. His later pathological loathing of the waltz perhaps had its origins in those memories of Matlock and his jealous isolation.

At the time no doubt his feelings were real and agonising. With his ready emotions, Byron was always to fall in love with extraordinary ease, and there are eyewitness accounts of him at Annesley in the throes of calf-love, moping around and shooting at the terrace door with his pistols. But there is something unconvincing about the way in which over the years Byron harps on his disappointed hopes of Mary Chaworth, making her the subject of elegy after elegy, claiming in the lines 'On Leaving England' of 1809 that she was his reason for abandoning his country:

> 'And I must from this Land begone,
> Because I cannot love but one.'

He even evokes the sacred memory of Mary Chaworth in a letter to his future wife, Annabella Milbanke, maintaining Mary to be the only other woman he has ever met to whom he would 'commit the whole happiness' of his future life.

The odd thing about this episode is that Mary Chaworth had never been a practical proposition for Byron. He was only fifteen; Mary Chaworth was engaged to someone else, the virile if unsubtle Jack Musters, the Nottinghamshire sportsman who in his prime 'could have leaped, hopped, ridden, fought, danced and played cricket, fished, swam, shot, played tennis and skated with any man in Europe'. Even without such competition, the ancient Byron–Chaworth enmity would probably have ruled out any permanent liaison. As Mrs Byron saw it: 'if my Son was of a proper age and the Lady *disengaged* it is the last of all connexions that I would wish to take place.'

A central role in the Byron legend has been accorded to the story of Mary Chaworth's disdainful comment to her maid, 'Do you think I could care anything for that lame boy?' This is supposed to have prompted Byron, when he overheard it or (in another version of the story) had it repeated to him late one night, to rush out of the house and hobble madly back to Newstead. It is a poignant tale, and one which Mary herself, questioned in later life, agreed was plausible. However, Byron's confidential friend John Cam Hobhouse treated the episode with the scepticism with which he had treated Byron's tales of old romances with Mary Duff and Margaret Parker, noting in his copy of Moore's *Life*, 'I do not believe this story.' Hobhouse recognised it for the construct it was, an episode exaggerated and embellished through the years to distract attention from Byron's real sexual predilections.

Byron himself comes nearest to the truth of Mary Chaworth in the beautiful and pessimistic poem 'The Dream', written in Geneva in the summer of 1816, after the disastrous ending of his marriage.

> 'I saw two beings in the hues of youth
> Standing upon a hill, a gentle hill,
> Green and of mild declivity.'

Mary, 'the Lady of his love', winds in and out of his long memories, here at last confronted as a fantasy and a chimera. He no longer portrays her, as in early elegies, simply as the girl who loved another. She has now emerged into something far more complex, the focus of his hopes for family and dynasty and sexual fulfilment within marriage: a future which Byron had half-begun to realise, even at the period when he first met Mary Chaworth, was likely to prove impossible to him.

Byron's ambiguity of appearance and character was evident to many contemporaries, who noted the particular turn of the neck; the almost translucent alabaster skin; the 'melting character' of his prominent eyes, 'frequently observed in females, said to be a proof of extreme sensibility'. The sculptor Sir Francis Chantrey remarked on the 'soft voluptuous character' of the lower half of Byron's face in contrast to the firmness of the upper part. The painter Sir Thomas Lawrence noted 'the full under-lip'. To Lady Blessington Byron's voice and accent were 'peculiarly agreeable, but effeminate'. James Hamilton Browne, with him on the voyage to Cephalonia in 1823, was transfixed, as were so many, by the 'irresistible sweetness of his smile, which was generally, however, succeeded by a sudden pouting of the lips, such as is practised sometimes by a pretty coquette, or by a spoiled child'.

Byron's looks reminded Douglas Kinnaird of those of his own mistress; Hobhouse reported from Malta that a female acquaintance 'picked out a pretty picture of a woman in a fashionable dress in Ackerman's Repository, and observed it was vastly like Lord Byron'. His friends agreed there was 'a great deal of the woman' about Byron: 'his tenderness, his temper, his caprice, his vanity'. His biographer Tom Moore, who knew him intimately, diagnosed an essentially female way of thinking, impatient of 'any consecutive ratiocination'. A much later biographer, Sir Harold Nicolson, himself discreetly homosexual, summed Byron up as 'a catalogue of false positions. His brain was male, his character was feminine.'

The best contemporary account of Byron's disconcerting but enchanting duality of temperament comes from George Finlay, the historian of Greece:

'It seemed as if two different souls occupied his body alternately. One was feminine, and full of sympathy; the other masculine, and characterized by clear judgment, and by a rare power of presenting for consideration those facts only which were required for forming a decision. When one arrived the other departed. In company, his sympathetic soul was his tyrant. Alone, or with a single person, his masculine prudence displayed itself as his friend. No man could then arrange facts, investigate their causes, or examine their consequences, with more logical accuracy, or in a more practical spirit. Yet, in his most sagacious moment, the entrance of a third person would derange the order of his ideas, – judgment fled, and sympathy, generally laughing, took its place. Hence he appeared in his conduct extremely capricious, while in his opinions he had really great firmness. He often, however, displayed a feminine turn for deception in trifles, while at the same time he possessed a feminine candour of soul, and a natural love of truth, which made him often despise himself quite as much as he despised English fashionable society for what he called its brazen hypocrisy.'

This duality in Byron's nature emerged in a painfully revelatory episode in 1803-4, his so-called Mary Chaworth summer, when Byron was almost certainly seduced by his Newstead tenant Lord Grey de Ruthyn.

Lord Grey had taken the lease on Newstead Abbey from January 1803, when he was twenty-three, paying £50 a year for the mansion and its park for the next five years, until Byron came of age. Mrs Byron had at first been rather scornful of his lineage: 'I cannot find Lord Grey de Ruthin's Title in the Peerage of England, Ireland or Scotland. I suppose he is a *new* Peer.' In fact his antecedents were impressive. The 19th Baron Grey de Ruthyn had inherited the title through his mother, a daughter of the 3rd Earl of Sussex. He had taken his seat in the House of Lords as a Whig. His real interests were more in shooting than in politics. His letters, and the comments of the Newstead steward Owen Mealey, show a truculent, unimaginative young man.

Through November 1803, when he should have been at Harrow, Byron stayed with him at Newstead. He became Lord Grey's collaborator in illicit shooting expeditions, and Mealey began complaining, 'they goe these moonlight nights and shuit pheasants as they sit at Roost'. Dark hints at more complex developments in their relationship are contained in letters from Byron to his half-sister Augusta, written after he left Newstead very suddenly. He tells her, in March 1804, 'I am not reconciled to Lord Grey, *and I never will*. He was once my *Greatest Friend*, my reasons for ceasing that Friendship are such as I cannot explain, not even to you my Dear Sister.' In November of that year, he was still sensitive about the subject of Lord Grey, 'whom I detest . . . I have a particular reason for not liking him.' He was keeping away from Nottinghamshire altogether to avoid the possibility of a meeting with his former friend.

The episode has generally been interpreted as a sexual overture that Byron had rejected. This does not, however, tally with the tenor of later correspondence between Byron and Lord Grey, in which Lord Grey claims still to be unable to account for Byron's peremptory breaking-off of friendship, while Byron himself adopts a sheepish half-apologetic tone. The most likely explanation is that Byron allowed himself to be seduced by Lord Grey and reacted with alarm only after the event. In commenting on the bland account in

Thomas Moore's biography of the 'intimacy' that 'soon sprung up' between Byron and his noble tenant, Hobhouse maintains that 'a circumstance occurred' during this intimacy 'which certainly had much effect on his future morals'. He pinpoints it as a central, if not *the* central, episode in Byron's sexual indoctrination.

In understanding the force of Byron's retrospective dismay at Grey's advances we need to be aware of the prevailing culture in late eighteenth- and early nineteenth-century Britain, when the male homosexual was viewed as a pariah. Even as a schoolboy Byron would have been aware that convictions for sodomy could lead to execution. Male homosexuality had been a capital offence in England since 1533, but it was only in the eighteenth century that the law against buggery began to be invoked with any frequency, following an increase in public comprehension of what sodomy actually was. It was unfortunate for Byron that his own dawning consciousness of his dual nature coincided with a period at which public feeling against homosexuals had become extreme.

Since sodomy itself was difficult to prove, requiring evidence of both anal penetration and emission, a lesser but almost as damaging charge of 'assault with the attempt to commit sodomy' had been evolved. Convicted men were punished by public exposure on the pillory, where they were liable to be stoned and vilified, pelted with mud and excrement, by an uproariously hostile crowd. Some were even killed by the homophobic mob. The level of intolerance forced even rich and intellectually distinguished homosexuals to flee the country rather than face the threat of criminal charges. One of these was William Beckford, author of the sodomitical dream novel *Vathek, an Arabian Tale*, to whom Byron reacted with the mingled fascination and revulsion that characterised his attitude to homosexuality at this early period.

At the end of January 1804 Byron at last went back to Harrow. His final year and a half there was more settled, taken up with an ever-widening circle of emotional involvements with other Harrow boys which he later remembered with great vividness: 'My School friendships were with *me* passions (for I was always violent).' Many records of these friendships survive from a period at which schoolboys corresponded copiously. The peculiarly touching letters from Byron's favourites, some childishly written and erratically spelt, are a window on to the close-knit society of early nineteenth-century Harrow, with its own language and behavioural codes.

Byron himself, apparently approvingly, explained the system of hierarchy:

'At every public School, the junior boys are completely subservient to the upper forms, till they attain a seat in the higher Classes. From this state of probation, very properly, no rank is exempt; but after a certain period, they command, in turn, those who succeed.'

Now it was Byron's turn to be a leader, a role in which he inevitably saw himself as a Highland chieftain surrounded by an obedient and adoring clan. He also described his throng of juniors as his Theban band.

With almost manic exactitude he listed and categorised these Harrow friendships: 'P. Hunter, Curzon, Long and Tatersall, were my principal friends. Clare, Dorset, C⁵. Gordon, De Bath, Claridge and Jⁿᵒ. Wingfield, were my juniors and favourites, whom I spoilt by indulgence.' Even within these groups there were sub-divisions. Byron, in a letter to Edward Noel Long, denied that his fag the Duke of Dorset had ever been 'a Friend' of his: 'I *petted* the *child*, but did not make him a *Friend*.'

Of all the well-bred young Harrow boys who vied for his attention, which was Byron's greatest favourite? Was it the Hon. John Wingfield? Or the future Sir John Claridge, who remembered sentimentally how Byron would carry him on his back when swimming and how, on the night before Byron left Harrow, they sat together on the Peachey Stone, a raised tombstone in the churchyard, famous feature of the Harrow landscape, taking a long farewell?

Was Byron's chief Harrow love the beautiful Earl Delawarr, not included in his list but described by him elsewhere as 'the most good tempered, amiable, clever fellow in the universe . . . If it were not for his sake, Harrow would be a desart'? Delawarr became the subject of one of those amatory quarrels over imagined insults, allegations of false pride, that blew up like a sirocco in the overheated atmosphere of Harrow. It took almost two years for them to be reconciled. Another favourite was William Harness, later assured by Byron, 'you were almost the first of my Harrow friends, certainly the *first* in my esteem.' Harness's lameness was a special bond between them. Byron successfully protected little Harness against the Harrow bullies with the love that expressed itself so easily as patronage and protectiveness.

In this floating world of superlatives Byron's schoolboy passions ebbed and flowed, peaked and petered out in jealousies and boredom. But certainly the most enduring of them all was with John Fitzgibbon, who had succeeded his father as 2nd Earl of Clare in 1802. He was four years Byron's junior. Byron described this as the Harrow school relationship that had 'begun one of the earliest and lasted longest'. In 1821, in Ravenna, the old friendship with Clare was still affecting Byron with a strength he found surprising. 'I never hear the word "*Clare*" without a beating of the heart – even *now*, & I write it – with the feelings of 1803–4–5 – ad infinitum.' By then he was defining Lord Clare as the only *male* human being for whom he felt true friendship: all his other ties were merely 'men-of-the-world friendships'. Since Clare's surviving letters are few and relatively guarded, it is difficult to gauge how far Byron's love for him had been reciprocated. Henry Drury, the master who knew both of them at Harrow, remarked interestingly on 'the total contrast, in every respect between him and Lord Clare'.

How physical were these relationships of Byron's? Again the subject is hidden in a cloud of obfuscation. The sex life of the English public school has been made mysterious not just by the silence of each new generation of boys, but by retrospective secrecy, protective codes of loyalty, extending beyond schooldays far into manhood. The long-term effects of this in forming over time an inbred and self-protective ex-public school society were brilliantly explored in Julian Mitchell's play *Another Country* of 1980. Byron's Harrow was itself another country, made still more impenetrable by those with vested interests who have wanted to obliterate all traces of his homosexual loves.

The ethos of boy worship at Harrow was encouraged by the classical studies that underpinned the curriculum. Byron and his contemporaries would have been familiar with heroic concepts of Greek love through their reading of Horace, Catullus, Virgil, Petronius: indeed in Byron's Cambridge circle the term 'Horatian' was used as a code word for homosexual. They were attuned to the ideal of the *eròmenos*, beautiful youths such as Ganymede or Hyacinth pursued by the Greek gods, and alerted by continual translation of the poets of the ancient world to the tempting image of the 'lightly-bounding boy', as he appears in Byron's post-Harrow translation from Anacreon, Ode 47:

> 'I love the old, the Jovial Sage,
> Whose Soul expands unchilled by Age,
> I love the lightly-bounding Boy,
> Whose hours the dance and loves employ.'

From the practical point of view sex between boys at an early nineteenth-century English public school was facilitated by long stretches of time spent unsupervised, as well as the custom of bed-sharing. A single bed often cost parents an additional fee. A letter to Byron from his friend John Tattersall, who left Harrow before him, indicates an almost claustrophobic intimacy: 'You say you shall miss me most damnably. I do not doubt it for who will you have to comfort you under afflictions, and (now for a sinking in poetry) to undress you when you go to bed . . . who to go bathe with you, in short who to do every thing with you.'

Although Byron often loved to mystify an audience, his obsessively precise accounts of his sexual experiences ring true and I think there is no reason to doubt the confidential confession he later made to Lady Caroline Lamb that he had practised homosexuality since boyhood and had indoctrinated three of his Harrow schoolfellows. According to Caroline, Byron's confessions culminated in his sacrificial conflagration of the portraits of his favourites. ('NB', wrote Byron's wife, in her appalled retelling of this story, 'two of their miniature pictures were burned with a curious remark.') John Cam Hobhouse was under no illusions about the physical nature of Byron's Harrow relationships, commenting in his diary, 'Certainly B had nothing to learn when he came from Harrow', and castigating Thomas Moore for real or feigned ingenuousness in his Byron biography: 'M knows nothing or will tell nothing of the principal cause & motive of all these boyish friendships.' 'Moore *said* he did not believe in the stories of his fancy for boys, but it looked as if he did believe it from his manner': so said Charles Fulke Greville, meeting a rather shifty biographer at a London dinner party in 1829.

In his final years at school and immediately after, Byron's experience of Harrow drifted into a series of deeply nostalgic, melancholy poems addressed to his favourites, some written as if to women, almost all with submerged or assumed identities. The most substantial of these is 'Childish Recollections', written in 1806 when Byron was ill in bed, and first published in his collection *Poems on Various Occasions*. It shows signs of the heightened awareness of illness, past and present conflating with a feverish intensity as Byron conjures up his Harrow idols one by one, disguising 'That *Madcap Tattersall*' as 'Davus', Delawarr as 'Euryalus', James Wynne De Bathe as 'Lycus', John Wingfield as 'Alonzo', with 'Clarus' as a not very opaque synonym for Clare. The underlying sadness of the poem, and his other Harrow verses, seems to spring from Byron's apprehension that the emotional candour of his youth will inevitably give way to adult posturings, hypocrisies, denials of natural sexual expressiveness. Leaving Harrow means bidding 'a long farewell to truth'. These poems are pervaded by world-weariness, a sense of life being half-over before it has begun, and by a consciousness of sexual differences that may in the end make England untenable to him. As he writes so presciently about Harrow:

> 'Ah! sure some stronger impulse vibrates here,
> Which whispers friendship will be doubly dear
> To one, who thus for kindred hearts must roam,
> And seek abroad, the love denied at home.'

*

At Harrow Byron's fascination with words, the power of language, the compulsions of the writer, first become apparent. Though he claimed to have found his formal lessons tedious, his exposure to the ancient texts had been long and intensive: 'Of the Classics', he admitted, 'I know about as much as most schoolboys after a Discipline of thirteen years.' These studies left him with a deep-seated, almost unconscious love of Ancient Greece, later to resurface dramatically in his support for the Greek War of Independence, and with a feeling for the austere grandeur of Greek tragedy. He admired especially Æschylus' *Prometheus*, one of the set texts he read three times a year at Harrow, and the *Medea* of Euripides, which would have introduced him to the vengeful woman, of whom there were to be several examples in his life.

Byron was reading widely throughout his time at Harrow. To keep up his pose of the anti-authoritarian idler he avoided being seen reading, but read while eating, or in bed, at times when no one else was reading, a secret addiction that stocked his mind with knowledge and helped him to develop a huge verbal facility. He boasted grandiosely that 'in the historical department' few nations 'exist or have existed with whose records I am not in some degree acquainted from Herodotus down to Gibbon'. He had rattled through biographies of kings, queens, emperors and generals, Julius Caesar, Cromwell, Marlborough, and inevitably Bonaparte; read the work of the philosophers Locke, Bacon, Hume and Berkeley, working up a detestation of Hobbes.

By the age of nineteen, Byron claimed to have read 'about four thousand novels, including the works of Cervantes, Fielding, Smollett, Richardson, Mackenzie, Sterne, Rabelais and Rousseau'. He knew all the British classic poets and most contemporary ones. Hobhouse felt that Byron exaggerated his breadth of reading. Walter Scott maintained that his knowledge was fairly superficial. But the proof of his reading is in the free use he makes of quotations from other writers, particularly Shakespeare, whose words are absorbed into Byron's own writing and remade as his own.

His early reading of the poets gave Byron his enormous sense of creative possibility. He realised the excitement of turning a phrase, of building up a stanza, arriving irresistibly at the final 'clinch'. He was already forming a grasp of the structure of a narrative. Assuming the schoolboy's protective stance of disdain, Byron found satiric poetry central to his taste. A copy of the works of Alexander Pope, the poet Byron most admired and most often emulated, was acquired by him during his Harrow schooldays. On the flyleaf of volume 2, he added his mark: 'Harrow on the Hill, Middlesex – AD 1803 – Given me by my Friend Boldero'.

Crucial also was his perception of the political power of language.

> 'But words are things, and a small drop of ink,
>   Falling like dew, upon a thought, produces
> That which makes thousands, perhaps millions, think.'

The ability of language to influence ideas and alter the course of society, as expressed so famously by Byron in *Don Juan*, began to dawn on him at Harrow. He put it into practice in pursuing a vendetta against the new headmaster, the Reverend Dr George Butler, who succeeded Drury in April 1805.

Byron had no real reason for such animosity towards Dr Butler. But his affection for Dr Drury and a natural resistance to change had made him the leader of the party in the school supporting the candidature of Mark Drury, Dr Drury's younger brother, and undermaster of Harrow. Butler was the Archbishop of Canterbury's appointment. Byron resented him as an upstart from outside, and once he was installed Byron was wilfully disruptive, though not to the extent that legend now has it. He did not lead a gunpowder plot against Dr Butler. But he wrote up on notices around the school, 'To your tents Israel!' Byron was the ringleader when Dr Butler's desk was dragged into the middle of the School House and set on fire. He pulled down the blinds of the study of Dr Butler's house, in which Byron was now lodging, and when asked his reason said, 'They darken the room.' Characteristically, when Butler reprimanded him, Byron 'cried and blubbered like a child'.

More seriously challenging to Butler were the poems Byron wrote in pursuing his campaign.

> 'Of narrow brain, yet of a narrower soul,
>   Pomposus holds you, in his harsh controul;
> Pomposus, by no social virtue sway'd,
>   With florid jargon, and with vain parade.'

These verses 'On a Change of Masters, at a Great Public School' were circulating round the school in summer 1805. His opposition to Butler, feeding on the controversy it had caused, swelled up into the longer and still more vitriolic 'Portrait of Pomposus' included in his 'Childish Recollections' and published in *Hours of Idleness*. Byron, playing innocent, claimed that he had kept this published version from the Harrow boys; but of course they read it all the same.

He attacked the headmaster as affected, ingratiating, overbearing, falsely boastful, pedantic and so socially lowly he should not be entrusted with the care of noble pupils. The assault was not just wounding to Butler personally. It attacked the whole basis of his economy, since early nineteenth-century head-masters grew rich on the fees they charged pupils. The success of the piece was a heady foretaste for Byron of the personal damage a poem could inflict.

At Harrow, amongst his contemporaries, Byron achieved integration of a kind. There was a side to him that craved acceptance. He was always to be as much insider as outsider, acquiring the double vision that made his social criticism so accurate. The relative equilibrium of his last few terms at Harrow was assisted by the sudden emergence in his life of an up-to-then shadowy figure, Byron's half-sister the Hon. Augusta Byron, child of Byron's father by his first wife Amelia D'Arcy, Baroness Conyers. After her mother's death Augusta had been brought up by her grandmother, Lady Holdernesse, who had herself died in 1801, leaving Augusta to lead the peripatetic existence common to lone women of her class. From then on Augusta did the ingratiating rounds of her aristocratic family relations, including Byron's guardian, the Earl of Carlisle.

Byron, avid for family, seized on Augusta as 'the *nearest relation* I have in *the world both by the ties of Blood* and *Affection*'. They met in the spring of 1803 at the house in Portland Place belonging to General (later 3rd Earl) Harcourt, when Byron was fifteen and she was twenty, tall, slim, full-lipped, weak-chinned with brown curling hair. Augusta, like Byron, had the family lisp and, in spite of her social poise, an underlying nervousness – the shyness of the ante-lope, so Byron called it: a trait he would always find attractive in a woman. She became surrogate mother as much as long-lost sister, with the added advantage that she listened sympathetically when Byron complained about his real mother; the growing warmth of their correspondence during Byron's final period at Harrow increased his confidence. In 1805, in his last term, he invited Augusta to Harrow Speech Day: 'I *beg Madam* you may make your appearance in one of his Lordships most *dashing* carriages, as our Harrow *etiquette* admits of nothing but the most *superb* vehicles, on our Grand *Festivals*.' The vision is alluring but Augusta never came.

By his last term his early antagonism towards Harrow had so completely altered that he counted each remaining day, dreading the thought of leaving. He made a little *tempus fugit* entry on the flyleaf of his *Scriptores Graeci* schoolbook: 'George Gordon Byron, Wednesday June 26th, AD 1805, 3 quarters of an hour past 3 o'clock in the afternoon, 3d school – Calvert, monitor, Tom Wildman on my left hand, and Long on my right. Harrow on the Hill.' Byron's strong sense of fate's strangeness would have revelled in the knowledge that Tom Wildman would eventually purchase Newstead Abbey. By 1805, according to school records, Lord Byron had become a monitor and third boy in the school.

The perspicacious Dr Drury had noted and encouraged Byron's innate theatricality. He 'had a great notion that I should turn out an Orator', wrote Byron, 'from my fluency – my turbulence – my voice – my copiousness of declamation – and my action'. Byron made star appearances at Harrow's public Speech Days in 1805, as he had done in 1804. One of his bravura performances was of King Lear's address to the storm. He went through the Harrow rituals of leaving his portrait, a formal frontal head and shoulders showing Byron in anything but ethereal mode, with his 'grand patron', ex-headmaster Dr Drury, and he incised his name alongside the dozens of old Harrow boys into the wooden wall-panels of the School House, the communal classroom in which they had been herded together for so many hours each day. Afterwards, on the steps, he met his friend Edward Long with his father and young brother. Byron bumptiously 'introduced an oath' into the conversation and the small boy asked his brother, 'Do boys at Harrow swear?'

Shortly after the end of his last term, Byron took part in an unofficial version of what was to become an important annual fixture in English social life: the Eton and Harrow cricket match. Cricket was a sport that Byron, by employing a runner, managed to take part in despite his lame leg. One of these runners was Henry Page, a Harrow wheelwright, who recorded:

> 'Oft at the famous game of cricket
> I've served his Lordship at the wicket.'

In the match on 2 August 1805, held in London, Eton beat Harrow easily. By Byron's ebullient account, in a letter to another Harrow boy, Charles David Gordon, he himself had scored eleven runs in the first innings and seven in the second, 'which was more than any of our side, except Brockman and Ipswich, could contrive to hit'.

The official scorebook shows this claim to be exaggerated: Byron's score in the first innings was actually seven, with two runs in the second. The captain of the team later commented ungraciously that Byron had played badly and would never have been in the eleven if his own advice had been taken. But in Byron's long memory the day remained a triumph, as in a sense it was, and the image of it also stayed with Stratford Canning, an opponent of Byron's in the Eton team. 'I had not forgotten the impression then made upon me by Lord Byron's appearance in his flannel jacket with bat over his shoulder,' he wrote when he met Byron again in Constantinople in 1810, by which time Byron was a published poet and Canning, later Viscount Stratford de Redcliffe, was an aspiring young diplomat.

5

Southwell
1803–1805

It was the violent extremes of Byron's experience that were to make him, as a writer, so remarkably versatile, equally at home with high and low and dark and bright. One of these contrasting experiences was Southwell, the small town of some three thousand citizens near Nottingham, which Byron found to his dismay to be full of 'old parsons and old Maids'. Southwell, polar opposite to mercantile and thrusting Aberdeen, gossipy contrast to Newstead's isolation, a town of quiet rituals, female to Harrow's maleness, was the nearest place in Byron's young adulthood to a settled home.

Byron was, at least officially, at Burgage Manor, the house in Southwell rented by his mother, from summer 1803, when he was fifteen, to winter 1808, when he returned to live temporarily at Newstead. Byron's period at Southwell spans both his later Harrow and his Cambridge years. Owen Mealey, the Newstead land agent, had reported favourably on the Manor: 'It is a handsome new house and very pleasantly situated. The rent for the House and Garden is 35 gns a year.' The house, built around 1780, is a fine example of Georgian provincial architecture, with a pretty classical pedimented façade, overlooking the open space of Burgage Green. A few minutes' walk away was the 'beautiful, well-kept Church and most elegant Chapter House, with its extraordinary gossamer-like carvings', as a contemporary visitor described Southwell Minster; such a well-built clean town, so the visitor went on, was the ideal retirement place for 'a quiet distressed Family'.

An acquaintance suggested that Catherine Byron would find the environment a dull one. But after years spent trailing her lame son from lodging house to lodging house during his school holidays, from Nottingham to Malvern to London, Cheltenham and Bath, trying to recapture the pleasures of the spa towns, she seems to have taken to the neighbourly existence of a small-town, church-orientated society, with its conventional mores and its ironic undertones, as so subtly described in the novels of Jane Austen. In Byron's personal mythology the little town resurges as the epitome of boredom: a '*Crater* of Dullness' and an 'Abode of Darkness', where his neighbours' only pleasures consisted of field sports. Complaining of heavy hours dragged along through month on month 'amongst the Mohawks' who inhabit Southwell's kraals, Byron poured out his invective upon the town, praying that it would be demolished by an earthquake, claiming that the time he spent there was 'a tedious *dream*', a blank out of his life. But how far to believe him? His resistance to Southwell was tied up with his resentment of his mother. There are signs he did not hate it as much as he pretended.

Byron made his first enduring female friend at Southwell. This friend was Elizabeth Pigot, five years older than Byron, who lived with her mother, the widow of a doctor, and her three brothers in the house opposite Burgage Manor, just across the Green. He was no doubt distantly remembering Elizabeth when he made the comment, in 1822:

'I have always laid it down as a maxim – and found it justified by experience – that a man and a woman – make far better friendships than can exist between two of the same sex – but *then* with the condition that they never have made – or are to make love with each other.'

Byron flourished in such friendships because they made no difficult demands on him, emotional or sexual. They were based on trust and liking. As in Byron's later non-sexual female friendships, with for instance Margaret Mercer Elphinstone and Lady Hardy, there was a robust sympathy, shared jokes, and give and take.

He met Elizabeth Pigot at a soirée given by his mother in April 1804 to introduce him to Southwell society. Byron had had high expectations of the party, as he reported to his half-sister Augusta in mock sophisticated style:

'My mother Gives a *party* to night at which the principal *Southwell Belles* will be present, with one of which although I don't as yet know whom I shall so far *honour having never seen* them, I intend to *fall violently* in love, it will serve as an amusement pour passer le temps and it will at least have the charm of novelty to recommend it.'

If nothing else, a doomed love affair would give him the materials for 'a pretty little Romance which shall be entitled and denominated the loves of Lord B. and the cruel and Inconstant Sigismunda Cunegunda Bridgetina &c. &c. princess of Terra Incognita – Don't you think that I have a Very Good Knack for *novel writing*?' But when the evening came Byron was seized by one of the fits of almost paralysing shyness that were always to assail him. His mother made three attempts before she was able to prise him from his room to join the young people of Southwell, decorously playing at a round game in the drawing room.

He made a poor first impression on Elizabeth. It is she who was responsible for the description of Byron as a fat bashful boy with unbecoming fringe that fixed his image at this period, gauche teenager before the transformation scene. The morning after the party his mother took him over Burgage Green on a visit to the Pigots, where 'he still continued shy and formal in his manner'. But Elizabeth, a well-informed, well-read, tactful girl, won him over with a reference to Gabriel Lackbrain, a character in *Life*, a comedy by Frederick Reynolds which Byron and his mother had seen recently at Cheltenham. Reynolds was later to adapt Byron's own dramas for performance at Drury Lane. 'Good-bye, Gaby,' said Elizabeth as he was bowing his goodbyes to her, and Byron gave a reciprocating grin.

From then on he spent much of his time with the Pigots when he was in Southwell, welcoming the escape from Burgage Manor. Elizabeth, like her mother, was a good watercolourist and one of her early acts of friendship was to make multiple copies of Byron's coat of arms for him to use as bookplates. He asked her to pay special attention to the twist in the tail of the mermaid. She was also to knit him a watch ribbon and a purse. They sang duets while Elizabeth played on the pianoforte: 'The Maid of Lodi' was one song which they both loved. There was an exchange of verses, written into her copy of the translation of Rousseau's *Letters of an Italian Nun and an English Gentleman*.

Elizabeth became his close confidante. He relied upon her steadiness, the counterpoint to his own gathering neurosis, as we see from the letters he sent her from Cambridge and from London, testing her out with accounts of his dissipations. Her letters to him stand out amongst those of the multitude of his female correspondents on account of their affectionate anxiety and their easy teasing tone: 'Our cottage is dull without you,' she tells Byron, 'and I sit down in my own armchair and wish it were *better filled* – not that I mean to say you are broader than me. Adieu!!' When Elizabeth's mother reassured an everanxious Mrs Byron that Elizabeth regarded him merely as a friend, seeing all his faults clearly and denying there was anything like love between them, she was not being entirely accurate. It was love of a sort, a deeply understanding friendship that offered vistas of parochial domesticity, which Byron half longed for but finally disdained.

Byron also made friends with John Pigot, Elizabeth's younger brother, then a medical student in Edinburgh. They coincided at Southwell in the holidays. John Pigot, too, was a reassuring presence for someone he described as 'even more shy than myself'. In summer 1806 they went to Harrogate together, travelling in grandeur in Byron's own carriage with his groom and valet, Francis Boyce, known as Frank. They took two of Byron's dogs with them, the bullmastiff Nelson and the Newfoundland Boatswain, who travelled on the box of the carriage with Frank. To Byron's grief they made the return journey without Nelson who attacked a horse so ferociously in the yard of the Crown Inn, where they were staying, that he had to be shot.

The Harrogate expedition was an anticlimax after their hopes of social success. Byron and Pigot dined in the public room but retreated soon after dinner to their own quarters, two bashful youths together, wondering if they could ever brave the ballroom. Like his sister, John Pigot became a stalwart defender of Byron, maintaining that few people understood him: 'but I know that he had naturally a kind and feeling heart, and that there was not a single speck of malice in his composition'. Pigot represents another antithesis to Byron, embodying those virtues that Byron chose to reject: the virtues of normal, decent, mainstream English professional life.

The longest stretch of time that Byron spent in Southwell was the year from summer 1806 to 1807. In these late teenage years, it was his place of growing up, of simple pleasures and, in other painful senses, of disillusionment. In February 1807 Byron sent a short résumé to his 'dearest' friend, Lord Clare:

'I have been *transporting* a servant, who cheated me, – rather a disagreeable event: – performing in private theatricals; – publishing a volume of poems (at the request of friends, for their perusal); – making *love*, – and taking physic. The last two amusements have not had the best effect *in the world*; for my attentions have been divided amongst so many *fair damsels*, and the drugs I swallow are of such variety in their composition, that between Venus and Æsculapius I am harassed to death.'

The cheating servant was Frank the valet, accused initially by Mrs Byron of stealing from her son. Byron, automatically loyal to his servants, had at first refused to believe the charge. But it was proved that Frank had stolen four pairs of black silk stockings from his mother, valued at 42 shillings, for which he was sentenced to seven years' transportation by the Southwell courts.

The Southwell 'theatricals' were a double bill, Richard Cumberland's comedy *The Wheel of Fortune* and Allingham's *The Weathercock*, performed in the dining parlour of the Leacroft family. Julia Leacroft, daughter of the household, was one of the Southwell belles with whom Byron flirted ostentatiously. He composed a prologue to *The Wheel of Fortune* in the carriage with John

Pigot en route home from Harrogate. Byron's interest in the theatre was already keen. He had seen the boy prodigy William Henry West Betty, known as 'Young Roscius', act several times in London. As well as directing the production, Byron cast himself in leading roles in both the Southwell plays.

An account of the proceedings written later by Miss Bristoe, daughter of a local clergyman, reflects almost uncannily the mood of the theatricals performed at Jane Austen's Mansfield Park, with its dramas within dramas and the sexual release experienced as actors entered into their unaccustomed roles. In spite of the forbidding presence at rehearsals of Miss Holmes, one of the Southwell maiden ladies, daughter of a deceased clergyman, Byron made advances to the naive Miss Bristoe, who was playing the part of Mrs Woodville to his Penruddock in *The Wheel of Fortune*. As she delightedly recalled it, 'Lord Byron requested to rehearse with me *alone*, for what reason I never knew, but I had cause to rejoice at his having made this request, as it prepared me for what I might expect on the Stage.'

Far from leading the life of the 'absolute Hermit' as he described it in an early letter to Augusta, Byron was now playing the field of Southwell belles. His blatant pursuit of Julia Leacroft, Emily Tempest to Byron's Penruddock in her home theatricals, resulted in formal remonstrations from her brother, who feared for his sister's reputation. Byron saw this as a ruse to trap him into marriage with a social inferior. He neatly turned the tables, replying to Captain Leacroft that 'as a young man very lately entered into the world, I feel compelled to state that I can permit no suspicion to be attached to my name with impunity'.

He became enraptured with the enticingly permissive Anne Houson, daughter of yet another local clergyman; he confided to John Pigot: 'She is a *beautiful Girl*, & I *love* her, nor do I *despair*, unless some *damned* accident intervenes, *secrecy* on this subject, my dear P. is requested, you will hear more Anon.' A further secret love of this period was Harriet Maltby, a normally outgoing and light-hearted girl who put on a façade of reserved silence to intrigue him. This policy paid off. He revelled in the small-town scandal he was causing, telling his old Harrow friend Edward Long that he had been accused of seducing 'no less than 14 Damsels, (including my mothers *maids*) besides sundry Matrons & Widows'. Hobhouse later made the comment that it was at Southwell where Byron learned his 'first lessons' in sexual relations with women, insisting that 'his Southwell recreations' were by no means as innocuous as Thomas Moore's biography makes out.

It is possible that Byron, at this period, fathered an illegitimate son. His collected *Fugitive Pieces* contains a sentimental six-stanza poem 'To My Son!', dated 1807, in which he hails the progeny of a girl of the labouring classes, now apparently deceased. In this morally defiant little poem he acknowledges the child and promises lifelong support for him:

'Why, let the world unfeeling frown,
Must I fond Nature's claim disown?
Ah, no – though moralists reprove,
I hail thee, dearest child of love,
Fair cherub, pledge of youth and joy –
A Father guards thy birth, my Boy!'

Whose was this child? Even Thomas Moore, so often gullible or guarded about Byron's sexual exploits, accepts the poem as autobiographical: 'it is not easy to suppose a poem, so full of natural tenderness, to have been indebted for its origin to imagination alone.' He cites the evidence of a friend of Mrs Byron's that Byron had asked his mother to look after the child then in the womb of the discarded mistress of his Harrow contemporary, the Hon. George Curzon. Whether or not she believed this complex story, Mrs Byron had agreed to raise the child. However, her generosity was never tested since the infant died soon after it was born.

Was Byron's putative Boy in fact a Southwell baby, or a child engendered on an escapade in London? This 'Fair cherub' is only one of several mystery children rumoured by Byron to have been his offspring: the child glimpsed by Samuel Rogers through the window of a house in Pisa near Byron's Palazzo Lanfranchi; the two children that he told Claire Clairmont had been born to Thyrza, a young girl of low birth he had seduced and abandoned before he went to the East. This girl then committed suicide and was 'buried in a cross road which was the reason he could not erect a stone to her memory'. His paternal instinct was always wayward, veering from fierce possessiveness to aristocratic nonchalance.

At Southwell emerge the first signs, still very tentative, of Byron's eventual literary fame. In July 1806 he was making preparations for his first book of poems, the volume entitled *Fugitive Pieces*. This was published privately in mid-to-late November, then suppressed and destroyed by Byron after local protests at its lewdness. Only four copies appear to have survived. A revised and toned-down collection, also published privately, came out in January 1807 under the title *Poems on Various Occasions*. A third volume, *Hours of Idleness*, with many further changes and additions, appeared in June 1807 and was Byron's first collection to be put on public sale and to receive serious professional reviews.

From the start this had been a largely local enterprise. The publishers were

Newark printers and booksellers, Samuel and John Ridge. Elizabeth Pigot transcribed the printer's copies of most of the poems from Byron's manuscripts, the first in a line of careful female scribes. John and Elizabeth Pigot read the proofs while Byron was in London after a particularly fierce quarrel with his mother, which had ended by her throwing the manorial firetongs at him. Some of the subject matter was scandalously local, with Anne Houson, Julia Leacroft and the rest of Byron's 'whole *Bevy*' of amorous females being clearly recognisable, even under disguised names. Outraged Southwell spinster ladies called Byron a '*young Moore*', finding parallels between his amorous suggestiveness and Tom Moore's titillating volume *The Poetical Works of the late Thomas Little*, published in 1801. This was perspicacious of them for Byron had indeed appreciated *Thomas Little*, reading the poems avidly when a boy at Harrow.

Chief censor of *Fugitive Pieces* was the Reverend John Thomas Becher, a rising local clergyman then in his early thirties. A relative of the Pigots, he was vicar of the Nottinghamshire parishes of Rumpton and Midsomer Norton. Becher is one of several equivocal parsons who emerge in Byron's history, living examples of his bitter jibes at hypocrisy within the Church of England. Becher seems to have welcomed Byron's private confidences about his sexual wildness whilst complaining officially of the immoral tenor of his verses. Byron's descriptions, he said, were 'rather too warmly drawn'.

Byron replied in verse to Becher in terms that would become his familiar battle cry: 'I seek not glory from the senseless crowd'. But nevertheless his obedient excisions include some of the liveliest of his early poetry, for example the lines addressed to Elizabeth Pigot on the miseries of wedlock:

> "Tis surely enough upon earth to be vex'd,
>   With wives who eternal confusion are spreading;
> "But in Heaven" (so runs the Evangelist's Text,)
>   "We neither have giving in marriage, or wedding."
>
> From this we suppose, (as indeed well we may,)
>   That should Saints after death, with their spouses put up more,
> And wives, as in life, aim at absolute sway,
>   All Heaven would ring with the conjugal uproar.'

For a boy of eighteen this is an impressive performance, not only on account of the confidence of its risky rhymes and risqué humour. Byron shows a precocious awareness of the dangers of early nineteenth-century sexual transactions, a subject he was to explore in his adult masterpieces *Beppo* and *Don Juan*.

*

An enduring image of the Southwell years is of Byron locked in combat with his mother. A letter to Augusta gives a treacherous description of their domestic situation.

'I am at this minute vis a vis and Tete a tete with that amiable personage, who is, while I am writing, pouring forth complaints against your *ingratitude*, giving me many oblique hints that I ought not to correspond with you . . . You may figure to yourself, for your amusement, my solemn countenance on the occasion, and the *meek Lamblike* demeanour of her Ladyship, which contrasted with my *Saintlike visage*, form a *striking family painting*, whilst in the background the portraits of my Great Grandfather and Grandmother, suspended in their frames, seem to look with an eye of pity on their *unfortunate descendant*, whose *worth* and *accomplishments* deserve a *milder fate*.'

Family portraits had been brought from Newstead to give Burgage Manor a more impressive air. In another letter Byron depicts sarcastically his '*wise* and *Good* mother (who is at this minute thundering against Somebody or other below in the Dining Room)'. How serious was the animosity between them? Certainly relations between them in Southwell were often desperately tense.

As he grew older Byron was more conscious of the embarrassing aspects of his mother, her lack of dignity and love of scandal, her blatant ogling of 'that detestable' Lord Grey de Ruthyn. She had 'a penchant for his Lordship,' he confided to Augusta, 'but I am confident that he does not return it, for he rather dislikes her, than otherwise . . . But she has an excellent opinion of her personal attractions, sinks her age a good six years, avers that when I was born she was only eighteen.' His mother's tendresse for the man who had seduced him was particularly galling for Byron since she kept pleading with him for the reconciliation that Lord Grey still desired. Intolerable too was the vituperation she unleashed on him whenever she was crossed; accusing him of behaving as badly as his father had, she prophesied that he would turn into 'a true Byrrone' – the ultimate among her insults. 'Am I to call this woman mother?' he protested to Augusta.

But the picture of unremitting animosity is not a true one. Even Byron admitted that there were calms between the storms. In good moods she would respond to Byron's teasing nickname 'Kitty Gordon'; at the time of the Southwell theatricals he was observed throwing open the drawing-room door and declaiming, 'Enter the Honourable Kitty', as the stately figure of his mother walked through. His Harrow friend William Harness remembered her specially bound collection of all the reviews of Byron's early poems with her own careful annotations in the margin: comments which struck Harness as very well-informed. From his vantage point across the Green, John Pigot was aware of their mutual dependence, despite the altercations: their concern for one another was reflected in the local story of both paying secret visits to the apothecary to make sure he was not supplying poison to the other.

Byron's worst diatribes against his mother occur in his letters to Augusta, whose sympathetic ear had the effect of encouraging him to ever-greater feats of vitriol. With accelerating glee he lays into 'the Dowager', his 'domestic Tyrant Mrs Byron'. He refers to her as 'this female Tisiphone', one of the furies; his 'tormentor' with the '*diabolical* disposition'. It is as if his pen has run away with him. Byron has become entrapped in a manner of expression, a habit of hostility, that bears no relation to the accurate or just. The depiction is as much fictional as realistic. Byron's real-life demons get subsumed into his narratives. Perhaps we should regard 'Mrs Byron furiosa' as one of Byron's greatest tragi-comic characters.

The clearest impression of Byron at this period is given by a series of twelve watercolour drawings, now in the University of Texas. These are Elizabeth Pigot's faux-naive story-book illustrations to her verse narrative 'The Wonderful History of Lord Byron & His Dog'. Byron's favourite dog Boatswain is central to the action, and the story has the motto 'Every Dog has his day'. A credible, endearing, curly-haired Lord Byron, mid-stage between boyhood and adulthood, emerges from her watchful and discriminating scrutiny. He wears top hat, ruffled shirt, pointed shoes, bright yellow trousers: the embryonic dandy. Byron is still plump, but evidently slimming. One of the drawings shows him sitting in a sweat-inducing warm bath, as directed by his local doctor, Benjamin Hutchinson, probably because Byron's weight was putting too much strain on his deformed leg.

Byron sent a fuller explanation of the regime in a letter to John Hanson:

'I wear *seven* Waistcoats, & a great Coat, run & play at Cricket in this Dress, till quite exhausted by excessive perspiration, use the hot Bath daily.'

He was allowed to eat meat only once a day, drink no 'malt Liquor' and very little wine. In three arduous months of violent exercise and fasting, he had lost eighteen pounds and, he assured Hanson, his clothes had had to be taken in 'by nearly *half* a *yard*'. A side effect was that Byron's figure became suddenly lissom, his face more beautiful and pallid. He kept up a more or less obsessive dependence on dieting and purgatives all through the years of his celebrity.

'He went into the house & sat down to writing,
And when he had done, Found Bosen was fighting'
A page from *The Wonderful History of Lord Byron and His Dog*, the affectionate verse
narrative written and illustrated by Byron's Southwell neighbour Elizabeth Pigot in 1807
when Byron was nineteen

His attitude to Southwell became that of distant fondness. He was later to
recommend it to Robert Charles Dallas, a family connection, as 'a large village,
or small town' where his family 'would have the advantage of very genteel
society, without the hazard of being annoyed by mercantile affluence'. In this
haven, he told Dallas, '*you* would meet with men of information and independ-

ence'. He had Southwell friends 'to whom I should be proud to introduce you'. But since Dallas was a prim and proselytising member of the Church of England there was probably a twist of irony in the suggestion. Byron himself occasionally felt a yearning for the life of the bookish country parson. Not for long. From his early days in the pretty town of minster bells and pleasant gardens, '*pigs, poultry, pork, pease*, and *potatoes*', he had realised that Southwell was far too small a stage.

6

Cambridge
1805–1807

Byron was admitted to Trinity College, Cambridge, on 1 July 1805 and took up residence on 24 October that year. He spent very little time in the town on 'that *oozy Helicon*': one term in autumn 1805; a few months from April to July 1806; another period of residence, with interruptions, from June to the end of December 1807. But Cambridge had an importance in his life far greater than the period he spent there. He arrived at seventeen, still gauche and immature, and in the candid view of his friend Hobhouse, without 'any reputation for superior attainments or extraordinary talents'. He left, at almost twenty, a poet of growing reputation, slimmed down and striking in appearance, with a circle of friends who remained (with one sad deletion) close to him for life. At Cambridge he began to measure himself against his contemporaries and felt, on the whole, that he could beat the competition. Here emerged the first signs of the iconic figure he became.

He went up to Cambridge with his usual misgivings about facing a new place. He had originally had his mind on Oxford, where several of his Harrow friends had gone. But there were no rooms vacant at Christ Church and his guardians, John Hanson and the Earl of Carlisle, had insisted upon Cambridge. He resented the enforced transition into adulthood, remembering how 'it was one of the deadliest and heaviest feelings of my life to feel that I was no longer a boy'.

But at least he was freed from Southwell and his mother, and he roused himself to make an ostentatious entry to Trinity. He told Hanson, 'Yesterday my appearance in the Hall in my State Robes was *Superb*, but uncomfortable to my *Diffidence*.' In his swirling dark green gown with encrusted gold embroidery Byron, the sole nobleman admitted in that term, stood out in his magnificence amongst the pensioners and sizars, financially dependent students, who made up the body of the college at that time.

Byron had been allotted '*Super*excellent Rooms', as he wrote excitedly to his half-sister Augusta. Their only disadvantage was that they adjoined the rooms of his tutor, the Reverend Thomas Jones, while on the other side was an old Fellow of the College, a possible dampener on his activities. The precise location of Byron's rooms has been a matter of dispute, but the most likely site is no. 1 I staircase on the north side of Nevile's Court. He bought furniture and planned to have the rooms papered and painted during the Christmas vacation 1805. When Byron's rooms, in his absence, were occupied by his friend Charles Skinner Matthews, their tutor Jones warned Matthews 'not to damage any of the moveables, for Lord Byron, Sir, is a young man of *tumultuous passions*'. Byron already had a sense of the value of belongings – of furnishings and decor, jewellery and clothes – in expressing personality.

Byron's Cambridge allowance of £500 a year, paid direct to him by Hanson, plus the upkeep of his servant and his horse, launched him on his career of conspicuous consumption. He told Augusta that he felt 'as independent as a German Prince who coins his own Cash, or a Cherokee Chief who coins no Cash at all, but enjoys what is more precious, Liberty'. He asked Hanson to send him down from London four dozen bottles of wine and a dozen bottles of port, sherry, claret and madeira, as well as a saddle for Oateater, his horse. The financial records show the exact extent of his expenditure at Trinity during that first term: for example, £75 for a joiner, £2 for a locksmith, £10 to the chandler, another £4 for coals and £20 17s 6d for Byron's perennial extravagance of books.

Included in his bill was 2 guineas due to the Head Lecturer. But did Byron attend any lectures? There was no pressure upon him to pursue formal studies since nobles were exempt from university examinations, and as Byron soon discovered the prevailing mood of Trinity was laziness and levity. He reported to Hanson: 'Study is the last pursuit of the Society; the Master eats, drinks and Sleeps, the Fellows *drink, dispute* and *pun*, the *employments* of the under Graduates you will probably conjecture without my description.' Byron was drawn into the licentious routine, part of a group of well-bred, lively, rich and philistine young men. The table in his rooms was awash with invitations. He dined and supped out riotously, his head 'confused with dissipation' the next day.

In his first term at Cambridge, relying on the familiar, Byron's friendship with Edward Long had deepened. At Harrow it was Long who had been the smooth one, 'sedate and polished' in contrast to Byron's gauche ferocity. At Cambridge, Byron's manners softened and Long's toughened, and they discovered a new compatibility, passing idyllic hours together swimming in the

River Cam, diving for plates, eggs and coins cast into the bottom of the deep water at the weir above Grantchester. Long was musical and Byron, whose responsiveness to music has been greatly underestimated, listened while he played the flute and cello in the evenings. With Long, he drank soda water rather than madeira. The books they read together included Thomas Moore's new volume *Epistles, Odes, and other Poems*. They shared a strong nostalgia for Harrow and Byron, with his sensitive antennae, detected an underlying melancholy in Long's nature, and a suicidal tendency, answering his own. The apparently unblemished companionship with Long coloured Byron's later reveries of Cambridge, where he spent 'the happiest, perhaps, days of my life'.

Cambridge was also the place of much darker recollections, memories of his tantalising homosexual love for the choirboy John Edleston, with its mingled feelings of guilt and ecstasy. At Cambridge Byron discovered an already thriving subculture of sodomy, with its own rituals and codes, into which he was indoctrinated by William Bankes, later defined by Byron as 'his collegiate pastor, and master', the 'father of all mischiefs', the young man who 'ruled the roost or rather the *roasting*' of Byron's Cambridge years.

Bankes was two years Byron's senior, and in many ways the opposite of Long: loquacious, touchy, highly intelligent and arrogant, brought up in the great English house of Kingston Lacy owned by his ultra-Tory father Henry Bankes, a long-serving MP who played an important role in directing government expenditure on the Napoleonic wars. Later a famous traveller and collector, William Bankes was to join the long line of English homosexual exiles. Already, at Cambridge, his taste for the esoteric was developed. He had fitted up some of his college rooms as a quasi-Catholic chapel, importing Cambridge choristers to serenade him. One observer reported: 'It was constantly asked "What the devil does Mr Bankes do with those singing boys?"' Byron's account of his meeting with the chorister, John Edleston, dwells upon the sound of him: 'his *voice* first attracted my notice, his *countenance* fixed it, & his *manners* attached me to him forever.' It has always been assumed that Byron heard him in the Chapel. But it is just as possible that their first encounter took place in the curiously furnished rooms of Bankes, the friend and mentor in whom Byron had 'implicit confidence' and in whom he 'used to confide all his iniquities'.

In meeting Edleston, the gentle, almost girlish fifteen-year-old chorister with his fair complexion, dark eyes and light brown hair, Byron reclaimed the idealism lost in the mindless drinking and whoring of his early Cambridge weeks. 'I took my gradations in the vices – with great promptitude,' he remembered with a shudder, 'but they were not to my taste – for my early passions though violent in the extreme – were concentrated – and hated division or spreading abroad.' In Edleston he found an emotional focus, though not without misgivings on the chorister's behalf for, as he explained the dilemma retrospectively, 'this very disgust and my heart thrown back upon itself – threw me into excesses perhaps more fatal than those from which I shrunk – as fixing upon one (at a time) the passions which spread amongst many would have hurt only myself.'

The obsession brought out Byron's deepest instincts for patronage and rescue, his sympathy for others in the orphan state. John Edleston was himself an orphan, parentless since the age of ten. Born in London, he had spent his boyhood in Cambridge, where his father appears to have been some kind of tradesman. Byron's love for Edleston, compared with his feelings for the younger boys at Harrow, had an extra dimension of class difference, the sexual frisson of *de haut en bas*. In this context John Edleston may well have had a predecessor. The existence of an earlier object of unequal adoration, probably a country boy, possibly a Newstead peasant who died young, is suggested by two earlier poems replete with an erotic condescension.

Byron loved mystification as much as he loved candour, and no doubt the element of enforced secrecy in his relations with Edleston increased his ardour.

> 'Ours too the glance none saw beside;
>   The smile none else might understand;
> The whisper'd thought of hearts allied,
>   The pressure of the thrilling hand.'

Their clandestine love united them against the world. It was a sentimental relationship of a kind enjoyed by many young men of his age and time; its excitements were related by Byron in confidential letters to Elizabeth Pigot back at Southwell. He and his '*musical protégé*' met every day, swimming, reading, singing, walking along the Backs, never tiring of one another's company. The lambent scenery of Cambridge, grey stone buildings, river shimmer, enhanced the forbidden intimacy. The tenderness between them is evoked in Byron's poem 'The Cornelian', describing the tentative gift of a gold ring mounted with a gleaming pale pink stone in the shape of a heart: 'He offered it with downcast look'. The boy too could do an underlook. The ring, a parting present at the end of Byron's first Cambridge term, is now in the collection at John Murray. It is poignantly small.

Byron spent the next few months in London. He had run through his allowance during that first term and was already nearly £1,000 in debt. He sent a pleading letter to Augusta: 'like all other young men just let loose, and especially one as I am freed from the worse than bondage of my maternal home, I have been extravagant, and consequently am in want of Money.' He asked her to help him to secure a loan from a Jewish moneylender. Since he was still a minor he needed somebody to vouch for him. Augusta, alarmed, offered to lend him money herself. But he could not bring himself to accept this and entered into complex arrangements with his London landlady Mrs Elizabeth Massingberd and her daughter, who acted as his mediators with moneylenders to raise a series of annuity loans. It was all too easy for Byron to raise money since the Byron estate was an unsettled one. Once Byron inherited, at the age of twenty-one, he would have absolute ownership of the estates and could pay his debts by mortgages secured on the property or, if the worst came to the worst, by selling his estates. Over the next few years the Massingberds, out of kindness or more dubious motives, signed a number of joint guarantor agreements for Byron, with repercussions that continued right up to the months before his death.

Returning to Cambridge in June 1807 his extravagances mounted. He bought a carriage necessitating horses and harnesses and servants in crimson livery. His munificence extended to a generous donation of thirty guineas towards a statue of William Pitt the younger, Prime Minister and a benefactor of Trinity who died in early 1806. Back in Cambridge his relations with Edleston resumed. His letters to Elizabeth Pigot suggest that a peak of fervour was reached in the ensuing weeks. By this time Edleston, whose voice would by now presumably have broken, had left the choir and would soon be leaving Cambridge altogether, 'to be stationed in a mercantile house of considerable eminence in the Metropolis' as Byron optimistically described it. In fact Edleston's future was to be that of a lowly clerk in offices in Lombard Street dealing with investments in the South Pacific.

Love was intensified by the imminence of parting: 'I certainly *love* him more than any human being, & neither *time* or Distance have had the least effect on my (in general) changeable Disposition.' And to Byron's delight the boy seemed even more attached to him than he to Edleston: the craving for adulation shows. Would Elizabeth Pigot have drawn the inference that Byron's interest in Edleston was sexual? Most probably her respectable upbringing in Southwell shielded her from such knowledge. Byron confessed to her his hopes for a permanent liaison. Once he came of age Byron would be able to finance Edleston's promotion to partner in his firm. They might even live together as a couple: 'In short, We shall put *Lady E. Butler*, & Miss *Ponsonby* to the Blush.' Here Byron was referring to the aristocratic cross-dressers Lady Eleanor Butler and Sarah Ponsonby, cousin of the Earl of Bessborough, known as the Ladies of Llangollen, who lived together in the mountains of Wales, so far socially accepted as to become a minor tourist attraction. But ideas that he and Edleston might be a nineteenth-century Jonathan and David, Pylades and Orestes, Nisus and Euryalus, legendary pairs of male lovers cited hopefully by Byron, were merest fantasy.

Over the period of his relationship with Edleston Byron's tendency to depression was increasing. When Augusta pressed him for the reasons for what she registered as a total change in temperament he replied evasively: 'I will not however pretend to say I possess that *Gaîté de Cœur* which formerly distinguished me, but as the diminution of it arises from what you could not alleviate, and might possibly be painful, you will excuse the Disclosure.' He was a little more forthcoming in a journal entry of the early 1820s:

'If I could explain at length the *real* causes which have contributed to increase this perhaps *natural* temperament of mine – this Melancholy which hath made me a bye-word – nobody would wonder – but this is impossible without doing much mischief – I do not know what other men's lives have been – but I cannot conceive anything more strange than some of the earlier parts of mine.'

We can relate his growing angst during his Cambridge years to his awareness of a hardening of public attitudes towards homosexuality in England as a whole. This had been intensified by resumption of the war against Napoleon in 1803. With possible invasion by French armies imminent, the mood in the country tended to hysteria. From 1805 onwards the rate of public hangings of convicted sodomists increased: six were carried out in 1806. More suspected offenders were being put to the pillory. The whole subject was shrouded in horrified innuendo and taboo. England labelled as degenerate the instincts that Byron experienced as natural. The sense of his departure from accepted sexual mores increased his tendency to automatic opposition. Letters from this period show him increasingly unhappy, isolated, alienated from an England where the future meant suppressing his private inclinations. The feeling of belonging to *no* country was beginning. Already at Cambridge Byron was planning to spend the next two years abroad.

When, years later, Byron thought back on the Edleston affair he called it 'a violent, though *pure* love and passion'. Is this to be believed? Was he lying in self-protection, or to protect his friends? Or had the liaison indeed been pure, in deference to Edleston's innocence, for fear of introducing him to criminal activities or to preserve their relations from Byron's earlier, more animal, experiences with Lord Grey de Ruthyn or the boys at Harrow School? Certainly the poems for Edleston lay stress on their chaste kisses. Maybe Byron preferred to keep relations between them on a more exalted plane. Surely he was thinking of Edleston in a later reply to a letter from Tom Moore: 'I don't know what to say about "friendship". I never was in friendship but once, in my nineteenth year, and then it gave me as much trouble as love.'

He parted from his '*Cornelian*' boy in Cambridge on 5 July 1807. He and Edleston had spent the evening together. Later that night, when he wrote to Elizabeth Pigot, a whole '*bottle* of *Claret*' was making his head muzzy, and tears were in his eyes.

When Byron came back to Cambridge in the summer of 1807, after a year's absence, he was physically changed. The boy who, at his heaviest, weighed 14½ stone had now, by a strict regime of dieting and fasting, reduced to 10 stone 13 lbs, weighed with his shoes. Even his closest friends had passed him in Trinity Walks, not recognising the willowy figure Byron had become. He was pleased with his new slimness, 'having *pared* off a sufficient quantity of flesh, to enable me to slip into an "*Eelskin*" & vie with the *slim* Beaus of modern times'. His only worry was that fashions had changed yet again and that the current mode amongst gentlemen was 'to grow *fat*'.

In June 1807 *Hours of Idleness* was published. This was another crucial development in the young Byron's metamorphosis. Compared with its predecessors *Fugitive Pieces* and *Poems on Various Occasions*, *Hours of Idleness* was a maturer, more substantial volume, from which Byron had carefully removed the most embarrassing of his youthful verse.

Though the book was once again printed by Ridge of Newark, who sold fifty copies in a fortnight to local enthusiasts before the advertisements were even out, this was the first of Byron's books to be available in London as well as in the fashionable watering places. With growing delight, as London booksellers reordered, Byron gloated over the books on display without revealing that he was the author, enjoying his '*fame* in *secret*'. One of his Scots cousins, Lord Alexander Gordon, staying in the same hotel in London, had told Byron that his mother, the Duchess of Gordon, had asked to be introduced to his 'poetical Lordship' as she had bought *Hours of Idleness*, 'admired it extremely, in common with the Rest of the fashionable world, & wished to claim her relationship with the Author'. A little exposure was going to his head.

Byron's attitude to professional publication was always to be ambivalent. With his keen sense of competition he relished the contest with his fellow poets and confrontation with literary reviewers at a period when critics gave no quarter. At the same time, partly as protection, he nurtured the dilettante status of the aristocrat-writer, the talented young lord throwing off a few verses in the night hours after his social events. Of the seventeen reviews Byron received for *Hours of Idleness*, the majority were encouraging. The only hostile and, to Byron, unexpected attack came from the most influential literary quarterly of the day, the *Edinburgh Review*.

The *Review*, irked by Byron's winsome preface to the poems in the persona of the diffident young lord, refused to let him have it all ways:

'It is a sort of privilege of poets to be egotists; but they should "use it as not abusing it"; and particularly one who piques himself (though indeed at the ripe age of nineteen), of being "an infant bard" – ("The artless Helicon I boast is youth") – should either not know, or should seem not to know, so much about his own ancestry.'

The critique wounded Byron doubly: as a Whig supporter, he had expected more leniency from a Whig review, and the Scot in him resented such cruelty from Edinburgh. He overreacted wildly when he read it, downing three bottles of claret after dinner and, according to Hobhouse, seriously contemplating suicide.

Byron responded to criticism in the way he knew best, answering attack with counter-attack. He began to feel much better as soon as he had written the first twenty lines of the retaliatory satire eventually published as *English Bards and Scotch Reviewers*. The chief object of his opprobrium was Francis Jeffrey, the *Edinburgh Review*'s editor, whom Byron had assumed to have written the review. Byron was never to discover that the anonymous author was Henry Brougham, the Scottish lawyer, whose championing of Lady Byron in the separation crisis gave rise to a bitter and very public feud.

By autumn 1807, with a second edition of *Hours of Idleness* in preparation, Byron set about improving and revising it, deleting more poems, adding others. Like all Byron's future publishers, John Ridge would be nerve-racked by his author's hectic way of composition, with second thoughts proliferating up to the last minute, long passages being augmented or deleted as Byron's personal likes and dislikes ebbed and flowed. One of the casualties of this second edition, published in March 1808 under the title *Poems Original and Translated*, was the long Harrow poem 'Childish Recollections', withdrawn after Byron's sudden reconciliation with the hated headmaster, Dr Butler, a typical example of the way his prejudices could be transformed to an equally extreme affection.

Byron, always an author with strong views on the appearance of his books in matters of paper, printing and binding, now proposed that his own portrait should be used as a frontispiece. He offered to order a plate in London from which the image could be engraved. Although the scheme was dropped in the hurry of production it shows clearly how Byron had already become conscious of the value of his own image in the selling of his work.

The most interesting of the new additions are the verses known as 'Stanzas', the final poem written for the volume, composed late in 1807 or early 1808. Several of the themes to be developed in *Childe Harold* are already evident in this wonderfully fluent lament for lost innocence:

> 'I would I were a careless child,
>   Still dwelling in my Highland cave,
> Or roaming through the dusky wild,
>   Or bounding o'er the dark blue wave.'

In this poem Byron, still not yet twenty, is playing with the cult of individual sorrow and alienation that lay at the heart of nineteenth-century Romanticism.

> 'Fain would I fly the haunts of men,
>   I seek to shun, not hate mankind,
> My breast requires the sullen glen,
>   Whose gloom may suit a darken'd mind.'

In these fifty-six lines of dramatically self-regarding pessimism the Byronic hero had made his entrance.

Byron had not planned to stay on in Cambridge for the autumn term of 1807. John Edleston was gone. Ned Long, addressed by Byron fondly as 'my dear *Standard Bearer*', was by then stationed at Chatham, wearing the scarlet regimentals of the Coldstream Guards: he was soon to distinguish himself in the military expedition to Copenhagen. William Bankes too was departing. It was a changed scene. But once back, intending only to dismantle his rooms and say his adieus, Byron found himself lingering. 'This place is wretched enough,' he told Elizabeth, 'a villainous Chaos of Dice and Drunkenness, nothing but Hazard and Burgundy, Hunting, Mathematics and Newmarket, Riot and Racing', but he became attuned to it and settled, as he had at Harrow in his final year.

The change of heart that brought about this determination to stay on at Cambridge for another term, to read for his degree, must partly be attributed to his new celebrity. With the publication of *Hours of Idleness* Byron was treated with sudden respect and circumspection by the Master and Fellows of his College, probably apprehensive of becoming the butt of his lampoons. He was cultivated by the new generation of Trinity College aristocrats. Of the six noblemen at Trinity in autumn 1807 four, including Byron, were Old Harrovians. The Marquis of Hartington, heir to the Duke of Devonshire, was one of these. 'Hart', when at Harrow, had been dismissed by Byron as a boy 'of a soft milky disposition and of a happy apathy of temper which defies the softer emotions'. The milksop had now grown up to be a member of the Cambridge Whig Club, which Byron too was invited by Lord Tavistock to join.

He was also, as he loved to be, the centre of attention in a wider, more rumbustious social circle, hosting parties of jockeys, gamblers, boxers, authors, clergymen and poets: 'A precious Mixture, but they go on well together, and for me, I am a *spice* of every thing except a Jockey, by the bye, I was dismounted again the other day.' His fascination with society at all levels, and especially with people on its doubtful outer edges, was already manifest as Byron gathered in professional jockeys from Newmarket and boxers from London. From his Harrow days Byron had been taking lessons from the fencing master Henry Angelo, a fashionable figure of the period with many raffish contacts in the London demi-monde. Byron's suggestion that Angelo should set up rooms in Cambridge to continue his tuition met with opposition from the Mayor, Mr Mortlake, who refused to countenance the holding of fencing classes in the Town Hall. 'We will yet *humble* this *impertinent Bourgeois*,' wrote a furious Byron to Angelo.

It is Angelo who gives us the most vivid picture of Byron at this period – almost a Hooray Henry of his day, arriving at the racecourse at Newmarket in his barouche, carrying a riotous party of friends. After the racing they had dinner at an inn in Cambridge where 'the glass and the joke made the evening pass swiftly; Lord Byron, by his affability and cordial reception, having greatly enhanced the pleasure of it'. Angelo and Theodore Hook, a London friend of Byron's, were seated on the top of the evening's mail coach, waiting for it to leave for London. Byron had sent out to St John's College for 'the good beer it was noted for'. He filled two tumblers and handed them up to Hook and Angelo, 'laughing at the many people that were wondering at his being so very busy waiting on the outside passengers'. The details of the scene remained with Angelo for ever, showing Byron at his most charming and vulnerable: 'his obliging condescension, our parting, the coach driving off, his huzzas, and the twirling of his hat'.

Now, in what turned out to be his final term at Cambridge, Byron made his most intimate male friendships, with John Cam Hobhouse, Scrope Davies and Charles Skinner Matthews, a group of young men on his own intellectual level who shared and indeed helped to perfect his sense of humour, the propensity to laughter which was Byron's saving grace. Though of the three only

Sketch by his Cambridge friend Scrope Berdmore Davies showing Byron as 'an Amatory Writer' beside an unidentified satirist. Above are, left, Charles Skinner Matthews and, right, John Cam Hobhouse, other members of Byron's Cambridge set

Matthews was overtly homosexual they provided a tolerant and sympathetic milieu in which all forms of sexual diversion could be openly discussed. The friendship was exclusive, almost conspiratorial: as Byron later wrote of Matthews: 'He, Hobhouse, Davies, and myself, formed a coterie of our own at Cambridge and elsewhere.'

John Cam Hobhouse was the son of Benjamin Hobhouse, a Liberal Whig MP created baronet in 1812. He was initially suspicious of Byron's affectations, disliking the way he went swanning around Cambridge wearing 'a *white hat*, and a *grey* coat' while riding 'a *grey* horse'. But he warmed to Byron on discovering that he wrote poetry. Hobhouse himself had literary aspirations. The friendship between the volatile and charismatic Byron and the dogged, faithful Hobhouse flourished through the years, surviving tiffs, domestic tragedies, political differences, so that Hobhouse, after Byron's death, could truthfully assert: 'I know more of B. than any one else & much more than I should wish any body else to know.'

Scrope Berdmore Davies, six years older than Byron, was an admired figure whose crucial influence has only recently been recognised. The son of a Gloucestershire vicar, he had been a scholar at Eton, and then, in 1805, became a Fellow of King's College, Cambridge. In that great age of conversation Hobhouse and Davies were already fine performers. Byron recalled their double act: 'Scrope was always ready – and often witty – H as witty – but not always so ready – being more diffident.' Davies's dry repartee was delivered with a stammer. Byron appreciated, and to some extent would emulate, the compulsive gambler and ardent womaniser, who excelled at reducing life to grand absurdity. It is Davies we must thank for the picture of 'the poet in bed with his hair *en papillotte*' which led him to exclaim, 'Ha, ha! Byron, I have at last caught you acting the part of the Sleeping Beauty.' The story is probably a fantasy. Byron's hair curled naturally. He had no need of curlers. But the story illustrates the strain of whimsicality that Byron loved in Scrope.

Of the three friends, Charles Skinner Matthews is the most enigmatic, described by Byron as 'a very odd & humerous fellow'. His temper was uncertain. In academic attainment he was far ahead of his contemporaries, a scholar and prizeman of Trinity who proceeded to win a fellowship at Downing. Though Hobhouse adored him and Bankes too had been close to him, Byron stood somewhat in awe of this 'Intellectual Giant', perhaps disliking the competition, claiming to detect a coldness in his temperament. But in matters sodomitical he depended upon Matthews as his 'guide, philosopher and friend'.

Matthews was known to his close circle as 'the man of Method', a reference to the codeword 'Methodiste' meaning homosexual. In fact his obsessive interest in this topic was probably more theoretical than practical. The iconoclastic Matthews was also nicknamed 'Citoyen': a revolutionary who might well cart you to the guillotine. He stood out as being stridently atheistical, even in a university town in which a mood of scepticism and free-thinking was well established. Byron found Matthews' doubts about God, salvation and the afterlife exhilarating. They reinforced his own.

Byron at Cambridge had a fourth friend, an ally he described as 'the finest in the world'. This was a tame bear. Byron was devoted to, and depended on, his animals for companionship and comfort, often preferring them to humans. Forbidden by the university statutes to bring a dog to Cambridge, he had circumvented the rules by importing a bear which he lodged not, as legend has it, in his rooms or high up in a turret in Trinity Great Court but in the stables in Ram Yard where he kept his horses and where the bear was evidently fed on bread and milk. When Ned Long heard the news that Byron had 'brought a *bear* to Grantchester' he wrote to ask him whether this was not 'carrying coals to Newcastle', adding, 'I make no doubt Bruin would receive a fellow of Trinity with a friendly hug.'

Long, well used to Byron's ways, had quickly grasped the point that his friendship with the bear was not simply showing off but contained a serious element of social protest. In boasting that his bear would be sitting for a fellowship Byron was attacking the low academic standards of the university and the widespread corruption associated with elections to fellowship, which resisted all attempts at reformation of the system. He had already made his disgust with Cambridge obvious in satiric poems in *Hours of Idleness*, in one of which – 'Granta, A Medley' – the poet is transported by a demon to the spire of St Mary's Church to view the inner workings of the colleges below:

> 'Then would, unroof'd, old Granta's halls
> Pedantic inmates full display;
> Fellows, who dream on lawn, or stalls,
> The price of venal votes to pay.'

In another poem, 'Thoughts Suggested by a College Examination', he pours scorn upon the small-minded vanity of the Cambridge elite, addicted to the footnote, terrified of aiming at the wider view. His reference to the Fellows' 'manners rude' contains a snipe at Richard Porson, violent and drunken Regius Professor of Greek at Trinity, who once attacked an undergraduate with a poker. Hobhouse later maintained that the victim had been Byron. When, having done no work and after three brief terms of residence, Byron was awarded an MA in July 1808, his worst fears about the laxity of Cambridge would be realised.

How big was Byron's bear? Unlike several of Byron's dogs, Bruin has no portrait. But it seems safe to assume that the bear was a small one, perhaps a former dancing bear. Byron felt a strong antipathy to all forms of coercion, and it is no coincidence that the British Parliament passed Wilberforce's bill to abolish human slavery in the year that Byron's bear arrived at Cambridge. The bear advanced the argument that animals too should be free and well treated.

Byron's notorious friendship with the bear drew hostile comment from Hewson Clarke, an embittered poor scholar of Emmanuel College, whose verses, published in the London monthly *The Satirist*, made the point that a Lord's patronage only made a bear subservient in a new way.

> 'Sad Bruin, no longer in woods thou art dancing,
> 　With all the enjoyments that Love can afford;
> No longer thy consorts around thee are prancing,
> 　Far other thy fate – thou art slave to a lord!
>
> How oft when fatigued, on my sofa reposing,
> 　Thy tricks and thy pranks rob of anger my breast;
> Have power to amuse me, to keep me from dosing,
> 　Or what's the same thing, they can lull me to rest.
>
> But when with the ardour of Love I am burning,
> 　I feel for thy torments, I feel for thy care;
> And weep for thy bondage, so truly discerning,
> 　*What's felt by a* Lord *may be felt by* a BEAR!'

Clarke's malicious implication that the bear was a sex toy may well be a veiled reference to Byron's love for Edleston.

Byron snapped back, attacking Clarke in a long footnote to *English Bards and Scotch Reviewers*, calling him 'a very sad dog, and for no reason that I can discover, except a personal quarrel with a bear, kept by me at Cambridge to sit for a fellowship, and whom the jealousy of his Trinity contemporaries prevented from success'. This prompted Mrs Pigot to write to Mrs Byron: 'I hope the poor Bear is well, I wish you could make him understand that he is *immortalised*, for if *four leg'd Bears* have any vanity it would certainly delight him.' The bear was to die at Newstead in 1810.

How far would Byron's history have differed if he had gone to Oxford rather than to Cambridge? If the episode of the bear itself, a superior sort of joke, has a particular Cambridge resonance in its comedy of logic taken to extremes, so Byron's interest in science and discovery owes as much to the Cambridge intellectual tradition as to his Southwell friendship with John Pigot, the medical student. He and Pigot exchanged views on the latest scientific advances. They discussed the findings of Sir William Herschel, the astronomer, who established a new view of the universe through the reflecting telescopes he designed and manufactured; the experiments of Johann Kaspar Lavater, the Swiss mystic, inventor of phrenology; Alfonso Galvani and his findings on animal magnetism and electricity. Byron was fascinated by the possibilities of galvanism and the scientific resuscitation of the dead. He and Pigot joked about Erasmus Darwin's *The Botanic Garden* with its intellectual speculation on the sex lives of plants. Byron himself was a disciplined observer. His great poem *Don Juan* is built upon a quasi-scientific analysis of the human condition, rejecting the half truths of sentimentality and cant.

For all his growing disillusionment and cynicism Byron did not lose his respect for truth or his capacity for wonder. A Cambridge spirit of Newtonian enquiry was still alive in him in Pisa in 1822 in a prophetic passage in which Byron posits the clash of interests between technological advances and morality:

'I suppose we shall soon travel by air-vessels; make air instead of sea voyages; and at length find our way to the moon . . . Where shall we set bounds to the power of steam? Who shall say "Thus far shalt thou go, and no farther"? We are at present in the infancy of science.'

Through her collaboration with Charles Babbage on the clockwork 'thinking machine' in the early 1840s Byron's daughter Ada was to become a pioneer of computer technology.

7

London and Brighton
1808–1809

By January 1808 Byron had finally left Cambridge and was lodging at Dorant's Hotel off Piccadilly. He would spend the next year flitting between Dorant's and Batt's Hotel in Jermyn Street, Gordon's Hotel in Albemarle Street, Reddish's Hotel in St James's Street, and lodgings at 8 St James's Street. He was addicted to hotels and the freedom they gave him, a sense of adventure which he recreated in the eleventh canto of *Don Juan* in which the foreigner of rank, on his secret mission, arrives in London for the first time, driving past the Mansion House, Westminster Abbey, Charing Cross and rattling up Pall Mall to look into 'one of the sweetest of hotels' in St James's, from the door of which 'a tide of well-clad waiters' streams to greet him. For Byron, more than ever rootless at this period, a hotel was more attractive than a home.

Byron's London life was focused on the streets round Piccadilly, an area where the aristocracy and the substrata of society which subsisted on serving them and selling to them coexisted cheek by jowl. The streets of St James's, with their network of small hotels, coffee houses, clubs, were – and still are – a male preserve. For the conspicuous consumer St James's Street was a heaven of shoemakers and tailors, hatters, hosiers and glovers, umbrella, cane and whip makers. In the Haymarket were specialist gun makers, saddlers and makers of equestrian accoutrements, cutlers and platemakers, hair cutters and wigmakers. Byron patronised the several booksellers of the area. He was a good customer of the chemists and druggists. Whole books have been written about his shopping habits; his expenditure was partly the expression of an indelible insecurity.

Byron was encouraged into gambling by his Cambridge friend Scrope Davies. 'Scrope Davies & I are members of the new Cocoa tree club & next week the dice will rattle.' It appears that Byron's gambling did not last long: even he could see the limits of his financial resources, and he may have been influenced by Hobhouse, his ever-protective friend, who feared it would do damage to Byron's reputation 'to be seen every night in the very vilest company in town'. But Byron had enough experience of the tables to understand the compulsion of it. He wrote later: 'I have a notion that Gamblers are as happy as most people – being always *excited*.'

For Byron excitement was a state of bliss, in all respects preferable to inertia. Each turn of the card and each cast of the dice created life-enhancing tension. A gambler always lived in hope. Byron remained entranced by the story of Scrope Davies going home, drunk, from the gaming house, having lost his money. Next day his friends discovered him still in his bed at two in the afternoon, sound asleep, without a nightcap, his bedclothes in disarray, with a chamber pot by the bed stuffed full of banknotes. Scrope had no idea where this largesse had arrived from, but it amounted to 'some thousand pounds'.

Byron was taking lessons in boxing from John 'Gentleman' Jackson, described in a note to *Don Juan* as 'my old friend and corporeal pastor and master, John Jackson Esq., Professor of Pugilism'. Jackson, former boxing champion of England, was a much admired figure in Regency England, with his well-developed chest, small waist, and 'large, but not too large hips', his 'balustrade calf and beautifully turned but not over delicate ankle' and firm foot. Byron went to the premises at 13 Bond Street which Jackson shared with Byron's fencing master Henry Angelo. These were also the headquarters of the Pugilistic Club. As well as the exercise, Byron liked the rumbustious society of 'the Fancy' and its vigorous slang.

It was only a short step from pugilism to duelling, clandestine pursuit of the aristocracy. Though banned by church and state, duelling and its ancient rituals of challenge and acceptance, as well as its real dangers, attracted Byron. His adrenalin rose at the proximity of death. Though this was to be denied by Hobhouse, Byron later claimed that he had taken part in 'many duels' as a second, and in two as principal. One of these 'many duels' may have been at the behest of Captain Wallace, a dissolute drinking companion of Scrope Davies. A scrawled cloak-and-dagger letter from Wallace was sent to Byron in autumn 1808: 'I now request if you can so far befriend me to be in readiness against a *certain* Colonel who at present I shall not name but *who* you have often heard me mention. Excuse haste.'

Byron lived in a louche atmosphere in which procurement flourished and desires merely hinted at could come to quick fruition. 'Bruiser' Jackson fetched his medicines, acted as his agent in the purchase of a pony, which had to be returned later as unsound, and searched for the pedigree greyhounds Byron fancied: 'You will get the greyhound from the owner at any price, and as many more of the same breed (male or female) as you can collect.' Byron had more dubious dreams of acquisition after attending an opera masquerade at Covent Garden. At the end of the performance he had supper behind the scenes in the apartments of the prima donna Madame Catalani – in company with seven whores, a bawd and James d'Egville, the ballet master and impresario. He confided to Hobhouse: 'I have some thoughts of purchasing D'egville's pupils, they would fill a glorious Harem.' Hobhouse later made the disapproving comment about d'Egville: 'This person was employed in a transaction not very creditable.'

In a letter written from Italy years later Byron himself refers to 'a little circumstance' which occurred when he was young in London:

'There was then – (& there may be still) a famous French "Entremetteuse" who assisted young gentlemen in their youthful pastimes. – We had been acquainted for some time – when something occurred in her line of business more than ordinary – and the refusal was offered to me – (and doubtless to many others), probably because I was in cash at the moment – having taken up a decent sum from the Jews, – & not having spent much above half of it. – The adventure on the tapis it seems required some caution and circumspection.'

There was a postscript to the invitation: 'Remember, Milor, that *delicaci ensure every Succés*.' We have no way of telling what exactly was the speciality on offer, male, female, hermaphrodite, adult or child, or even whether he availed himself of it. But there is evidence that Byron, at this juncture, was experimenting with sexual partners in varied permutations.

'You have heard of one *nymph*,' he told an envious Hobhouse. 'Rumour has been kind in this respect, for alas! I must confess that *two* are my *property*.' A fortnight later he wrote to the Reverend John Becher: 'I have three females (attendants included) in my custody.' Simultaneously, he was amusing himself with 'the "chere amie" of a French Painter in Pall Mall, a lively Gaul; – and occasionally an Opera Girl from the same Meridian'. Byron had made one 'of a party of ten at a house of Fornication'. The numbers rise and rise. His pious relation Robert Dallas was not far off the mark when he wrote of Byron at this time: 'Unaccustomed to female society, he at once dreaded and abhorred it; and spoke of women, such I mean as he neither dreaded nor abhorred, more as playthings than companions.' There was safety in the numbers of Byron's female concubines in a society proscribing relations with boys.

Besides, Byron was already intent on living up to his self-made image of 'the votary of Licentiousness, and the Disciple of Infidelity', taunting Dallas with his iconoclastic views: 'I hold virtue in general, or the virtues severally, to be only in the Disposition, each a *feeling* not a principle. – I believe Truth the prime attribute of the Deity and Death an eternal sleep, at least of the Body. – You have here a brief compendium of the Sentiments of the *wicked* George Ld. B.'

The summer of 1808 was one of record-breaking temperatures. On a famous 'Hot Wednesday' in July the thermometer reached 99°F. For much of the summer Byron was in Brighton. He liked the south coast, having spent some happy weeks at Littlehampton with Ned Long and his family, and his own dog Boatswain, two years before. Brighton was a larger, more fashionable resort, by then almost a Piccadilly on sea. It had expanded under the patronage of the Prince of Wales, whose summer residence it was. The Prince's gross extravagance made Byron's look like child's play, and his ostentatious onion-domed Pavilion, rising high over Byron's humbler lodgings at 1 Marine Parade, gets a side-swipe in *Don Juan*:

> 'Wealth had done wonders – taste not much; such things
>   Occur in orient palaces, and even
> In the more chasten'd domes of western kings.'

By the time he got to Brighton Byron was already dreaming of oriental excursions of his own.

Scrope Davies and Hobhouse were with Byron in Brighton, idling and squabbling through the sultry summer, gambling and getting troublesomely drunk. They went bathing, stripping and plunging into the sea, and back at their lodgings emerging in their dressing gowns 'to discuss a bottle or two of Champaigne and Hock (according to choice)'. One stormy day one of the group, the Hon. Lincoln Stanhope, got into difficulties in the water. Byron swam over to him, shouting encouragement, watched by an anxious crowd gathered on the beach, until they were both rescued by boatmen with safety ropes round them, who dragged them from the sea. That summer Byron was becoming a keen sailor. James Wedderburn Webster, another Brighton crony, was surprised by the graceful movement with which he managed to get into his sailing boat: 'While standing on the beach I once saw him vault into it with the agility of a harlequin, in spite of his lame foot.'

In Brighton too was Byron's 'Blue-eyed Caroline', most permanent and most resourceful of his several concubines. Caroline Cameron was a sixteen-year-old prostitute, formerly employed by a London bawd called Mrs Durville. In February Byron was gloating that his Caroline had 'been lately so *charming*, that though we are both in perfect health, we are at present commanded to *repose*, being nearly worn out', explaining in more graphic detail to Hobhouse:

'I am at this moment under a course of restoration by Pearson's prescription, for a debility occasioned by too frequent Connection.' Pearson the physician warned him he had had enough sex in the previous ten days to undermine his constitution.

Byron had taken lodgings with Caroline in Queen Street, Brompton, an arrangement which shocked his more conventional friends. Tom Wildman, invited to breakfast, was put out when Byron summoned Miss Cameron to join them, while noting with prurient interest that he and his mistress slept in separate beds. This, Wildman added, was Byron's habit with all his women. If so, one reason could have been his shame at his deformity. That Caroline was a cut above the normal London prostitute is suggested in Byron's comment to Hobhouse: 'I am still living with my Dalilah, who has only two faults, unpardonable in a woman, – she can read and write.'

Byron's importation of Caroline to Brighton was still more outré. Dressing her in boy's clothes, he passed her off as his brother Gordon, explaining later that this had been a subterfuge to prevent his mother hearing that he had 'such a female acquaintance'. It was also surely a complex form of sex game, a titillating masquerade of boyish girls, pages and their masters, which would be resurrected on a more sophisticated level in his affair with Lady Caroline Lamb. Blue-eyed Caroline played along with the deception. When Lady Perceval, staying in Brighton that same summer, suspiciously examined the girl dressed as a boy, admiring the 'very pretty horse' which he was riding, she received the reply, 'Yes, 'twas *gave* me by my brother.'

The disguise was penetrated at some point in the summer when Caroline, then pregnant, had returned to London where, according to a scandalous report, 'the young gentleman miscarried in a certain family hotel in Bond Street, to the inexpressible horror of the chambermaids and the consternation of all the house'. To Hobhouse's alarm, Byron seems to have contemplated marrying her. Young men of their social class did not marry prostitutes. But by July he and Caroline were no longer together. 'I have parted with Miss Cameron, & I beg she may have her Clothes & the trunk containing them,' wrote Byron from Brighton to Mrs Massingberd, his moneylender and occasional landlady in London. It is clear she had colluded in his liaison with Caroline. In all respects they were on confidential terms.

Byron left the seaside in August 1808, and we now lose sight of Caroline, except for the strange little report from Scrope Davies that he had seen her at the theatre in London 'parading the Lobby', where she launched 'the most violent attack on Hobhouse' he had ever witnessed. Now cast back upon her old world of disrepute, she clearly blamed Hobhouse for the break with Byron.

The story of Byron's liaison in Brighton with 'a young Female, dressed as a Youth' was still doing the rounds of the London gossips five years later and contributed to his by then enlarging reputation for dark, bizarre behaviour.

In Brighton Byron found John Cowell, a rival to Caroline and, more pertinently, a substitute for Edleston. This new John was very similar in background, son of a tradesman or, as Byron preferred to describe Cowell's father, 'a citizen of London'. John Cowell was thirteen when they met. He had been in the habit of playing on the seashore with Byron's dogs, bonding closely with the 'faithful and gentle' Boatswain. A few short letters to his patron in Cowell's well-formed copperplate attest to the progress of a relationship which the boy evidently found immensely flattering. 'The notice with which you honoured me at Brighton, makes me wish to know that your Lordship is well, & I hope it will be an excuse to you, for the liberty I take, as a little boy, of trespassing thus on your time.' Cowell wrote this letter to Byron in October and his family delightedly encouraged the liaison.

It followed a pattern which becomes familiar in Byron's relationships with adolescent boys: the mingling of love with practical assistance. He entreated his Harrow tutor Henry Drury, with whom Byron was now reconciled, to find the boy a place at Eton, where Drury's brother was a master. Byron followed John Cowell's progress through the school, writing to remind him to watch his prosody and tipping him generously when they met. Byron later encouraged his protégé to enter his own college, Trinity in Cambridge, keeping up a degree of emotional involvement: 'Cowell is & always was a fine fellow – I don't like anybody much – but him as well as most.' When Tom Moore met Cowell, then in his early thirties, while doing the research for his biography of Byron, he noted how much Cowell resembled his old patron: 'Cowell's imitation of his look & manner very striking', as if Byron's personality had subsumed his own.

In the autumn of 1808 Byron returned to live at Newstead. Lord Grey de Ruthyn had left the Abbey once his lease expired in June and Byron swept aside ambivalent and troubling memories with an intensive programme of renovation. 'I am now fitting up the *green* drawing room, the red (as a bedroom), and the rooms over as sleeping rooms,' he told his mother, using the presence of so many workmen as an excuse to keep her away. The Hansons too were rejected, sent off to lodge in Mansfield, while Byron decorated and furnished his apartments in the fashionable anglicised French Empire style. He installed the opulent chinoiserie four-poster ornamented with coronets on all four corners, with which he had impressed his friends at Trinity, in his own suite in the north-west wing, adjoining the ruined Abbey front, and he refurbished some guest rooms in the south-east wing, at a strategic distance from his own.

Byron was skilled at making the most of his resources. These rooms were an oasis of splendour in a building otherwise still neglected and decayed. The Great Hall, more or less empty, was used for shooting practice and the Great Dining Room for exercise with fencing foils and singlesticks. A journalist who visited the building some years later viewed Newstead as revealing 'more of the brilliant conception of the poet than of the sober calculations of common life'. Many of the rooms

'he had superbly furnished, but . . . he had permitted so wretched a roof to remain, that in about half a dozen years the rain had visited his proudest chambers, the paper had rotted on the walls, and fell, in comfortless sheets, on the glowing carpets and canopies, upon beds of crimson and gold, clogging the wings of glittering eagles and destroying gorgeous coronets.'

Byron may have been a perpetrator of façadism but his Newstead, while it lasted, gave a lovely light.

At this stage Byron began assembling his close entourage of servants, the biddable, familiar faces who made him feel secure. His valet, William Fletcher, originally a farm worker on the Newstead estate, was employed first as a groom and then as Byron's personal servant, replacing the discredited Frank Boyce. Immensely loyal, the accident-prone, self-indulgent, superstitious Fletcher, Byron's 'Cameriero', with his Nottingham accent and his amiable, lazy physiognomy, rivalled Hobhouse as repository of Byron's confidences. The 'Ursine Sloth' in the menagerie at Exeter Exchange, so Byron commented, had 'the very voice and manner' of his valet. But Fletcher was by no means as stupid as Byron liked to claim. Shelley once compared him to a shadow, waxing and waning 'with the substance of his master'. He was at Byron's side from 1804, when Byron was sixteen, almost without interval until his master died.

Old Joe Murray was recalled from an unhappy exile from Newstead and became Byron's chief servant. 'Joseph Murray is at the head of my household, poor honest fellow!' he wrote sentimentally to his sister Augusta, who was now married to her cousin Colonel George Leigh. 'I should be a great Brute, if I had not provided for him in the manner most congenial to his own feelings, and to mine.' Joe Murray, at seventy, was a prodigious link with the past, having entered service with 'the Wicked Lord' back in the 1760s, enduring the dismal days of his reclusiveness when his Lordship dined alone and was every day served with the same bottle of claret, uncorked but never touched. Although outwardly respectable in appearance Old Joe retained his talent for singing ribald songs. Byron petted him, liking to hand him a tumbler of madeira over his shoulder at dinner, saying 'with a cordiality that brightened his countenance, "Here my old fellow"'. He treated his servants with a real affection.

Robert Rushton was a new recruit to Byron's household. His father rented one of the farms on the Newstead estate. A local woman later told the tale that Byron had watched Fletcher and Robert ploughing the elder Rushton's fields, taken a fancy to them both and hired them for his household. If this picturesque story is true, Robert was first sighted when little more than a child. In 1808 he was a fresh-faced light-haired adolescent, of an age to be employed as Byron's official page. As with Edleston and Cowell, Byron's role vis-à-vis Rushton was protective, educative. 'I like him', he told his mother, 'because like myself he seems to be a friendless animal.'

At Newstead Rushton slept in a little cubbyhole adjoining Byron's bedroom. The probability that his services included sex emerges in the encoded exchange of correspondence between Byron and Hobhouse over the well-known portrait by George Sanders showing Byron and Rushton standing in a rocky landscape preparing to embark together on a sailing boat. Hobhouse teases Byron for his sexual recklessness, implying that he might get shot for criminal connection with the young seafarer. It is doubtful if this painting would have entered the Royal Collection had the esoteric innuendo been fully understood.

Byron had grand ideas of playing the host at Newstead. That autumn he began to issue invitations. First of his guests was Hobhouse, at Newstead through October when Byron the theatrical entrepreneur directed a performance of Young's *The Revenge*. The two of them attended the Infirmary Ball in Nottingham, and Hobhouse accompanied him on a more delicate mission to Annesley Hall to dine with Mary Chaworth, now Mrs Musters. She had married her sportsman and tactlessly paraded her two-year-old daughter for Byron's admiration.

The dinner was an agony, as Byron relived the chagrin of his callow love for Mary: 'I forgot my valour and my nonchalance, and never opened my lips even to laugh, far less to speak, & the Lady was almost as absurd as myself.' The horror of the evening propelled him into desolate reflections on the cycles of hunger and distaste in his relations with women eerily prophetic of his own disastrous marriage: 'What fools we! We cry for a plaything, which like children we are never satisfied till we break it open, though unlike them, we cannot get rid of it, by putting it in the fire.'

Hobhouse stood by his friend through another ordeal, the death in November of Byron's dog Boatswain. The huge Newfoundland had had a fit.

The signs are those of rabies, a virulent form of canine madness. Byron wiped the spittle from the poor dog's lips as he went into his final paroxysms. 'Boatswain is dead!' Byron announced dramatically. 'I have lost every thing except Old Murray.' He made up his mind to be buried with his dog, originally specifying a vault in the ruined Abbey church, close to the high altar, but finally deciding to erect a monument to Boatswain in the gardens at Newstead. For this tomb he composed an adulatory epitaph in the style of Alexander Pope:

> 'To mark a Friend's remains these stones arise;
> I knew but one unchang'd – and here he lies.'

When Byron died he intended that his body should be inserted in the tomb alongside Boatswain, without disturbing the dead dog's bones.

Byron was relieved when Hobhouse finally left Newstead. His longing for company alternated with a stronger desperation to be rid of it. Hobhouse's stalwart devotion sometimes grated; as he told Augusta, 'I could not bear the company of my best friend, above a month.' He did not return the calls of the neighbouring nobility and gentlefolk. He demurred when his mother compared him to Jean-Jacques Rousseau: 'I can't see any point of resemblance – he wrote prose – I verse – he was of the people – I of the Aristocracy.' But in his capacity for withdrawal, and his questioning of the social conventions, the young Byron was indeed a little Rousseauesque.

He mooned around Newstead, contemplating mortality. When one of the gardeners brought in a human skull Byron, like Hamlet scrutinising the skull of Yorick, decided it had 'probably belonged to some jolly friar or monk of the abbey about the time it was dis-monasterised'. The skull was a particularly large one, and he sent it to London to have it mounted in silver as a drinking cup. It came back highly polished 'and of a mottle colour like tortoiseshell'. In ghoulish celebration Byron wrote 'Lines inscribed upon a Cup formed from a Skull'.

> 'I lived – I loved – I quaff'd like thee;
> I died – let earth my bones resign.
> Fill up – thou canst not injure me;
> The worm hath fouler lips than thine.'

He amused himself within his own domestic circle, with results made public at the start of the next year when he sent news to Hobhouse that 'Lucinda' (Lucy, the housemaid) 'is pregnant', and that Robert Rushton had 'recovered of the Cowpox', with which it had pleased his master to infect him. He enlarged upon the situation in a letter of instructions to John Hanson on dispersing the staff after Byron left for London: 'You will discharge my Cook, & Laundry Maid, the other two I shall retain to take care of the house, more especially as the youngest is pregnant (I need not tell you by whom) and I cannot have the girl on the parish.'

Byron's attitude to sexual relations with housemaids shows much of the droit de seigneurism of his age. Servants were fair game. Witness the tone of gentlemanly complicity with which he later wrote to Sir Walter Scott describing the 'tremulous anxiety with which one sometimes makes love to a beautiful woman of our own degree with whom one is enamoured in good earnest; – whereas we attack a fresh-coloured housemaid without . . . any sentimental remorse or mitigation of our virtuous purposes'. But Byron was more enlightened than the norm in his refusal to have Lucy thrown out to subsist on parish charity. The way this prospect haunted him is shown in the touching little portrait in *Don Juan* of

> 'a country girl in a close cap
> And scarlet cloak (I hate the sight to see, since –
> Since – since – in youth, I had the sad mishap –
> But luckily I have paid few parish fees since)
> That scarlet cloak, alas! unclosed with Rigour,
> Presents the problem of a double figure.'

Confiding in Hanson about the maid enceinte, Byron at first proposed to make a will leaving the baby what the lawyer considered a ridiculously high proportion of his prospective inheritance. Finally, caution ruled and he settled on a more modest but still, by the standards of the time, generous annuity of £100 for Lucy and the child.

What happened to this baby? We do not know what sex it was. It was not, apparently, with Lucy when she was reinstated as chief of Byron's maidservants after he returned from his travels two years later. Maybe it was raised by relatives. Later Byron is said to have commented to his wife that he had *two* natural children to provide for: if one was Claire Clairmont's daughter Allegra, the other could have been the housemaid Lucy's child. A distant memory of Lucy, from another Newstead servant, was of a beautiful page boy 'which the housemaids said was a girl . . . she was a great favourite with Lord Byron, and had been much noticed by him, and began to have high notions.' It seems that Byron's Lucy cross-dressed for him as well.

When Byron came of age on 22 January 1809 a feast was planned at Newstead: 'the tenants are to have a good dinner and plenty of Ale & Punch, and the *Rabble* will have an Ox and two Sheep to tear in pieces, with *Ale*, and *Uproar*.' Byron himself was absent, having asked John Hanson to stand in for him, and spent the day alone at Reddish's Hotel where Robert Dallas, calling on him, found him 'in high spirits; indeed, so high as to seem to me more flippant on the subject of religion, and on some others, than he had ever been before'.

Byron's flippancy, so often the sign of deep disquiet, masked his anxieties at his uncertain future. Much was expected of him. His mother had written hope-fully: 'his Heart is good and his *Talents* are *great* and I have *no* doubt of his being a great Man.' Byron had tremendous expectations of himself, and a certain sense of national obligation. He admitted to Augusta his 'portion of Ambition, and a conviction that in times like the present, we ought to perform our respective duties'. But what was Byron's duty?

In 1803, when the war between Britain and France had been renewed, Byron had courted unpopularity at Harrow by ostentatiously defending his bust of Napoleon against the more conventionally patriotic boys. Since then, in spite of the British naval victory at Trafalgar, Napoleon had made spectacular progress on land: Austerlitz in 1805 brought the defeat of Austria and retreat of the Russian forces; in 1806, with the battles of Jena and Auerstadt, Prussia in turn was crushed. By 1807 Napoleon commanded the largest European empire since the days of Rome. Byron's response was, as usual, much more complex than the jingoism felt against Napoleon in the country as a whole. He was thrilled by Napoleon's grand vision and his effrontery in implementing it, whilst being dismayed by the widespread savagery that the Napoleonic wars unleashed. This ambivalence of attitude was shared by the more Whiggish members of his circle. Hobhouse too was a fervent admirer of Napoleon.

The mood in the country had become more aggressively militaristic in the years of the Peninsular War. The death of Byron's Harrow and Cambridge friend Ned Long early in 1809, drowned in a transport ship on the way to Lisbon to join the British expeditionary force against Napoleon, convinced him more than ever of the horrors of senseless carnage in a doubtful cause. How was he to channel his talents and ambitions in a country with whose politics and morals he was increasingly at odds?

Coming of age had not solved Byron's financial problems. Mrs Byron attacked the problem with realistic vigour: 'I have no doubt of his being a great speaker and celebrated public character, and *all* that; but that *won't add* to his fortune, but bring more expenses on him, and there is nothing to be had in this country to make a man rich in his line of life.' Locked into his cycle of expend-iture and loans, Byron's debts had now risen to about £12,000, mainly secured on his life interest in his properties. These loans were due to be repaid once Byron came of age.

He could now sell his land. But the estates in Norfolk were of no great value, whilst the estates in Lancashire were still tied up in long-running legal disputes and were not negotiable. Byron set his mind completely against selling Newstead, although this was urged by Hanson. He now identified himself personally with the flawed but beautiful estate: '*Newstead* and I *stand* or fall together, I have now lived on the spot, I have fixed my heart upon it, and no pressure present or future, shall induce me to barter the last vestige of our inheritance.'

Byron's hope was to raise a mortgage on Newstead, to pay off his debts and finance him until Rochdale could be sold. Mrs Byron's more pragmatic view was that he should improve his prospects 'in the old and usual way by marrying a woman with two or three thousand pounds' a year. As she told John Hanson, 'Love matches is all nonsense. Let him make use of the Talents God has given him. He is an English Peer, and has all privileges of that situation.' Byron's response to this scenario was one of horror: 'I suppose it will end in my marrying a *Golden Dolly* or blowing my brains out, it does not matter which, the Remedies are nearly alike.' As Dallas had noted, Byron had no real concept of domesticity.

Byron the hereditary peer took his seat in the House of Lords on 13 March 1809. A political career was now one of his options, though in some ways he would have preferred the less lethargic House of Commons: '*our* house is not animating like the hounds of the commons – when in full cry. – Tis but cold hunting at best in the Lords.' He took his seat somewhat reluctantly, pale with performance nerves, as he had been on Harrow Speech Days. Dallas, who accompanied him, watched his progress through the chamber, passing the woolsack without looking round and advancing to the table to take the oaths. 'When he had gone through them, the Chancellor quitted his seat, and went towards him with a smile, putting out his hand warmly to welcome him.' Byron rebuffed Lord Eldon, making a stiff bow and merely touching with his finger-ends the Tory Chancellor's outstretched hand. He then sat slumped for a few minutes on one of the empty benches to the left of the throne, normally occupied by the Lords in opposition. The image is already that of the outsider, arrogant and dissident.

Byron's natural home in politics was with the Whigs, the party of patrician revolution. The Whigs had been, like Byron, born to opposition, agents of the coup which had ousted the Roman Catholic monarch James II in 1688. The young Byron, former member of the Whig Club in Cambridge, which his friend Hobhouse had founded, was the fervent admirer of more recent Whig luminaries, Richard Brinsley Sheridan and Charles James Fox, writing in 1807: '*these* are *great* names, I may imitate, I can never equal them.' His serious interest in the Whig tradition is suggested by the inclusion in his reading list for this period of parliamentary debates from 1688 to the mid-eighteenth century. He made seven appearances at the House of Lords before he left on his travels in the summer of 1809. But Byron was never a committed member of the Whig or indeed of any other organised party. He was always to consider himself as independent, taking the wider internationalist view, speaking for humanity. The lack of conviction with which he took his seat was a small presage of the political maverick that he became.

There was a sub-plot to Byron's entrance to the House of Lords. He had written to his guardian Lord Carlisle to tell him he would be taking his seat, in the expectation that Carlisle would introduce him personally to the House. Lord Carlisle sent him a letter with some technical instructions, but made no offer to accompany him. Byron was devastated by what he regarded as the ultimate insult in their chequered history. 'I have *lashed* him in my *rhymes*', he told his mother, 'and perhaps his Lordship may regret not being more conciliatory.' Byron took his revenge in ferocious lines inserted in his now almost completed satire *English Bards and Scotch Reviewers*:

> 'No muse will cheer, with renovating smile,
> The paralytic puking of CARLISLE …
> What heterogeneous honours deck the Peer!
> Lord, rhymester, petit-maitre, pamphleteer!'

The insult was even worse than Byron had intended, for by the time of its publication his guardian had indeed been stricken with a form of paralysis.

Through all Byron's vicissitudes it was work that drove him, challenged him and steadied him, took him out of himself into a condition of total concentration in which the prevailing values were the literary ones. When he calls himself a 'mighty Scribbler' he acknowledges his need for the regular discipline of composition. He had started a first version of *English Bards* while still at Cambridge and continued to enlarge and recast it during 1808. He worked on the poem systematically in the quiet of a snowy winter month at Newstead Abbey, getting up in the evening, writing through the night and going to bed again at dawn. By January 1809 he had completed 624 lines of it, and was still going strong. The poem, bulging with his animosities and prejudices, stood at over a thousand lines when it was published anonymously in March 1809.

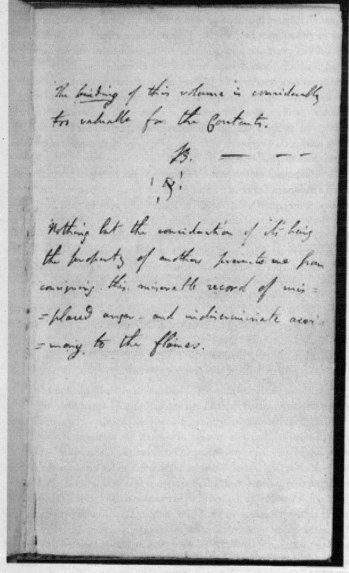

Remorseful inscription by Byron in the front of the 1811 edition of his satire
English Bards and Scotch Reviewers

English Bards was an almost manic act of courage in which Byron took on the entire British literary establishment. He declared it as his object 'not to prove that I can write well, but, *if possible*, to make others write better'. The tone is one of unremitting ridicule, remarkable even in that remorseless age of personal vindictiveness. Byron's sense of the grotesque in human nature has its counterpart in James Gillray's political cartoons, emphasising the physique and personal foibles of his victims, puncturing their pretensions and moral dignity. Although some of Byron's targets have now lapsed into obscurity the poem is still, at its best, extremely funny, not least when he attacks Wordsworth and Coleridge, the poets with whom, as leading protagonists of Romanticism, Byron is now inevitably parcelled in histories of English literature. His derision of the 'ballad-monger' Robert Southey, soon to be appointed Poet Laureate, fuelled a lifelong antagonism.

There is a compelling sense of immediacy in the poem, as Byron added impulsively what was uppermost in his mind. A grief-stricken reference to his friend, the 9th Viscount Falkland, who died of wounds received in a duel at Golders Green after a drunken quarrel, overflows into a footnote:

'On Sunday night I beheld him presiding at his own table, in all the honest pride of hospitality; on Wednesday morning, at three o'clock, I saw stretched before me all that remained of courage, feeling, and a host of passions.'

Byron cut a lock of hair from the corpse, a wan memento that is still in the collection of his relics. He made the pertinent comment in the footnote that if Falkland had died equally bravely on the deck of the frigate to which he had just been appointed he would have been acclaimed a national hero.

Byron's angry defence, in *English Bards*, of the traditional literary values of Dryden, Pope and such contemporary poets as Thomas Campbell and Samuel Rogers against fashionable hacks and ill-equipped reviewers, brought him his first glimmerings of serious success. In spite of the volume's anonymity, the secret of its authorship was soon out. Hatchard's, the Piccadilly bookseller, confessed to Byron that 'notwithstanding our precautions, you are pretty generally known to be the author.' The poem overwhelmed his Southwell admirer Mrs Pigot, who found in it 'all the fire of ancient genius'. It was praised in the more worldly setting of a dinner party in Kensington attended by the Princess of Wales whose lady-in-waiting Lady Charlotte Bury reported in her journal that the gathered company 'declared they were surprised it had not made more noise, as it was the cleverest thing ever was written. They added that it was wonderful it should be so, because his "Hours of Idleness" was remarkably weak and poor.'

The poem won the good opinion of William Gifford, one of the few critics Byron then respected. Within a few weeks the first edition of 1,000 had sold out and the publisher, James Cawthorn, was preparing a second edition, this time under Byron's name. More insults were piled on, a parting salvo. By the time *English Bards* had hit its targets, Byron calculated he would be beyond the Bosphorus.

It is hard to keep track of Byron's fluctuating travel plans. There is a strong pattern in his life of journeys planned and then postponed, almost as if the planning were a substitute for action, with travelling companions left stranded in his wake. As early as summer 1805 he had intended making a tour of the Highlands and the Hebrides with a party of his friends 'engaged for the purpose'. The following year, waiting to leave Cambridge, he envisaged taking a long journey with a tutor through Germany and Russia, visiting the Courts of Berlin, Vienna and St Petersburg. In 1807 he was once again all set to see the Highlands and, attracted by the unpredictable drama of the volcano, travel on to Iceland 'to peep at Hecla'. Only two months later Byron was announcing his intention of going to sea for four or five months with his cousin Captain George Edmund Byron Bettesworth, one of the famous seafaring Byrons, who commanded the *Tartar*, 'finest frigate in the navy', and who had in his possession a letter from Lord Nelson attesting that Bettesworth was the only officer in the British navy who had more wounds than Nelson himself. Byron planned to sail with Bettesworth to the Mediterranean, or to the West Indies, 'or to the Devil'. This plan to 'look at a naval life' had proved abortive too.

By 1808 his travel plans went far beyond the conventional Grand Tour through France and Italy taken by young English aristocrats, a route Byron dismissed as 'the common *Turnpike* of coxcombs & *virtuosos*'. The war in any case made journeying through France impossible. Byron was now attracted by the prospect of Greece and Turkey, countries which he felt 'a singular propensity to investigate' partly, if not mainly, because homosexual relations in the East had none of the stigma they bore in his own country. By October 1808 his plans were focused upon Persia. In November he had changed his destination to India, 'if nothing particularly obstructive occurs'.

On 8 April 1809 he had actually booked a passage on the Malta packet for the following month, paying a deposit and forwarding some of his baggage. There is a sudden note of urgency in Byron's letter to John Hanson written on 16 April: 'If the consequences of my leaving England were ten times as ruinous as you describe, I have no alternative, there are circumstances which render it absolutely indispensable, and quit the country I must immediately.' Why this sudden panic? Byron makes it clear that the reason was not simply financial desperation, clamorous as his debtors were becoming. He returns to the subject in a later letter: 'I never will live in England if I can avoid it, *why* must remain a secret.'

The secret is still a secret. Byron's defensive shiftiness suggests some sort of homosexual threat which has encouraged the convenient explanation that he was escaping a burgeoning scandal involving John Edleston. This is, in my view, based on a misreading of an entry for 6 June 1810 in Hobhouse's manuscript diary, now in the British Library. The confusion is one of orthography. The phrase that twentieth-century interpreters seized on – 'the *Edleston* accused of indecency' – is in fact a less sensational reference to Hobhouse's recently published book of poetry, *Miscellany (Imitations and Translations)*, 'the *collection* accused of indecency'. Byron would have been amused.

Now that his journey was at last becoming a reality, he assembled a party of his friends at Newstead. He travelled down from London with Charles Skinner Matthews, 'talking all the way incessantly upon one single topic': no doubt their shared interest in Horatian affairs. At the Abbey, Byron, Matthews, Hobhouse, James Wedderburn Webster and imported Newstead neighbours all dressed up in monks' clothes ordered from a masquerade warehouse and sat up through the night in the sepulchral gloom quaffing burgundy, claret and champagne out of Byron's skull cup and addressing him as 'Abbot'. They went careering round the house in their 'conventual garments'. Matthews hid himself in a stone coffin in the Long Gallery, rising up in his cowl to startle Hobhouse in the night. Legend later inflated these cavortings into orgies on a par with Sir Francis Dashwood's at West Wycombe, an impression reinforced by Byron's own descriptions in *Childe Harold* of singing, smiling 'Paphian girls' leading the monks astray. Hobhouse later agreed that there had been a lot of drinking but denied the debauchery.

Byron had been gradually gravitating back to Harrow. With a characteristic reversal of emotions his relations with Henry Drury, Dr Drury's son and Byron's one-time housemaster, had now changed to warm and confidential friendship. After Henry Drury's marriage, in December 1808, to Anne Caroline Tayler whose sister was later to marry Byron's friend Francis Hodgson, Drury's house became a more welcoming place. Byron was present at two Harrow Speech Days in summer 1809, before his departure for the East. The senior boys had been reading *English Bards and Scotch Reviewers*. Byron had already become a Harrow hero. Drury jovially blamed the influence of his incendiary poetry for an outbreak of rebelliousness among the boys. Ned Long's younger brother Henry was picked out as Byron's companion on these nostalgic visits to the school. Byron was still adept at tipping his small favourites: on parting after a visit to Byron at a hotel in Albemarle Street, so Long later remembered, 'Lord Byron in shaking my hand very cordially, left in it a piece of crumpled paper, which I being totally unversed in these matters was very nearly letting drop, but I looked at it as we were going down the stairs.' The piece of crumpled paper was a £5 banknote. On another occasion, on a visit by Byron to Harrow, five golden guineas were dropped surreptitiously into the boy's hand.

In a mood of nostalgia, Byron now commissioned a small series of portraits of the boys who were his Theban band at Harrow, to be exchanged for portraits of himself. As he wrote to William Harness on 18 March, 'I am collecting the pictures of my most intimate Schoolfellows, I have already a few, and shall want yours or my cabinet will be incomplete.' Dallas noticed these miniatures, 'by capital painters . . . elegantly framed, and surmounted by their respective coronets', sentimentally assembled in Byron's London rooms. With departure imminent, he was more than ever sensitive, distraught because Lord Clare, the day before Byron left London, went out with his mother to the milliner's, too preoccupied to take proper leave of him.

The Byron portrait of this period most resonant with meaning is of course George Sanders' *Byron and Robert Rushton*, intended as a parting present for his mother. The late delivery of the Sanders portrait was to form a plaintive theme in Byron's letters home. The mood of pent-up anticipation in the painting, young man standing on the seashore, arm outstretched and necktie flying, fixes Byron in his persona of Romantic wanderer, and so the portrait was seen, in its many engraved versions, throughout the nineteenth century.

But to Byron's contemporaries the depiction had other, still more powerful connotations. The young man was the potential naval hero, in the pattern of his grandfather Captain John Byron, 'Foulweather Jack', explorer of the Patagonian shores. Byron's stance is also visibly that of a young Nelson: the pose in the portrait, self-confident adventurer with admiring boy attendant, is strikingly parallel to that in Guy Head's celebratory painting *Nelson Receiving the French Colours at the Battle of the Nile*. Byron admired Nelson: '*Nelson* was a hero,' he wrote later. Compared with Nelson, Wellington was 'a mere Corporal'. Sanders' magnificent portrait sets up Byron as incipient world-warrior. The comparison not only with Nelson but still more with Napoleon is already in the air.

When the painting eventually reached his mother she remarked: 'the countenance is *angelic* and the finest I ever saw and it is very like.' Certainly it expresses Byron's mood of mixed excitement and defiance in summer 1809: 'the world is all before me, and I leave England without regret.'

8

Mediterranean Travels
1809

Byron and Hobhouse, his companion on his travels, were given a sumptuous send-off from London by Charles Skinner Matthews, 'a most splendid entertainment' to which they did 'ample justice'. Byron left a trail of loans behind him, including £6,000 pledged by Scrope Davies at the usurers on his friend's behalf. They arrived in the Cornish port of Falmouth by 21 June 1809, lodging at Wynn's Hotel. Now in Cornwall, Byron felt he was already in a foreign country. Falmouth was a place of wonder where the young male and female inhabitants struck him as 'remarkably handsome . . . The Claret is good, and Quakers plentiful, so are Herrings salt & fresh.' He notices how Falmouth oysters have a taste of copper, given them by the metallic soil of mining country; how the garrison fort off St Mawes is commanded by 'an able-bodied man of eighty years old'. He watches with fascination the public flogging through the Falmouth streets of a woman who had stolen a cockerel and poured scorn on the authorities: 'she was much whipped but exceeding impenitent.'

Removed from his anxieties and responsibilities, a wave of joy came over him. From his letters one can sense his inhibitions falling away. He tells Henry Drury, in the new tone of jocular intimacy with which he addresses his former Harrow housemaster, that he intends to add a chapter 'on the state of morals' to the record of their travels which Hobhouse planned to write, 'and a further treatise on the same to be entitled "Sodomy simplified or Paederasty proved to be praiseworthy from ancient authors and modern practice"'. He adds a sentence about Hobhouse, whose sexual diffidence in comparison with Byron's voracious carnality was a running joke amongst their friends: 'Hobhouse further hopes to indemnify himself in Turkey for a life of exemplary chastity at home by letting out his "fair bodye" to the whole Divan.'

This mood of Eastern promise becomes even more explicit in a letter from Falmouth to Charles Skinner Matthews, started by Hobhouse and continued by Byron:

'My dear Mathieu – I take up the pen which our friend has for a moment laid down merely to express a vain wish that you were with us in this delectable region, as I do not think Georgia itself can emulate in capabilities or incitements to the "Plen. and optabil. – Coit" the port of Falmouth & parts adjacent. – We are surrounded by Hyacinths & other flowers of the most fragrant nature, & I have some intention of culling a handsome Bouquet.'

The code phrase 'Plen. and optabil. – Coit', used by Byron again in later letters, is a corruption of the phrase in Petronius' *Satyricon*, 'coitum plenum et optabilem' – as much full intercourse as one could wish for. The context in Petronius is that of overcoming an uninitiated boy's reluctance. Byron's use of the word 'Hyacinth' refers to the beautiful Laconian youth loved by Apollo who, killed accidentally in a game of quoits, was changed into a flower. We are in the punning, teasing sexual language of botany. 'One specimen I shall certainly carry off, but of this hereafter. – Adieu Mathieu!' From Athens Byron later writes of 'L'Abbe Hyacinth at Falmouth', apparently the boy he made a conquest of, comparing l'Abbé Hyacinth's inefficiency at swimming with that of the Italian boy companion he had by then acquired.

Matthews responded with enthusiasm to Byron's news from Falmouth, writing revealingly to Hobhouse: 'if he "can never love but one" I presume he means not more than one at a time, as I take him to be a pretty general lover. At least in that *quarter of the world* which he has selected for his erotic [*sic*]. A passage in his part of the letter from Falmouth raised my curiosity & expectation considerably.' In a letter to Byron, Matthews sent further coded messages of encouragement:

'If you should find anything remarkable in the botanical line, pray send me word of it, who take an extreme interest in your anthology; and specify the class and if possible the name of each production . . . as grand founder and arch-Patriarch of the Methode I give your undertaking my benediction, and wish you, Byron of Byzantium, and you, Cam of Constantinople, jointly and severally, all the success which in your Methodistical fantasies, you can wish yourselves.'

Here again the reference to Hobhouse is ironic. Although an interested observer of his friends' Methodistical pursuits there is no evidence of Hobhouse's participation; his journals merely bear record of frequent recourse to female whores.

Besides Hobhouse, Byron's entourage in Falmouth consisted of four servants: Old Joe Murray, whose departure from Newstead was viewed by Byron's mother, now in charge there, with some relief; Friese, a German servant with experience of Persia, recommended by Byron's new ally Dr Butler of Harrow; William Fletcher, the valet, who left his wife Sally and two small boys at Newstead; Robert Rushton, the page. The two latter had been out of favour with their master after an escapade in which Fletcher had taken Rushton with him to a London prostitute. The valet was reprimanded both for committing adultery and for 'depraving the mind of an innocent stripling'. There is an undercurrent of proprietorial jealousy. Fletcher was threatened with dismissal and only reinstated just in time to sail.

The original plan to take the Malta packet was abandoned when the ship for Malta was delayed for several weeks. Instead they decided to sail to '"that there *Portingale*"', as Byron's Nottinghamshire servants called it, taking the *Princess Elizabeth* to Lisbon. There were eighteen passengers, including Byron's party: two officers' wives, three children, two waiting maids, two army subalterns going to join the British troops in Portugal, three Portuguese. The ship was commanded by a 'gallant' Captain Kidd. As they were departing on 2 July 1809 Byron sent some verses to their old friend Francis Hodgson. His excitement is almost tangible:

> 'Huzza! Hodgson, we are going,
>   Our embargo's off at last,
> Favourable Breezes blowing
>   Bend the canvass o'er the mast . . .
> Fletcher, Murray, Bob, where are you?
>   Stretched along the deck like logs.
> Bear a hand – you jolly tar you!
>   Here's a rope's end for the dogs.
> Hobhouse muttering fearful curses
>   As the hatchway down he rolls,
> Now his breakfast, now his verses
>   Vomits forth and damns our souls.'

The presence of Rushton was also, more privately and tenderly, recorded in lines about Byron's 'guilty henchman page' written for and afterwards censored from *Childe Harold*:

> 'Him and one yeoman only did he take
> To travel Eastward to a far countree
> And though the boy was grieved to leave the lake

On whose fair banks he grew from Infancy
Eftsoons his little heart beat merrily
With hope of foreign nations to behold
And many things right marvellous to see.'

The expectant travellers arrived at the mouth of the Tagus after a journey of four and a half days.

Byron was to be away from England for two years. Hobhouse was with him for the first year, returning home from Greece in July 1810. For the time they were together it is Hobhouse who provides the factual details of their travels. Hobhouse too was a rising literary figure, though he was never to approximate the fame of Byron, a disparity that sometimes led to tensions between them. He intended to write a travel book on his return, the book that became *A Journey through Albania*, and Byron slyly noted the 'wordy preparations' for this task, the '100 pens two gallons Japan Ink and several vols best blank' paper for recording his impressions. Against Hobhouse's conscientious narrative Byron's letters stand in brilliant counterpoint. He begins to see the uses of the letter as performance, an act he would perfect in Venice later on.

He writes from Lisbon to Hodgson, ecstatically childish:

'I am very happy here, because I loves oranges, and talk bad Latin to the monks, who understand it, as it is like their own, – and I goes into society (with my pocket pistols), and I swims in the Tagus all across at once, and I rides on an ass or a mule, and swears Portuguese, and have got a diarrhoea and bites from the mosquitoes. But what of that? Comfort must not be expected by folks that go a-pleasuring.'

We are dependent for our text of this letter on Tom Moore, notorious for the extent of his deletions of words he felt the public should not be exposed to. In its printed version this passage peters out in asterisks.

Travel in Europe was extremely problematic at this period of the Napoleonic wars. Had Byron and Hobhouse stuck to their original plan of sailing to the East via Malta they would have been less aware of the movements of the warring armies. The British navy had dominated the Mediterranean sea since Nelson's victories at Aboukir Bay, and then Trafalgar. But Byron and his party arrived to find Portugal and Spain in the throes of the Peninsular War. The French invasion of 1807 had been followed by fighting from the Spanish resistance and the arrival of a British Expeditionary Force. Only three months earlier, in April 1809, Sir Arthur Wellesley (soon to be the Duke of Wellington) had arrived in Lisbon to take command and, in May, had defeated the French at Oporto. The fighting was now moving eastwards into Spain. The atmosphere of activity and danger was part of the attraction for the young men.

The Lisbon they arrived at was a place of filth and uproar. A hundred and fifty British transport ships were packed into the harbour. They watched a review of British troops commanded by General Crauford on 10 July. Sir Arthur Wellesley was already on the Spanish frontier at the head of the British army, and as Byron wrote to Hanson, 'a battle is daily expected'. This was the battle of Talavera, fought on 27 and 28 July, in which Wellesley defeated the French Marshal Victor. Marauders thronged the town, hence Byron's pocket pistols. He and Hobhouse were threatened by four ruffians who surrounded their carriage on the way to the Rua dos Condes theatre, whose performances consisted mainly of Iberian dances of extreme lasciviousness.

They chose the least squalid of Lisbon's insalubrious hotels, the Buenos Ayres, kept by an Englishman called Barnewell, and frequented by British visitors. Hobhouse assiduously noted the unprepossessing sights in a city he judged to be a hundred years behind that of the English in its level of civilisation: a man sitting in a doorway in the street extracting lice and fleas from his clothes and cracking them in dozens on the steps, three or four monks indecently assaulting a woman in a church, while another woman knelt in prayer. Byron found enormous pleasure in the scene, even as they paddled through the human excrement heaped up along the pavements of the stinking city. The great thing about Lisbon was that it was abroad.

From Lisbon they made an expedition out to Cintra, a village set in a mountain range some fifteen miles north of the city. Byron was so struck by it he judged it 'perhaps in every respect the most delightful in Europe': this in what was only his first week on the continent. He responded to Cintra's luxuriant combination of natural and artificial beauty: 'Palaces and gardens rising in the midst of rocks, cataracts, and precipices, convents on stupendous heights'. He describes it as uniting the wildness of the Western Highlands with the lusher greenery of somewhere he had never been, the South of France. There is a dreamlike quality in Byron's writing of his travels as the real scenes before him merge with scenes imagined, scenes already in his mind from his reading, his immersion in the history of place. His description of the landscape of Cintra in *Childe Harold* – 'The horrid crags, by toppling convent crown'd' – is quintessential Byron, Romantic landscape glorified and, in its exaggeration, subtly undermined.

The place in Cintra with the strongest resonance for Byron was the overgrown garden and deserted house of Montserrate, once the place of exile of

William Beckford, who was still renowned there as the English sodomite. By a strange coincidence Byron had changed horses on his journey down to Falmouth only the month before at the inn on Hartford Bridge where 'the great Apostle of Paederasty Beckford!' had been staying for the night. He told Hodgson excitedly: 'we tried in vain to see the Martyr of prejudice, but could not.' Even Byron had been startled by the effrontery with which Beckford, already the subject of so much scandal, travelled with his younger lover William, Viscount Courtenay, following him only a little way behind. Byron already identified himself with Beckford's history and the sight of Montserrate started fresh ruminations on English prejudice and the ruin of great men:

> 'Unhappy Vathek! in an evil hour
> Gainst Nature's voice seduced to deed accurst,
> Once Fortune's minion, now thou feel'st her Power!
> Wrath's vials on thy lofty head have burst,
> In wit, in genius, as in wealth the first
> How wondrous bright thy blooming morn arose
> But thou wert smitten with unhallowed thirst
> Of nameless crime, and thy sad day must close
> To scorn, and Solitude unsought – the worst of woes.'

These lines were cancelled from the published version of *Childe Harold* and replaced by a much more anodyne lament.

Cintra had also prompted Byron's sardonic comment – lines which again were deleted from *Childe Harold* – on the so-called Convention of Cintra negotiated in 1808 between the then British commander Sir Hew Dalrymple and the French General Junot, allowing the French to withdraw from Portugal with their arms and artillery intact. The agreement had not actually been signed in Cintra, as Byron imagined, but at Torres Vedras: it was later despatched from Cintra. His lines on the treaty, in which the British reneged on their obligations to the Portuguese, show Byron in ferociously anti-governmental mode.

On these European journeys we see the early signs of Byron's apotheosis as a public figure. Meeting him in Lisbon John William Ward, later 1st Earl of Dudley and Ward and Foreign Minister in Canning's administration, identified him as 'a person of no common mind', though this did not prevent him from overcharging Byron grossly for some English saddles. Byron, to his chagrin, was always to retain a streak of gullibility. Byron's swimming of the Tagus, from the south bank to the north at the fort of Belém in just two hours, was a public demonstration of prowess, first of his famous series of European swims. Hobhouse maintained that this crossing, made in windy weather with a tide and counter-current, was more dangerous than his later heroic swim across the Hellespont.

After two weeks in Lisbon they set off on horseback to Seville and Cadiz, riding at a rate of seventy miles a day in steamily hot weather. He and Hobhouse wore English regimental uniform, claiming this to be the safest way to travel through the war-torn border countryside of Portugal and Spain. Byron appreciated the kudos that it gave him, reporting to his mother that 'an English nobleman in an English uniform is a very respectable personage in Spain at present'. They were made constantly aware that they were travelling in a war zone. At the fortified Spanish frontier town of Elvas they were requested to present their passports to the governor, and there were further passport checks en route, one made by an official unable to read. They met a troop of two thousand well-equipped Spanish patriot soldiers and fended off an attempt by a government official to requisition their horses. On the road through the Sierra Morena they registered the large batteries stationed on the hills waiting to repel a French attack. Byron describes these defences in *Childe Harold*:

> 'At every turn Morena's dusky height
> Sustains aloft the battery's iron load.'

Near Seville they overtook French prisoners and a spy being taken to the city to be hanged.

Seville's population had swollen from 70,000 to 100,000 now that the Grand Junta, the provisional Spanish government allied with the British against Napoleon's forces, had been established there. After Lisbon it seemed a lovely city, clean and tranquil, with its narrow streets and houses built around square courtyards over which, in sunny weather, canvas awnings would be stretched. Byron and Hobhouse, on the recommendation of the British Consul, lodged with two unmarried Spanish ladies, Donna Josepha Beltram and her younger sister. To their surprise all four slept in one room.

Donna Josepha, a fine figure of a woman who claimed to be engaged to an officer in the Spanish army, made advances to Byron. He boasted to his mother, 'The eldest honoured your *unworthy* son with very particular attention, embracing him with great tenderness at parting (I was there but 3 days).' The Donna reproached him for not having accepted her suggestion that he should join her in bed at two o'clock that morning. 'Adio tu hermoso! me gusto mucho,' she said in parting: 'Adieu you pretty fellow you please me much.' Donna Josepha then cut off a lock of Byron's hair and gave him in exchange a tress of her own hair about three feet in length. He sent this trophy to his mother. It is now in the collection at John Murray, thick, glossy, very springy, of a rich dark brown. Later, in Venice, Byron wrote a prose story about a young Andalusian nobleman whose lover, Donna Josepha, bears his son and continues to pursue him. Moore printed an extract from this story in his *Life*. Hobhouse noted in his copy that the tale was based upon Byron's own experiences.

The phenomenon of women throwing themselves at Byron was repeated at Cadiz, where he was taken to the opera by Admiral José de Cordova, veteran of the Spanish defeat by the British navy in the battle of St Vincent a decade before. Byron found the Admiral's daughter 'very pretty in the Spanish style', with the appealing national attributes of 'dark languishing eyes, *clear* olive complexions, and forms more graceful in motion than can be conceived by an Englishman used to the drowsy listless air of his countrywomen'. Signorita Cordova beckoned Byron to come and sit beside her in the box, displacing an old woman, an aunt or duenna. He would always love the way in which boxes at the theatre set up their own rival performances, becoming small-scale private stages of intrigue. Hobhouse made a grumpy note in his diary about Byron's propensity to fall in love at short notice. He had taken himself off to the whorehouse in defence.

After their 'gentle Gallop of four hundred miles without intermission' from Lisbon they reached the port of Cadiz on 29 July. The next day, at Puerto Santa Maria across the bay, they watched a bullfight which aroused mixed emotions in Byron: excitement at the drama, horror at the torments of the toreador's dying horse. The Englishmen went on to the Seraglio, a music-hall brothel in Cadiz, to recover. On 1 August they were woken by the cannon firing in celebration of the victory at Talavera and the landing at Cadiz of Wellesley's brother, Richard Colley, Marquis of Wellesley, newly appointed British ambassador to the Spanish junta. Victorious crowds drew his carriage through the streets of Cadiz. The next day Hobhouse and Byron dined on board the *Atlas*, a warship anchored in Cadiz harbour, with Admiral Purvis who arranged their passage onwards to Gibraltar in the frigate *Hyperion*. At all stages their travels in Europe were facilitated by a network of highly placed English acquaintances.

Passing Cape Trafalgar and glimpsing the coast of Africa, they landed in Gibraltar on 4 August 1809. The town appeared to them dirty and detestable; they set up at the bug-infested Three Anchors, alias the British Hotel. Byron's servants had sailed round from Lisbon to meet them. But Byron by now had decided to send Old Joe Murray and Robert Rushton back to England, Joe because of old age and his page for other reasons: 'I have sent Rushton home', he told John Hanson, 'because Turkey is in too dangerous a state for boys to enter', providing the further explanation for his mother: 'you *know boys* are not *safe* amongst the Turks.'

He told his mother to treat Robert with special kindness 'as he is my great favourite', and asked her to explain the reasons for his return to Rushton's father 'who may otherwise think he has behaved ill'. Already, in the will drawn up at his departure, he had left Rushton £25 per annum, so that if he died the boy would be independent. Now, paternalistically, he allocated an immediate £25 a year for Rushton's education back in England. The page was pathetically unwilling to leave his master. It seems that the German servant Friese departed at this point too.

Byron was observed in Gibraltar by John Galt, a Scotsman – failed commercial entrepreneur turned literary hack whose novel *The Annals of the Parish* was later to bring him popular success. He was now on a doubtful mission investigating ways of circumventing Napoleon's embargo on the import to Europe of British goods. Galt's *Life of Lord Byron*, published in 1830, is long-winded and often inaccurate. But his remembered sightings of Byron in these early stages of his European travels have a certain bloom of authenticity. Galt was reading in the military garrison library, having retreated there from the blaze of a hot day:

'while sitting there, a young man came in and seated himself opposite me at the table. Something in his appearance attracted my attention. His dress indicated a Londoner of some fashion, partly by its neatness and simplicity, with just so much of a peculiarity of style as served to show, that although he belonged to the order of metropolitan beaux, he was not altogether a common one . . . His physiognomy was prepossessing and intelligent, but ever and anon his brows lowered and gathered; a habit, as I then thought, with a degree of affectation in it, probably assumed for picturesque effect and energetic expression; but which I afterwards discovered was undoubtedly the occasional scowl of some unpleasant reminiscence: it was certainly disagreeable – forbidding – but the general cast of his features was impressed with elegance and character.'

Galt sailed on the ship, the *Townshend* packet, that took Byron to Sardinia. He observed Byron closely on that journey: supervising the embarkation of his luggage with aristocratic impatience; leaning on the rail of the ship in the twilight, ostentatiously apart from the other passengers and gazing out to sea; then suddenly becoming sociable and playful, supplying the pistols for shooting at bottles, at which Byron himself proved the best shot, 'but not very preeminently so'. Once they entered calm waters a small jolly-boat was lowered, from which Byron and the captain caught two turtles. A shark was also caught, part of which was eaten for breakfast, without enthusiasm.

When the ship reached Cagliari on the southern tip of Sardinia Byron and the ship's captain rode out into the country. Sardinia, like Malta, had avoided direct involvement in the wars, thanks to the British navy's domination of the Mediterranean. Byron reported nothing of interest except three heads nailed to a gallows. The social life of the fortified port town was more enticing. Byron had had 'a most superb uniform as a court dress' made for him in Gibraltar at a cost of fifty guineas in the expectation of being presented to King Vittorio Emanuele I of Sardinia. Hobhouse too wore his 'best suit of red' when they dined with the British Minister, Mr Hill. The party proceeded to the theatre where Hill showed off his young compatriot to the audience, including the assembled royal family, sitting with Byron in a highly visible box *à deux*. At the end of the evening Byron made an effusive speech of thanks to the minister, at which Hobhouse jeered. On the way back to their lodgings Byron, 'on account of his lameness, and the roughness of the pavement', took hold of John Galt's arm, asking for reassurance that his thanks had been appropriate. When teased or challenged, his confidence could completely disappear.

On 20 August they embarked for Malta, still in the *Townshend* packet, sailing past the southern coast of Sicily. Byron, 'overflowing with glee and sparkling with quaint sentences', joined the other travellers in uncorking and drinking some very fine champagne. From the coast they saw on the hill the columns of the ancient temple city of Agrigento. Byron and Hobhouse, by this time getting on the nerves of the other passengers, were sent off together in a smaller boat to deliver the post to the Captain of Port, a solitary figure living in a large desolate house on the coast. He received them dressed in his official uniform of sky-blue coat and and gold epaulettes. After this diversion they sailed back to the packet.

By noon on 31 August they were approaching Malta harbour, described by Hobhouse as 'very grand & surpassing every conception of that place'. Byron had sent a message to the Governor, Sir Alexander Ball, to give him notice that he would be arriving. Byron and Hobhouse stayed on board while the others went ashore, apparently expecting a salute of welcome from the guns of the garrison. In this they were disappointed, and they made a rather ignominious entrance to the city late that afternoon.

Eventually the Governor received them with the attentiveness Byron felt his due, arranging for them to lodge in a fine house in Strada di Forni in Valetta belonging to a Dr Moncrieff. They were quickly absorbed into the military and merchant community in Malta, invited out to gossipy dinners, initiated into eating quail and 'a curious fish found in a shell', resembling a mussel enclosed in a rock. They went to bathe 'in a well constructed bath': on their travels Byron's attention to cleanliness was obsessive, Hobhouse's much less so. They attended the opera, and Byron bought an Arabic grammar for a dollar, in preparation for his journeys further east. He found a tutor in Arabic to give him lessons. But Byron was susceptible to distraction. He recognised this fallible pattern to his life, recollecting wryly, 'I set in zealously for the Armenian and Arabic – but I fell in love with some absurd womankind both times before I had overcome the characters and at Malta & Venice left the profitable Orientalists – for – for – (no matter what –)'

The 'absurd womankind' in Malta was 'la Celebre Mrs Spencer Smith', as Hobhouse designated her, 'a tall pretty woman, with fat arms, well made'. Constance Spencer Smith, at twenty-four, was already notorious in diplomatic circles. She was the daughter of Baron Herbert, Austrian Ambassador at Constantinople, and wife of the British Minister at Stuttgart. In 1806 she had been arrested by the Napoleonic government in Venice and, on the way to prison at Valenciennes, she was abducted by an admiring Sicilian nobleman, the Marquis de Salvo, from an inn in Brescia, in a dramatic rescue involving disguises, elongated ladders and boats hired to cross Lake Garda. As Byron summarised it: 'her life has been from commencement so fertile in remarkable incidents, that in a romance they would appear improbable.'

Constance was now in Malta en route to join her husband, John Spencer Smith, in England. Byron was introduced to her at the theatre and was immediately intrigued. He felt the allure of her celebrity. Maybe his interest was quickened by the fact that she had made her midnight escape from the inn wearing male clothes. He was certainly impressed by the fact that Napoleon was 'so incensed against her' that her life would be in danger if she were recaptured. He told his mother that since meeting this 'very extraordinary woman' they had been almost inseparable. 'I have found her very pretty, very accomplished, and extremely eccentric.' It is interesting that several of the women Byron was to be involved with stand out as unconventional for their period.

He went through all the motions of *grande passion* for 'Calypso', as he refers to her in stanzas in *Childe Harold*. She is also the addressee of his yearning 'Lines to Florence'. In 1812 Byron was to give an account to Lady Melbourne of the '*everlasting* passion' for Mrs Spencer Smith which seized him in the Mediterranean in 1809 and how they were on the brink of an elopement, only prevented when their destination, the Friuli mountains north of Venice, were suddenly discovered to be under French control.

In 1821, in Ravenna, Byron was still reminiscing about Mrs Spencer Smith in his journal: 'I was once *so desperately* in love with a German woman, Constance.' But John Galt, astute spectator, judged Byron's Malta passion to have been an affectation, in reality 'Platonic'. This is partly borne out by a letter from Byron written the next year, referring to a duel he had narrowly escaped fighting over Mrs Spencer Smith's honour with an insolent English aide-de-camp. He told his friend Scrope Davies: 'When I was in Malta last – I fell in love with a married woman, and challenged an officer, but the lady was chaste, and the gentleman explanatory, and thus I broke no commandments.' Hobhouse too denied that Byron had been in love with Constance: 'the notion of his being in love was but a dream.' Certainly the woman's passion long outlasted Byron's, a pattern frequently repeated in his history.

They were now in the final phase of their planned journey to the East. On the recommendation of the Governor of Malta, Hobhouse organised their passage on the British warship *Spider* which was escorting a convoy of British merchant ships to Prevesa. The ship was routed via the Greek city of Patras, on the northern tip of the Peloponnese. The *Spider*, commanded by Captain Oliver, sailed in convoy with fifty or so smaller ships, depicted by Byron in *Childe Harold* as 'spread like wild swans in their flight'. On the morning of 23 September 1809, as they travelled up the channel between Cephalonia and Zante (now Zakynthos), Byron and Hobhouse had their first sight of the Ancient Greece of their imagination.

It was an eventful journey. They were in territory of great political complexity. The Ionian Isles were then in the possession of the French, though imminently to be taken over by the British. Britain was in a state of hostility with Russia, as was the Turkish Ottoman Empire. The Ottoman Turks were in control of Greece, an oppressive domination which had been in place since the fall of Constantinople, in 1453. Warships of many nations were in the area. Near the Gulf of Corinth the *Spider* chased and captured a small boat laden with currants and fitted her out as a privateer. Byron, Hobhouse, the surgeon, the midshipman and ten sailors set off in this makeshift gunboat, hoisting the British flag, pursuing and boarding two other boats, then capturing an aggressive Turkish brig of seventy tons, which had opened fire on the British vessel, probably mistaking it for a French one. In the ensuing gun battle one of the men was wounded and a bullet passed within an inch of Hobhouse's ear. The *Spider* later captured a boat from French-occupied Ithaca and a second Turkish ship which Byron rummaged, finding nothing but some worthless arms. As described in Hobhouse's diaries these episodes have the feel of young men's irresponsible adventures rather than the serious pursuit of war.

They sailed up the Gulf towards Patras on 26 September with light breezes blowing and dawn breaking over the mountains to the east. As they reached Patras the sun rose and they saw 'the greenest fields and groves rising up the mountain sides'. The minarets glittered in the light. They went ashore briefly.

Byron and Hobhouse spent their first hours on Greek soil shooting pistols in a currant field to the north of Patras. They were 'very much struck' to see Turkish soldiers of the occupying Ottoman forces standing at the landing place with pistols and daggers stuck in their belts. As they sailed back north-west towards Prevesa they passed the town of Missolonghi 'with a curious double shore at the foot of the mountains which rise one above the other as far as the eye can reach'. It is strange to see Byron, as a young man, glimpse the places to be most associated with his memory.

Passing the southern shore of the Isle of Ithaca and, on Lefkadha, the cliff face known as 'Sappho's Leap' they sailed up the west coast of Greece towards Albania and landed at Prevesa on 29 September. Up to now their travels had been relatively tame, made through territory familiar to the British, cosseted by the easy social rituals of early nineteenth-century expatriate life. Albania was a more truly foreign country, remote on account of its mountainous terrain, the reputed 'savage character' of its natives and its eruptive and complicated politics. At the time Byron arrived there Albania, nominally part of the Ottoman Empire, was ruled by the former robber chieftain Ali Pasha, who had created his own despotic fiefdom. After a long series of ruthless coups Ali Pasha was now in control of a vast empire, extending from northern Albania south into Greece and east into Macedonia and Thessaly. His son Veli Pasha was installed in the Peloponnese.

Byron was later to claim that he had seen more of Albania than any other Englishman except for William Leake, the British Resident in Janina, Ali Pasha's capital. This was not completely true, but Byron's incursions into these rugged lands have all the zest of new discovery. On that first morning in Prevesa Byron and Hobhouse, in their scarlet regimental uniforms, walked through a violent shower of rain to the Consul's house where, in rooms furnished with low sofas *à la Turque*, they dined on rice soup containing chicken 'boil'd to rags', highly seasoned mutton, broiled fish, fish roes and fruit, served with 'decent' country wines and a bottle of good port. The privy at the Consul's house caused some consternation, being simply a triangular hole in the floor with a semicircular opening above it cut into a long bench, stretching right across the room. Mystified by this, Byron sat straight down on the edge of the hole in the floor in 'a most distressing posture', with his knees to his nose. Their first impressions of Albania were not encouraging. 'Had the commander of the brig been very pressing, I believe that we should have consented to go back to Patras,' Hobhouse later wrote.

However, they now braced themselves to travel overland to Janina (or Ioannina), making a three-day journey north through wild mountains with ten horses and their weighty baggage: seven trunks, beds and bedding, a canteen, all packed in saddlebags. Janina was a city of romantic beauty with its domes and minarets rising high above a large pellucid lake. But as they neared the city they found, hanging from a tree, an arm torn from the body of a rebellious priest, a sight of savagery that made both Byron and Hobhouse 'a little sick'.

Sir Alexander Ball, the Governor of Malta, had provided an introduction to William Leake. It seems that Leake had alerted Ali Pasha to the young Englishmen's arrival. Ali Pasha himself was not in Janina. He left profuse apologies but had been 'obliged to leave his city to finish a little war'. His army was besieging a local warlord, Ibrahim Pasha, in the castle of Berat further north. He entreated the highly flattered English travellers to follow him and meet him at his residence in Tepeleni, south of Berat; he had meanwhile made arrangements for them to stay in Janina in luxury, at his expense. The city was a mixed community of Greeks and Turks. Hobhouse investigated local sexual customs: 'the unmarried women are never seen, the bridegroom never sees his future wife till he puts on the ring – there are consequently no amours except with married women – and now and then a little contrabande ... This is some excuse for paederasty; which is practised underhand by the Greeks, but openly carried on by the Turks.'

In Janina Byron and Hobhouse were presented to two of Ali Pasha's grandsons, Hussein Bey and Mahmout Pasha, whose precocious chatter and flirtatiousness prompted Byron to describe them to his mother as 'totally unlike our lads'. He was transfixed by these children's 'painted complexions like rouged dowagers, large black eyes & features perfectly regular. They are the prettiest little animals I ever saw.' Hussein Bey, ten-year-old son of Mouchtar Pasha, Ali Pasha's eldest son, showed them around his father's palace, covertly admiring Byron's sword. His slightly older cousin Mahmout, son of Veli Pasha, impressed Byron with his breadth of knowledge by asking whether Hobhouse and he were in the upper or lower House of Parliament: 'It may be doubted if an English boy at that age knows the difference of the Divan from a College of Dervises.' Byron formed a particular rapport with Mahmout, who hoped to see him again: 'we are friends without understanding each other, like many other folks, though from a different cause.'

They rode on north towards Tepeleni and Ali Pasha through worsening weather. In the evening of 11 October, Hobhouse arrived with an advance party at Zitza, a precipitous mountain village. It was dark, the rain was pouring down in torrents. Byron, following with the servants and baggage, was nowhere to be seen. Getting anxious, Hobhouse ordered fires to be lit on the hill above the village and muskets to be fired to show Byron where they were. Hobhouse lay down in his greatcoat, but sleep was impossible with the storm raging, dogs barking, shepherds shouting to each other across the mountainsides.

Shortly after midnight a man arrived, pale, panting, drenched with rain, to tell them that Byron's party had got lost en route, their baggage horses having stumbled on the treacherous ground. Men, carrying pine torches, were sent off with more horses. Byron, with a Greek priest and the servants, had spent much of the night beside a group of Turkish tombstones and a torrent, illuminated dramatically by the lightning flashes. When they finally reached Zitza at three in the morning they had been out in the storm for nine hours.

They got up late the next morning, had breakfast and strolled out into the extraordinary village which, like the goats they had read about in Virgil, seemed to be perched dangerously on the edges of the rock. Now a veteran traveller, Byron acclaimed Zitza as 'in the most beautiful situation (always excepting Cintra in Portugal) I ever beheld'. They visited the monastery on its little green hill, where the Prior sustained them with hand-pressed white wine, walnuts and some coffee. Fletcher complained that the 'benevolent faced clergyman' had been teaching him Greek and kissing him.

After nine days of hard riding through swelling mountain torrents they reached Ali Pasha's palace in Tepeleni at sunset on 19 October. Though the kilts were not identical, the scene reminded Byron of a Highland novel by Walter Scott:

'The Albanians in their dresses (the most magnificent in the world, consisting of a long *white kilt*, gold worked cloak, crimson velvet gold laced jacket & waistcoat, silver mounted pistols & daggers), the Tartars with their high caps, the Turks in their vast pelises and turbans, the soldiers & black slaves with the horses, the former stretched in groupes in an immense open gallery in front of the palace, the latter placed in a kind of cloister below it, two hundred steeds ready caparisoned to move in a moment, couriers entering or passing out with dispatches, the kettle drums beating, boys calling the hour from the minaret of the mosque, altogether, with the singular appearance of the building itself, formed a new & delightful spectacle to a stranger.'

Both Hobhouse and Byron were delighted by the fineness and exoticism of the Eastern clothes. An entry in Hobhouse's diary shows him getting up at ten o'clock and trying on 'Albanian suits', while Byron writes to his mother telling her he has bought some 'very "magnifique"' Albanian dresses, an extravagance at £50 each.

Byron and Hobhouse had been assigned a fine apartment in the palace. They noticed English carpets in the rooms used in winter, whilst the long gallery reminded them of the top storey of an English inn. The day after they arrived they were received by Ali Pasha, Byron having dressed for the occasion 'in a full suit of staff uniform with a very magnificent sabre &c.' The state room was paved with marble, with a fountain in the centre. Scarlet ottomans were placed around the walls. The Vizier, in his late sixties, 'very fat, & not tall, but with a fine face, light blue eyes and a white beard', paid Byron the compliment of receiving him standing, then invited him to sit down on Ali Pasha's right. The polite small talk began with the question of why Byron had left his country at such an early age.

Why was this powerful despot so attentive to Lord Byron? Ali Pasha was a devious, sophisticated potentate, intent on playing his own diplomatic power games with the British and French, as well as with the Turks. He may have imagined that Byron could be useful in his delicate manoeuvres. At this juncture his interests coincided with English policy in the Ionian Isles, which was aimed at dislodging the French. Captain Leake had informed him that Byron came of an important aristocratic family. He may have overestimated his political influence. Besides, to this elderly and self-indulgent tyrant, Byron's person was evidently irresistible.

Hobhouse noted how he looked a little leeringly at Byron, asking how he could have had the heart to leave his mother. Caressingly he told the young man that he could tell he was well born because he had 'small ears, curling hair, & little white hands'. He had observed already the peculiarity of Byron's ears, which had almost no lobes. Ali Pasha was effusive about Byron's looks and clothes and told him to regard him as a father while he was in Turkey. 'Indeed', Byron told his mother, 'he treated me like a child, sending me almonds & sugared sherbet, fruit & sweetmeats 20 times a day. He begged me to visit him often, and at night when he was more at leisure.' That first meeting ended with coffee and Turkish pipes.

Byron saw Ali Pasha three more times. It has been suggested that Ali Pasha made a conquest of Byron. This is unlikely. Byron was not susceptible to older men. But he was certainly responsive to the flattery of such a powerful figure and held by the ferocious strength of will behind Ali Pasha's urbanity of manner: 'he is a remorseless tyrant, guilty of the most horrible cruelties, very brave & so good a general, that they call him the Mahometan Buonaparte.' There was a horrid fascination in Ali's most un-English practice of impaling and then roasting his enemies.

Even in the early weeks of Byron's travels he was referring to them as a pilgrimage. A pilgrim's journey it had now indeed become as he explored both his inner nature and the landscape and history, psychology and politics of other countries in Europe and the East. Captain Leake in Janina was aware of his propensity to turn aside 'from the contemplation of nearer objects and from the conversation of those about him, to gaze with an air *distrait* and dreamy upon the distant mountains'. This impression may have been romanticised by hindsight, but there is evidence that Byron's poetic travelogue *Childe Harold's Pilgrimage* was gestating at this time.

At the end of October, soon after they left Ali Pasha's palace, Hobhouse's journal tell us: 'Byron is all this time engaged in writing a long poem in the Spenserian stanza.' Byron himself gives an official starting date of 31 October, by which time they had returned to Janina. He had now embarked on his own more ambitious counterpart to Hobhouse's journals, a verse narrative written 'amidst the scenes which it attempts to describe'. These scenes are filtered through the tormented sensibility of the young traveller, originally named 'Childe Burun', responsive to yet alienated from his surroundings by some undisclosed and undisclosable wrongdoing. This was to be a pilgrimage of the divided self.

But while Byron was describing his journeys he was also, at Hobhouse's insistence, covering his tracks. In Albania, as regards his records for posterity, there was loss as well as gain. On one of their stops while they were on their travels, a pile of manuscript sheets fell out of Byron's portmanteau. Hearing that this was an account of Byron's early life, presumably including reminiscences of his love for Edleston, the wary Hobhouse persuaded him to burn it. 'For', he warned, 'if any sudden accident occur they will print it, and thus injure your memory.' Later, Byron appears to have regretted this destruction, telling Thomas Moore that the loss of the manuscript had been 'irreparable'.

In early November Byron and Hobhouse were travelling south again, heading towards Greece, with an enlarged entourage. Besides Fletcher and Andreas Zantakis, his Greek interpreter, he now acquired an Albanian servant, Vassily (or Vasi), assigned to him in Tepeleni by Ali Pasha, and a young Muslim, Dervise Tahiri, one of the guard of forty or so Albanian soldiers whom Ali Pasha had directed to accompany Byron and his party to protect them from the robbers in the region. Byron thought highly of his two Albanian servants, who stayed with him throughout his travels in the East.

Fletcher, on the contrary, was turning out to be a burden. He was not a resilient traveller. Ali Pasha had provided an armed galliot to take them by sea from Prevesa to Patras. The crew was incompetent. A storm drove them off course.

'Fletcher yelled after his wife, the Greeks called on all the Saints, the Mussulmen on Alla, the Captain burst into tears & ran below deck telling us to call on God, the sails were split, the mainyard shivered, the wind blowing fresh, the night setting in, & all our chance was to make Corfu, which is in possession of the French, or (as Fletcher *pathetically* termed it) "a *watery* grave".'

Byron did what he could to comfort his valet before wrapping himself up in his Albanian capote and stretching out on deck philosophically to await the worst. In his letters to his mother he turns his grumbling valet, so out of his element and so determinedly unresponsive to the pleasures of the East, into another of his great comic characters, the embodiment of English insularity.

'He has suffered nothing but from *cold*, heat, & vermin which those who lie in cottages & cross mountains in a wild country must undergo, & of which I have equally partaken with himself, but he is not valiant, he is afraid of robbers & tempests.'

Fletcher, like Hobhouse, has his role as Byron's plodding alter ego. The emotional bond between the two of them was strong.

The ship finally managed to anchor on the rocky coast near Parga. They now travelled overland, protected by Ali Pasha's guard as they journeyed some 100 km from Parga to and then through the forest of Akarnania. On 20 November the party was safely in Missolonghi where the British Consul met them, mistaking Byron for a new ambassador and insisting on talking French to him. They were delayed the next day by bad weather. Byron was to see much more of Missolonghi rain. On 22 November they hired a *tribaculo*, a large boat with ten oarsmen, which took them to Patras. From there they travelled east over bad roads along the Gulf of Corinth. On 5 December they could make out, in the distance, a snow-covered Mount Parnassus. On 14 December they crossed to the north coast of the Gulf and reached Salona by midnight. Fletcher subsided with toothache and a headache. Next day they visited Delphi. Their hearts raced to see these ancient sites, so familiar from their knowledge of the classical writers. Hobhouse had been reading Thucydides on the ancient Grecian character 'to see how much the present Albanians and the freer Greeks resemble their forefathers'. They practised some gymnastics and their own modern version of the Olympian games.

On the southern shore near Vostitsa (now Aiyion), Byron had shot a young eagle. It was only wounded and he did his best to save it; 'the eye was so bright; but it pined and died in a few days'. He swore that he would never willingly kill another bird. A week later, riding from Khryso to Delphi, he saw an unusually large flight of eagles in the air: his accounts vary as to whether there were six or twelve. The previous day he had composed the lines to Parnassus which appear in *Childe Harold*:

> 'Oh, thou Parnassus! whom I now survey,
> Not in the phrenzy of a dreamer's eye,
> Nor in the fabled landscape of a lay,
> But soaring snow-clad through thy native sky,
> In the wild pomp of mountain-majesty!'

When he saw the eagles he hoped it was an omen, a sign that his homage was accepted by Apollo, and that he would achieve a poet's name and fame.

He and Hobhouse were no longer in undiscovered country. As they approached Athens they saw evidence of other British enthusiasts for Greece. The British revival of interest in Greek culture dated back to the mid-eighteenth century. The work of the German art historian Johann Joachim Winckelmann, translated into English by the painter and critic Henry Fuseli, spread the appreciation of Greek art, particularly sculpture. Greece especially attracted antiquity-seeking British travellers at a time when much of Europe was inaccessible because of the Napoleonic wars. In a monastery chapel in an olive grove near Delphi Byron and Hobhouse found two names scratched on a pillar: H.P. HOPE 1799 and ABERDEEN 1803. Henry Philip Hope was the younger brother of Thomas Hope, connoisseur of the East and member of the Society of Dilettanti which laid the foundations for the scientific study of Greek archaeology. The old Harrovian connoisseur, the 4th Earl of Aberdeen, was already one of Byron's targets in the satire *English Bards and Scotch Reviewers*. However, Byron and Hobhouse inscribed their names as well.

English enthusiasm for Greek culture resulted in blatant acquisitiveness. When they were in Malta Hobhouse noted in his diary the rumours they had heard that the noted collector Thomas Bruce, 7th Earl of Elgin, Scottish peer and former ambassador to Constantinople, had defaced many fine columns at Athens 'to get at the releivos', the sculptural reliefs. At Orchomenus, the site of an ancient city near Livadia, they found evidence of further depredations by their countrymen. Only a few ancient inscriptional marbles remained in the monastery: Hobhouse's explanation was that 'my Lord Elgin or some Englishman loaded mules with other inscripteae stones' and carried them away.

They were now travelling south-east, heading for Thebes. They stopped at a poor hill village called Mazi. In appalling lodgings Byron was inspired to decapitate a goose, using his sabre, providing the travellers with 'a delicious roast'. They noticed how the women in this desolate area strung their hair with coins, to show prospective suitors the dowry they could offer. Hobhouse and Byron galloped into Thebes on 20 December, through downpours of rain. They were disappointed to find no visible signs of the ancient city, still less any reminders of its former glory. They were now beyond the regions ruled by Ali Pasha, and no longer received preferential treatment. Confronted with the local bureaucracy, they were delayed by a squabble over coach horses and finally set off for Athens on 24 December.

Still travelling south-east, they broke the journey at Skourta, 'a miserable deserted village, where half the houses were shut up', and they spent Christmas Eve 1809 in the worst hovel they had encountered on their travels. The room contained a manger, a seasonal reminder of the nativity of Christ. They were up before daylight for the last phase of their journey towards Athens. Crossing a broad plain, they took a stony path through pine woods rising up the hills, their horses 'tumbling as if by consent one after the other'. From the summit, near Fort Phyle, a spot remote and lonely enough to have appealed to Timon the misanthrope, they had their first distant view of Athens: 'the plain of Athens, Pentelicus, Hymettus, the Ægean, and the Acropolis, burst upon the eye at once; in my opinion, a more glorious prospect than Cintra,' Byron later wrote.

Approaching the town of Chasia (now Fili), half-way point of that day's journey, the route became 'every moment more romantic over steep hills clothed with more noble pine trees'. Passing under the walls of an ancient fortress, they emerged from the wooded landscape on to a huge plain cultivated with vineyards and olive groves. The mosque of a far-off town was tipped with the last rays of the setting sun. Turning the corner of a little hill, they saw the Acropolis before them, now quite close. Riding on for another hour down a straight broad road, they made their entrance through the archway to the city of Athens at half-past eight on Christmas night.

9

Greece and Constantinople
1809–1810

Byron and Hobhouse spent the next ten weeks in Athens. This was Byron's first protracted stay in the country for which he was to feel his closest emotional attachment, his 'dearly beloved Greece', the land of azure skies and incomparable landscapes: ultimate contrast to England's foggy shores.

Athens was then an undistinguished provincial town ruled by a resident Turkish governor, known as the Voivode, appointed by the chief of the Black Eunuchs in Constantinople. The ramshackle houses, mostly huddled to the north of the Acropolis, were surrounded by a ten-foot wall which Hobhouse strode around in forty-seven minutes. Of a population of around ten thousand, Turks and Albanians outnumbered the subjugated Greeks. There was a small foreign colony of a dozen or so families, officials and merchants, in which the French and English mingled on amicable terms.

Byron took lodgings in one of these households, with Madame Tasia Makri, widow of the Greek-born British Vice-Consul in Athens. His sitting room and two bedrooms opened out on to a courtyard fragrant with lemon trees which flavoured the pilaff Madame Makri served to lodgers. A flagpole on which the British flag once fluttered still stood outside the house. Hobhouse stayed in an adjoining house which was connected for easy interchange by a doorway made in the wall. Madame Makri had three beautiful, well-educated daughters, Katinka, Mariana and Teresa, trained to be assiduous to their mother's clients. A later visitor described the trio as 'of middle stature. On the crown of the head of each is a red Albanian skull-cap, with a blue tassel spread out and fastened down like a star.' Their outer robes, edged with fur, hung loose down to the ankles; underneath they wore a muslin bodice, then a striped silk or muslin gown 'with a gore round the swell of the loins, falling in front in graceful negligence'. The ensemble was completed with white stockings and yellow slippers. The youngest, Teresa, only twelve years old but in

Hobhouse's view 'quite "nubilis"', was the Maid of Athens made famous by Byron's poem.

What was Byron's view of Greece and of the Greeks during those early weeks in Athens? His impressions were still relatively raw, compared with the much greater understanding he showed of Greek life and culture when he returned to Athens for a longer period the next year. But his clear-eyed affection and admiration were strong. 'I like the Greeks,' he told Henry Drury, 'who are plausible rascals, with all the Turkish vices without their courage. – However some are brave and all are beautiful, very much resembling the busts of Alcibiades.' The women were not quite so handsome as the men.

Already there are signs of his awareness of the cause of Greek independence from the Turks. On the way to Athens, when he and Hobhouse stopped at Vostitsa on the south side of the Gulf of Corinth, they stayed at the house of the local governor or 'elder', a Greek, Andreas Londos, who was in fact only nineteen years of age. This exuberant boy, easily encouraged to throw off his robes of office and perform feats of gymnastics, bounding across the chairs, was an ardent Greek patriot, in spite of his employment by the Turks. He told stories of the nationalist Velestinlis Rigas, killed by the Turks in 1798 after his attempts to bring about a Greek revolution.

One evening Londos, playing chess with Hobhouse and overhearing the name Rigas, 'jumped suddenly from the sofa, threw over the board, and clasping his hands, repeated the name of the patriot with a thousand passionate exclamations, the tears streaming down his cheeks'. Through Londos Byron came into direct contact with the suppressed emotionalism of the Greek cause, writing his own version of Rigas's famous war song 'Sons of the Greeks, arise!' Years later, when Londos had become one of the leaders of the Greeks in the War of Independence, Byron wrote to him, full of nostalgia for their early meetings: 'Greece has ever been for me, as it must be for all men of any feeling or education, the promised land of valour, of the arts, and of liberty throughout all the ages.'

In Athens Byron and Hobhouse played the grand tourist, exploring the sites round the Acropolis. They saw the Temple of Theseus, near their lodgings in present-day Odos Agias Theklas in Monastiraki. The temple, by then a church, was well preserved, except for some columns displaced by earthquake movement, but the door was pierced full of pistol and gun holes probably by soldiers using it for target practice. They walked out to the hills of the Areopagus, the Pnyx and the Muses, and were able to discern the little hill surmounted by the rock from which Xerxes surveyed his defeat at the battle of Salamis. They viewed the remains of the Odeum, the Theatre of Dionysius, the

Monument of Lysicrates. They saw the sixteen columns, all that remained of the original 150, of the Temple to Olympian Zeus. Finally, after the statutory negotiations involving gifts of tea and sugar to the Turkish officer, the Disdar, in command of the fortress, they ascended to the Acropolis itself.

> 'Sun of the morning rise! approach you here!
> Come – but molest not yon defenceless urn:
> Look on this spot – a nation's sepulchre!
> Abode of gods, where shrines no longer burn.'

The second canto of *Childe Harold* reflects Byron's dismay at the ruination of Athens. He had seen himself the neglected and pillaged ancient buildings of the Propylaea, the Erechtheum and, most melancholy of all, the Parthenon. The temple where Athena's statue had been revered now stood ruined and roofless, dismembered of its columns which lay strewn over the ground. The scene of tragic mutilation led him to sad reflections on the impermanence of even the most admirable human institutions, and the ultimate futility of human speculation. Faced with the ruined Acropolis Byron quotes the words of Socrates, 'All that we know is nothing can be known'.

In these first few weeks in Athens he and Hobhouse rode out on explorations far beyond the city walls, often guided by the erudite French Consul, Louis-François-Sébastien Fauvel, travelling westward to Eleusis, east to Mount Hymettus and Mount Pentelicus, where they saw the marble quarries which provided the stone from which many of Athens' monuments had been built. On one of their rides, to the Piraeus, Hobhouse and Byron were insulted by a 'renegado Spaniard'. When they reported this to the governor the man was bastinadoed with fifty strokes on the feet in the presence of Fletcher; he 'roar'd most abundantly & shit his breeches – the Waiwode continued smoking his pipe most calmly in spite of music & stench'. Hobhouse's comment on this barbarous scene was laconic: 'Whatever I may think of it at home, abroad autocracy has its advantages.'

Byron was at his best, stimulated by new scenes, strange people, outlandish foods. On the shore at Rafti, their Greek servant Demetrios Zografos (or, in Byron's version, 'Demetrius Zograffo') fried fresh fish for them, including a mysterious 'dried fish with 8 legs in rings', known as the 'octopodes', about the size of a small lobster. Hobhouse appreciated his companion's 'quickness of observation and ingenuity of remark', combined with 'that gay good humour which keeps alive the attention under pressure of fatigue, and softens the aspect of every difficulty and danger'. On these travels Byron was all charm. While Hobhouse, more pedantic, pottered around the sites with map and compass, measuring and taking notes, Byron rode about on his mule making broader connections, delightedly aware that these pines, these eagles, these vultures and owls were descended from those Themistocles and Alexander had seen.

At Cape Colonna, which they reached on 23 January 1810, the day after Byron's twenty-second birthday, he registered not only the overwhelming beauty of the Temple of Poseidon (at that time thought to be the Temple of Minerva) on the sea edge overlooking the Aegean isles. He was also aware of this as the supposed scene of Plato's conversations. An added bonus for an Englishman was that Cape Colonna was 'the actual spot' of the disaster described in William Falconer's popular poem *The Shipwreck* of 1762. It is the accumulated layers of meaning that give such depth and splendour to Byron's poetry of liberty.

Next day, he and Hobhouse reached the plain of Marathon, and Byron was once again overwhelmed by the historic reverberations. Marathon had been the place of the Greeks' heroic victory of 490 B C when the Athenian army, commanded by Miltiades, outmanoeuvred the much larger Persian force that threatened to invade them. Years later, in *Don Juan*, with a tinge of irony, he recaptured the intensity of his own response as a young man:

'The mountains look on Marathon –
And Marathon looks on the sea;
And musing there an hour alone,
I dream'd that Greece might still be free.'

In contemplating Greece as a ruined country, a sad relic of its former days, Byron's grief and anger were directed not simply at tyrannous Turks and supine Greeks but at the arrogant behaviour of the British in purloining Greek antiquities. On their first day in Athens they received a visit from Lord Elgin's agent, Giovanni Battista Lusieri, a Neapolitan originally employed as a painter in Lord Elgin's entourage. Lusieri was now supervising the despatch to England of the last of the marble sculptures which Lord Elgin had been accumulating for the past decade. The evidence of piracy, most obvious in Athens at the Erechtheum and the Parthenon, continued as Byron and Hobhouse travelled further in Greece. On the way to Cape Colonna they had explored a cavern, 'a splendid dome of crystals', from which several cartloads of the pure white crystal had recently been removed by 'the Inglese'. In the harbour at Piraeus they saw fifty crates of Lord Elgin's marbles ready to be loaded. The traffic in Greek marbles was almost an industry.

Byron had of course been aware of the arrival in England of earlier consignments of Greek sculptures. These were put on show in London in 1807 in an unprepossessing amateur museum, 'a damp, dirty penthouse', opened by Lord Elgin at his house in Park Lane. Byron had mocked Lord Elgin's enterprise in passing in his satire *English Bards and Scotch Reviewers*:

> 'Let ABERDEEN and ELGIN still pursue
> The shade of fame through regions of Virtu;
> Waste useless thousands on their Phidian freaks,
> Mis-shapen monuments, and maimed antiques;
> And make their grand saloons a general mart
> For all the mutilated blocks of art.'

At the time it was a routine, relatively uninformed attack. But now, seeing the marbles being wrenched from their Greek context and becoming aware of the value and beauty of the sculptures themselves, Byron entered more seriously into the controversy. He was unconvinced by Elgin's arguments that Athens' ancient buildings were deteriorating rapidly and that he was rescuing the marbles for posterity from Turkish ignorance and gross neglect. Byron was unaffected both by his valet Fletcher's chauvinistic view that the British had a right to any foreign spoils they fancied and by Hobhouse's more sophisticated argument that British architects and sculptors would benefit from having these remarkable works accessible in London. To the Hobhouse school of thought Byron answered: 'I opposed, and will ever oppose, the robbery of ruins from Athens, to instruct the English in sculpture (who are as capable of sculpture as the Egyptians are of skating)'.

What he saw as Elgin's crass acquisitiveness prompted him to launch a passionate attack on British cultural imperialism:

'when they carry away three or four shiploads of the most valuable and massy relics that time and barbarism have left to the most injured and most celebrated of cities; when they destroy, in a vain attempt to tear down, those works which have been the admiration of ages, I know no motive which can excuse, no name which can designate, the perpetration of this dastardly devastation.'

The pros and cons of British possession of the Parthenon marbles, now in the British Museum, are still argued over in the twenty-first century. Byron's eloquent protest did not prevent him becoming an intimate friend of Elgin's agent, the loose-living Lusieri, nor did his respect for Greek antiquities restrain him from inscribing his name on one of the pillars of the temple at Sunium, or defacing a life-size bas-relief of a human figure carved into the rock of the Paneum, a sculptured cave near Vari, by writing 'Byron' just above the nose.

*

Athens was already taking shape in Byron's mind as 'a place which I think I prefer upon the whole to any I have seen'. He loved its contrasts of ancient gravity and modern gossip, the way it brought together the sacred and the lewd, as in Fauvel's own cabinet of curiosities which the French Consul had accumulated on his travels. This included a statue of Flora whose underskirt of fruits was supported by an enormous penis, 'by which it appears', as Hobhouse noted pedantically, 'that the ancients were acquainted with the sexes of plants', and a Silenus supporting his cup of wine on his erect member. The Athens carnival was a dreamlike scene of role-changing and cross-dressing, Hobhouse dancing with the servant Demetrius Zograffo, Byron appearing in female attire. There were titillating evenings of sport and masquerading, with a Greek girl dressed in Hobhouse's Albanian clothes. The mood of freedom of the pre-Lenten carnival in Athens held an element of political wish-fulfilment as Greeks dressed up to represent the Voivode, the Cadi and other Turkish rulers of the city and paraded the streets with their servants, also impersonating Turks.

It was in the course of this uninhibited atmosphere of carnival that Hobhouse noted in his diary: 'Theresa 12 brought here to be deflower'd, but B would not.' The implication is that the girl, presumably with the collusion of her mother, had been taken next door to Hobhouse's lodgings for an initiation in which Byron refused to co-operate. To other English visitors Teresa's mother, Madame Makri, appeared 'a respectable person'. The evidence of Byron himself suggests that the impoverished widow of the British Consul was all too eager to sell her youngest daughter, the 'pale and pensive looking girl with regular Grecian features', to an English lord. Byron later wrote to Hobhouse: 'the old woman Teresa's mother was mad enough to imagine I was going to marry the girl, but I have better amusement'; and, in another letter, 'I was near bringing away Theresa but the mother asked 30,000 piastres!' Perhaps his failure to acquire her was more a matter of price than principle: he had little ready money and he hated the idea of being overcharged.

There is no doubt that Byron had seriously contemplated purchasing Teresa. John Galt was another witness to the fact. As future episodes would show, he was always attracted to the idea of acquiring a beautiful, willing, totally dependent girl-child for his entourage. In his way, moved by her innocence, he loved the Greek girl. Though the poem has a sordid undercurrent unsuspected by its Victorian readers there is a certain emotional truth in Byron's stanzas:

'Maid of Athens, ere we part,
Give, oh, give me back my heart!'

He evidently had his eye on a second Makri sister, writing to his old Harrow master Henry Drury: 'I almost forgot to tell you that I am dying for the love of three Greek Girls at Athens, sisters, two of whom have promised to accompany me to England, I lived in the same house, Teresa, Mariana, and Katinka, are the names of these divinities all of them under 15.' It was Byron's own personal involvement in such episodes that gives a sardonic edge to his poetic accounts of the human traffic in female flesh.

Byron's early travels were made at a time of rising European interest in the Middle East and Orient, a response to the political disruption of Europe as well as to the shifting balance of world trade. British orientalism had been stimulated by scholarly studies, travel literature, artistic fashion for the sublime and picturesque. The cult of the Turk in particular is obvious in British portraiture of the eighteenth and early nineteenth centuries, with both men and women posing in oriental dress. With his love of the exotic and his penchant for disguises, Byron had succumbed to 'Turkomania' at an early age. He was fourteen when he attended a Christmas masquerade in Bath dressed as a Turkish boy. Six years later, a bill from a Nottingham tailor includes charges for a 'Masquerade Jackett with belt and rich Turban', evidently ordered for a Newstead entertainment.

When he set out from England Byron always intended to visit Turkey proper. Part of the attraction of course was sexual: he tantalised Matthews with the prospect of 'the exotics we expect to meet in Asia'. He was overcome with excitement at the prospect of a real Turkish bath. Byron and Hobhouse sailed from Athens on 5 March 1810, in the British sloop of war *Pylades*, travelling to Smyrna. With them, as well as the desperately homesick William Fletcher, were the two Albanian soldiers and Andreas Zantakis, the Greek interpreter Byron had taken on in Patras. On board they found the young Dr Francis Darwin of the scientific dynasty, son of Erasmus, author of *The Botanic Garden*, and uncle of Charles, who was to write *The Origin of Species*. As they sailed into Smyrna Darwin pointed out the accumulation of shoals in the water and predicted that in time the Gulf of Smyrna would become dry land.

Smyrna (now Izmir) was a large cosmopolitan city, then commercial capital of the Turkish Empire. Byron and Hobhouse lodged with the British Consul, Francis Werry, a fierce, tall, well-preserved expatriate of the old school. They spent five weeks in Smyrna in the languid early spring. Writing home from Asia Minor Byron's letters become more recklessly amusing. He observed to Drury:

'I see not much difference between ourselves & the Turks, save that we have foreskins and they none, that they have long dresses and we short, and that we talk much and they little. – In England the vices in fashion are whoring & drinking, in Turkey, Sodomy & smoking, we prefer a girl and a bottle, they a pipe and pathic.'

He sent a meaningful message to Rushton via Mrs Byron: 'tell the boy it is the most fortunate thing for him that he did not accompany me to *Turkey*.' His mother would have grasped the inference.

Posing as the idle and dissipated traveller Byron describes himself as smoking and staring at mountains and twirling his moustachios. He had developed a taste for Turkish tobacco and for chewing mastic, a device he used to stave off hunger on his travels. He had let his facial hair grow, as he was usually to do when out of England, a gesture of defiance to his unenlightened country, a symbol of his openness to new experience. As he and Hobhouse made the journey out from Smyrna to the site of ancient Ephesus, the new scenes and sounds of Turkey – nesting storks, howling jackals, croaking frogs – were imprinting themselves on his imagination. The mere sight of a camel three years later, back in London, at the Exeter Exchange menagerie, made him 'pine again for Asia Minor'. Turkey was to bring him 'some of the brightest and darkest but always the *most living* recollections' of his life.

Midway on the journey from Smyrna to Ephesus, an area of marshy wilderness strewn with the broken columns of ancient temples and ruins of more recently abandoned mosques, Hobhouse's sudden illness forced them to stop in a lonely Turkish cemetery. Poor Hobhouse, who had caught the clap in Cadiz, was now afflicted with deafness as well as with diarrhoea. The incident, magnified and made more sinister, provided Byron with the subject for his tale on the famous night when he, the Shelleys and Dr Polidori exchanged ghost stories at the Villa Diodati, Mary Shelley contributing the earliest version of *Frankenstein*. In Byron's Turkish story, which he never finished, the temporarily ailing Hobhouse of real life is transformed into Augustus Darvell, a character mysterious, aristocratic and terminally ill. In this doomed figure of the 'turbaned tombstones', with his 'shadowy restlessness' and 'cureless disquiet', there is less of John Cam Hobhouse than of Byron himself.

John Galt, catching up with him again in Smyrna, was aware of a change in Byron's manner since he had left Athens. He demanded deference and sulked when contradicted. He now seemed uncertain about his future plans, considering returning home from Constantinople. His moodiness may have been partly sexual disappointment: dinner parties at the Werrys' were decorous compared with his imagined marble palaces of sodomy and sherbet. He was anxious about his financial affairs, having written to John Hanson from every seaport since Lisbon with, he complained, no response in the form of letters 'nor (what is of more importance) further remittances'. What had happened to the sale of the Byron lands in Norfolk, to the Lancashire lawsuit? He was showing signs of paranoia, still brooding over Lord Clare's parting slight.

Byron had been away from England now for almost a year with not one letter from a friend, except for the tediously faithful Francis Hodgson: his longing to shed ties was, as usual, balanced with a terror of being out of circulation. He was feeling a more general discontent at his own failure to find a public role that answered to his talents and position in the world. Though he tried hard to conceal it he had a strong belief in virtue, honour, reputation. The sense of real purpose was missing from his life. In Smyrna he completed Canto II of *Childe Harold*. But he was still seeing the writing of poetry less as a serious professional occupation than as a diversion, a knack, a self-indulgence. In the scale of human achievement, as he viewed it at this time, rhyming did not count.

They left Smyrna on 11 April. Mrs Werry, the Consul's wife, cried at parting with her guest, cutting off a lock of Byron's hair. Hobhouse noted nastily, 'pretty well at 56 years at least'. They were now sailing on HMS *Salsette*, a thirty-six gun frigate which two years earlier had been fighting in the Baltic, supporting Sweden against Russia in the war that resulted from the Franco-Russian Treaty of Tilsit. The *Salsette* had spent the winter of 1808–9 stranded in an ice floe with the crew nearing starvation. The ship had then taken part in the disastrous expedition to Walcheren on the Scheldt estuary which was abandoned in October 1809 after thousands of men had died from fever. The *Salsette* had reached Gibraltar, and had taken part in operations off Toulon, before being despatched to Constantinople. Her commander was Captain Bathurst, 'a fat short pockmark'd stuttering man', with whom Byron had already had some acrimonious exchanges across the Consul's dinner table. Bathurst was to die, one of the few English casualties, in the battle of Navarino.

Byron made a protégé of Frederick Chamier, a fourteen-year-old midshipman who looked even younger. The boy had been sitting in the forecastle, puzzling over the ship's longitude, when Byron demanded an orange from the steward, who was unable to provide one. Chamier ran below and 'brought forth two ripe Smyrna oranges' from the inner compartment of his travelling chest.

The midshipman was released from official duties to go ashore with Byron to see the plains of Troy. Already for some hours, as the ship approached the Troad, the north-west promontory of Asia Minor, Byron had been gazing through his telescope. Once the ship had anchored off the island of Tenedos they set off in a small boat, taking the two Albanian guards. According to

Chamier, 'Troy and its plains were hallowed ground to his Lordship, which I ventured to profane, by blazing away at every bird I saw.' They had a long walk round the ancient walls, alive with lizards, at the end of which Byron 'brought himself to anchor' on the tomb of Patroclus and immersed himself in the copy of Homer he had brought with him from the ship.

With the *Salsette* held up offshore awaiting official permission to enter the Dardanelles, Byron returned to Troy again and again. As he recollected, 'I have stood upon that plain *daily*, for more than a month in 1810.' He refused to be diverted by the arguments then raging over the exact site of Homer's city and indeed the veracity of the Trojan War itself. Doubts had first been raised by Jacob Bryant in his *Dissertation concerning the War of Troy: and the expedition of the Grecians, as described by Homer; showing that no such expedition was ever undertaken and that no such City of Phrygia existed*, published in 1796. This had resulted in scholarly disputes which Hobhouse took all too seriously. Characteristically Byron suspended disbelief:

'I still venerated the grand original as the truth of *history* (in the material *facts*) and of *place*. Otherwise, it would have given me no delight. Who will persuade me, when I reclined upon a mighty tomb, that it did not contain a hero? – its very magnitude proved this. Men do not labour over the ignoble and petty dead – and why should not the *dead* be *Homer's* dead?'

On the plains of Troy there was a dramatic episode, of the kind which Byron drew on for his Eastern tales, when the English foragers suddenly came face to face with a squadron of mounted Turks. Imagining the Englishmen were Russians they drew their sabres. According to the terrified midshipman Chamier, 'the foremost of the hot-headed Turks waved their sparkling cimeters over their turbaned skulls, whilst those in the rear drew forth their splendid pistols, and cocked them.' Byron, good in an emergency, seems to have persuaded them that the Englishmen were friendly: 'had it not been for Lord Byron's coolness we should have been minus a head or two before long.'

On 3 May, after one failed attempt, Byron succeeded in the exploit he maintained meant more to him than any other kind of glory, 'political, poetical or rhetorical'. He swam across the Hellespont from Sestos, on the European shore, to Abydos, on the Asiatic, a mile or so south. The *Salsette* had been delayed again, this time for lack of wind, and was anchored near Abydos, at the town of Chanak-Kalessi. Byron made the crossing with William Ekenhead, Lieutenant of Marines on the *Salsette*.

The strong current made the exploit very treacherous. Halfway across, the swimmers were alarmed to encounter some large fish. They completed the swim in one hour ten minutes, emerging from the water very chilled. The crossing had been made in conscious imitation of the legendary swimmer Leander, whose nightly expedition to visit his lover Hero, the priestess of Aphrodite, was a famous subject of myth. The feat was so demanding that Byron wondered whether 'Leander's conjugal powers must not have been exhausted in his passage to Paradise'.

Byron and Hobhouse first saw Constantinople in the afternoon of 13 May 1810 as the *Salsette*, in very windy weather, tacked around Seraglio Point. The white minarets of Santa Sophia and the mosque of Sultan Ahmed, which reminded Hobhouse of King's College Chapel, were distantly visible through the encroaching gloom. Next day, as they were towed, now in the Captain's boat, along the walls of the Seraglio towards the harbour of the Golden Horn, the midshipmen's telescopes were trained on to the peepholes, spying out imprisoned beauties. In the Seraglio gardens there was the macabre spectacle of two dogs gnawing a human body, a scene that Byron resurrected in *The Siege of Corinth*. They took 'very decent' rooms in the inn at Pera on the east side of the city, where they ate the best dinner they had had since leaving London. Hobhouse had a tooth extracted by the Jew who was official dentist to the Turkish Sultan Mahmoud II, a satisfactory end to many months of misery.

The arrival in Constantinople was in many respects the culmination of all Byron's expectations of the East. He was overwhelmed by the intrinsic drama of the city, describing vividly in a letter to his mother a ride he took around the walls of the city: 'imagine, four miles of immense triple battlements covered with *Ivy*, surmounted with 218 towers, and on the other side of the road Turkish burying grounds (the loveliest spots on earth) full of enormous cypresses.' Exaggerating unashamedly he wrote: 'I have traversed a great part of Turkey and many other parts of Europe and some of Asia, but I never beheld a work of Nature or Art, which yielded an impression like the prospect on each side, from the Seven Towers to the End of the Golden Horn.'

The juxtapositions of the ancient and the new were even more striking than they had been in Athens. Here the city's ancient monuments, the aqueducts and cisterns, loomed alongside busy covered bazaars, crowded with women and exotic merchandise, coffee houses with marble seats and fountains playing, 'cabab' houses serving 'little pieces of fried mutton with milk and butter' which, according to Hobhouse, were very good indeed. Byron was spotted *en flâneur* in the city by an Englishman resident in Constantinople, who published his anonymous recollections in the *New Monthly Magazine* after Byron's death. This Englishman had first recognised Byron by his lameness. He was in a shop selecting pipes, wearing the gold-embroidered scarlet dress uniform of the English aide-de-camp, an ostentatious yet vulnerable figure with his remarkably delicate features which 'would have given him a feminine appearance but for the manly expression of his fine blue eyes'. He took off his feathered cock hat in the inner shop, revealing a head of curly auburn hair that emphasised the 'uncommon beauty' of his face. The unknown observer was haunted by this glimpse of him: 'The impression which his whole appearance made on my mind was such, that it has ever since remained deeply engraven on it.'

Until recently Turkey had been at war with England. In 1806, the British had sent a fleet against Turkey in support of Russia, their then allies. Now following the Treaty of Tilsit, in which the British-Russian alliance was severed, peace with Turkey had been restored. The Treaty of the Dardanelles between Britain and Turkey, negotiated by an English mission headed by Robert Adair, was signed in January 1809. Adair had subsequently become Ambassador to the Turkish Porte. He was now being recalled, and the *Salsette* had been sent to take him back to England. Perhaps not before time: local diplomatic rumour suggests that Adair, while in office, had gone native. According to one eyewitness his sign-language dialogue with a Greek lady in a house across the street from the Embassy had culminated in the display of his penis on a plate balanced precariously on the window sill.

The mood of mutual compliment surrounding Adair's departure benefited Byron. The Grand Signior, Sultan Mahmoud II, had granted special dispensation to privileged foreigners to view the mosques, and on 15 June Byron saw Santa Sophia, Little Santa Sophia and the royal mosques of Ahmed, Osman and Suleiman. Byron and Hobhouse attached themselves to an official visit made by the *Salsette* officers to the Arsenal to inspect the Turkish fleet. Not so officially they explored the lurid low life of the city, learning the distinction between whirling dervishes, bona fide mystics who performed ecstatic dances, and the cruder howling dervishes, entertainment artistes yelling, grunting, jumping and jogging themselves into sexual trances. They were fascinated by the nearly naked wrestlers, the female pavement entertainers ('pedestrian Paphians' as Byron calls them in *Don Juan*), the long-haired boy dancers of a wine house whose 'indescribably beastly' technique was to stand almost still 'making a thousand lascivious movements' with thighs, loins and belly. When Hobhouse asked one of the British Ambassador's bodyguards, a Turk who spoke English, whether these boys would not be hanged in England the answer was yes: 'de Turk take & byger dem d'ye see?'

Within the city of such beauty there were sudden sights of horror: heads of criminals exhibited in the Seraglio gardens; a dead body, that of a Christian priest, being drawn in procession through the streets with his face and hands uncovered, his eyes open and the rheum running from one of them. Chamier describes Byron's appalled reaction when he arrived at the scene of execution of a Greek elder accused of trafficking with Russians. The body was left abandoned in front of the place of execution, the head stuck between the legs as a sign of disgrace. Scavenging dogs began lapping up the blood that still oozed from the severed neck. Crying out 'Good God!', Byron turned abruptly away. It was scenes like this, so macabre as to be comic, that gave his writing what he called its 'Oriental twist'.

As in Athens he and Hobhouse travelled out beyond the city. They were taken up the Bosphorus in the Ambassador's barge as far as the edge of the Black Sea. On another expedition Byron could not resist scrambling dangerously up the Symplegades, the clashing rocks through which Jason's ship the *Argo* had passed. At the summit Byron made an instant translation of Euripides' lines from the *Medea*, which he sent to Henry Drury:

> 'Oh how I wish that an embargo
> Had kept in port the good ship Argo!'

On the European side of the Bosphorus they visited the village and forest of Belgrade, finding the site of the house where the poet and wit Lady Mary Wortley Montagu had lived when her husband was ambassador to Turkey early in the eighteenth century. 'The charming Mary Montagu' was a heroine of Byron's, partly because of her connection with Pope but also because of the asperity of her observation. Her courageously frank and amusing 'Turkish Letters', published after her death in 1763, had an obvious influence on Byron whose view of the East was filtered through her eyes.

Byron's favourite ride was through the valley known as 'Sweet Waters' between the port of Constantinople and the resort town of Buyükdere. These riverside gardens had been laid out by a Frenchman in the formal style of Versailles or Fontainebleau. However, in stark contrast, on the hills above the plain was a melancholy landscape, aftermath of the recent revolution in Turkey in which the former Sultan Selim III, cultivated as an ally by Napoleon, had been assassinated by opponents of the French. Byron's memories of the 'grandeur of desolation' of the Sultan's decayed palace were still vivid when he described it three years later in a letter to his future wife Annabella Milbanke: 'Streets in ashes – immense barracks (of a very fine construction) in ruins – and above all Sultan Selim's favourite gardens round them in all the wildness of luxurient neglect – his fountains waterless – & his kiosks defaced but still glittering in their decay.' This has all the force of the Byronic double vision: painted, operatic villas strung along the Bosphorus, parties picnicking in the shade with tablecloths and servants, and in the hills nearby the ruins of a once powerful political regime.

What is remarkable in Byron's response to the Turks is its intelligent curiosity. There is little of the automatic derision common amongst his English contemporaries. In an extended note to *Childe Harold* he argues cogently and wittily that 'the Ottomans, with all their defects, are not a people to be despised', pointing out the excellence of their educational system, their straightforwardness and honesty in financial transactions, their sophisticated culture and standard of living, the quality of their manufactured products. 'Is a Turkish sabre inferior to a Toledo? or is a Turk worse clothed or lodged, or fed or taught, than a Spaniard? . . . I think not.'

All the same Byron's behaviour in Turkey was erratic. John Galt was aware of the same gloomy self-absorption he had noticed earlier in Smyrna, the 'caprice and feline temper', the acute sensitivity over questions of rank. Other foreign residents in Constantinople were so baffled by his swings of mood, from friendliness to hostility, that they began to wonder if the English lord was mad. A climax came when Byron felt he had been slighted in the line-up for the procession assembling at the Embassy to accompany Adair on his visit to take leave of the Camican, the Turkish official standing in for the Grand Vizier who was absent, preoccupied with the Russian wars. Byron, arriving in his scarlet regimentals, objected to processing behind Stratford Canning, his old schoolfellow at Harrow, now First Secretary in the British Embassy. When he learned that no departure could be made from the usual rules of Turkish etiquette, by which diplomats took precedence over their visiting countrymen, he left abruptly. Canning watched him limping, 'with as much swagger as he could muster', through the hall and cocking a foreign military hat on his head. It took Byron three days to recover from this contretemps. Stratford Canning dined out on the story for years.

Typically, once his anger had blown over, Byron wrote a charming, deferential letter to Adair offering to make amends by following not only His Majesty's Ambassador but also his servant, his maid, his ox, his ass. 'The fact is', he added, 'that I am never very well adapted for or very happy in society, and I happen at this time from some particular circumstances to be even less so than usual.' He may, at this point, have been preoccupied by news of serious financial problems at home. Byron's debts, still over £10,000, included a £1,600 bill for furnishings at Newstead, for payment of which an execution was threatening. His edginess had prompted him to give Fletcher his notice and to request Captain Bathurst to supply him with a substitute valet, a lad from the *Salsette*. The dismissal was later rescinded, in the cycle of irritation and mutual dependence that was the basis of Byron and Fletcher's long relationship.

On 10 July Byron was received by Sultan Mahmoud II in his palace. This time his behaviour was impeccable. Canning describes him as 'delighting those who were nearest to him by his well-bred cheerfulness and good humoured wit'. Byron makes less of this occasion in his letters than he does of his reception by Ali Pasha at Tepeleni, probably because this time he got less preferential treatment. But the glamour of the ceremony could not have been lost on him. Hobhouse provides a wonderful description of the young sultan sitting on his jewelled throne:

'He was dressed in a robe of yellow satin, with a broad border of the darkest sable; his dagger, and an ornament on his breast, were covered with diamonds; the front of his white and blue turban shone with a large treble sprig of diamonds, which served as a buckle to a high, straight plume of bird-of-paradise feathers.'

According to Hobhouse, the Sultan sat immobile, a hand on each knee, not appearing to direct his eyes on anybody present, not even the Ambassador. But it appears that Sultan Mahmoud noticed Byron. He was later to insist that the English lord who had attended his audience had in fact been a woman in man's clothes.

Byron left Constantinople on 14 July, sailing with Hobhouse and Adair on HMS *Salsette*, now on the first leg of its journey home. In tribute to their moody but charismatic passenger the officers of the *Salsette* had, a few weeks earlier, put on a performance of *The Rival Candidates*, a two-act comic opera, in which the chief protagonist had the name of Byron. This was followed by a comic entertainment with songs and hornpipes entitled *Prick on Prick*.

In the harbour at Zea (now Kea), a small island port hemmed in by steep and rocky terraced banks, Byron and Hobhouse parted, Hobhouse to return to England via Malta, Byron to proceed to Athens. The scene was recorded emotionally by Hobhouse: 'Took leave, *non sine lacrymis*, of this singular young person, on a little shore terrace at the end of the bay, dividing with him a little nosegay of flowers; the last thing perhaps that I shall ever divide with him.' Byron refused to be drawn into all this tearfulness: 'Your last letter', he told Hobhouse, 'closes pathetically with a postscript about a nosegay, I advise you to introduce that into your next sentimental novel.' After a year together, his travelling companion had been getting on his nerves.

Hobhouse was affronted when, twenty years later, he read the account of his parting with Byron which is given in Moore's *Life*. The words 'even the society of his fellow traveller . . . grew at last to be a chain and a burthen to him' drew the expostulation in the margin, 'What authority has Tom got for saying this?

He has not the remotest guess at the real reason which induced Lord B. at that time to prefer having no Englishman immediately or constantly near him.' The implication is that Byron had made a kind of treaty with Hobhouse to leave him to his own devices, with no friendly witnesses to inhibit his behaviour.

His intentions are made plain in a verse message to Matthews, sent via Hobhouse at the time of his departure:

> 'Tell him, that not in vain I shall essay
> To tread and trace our "old Horatian way",
> And be (with prose supply my dearth of rhymes)
> What better men have been in better times.'

That there was indeed a difference between the travels Byron made in company with Hobhouse and the period he spent independently in Athens, from late summer 1810 to April 1811, is emphasised in an entry in his journal three years later: 'H. doesn't know what I was about the year after he left the Levant; nor does any one – nor – nor – nor – '

He did not return to Turkey. But he was profoundly affected as a writer by oriental life, with its mixture of languor and fierce passion, confessing two years later: 'I can't empty my head of the East.' The idea of devoting his life to becoming a good oriental scholar was one of his recurring dreams. 'I shall retain a mansion in one of the fairest islands, and retrace, at intervals, the most interesting portions of the East.' He calculated that the amount of money needed to make him merely comfortable at home would, in the favourable economy of Turkey, buy him a principality.

10

Athens

1810–1811

Byron arrived back in Athens on 18 July 1810, in blazing heat. '*You northern Gentry* can have no conception of a Greek summer,' he told his mother. Nottinghamshire seemed more than ever remote. Now, embarking on his second, and longer, stay in Athens, Byron immersed himself more thoroughly in Greek history and culture, and as he experienced day-to-day life in Greece, there emerged the first signs of his growing involvement in its politics.

Byron's sense of liberty was not merely theoretic. There was a personal dimension to his philhellenism which resulted from his always passionate response to the places and people that he knew – a facet of the peculiar intelligence that made him a great poet: pessimism at the human condition tempered by delight in individual human vagaries. In Greece, as later in Italy, Byron's identification with an oppressed minority was partly the product of his own resistance to authority, the outcast allying himself with the intransigents. But it shows, too, the quality his male friends valued in him: a generous, immediate human sympathy.

Having shed one travelling companion he soon acquired another. Three days after he reached Athens he was off again, persuaded by the Marquis of Sligo to make an expedition to the Peloponnese. He and Sligo, then Lord Altamont, had been at Cambridge together. They had other points of contact: Sligo had been a patron of blue-eyed Caroline in Mrs Durville's brothel before Byron extracted her. This raffish young aristocrat, following the English dilettante trail, had arrived in Athens while Byron was in Turkey. Sligo was soon cast as one of Byron's cartoon characters: epitome of hopelessness, proprietor of 'a brig with 50 men who wont work, 12 guns that refuse to go off, and sails that have cut every wind except a contrary one, and then they are as willing as may be'. He would soon be in more serious trouble, on a charge of kidnapping seamen from a British naval ship.

The two English lords travelled together as far as Corinth. In the unruly suite of 'the Marchesa', as Byron referred to Sligo, were a sea captain, an Italian painter brought along to sketch the landscapes, a 'Gentleman misinterpreter' given to sparring with the painter, besides men Byron described as 'sundry idle English Varlets'. They took twenty-nine horses. Tempers frayed as the thermometer registered 125°F. Two of Sligo's servants perspired in leather breeches. At Megara Fletcher trapped his foot inside a boiling tea-kettle. When they went their separate ways, Sligo to travel on to Tripolitza (now Tripolis), Byron to make for Patras, it was with some relief. Byron felt a wave of nostalgia for Hobhouse, writing to assure him: 'You cannot conceive what a delightful companion you are now you are gone', and adding the tantalising information that Sligo had told him 'things that ought to set you and me by the ears, but they shan't, and as a proof of it, I wont tell you what they are till we meet'.

Byron had acquired a new boy follower, of a very different style from Midshipman Chamier. Eustathius Georgiou, as Byron called him, was a volatile young Greek who had attached himself to Byron on his visit to Vostitsa the previous year. There had then been a plan that he should join Byron in Athens but the boy's illness had prevented this. Now, returning to Vostitsa, Byron found his 'dearly-beloved Eustathius' eagerly awaiting him, ready to follow him 'not only to England, but to Terra Incognita' if his master's compass pointed that way. The day after their reunion Eustathius appeared on horseback, dressed 'very sprucely in Greek Garments', with his 'ambrosial curls' cascading down his back. To Fletcher's horror and Byron's embarrassment Eustathius was carrying a parasol to protect his complexion from the sun.

Though Byron was very much taken with the boy, maintaining he had never in all his life tried so hard to please, there were frequent clashes of temperament between them. In the disapproving view of Samuel Strané, British Vice-Consul at Patras, Byron spoilt Eustathius and 'the child was as forward as an unbroken colt'. After a full-scale quarrel they parted with 'as many kisses as would have sufficed for a boarding school, and embraces enough to have ruined the character of a county in England', only to make up the next day. Byron provided Eustathius with sal volatile to cure a headache and persuaded him to exchange the 'effeminate parasol' for a green eyeshade. He gave Matthews a self-mocking description of the strangeness of his entourage as he travelled through Greece with William Fletcher, two Albanian servants, one Greek, one Tartar, and his new effusive boy-lover prancing by his side.

As we see from the code language used by Byron in the messages sent on to Matthews via Hobhouse, Eustathius was already sexually proficient: 'in *other* matters he was very tolerable, I mean as to his *learning*, being well versed in the

Ellenics.' But his whims wore Byron out and his health was an anxiety: the boy was subject to epileptic fits which, from the way Byron describes them to Matthews, appear to have had a connection with sex. Maybe the decision to send Eustathius home, instead of taking him back to Athens, was also influenced by a distraught letter from the boy's mother to the Vice-Consul at Patras, asking that the noble milord, referred to as 'the godfather', should return her son.

Eustathius was apologetic about his failure to travel on with Byron in a letter written in Vostitsa the following year, in which he begs Byron to remember him 'and love him as one who is entirely his'. In view of his father's misfortunes he asks Byron to send him 200 piastres, or authorise payment through the British Consul, so that he can have a set of clothes made to please his lord and patron. In a final woeful letter dated 20 March 1813, he states that he is unable to repay the money Byron sent him. The boy with the parasol had fallen on hard times.

Byron's obvious openness to homosexual experience landed him in situations even he found hard to handle. At Tripolitza, in early August 1810, he received unexpected, and not entirely welcome, overtures from Veli Pasha, son of Ali Pasha, ruler of the Peloponnese. Veli received him 'even better than his Father did', providing Byron with 'a very pretty house' and giving him a stallion. He also issued 'a most particular invitation' to Byron to meet him at Larissa, addressing him as a brave youth and a beautiful boy, and suggesting that as they were both young men it would be appropriate for them to live together. Byron, complaining that far from being a young man Veli Pasha had 'a *beard* down to his middle', shrank from these demonstrative approaches, particularly what he described as Veli's 'awkward manner of throwing his arm around one's waist and squeezing one's hand in *public*'. The tone is, for once, that of an outraged English citizen. He was all the more embarrassed because Vice-Consul Strané was an inquisitive witness to the scene.

By late August Byron had returned to Athens, leaving his now problematic lodgings with the Makris and moving into the Capuchin monastery, a typically hybrid Athens edifice constructed around the fourth-century monument to Lysicrates at the base of the Acropolis. The monastery, housing a friar and his six boy pupils along with Byron's retinue, was the scene of what Byron refers to wonderingly as his 'fantastical adventures'.

As usual, new surroundings sharpen Byron's prose style. He wrote to the surely envious Francis Hodgson:

'I am living in the Capuchin Convent, Hymettus before me, the Acropolis behind, the temple of Jove to my right, the Stadium in front, the town to the left, eh, Sir, there's a situation, there's your picturesque! nothing like that, Sir, in Lunnun, no not even the Mansion House. And I feed upon Woodcocks & red Mullet every day.'

The setting encouraged multiple amatory intrigues: Byron's servants got drunk and acquired new mistresses; the Albanian washerwomen in the monastery garden amused themselves in their leisure hours 'by running pins into Fletcher's backside'. Byron himself was awakened every morning by the six boy 'Sylphs', three Catholic, three Greek, shouting 'venite abasso'. From then on there was 'nothing but riot from Noon till night': playing, flirting, swimming. He noted that the Turks retained their lower garments when bathing, as Byron did himself, but the young Greeks did not. He was 'vastly happy and childish' at the Convent, where the lascivious chaos, the 'scamperings and eating fruit and pelting and playings', took him back to his days at Harrow School, and he told Hobhouse to expect 'a world of anecdotes' for him and for 'the Citoyen'.

Byron's chief devotee amongst the friar's students was Nicolas or, as Byron called him, Nicolo Giraud. He was brother to Lusieri's French wife, a connection which may have encouraged Byron to make a new ally of Lord Elgin's Athens agent. Byron knew Nicolo from his last Athenian visit. Old intimacies are suggested by the way in which his name is bracketed with Eustathius Georgiou's in one of Byron's confidential letters home. The boy had been born in Greece, though his parents were French. He also spoke fluent Italian, and his first assignment at the monastery was to teach Italian to Byron, giving him the love of that mellifluous language which increased during his years in Italy. 'I am his "Padrone" and his "amico" and the Lord knows what besides,' Byron informed Hobhouse. He had been employed for most of the day in conjugating the verb 'to embrace'. He would write to inform Matthews as soon as he arrived at 'the pl & opt C'. Six weeks later the message to 'the Citoyen' from Byron was that he had achieved 'above two hundred pl & opt Cs', the first having taken place at the monastery of Ayii Asomati at the foot of Mount Pendeli, vulgarly called Mendeli. He was already 'almost tired of them'.

Scandalous stories spread locally. The Albanian servant Vassily was the source of rumours that Byron had consulted an English doctor passing through Athens about an anal rupture from which Nicolo was suffering, common amongst ancient Greek and Roman concubines. The doctor was almost certainly Charles Lewis Meryon, then travelling with Lady Hester Stanhope and Michael Bruce, who gives an account in his memoirs of Byron's anxious consultation on the ailments of a young Greek, 'about whom he seemed much interested'.

Michael Bruce and Lord Sligo, two witnesses later questioned by Tom Moore about Byron's relationship, gave disparaging accounts, both probably self-serving. Bruce remembered Giraud as 'a miserable looking creature'. But Byron, quoting Horace, compares him with Lycus, 'beautiful for his black eyes and black hair'. In fact the lock of his hair still in the Murray archive is a rich mid-brown. His letters suggest a boy of intelligence and spirit. Nicolo was Byron's major-domo on a second expedition to the Peloponnese in September 1810 and nursed him heroically when Byron was bedridden in Patras with a fever. The illness was so bad he felt he could be dying. He told Lady Melbourne that, surprisingly, his sexual desires were unaffected and he nearly expired whilst in the sexual act. Lady Melbourne would have understood his partner to be female. Nicolo, almost inevitably, caught the fever, which attacked him in an even more virulent form.

Byron's Patras fever, which he calls a 'tertian fever', was probably malarial. At first he resisted being treated by the two untrained and inexperienced doctors called in by Samuel Strané the Vice-Consul and by the anxious Tartar servant and Albanian bodyguards; William Fletcher had been left behind in the Athens monastery. But, enfeebled by his illness, Byron finally gave in and the physicians 'vomited and glystered' him, prescribing emetics, bloodletting and bark. Byron still managed to compose himself joke epitaphs, one showing an advanced commercial acumen:

> 'Odious! in boards, 'twould any Bard provoke,
> (Were the last words that dying Byron spoke).
> No, let some charming cuts and frontispiece
> Adorn my volume, and the sale increase;
> One would not be unpublished when one's dead,
> And, Hobhouse, let my works be bound in *Red*.'

His vanity told him that the pallor of illness suited him. Returning to Athens and seeing himself in a looking-glass he exclaimed to Lord Sligo: 'How pale I look! – I should like, I think, to die of a consumption.' When asked why, Byron answered: 'Because then the women would all say "See that Byron – how interesting he looks in dying!"' The future Prime Minister Robert Peel felt certain he had seen Byron in St James's Street when in fact he was desperately ill in Patras: by no means the last example of the Byronic ghost.

Shortly before he left for the Peloponese Byron had encountered Lady Hester Stanhope. Indeed the two events may have been connected, for the sharp, erudite, worldly Lady Hester, niece of William Pitt the younger, now in her mid-thirties, was the type of woman Byron was most alarmed by. He wrote to Hobhouse: 'I saw the Lady Hesther Stanhope in Athens, and do not admire "that dangerous thing a female wit".' Hobhouse, who had encountered her himself in Malta only a few weeks earlier, described her in even more anti-pathetic terms as 'a masculine woman, who says she would as soon live with packhorses as women . . . She seems to me a violent, peremptory person.'

Lady Hester was travelling eastwards with her much younger lover Michael Bruce, a Cambridge contemporary of Byron's. When they first saw Byron he was at the Piraeus, diving off the pierhead of the harbour where he took his daily swim. He dressed quickly and met them on the shore. They met again more formally in Athens and Lady Hester attacked him for his low opinion of female intellect. Byron later claimed that he had had the upper hand, telling Hobhouse he avoided her attempts to 'argufy' with him by either laughing or yielding: 'I despise the sex too much to squabble with them.' Michael Bruce told a different story, recalling that Byron 'had no chance with her, but took refuge in gentlemanlike assent and silence'.

Byron, whose view of women was basically conventional, found Lady Hester's freewheeling conversation and her open liaison with Bruce discon-certingly unfeminine. She thought Byron affected, mimicking him cruelly, maintaining that, with his close-set eyes and his contracted brow, he 'had a great deal of vice in his looks'. But from an initial dislike and suspicion, they reached a kind of mutual respect.

Just as interesting is Byron's brief encounter in Athens with Michael Bruce. After his protracted travels in the East Bruce was to become famous for his part in the Lavalette affair: so much so he became known as 'Lavalette Bruce'. Count Lavalette, an aide of Napoleon's, was condemned to the guillotine by the Bourbons when they returned to power in 1815. The Count escaped from prison disguised in his wife's clothes and, in an exploit comparable with those of the Scarlet Pimpernel, Bruce managed to smuggle him across the border before being arrested and imprisoned himself. Byron was to rate Michael Bruce, along with the 'stupendous traveller' William Bankes, as one of his con-temporaries whose achievements he admired most.

Bruce too was bisexual, a fact made clear by Hobhouse, quoting Horace, when he says that Bruce like Byron is 'much upon the "nil admirari" plan: in other words "wonder at nothing"; he is not quite the "Nissus" he was formerly but still, in my mind, very handsome.' It appears that Bruce made a sexual overture to Byron on his last night in Athens, as he and Lady Hester were about to board ship at the Piraeus. Byron found this startling, feeling he had done nothing to encourage it. 'Seriously I can't think for the soul of me, what possessed Michael,' he told Hobhouse. They had dined together, so Byron knew he was not drunk: 'but the truth is, he is a little chivalrous & romantic, and is smitten with unimaginable fantasies ever since his connection with Lady H. Stanhope.' Byron was feeling too old to make a new 'eternal friend', and resisted their pressing invitation to travel on to Constantinople.

Byron stayed in Athens in relative tranquillity through the winter of 1810–11, developing a more intimate, more solemn view of Greece. He was scornful of the pedantic English dilettantes, John Nicholas Fazakerly, the Hon. Frederic North and Henry Gally Knight, all of whom attempted to cultivate Lord Byron. North, who later founded the Ionian University and who insisted, as its chancellor, on wearing ancient classical costume, was denounced by Byron as 'the most illustrious humbug of his age and country'. But he now became friendly with the English architect-explorer Charles Robert Cockerell and, after an initial contretemps over a horse, with Cockerell's scholarly collaborator John Foster who was later to design many of Liverpool's fine neo-classical buildings. Byron liked these young men for their physical energy as well as their enquiring minds. He also got to know a group of young continental archaeologists and artists, most notably Karl Freiherr Haller von Hallerstein, architect to Prince Louis of Bavaria, and the Estonian Otto Magnus Freiherr von Stackelberg. These were scholars who took seriously not only the ancient but also the modern Greeks.

Byron commissioned a number of Greek landscapes from the Württemburg painter, Jacob Linckh, and took lessons in the contemporary Romaic Greek language from a tutor, Ioannis Marmaratouris, a Greek patriot, who brought him into closer contact with the movement for Greek regeneration. Freed from his symbiotic relationship with Hobhouse it was easier for Byron to move independently within Athens' cosmopolitan society, attending the foreign colony's masquerades and dinners, making love to 'a number' of Greek and Turkish women. 'Here I see and have conversed with French, Italians, Germans, Danes, Greeks, Turks, Americans, etc., etc., etc., and without losing sight of my own, I can judge of the countries and manners of others.' He was still a young man: his twenty-third birthday took place in January 1811. He was still learning and absorbing. This winter in Athens was an essential phase in his emergence as a citizen of the world.

The strange scenes and mysterious moral dramas perpetrated by this multi-cultural society worked on his imagination. Returning from one of his rides to the Piraeus Byron came upon a lugubrious procession carrying a girl sewn into a sack. In accordance with Islamic law she had been condemned to be drowned for immorality. Byron drew on this encounter for the haunting central episode in his poem *The Giaour*, implying a personal involvement in the scene which made it impossible to do full justice to the real horror: 'to describe the *feelings* of *that situation* were impossible – it is *icy* even to recollect them.'

Intriguingly, there are two versions of the story. The first, and closest to the tale as related in *The Giaour*, is the one Byron himself had often told Tom Moore: he knew the girl and their affair had been the reason for her sentencing. He said he had imagined her to be a Greek, although in fact she turned out to be a Turk. The sentence had been carried out, and when Byron met the procession on the shore the girl in the sack was already dead.

The second, more uplifting version, is a later one given by Lord Sligo, who arrived in Athens a few days after the event. According to Sligo, Byron had intercepted the procession on its outward journey to the shore, drawing his pistol on the leader of the force accompanying the condemned girl, and making him return with his prisoner to the Voivode's house in Athens where Byron threatened, cajoled and bribed the governor, eventually achieving the girl's release on condition she left Athens. He took her to the safety of the Capuchin monastery, and from there sent her off by night to Thebes.

This later story was the approved account, given in a letter written in 1813 by Lord Sligo at Byron's request and circulated around his influential friends. The picture of Byron as Romantic hero, dashingly heterosexual, was intended to counteract rumours being spread by a malicious Lady Caroline Lamb about his male liaisons in the East. It was further embellished by Sligo who suggested in conversation that Byron 'might have had' the girl after the event. Ten lines are heavily deleted in the Sligo letter. Byron himself insisted that they 'contained merely some Turkish names, and circumstantial evidence of the girl's detection, not very important or decorous'. But if so innocuous, why were they scored out? The deletions have so far withstood all attempts to decipher them by the most advanced methods of modern technology.

On these early journeys Byron had been seeing Turkey from the viewpoint of an enlightened traveller. His responses to Greece were more emotional, more personal, and were the underlying cause for his eventual involvement on the Greek rather than the Turkish side in the Greek War of Independence. Byron was already indignant that almost four hundred years of thraldom to the Turkish Ottoman Empire had stultified the natural growth of the Greek people. His developing consciousness of Greece as a nation with a complex, peculiarly evocative past history, a nation deserving of a more optimistic and independent future, gave his writing a new urgency. His last few months in Athens were a productive time in which he wrote and revised over seven hundred lines of a new satire, *Hints from Horace*, intended as a sequel to *English Bards* and based on Horace's epistle on the 'Art of Poetry' – Byron had come across a copy of Horace in the Capuchin monastery. He also began *The Curse of Minerva*, his homage to the city of Athens itself and the most vehement of his attacks on Elgin. He added some long prose notes to *Childe Harold* which have the immediacy of policy in progress, his views on the liberation of Greece written down at the moment these are forming in his mind. What Byron envisaged at this period was not total independence: he thought it unrealistic to imagine that the Greeks would rise again 'to their pristine superiority'. The best he could foresee was their liberation from the Turks by some other foreign power, allowing Greece to become a 'useful dependency, or even a free state with a proper guarantee'.

In those final weeks in Athens, writing in the monastery that now held so many strangely assorted memories, Byron added three new stanzas to *Childe Harold*, verses that epitomised his feelings and his hopes:

> 'Where'er we tread tis haunted, holy ground;
> No earth of thine is lost in vulgar mould,
> But one vast realm of wonder spreads around,
> And all the Muse's tales seem truly told,
> Till the sense aches with gazing to behold
> The scenes our earliest dreams have dwelt upon:
> Each hill and dale, each deepening glen and wold
> Defies the power which crush'd thy temples gone:
> Age shakes Athena's tower, but spares gray Marathon.'

With such lines Byron was forging an identity for Greece, and an eventual mission for himself.

In April 1811, as uncertainties over his financial affairs deepened, he abandoned all plans to travel on to Jerusalem and Egypt, for which he had received special permission from the Turkish Porte, and decided to return temporarily to England. He had already despatched Fletcher home with documents needed for the slow-moving negotiations for the sale of his lands in Norfolk and Lancashire together with instructions to John Hanson that, whatever happened, Newstead must not be sold. Byron claimed not to have missed his valet 'unless it be by having less confusion than usual in my wardrobe & household'. It had been a relief to be free of William Fletcher's 'perpetual lamentations after beef and beer, the stupid bigotted contempt for everything foreign, and insurmountable incapacities of acquiring even a few words of any language' that had made him, like all other English servants, 'an incumbrance'. Fletcher was to be taken back into Byron's employment after his return.

Byron now arranged to travel home on the transport ship *Hydra*, the very ship that was carrying the final load of Elgin's purloined marbles back to London. On the first stage of the journey Elgin's agent Lusieri travelled with them, giving Byron a letter to deliver to Lord Elgin when he arrived in London. Byron remarked on the irony of this. He embarked his own booty, in the form of four live tortoises and four skulls, 'all taken out of ancient Sarcophagi', a phial of Attic hemlock, destined for John Murray, and the two middle-aged Greek servants, Demetrius Zograffo and 'Spiro Saraci', more correctly Spyridon Sarakis, whom Byron was planning to redeploy at Newstead. He also brought some Greek marbles on Hobhouse's behalf. He paid off his Albanian servants before leaving. Vassily awkwardly took his bag of piastres. Dervise Tahiri, according to Byron, took the money 'but on a sudden dashed it to the ground; and clasping his hands, which he raised to his forehead, rushed out of the room weeping bitterly'. Byron was deeply moved by Tahiri's laments, which lasted till the moment of embarkation.

Held up by contrary winds, the *Hydra* remained a further night in the harbour at Piraeus. Four of Byron's closest Athens friends, John Foster, Cockerell, Haller and Linckh sailed out in their open boat. Passing under the stern they serenaded Byron with a favourite song of his. He appeared at the window and invited them aboard to drink a glass of port.

The ship finally arrived at Malta on 30 April. Here Byron spent a melancholy month of May on an island resembling an 'infernal oven'. The fever he had suffered from in Patras recurred, with the added discomfort of piles and the gonorrhoea Byron had caught in Athens. The army surgeon Tucker could do nothing to control the malarial spasms that came on him every other day, shaking his whole frame and working him 'up to a Vesuvian pitch of fever'. His sweating was so bad he kept a servant in attendance to change his linen at night.

On top of this he had to negotiate two delicate farewells, the first with Constance Spencer Smith. His own interest had waned not long after he left her in Malta in September 1809.

> 'The spell is broke, the charm is flown!
>   Thus it is with life's fitful fever:
> We madly smile when we should groan;
>   Delirium is our best deceiver.'

This worldly-wise little poem written in Athens four months after their parting probably signified the end of the affair in Byron's mind; it had not done so in

Mrs Spencer Smith's. She pursued him with letters, some of which show clearly the bleak disparity in relations between Byron and his female lovers. Constance was still writing hopefully only weeks before Byron's reappearance in Malta: 'I should feel happy to repeat to you how much I am sincerely yours.' They finally met at the Governor's Palace for what Byron called 'the most diabolical of explanations', carried through in the soporific gloom of the sirocco, the mere memory of which caused Byron to perspire.

Byron's diminutive major-domo Nicolo Giraud, who had come with him from Athens, was also left behind in Valetta. Byron had arranged for Nicolo to attend a monastery school there, with the approval of his family and gratitude of Nicolo, who wrote Byron dutiful letters, some in painstaking English, some in Greek. After a year he was suspended for attending the theatre with Byron's architect friend Charles Robert Cockerell. Cockerell too was known for his penchant for boys. Expulsion did not displease Nicolo: he told Byron he had had enough of monks.

In a will drawn up soon after Byron was back in England he left Nicolo Giraud £7,000, to be paid when he was twenty-one, a startlingly large sum: however, the will was later cancelled. Nicolo continued to write despite the fact that Byron rarely answered. In January 1815 – the month, unknown to Nicolo, of Byron's marriage – he wrote stiffly in English with a less inhibited postscript in Greek which reads, in translation:

'My most precious Master, I cannot describe the grief of my heart at not seeing you for such a long time. Ah, if only I were a bird and could fly so as to come and see you for one hour, and I would be happy to die at the same time. Hope tells me that I shall see you again and that is my consolation for not dying immediately. It is two years now since I spoke English. I have completely forgotten it.'

Byron left Malta for England on the *Volage*, a frigate returning victorious from its recent battle with the French and Italian squadron off Lissa, on the Dalmatian coast. With them sailed another English warship, the *Amphion*, and two French frigates they had taken captive. Debilitated by his illness and uncertain of the future, Byron was gloomy, his mood not improved by the presence in his cabin of General Oakes's staff apothecary, 'a teller of tough stories, all about himself'. Byron complained: 'I can make no more of him than a Hedgehog, he is too dull to be ridiculous.' As they made their slow progress towards England, exactly two years after Byron had left Falmouth, he felt he was returning home 'without a hope, & almost without a desire', in a kind of numbness of apprehension.

THE MAKING OF A LEGEND

St James's

1811–1812

The *Volage* arrived in Portsmouth but was then redirected, with its troops still on board, to Sheerness on the Isle of Sheppey, where it docked on 14 July 1811. Byron went on to London, staying at Reddish's Hotel, St James's Street, back at the very centre of the 'tight little island', land of mists, drizzles and terrible expenditure. Byron, now aged twenty-three, saw England as a country of preposterous pretences. He had had a premonition, while he was abroad, of his schoolfellows having gone out into the world and walking about 'in monstrous disguises, in the garb of Guardsmen, lawyers, parsons, fine gentlemen, and such other masquerade dresses'. He was soon to be drawn into the masquerade himself, in the guise of the great lover of the age.

These were the years of 'Byromania', the period of unprecedented personal success that sprang from the publication of the poetry Byron brought back with him from the East. Of the 4,000 lines in manuscript it was not, as Byron thought, his satire based on Horace that would confirm his reputation but the long Spenserian narrative to be known as *Childe Harold's Pilgrimage*. Robert Charles Dallas, Byron's eager man of business, who had come hurrying round to greet him on his second day in England, watched as he diffidently unpacked the manuscript from a small trunk in his rooms in Reddish's Hotel. Dallas took it home with him and recognised its quality immediately, writing to the author: 'You have written one of the most delightful poems I have ever read . . . I have been so fascinated with Childe Harold, that I have not been able to lay it down.'

Once persuaded that *Childe Harold* was publishable, Byron was intent on finding a more prestigious outlet than Cawthorn, the publisher of *English Bards*. At his suggestion Dallas first took the manuscript to William Miller who not surprisingly, as Lord Elgin's publisher, turned down a poem strong in its condemnation of the peer. *Childe Harold* was then offered to John Murray, a genial Scotsman in his early thirties, already influential as publisher of the Tory

Quarterly Review. Murray was ambitious on his own account, but he had a larger purpose to raise the status of the publisher from that of tradesman-bookseller to serious literary entrepreneur. His gift for friendship with his authors was to be the basis of his great success.

The agreement that Murray should publish *Childe Harold* was made before the end of Byron's first month back in England. Murray would print the poem at his own expense, sharing any profits with Dallas. Though his views would alter later, Byron's aristocratic principles prevented him from claiming a financial interest. Byron's first letter to Murray is dated 23 August 1811: 'My friend Mr Dallas has placed in your hands a manuscript poem written by me in Greece, which he tells me you do not object to publishing.' From now on Byron's reputation and his publisher's would be closely intertwined.

After Byron arrived in England one of his first reunions was with Hobhouse, now disguised as Captain Hobhouse of the Royal Cornwall and Devon Miners. A career in the militia was the most obvious option for young men of their generation. Even the anti-militarist Byron, in a moment of despair about his future on the journey home, had contemplated seeking an appointment on the staff of Lord Wellington or General Graham. Hobhouse was now at Dover, awaiting embarkation with his regiment to Ireland. He and Byron arranged to meet at Sittingbourne in Kent where they spent three days together. The two Greek servants came with Byron. The friends visited Canterbury Cathedral and saw Thomas Becket's tomb. Hobhouse caught up on Byron's Athens exploits: 'none female nor under ten nor Turk'. Since Byron had boasted of sleeping with Greek women presumably 'none female' means no young girls.

Hobhouse was in a mood to urge the need for discretion. Public events had been causing alarm to the Cambridge 'Methodists'. Earlier that year Matthews had sent Byron an all too vivid account of the so-called Vere Street affair, a police raid on the White Swan tavern in Vere Street, off Bond Street, where homosexuals were known to congregate in the back parlour. Of the men charged with 'assault with the intention to commit sodomy', six were sentenced to be pilloried in the Haymarket. 'Your Lordship's delicacy', wrote Matthews, 'would I know be shocked by the pillorification (in the Hay M.) of a club of gents who were wont to meet in Vere Street (St Clement's) – how all London was in an uproar, on that day, how the said gents were bemired and beordured.' The highly publicised Vere Street arrests aroused a savage public outcry against homosexuals.

Matthews and Scrope Davies had been to see two prisoners in Newgate, a Lieutenant Hepburn and Thomas White, a sixteen-year-old drummer boy, who as a result of the Vere Street prosecutions now lay under sentence of death. Davies had agreed with Matthews 'that the lieutenant's piece was hardly worth hanging for'. But this was bravado. Matthews' ghoulish little sketch of a convicted man suspended from a gallows conveys a fearful message, on Byron's as well as on his own account. Hobhouse too sent alarming letters to Byron, one of which, written from Dover, warned him to keep 'the Mendeli Monastery story and every thing' entirely to himself.

Byron's homecoming from Athens, in some ways so propitious, was also a time of increasing depression for him, with sexual isolation once again imping-ing and news of the deaths of people close to him arriving in a spiral of catas-trophe. First there was Hargreaves Hanson, eldest son of John Hanson, old family friend and Byron's Harrow schoolfellow. He had died rapidly of con-sumption at the age of twenty-three. Byron was now also told that a much closer Harrow friend, the Hon. John Wingfield, had died of a fever during mili-tary service with the Guards at Coimbra in May 1811, while Byron was abroad. He added a lament for Wingfield to *Childe Harold* and attached the note: 'I had known him ten years, the better half of his life, and the happiest part of mine.' They had played cricket, fished and swum together. With Wingfield's death the remembered landscape of Harrow clouded over.

Byron had looked forward with mixed feelings to the reunion with his mother. In his absence, Mrs Byron, acting chatelaine at Newstead, had been heroically but ineffectively attempting to fend off Byron's creditors. With des-perate ingenuity Old Joe Murray had covered over with brown paper the bills on the Abbey doors announcing the execution on Byron's property, but at least four bailiffs were installed in the house.

When Byron had written to his mother from the *Volage* it was with fond intentions. He had told her he had brought her a shawl and 'a quantity of Ottar of Roses'; he asked her to prepare his apartments for his arrival and gave precise dietary instructions: 'I must only inform you that for a long time I have been restricted to an entire vegetable diet neither fish or flesh coming within my regimen, so I expect a powerful stock of potatoes, greens, & biscuit, I drink no wine.' But rather than setting off immediately for Newstead Byron lingered in London, sending her excuses. On 1 August, more than a fortnight after his arrival back in England, he was shocked to be told that she was gravely ill.

He had not known, or had not wanted to register the fact, that Mrs Byron's health had been deteriorating badly while he was abroad. He borrowed £40 from Mrs Hanson to finance his hasty journey north. Byron left London on 2 August. Robert Rushton was despatched from Newstead to waylay Byron at

Newport Pagnell with the news that his mother had died the day before. Probably the death of obese, lonely Mrs Byron, at the age of forty-six, had been accelerated by accumulating anxieties on her son's behalf.

Byron was overcome by the sudden loss. En route he sent a letter to their old Southwell friend John Pigot, quoting the poet Thomas Gray: 'I now feel the truth of Mr Gray's observation, "That we can only have *one* mother" – Peace be with her!' When he arrived at Newstead he went straight up to Mrs Byron's room where her servant later found him still sitting in the dark beside the body, pondering the mystery of his loss. He wrote to Hobhouse in those days of grief:

'There is to me something so incomprehensible in death, that I can neither speak or think on the subject. – Indeed when I looked on the Mass of Corruption, which was the being from whence I sprang, I doubted within myself whether I *was*, or She *was not*.'

He made arrangements for the ceremonial burial in the family vault at Hucknall Church, ordering black mourning coats, hat bands and gloves for himself and the male servants, specifying the wording of the plate on her coffin, 'Mother of George Lord Byron and lineal descendant of the Earl of Huntley and Lady Jean Stuart, daughter of King James 1st of Scotland'. But when the day came he could not bear to attend the funeral, staying at Newstead sparring with Robert Rushton in a desultory way.

The desolating sequence was by no means over. On 7 August Byron had written to Scrope Davies: 'Some curse hangs over me and mine. My mother lies a corpse in this house: one of my best friends is drowned in a ditch. What can I say, or think, or do?' Byron's intimate Cambridge friend Charles Skinner Matthews had drowned in the River Cam. He had gone out to bathe alone and had become entangled in a deep bed of weeds on a bend in the river close to Freshmen's Pool. According to the one eyewitness of the tragedy, Thomas Hart, who did his best to rescue Matthews, his arms 'were locked in weed; so were his legs and thighs'. Matthews had been crying for help but his immersion in these treacherous waters may initially have been intended as suicide.

For Byron the death of Matthews held a double horror. This was someone he had genuinely admired, with a respect he allowed to few of his contemporaries: 'In ability who was like Matthews? How did we all shrink before him.' The erudite, witty Matthews was a parliamentary candidate for Cambridge in the forthcoming election. He had seemed on the brink of a considerable future. His death brought Byron a particular and personal agony since Matthews sympathised with and actively encouraged his sexual predilections: they had shared the coded language of the Cambridge 'Methodistes'. His heart went out to Hobhouse who would feel the loss of Matthews even more than he did. Sitting in his study at Newstead, surrounded by his antique skulls, there were times when his grief erupted into what he described as 'a kind of hysterical merriment, which I can neither account for, or conquer, but, strange as it is, I do laugh & heartily, wondering at myself while I sustain it'. The resilience of laughter was Byron's most powerful inner resource.

Finding himself craving company, he invited a former Harrow favourite John Claridge to visit him at Newstead. But Claridge was not Matthews: 'now here is a good man, a handsome man, an honourable man, a most inoffensive man, a well informed man, and a *dull* man, & this last damned epithet undoes all the rest.'

Religion was no comfort. When his friend Francis Hodgson, who was soon to be ordained, seized the opportunity to preach about the afterlife, Byron sent a strong rebuff: 'I will have nothing to do with your immortality; we are miserable enough in this life, without the absurdity of speculating upon another. If men are to live, why die at all? and if they die, why disturb the sweet and sound sleep that "knows no waking"?' Byron's own intermittent contemplations of suicide were directed at eternal oblivion. His travels in the East had strengthened his resistance to the Christian religion and the sanctimonious platitudes of the English vicarage:

'I am no Platonist, I am nothing at all; but I would sooner be a Paulician, Manichean, Spinozist, Gentile, Pyrrhonian, Zoroastrian, than one of the seventy-two villainous sects who are tearing each other to pieces for the love of the Lord and hatred of each other. Talk of Galileeism? Show me the effects – are you better, wiser, kinder by your precepts?'

He could find superior virtues in 'ten Mussulmans'.

The financial troubles in which Byron found himself on his return to England focused his mind on two possible remedies: persuading a 'wealthy dowdy to ennoble the dirty puddle of her mercantile Blood' by marriage to a Baron, and making the most of his 'coal concerns' in Lancashire. Early in September, dragging himself out of the inertia of mourning, he set out for Rochdale with John Hanson. The long-running case over the recovery of Byron's legal rights to the coal mines had been in abeyance while Byron was abroad, and Byron was now hoping that progress could be made towards either the selling or preferably the working of the collieries. He calculated that this could bring in an income of £4,000 a year. Hanson saw further possibilities in the economic exploitation of Byron's manorial rights, extending over 8,000 acres of the county. But the recurring problem was the lack of capital.

When it came to commercial strategy Byron's attention span was short, and he was easily distracted on his first and last visit to his lands in Lancashire: 'unluckily receiving an Invitation to a pleasant country seat near Rochdale full of the fair & fashionable sex, I left my affairs to my agent (who however managed better without me) never went within ken of a coalpit, & am returned with six new acquaintances but little topographical knowledge.' He had gone to stay at Hopwood Hall with Robert Hopwood and his wife Cecilia. His fellow guests were two of Cecilia's sisters and her cousin Mary Loveday, a middle-aged woman confident enough to have told Byron, when he made an irreligious remark, that she pitied him from the bottom of her heart. 'Do you indeed?' was his response.

Mary Loveday's journal gives an intimate picture of Byron at this period, strikingly peculiar and already charismatic just before the years of full-blown fame. He arrived at Hopwood Hall at four in the afternoon, claiming to be shy and in dread of meeting so many beautiful members of the family. He refused to come down to dinner, saying it was his starving day. When Miss Loveday warned him of the baneful effects of vinegar consumed as a slimming aid, he told her he would rather not exist than be large: 'and so he is a pale, languid-looking young man who seems as if he could not walk upright from sheer weakness. He has a fine large blue eye, but it is so wild and odd that I have no doubt, if he lives, he will be mad.' She watched him endlessly prowling about the two sitting rooms, picking up many books and reading little bits in each of them, always conscious of being observed.

She decided that she liked rather than disliked Byron: 'but his fidgeting manner sets my heart beating'. She noted that one of his legs was shorter than the other 'and the high clumping shoe he wears on it sounds bad'. He dressed in long white linen pantaloons and wore a long gold chain around his neck. His embroidered shirts had 'a foreign look'. When the house guests were being entertained one morning with a reading from Mary Brunton's novel *Self-Control* Byron 'came in very often and smiled at "the cant of it" as he termed all the serious parts'.

Byron returned to Newstead to the worst blow of all, the death of John Edleston. He had heard a report at Malta, on his way back to England, that Edleston was well. He does not appear to have sought a meeting on his return, probably scared off by Hobhouse's admonitions. Now Ann Edleston wrote to inform Byron that her brother had died of consumption four months earlier, on 16 May 1811. This new grief was too much for him, in his already weakened state. He wrote to Hodgson on 10 October:

'I heard of a death the other day that shocked me more than any of the preceding, of one whom I once loved more than I ever loved a living thing, & one who I believe loved me to the last, yet I had not a tear left for an event which five years ago would have bowed me to the dust; still it sits heavy on my heart & calls back what I wish to forget, in many a feverish dream.'

This feeling of inability to respond with proper gravity to an event of such great consequence recurs in a letter to Dallas. It conveys the sense of a life unfurling far too quickly: 'It seems as though I were to experience in my youth the greatest misery of age. My friends fall around me, and I shall be left a lonely tree before I am withered.' Other people could take refuge in their families; it seemed to Byron that his sorrow could only be turned in upon itself.

Byron's letters to Hodgson and Dallas are self-consciously generalised, referring to 'a death', without a name, without a sex. When Byron forwarded to Dallas a stanza of mourning to be inserted in *Childe Harold* he was careful to claim that 'this stanza alludes to an event which has taken place since my arrival here, and not to the death of any *male* friend'. The secret nuances of grief are revealed only to Hobhouse, now in Ireland with his regiment: 'you remember *E* at Cambridge – he is *dead* . . . now though I never should have seen him again, (& it is very proper that I should not) I have been more affected than I should care to own elsewhere.'

He could unburden to Hobhouse the symptoms of his mourning: loss of appetite, imperviousness to alcohol, the alternation of restlessness and lassitude, inability to concentrate, the torment of revisiting remembered scenes. When he writes from Cambridge in mid-October on a visit to Scrope Davies, the sense of Edleston's loss is even more intense: 'Wherever I turn, particularly in this place, the idea goes with me, I say all this at the risk of incurring your contempt, but you cannot despise me more than I do myself.' Byron's dismay emboldened him to write to Mrs Pigot, at Southwell, with 'the most selfish & rude of requests'. He asked her to intercede with her daughter to return the Cornelian ring which Edleston had given Byron and Byron then passed on as a present to Elizabeth.

This ring, 'the pledge', is a recurring motif in the series of elegies, known as the 'Thyrza' cycle, written over the six months after the death of Edleston. One of these is entitled 'On a Cornelian Heart Which Was Broken', the brittle juxtaposition of human heart and jewel heart conveying the bleakness with which Byron confronts his memories of a relationship which in itself amounted to so little, the brush of a hand, the sound of Edleston's pure voice.

> 'Sweet Thyrza! waking as in sleep,
>   Thou art but now a lovely dream;
> A star that trembled o'er the deep,
>   Then turn'd from earth its tender beam.'

The theme is always the evanescence of perfection.

Six of these elegies were to be published as additions to the first and second editions of *Childe Harold*. They were read attentively. These were poems which gave the reader admittance to what appeared to be the poet's private world. The name Thyrza, which Byron had taken from Solomon Gessner's *The Death of Abel*, was assumed to be a woman's, and part of the grand irony was the alacrity with which Byron's female readers sympathised with his desolation, imagining themselves as potential Thyrza substitutes. A seventh elegy, written in Latin, not discovered in the Murray archives until 1974, is addressed without pretence 'Te, te, care puer!': to the beloved boy. The three words 'Edleston, Edleston, Edleston' are written over the top of the manuscript, like an agonised refrain.

> 'I must not think, I may not gaze
> On what I am, on what I was.'

It seems the death of Edleston shocked Byron into caution. Early in November he shows signs of paranoia in a letter to Hobhouse, reporting James Wedderburn Webster's indiscreet reference to a boy, a 'Hyacinth', at an evening gathering in London which Hodgson had also attended: 'He made one cursed speech which put me into a fever . . . & made Hodgson nearly sink into the earth.' There is an implication that the boy had been for sale for £200 a year. 'Bold' Webster threw in reckless comments on his brother-in-law Lord Valentia, a known homosexual. The scene prompted Byron to make anxious enquiries as to the whereabouts of the boastful letters of male sexual conquest he had written from the monastery in Greece.

Hobhouse was reassuring: 'Your Greek letters are all safe with me.' But he was alarmed at Byron's reports of 'the beastly talk of that fool of fools Bold Webster – Why you do not cut him dead I do not understand.' He was also disapproving of the reappearance of Byron's one-time Harrow favourite Sir James Wynne De Bathe. 'Why this my dear Lord is returning, like a dog to his vomit, to every thing before cast up and rejected.' When Hobhouse himself had met De Bathe in Oxford Street he had treated him 'as the

Pharisee did the good Samaritan', avoiding him by crossing over to the other side.

Byron listened to the warning voices. Between 1811 and 1816, when he again left England, his friendships with younger men were to be muted. Conversely his attentions to women were to be frenetic over these five years, with an element of cruelty engendered by the knowledge that he was being false to his own heart. Out of these emotional contortions came the language we have come to recognise as quintessentially Byronic, a camp language of defiance, the bravura self-mockery of someone forced to recognise his outlaw state.

A day or two after receiving the news of the death of Edleston he sent Francis Hodgson an 'Epistle to a Friend'. The poem ends:

> 'The world befits a busy brain, –
> I'll hie me to its haunts again.
> But if, in some succeeding year,
> When Britain's "May is in the sere",
> Thou hear'st of one, whose deepening crimes
> Suit with the sablest of the times,
> Of one, whom love nor pity sways,
> Nor hope of fame, nor good men's praise,
> One, who in stern ambition's pride
> Perchance not blood shall turn aside,
> One rank'd in some recording page
> With the worst anarchs of the Age,
> Him wilt thou *know* – and *knowing* pause,
> Nor with the *effect* forget the cause.'

The well-meaning Hodgson deleted these lines from the copy of the poem later sent for publication with the comment, 'NB. the poor dear Lord *meant* nothing of this.'

Through autumn 1811 Byron's ties with his publisher John Murray strengthened as *Childe Harold* was prepared for publication. When founded in Fleet Street by Murray's father, also John Murray, an émigré Scot, in 1768, the firm was primarily a bookselling business. But it had been expanded with great flair into a broad-based publishing enterprise. Besides Byron, John Murray II's authors would include Jane Austen, Robert Southey, Madame de Staël, James Hogg, Thomas Moore and Thomas Malthus. The literary, experimental aspects of Murray's list were underpinned by such staples as medical handbooks, Admiralty publications and the Navy lists. Byron was to joke about the catholicity of Murray's interests:

> 'Along thy sprucest bookshelves shine
> The works thou deemest most divine –
> The "Art of Cookery" and Mine
> My Murray.'

Mrs Rundell's *Domestic Cookery*, a practical instruction manual for housewives, published in 1806, had been John Murray's most successful speculation yet.

Sixty-five stanzas of the first canto of *Childe Harold* had been printed by 17 November. 'Good paper, clear type, & vast margin as usual,' he told Hobhouse contentedly. He took to calling in at John Murray's Fleet Street premises while the sheets were passing through the press. Samuel Smiles's memoir of John Murray recounts how, coming straight from Angelo and Jackson's fencing rooms, Byron

'used to amuse himself by renewing his practice of "Carte et Tierce" with his walking-cane directed against the book-shelves, while Murray was reading passages from the poem, with occasional ejaculations of admiration; on which Byron would say, "You think that a good idea, do you, Murray?" Then he would fence and lunge with his walking-stick at some special book which he had picked out on the shelves before him.'

Murray would often feel relieved when his over-active author left.

Byron was certainly the most difficult of Murray's authors, his liking for practical involvement alternating with bursts of aristocratic hauteur. The conservative Murray's misgivings about some of Byron's controversial political and religious views are addressed in an early letter to his author on the subject of *Childe Harold*, written in the silken tones of the diplomatic publisher:

'There are some expressions too concerning Spain & Portugal – which however just, and particularly so at the time they were conceived, yet, as they do not harmonize with the general feeling, they would so greatly interfere with the popularity which the poem is, in other respects, so certainly calculated to excite, that, in compassion to your publisher, who does not presume to reason on the subject, otherwise than as a mere matter of business, I hope your Lordship's goodness will induce you to obviate them – and, with them, perhaps, some religious feelings which may deprive me of some customers amongst the *Orthodox*.'

Byron agreed to minor changes but defended his authorial independence concerning 'the political & metaphysical parts' in a strongly worded letter in which he reminded Murray that even the *Æneid* was a political poem, written for a political purpose, and warning him that 'anything from my pen must expect no quarter'. This was a dialogue which, in its essence, continued through the years, and it is a tribute to the personal affection that soon grew up between them that their productive partnership continued for so long.

Byron had an ally within the Murray firm, in some ways a surprising one. William Gifford was an arch Tory satirist and critic who had edited the *Anti-Jacobin* review and was now the editor of Murray's conservative *Quarterly Review* as well as chief literary adviser to the firm. Though Byron was completely opposed to Gifford's politics he admired the fastidiousness with which Gifford upheld classical eighteenth-century literary values, the Augustan precision of Pope, Addison, Steele and Swift, against the shoddiness of contemporary writing. Byron, with his innate contrariness, had warmed to Gifford because he was by then unfashionable. Searching for a copy of Gifford's once popular satire *Epistle to Peter Pindar* Byron had discovered that his bookseller's copies had been cut up for wastepaper, the nineteenth-century equivalent of pulping. William Gifford had been one of very few contemporary poets to escape Byron's censure in *English Bards*.

When he discovered that John Murray had proposed sending the manuscript of *Childe Harold* for Gifford's approval, Byron had been enraged. This was no doubt partly nerves at the prospect of exposure to the most implacable literary critic of the age. But Gifford approved strongly of *Childe Harold*. Byron, easily mollified by praise, withdrew his defences, accepting Gifford's editorial interventions more or less graciously from then on, going so far as to send a message by John Murray: 'From Mr G any comma is an obligation for which thank him in my name and behalf.' Towards the end of his life Byron was claiming, 'I always considered Gifford as my *literary* father – and myself as his "*prodigal* Son".' There was an additional reason for rapport. William Gifford, a determinedly self-made man, was an orphan and a cripple, described by Walter Scott as 'a little man, dumpled up together, and so ill-made as to seem almost deformed, but with a singular expression of talent in his countenance'. It was a league of the physically maimed.

Byron claimed to dislike the company of other writers. Some of this was simple snobbery: the unwillingness of the peer of England to associate himself with mere professionals. He was also dogged by misgivings about the intrinsic value of writing as an occupation and a very real fear of being bored by the literary in-crowd of his time:

'I do think ... the mighty stir made about scribbling and scribes, by themselves and others – a sign of effeminacy, degeneracy, and weakness. Who would write, who had anything better to do?'

He preferred the wittier, more urbane society of the dandies at the exclusive Watier's Club at the corner of Bolton Street in Piccadilly, founded in 1807 by Jean-Baptiste Watier, the Prince of Wales's chef, frequented by 'Beau' Brummell, Lord Alvanley and their gambling friends. Though Byron later denied being officially a dandy, his mode of dress at this period, fastidious without being outré, was the fashionable London dandy style.

But however reluctantly, in the winter of 1811–12 Byron gravitated into London literary circles. At this period Byron had the opportunity of making friendships with the so-called Lakeland poets. He was to meet both Wordsworth and Southey, Wordsworth at a party given by Samuel Rogers, Southey at a reception at Holland House where Byron viewed him as 'the best looking bard I have seen for some time – To have that Poet's head and shoulders, I would almost have written his Sapphics.' Byron was spied, muffled up and semi-incognito, attending at least two of Coleridge's famous series of lectures on Shakespeare and Milton, given in Scots Corporation Hall in Fleet Street in December 1811 and January 1812. Significantly, however, the young Byron chose to align himself in London with poets who had made their reputation decades earlier, whose works he had read with pleasure in his youth, rather than the poets then at the height of their powers.

An early contact was with Samuel Rogers, middle-aged bachelor, poet and connoisseur, whose best-known work, a long nostalgic poem *The Pleasures of Memory*, in which the author roams around the villages he knew in childhood, had been a popular success of 1792. Rogers was an ex-banker, wealthy, elegant, malicious, with what Byron described as a 'Dew Drop' chin. His breakfast parties, held in his immaculately decorated house in St James's Place, over-looking Green Park, had become a cultural institution.

On 11 November Rogers held a dinner party at which Byron was chief guest. Also present was Thomas Campbell, another formalist poet of an older gener-ation, whom Byron had acknowledged along with Rogers as a shamefully neglected genius.

Thomas Moore was the third person at Samuel Rogers' dinner, and indeed its *raison d'être*. This meeting marked the end of a misbegotten feud between Byron and the Irish poet whose risqué poems had entranced him in his youth. The feud was farcical, on the subject of a duel which almost provoked another. Byron's sneering references in *English Bards* to an abortive duel between Moore and Francis Jeffrey, editor of the *Edinburgh Review* and Byron's *bête noire*, provoked Moore to issue his own challenge to Byron. The challenge lay undelivered while Byron was abroad. By the time he returned two years later the heat had gone out of the affair and Moore was glad to accept Byron's explanation that he felt no personal animosity towards Moore.

Rogers stage-managed the reconciliation carefully. When Byron arrived at St James's Place Rogers received him in the drawing room alone, before calling in Moore and Campbell and introducing them to Byron, 'naming them as Adam named the beasts'. Campbell knew Byron by sight, but none of the three had actually met him before. Tom Moore recalled the scene in terms of rapt emotion. Byron was still in mourning for his mother, his sombre clothes as well as his dark, glossy, curling hair offsetting 'the pure, spiritual paleness of his features'. Moore was aware of the extreme mobility of Byron's facial expressions in the throes of conversation, 'though melancholy was their habitual character, when in repose'.

At dinner the talk was lively as the writers weighed the reputations of their rivals, including Joanna Baillie and Walter Scott. Byron was at his most ingratiating, taking an immediate liking to sprightly sentimental Moore who, when he sang his Irish melodies in London drawing rooms, could easily reduce the company to tears. It was an important meeting for Byron as much as for his future biographer. Moore was almost immediately accepted into the inner circle of his close male friends. Byron saw, but was amused by, Moore's great gift for social climbing, making the comment that Tommy loved a Lord. The person who was less amused by Moore was John Cam Hobhouse, who resented him not just as a lightweight and a *parvenu* but as a rival for the affections of his friend. This battle for the ownership of Byron was to increase in bitterness over the years.

There is a postscript to this historic dinner, for it was here that a favourite Byron story had its origins. Byron was offered soup by Rogers but refused it; he then refused the fish, the mutton and the wine. When Rogers asked in desperation what he did eat and drink, Byron replied, 'Nothing but hard biscuits and soda-water.' These Rogers was unable to provide. But Byron finally compromised and dined upon 'potatoes bruised down on his plate and drenched with vinegar'. When Rogers met Hobhouse in the street a few days later Rogers asked how long he thought Byron would continue with this austere diet. 'Just as long as you continue to notice it,' said Hobhouse. According to Rogers it later transpired that on leaving his house Byron had been seen eating 'a hearty meat dinner' in a club in St James's Street.

This is improbable. Byron's avoidance of meat was not simply an ostentatious whim. On medical advice he had been eating abstemiously since the Southwell years and, as we have seen, he had been strictly vegetarian since returning, with a delicate digestion, from the East. He told Dallas he felt 'lighter and livelier' for his restricted diet. Soon after Rogers' dinner he had watched with horror as Moore, opposite him at the table, devoured a beef-steak, asking, 'Moore, don't you find eating beef-steak makes you ferocious?' He distrusted the effect of meat upon the mind. The way that Byron's eating habits entered the realms of legend, with inaccuracy growing each time the tale was told, shows how prone he was becoming to the tittle-tattle of celebrity.

Through autumn 1811 Byron had been making changes to the household at Newstead, gathering his 'little sensual comforts together', dismissing the servants whose appearances displeased him, replacing these with more promising material. Instead of a thirty-five-year-old maidservant with 'a flat face and a squeaking voice' he recalled Lucy, the housemaid he had impregnated two years earlier, from her home in Warwickshire to be commander 'of all the makers and unmakers of beds in the household'. By the middle of November he had also acquired Susan Vaughan, 'a very pretty Welsh girl', and a local Nottingham girl, Bessy. These, he assured Hobhouse, were 'all under age, and very ornamental'. Byron issued directives that maidservants' caps should be abolished; hair should not be cut 'on any pretext'; stays were permitted 'but not too low before'; and full uniform should be worn by servants in the evening. Though he maintained that because his diet was so meagre he could 'carry on nothing carnal', this does not appear to have been the case.

He had hoped Hobhouse and Moore would come to Newstead for Christmas. But in the end Francis Hodgson and Byron's lame young Harrow friend William Harness, now at Cambridge, were his only guests. Byron, it seems, was attempting to rekindle another old Harrow alliance, as he had with John Claridge: he informed Hodgson, 'Master William Harness and I have recommenced a most fiery correspondence; I like him as Euripides liked Agatho, or Darby admired Joan, as much for the past as the present.' In spite of, or because of, the death of Edleston the idea of the long-standing male relationship still had a powerful hold on him. Just before Christmas he had caught a wistful glimpse of Clare and Delawarr together at the theatre in London watching John Kemble playing Coriolanus. 'By Good luck,' he told Harness, 'I got an excellent place in ye. house which was more than overflowing. Clare & Delawarr who were there on ye. same speculation were less fortunate. – I saw them by accident, we were not together.' He judged Kemble's performance glorious.

Byron's latest 'Carissimo Amico' Harness left an atmospheric account of his three weeks' stay at Newstead:

'It was winter – dark, dreary weather – the snow upon the ground; and a straggling, gloomy, depressing, partially inhabited place the Abbey was. Those rooms, however, which had been fitted up for residence were so comfortably appointed, glowing with crimson hangings, and cheerful with capacious fires, that one soon lost the melancholy feeling of being domiciled in the wing of an extensive ruin.'

Byron was working on the proof sheets of *Childe Harold*. Hodgson was continuing with his self-appointed task of convincing Byron of the true principles of Christianity, 'often speaking with tears in his eyes'. There were alternative activities, unmentioned by Harness, as Byron became 'tolerably enamoured' of the new Welsh servant Susan Vaughan.

The Welsh girl, nicknamed Taffy, was an uninhibited correspondent and it is from her high-spirited letters to Byron that we can best gauge the mood of their affair, with Byron creeping up the stairs to the servants' room which Susan shared with Bessy and with Fletcher's two young sons, William and George, and locking them all in. Young George Fletcher was a wide-eyed observer of the scene: 'Don't you remember, Susan, the Lord putting his hand so nicely over your *bosom*? . . . The D—l may have George Fletcher if he did not *kiss* you besides, and Bessy too.'

If Byron was predatory towards his female servants this was standard practice amongst noblemen and landowners of his age. Byron treated Susan Vaughan as he had treated Lucy before her with an irresponsibility born of inequality, as allowable entertainment. But he also displays surprising vulnerability, writing to her three times on his journey south to London and sending her a locket containing a curl of his hair. For her part Susan shows all the signs of *folie de grandeur*, putting on airs which annoyed the other servants, demanding that Byron should go abroad and take her with him: 'Then I'd show you my dear Ld Byron the dangers I'd expose myself to was there occation for you my dear and only friend I have in this world.'

While he was away Susan held a party at Newstead for her twenty-first birthday, which exactly coincided with Byron's twenty-fourth. She saw it as a celebration for them both. She went to great lengths, decking out the parlour with long trails of ivy, turning the room into a bower with green branches hung around the walls and making the central pillar into a Jack-in-the-Green. She arranged a lavish supper for the servants: spare rib of pork, apple pie, mince pies and custards, a nice plum cake. Old Joe Murray drank his absent master's health. There were three cheers for Lord Byron. It was a convivial evening of which Susan slyly reported secret undercurrents:

'All the *pure virgins* was in white two in particular shining out to see which cut the dash in *gold chains*. Now laugh again, when I tell you how spitefully I look'd at Lucy's and she at mine.'

Though Harness later claimed to have had his suspicions, Byron seems to have been genuinely shocked and dismayed when it emerged that, in his absence, perhaps on the very night of Susan's party, she and Lucy had both been unfaithful with Robert Rushton. The denouement was the more painful because of the involvement of Byron's much loved page. Though Rushton was forgiven both girl servants were dismissed, and it may have been at this stage that Byron altered the terms of Lucy's maternity allowance, reducing her £100 to £50 per annum, the remaining £50 to be paid directly to the child.

He wrote despondently to Hodgson, with an echo of his old rejection by Mary Chaworth: 'I do not blame her, but my own vanity in fancying that such a thing as I am could ever be beloved.' To Susan herself he said wanly, 'All is over – I have little to condemn on my own part, but credulity; you threw yourself in my way, I received you, loved you, till you have become worthless, & now I part from you with some regret, & without resentment.' When Susan sent a letter to him the following September from an address in Pimlico she was evidently destitute. She wanted Byron to vouch that an expensive dress, which she intended to sell, had been a gift from him, in case she was suspected of having stolen it. Her letter is despairing, all Taffy's old ebullience reduced to words of dread: 'how miserable afraid afraid'. She signs herself 'in disgrace'. Was she, too, pregnant? There is no evidence that Byron answered her.

A final episode is hinted at in the Murray archive. In 1811 she had given (or Byron had taken) a curl of Taffy's strawberry blonde hair. Two years later, in 1813, she sent a larger sample by post from Doncaster with a pencilled note:

'My dear Lord Byron

I should have been exceedingly pleased to have seen you before I had sailed. Indeed I take it very unkind I never saw any one else ashamed at me. It is impossible to say how happy it would make me to see you again at sweet Newstead or anywhere else.'

Where was Susan sailing to? Was she emigrating? Had she even been transported? We shall never know.

By early 1812 Byron was being drawn into the Whig palaces of power, becoming an habitué of Holland House, in leafy Holland Park a few miles from central London. Lord Holland, the 3rd Baron, was the nephew and protégé of the great libertarian Whig statesman Charles James Fox. Holland House, with its easygoing grandeur and fine library, was now the intellectual and social centre of the Foxite Whigs. The hospitable Lord Holland, a good classical scholar, was a bald-headed bullish-looking man, Napoleonesque in the impression he gave of immense reserves of power, and indeed Napoleon, soon to embark on the invasion of Russia, was an admired figure at Holland House, giving it the reputation, among the Tories, of being a den of subversion.

Lady Holland, born Elizabeth Vassall, the daughter of a Jamaica planter, had married Lord Holland two days after her first husband, Sir Geoffrey Webster, had divorced her, citing Lord Holland as co-respondent. This scandal of fifteen years before had left a lingering air of raffishness and daring over the assemblies at Holland House. Byron was beginning to develop his skills in cultivating middle-aged *grandes dames* with a past. A rapport soon grew up between him and Lady Holland, his teasing deference flattering the youthful memories of a woman who became so badly crippled by arthritis she spent many of her days supine on her sofa. As she readily admitted later, she was Byronised: 'He was such a loveable person – I remember him sitting there, with that light upon him, looking so beautiful!' His grace and charm of manner stayed ineradicably in Lady Holland's mind.

From Byron's point of view the patronage of the Hollands gave him the entrée into social circles where, while affecting to despise them, he craved to be admitted. On being given to understand that his new friends objected to the pejorative remarks in *English Bards* on Holland House and on Lady Holland in particular – 'My Lady skims the cream of each critique' – Byron was easily persuaded to suppress the fifth edition of the poem then being printed and to forbid any future editions, though pirated versions continued to appear.

Part of Lord Holland's motivation in cultivating Byron was to procure a new, young, handsome and articulate spokesman for the Whig opposition in the House of Lords. He groomed him for his maiden speech on 27 February 1812, in which Byron opposed the Tory Frame Work Bill, commonly known as the 'Frame-breaking Bill', then being given its second reading in the House. This was a measure intended to suppress the rioting that had broken out amongst the unemployed stocking weavers of Nottingham, whose livelihood was being threatened by increasing mechanisation of the trade, in particular the introduction of the new 'wide frames' that enabled more than one piece of material to be knitted at a time. The Bill sought to make the Luddite destruction of these frames, an increasing local problem, a capital offence.

In arguing the case for a more humane approach towards the rioters Byron was taking up a cause very close to home. He had been aware of the ructions in Nottingham while he was at Newstead over Christmas, and indeed the unrest had been the subject of one of the most engaging of the letters he received from Susan Vaughan, a mock-rustic dialogue between the gamekeeper Whitehead and a local labourer:

'"Nah, Billy Whitehead these be sad times." He answered with a sigh "Nah indeed they bee. One dunnot know how to get on."'

They speculated as to whether Byron would be going 'up to that Lunnon to speak for the goode of the Nation' or if he would be presenting a petition. In fact Byron assured Lord Holland, 'The few words I shall venture to offer on Thursday will be founded upon these opinions formed from my own observations on ye spot.'

What Byron observed locally was that the skilled stocking and glove makers of Nottingham were 'a much injured body of men' exploited by cynical entrepreneurs who, by bringing in new machines capable of doing the work of six or seven men, were flooding the market with inferior goods. The summary of the speech he intended to deliver, as given in Byron's letter to Lord Holland of 25 February, is sensible and measured, a foretaste of the humanitarian arguments marshalled against unrestricted technological advance by such critics as Carlyle and Ruskin in the coming age: 'we must not allow mankind to be sacrificed to improvements in Mechanism. The maintenance & well doing of ye. industrious poor is an object of greater consequence to ye. community than ye. enrichment of a few monopolists.'

Lord Holland might have been warned by a postscript to this letter: 'I am a little apprehensive that your Lordship will think me too lenient towards these men, *half a framebreaker myself*.' The speech which Byron made went far beyond the résumé he had given to Lord Holland, beginning relatively soberly but ascending into an abusive peroration. Already in his poem *The Curse of Minerva* Byron had attacked the economic consequences of cynical warmongering:

> 'The idle merchant on the useless quay,
> Droops o'er the bales no bark may bear away;
> Or back returning sees rejected stores
> Rot piecemeal on his own encumber'd shores:
> The starv'd mechanic breaks his rusting loom,
> And desperate mans him 'gainst the common doom.'

Now he confronted his fellow members of the House of Lords with an overwrought vision of a nation reduced to a state of potential anarchy:

'How will you carry the bill into effect? can you commit a whole county to their own prisons? will you erect a gibbet in every field to hang up men like scarecrows? or will you proceed (as you must to bring this measure into effect) by decimation, place the country under martial law, depopulate & lay waste all around you, & restore Sherwood Forest as an acceptable gift to the crown in its former condition of a royal chace & an asylum for Outlaws? Are these the remedies for a starving & desperate populace?'

Byron felt satisfied that he had gone too far, boasting to Hodgson that he had spoken 'very violent sentences with a sort of modest impudence, abused every thing & every body, & put the Ld. Chancellor very much out of humour'. When Dallas met him in the passage coming out of the Great Chamber he was in a state of euphoria, 'glowing with success', admonishing Dallas for giving him his left hand to shake because his right hand was still holding an umbrella. 'What give your friend your left hand upon such an occasion?' Dallas quickly changed the umbrella round.

But later views of Byron's performance were more critical. Lord Holland judged it as too self-consciously rhetorical: 'His speech was full of fancy, wit and invective, but not exempt from affectation nor well reasoned, nor at all suited to our common notions of Parliamentary eloquence.' His approach was that of the poet and the writer. He could not embrace the humdrum, workaday language of professional politicians. When Byron made his second House of Lords speech, on 12 April, in support of another minority cause, Irish Catholic Emancipation, this impression was confirmed and Byron was accused of speaking in the sing-song style 'contracted at most of the public schools, but more particularly, perhaps, at Harrow'. In the end Byron himself was forced to acknowledge that his public debut had been less than a success.

Defensively he would claim that he had never really tried to be an orator, never settled '*con amore*' to a life in politics. The formalities of House of Lords protocol, the 'parliamentary mummeries', annoyed him. He was too impatient to listen to so many bumbling speakers and was easily tempted to slip out of the chamber to attend a ball. He hated the regimentation and the currying of favour endemic in early nineteenth-century party politics. He could not face the necessary trimming of opinion in what he came to see as the sickbed of the nation, explaining a few years later to Leigh Hunt:

'if you knew what a hopeless & lethargic den of dullness & drawling our hospital is – during a debate – & what a mass of corruption in its patients – you would wonder – not that – I very seldom speak – but that I ever attempted it – feeling – as I trust I do – independently.'

Byron's political career was in any case overtaken by events. On 3 March 1812, the week after his maiden speech in the House of Lords, John Murray published the first two cantos of *Childe Harold*. An early reader, Walter Scott, described it as 'a poem of most extraordinary power' which 'may rank its author with our first poets'. In effect Byron had exchanged one sort of power for another, political persuasion for the influence of writer upon reader, the effect of the written word on hearts and minds.

In May 1812 William Wordsworth took a walk across the fields to Hampstead with Henry Crabb Robinson, lawyer and literary hanger-on. They spoke, not entirely approvingly, of Byron. 'Power' was the word used of him by Wordsworth too. According to Robinson: 'Wordsworth allowed him power, but denied his style to be English. Of his moral qualities we think the same. He adds that there is insanity in Byron's family, and that he believes Lord Byron to be somewhat cracked.'

Like it or suspect it, *Childe Harold* was a phenomenon which, in the spring of 1812, could not be ignored. Its power was not just the splendid surge of Byron's language, exhilarating as this was, but its energy in questioning accepted moral values. It was the archetypal, one might even say the necessary, poem of the aftermath of the French Revolution, expressive of new freedoms, and with them a new angst, as people searched for a framework within which to lead their lives. As seen by his near contemporary Moore, Byron was 'as much the child and representative of the Revolution, in poesy, as another great man of the age, Napoleon, was in statesmanship and warfare'. Both were upheavers of the static, denigrators of the known.

Childe Harold was compulsively, convincingly subversive, and with it Byron started a long process that continued by fits and starts throughout the next century: the Romantic and creative subversion of authority, with its final consequence, the end of deference.

12

Melbourne House

1812

'The subject of conversation, of curiosity, of enthusiasm almost, one might say, of the moment is not Spain or Portugal, Warriors or Patriots, but Lord Byron! ... This poem [*Childe Harold*] is on every table, and himself courted, visited, flattered, and praised wherever he appears. He has a pale, sickly, but handsome countenance, a bad figure, animated and amusing conversation, and, in short, he is really the only topic almost of every conversation – the men jealous of him, the women of each other.'

Elizabeth, Duchess of Devonshire's account to her expatriate son Augustus Foster shows the degree of celebrity that overtook Lord Byron in the spring of 1812.

He had disapproved of John Murray's decision to publish *Childe Harold* in a large format quarto edition, calling it 'a cursed unsaleable size'. The approximate price of a bound copy, 50 shillings, has been assessed by the literary economist William St Clair as equivalent to 50 per cent of the weekly income of a gentleman. However, in three days the first edition of 500 copies had all gone. Dallas, who had reviewed the poem in advance, found Byron in his rooms at 8 St James's Street 'loaded with letters from critics, poets, authors, and various pretenders to fame of different walks, all lavish of their raptures'. Murray then brought out an edition in octavo, smaller in size and approximately half the price, though still relatively expensive. The first two cantos of *Childe Harold* were reprinted eight times in octavo over the next six years and an estimated 20,000 copies sold. As well as making Byron instantaneously famous, the poem that Murray's shopman persisted in calling the 'Childe *of Harrow's* Pilgrimage' consolidated John Murray's own position. On the strength of its success Murray moved that same year from Fleet Street to the more fashionable Albemarle Street, taking over the premises of William Miller who had made the mistake of rejecting Byron's poem.

Because of its cost *Childe Harold*'s readership was confined more or less to the aristocracy, the gentry and the entrepreneurial classes. Byron had not yet achieved the widespread influence that would follow publication of the cheap editions of *Don Juan*. But amongst the *bon ton* and those with social aspirations its success was a phenomenon only partly explicable by the public hunger for romantic narratives with magnificent and unfamiliar settings. The literary sensation of 1810 had been Walter Scott's *The Lady of the Lake*, in which the hero was a similar roaming knight of mysterious origins. But *Childe Harold* had another compelling dimension well analysed by Hobhouse, who ascribed it to the daring of its author in giving utterance 'to certain feelings which every one must have encouraged in the melancholy & therefore masked hours of his existence, and also to the intimate knowledge which he has shown of the turns taken by the passions of women'. Byron's own view two years after publication was 'If ever I did anything original it was in C—d H—d – which *I* prefer to the other things always after the 1st week.'

How far was Childe Harold a self-portrait? After all, Childe Harold had been called 'Childe Burun' in the original version of the poem. Byron later became anxious to distance himself from his misanthropical hero, telling Dallas: 'I by no means intend to identify myself with *Harold*, but to *deny* all connexion with him. If in parts I may be thought to have drawn from myself, believe me it is but in parts, and I shall not own even to that . . . I would not be such a fellow as I have made my hero for the world.' But Byron was being naive if he thought that he could separate the author from the poem. Its success was deeply implicated with the avid public speculation about the twenty-four-year-old Lord Byron, the hitherto obscure young aristocrat who had himself only recently returned from two years of travel in the East. His beauty and his lameness only added to the aura. What was Byron's secret history? Older men, a little jealous, clucked over the world-weariness they found in Byron's poetry. How could such a young man have experienced so much?

Tom Moore, often with him at this period, attributes the growth of 'Byromania' to Byron's unique combination of 'vast mental power' and personal desirability. It was almost as if London society had been waiting for a Lord Byron to lionise: 'The effect was, accordingly, electric; – his fame had not to wait for any of the ordinary gradations, but seemed to spring up, like the palace of a fairy tale, in a night.' Suddenly all doors were open to him. Besides the Hollands, Byron was now mixing with the aristocratic elite: the Jerseys, the Cowpers, the Ossulstons, the Abercrombies. He had attained to a new level of social intercourse and political power. The Countess of Jersey, in spite of, or because of, having been the Prince of Wales's mistress, was looked up to as the most exacting of hostesses. It was Byron's poetry, so Lord Holland remarked, that gave him the entrée to the highest echelons of society, not his minor title, which Lord Holland had imagined to have been extinct. One evening at the Hollands, as Byron and Thomas Campbell were standing in an antechamber off the main saloon, Lord Holland entered bearing 'a vessel of some composition similar to that which is used in catholic churches'. He exclaimed jovially, 'Here is some *incense* for you.' Campbell answered, rather edgily, 'Carry it to Lord Byron, *he is used to it.*'

In June 1812, at an evening party given by a London hostess, Miss Johnson, Byron was summoned to meet the Prince Regent. This could have been a problematic encounter, since Byron's bitter little poem 'Lines to a Lady Weeping', upbraiding the Prince of Wales for abandoning the Whigs once he had assumed the Regency, had appeared anonymously in the *Morning Chronicle* only three months earlier. Evidently the Prince, if he had read the poem, had not penetrated the poet's identity since his conversation with Byron was altogether affable; 'for more than ½ an hour HRH conversed on poetry and Poets, with which he displayed an intimacy & critical taste, which at once surprised & delighted Lord B . . . He quoted Homer & some of the obscure Greek poets even, & appeared as Lord B supposes to have read more poetry than any prince in Europe,' John Murray reported to Walter Scott, the Prince of Wales's favourite contemporary writer. The encounter had the further consequence of reconciling Byron and Scott, who was yet another of the writers whom Byron had insulted in *English Bards*. Soon after the royal interview Dallas discovered Byron in his rooms prepared to attend a palace levée, dressed in a full dress court suit 'with his fine black hair in powder'. Disappointingly, the levée was postponed.

Byron himself achieved a quasi-royal charisma in the period he would later refer to as his '*reign*', the spring and summer season of 1812 when women in particular went 'stark mad' about *Childe Harold* and its author. Samuel Rogers wrote sardonically of 'the manoeuvres of certain noble ladies' to gain access to Byron through him. Their frenzies were accelerated by his remoteness, the 'sort of moonlight paleness' of his countenance, and the *noli me tangere* impression he gave to people whom he did not know. 'Lord Byron, the author of delightful *Childe Harold* (which has more *force, fire* and *thought* than any-thing I have read for an age) is cold, silent, and reserved in his manners,' wrote Lady Morgan, meeting him that summer. Byron learned to manipulate his fame, avoiding appearing in public in the morning, steering clear of situations where his lameness would show him at a disadvantage.

His peculiar impact upon women can be seen in the episode of Lady Falkland, widow of the friend whose death after a duel had grieved Byron so greatly before he left England in 1809. Byron had agreed to be godfather to Falkland's posthumous child, Byron Cary, and donated £500 towards the upkeep of the now destitute family, leaving a cheque tucked surreptitiously into a teacup. Lady Falkland wrote to him on his return, complaining of neglect and asking for a meeting, a demand which Byron parried on the grounds that this might lead to a scandal. After the publication of *Childe Harold* Lady Falkland wrote again, by now convinced that Byron was in love with her and, a final twist of irony, convinced that his poems to Thyrza were really addressed to her. And not only Thyrza: she imagined herself to have been the real subject of his stanzas to the Maid of Athens and to Constance Spencer Smith, assuring him: 'It is not a loveless heart I offer you, but a heart where every throb beats responsive to your own.' Byron disposed of poor deluded Lady Falkland, firmly but not unkindly. Importunate and often fantasising women, excited and emboldened by Byron's poetry to seek out its originator, were the curious by-product of his fame.

Byron's effect upon women of differing ages and varied social classes is shown by an extraordinary cache of letters in the Murray archive addressed to the author of *Childe Harold* by his female fans. 'My Lord,' writes Miss Horatia Somerset, giving as her address Post Office, Clifton, near Bristol, 'I can resist no longer, how I could have remained so long silent after reading your poetry astonishes me.' Sarah Agnes Bamber of Alphington, near Exeter, addresses him: 'Sir, I have just finished the perusal of your incomparable works – an impulse grateful as irresistible impels me to acknowledge your Pen has called forth the most exquisite feelings I have ever experienced.' Another correspondent, who signs herself 'MH' and describes herself as 'a woman – certainly a young, and I trust not a disagreeable one', assures him that 'upon perusing "Childe Harold" & its accompanying poems' she became 'as it were animated by a new soul, alive to wholly novel sensations and activated by feelings till then unknown'.

These often anonymous women beseech Byron for a sample of his handwriting, signed copies of his works, a lock of his hair, 'an occasional place in your lordship's thoughts'. Some are bold enough to request a meeting with him. The letters are shot through with furtiveness and melodrama: 'You must excuse this madness'; 'instantly destroy what was intended for *your eye only*'. The correspondence shows the remarkable capacity of Byron's more neurotic female readers to construct their personal scenarios around him, convinced by the intense emotionalism of his poetry that they are addressing 'a feeling

Heart'. Some of Byron's female fans even send him their own verses, poignant poetry of amorous illusion:

> 'I count the hours, which slowly move
> Fond expectation nigh,
> When listening for thy carriage wheels
> That welcome rattle by.'

One of these recklessly conspiratorial letters, written in elegant brown copperplate, comes from Isabella Lanchester of Strawberry Cottage, Fulham. It is dated 6 May 1812 and opens in the usual apologetic manner: 'You will no doubt be astonished that a young person should in a clandestine manner apply to a Gentleman of your rank but I trust the goodness of your Heart will excuse the impropriety I am now guilty of.' Byron had evidently already met this girl, whose mother had brought her up 'in the strictest rules of Virtue' and given her a superior education in the hope that she would find employment as a governess, but had then had a change of heart. After a disaster in business and influenced by a 'wicked female friend', Isabella's mother had suppressed her 'feelings of nature' – so much so that Isabella had been offered to Lord Byron, who apparently declined to pursue the proposition. The desperate girl was now writing to ask for Byron's protection in her 'Friendless situation', relying perhaps over-optimistically on 'the Honour of an English Gentleman'.

These letters disclose a whole small world of early nineteenth-century female isolation. The fact that Byron was intrigued and flattered by such dramas is suggested by the way in which he hoarded this clandestine correspondence. Dallas noted that although he pretended to despise the society of women yet, in summer 1812, 'female adulation became the most captivating charm of his heart'. His power over women freed him from his consciousness of being the derided cripple, and distracted him from the homosexual instincts he was straining to repress. A decade later he was still talking about the phenomenon of fandom, as Lady Blessington rather acidly recalled: 'Byron says that the number of anonymous amatory letters and portraits he has received, and all from English ladies, would fill a large volume. He says he never noticed any of them; but it is evident he recurs to them with complacency.' His last Italian mistress, Teresa Guiccioli, kept a large boxful of letters from his female adorers, a dubious comfort after Byron's death.

Towards the end of March 1812 Byron acquired the fan to end all fans, Lady Caroline Lamb, the woman he would call his 'evil Genius'. Mischief-making Samuel Rogers had been their Pandarus, telling Lady Caroline that she should know 'the new poet' and giving her a proof copy of *Childe Harold*, which Byron had sent to him, to read. Her response was instantaneous: 'I read it, and that was enough.' She was undeterred by Rogers' warning that Lord Byron had a club-foot and bit his nails. 'If he was ugly as Æsop I must know him.' Lady Westmoreland undertook to introduce them at her soirée, leading Lady Caroline up to the poet who was, as usual, surrounded by women 'all throwing their heads at him . . . I looked earnestly at him, and turned on my heel.' It was after this encounter that she set him down in her journal as 'mad – bad – and dangerous to know', a comment which instinctively acknowledged the parity between them. The clever and highly neurotic Lady Caroline shared Byron's capacity for treachery.

Caroline Lamb, three years older than Byron, was born Caroline Ponsonby, daughter of the Countess of Bessborough, granddaughter of Earl and Countess Spencer. Her mother's sister Georgiana had married the 5th Duke of Devonshire. As Byron would later boast to his publisher, the liaison with Lady Caroline connected him with one of the first families in the land. In Caroline's childhood her mother had been paralysed by a stroke and she was brought up with her cousins in the welcoming but random atmosphere of Devonshire House in Piccadilly described in her later memoir for a friend, Lady Morgan: 'children neglected by their mothers – children served on silver in the morning, carrying down their plate to the kitchen – no one to attend to them – servants all at variance – ignorance of children on all subjects – thought all people were dukes or beggars – or had never to part with their money – did not know bread, or butter, was made – wondered if horses fed on beef – so neglected in her education, she could not write at ten years old.' Perhaps the lack of formal education encouraged her creativity. Her early commonplace books overflow with drawings, poems. Her original and wayward personality was marked by the number of her nicknames: 'Sprite', 'Young Savage', 'Ariel', 'the little Fairy Queen'.

In 1805 Lady Caroline had married the rising politician William Lamb, adherent of Charles James Fox and 'friend of Liberty'. She loved him, as she loved Byron, before she even saw him, since reading his poems at the age of twelve. William Lamb was the son of Lord and Lady Melbourne, a handsome, well-bred, watchful, self-indulgent man who eventually became the young Queen Victoria's adored Prime Minister. After their marriage '*les agneaux*', as Byron called them, moved into Melbourne House, opposite the Banqueting House in Whitehall. The building had been splendidly reconstructed with a pillared, domed rotunda by the architect Henry Holland for its previous occupant the Duke of York. The house was now one of the great Whig mansions of the period, central London counterpart of Holland House in Kensington.

The domestic geography was conducive to intrigue. The Lambs' rooms were on the first and second floors of the building while Caroline's parents-in-law, Lord and Lady Melbourne, resided on the floor below. Caroline's pregnancies had been problematic. Her first child, a girl, had been stillborn. But a son, Augustus, was born in August 1807. The christening, a grand affair, was held at Melbourne House. The glittering assembly demonstrated the cynical sexual networks of the age. The guest of honour, and the baby's godfather, was the Prince of Wales, former lover of the child's paternal grandmother, Lady Melbourne. Another of the well-wishers was the politician and playwright, Richard Brinsley Sheridan, whose tempestuous liaison with Augustus's other grandmother, Lady Bessborough, had been a source of scandal for years. Such complex sexual undercurrents were characteristic of that society where, once an heir was born, discreet adultery was more or less *de rigueur*. Despite the fact that this was a period of serious conflict in Europe the personal intrigues of the English social and political elite continued unabated. Indeed the Napoleonic wars appear to have acted as a stimulus to amatory activity in the circles in which Byron was now mingling. The young Lambs were living at the centre of a luxurious, power-loving milieu.

Byron and Lady Caroline were first to meet properly at Holland House. This meeting place had its overtones of irony, since Caroline had recently been having a flirtation with Sir Godfrey Vassall Webster, Lady Holland's son by her previous husband, also Sir Godfrey Webster. Lady Caroline had paid a daytime visit to the house in Kensington and was sitting with Lord and Lady Holland when Byron was announced. 'Lady Holland said "I must present Lord Byron to you". Lord Byron said "That offer was made to you before; may I ask why you rejected it?"' The reason was that he had been 'suffocated' with women at Lady Westmoreland's. She had not wanted to be one of the throng.

Byron asked if he could come and see her the next day. When he arrived at Melbourne House she was sitting on the sofa, hot and sweating having just come in from riding, with Samuel Rogers and Thomas Moore in attendance. She ran out of the room to wash, at which Rogers made a typically disobliging remark about the preferential treatment she was giving to Lord Byron who then took the initiative. According to her later narrative of their affair, 'Lord Byron wished to come and see me at eight o'clock, when I was alone; that was my dinner hour. I said he might. From that moment, for more than nine months, he almost lived at Melbourne House.'

This was an exaggeration, like so many of the statements of the person Byron called 'an exaggerated woman'. But he was a frequent visitor in 1812. Melbourne House was certainly to give him a new axis, a new worldliness and confidence as a member of London's social and intellectual elite. Its mingling of aristocracy and statesmen, writers, connoisseurs, country gentry, hangers-on, began providing him with the breadth of social observation that is the basis of *Don Juan*. As far as Byron was concerned Melbourne House's emotional ramifications were widespread, involving not only Lady Caroline herself but her mother, Lady Bessborough, her mother-in-law Lady Melbourne and her husband's cousin Anne Isabella Milbanke, the future Lady Byron: a quartet of aristocratic women with whom he soon became enmeshed.

Melbourne House was physically as well as sexually perilous, with its elevated public spaces and 'dark and winding passages and staircases' behind them, spreading confusion among visitors. Byron stumbled as he was ascending the curved stairway from the hall to a morning assembly on his first visit there on 28 March 1812, commenting to his companion Tom Moore that this should probably be read as a bad omen. Lady Caroline is said to have ordered rope handrails to be fitted to assist him to the upper floors.

Morning dancing parties at Melbourne House were then an institution, dedicated to the practice of the quadrille, recently imported from France, and the even more popular German waltz. Forty or fifty people, the cream of the *bon ton*, came for daily waltzing, starting at midday. Dancing took place in the grand saloon, with a restorative cold dinner served in one of the back drawing rooms. It was not a scene to bring delight to Byron, the non-combatant whose innate disgust at these newly fashionable intimacies between men and women is made clear in the poem 'The Waltz: An Apostrophic Hymn' written later that same year. Other dances may be lewd, the waltz was worse:

> 'Waltz – Waltz – alone both arms and legs demands,
> Liberal of feet – and lavish of her hands;
> Hands which may freely range in public sight,
> Where ne'er before – but – pray "put out the light".'

The daily dances had been a source of pleasure to the gamine, agile Lady Caroline, lauded in the London *Morning Post* as 'a *correct* & *animated* Waltzer'. But, as she remembered sadly, 'Byron contrived to sweep them all away.'

At the party on that fatal first morning was Lady Melbourne's niece, the daughter of her brother Sir Ralph Milbanke. Anne Isabella, known as Annabella, Milbanke was piquant, pretty and, compared with her cousin-by-marriage Caroline, a level-headed, unsophisticated country girl, whose father owned estates in County Durham and was reputed to be rich. She fancied herself as an analyst of character and, already intrigued by Byron's reputation, focused her attention on the drama unfolding before her, reporting to her mother, 'Lady C has of course seized on him, notwithstanding the reluctance he manifests to be shackled by her.' Annabella, with a determined detachment which in retrospect has an appalling irony, saw how 'all the women were absurdly courting him and trying to *deserve* the lash of his Satire. I thought *inoffensiveness* was the most secure conduct, as I am not desirous of a place in his lays ... I made no offering at the shrine of Childe Harold, though I shall not refuse the acquaintance if it comes my way.'

Byron was in fact more responsive to Caroline's overtures than Annabella had imagined; he returned to Melbourne House three days later bearing a rose and a carnation. Caroline was to remember him saying 'with a sort of half sarcastic smile ... "Your Ladyship, I am told, likes all that is new and rare for the moment."' Her reply, dated Good Friday 1812, written on ornate blue-edged paper with white embossed decoration, sets the style for a remarkable sequence of love letters in which Lady Caroline's originality and fluency often outdoes Byron's. 'The Rose Lord Byron gave Lady Caroline Lamb died in despight of every effort made to save it: probably from regret at its fallen fortunes. Hume at least who is no great believer in most things, says that many more died of broken hearts than is supposed.' The dying rose was part of their shared fantasy. She hoarded it for years.

Byron was temporarily overwhelmed not just by Lady Caroline's social position but by her vivacity, the depth and expressiveness of her large dark eyes, the 'soft, low, caressing voice' which, as described by her friend Lady Morgan, 'was at once a beauty and a charm, and worked much of that fascination that was particularly hers; it softened her enemies the moment they listened to her.' It reached out to Byron, susceptible as he was to the honeyed words of female admirers. He loved her directness, her own lack of cant. Lady Caroline amused him and, at a deeper level, he responded to her vicissitudes, the 'mixture of good & bad – of talent and absurdity' that mirrored the extreme contradictions in him. 'I have always thought you the cleverest most agreeable, absurd, amiable, perplexing, dangerous fascinating little being that lives now or ought to have lived 2000 years ago,' he wrote to her soon after the start of their affair.

He does not at first appear to have been conscious of Lady Caroline's unstable history. When she was a child in the nursery at Devonshire House a doctor had to be called in to advise on the treatment of her violent tantrums; her Devonshire and Lamb connections tended to keep the volatile Caroline at arm's length. 'Caro is a little less mad than usual,' wrote William's sister-in-law with typical dismissiveness the year before the relationship with Byron began.

The dynamics of her marriage to William Lamb were themselves unsettled, a cycle of quarrellings and makings up. Enraged she would throw the fire-irons or tea things at him; then they would embrace and settle down to spillikins. Beneath the bland and pleasant exterior Lamb, as it later emerged, was a flagellator, addicted to *le vice anglais*. Caroline would claim to have been beaten by her husband, and unusual sexual demands are suggested in a letter to her mother-in-law, Lady Melbourne, written in 1810, describing William's assaults on her girlish innocence:

'He called me prudish – said I was strait-laced, – amused himself with instructing me in things I need never have heard or known – & the disgust that I at first felt for the world's wickedness I till then had never even heard of – in a very short time this gave way to a general laxity of principles which little by little unperceived of you all has been undermining the few virtues I ever possessed.'

Her love affair with Byron was made more fraught by a continuing sense of strong attachment to her husband and her accelerating guilt. Her nervousness was worsened by anxieties over her son Augustus, who was diagnosed to be

Lady Caroline Lamb with her autistic son Augustus,
the '*little pet lamb*' to whom she was devoted
Self-portrait in her sketch book

what we should now term autistic. His backwardness and fits were a torment to his mother, who remained tenderly devoted to the child. Byron was kind to Augustus. One of the most endearing descriptions of this period is of the celebrated poet in the upper floor nurseries at Melbourne House holding the ungainly child on his lap.

But soon Caroline's indiscretion began to put Byron in a panic. In one of his first letters he is already upbraiding her for 'a total want of common conduct' and teasing her for emotional eruptiveness: 'Then your heart – my poor Caro, what a little volcano! that pours *lava* through your veins.' He seems to feel he has taken on more than he had bargained for. In another letter, written a few weeks later, he complains about the gossip: 'people talk as if there were no other pair of absurdities in London.' He tries to calm her down, telling her that 'this dream this delirium of two months must pass away, we in fact do not know one another, a month's absence would make us rational.' But by this time the affair had developed a momentum of its own.

In the public perception it was she who made the running. Her Devonshire relations were aghast. In May 1812 Caroline's cousin Harriet reported to her brother 'Hart', who had now become 6th Duke of Devonshire: 'Lord Byron is still upon a pedestal and Caroline William doing homage.' (She was known as Caroline William to distinguish her from her sister-in-law Caroline George.) 'Your little friend, Caro William, as usual, is doing all sorts of imprudent things for him and with him,' the Dowager Duchess of Devonshire reported to her son. The chatterbox Samuel Rogers circulated more lurid rumours of the way Lady Caroline 'absolutely besieged' Byron, waiting in the street for him to return from parties late at night. One night after a great ball at Devonshire House, to which Lady Caroline had not been invited, a sign of her family disgrace, Rogers 'saw her, yes saw her, talking to Byron with half her body thrust into the carriage into which he had just entered'. An important element in the Byron legend, as it now developed, was just this capacity to provoke women to physical excess.

It is hard to accept Rogers' view that there was 'nothing criminal between them'. But Byron showed a certain lukewarmness in response. According to the account given by Caroline's friend Lady Elisabeth Auckland to Byron's biographer Tom Moore, Byron 'had no passion – used to keep Lady Caroline off, she by her own expression, being always making an offer of herself to him'. He would make excuses: 'No – no – not this evening – you have been dining at Holland House, and it would not now be *beau*.' He kept reminding her of her wifely obligations and the great crime adultery would be. When the evening of consummation finally came the 'apparatus with which he surrounded the evening' was 'almost incredibly absurd – her head resting upon a skull, a case of loaded pistols between them'. Was Byron's confidence boosted by this setting of Jacobean tragedy?

There is a strange staginess in their love affair as it developed through the early summer of 1812. They began to be seen together in public, accepted almost like a married couple. William Lamb was playing the complaisant husband. But they also spent much time alone, ensconced in the upper rooms at Melbourne House; according to Caroline, 'he liked to read with me & stay with me out of the crowd'. As with Byron's earlier 'blue-eyed Caroline', their relations were sustained by sexual tricks and stratagems. Lady Caroline's interests were not at all straightforward. She seems to have shared the lesbian tendency evinced by her relation Sarah Ponsonby, one of the ladies of Llangollen. She was to alarm the actress Madame Vestris with 'certain testimonies of personal admiration, such as squeezing etc.' while making arrangements for the two of them to go to a masquerade. She also had a predilection for her pages, a taste she shared conspiratorially with Byron, and for dressing in her pages' scarlet and sepia livery, a uniform she had carefully designed for them herself.

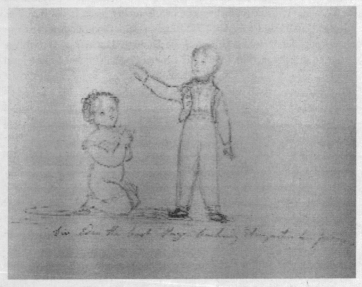

'Sir Eden the least Page teaching Augustus his prayers'
Sketch in Lady Caroline Lamb's scrapbook

Cross-dressing became a complex game between them. Lady Caroline enlisted the help of William Fletcher, telling him to receive 'the little Foreign Page' she was sending to see Byron: 'do not tell him beforehand, but, when he comes with Flowers, shew him in. I shall not come myself only just before he goes away: so do not think it is me. Besides, you will see this is quite a child.' The page was obviously the small, slim, boyish Lady Caroline. Robert Dallas also caught a glimpse of this enigma when 'the lady's *page*' delivered a letter to Byron in his rooms: 'He was a fair-faced delicate boy of thirteen or fourteen years old, whom one might have taken for the Lady herself.' The bearer of the letter was dressed in a scarlet hussar jacket and pantaloons. According to Dallas, who suspected the disguise although Byron remained discreetly silent, the messenger had 'light hair curling about his face, and held a feathered fancy hat in his hand'. Caroline played up these disguises as a secret bond between them, telling Byron: 'Women who walk in the streets alone in Pages cloathes must expect insults & barbarity but from you.'

Their shared fascination with sexual oddities emerges in a letter from Lady Caroline to Byron on the subject of a baby taken in by her charitable mother, Lady Bessborough. The baby was evidently a hermaphrodite: 'it is of both sexes and a remarkably fine interesting child about six months old perfect in every respect. Shall it pass for a male or female – which be the safest? If you can throw any light upon the subject do but for your life do not name it to anyone . . . it will appear a mighty strange sort of topic of discussion from me to you – so be discreet.' Lady Caroline's wariness might be explained by the fact that she had just had a letter from her mother-in-law, Lady Melbourne, who had heard the new rumour, which she claimed to disbelieve, that Caroline now had a female page. Lady Melbourne made it clear that she took such rumours seriously: 'You always think you can make people laugh at your follies but these are *crimes*.'

Not only was Lady Caroline impersonating pages, she was apparently also procuring them. A letter to Byron only very recently discovered in the Murray archive, written in French, with the watermark date of 1812, announces that 'Antoinette et Georgine sont tous les deux a votre service – Le Pere et la Mere souhaitant beaucoup que vous en prenez une.' Caroline's recommendation is for Antoinette the younger girl, who is the more robust in health and of an exceptionally devoted disposition: 'La petite te suivera te soignera et te sera fidele – aimes la pour moi.' Whichever applicant he does not want is to be returned to her. Caroline ends her letter, 'Adieu mon cher Maitre'.

An intricate masquerade of male and female, page and master, creature and possessor, was fundamental to the highly charged relationship. One of Lady

Caroline's own pages was renamed Rushton, after Byron's Newstead servitor. As she later assured Byron: 'I lov'd you as no woman ever could love because I am not like them but more like a beast who sees no crime in loving & following its Master – you became such to me – Master of my soul.' But Byron eventually castigated her for her lack of conventional female attributes, the sexual ambiguity he had originally found intriguing and attractive. 'Such a monster as that *has no sex*, and should live no longer.' The masculine-feminine gamesplaying rebounded upon Caroline at the end of the affair.

In early nineteenth-century London there was a striking contrast between the brittle politesse of social life and the violence that so frequently and suddenly impinged on it. This was the more obvious because of the then relatively small scale of the city. The frequent clash of moods exhilarated Byron, poet of extremes. He had been determined to watch the public hanging, on 18 May 1812, in front of Newgate prison, of John Bellingham, a political dissident who had murdered Spencer Perceval, First Lord of the Treasury and Chancellor of the Exchequer, shooting him through the heart on the steps outside the House of Commons the week before. Byron hired a room with a window opposite the gallows. Such proximity with death excited and unnerved him. He appeared 'pale and exceedingly agitated' when he went to visit Lady Caroline Lamb at Melbourne House the night before the hanging, saying he 'must' see Bellingham die.

An episode that night near Newgate disconcerted him still further. Byron had arrived with two old Harrow friends to take up his position at about 3 a.m. Stumbling across a poor woman lying in a doorway Byron had offered her a few shillings. She pushed his hand away and 'starting up with a yell of laughter, began to mimic the lameness of his gait'. But he seemed calm again by the time he returned to Melbourne House for breakfast after Bellingham's execution. 'I have seen him suffer', he told Caroline, 'and he made *no confession*.'

Lady Caroline was becoming conscious that Byron was already eager for distractions. To her irritation he had been reading and admiring William's cousin Annabella Milbanke's poems: 'They display fancy, feeling, & a little practice would very soon induce facility of expression . . . She certainly is a very extraordinary girl, who would imagine so much strength & variety of thought under that placid countenance?' When Byron went to Newstead with Hobhouse in June 1812 they were pursued by a page bringing letters from Lady Caroline. 'Dreadful body,' comments Hobhouse in his journal. Could this have been the angular Lady Caroline in person? Hobhouse adds, two days later, 'this whole week passed in a delirium of sensuality.'

Lady Bessborough began to intervene in an affair that was bringing her daughter such unhappiness and strain. While Caroline was lavish in her love for the loyally affectionate Lady Bessborough, Byron disliked her greatly, calling her 'Lady Blarney', after the loquacious society lady in Goldsmith's *The Vicar of Wakefield*, or, at his most abusive, 'The hack whore of the last half century'. He blamed her, not unconvincingly, for setting the whole affair in motion by assuring Byron that her daughter did not love him, information that had piqued his vanity.

In desperation Lady Bessborough approached not Byron, but his ally John Cam Hobhouse, who had now returned to London. We find this entry in his diary for Tuesday 30 June: 'heard bad news of Byron this day about his O O.' He used the code O O for Byron's illicit liaison. 'Came home & found an odd note from Lady Besborough.' On 2 July: 'called on Lady B – a very curious scene.' On 3 July: 'received note from Lady B – went to B who agrees to go out of town.' On 8 July Byron accompanied him to Whitton Park in Hounslow, Hobhouse's family mansion, but soon returned. By Thursday 16 July the plot had thickened: 'walked by desire to Lady B's Cavendish Square in midst of our conversation in comes Lady C L – who talked of Lady B and myself looking *guilty* – here's a pass for the world to come to.' Part of Hobhouse's difficulty as a go-between was that, being in Byron's confidence, he knew that the affair was much further advanced than Lady Bessborough imagined. On Wednesday 29 July, in a scene containing farce as well as tragedy, Byron and Lady Caroline attempted to elope.

Byron entered into the preplanned elopement with the same lack of enthusiasm with which, two years later, he would embark on marriage. On 29 July he had arranged to go with Hobhouse on a visit to Harrow, 'a scheme he had resolved on to avoid the threatened visit of a Lady'. At midday they were both in Byron's rooms at 8 St James's Street, just about to leave, when 'several thundering taps were heard at the door'. A crowd collected and 'a person in a most strange disguise walked upstairs'. This was Lady Caroline, having arrived from Brocket Hall, the Melbournes' country seat in Hertfordshire. Seeing Hobhouse she ran up the garret stairs. With admirable coolness Hobhouse then descended to the shop below, Mr Dollman's fashionable hatters, and ordered himself a hat. Returning upstairs again he prepared to leave, but thought better of abandoning Byron in such a potentially scandalous situation. Mr Dollman had told him that everyone in the house, including the servants, knew the identity of the lady in disguise.

By now Lady Caroline was in the bedroom, removing her outlandish over-garments, presumably an enveloping cloak or cape, to reveal the page's livery she wore beneath them. Byron was in the bedroom too but kept coming in and out, 'so that nothing', wrote Hobhouse, 'could possibly have happened, besides which, both parties were too much agitated to admit a doubt of their conduct at that time'. Mr Dollman the hatter, surreptitiously enlisted by Byron as his messenger, now entreated Hobhouse to get rid of Lady Caroline who was eventually persuaded to redisguise herself by putting on a habit, bonnet and shoes belonging to a servant in the house. She still refused to leave. 'Then', said Byron, 'we must go off together, there is no alternative.' Hobhouse, determined to prevent the elopement, continued to order her to leave the house, at which she threatened that 'there will be blood spilt'. 'There will indeed', returned Hobhouse, 'unless you go away.' She was incensed to see Byron nodding his agreement. 'It shall be mine then,' said Lady Caroline.

She now became 'quite wild' and struggled. Seeing Byron's dress sword lying on the sofa she made an attempt to grab it, but Byron held her back. Hobhouse left the room, hoping that this would calm her. He pacified the agitated Mr Dollman, preventing him from taking any 'violent measures', and placed Byron's valet Fletcher on guard in Byron's bedroom to forestall the possibility or even the suspicion of adultery. By the time he returned to the sitting room Lady Caroline had indeed become more tranquil and now agreed to go on condition she could see Byron once again before she left London at the end of the week.

There was still a practical difficulty. Where could she change back into her own clothes, which she had with her 'in a bundle', before returning home in her carriage? If she changed at 8 St James's Street she would be recognised. Hobhouse, ever resourceful, suggested she should take a hackney coach, still in her borrowed servant's garments, to his own lodgings at 4 Manchester Buildings, Westminster, where she could put on her own clothes and then proceed in another hackney coach either to her carriage or to a friend's house.

Caroline now had a new strategy. She said she would agree to this if Byron went with her. Hobhouse answered: 'I cannot consent to let you and Byron be in my rooms together – such a conduct would not be consistent with what I owe to both of you, to your mother and to myself.' She entreated. Hobhouse refused, and Byron backed him up. At last Lady Caroline left in the coach, having wheedled the concession that Byron should travel with her as far as Westminster. While Byron and Caroline were driving in the hackney around St James's Park, Hobhouse hurried down St James's Street and cut across the park to Westminster. He opened his front door and was waiting at the corner of the street to intercept the coach and make certain that, before it reached the Buildings, Byron did indeed get out.

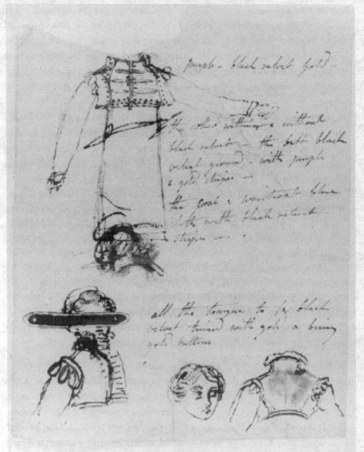

Lady Caroline Lamb's detailed instructions to her tailor for a costume
for a ball similar to the uniform worn by the pages of her household

Through all these alarums and excursions, what was going on in Byron's
mind? Why did he collude, albeit reluctantly, in her dangerous fantasies
and plans? Why could Hobhouse neither extricate him from London nor
prevent him from continuing to correspond with Caroline? Even Hobhouse
saw the problems: 'it was not strange he should not take my advice when the
lady was so exigeante.' Embarrassed as Byron was by her reckless histrionics,

there was a unique and curious sexual bond between the two of them. There was also a streak of indolence in Byron that made it hard for him to discard people, however wearing, who attached themselves to him. He saw fatality in his relationship with Caroline: they were matched in their uncompromising attitude to life. Besides, at the time he was preoccupied with plans for the auctioning of Newstead Abbey, the decision he had been dreading and fending off for years.

One of her many plaintive letters of this period refers to the sale: 'Newstead – that is pity – why not have kept it & taken Biondetta there & have lived & died happy?' Biondetta, his bounding antelope, was the most poetic of loving pseudonyms Byron bestowed on Lady Caroline. She attached a small packet of her auburn pubic hair, tinged with her blood, and demanded he reciprocate: 'I asked you not to send blood but yet do – because if it means love I like to have it. I cut the hair too close & bled much more than you need – do not you the same & pray put not scizzar points near where quei capelli grow.' Another note, dated 9 August 1812, bearing the symbols of a cross and two joined hearts, refers wistfully to Thyrza:

> 'Caroline   Byron –
> next to Thyrsa Dearest
> & most faithful – God bless you
> own love – ricordati di Biondetta
> From your wild Antelope.'

On 12 August, only days before she was due to leave for Ireland with her mother and her husband, Caroline disappeared. That morning Lady Bessborough sent a frantic letter to her lover Lord Granville Leveson-Gower, now married to Harriet Cavendish, her niece, exclaiming, 'Oh G! Caroline is gone! It is too horrible! She is not with Byron, but where she is, God knows!' It emerged that there had been a scene at Melbourne House in which Caroline was castigated for her bad behaviour by the usually tolerant Lord Melbourne. She answered 'so rudely, so disrespectfully' that her mother, who happened to have called at Melbourne House, was frightened enough to go and look for Lady Melbourne. By the time they returned together Caroline had run out of the house so fast that the servants, who pursued her, could not tell which way she had gone.

Lady Bessborough drove up and down Parliament Street 'in every direction'. Since Caroline had made a threat to Lord Melbourne that she would be going to Lord Byron, eliciting the retort from her father-in-law that he doubted if Lord Byron would take her, the two distraught *grandes dames* Lady

Melbourne and Lady Bessborough appeared together at 8 St James's Street. Byron appeared to be 'as much astonished and as much frightened' by the news as they were, and promised to bring her back if she made contact with him. Later in the day he wrote a little slyly to Lady Melbourne, with whom he was by now on confidential terms: 'As I am one of the principal performers in this unfortunate drama I should be glad to know what my part requires next?'

Caroline had in fact run all the way up Pall Mall, hiding in a chemist's shop until she thought pursuit was over. She sold a ring to get money to hire a hackney coach, which took her to Kensington. Here she borrowed a further twenty guineas on the strength of a fine opal ring, and booked a place in a stage-coach to Portsmouth. Her intention was to embark on the first boat to set sail. Taking temporary refuge in a surgeon's house in Kensington she sent the hackney coachman back into central London with a packet of letters of farewell and a note for Byron's servant, telling him to inform Byron that he would find a letter from her at the Bessboroughs' house in Cavendish Square.

Byron followed the hackney coachman, threatening and bribing him to take him back to Caroline. She had given instructions that no one was to enter the surgeon's house, where she had told the story that she was a fugitive from treacherous friends. Byron made his way in, pretending to be her brother, and practically forced her back to Cavendish Square. Here he finally persuaded her to return with Lady Bessborough to Melbourne House. The long-suffering William received her and forgave her. Lord and Lady Melbourne were affable, relieved. Plans to remove Caroline to the family estates in Ireland were resumed. But when her daughter, in a final dramatic coup, announced that she was pregnant and a journey to Ireland might lead to a miscarriage, Lady Bessborough herself, not surprisingly, collapsed, spitting up alarming quantities of blood.

Having returned her to her family, Byron wrote his farewell letter:

'My dearest Caroline – If tears, which you saw & know I am not apt to shed, if the agitation in which I parted from you, agitation which you must have perceived through the *whole* of this most nervous *nervous* affair, did not commence till the moment of leaving you approached, if all that I have said & done, & am still but too ready to say & do, have not sufficiently proved what my real feelings are & must be ever towards you, my love, I have no other proof to offer; God knows I wish you happy, & when I quit you, or rather when you from a sense of duty to your husband & mother quit me, you shall acknowledge the truth of what I again promise & vow, that no other in word or deed shall ever hold the place in my affection which is & shall be most sacred to you, till I am nothing I never knew till *that moment*, the *madness* of – my dearest & most beloved friend – I cannot express myself – this is no time for words – but I shall have a pride, a melancholy pleasure, in suffering what you yourself can hardly conceive – for you do not know me. – I am now about to go out with a heavy heart, because – my appearing this Evening will stop any absurd story which the events of today might give rise to – do you think *now* that I am *cold & stern*, & *artful* – will even *others* think so, will your *mother* even – that mother to whom we must indeed sacrifice much, *more* much more on my part, than she shall ever know or can imagine. – "Promises not to love you" ah Caroline it is past promising – but I shall attribute all concessions to the proper motive – & never cease to feel all that you have already witnessed – & more than can ever be known but to my own heart – perhaps to yours – May God protect forgive & bless you – ever & even more than ever

yr. most attached

BYRON

P.S. – These taunts which have driven you to this – my dearest Caroline – were it not for your mother & the kindness of all your connections, is there anything on earth or heaven would have made me so happy as to have made you mine long ago? & not less *now* than *then*, but *more* than ever at this time – you know I would with pleasure give up all here & all beyond the grave for you – & in refraining from this – must my motives be misunderstood – ? I care not who knows this – what use is made of it – it is to *you* & to *you* only that they owe yourself, I was and am *yours*, freely & most entirely, to obey, to honour, love – & fly with you when, where, & how you yourself *might* & *may* determine.'

Doubts have been cast on the authenticity of Byron's letter. It has even been suggested that Caroline had written it to persuade herself and others of the depth of Byron's love for her. But this is nonsense. With its beauty of phraseology, magnificent but totally unrealistic statements, its general sense of emotional confusion and defensive mystification – 'for you do not know me' – it is Byron through and through.

Caroline eventually left for Bessborough House near Fiddown, southern Ireland. Her cousin Harriet, seeing her en route, was alarmed that she was now 'worn to the bone, as pale as death and her eyes staring out of her head'. Her resilient husband William meanwhile 'laughs and eats like a trooper'. No more was heard of the putative pregnancy. With Caroline's departure the complex emotional geography within Melbourne House was changed as Byron's attention shifted from the daughter-in-law in the upper apartments to the mother-in-law in her state rooms on the ground floor. 'I presume that I may now have

...ron and Robert Rushton, oil by George Sanders. The portrait of Byron and his page was painted in 1807–8,
...ly before the twenty-one-year-old Byron set out on his expedition to Greece, Albania and Turkey.

2 Mrs Catherine Gordon Byron, oil by
Thomas Stewardson. Byron's relations with his
possessive, irascible mother were always problematic. But he was grief-stricken when she
died in 1811.

3 Captain John Byron. Byron's absentee
father, known as 'Mad Jack', was glamorous but
dissolute. He died in penury in France,
a suspected suicide, when Byron was a child.

The Castle of Gight at Fyvie, inherited by Mrs Byron as 13th Laird in 1785 but sold two years later to pay family debts. It had become a ruin in Byron's time.

Brig o'Balgounie, the ancient stone bridge over the Don in Aberdeen to which the lame boy used to ride a Highland pony. It was probably here he learned to swim.

6   Newstead Abbey, Nottinghamshire. The Gothic mansion, originally an Augustinian priory, with large estates was inherited by Byron at the age of ten on the death of the 5th Baron Byron, his great-uncle.

7   Byron aged seven, engraving by Edward Finden from William Kay's watercolour of 1795. Foliage obscu the child's malformed foot.

8   Old Joe Murray, oil by T. Barber. Byron inherited his chief Newstead servant from the 5th Lord. Joe's death in 1820 seemed 'the end of Newstead itself'.

Mary Chaworth of Annesley Hall, neighbouring estate to Newstead, with whom Byron was 'distractedly in [love]' at the age of fifteen. Miniature by John Hazlitt, 1805.

The Earl of Clare aged fourteen. Harrow School miniature of Byron's Harrow protégé, four years his [juni]or, whom he later claimed to love better than 'any *male* thing in the world'.

The Peachey Stone in Harrow Churchyard, legendary site of Byron's schoolboy reveries. Byron began [writ]ing poetry at Harrow and by the end of the century was being cited as 'by far her greatest son'.

Edleston
Edleston
Edleston

Te, te, care puer! veteris si nomen amoris
Jam valeat, socium semper amare voco.
Te, ~~fatumque~~ tuum, quoties carissime! plange
Et toties haeret fortior ipse dolor.
Dulcis at ipse dolor, quam dulcis! dulcior am...
Vanus amor, ~~credens~~ te ~~revocare gradum~~
Me miserum! frustra pro te vixisse precatu...
Cur frustra volui te moriente mori?—
Heu quanto minus est jam serta, unguenta, ...
Carpere cum reliquis quam meminisse tu...
Quae mihi nunc maneant? gemitus, vaga somnia ...
Aut sine te ~~vacuo~~ lacrymis pervigilare toro.
Ah Libitina veni, invisa mihi parcere Parca!
Mortua amicitia Mors sit amica ...

12 'Edleston, Edleston, Edleston'. Byron's anguished inscription on the manuscript of his Latin elegy on death of John Edleston, the chorister he had loved at Cambridge.

13   Trinity College, Cambridge, where Byron was in residence, with many interruptions, from October 1805 to December 1807. He made lasting friendships here and brought a bear as a companion.

14   Entrance to I Staircase in Nevile's Court at Trinity, probable location of Byron's '*Super*excellent' Cambridge rooms.

15   John Cam Hobhouse, most loyal and long-suffering of Byron's friends, companion on his travels to the East in 1809. Hobhouse, later Baron Broughton de Gyfford, had a distinguished career as a Radical reformer and Whig statesman. Miniature by W. J. Newton.

16 The Torre de Belém in Lisbon. The first of Byron's heroic swimming exploits was his crossing of the Tagus in July 1809.

17   Deserted Monastery of the Capuchos. Byron drew on the wild mountain landscape around Cintra for *Childe Harold*, Canto I.

18   The Capuchin Monastery at the foot of the Acropolis, built in 1669 around the Choregic Monument of Lysikrates and scene of Byron's 'fantastical adventures' in the summer of 1810.

Childe Harold's Pilgrimage. a Romaunt

Canto 1st

1.

Whilome in Albion's isle there dwelt a youth
  Who ne in Virtue's ways did take delight
But spent his days in riot most uncouth ~~& ~~,
  And vexed with mirth the drowsy ear of Night,
Ah me! in sooth he was a shameless wight
  Sore given to revel, & ~~ungodly glee~~
He shunned the lad, & did the good affright
  With concubines & carnal compan~~ye~~
And flaunting Wassailers, of high & low degree. —

Harold 2.

Childe ~~Harold~~ was he hight, — but whence his name
  And lineage long, it suits me not to say.
Suffice it, that perchance they were of fame
  And had been glorious in another day,
But one sad losel soils a name for aye
  However mighty in the older time
Nor all that heralds rake from coffined clay,
  Nor florid prose, nor honied lies of rhyme
Can blazon evil deeds, nor consecrate one crime. —

First page of manuscript of *Childe Harold*, Cantos I and II. In the original draft the hero's name is 'Ide Burun', later amended to Harold. Though Byron attempted to deny it, the darkly disconsolate im of the poem bore a marked resemblance to the author.

20 Manuscript of *Childe Harold* with multiple corrections showing the practical problems
being Byron's publisher. He continued to make alterations and long additions even after his
poems had been set up in type.

Those large blue eyes, fair locks & snowy hands,

...shines in his maddest spiteful mood,
Strange pangs would flash along Childe Harold's brow,
Of the Memory of some deadly feud,
Disappointed passion lurked below,
~ this None knew, or haply cared to know,
his was not that open artless soul,
t feels relief by bidding Sorrow flow,
Nor sought a friend to counsel or ~~condole~~,
                                       condole
steer this grief mote be, which he could not
                                         controul.

None did love him ~~though~~ ~~to me~~ cowed
~~He~~ He gathered revellers from far, and nigh
~~And~~ ~~some just bordering on a~~ ~~steer~~
knew them flatterers of the ~~festal hour~~,
They heartless Parasites of present cheer:
~~he deemed no mortal with~~
None did love him not his Lemans
~~the Dames still by~~ dear, ~
                                 alone
But pomp & honour, are Woman's care
where these are Let no Pretensor fear
Maidens like Moths are ever caught by
and Mammon, ~~wins~~ where Angels might despair.

Four days are sped but with the fifth anon,
New shores desired make every bosom gay

21 Ali Pasha, despotic ruler of the southern region
of Albania. He gave Byron an enthusiastic reception
at Tepeleni in 1809.
22 Teresa Macri, the young Greek girl
who was the subject of Byron's famous
'Maid of Athens' poem.

23 Drawing of Byron by G.H. Harlow c.1815.
This portrait, dating from the time of his marriage,
became one of the defining images of Byron;
see no. 75.

Breakfast at Samuel Rogers's Residence, mid-nineteenth-century engraving by Charles Mottram after John [...], showing Byron at the centre of the London literary scene in his 'curled darling' years of 1812–15. His [...] the poet Samuel Rogers, sits on Byron's left; opposite are William Wordsworth, Byron's biographer-to-[...] [T]homas Moore, Samuel Taylor Coleridge and Walter Scott.

Drawing Room at Fifty Albemarle Street. Watercolour by L. Werner c.1850 reconstructing the scene of [...] Murray's momentous introduction (on the right of the picture) of Byron to Walter Scott on 7 April 1815.

26   Melbourne House in Whitehall, now the Scottish Office. The Melbourne family's London residence was frequented by Byron in 1812–13, the period of his complex intertwined relationships with Lady Melbourne and her daughter-in-law Lady Caroline Lamb.

27   Lady Melbourne painted by Thomas Lawrence in her social and political heyday. She was just over s when she became Byron's confidante. His most brilliantly indiscreet letters were addressed to her.

28   Lady Caroline Lamb, portrait miniature from oil painting by Thomas Phillips. Her highly public affa with Byron took place in 1812. She was fond of dressing up in page's uniform.

Lady Frances Webster. Byron was pursuing the wife of his London gambler crony James Wedderburn
ster in autumn 1813. She was the subject of his sonnets 'To Genevra'.

yron by Thomas Phillips. This portrait of Byron at the height of his fame was first shown at the Royal
emy Exhibition in 1814. Subsequent copies and engravings made it one of his most influential images.

ne Elizabeth, Countess of Oxford, by John Hoppner c.1800. Byron's affair with the voluptuously middle-
Lady Oxford preoccupied him in winter 1812–13. She was highly intellectual and politically engaged.

ady Charlotte Harley, the Countess of Oxford's eleven-year-old daughter to whom he addressed the
as 'To Ianthe' in *Childe Harold*. Byron contemplated marrying her when she was old and bad enough.

33 The Byron Screen. Collage screen made in 1814 by Henry Angelo and reputedly Byron himself for h[is]
Albany apartments, reflecting his great enthusiasm for the theatre. Central figures are Mrs Siddons and
Byron's most admired actor Edmund Kean. The reverse of the screen displays famous pugilists.

34 Pastel portrait of the Hon. Douglas Kinnaird, Byron's friend and later his business manager. Kinnair[d]
chose to be depicted with the bust of Napoleon and a version of Richard Westall's 1813 portrait of Byron
He is holding Byron's poem *Parisina*.

35 John Murray, oil portrait by W.H. Pickersgill. The second John Murray was the great publishing
entrepreneur of his period. After the immediate success of *Childe Harold* his fortunes and Byron's becam[e]
interlinked. His own copy of Bertel Thorwaldsen's marble bust of Byron is included in the portrait.

access to the lower regions of Melbourne House from which my *ascent* had long excluded me,' Byron wrote to Lady Melbourne later in the year.

In 1812 Elizabeth Melbourne was a little over sixty, still with much of the magnetism and self-confidence suggested in Joshua Reynolds' early portraits. She had had an adventurous and, to Byron, an alluring history. Bosom friend of Georgiana, Duchess of Devonshire, with whom she posed for Daniel Gardner's famous portrait of the soothsayers from *Macbeth*, *Witches Round the Cauldron*; veteran campaigner for Charles James Fox in the Westminster election campaigns of 1784, Lady Melbourne was also the unscathed survivor of affairs not only with the Prince of Wales but with Lord Egremont, reputed to be William Lamb's father, and with the Duke of Bedford. She had the quick wit and practised confidence of the consort of great men.

Her malicious tongue caused Lady Bessborough to nickname her 'The Thorn', and Caroline made the true comment that Lady Melbourne lacked the quality of softness, the 'Vieille Cour' manner, possessed by Lady Bessborough and by Byron himself, living as she did by the principle of dog eat dog. Her worldly wisdom, bracing kindness and equable temperament came as a relief to Byron after Caroline's demented vacillations. When he asked Lady Melbourne to 'undertake' him he revealed his innate hatred of decision making: 'I am always but too happy', he told her, 'to find one to regulate or misregulate me, & I am as docile as a Dromedary & can bear almost as much.'

Byron and his female mentor were both naturally devious. Lady Holland was not the only person who compared Lady Melbourne with the conniving Madame de Merteuil in Pierre Choderlos de Laclos' novel *Les Liaisons dangereuses*. Horace Walpole also likened her to Diane de Poitiers, Duchess of Valentinois, skilfully intriguing mistress of Henry II. Byron had enlisted her sympathetic interest in his schemes for writing Caroline 'the greatest absurdities' to 'keep her "gay"' in Ireland, forestalling her from making further scenes or, still worse, from returning. He wrote to Lady Melbourne in the middle of September: 'C is suspicious about our counter plots, & I am obliged to be as treacherous as Talleyrand, but remember *that treachery* is *truth* to you.'

In an age of letter writing the conspiracy between them was sustained by their exchange of others' confidential letters. As Caroline sent confessional missives to her mother-in-law, Lady Melbourne passed these on to Byron. Some of those letters contained extracts from the letters Byron had originally sent to her. Even the Prince of Wales expressed horror at this practice: 'I never heard of such a thing in my life, taking the Mothers for confidantes!' Before she left for Ireland Caroline had found a page of what turned out to be an indiscreet letter from Byron to her mother-in-law lying on the floor of the Lambs' upper apartments at Melbourne House. Weeks later, Caroline was still upbraiding him for this. Byron turned the tables, in a postscript to a letter which gives the exact flavour, teasingly flirtatious, of his burgeoning friendship with 'Lady M'. He blames Lady Melbourne for the planting of the letter:

'but *who* was careless? ma tante – methinks that reproach was somewhat misplaced – If you left it in ye. way on purpose – it had a blessed effect – it is but adding another *winding* to our *Labyrinth* – she quotes from it passages which I recollect – how could you Lady M – how could you "wear a pocket with a hole?"'

The intimacy between them was wonderfully verbal. Byron once told Lady Melbourne that her conversation was 'Champaigne' to his spirits. He spoke and wrote to her with an effervescent freedom that surprised even Hobhouse: 'Very extraordinary productions they are, such confessions!' he exclaimed when he read Byron's letters to 'la tante' in 1827, after Byron's death. Byron, always so wary of commitment to a woman, felt the age gap between them as a liberation. 'Lady M,' he said later, 'who might have been my mother, excited an interest in my feelings that few young women have been able to awaken.' He called her 'a sort of modern Aspasia, uniting the energy of a man's mind with the delicacy and tenderness of a woman's'. Aspasia was Pericles' formidable mistress, intellectual enough to have held her own with Socrates. Byron maintained that 'with a little more youth' Lady Melbourne might have turned his head as she so often turned his heart.

Their correspondence is certainly sexually charged. Is it possible that they had a physical relation? According to one of the statements circulated at the time of Byron's separation, Lord Byron told his wife 'that in 1813 he had absolute *criminal* Connection with an *old Lady*, at the same time as with her Daughters-in-law – that *She* absolutely *proposed it* to *him* – and that he said "She [was] *so old* he hardly knew how to set about it".' The last quip at least sounds authentically Byronic. But if true, this must have been only a temporary skirmish. At the basis of Byron's love for 'Lady M' was the security of a sexually undemanding friendship: 'She was my greatest *friend*, of the feminine gender: – when I say "friend", I mean *not* mistress, for that's the antipode.' Though it flattered her sense of sexual possibility, Lady Melbourne's devotion to Byron was essentially that of the voyeur.

The young Byron basked in her sophisticated knowingness. Caroline never forgave Lady Melbourne for supplanting her. Her always acute powers of observation were heightened by her grief when she came to confront Byron with the painful reality of her 'extraordinary' situation: 'my mother-in-law actually in the place I held – her ring instead of mine – her letters instead of mine – her heart – but do you believe either she or any other feel for you what I felt – ugly & thin & despised as I am.'

But even Caroline was never aware of the full ramifications of that correspondence of autumn 1812. On 13 September Byron told 'la tante' that his affair with Caroline was now definitely over and that his real object of attachment was Annabella Milbanke, daughter of Lady Melbourne's brother Ralph – 'one to whom I have never said much, but have never lost sight of'. The effects of this confession, possibly as unexpected to Byron as it was to Lady Melbourne, were to reverberate through the coming winter, over the next decade and indeed on into the centuries to come.

13

Cheltenham and Eywood
1812–1813

In September 1812, the month Napoleon entered Moscow, Byron was in Cheltenham, the spa town he had first visited with his mother as a boy in 1801 when the fortune-teller told her he would be married in his 26th year and die in his 37th. This prophecy was not to be far out.

Newstead had now, at least theoretically, been sold. Though the house and estate had failed to reach a satisfactory price at auction on 14 August and, on Hanson's instructions, had been bought in, another buyer, Thomas Claughton, materialised next day and his offer of £140,000 had been accepted. Byron was a homeless animal again. Anxious to escape London at 'this very *unwholesome* season' of the year, and to put himself well beyond the reach of Caroline, he had toyed with an invitation from Margaret Mercer Elphinstone, an intelligent, candid and beautiful young heiress whom Byron much admired, to join her in a party at Tunbridge Wells. He had finally settled on Cheltenham instead, back within sight of the Malvern Hills he had first come to love on his holiday visits as a boy.

Cheltenham was now emerging as one of the most fashionable of English spa towns, busy with the building of its colonnades and crescents, parades and squares to accommodate the influx of wealthy visitors. One of the attractions for Byron was the presence of a number of his friends from the London political circles in which he now moved: amongst what he termed 'a very pleasant set' were 'ye. Jerseys Melbournes Cowpers & Hollands', as well as Lord and Lady Rawdon and Lord and Lady Oxford. The *Cheltenham Chronicle* for 3 September announced: 'Lord Byron, the envied and successful Bard, is present amongst our visitants.' He spent his first few weeks in lodgings in the High Street before moving to the house, Georgiana Cottage, where the Hollands had been staying, a building with elegant iron balconies and verandas and a beautiful long garden. '"By the waters of Cheltenham I sate down

& *drank*, when I remembered thee oh Georgiana Cottage!"' The words of the Psalmist echoed in his mind.

For some months, Byron had been suffering from a painful complaint diagnosed to be a kidney stone. He had been 'cupped on the loins, glystered, purged & vomited' but, after a temporary respite, the problem had recurred. Another of his reasons for coming to Cheltenham had been to seek further treatment for his 'teazing maladies'. He consulted Dr Henry Charles Boisragon, a highly regarded Cheltenham practitioner, extra physician to the Prince of Wales. Besides drinking the 'very medicinal & sufficiently disgusting' waters of the spa, Byron was 'diluted to the throat' with supplementary medicines prescribed by Dr Boisragon. But painful attacks continued into the next year.

In autumn 1812, while Byron was in Cheltenham, *Childe Harold* was going into its fifth edition. For the frontispiece John Murray had commissioned an engraving of a miniature portrait of the author by George Sanders. Byron had approved of Sanders' original, a painting depicting him full-face, looking lordly in a draped pelisse with sable border. He had however become acutely conscious of the importance of his public image and was less enthusiastic about the engraved version by Henry Meyer, submitted by John Murray for his approval. 'I have a *very strong objection* to the engraving of the portrait & request that it may on no account be prefixed, but let *all* the proofs be burnt, & the plates broken,' he instructed Murray. His publisher obediently, though reluctantly, committed the engraving of the portrait to the flames where, he told Byron, he 'had some consolation in seeing it ascend in sparkling brilliancy to Parnassus'. Byron insisted that the plate itself should be broken, but Murray pleaded with him to be allowed to keep one copy of the offending engraving, the only example known to be extant.

Murray was anxious to galvanise his celebrated poet into action again, offering him a thousand guineas for a new poem, though saying, 'I will sacrifice my right arm (your Lordship's friendship) rather than publish any poem not equal to Childe Harold – without a conscriptive Command.' That September, in the formal elegance of Cheltenham, Byron started *The Giaour*, a long narrative which drew on the dark-bright memories of his exotic travels, the landscape still agonisingly vivid in his mind. In recreating the real story of the slave girl in the sack, sentenced to be thrown into the sea by her Turkish lord Hassan, Byron brings to the grand themes of freedom and oppression his authentic Eastern twist.

The slave girl Leila encapsulates his liking for the lithe, dark-skinned, dark-eyed, docile style of Eastern beauty. When he returned from Turkey he had found it difficult to adapt himself to Englishwomen: 'they were so fair, and unmeaning, and *blonde*'. The character of the Giaour, as Byron was freely to admit to Lady Melbourne, bore a very close relation to his own state of mind at the time he wrote the poem. Here is another dark, glamorous, intemperate outsider, an infidel racked by guilt 'For some dark deed he will not name'. Byron, whose mobile mind made him impatient with many of his heroes, was to retain a fondness for the Giaour, defending him against detractors: 'The Giaour is certainly a bad character – but not dangerous.'

It was now, while at Cheltenham, that Byron became more closely involved with the theatre, one of the ruling passions of his life, the ephemeral excitements of performance answering the changeable emotionalism of his temperament. The Kembles were acting at the Theatre Royal. His comments on William Betty, the former child prodigy 'Young Roscius' whom Byron once admired, show him at his most abusive as a drama critic:

'Betty is performing here, I fear, very ill, his figure is that of a hippopotamus, his face like the Bull and *mouth* on the pannels of a heavy coach, his arms are fins fattened out of shape, his voice the gurgling of an Alderman with the quinsey, and his acting altogether ought to be natural, for it certainly is like nothing that *Art* has ever yet exhibited on the stage.'

In October 1812 Byron and the famous clown Joseph Grimaldi were fellow guests of Colonel Berkeley at Berkeley Castle in Gloucestershire. Byron greeted Grimaldi pantomimically, giving him a series of low bows and expressing his 'great and unbounded satisfaction in becoming acquainted with a man of such rare and profound talents'. Grimaldi bowed back even more elaborately, turning round to make a face at Colonel Berkeley 'expressive of mingled gratification and suspicion, which threw those around into a roar of laughter'. Charles Dickens, when he came to edit and to some extent to ghost Grimaldi's memoirs, was clearly enchanted by this meeting of the clowns, giving the scene the mad vitality of a great comic novel. Grimaldi has been told to accept by way of eat and drink whatever Byron suggests:

'Towards the end of the repast his Lordship invited him to eat a little appletart. He therefore acquiesced with many thanks, and the tart being placed before him, began operations.

"Why, Mr Grimaldi, do you not take soy with your tart?"

"Soy, my Lord?"

"Yes, soy: it is very good with salmon, and therefore it must be nice with apple-pie."

He bowed assent to Byron's proposal and proceeded to pour some of the fish-sauce over the tart. After one or two vain attempts to swallow a mouthful of the vile mess, he addressed Lord Byron with considerable formality begging to observe that he really trusted he would forgive his declining to eat the mixture as, however much the confession might savour of bad taste, he really did not relish soy with apple-tart.'

While Byron was still in Cheltenham Lord Holland, now returned to London, wrote asking him to compose an address to celebrate the reopening of Drury Lane Theatre, which had been rebuilt after its destruction by a fire in 1809. Byron had watched the blaze himself from the upper storey of a house in Covent Garden. Lord Holland, on behalf of the committee of management, had originally invited Byron to enter a competition for the address. This Byron disdained to do: 'as all Grubstreet seems engaged in the Contest, I have no ambition to enter the lists.' When he found there were rival contenders he threw his verses in the fire. The entries were, however, of such poor quality that Byron was then commissioned outright.

His 'Address, spoken at the Opening of Drury-Lane Theatre Saturday, October 10th, 1812' was written as a stirring celebration piece, commemorating Shakespeare and Sheridan, praising Mrs Siddons, David Garrick and the powerful English theatrical tradition of which Drury Lane had been so much a part. John Murray, already in the role of Byron's loyal representative, attended the opening, writing to assure him that his address had been received with 'applauding satisfaction', and enclosing a copy of the poem carefully marked by him to indicate the passages that had been most noisily appreciated. The more disquieting news was that Mr Elliston's delivery had been 'exceedingly bad – indeed his acting exhibits nothing but conceit'.

The Drury Lane address confirmed Byron as a leading and, by now, controversial public figure. He was sufficiently recognisable for George Cruikshank to depict him with Lord Holland in a vitriolic cartoon satirising Drury Lane, *Management – or – Butts and Hogsheads*, the implication being that Lord Holland had traded the commission for the address for Byron's support for Whig policies in the House of Lords.

Byron's involvement in contemporary theatre was soon to be eclipsed by the dramas of his private life. Earlier in 1812 he had been dismissive of Annabella Milbanke. In a letter to Caroline Lamb he had asserted: 'I have no desire to be better acquainted with Miss Milbank, she is too good for a fallen spirit to know or wish to know, & I should like her better if she were less perfect.' What had happened between May and September of that year, by which time he was seriously contemplating marrying a woman who, on his own admission, he scarcely knew?

It appears that by degrees Annabella had grown on him. Though he pretended an aversion to well-educated women this was not so in practice: all his important female liaisons – Caroline Lamb, Lady Oxford, Teresa Guiccioli – were with women of more than usual intelligence. Miss Milbanke seemed a marriageable proposition because she was 'a clever woman, an amiable woman' and also a woman 'of high blood'. Byron freely admitted that he shared his mother's snobbery: 'I have still a few Norman & Scotch inherited prejudices on that score.' Annabella's connection with the extended family of Lady Melbourne was a definite advantage. He told her: 'I am perfectly convinced that if I fell in love with a woman of Thibet she would turn out an *emigré cousin* of some of you.' In pursuing Annabella, Byron was willing to overlook the fact that she was not immediately in the 'golden dolly' category, though she had expectations of an inheritance from her childless uncle, Lord Wentworth. Her father, Sir Ralph Milbanke, was in financial trouble after overspending on local electioneering in Durham. But, believing that he had sold Newstead and still hoping that his Rochdale affairs would soon resolve themselves, Byron felt confident he could support them both.

Annabella's air of quizzical detachment appeared the more attractive after Lady Caroline Lamb's impulsiveness. The decorous, thoughtful Annabella was in many ways the direct opposite of the 'little maniac', who was still besieging him from Ireland: '*A T T H I S moment*', he wrote on 28 September, 'another *express* from Ireland!!! more Scenes!' He was feeling that nothing but a very rapid marriage could save him from Caroline's continuing pursuit. In a letter to Lady Melbourne he assesses his position, analysing Annabella with devastating candour:

'As to *Love*, that is done in a week, (provided the Lady has a reasonable share) besides marriage goes on better with esteem & confidence than romance, & she is quite pretty enough to be loved by her husband, without being so glaringly beautiful as to attract too many rivals.'

He puts himself over as cynically eager to play the high society marriage game. But behind this bravado there was, however short-lived, a genuine longing for the settled existence that a good marriage would bring him, allaying any rumours of his troubled past. 'Whatever you may think,' he told Lady Melbourne, 'I assure you I have a very domestick turn.' In his imagination Byron could project himself into a secure and tranquil future, the opposite of his so far fragmented existence: the country house, the town house, the genial friends, the children. One anxiety remained: 'Does Annabella *waltz*?'

By the end of September the fashionables had all left Cheltenham. Byron was feeling lonely and depressed, complaining: 'Cheltenham is a desart, nothing but the Waters detain me here.' His long-distance courtship of Annabella Milbanke was interrupted by the rumour that she was already engaged to the Hon. George Eden. Though reassured that she was so far uncommitted he was nervous about broaching the question of marriage, 'never having made a proposal' in his life and still conscious of his humiliation over Mary Chaworth. Lady Melbourne, seeing an engagement to Annabella Milbanke as a means to retrieve Lady Caroline, agreed to approach her niece with a tentative proposal of marriage on Byron's behalf. When he was rejected his response was apparently philosophic: 'My dear Ly. M. marry – Mahomet forbid! – I am sure we shall be better friends than before.' Valiantly Byron quoted, indeed slightly misquoted, Colley Cibber's Lord Foppington: '"I have lost a thousand women in my time but never had the ill manners to quarrel with them for such a trifle."' Annabella, he maintained, had been absolutely right.

Why, at this juncture, did she refuse Lord Byron? She had certainly been drawn to him from the time of their first conversation, in April 1812, when they had discussed the Milbankes' protégé, the young cobbler-poet Joseph Blacket. Byron must have been making an extraordinary effort, since rural poets were anathema to him. No doubt she was taken by surprise by this unexpected and impersonal proposal. She had had other suitors besides the highly eligible George Eden, heir of the 1st Lord Auckland. Annabella's analytic cast of mind had been noted by Elizabeth, Duchess of Devonshire: 'She really is an icicle.' Her temperament was one of cool appraisal not of rash decision on the subject of her marriage. But her immediate response to the proposal, to sit down and write a 'Character of Lord Byron', a careful assessment of the way in which Byron's passions had since childhood exercised a 'tyrannical power' over his intellect, suggests an accelerated interest in her suitor, and when their correspondence resumed in August 1813 it was Annabella who took the initiative.

Byron was always well insured against rejection. While he was entrusting 'Lady M.' with his proposal he was doing his best to fall in love with 'a new Juliet, who sets off for London in the long Coach tomorrow to appear on (not in) Covent Garden'; with an Italian songstress and Welsh seamstress; with his agent's wife and daughter (the Hansons were in Cheltenham); as well as with 'a picture of Buonaparte's Empress who looks as fair & foolish as he is dark & diabolical'. Byron's valet also pressed the claims of a very pretty Dutch widow 'of great riches & rotundity', with whose maid Fletcher was himself involved.

Of Byron's Cheltenham flirtations it was 'La Pulcella', the dark-eyed, dusky skinned Italian opera singer, who attracted him most. They conversed in Italian since she could speak no English: 'a great point', Byron told Lady Melbourne, 'for from certain coincidences the very sound of that language is Music to me'. Though he withheld the details, the coincidence is clear: 'La Pulcella' recalled Nicolo Giraud and the lessons in Italian in the Athens monastery. She 'reminds me of many in the Archipelago I wished to forget, & makes me forget what I ought to remember, all which are against me'. In making such a semi-confession Byron was, as always, sailing close to the wind. A rather less romantic aspect of 'La Pulcella' was her propensity for guzzling huge suppers: chicken wings and sweetbreads, custards, peaches and port wine. His fastidious dislike of women's physicality meant that women in the act of eating were repulsive to him. He elaborated on this to Lady Melbourne: 'a woman should never be seen eating or drinking, unless it be *lobster sallad* & *Champagne*, the only truly feminine & becoming viands. – I recollect imploring one Lady not to eat more than a fowl at a sitting without effect, & have never yet made a single proselyte to Pythagoras.'

According to Hobhouse, Byron was not too shaken by Annabella's refusal of his offer of marriage: 'Perhaps it may be said that he did not pretend to regret it at all.' He did his best to rise above it in his usual manner, gently jeering at his 'amiable *Mathematician*': 'Her proceedings are quite rectangular, or rather we are two parallel lines prolonged to infinity side by side but never to meet.' By November 1812 he had come to congratulate them both on their mutual escape: 'That would have been but a *cold collation*, & I prefer hot suppers.' By this time Byron was in his new lover Lady Oxford's more voluptuous arms.

A few weeks later Byron was paid a visit by his old Cambridge intimate William Bankes who confessed to him tearfully that his recent proposal of marriage to Annabella Milbanke had been rejected. Byron burst out laughing at the thought that his one-time pastor, master and inductor into Cambridge pederasty, should have been turned down by Annabella too.

On 19 October 1812 Napoleon was beginning the retreat from Moscow which he had taken a month earlier. The Russians had abandoned and burned the city, and still refused to make peace. The ignominious reversal in Napoleon's fortunes was causing consternation to his English admirers. That day Hobhouse wrote to Byron: 'The world is certainly bewitched.' A week later Byron left Cheltenham for Eywood, country seat of Lord and Lady Oxford, in wild and lovely countryside in Herefordshire, near Presteigne. In accepting her flatteringly eager invitation Byron was aiming to play off Lady Oxford against Lady Caroline, as he confided to Lady Melbourne, his 'dear Machiavel'.

Lady Oxford's importance to Byron has been greatly underestimated partly because of the paucity of letters between them. They corresponded little because they were virtually living together through the autumn of 1812 to spring 1813, a liaison more or less accepted by her husband, Edward Harley, 5th Earl of Oxford, who was well trained in complaisance by his wife's already long sequence of affairs. Lady Oxford was then forty to Byron's twenty-four. The age difference between them was part of the attraction. In a later account of this love affair he even raised her age to forty-six. Compared with the indiscreet intensities of Lady Caroline, Byron found the 'autumnal charms' of Lady Oxford soothing, likening her to a Claude Lorrain landscape with a setting sun.

He would claim that he never felt a stronger passion, which she returned with equal ardour. Their sexual compatibility was partly a matter of emotional ease between them. Lady Oxford was a woman of sophistication and experience who, to start with at least, knew not to make demands. Byron referred to her as his 'Enchantress', drawing a parallel between their own disportings and those in the print of Rinaldo and Armida which adorned his apartment at Eywood. Armida was the sexually charismatic woman whose magic detained the young Crusader Rinaldo in Torquato Tasso's sixteenth-century epic *Gerusalemme liberata*. This great moralistic fable of the First Crusade draws its force from a sense of shifting sexual boundaries, and there is indeed an element of role reversal in the love between strong-minded intellectual Lady Oxford and her beautiful, effeminate young protégé.

Lady Oxford, born Elizabeth Jane Scott, was a highly political creature. She was a rector's daughter, brought up in the fervour of French revolutionary optimism, living according to her own ideals of freedom in politics and love. In her own right she was an influential figure on the radical wing of the Whig party. She consorted with the pamphleteer John Horne Tooke and his reformist associates. She had been the mistress of Sir Francis Burdett, courageously populist spokesman in the House of Commons. To Hobhouse, political liberal though he was, Lady Oxford's links with the radical extremists of the Hampden Club put her beyond the pale. Besides his amorous education Lady Oxford exerted herself to politicise Byron, as he acknowledged: '*There* is a woman, who amid all her fascination, always urged a man to usefulness or glory.' In encouraging him to enter active politics, particularly in taking up 'the cause of weakness', she developed his consciousness of obligation and gave Byron a new sense of his potential influence.

He remained at Eywood through most of November 1812, lapped in her affections. A year later he remembered how she said to him, '"Have we not passed our last month like the gods of Lucretius?" And so we had. She is an adept in the text of the original (which I like too).' There was an aura of magic about Eywood, the classical mansion rising in pedimented, porticoed splendour in the midst of untamed country on the borders of Wales. Lord Oxford's mother and sisters seemed as ancient as Owen Glendower. For Byron the often impassable roads gave Eywood an added attraction. The fear of Lady Caroline's sudden arrival was still an ever-present threat. He secreted himself happily in the famous library assembled by the 1st Earl of Oxford, Robert Harley. A collection of the manuscripts belonging to this library was published in 1744 under the title *The Harleian Miscellany*. Wits around London now applied this title to Lady Oxford's six children in view of their reputedly miscellaneous parentage.

The regime at Eywood was pleasantly easygoing. It suited Byron better than the more formal luxury of Middleton Park, where he was entertained at this same period by Lady Jersey, another mature aristocratic female admirer. Lady Oxford's ideals of liberation permeated her whole household. She reared her family as children of nature with a watchful indulgence inspired by the tenets of Jean-Jacques Rousseau. Byron himself spent hours reading, joking and playing Blind Man's Buff with them, reverting to childish pleasures in the way he did so easily. With the Harley children he roamed through the countryside. As they explored the site of an old Roman encampment at the top of Wapley Hill a stone thrown accidentally – or possibly on purpose – by three-year-old Alfred at his mother's paramour struck Byron in the face, very near the eye. The wound bled alarmingly and he fainted from the pain. He soon recovered but was left with a small scar. 'Never mind, my Lord, the scar will be gone before the *season*,' said his valet William Fletcher, conscious of how essential Byron's appearance was to his social success.

In fact he fattened with contentment while at Eywood, promising that he would diet himself back to thinness later. He planned to let his moustachios grow again, as he had done abroad. In November 1812, at Lady Oxford's suggestion, he took a house at Kinsham, five miles away from Eywood, on an isolated, thickly wooded hillside high above the valley of the River Lugg. Kinsham Court was a jointure house belonging to the Oxford family. Byron's negotiations with Lord Oxford for the property were not without their tensions. Oxford's father, the Bishop of Hereford, had lived there. A small church adjoined the property with a churchyard said by Byron, connoisseur of gravestones, to be full of 'the most facetious Epitaphs' he had ever read. Byron, still imagining that the sale of Newstead would soon be finalised, came to regard Kinsham as his new, more modest but potentially much more comfortable country seat and he began to issue invitations to his house in 'the *wilderness*'.

The name 'Byron', etched on to one of Kinsham's upper windows, may be an early mark of his proprietorship.

Lady Caroline's frantic letters followed him to Eywood. The situation was particularly poignant since Caroline had once been an intimate friend of Lady Oxford's, an admirer of her independent cast of mind. They had corresponded on such esoteric subjects as whether learning Greek purifies or enflames the passions. But now Lady Oxford was at war with Lady Caroline, enlisted in Byron's defence, mocking her letters, helping Byron to reply to them. Byron was the more incensed with his discarded lover since, with her instinct to make contact with those closest to him, she had been meddling with the Earl of Clare.

On their way back from Ireland early in November, her mother brought Caroline a letter from Byron with a coronet on the seal. The initials beneath the coronet were Lady Oxford's. It seems likely that this letter, made public later in Caroline Lamb's novel *Glenarvon*, published in 1816, was composed under Lady Oxford's approving eye:

'I am no longer your lover; and since you oblige me to confess it, by this truly unfeminine persecution, – learn, that I am attached to another; whose name it would of course be dishonourable to mention. I shall ever remember with grati-tude the many instances I have received of the predilection you have shewn in my favour. I shall ever continue your friend, if your Ladyship will permit me so to style myself; and, as a first proof of my regard, I offer you this advice, correct your vanity, which is ridiculous; exert your absurd caprices upon others; and leave me in peace.'

Since their amour had been so sexually ambivalent the complaint of Lady Caroline's lack of femininity was particularly heartless. The letter unhinged her. She collapsed and was forced to interrupt her journey at the 'filthy Dolphin Inn' at Rock in Cornwall, where she was bled and leeched. She began sending dis-traught letters direct to Lady Oxford, threatening to write to Lord Oxford as well – a development that Byron dreaded, with the chain of repercussions through the Oxford and Lamb families that would inevitably result.

In December Lady Caroline staged a terrible and imaginative revenge, ordering a bonfire to be lit in the grounds of Brocket Hall, the Melbourne house in Hertfordshire. She instructed a group of village girls from Welwyn, dressed in white, to dance around the bonfire. One of her pages recited the lines she had composed, celebrating the burning in effigy of Byron, an Englishman as traitorous as Guy Fawkes himself. Into the flames she cast a replica of his miniature, copies of his letters, chains and rings, flowers and feathers, tawdry ornaments of love:

'Burn, fire, burn, while wondering boys exclaim,
And gold and trinkets glitter in the flame.'

Hobhouse wrote sympathetically to Byron: 'Your tale of the Brocket bon fire is almost incredible – well may you say with Horace, "Me Phryne macerat" adding at the same time "nec uno contenta" [Phryne, not satisfied with one man, torments me].' Phryne, Horace's Roman courtesan, was one of the names Caroline adopted in her letters to Byron in happier days.

Byron spent Christmas 1812 *en famille* with the Oxfords, glad to be marooned at Eywood by the avalanches of January snows and feeling 'very *qualmish*' at the prospect of returning to town. Back in London, he took lodgings at 4 Bennet Street, St James's. Lady Oxford, a friend and supporter of the Princess of Wales in her acrimonious separation from the Prince, now introduced Byron into Princess Caroline's close circle. The Prince had married the former Caroline of Brunswick to pay off his huge debts and to provide an heir, thus safeguarding the succession. Since the birth of their daughter, Princess Charlotte, they had kept separate establishments. In 1806 there had been a parliamentary enquiry into charges of immorality against her, fuelled by rumours that she had had an illegitimate child. She had been exonerated, but sympathisers claimed she was still being unjustly victimised.

At the time Byron met her Princess Caroline was being cultivated by the more libertarian Whigs, who were using her as the focus for their opposition to the Prince who they felt had reneged on them when he became Regent. By 1812 the Princess's residence in Kensington had become a focal point for the politically disaffected and the louche. Byron and Lady Oxford were invited there together for dinners that sometimes went on until dawn. On one of these evenings, according to his hostess, Byron 'really was the hero of the party, for he was in very high spirits, free like a bird in the air, having just got rid of his chains'. Presumably this was because he had discarded Lady Caroline. He was still talking of going abroad again.

Lady Oxford had hoped that Byron would take up the Princess's cause in the House of Lords. But he was not so tractable as she expected, confiding disloyally to Lady Melbourne: 'M'amie thinks I agree with her in *all* her politics, but she will discover that this is a mistake.' Byron felt that in her championing of Princess Caroline Lady Oxford was morally on very shaky ground: 'She always insists upon the P's innocence; but then as she sometimes reads me somewhat a tedious homily upon her own, I look upon it in much the same point of view as I should on Mary Magdalen's vindication of Mrs Joseph, or any other *immaculate riddle*.' There are signs that Lady Oxford's political tutelage had become a little wearisome, as his sexual interest began to wane. Princess Caroline watched the affair with fascination, doubtful if Lady Oxford could succeed in capturing him permanently. On one of their evening visits 'Lord Byron was so cross to her (his Lordship not being in a good mood), that she was crying in the ante-room'.

In spring 1813 in London Byron was in the grip of one of his cycles of depression, veering between lassitude and hyperactivity, haunted by nightmare images and assailed by a sense of the uselessness of human endeavour. He was still writing *The Giaour*. Reading excerpts aloud to Dallas he told him that the verses on the self-annihilating scorpion had come to him in his sleep:

> 'The Mind, that broods o'er guilty woes,
>   Is like the Scorpion girt by fire,
> In circle narrowing as it glows
> The flames around their captive close,
> Till inly search'd by thousand throes,
>   And maddening in her ire,
> One sad and sole relief she knows,
> The sting she nourish'd for her foes,
> Whose venom never yet was vain,
> Gives but one pang, and cures all pain,
> And darts into her desperate brain. –
> So do the dark in soul expire,
> Or live like Scorpion girt by fire.'

The suicidal impulses were never far away.

Domestic anxieties piled up on him. Claughton, the prospective purchaser of Newstead, had paid only £5,000 of the agreed down-payment for the property. Byron was embarrassed at being unable to settle his debt to Scrope Davies, who was now desperate for money. He was also unable to satisfy the many creditors pursuing him under the impression that Newstead had been sold. Nevertheless he lent £500 to his old friend Francis Hodgson in a fit of typically irresponsible generosity.

Caroline Lamb was now virtually stalking him. She was threatening to ruin him by making public what he had confessed to her of his homosexual past. He told her, 'it is in a great measure owing to this persecution – to the accursed things you have said' that he was feeling impelled to leave the country. Byron had learned the hard way that 'an incensed woman is a dangerous enemy'.

She arrived in his Bennet Street apartments one day when he was out. William Beckford's *Vathek* was on his table. Exploiting her secret knowledge of his own links with Beckford the sodomist she wrote on the first page of the book, 'Remember me!' When Byron returned and discovered this attempt at none too subtle blackmail, he riposted, in what he called 'the irritability of the moment', by inscribing underneath his own two stanzas, carrying a bitter echo of her words:

> 'Remember thee, remember thee!
>   Till Lethe quench life's burning stream,
> Remorse and shame shall cling to thee,
>   And haunt thee like a feverish dream!
>
> Remember thee! Ay, doubt it not;
>   Thy husband too shall think of thee;
> By neither shalt thou be forgot,
>   Thou *false* to him, thou *fiend* to me!'

In another episode showing her anguished ingenuity Lady Caroline copied Byron's handwriting and signature in order to extract his miniature from John Murray. 'Car L has been *forging letters* in my name & hath thereby pilfered the best picture of *me* the Newstead miniature!!! Murray was the imposed upon.' His fury is mingled with a grudging admiration at her effrontery. The 'Newstead miniature' was the portrait by George Sanders, the original of the engraving Byron had disliked and ordered to be destroyed. So desperate had Caroline been to acquire the miniature she had followed up the letter by appearing in person at John Murray's to collect it. Byron rebuked his publisher for such gullibility, instructing him not to allow anything of Byron's to pass from his hands without his seal as well as signature. Using Lady Melbourne as his intermediary he retrieved the miniature a few months later. Lady Melbourne had had a copy made for her errant daughter-in-law.

When Caroline beseeched Byron for a lock of his hair he sent her, via Lady Melbourne, a lock of Lady Oxford's: 'it was a lucky coincidence of colour & shape for my purpose.' He surmised that Caroline would never know the difference. It could have been a revenge from a Jacobean tragedy.

Spring snows were falling at Eywood when Byron returned there in April 1813. He seized the few fine days to go out on expeditions on the water or in the woods, 'scrambling and splashing about with the children' or in contented solitude. But his kidney trouble was recurring painfully as we see from his urgent instructions for a bottle of 'Adam's Solvent for the Stone' to be sent immediately from London by the Leominster coach. Lady Oxford's bower had begun to lose its hold on him: he complains about waiting for her in Ledbury 'like a dutiful Cortejo'. The idleness of the life of the attendant lover irked him. He could not bear to be a man without a real role.

It was in this restless mood that his affections to some extent transferred from the mother to the daughters, beautiful, well read, precocious children whose education Lady Oxford had supervised herself. When he met her in London Hobhouse had been bowled over by the attractions of the eldest daughter, Lady Jane Harley, then sixteen, describing her in his diary as 'a delightful creature, but un peu libre'. She could recite the entire works of Shakespeare by heart. Byron too admired Jane but his favourite was her younger sister Lady Charlotte, generally believed to be Lady Oxford's daughter by Sir Francis Burdett. Charlotte, at eleven, was at the age of promise which most moved him, the child on the edge of puberty.

He became temporarily obsessed with Charlotte just as, a few months later, he was fleetingly besotted with his '*petite cousine*', seven-year-old, black-eyed, black-haired Eliza Byron, plotting to buy toys for her and take her to the theatre. Lady Oxford's daughter Charlotte is the subject of the famous and much anthologised five stanzas 'To Ianthe', fragile flower of the narcissus. He addresses her as his 'Young Peri of the West!' In these stanzas, published as a preface to the seventh edition of *Childe Harold*, Byron celebrates the girl's evasive charm and addresses the painful ambiguities of their relationship:

> 'Oh! let that eye, which, wild as the Gazelle's,
> Now brightly bold or beautifully shy,
> Wins as it wanders, dazzles where it dwells,
> Glance o'er this page; nor to my verse deny
> That smile for which my breast might vainly sigh,
> Could I to thee be ever more than friend:
> This much, dear maid, accord; nor question why
> To one so young my strain I would commend,
> But bid me with my wreath one matchless lily blend.'

Byron arranged for Richard Westall to paint Lady Charlotte's portrait, suggesting that John Murray, in the new edition, could use an engraving taken from the picture of 'the pretty little girl' Murray had seen the other day. In a further act of revenge on Lady Caroline he gave the child as playthings the rings she once gave Byron, including the wedding ring she ordered for herself from a Bond Street jeweller, insisting that Byron should place it on her finger. In reporting this black comedy to Lady Melbourne he confided his tendresse for Lady Charlotte, 'whom I should love forever if she could always be only eleven years old – & whom I shall probably marry when she is old enough & bad enough to be made into a modern wife'.

At Eywood he acted out the fantasy of educating Charlotte Harley as the future Lady Byron, supplanting her mother as tutor, laughingly imagining himself as poor duped Moody, the middle-aged character in Garrick's *The Country Girl* whose designs on his young ward, brought up in rural innocence, misfire when she outwits and abandons him. Byron's concentrated sessions *à deux* as Lady Charlotte's tutor evidently went too far. One of Lady Byron's separation statements reads: 'He told me that at the time of his connextion with Lady O she detected him one day in an attempt upon her daughter, then a Child of thirteen, & was enraged with him to the greatest degree.'

How seriously should we take this accusation? Lady Byron's statements, assembled to build up the case against her husband, have a note of hysterical vindictiveness. This particular statement was one of those dictated to Mrs Clermont, her one-time governess and her close ally, whose malevolence towards Byron was not conducive to accuracy. In this statement, for example, Lady Charlotte's age is given as thirteen when in fact it was eleven. Though there are many signs in Byron's history of his predilection for young girls there is no evidence of sexual attacks on them. He had, after all, rejected the Maid of Athens when she was on offer. If he had attempted to rape her daughter Lady Oxford, an unusually fond mother, rather than simply remonstrating with him, would surely have ejected Byron from her house. It seems likely that the 'attempt' on Lady Charlotte went no further than an unwisely ardent embrace. Nevertheless, amongst the curious collection of Byron's trophies and mementoes in the John Murray archive, two small packets contain samples of Lady Charlotte Harley's nut brown hair.

Less in thrall to Lady Oxford, Byron was vacillating. Weak-mindedly he finally agreed to the interview in London which Caroline Lamb had been demanding. She wanted to 'bid him adieu', knowing he was intending to leave England again soon. Byron made it a condition that she would not also insist on seeing Lady Oxford. He was probably alarmed, and with reason, that she would divulge his unwise confidences on the subject of his homosexual affairs. When he met Lady Caroline, Byron melted: 'He asked me to forgive him; he looked sorry for me; he cried.' His eyes, his looks, his words, his manner were as intimate as ever. She could not believe that he did not love her still.

Byron's natural empathy was his most dangerous asset. The responsiveness that gave such depth and meaning to his writing caused havoc in his emotional life. Now, beset by Caroline, still adored by Lady Oxford, he reacted to confusion by inviting yet more of it. When he encountered Annabella Milbanke at a

London party her obvious agitation transferred itself to him. She offered him her hand and Byron turned pale as he pressed it. She later identified this as the moment when their engagement was formed, at least on her own side.

Lady Oxford was attempting to regain his attention. In April 1813 he wrote to Lady Melbourne: '*We* are at present in a slight perplexity owing to an event which certainly did not enter into my calculation – what it is – I leave to your own ingenious imagination.' Presumably Lady Oxford had given Byron warning of a possible addition to the Harleian Miscellany. In mid-May he sent news that Lady Oxford, then in Cheltenham, had burst a small blood-vessel and was weak and ill, 'all which she attributes to "me & my *friends* in town"!! – I presume it will end in an indisposition which however unpleasant for a time – would eventually be a great *relief* to both.' Perhaps the unscheduled pregnancy ended in miscarriage. In any case Byron suspected that the malady had been a ruse.

There are signs of Lady Oxford's lingering influence in two episodes that summer. The first was his series of visits to the poet and essayist James Henry Leigh Hunt, then in Horsemonger Gaol in Farringdon Road on charges of libelling the Prince Regent in his radical paper the *Examiner*. As a political prisoner Leigh Hunt was treated well and given facilities for entertaining visitors. Tom Moore, a mutual friend who had arranged the meeting, stipulated 'plenty of fish and vegetables for the noble bard'. They got on well together. Byron, already an admirer of Hunt's writing, viewed him as 'an extraordinary character, and not exactly of the present age. He reminds me more of the Pym and Hampden times – much talent, great independence of spirit, and an austere, yet not repulsive, aspect.' He saw Hunt as part of the long and impressive English tradition of reform. Hunt was willingly seduced by Byron's charm, touched by his thoughtfulness in bringing Hunt books he knew would interest him, entering the prison with 'a couple of quartos' tucked nonchalantly under his own arm instead of giving orders to his footman to deliver them. As Hunt saw it, 'He was a warm politician, and thought himself earnest in the cause of liberty.' As always with Hunt there is a sting in the tail.

Ten days after the first of his visits to Leigh Hunt Byron made his final speech in the House of Lords. This was his Presentation of Major Cartwright's Petition, on 1 June 1813. John Cartwright was a veteran Radical campaigner, the most active member of the Hampden Club with which Lady Oxford was closely associated and to which Byron himself belonged. Cartwright had recently been arrested in his attempts to gather signatures for his latest petition for the rights of representatives of the people to put the case for parliamentary reform.

It was a courageous and almost a lone performance. Byron's parliamentary swansong, as he knew, was doomed to failure. The Radical Whig leader, Samuel Whitbread, had already refused to support Cartwright's Petition in the House of Commons. Byron's only ally in the upper house was Earl Stanhope, the elderly Jacobin whose support for the French Revolution had made him a deeply unpopular figure in Parliament. Though free speech was a cause he passionately believed in, Byron's own address, a relatively short one, has little of the imaginative eloquence of his speech in opposition to the Frame-breaking Bill. After it was over Byron called at Moore's lodgings. Moore was dressing for dinner. Byron strode up and down the next room declaiming, 'in a sort of mock-heroic voice', extracts from the speech he had just been delivering. '"I told them", he said, "that it was a most flagrant violation of the Constitution – that, if such things were permitted, there was an end of English freedoms, and that –"' When Moore interrupted him and asked what the dreadful grievance was, he pretended to have forgotten. The things he cared about most received a throwaway response.

'Ly. O arrives in town tomorrow – which I regret – when people have once fairly parted – how do I abhor these partings! – I know them to be of no use – & yet as painful at the time as the first plunge into purgatory.' The Oxfords were soon leaving for the continent, with gambling and other debts said to amount to £200,000. Byron had at one stage planned to sail with them to Sicily or join them in Sardinia. Now he was not so sure. In the last uneasy weeks before their embarkation he stayed with them in lodgings near Portsmouth. Lord Oxford began showing his resentment, a development with which his wife as usual dealt coolly: 'The Devil – who ought to be civil on such occasions has at last persuaded Ld. [Oxford] to be so too – for on *her* threatening to fill up my "carte blanche" in her own way – he quietly ate his own words & intentions – & now they are to "live happy ever after" – & to sail in the pleasing hope of seeing or not seeing me again.' Byron suggested flirtatiously to Lady Melbourne that the way was now clear for their own elopement, an event which would cause a greater sensation than any since Eve ran away with the apple. In fact Lady Oxford's departure left him feeling more '*Carolinish*' about her than he had expected. But it was emptiness mixed with some relief.

In later years Lady Oxford scandalised Italian women by walking about Naples with a miniature of Byron in her girdle. Byron reciprocated by hanging her portrait on one side of the chimney piece in his lodgings balanced by a picture of Lady Caroline. 'A woman is only grateful for her *first* and *last* conquest. The first of poor dear Lady O's was achieved before I entered on this world of care, but the *last* I do flatter myself was reserved for me.' This was his considered verdict on the affair.

The acclaim for *Childe Harold* had had a beneficial effect on Byron. John Galt, who noted how Byron had been 'soothed by success' in 1812, diagnosed that one reason for his nervous aggressiveness in spring 1813 was that 'he had risen in his own estimation above the honours so willingly paid to his genius, and was again longing for additional renown.' Byron's hunger for celebrity was satisfied, at least temporarily, by publication of *The Giaour*.

This poem, first of Byron's four popular 'Eastern tales', was published in June 1813 with a dedication to Samuel Rogers. By the end of the year it had gone into eight editions, each of which gave Byron the chance to make additions to what he calls 'this snake of a poem – which has been lengthening its rattles every month'. What had started as a poem of 685 lines eventually increased to 1,334. Jeffrey praised *The Giaour* in the *Edinburgh Review* for its highly original fragmentary structure, its fluency of verse, the convincing energy with which the aristocratic Venetian hero is delineated. Byron's friend 'Bold' Webster wrote admiringly from Yorkshire: 'You are indeed ye Idol Poet of ye Day.'

How was 'Giaour' pronounced? This mystery was part of its peculiar appeal. 'The "*Giaour*" has never been pronounced to this day,' Byron wrote to John Murray in 1817. The debate entered fiction in Jane Austen's *Persuasion* when Anne Elliot and Captain Benwick discuss not only the pronunciation of Byron's title but also his poetic depiction of hopeless agony and broken hearts. Anne Elliot, alarmed by the 'tremulous feeling' with which the apparently shy and inhibited Captain launches into quotation from Byron, 'ventured to hope he did not always read poetry; and to say, that she thought it was the misfortune of poetry, to be seldom safely enjoyed by those who enjoyed it completely; and that the strong feelings which alone could estimate it truly, were the very feelings which ought to taste it but sparingly'. This passage from *Persuasion*, written in 1815–16 and published two years later, summarises nicely the anxious fascination which greeted Byron's poetry in his own age.

14

Six Mile Bottom

1813–1814

Since 1812 the war had gone badly for Napoleon. The disastrous retreat from Moscow, which decimated the French army, was now being followed by decisive British victories in the Spanish Peninsula. In July 1813 London was in the throes of celebration of the victory, a few weeks earlier, of Wellington's armies over the French forces at Vitoria. 'This victory! – sad work – nothing but Conquest abroad & High health at home,' Byron lamented to Lady Melbourne, demonstrating his shock at his hero's turn of fortune and his horror of the self-congratulatory tone of the British celebrations. A Grand National Fête in Vauxhall Gardens was preceded by the Prince Regent's banquet, at which Wellington was toasted. Byron, with his jaundiced view of the proceedings, was delighted when the illuminations at Woolwich conflagrated, causing a huge fire. 'We are just recovering from tumult and train oil, and transparent fripperies, and all the noise and nonsense of victory,' he wrote to Tom Moore wearily, adding the news that his sister Augusta had arrived in town.

Circumstances conspired to make Byron susceptible to what became his closest and most perilous liaison. His political disillusionment was total. Lord Liverpool's aristocratic and conservative ministry, which had resumed power in summer 1812, was anathema to Byron. Its priorities were the defeat of Napoleon and the preservation of order in England under the shadow of the madness of King George III. Byron was bitter that this was a government with no sense of vision, no urge to ameliorate the conditions of the poor. His own lack of occupation was so desperate that he was driven to contemplate taking holy orders. Still enmeshed by his old debts and guilty memories, he told Lord Holland: 'the sins of my nonage sit heavy upon my majority.' Over the past year Byron had been exhausted by the relentless pursuit of Lady Caroline and the frenzied admonitions of her mother. The departure in late June of his enchantress, Lady Oxford, had left a sudden vacuum in his life. The rediscovery of his half-sister Augusta, after four years' separation, brought the joy of the familiar together with the frisson of new possibility: 'never having been much together, we are naturally more attached to each other.' For the three weeks that Augusta was in London brother and sister were almost inseparable.

Sketch of Colonel George Leigh, described by Byron as his
half-sister Augusta's 'drone of a husband'

Augusta had been married since 1807 to her cousin George Leigh, a Colonel in the fashionable 10th Hussars and former equerry to the Prince of Wales. The marriage, which Augusta had held out for in spite of the disapproval of his family, had only been a partial success. George Leigh, man about town and gambler, proved an absentee husband in the mode of Augusta's father 'Mad Jack' Byron. In 1810 there was a scandalous rift between Colonel George and his royal patron, the gist of which Mrs Byron had reported to Byron while he was travelling abroad: 'The cause of Colonel Leigh's quarrel with the Prince is that he cheated him in selling a horse for him, as he *retained* for *himself* part of the purchase money.' In spite of his neglect and fecklessness Augusta remained obstinately devoted to her husband and fiercely protective of their three small children. They still lived in the house the Prince of Wales had given them, the Lodge at Six Mile Bottom, a hamlet in horse-racing countryside near Newmarket. The name Six Mile Bottom inspired Lady Caroline Lamb to flights of Shakespearean ribaldry.

'Let me know when you arrive – & when & where & how you would like to see me – any where in short – but at *dinner*.' To begin with, in his eagerness, Byron wanted their reunion to take place alone. But he soon began to find an additional excitement in being seen in public with his sister. 'I think our being together before 3d. people will be a new *sensation* to *both*,' he suggested, proposing she should accompany him to a reception being given by the society hostess Lady Davy, wife of the chemical scientist Sir Humphry, where he would watch over her as if she were an unmarried woman in danger of remaining so. Part of the rapport between Byron and Augusta was the simple intimacy of their jokes. As an added inducement Byron threw in the prospect of a meeting with Madame de Staël at Lady Davy's. The formidable French intellectual, exiled by Napoleon, was being lionised in London in the summer of 1813.

A few days later Byron was begging Lady Melbourne for 'a *she* voucher for a ticket' for the Almack's Masque. Almack's were the magnificent assembly rooms in King Street, St James's, with a hundred-foot ballroom. Entry was selective. Tickets for the weekly balls there were controlled by a committee of aristocratic patronesses. In asking her to procure a ticket for his sister, Byron told Lady Melbourne he had begun to wish Augusta could live with him as his housekeeper. Lady Melbourne, used as she was to Byron's private ways, could surely read between the lines.

As Byron and his sister exchanged endearments together on the sofa at these London summer parties, people began to talk. The eagle-eyed Madame de Staël was suspicious, whilst the shows of public affection with Augusta provoked Caroline Lamb to further extremes of jealousy. At 'a small Waltzing Party' held by Lady Heathcote on 5 July, she made what was generally interpreted as a botched suicide attempt. Caroline herself denied it. According to her own account, seeing Byron at the party, feeling freed by his behaviour from her enforced promises that she would never waltz again, she had whispered to him: 'I conclude I may waltz *now*.' Byron answered sarcastically: 'With every body in turn – you always did it better than any one. I shall have a pleasure in seeing you.' Having waltzed, and feeling faint with emotion, she retreated to the small inner supper room. Byron later came in with Lady Rancliffe. He said to Caroline, taunting her for her agility at dancing, 'I have been admiring your dexterity.' She picked up a table knife, 'not intending anything'. He encouraged her to action, saying, 'Do, my dear. But if you mean to act a Roman's part, mind which way you strike with your knife – be it at your own heart, not mine – you have struck there already.' Exclaiming 'Byron', Caroline ran out of the room still brandishing the knife. She was adamant she did not stab herself.

Byron told a different story. Caroline, he asserted, had taken hold of his hand as he passed, after their acrimonious words about the waltz, and had pressed 'some sharp instrument' against it, saying, 'I mean to use this.' But he maintained to Lady Melbourne that he had not taken Caroline's threat seriously, assuming it to be one of her 'not uncommon *bravadoes*'. He denied that there had been an altercation in the supper room. He had stayed at Lady Heathcote's until nearly 5 a.m., only hearing of the 'cursed scarification' the next day as proliferating versions embroidered all the details. Lady Caroline had stabbed herself with a pair of scissors. She had attempted an incision in the jugular with a broken jelly glass, 'to the consternation of all the dowagers'. She had whipped out a knife and rammed it in her side, serious injury only being prevented by her stays. Byron kept his invitation card from Lady Heathcote as a curiosity and warning, a relic of the Ball at which 'Ly. Caroline L. performed ye. dagger Scene of indifferent memory'.

Caroline could hardly have evolved a scene better designed to accelerate Byron's dependence on Augusta. He hated other people's histrionics. He was deeply disconcerted and embarrassed by a lack of public decorousness in women. Augusta was still shy, perhaps as shy as Byron: this was another of the bonds between them. But she had the natural good manners of her class and a certain surface polish acquired during her upbringing in some of the grandest aristocratic households in the land. Augusta was amiable, forthcoming and amenable. She knew how to behave.

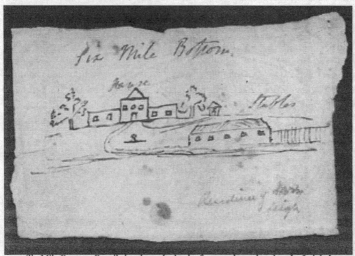

Six Mile Bottom. Pencil sketch on the back of an envelope showing the Leighs' establishment near Newmarket

In July and early August Byron made two visits with her to Six Mile Bottom, boxing and coxing it with George. He had always imagined Six Mile Bottom as 'that bleak common near Newmarket'. However, the setting of the lodge, with its stable block and paddocks, was picturesquely rural. The house, though small and cramped compared with Eywood, had for Byron the same quality of difference and enchantment, an erotic world-apartness. Here in her own domain his feelings for Augusta were confirmed.

The lingering impression that Byron's half-sister was 'dowdy' relies on a somewhat malicious comment from Lady Shelley, the diarist and socialite whose husband, Sir John Shelley, was a racing colleague of George Leigh's. Frances Shelley visited Six Mile Bottom at a time when Augusta was pregnant. Although she was not outstandingly beautiful nor a showy dresser, her portraits suggest Augusta's prettiness and sweetness. She had a maternal manner, a domestic radiance Byron always found attractive since it had been so lacking in his early life. Their love was rooted in childish affections and memories, nicknamings and teasings. Augusta was the person who could call him 'baby Byron'. He shortened her name to 'Gus', rapidly transformed into 'Goose'.

He was fond and indulgent with Augusta's own children. At the time of his first visits George Henry was a baby, Augusta Charlotte two and a half, Georgiana nearing five. Byron liked to claim an antipathy to children. He had once written to Augusta: 'I abominate the sight of them so much that I have always had the greatest respect for the character of *Herod*.' This was not really so. Byron's sense of himself as an orphan impelled his endless search for a replacement family, as for instance in the easy, perhaps too easy, camaraderie he experienced with Lady Oxford's children. At Six Mile Bottom, at close quarters with Augusta's infants, he seems to have been forbearance itself. As Lady Shelley noticed later: 'He was very patient with Mrs Leigh's children, who are not in the least in awe of him. He bore their distracting intrusions into his room with imperturbable good humour.' This was at the time he was writing *The Corsair*.

At some stage in their renewed relationship Byron and Augusta began to sleep together. What evidence do we have for this? There are Byron's confessions to Lady Melbourne, sometimes jauntily defiant, sometimes cagey and tormented, referring to Augusta in his letters as 'A' or with a blank. There is Byron's observation to Tom Moore, not entirely obliterated by Moore's censoring asterisks, on 22 August 1813: 'the fact is, I am, at this moment, in a far more serious, and entirely new, scrape than any of the last months, – and that is saying a great deal * * *.' There is Hobhouse's conspiratorial reference in his diary the following May to a conversation with Douglas Kinnaird held in the midnight hours as they walked home after a performance of Edmund Kean's Othello: 'We made mutual confessions of frightful suspicions.' They are borne out by Hobhouse's later knowing annotations in the margins of Moore's *Life*.

Most persuasively of all, we have Byron's own words of love and guilt and desperation addressed to his sister over the course of their affair and through the years of separation after it had ended. He wrote to her unmistakably from Venice six years after he first visited her at Six Mile Bottom:

'we may have been very wrong – but I repent of nothing except that cursed marriage – & your refusing to continue to love me as you had loved me . . . It is heart-breaking to think of our long Separation – and I am sure more than punishment enough for all our sins – Dante is more humane in his "Hell" for he places his unfortunate lovers (Francesca of Rimini & Paolo whose case fell a good deal short of *ours* – though sufficiently naughty) in company – and though they suffer – it is at least together – If ever I return to England – it will be to see you – and recollect that in all time – & place – and feelings – I have never ceased to be the same to you in my heart.'

Proximity was always a powerful inducement to Byron: Augusta attracted him because she was close and, at the time, available. This was reinforced by their consanguinity. Byron's love for Augusta answered to his highly developed instinct of tribalism and aristocratic pride. It brought with it the pleasures of illicitness. Their private endearments constituted a grand gesture of social defiance. In the early nineteenth century incest, unlike homosexuality and bigamy, was not legally a criminal offence in England. It was punishable only by the ecclesiastical courts whose sentences, from 1813, were limited to six months' imprisonment. But although it was by no means uncommon, at every level of society, reputedly even in British royal circles, the mere suspicion of incest was likely to result in scandal and social ostracism.

In entering this forbidden territory Byron was conscious of his literary antecedents, the black and tragic treatments of incest in the plays of the Italian Vittorio Alfieri and the German Friedrich von Schiller. 'Incest is like many other *incorrect* things a very poetical circumstance. It may be an excess of love and hate,' wrote Shelley, who himself pursued the theme of sibling incest in *Laon and Cythna*, his original version of *The Revolt of Islam*. Byron's incest with Augusta was part of a much wider Romantic culture of excess.

Did Byron let Augusta into the secret of his earlier homosexual affairs? It seems probable. One of the accusations later levelled at Augusta by Lady Byron after the separation was that, knowing what she did, Augusta did nothing to prevent the marriage. Byron said later to Lady Blessington:

'Augusta knew all my weaknesses, but she had love enough to bear with them. I value not the false sentiment of affection that adheres to one while we believe him faultless; not to love him would then be difficult: but give me the love that, with perception to view the errors, has sufficient force to pardon them, – who can "love the offender, yet detest the offence"; and this my sister had.'

If indeed he had told her of his love for boys the confession would have made an extra bond between them, Byron weaving her into the emotional complexities of his Harrow friendships, his Cambridge obsession, his adventures in the East. In 1820 Byron wrote to his ex-wife from Ravenna with superfluous cruelty telling her, of Augusta, 'She & two others were the only things I ever really loved.' It is not difficult to guess that the two others were John Edleston and the Earl of Clare.

We cannot be certain when incestuous relations between Byron and Augusta began. Was it in London or, more likely, the seclusion of Six Mile Bottom in George Leigh's absence in the late summer of 1813? On 11 August Byron wrote to Lady Melbourne of the 'two or three *Gordian* knots' tied round him: 'I shall cut them', he said, 'without consulting anyone – though some are rather closely twisted round my *heart*.' Perhaps significantly, five days later he gave George Leigh £1,000. Byron later implied to Lady Melbourne that he was the initiator of the sexual relationship: 'it was not her fault – but my own *folly* (give it what name may suit it better) and her weakness', and in another letter he claimed that Augusta 'was not aware of her own peril – till it was too late'.

Hobhouse's departure in June 1813 on a European tour of the Baltic and the Adriatic and back to Vienna, skirting round the countries in Napoleon's control, sharpened Byron's own longing for departure from a triumphalist England he was finding increasingly unsympathetic. Through the summer he had contemplated a return to Greece but had been finding it difficult to arrange a passage on any ship of war. 'They had better let me go,' he wrote to Tom Moore in July, 'if I cannot, patriotism is the word – "nay, an' they'll mouth, I'll rant as well as they".' Now, in August, he was planning to take Augusta with him on his much-postponed departure for the continent, giving as the official reason 'her Lord's embarrassments'. The Colonel could reorder his affairs in his wife's absence. Their proposed destination was Sicily, where Byron had imagined himself with Lady Oxford only a few months earlier. Augusta was apparently enthusiastic: 'she appears to have still less reluctance at leaving this country than even myself,' Byron confided to 'la tante'.

It is interesting that Augusta, so conventionally religious, shows little of Byron's own sense of having sinned. She may have rationalised the situation:

she was only his half-sister. There is a certain element in Byron's own responses of Calvinist breast-beating, of manufactured doom. However, her relations, consulted by Augusta, disapproved strongly of the proposed journey. Lady Melbourne was greatly alarmed by the idea. The voyage to Sicily was abandoned after news was received of a plague sweeping through the Mediterranean lands. Byron had in any case lost interest once Augusta insisted on travelling with one of her children, presumably the infant George. Children in transit made Byron irritatable: 'it is so superfluous to carry such things with people – if they want them why can't they get them on the Spot?'

At the beginning of September, shaken by the terror of his feelings for Augusta, Byron attempted to justify such overwhelming emotional states:

'The great object of life is Sensation – to feel that we exist – even though in pain – it is this "craving void" which drives us to Gaming – to Battle – to Travel – to intemperate but keenly felt pursuits of every description whose principal attraction is the agitation inseparable from their accomplishment.'

The recipient of this outburst of philosophy, a view soon to be seen as quintessentially Byronic, was, ironically enough, Byron's future wife Annabella Milbanke with whom he was once again in correspondence. She sent a thoughtful and unsympathetic response.

Through the autumn of 1813 he was drumming up multiple distractions from Augusta, attempting to vanquish what he called his 'demon'. Besides Annabella he now had a new inamorata, Lady Frances Wedderburn Webster, a slender pale young woman whose tinge of well-bred English melancholy is nicely caught in Byron's 1813 sonnet 'To Genevra':

> 'Thine eyes' blue tenderness, thy long fair hair,
>> And the wan lustre of thy features – caught
>> From contemplation –'

Lady Frances in the guise of Queen Guinevere.

Complex personal relationships stimulated Byron. Lady Frances, highly pedigreed daughter of the 1st Earl of Mountnorris and 8th Viscount Valentia, was married to Byron's buffoonish friend 'Bold' Webster. They had asked him to be godfather to their first child. The mansion which the Websters were now renting, Aston Hall in South Yorkshire, was believed by Byron to have been the very house where his father Captain John Byron had 'adulterated' with Lady Carmarthen after they eloped: this was probably erroneous, but it added excitement to the pursuit. Byron was even considering taking a house of his own in the vicinity now that Kinsham Court had fallen through. To add to the concentration of coincidence, Byron's page Robert Rushton, whom he had recommended to Webster, imagining he himself would soon be travelling abroad, had entered Webster's 'Agricultural establishment' and would presumably have been at Aston by the time Byron arrived on his first visit in the middle of September. Augusta was invited to join the house party but she declined.

The bitter-sweetness of the whole Mozartian ensemble comes over in the sequence of brilliantly detailed bulletins Byron sent to Lady Melbourne from this seat of the 'Blunderhead family' near Rotherham. His beloved Lady M was back in her role of treacherous voyeur, aiding and abetting Byron in his schemes for transferring his affections from one woman to another. Compared with his liaison with Augusta, Byron's attempted seduction of his host's wife seemed a harmless escapade. 'The place is very well & quiet', he reported on arrival, '& the children only scream in a low voice.'

When Byron had observed Lady Frances in 1811 in London he predicted that her husband would be 'a noble subject for Cuckoldom in three years'. He suspected that she already despised her foolish husband. Now, with the predicted time-span almost up and in spite of Webster's blatant and embarrassing unfaithfulness, Byron found her less co-operative than he had imagined. Although cold to her husband, she showed no immediate signs of being willing to deceive him. When Webster preached a sermon praising Lady Frances' virtues, 'concluding by an assertion that in all moral and mortal qualities she was very like *Christ*!!!', Byron felt a comparison with the Virgin Mary would be more appropriate. Lady Frances' apparent lethargy may in fact have been connected with an illness. Descriptions of her pallor, unnatural thinness and lack of appetite suggest some form of anorexia. Byron found her 'in delicate health & I fear going – if not gone – into a decline'.

Subtly he succeeded in arousing his hostess's interest, informing Lady Melbourne: 'she evidently expects to be attacked – & seems prepared for a brilliant defence – my character as Roué had gone before me – & my careless & quiet behaviour astonished her so much that I believe she began to think herself ugly – or me blind – if not worse.' He left Aston for London early in October and returned a few days later. Passing Stilton he sent his publisher John Murray the present of a local cheese.

Lady Frances had softened. On 8 October Byron reported in some triumph that he had had 'a good deal of conversation with an amiable person – whom (as we deal *letters* – & initials only) we will denominate *Ph*'. He had made his first amatory overtures and they had been returned. This conversation took place in the billiard room at Aston, the tip-tapping of the billiard cues concealing the erotic tension of the exchange. He told Lady Melbourne: 'I also observed that we went on with our game (of billiards) without *counting* the *hazards* – & supposed that – as mine certainly were not – the thoughts of the other party also were not exactly occupied by what was our ostensible pursuit.'

In a moment of frustration with the spoken word Byron got out pen and paper and 'in tender & tolerably timed *prose* periods (no *poetry* even when in earnest)' wrote an imprudent letter which Lady Frances stuffed into her bodice. This was, needless to say, the point at which her husband entered the billiard room. She showed no sign of guilt or panic, and Byron kept his composure as well as he could. As Byron was writing this account to Lady Melbourne, the 'Marito' made another unexpected entrance, bringing in a political pamphlet in manuscript for his friend's approval. Byron's telling of the story in letter form brings out his fascination with the balance of the real and the theatrical: he constructs his own pursuit of Lady Frances almost as a play within a play.

Byron and 'Bold' Webster now decamped to Newstead Abbey where Webster, to Byron's scorn, was involved with 'a foolish nymph', apparently one of the servant girls. Claughton's negotiations for the purchase were still hanging fire. Byron accused Claughton of robbing the cellar in his absence, but there were still sufficient stocks for Byron and the friend he hoped to cuckold to sit opposite one another in 'the melancholy mansion' of his fathers with, between them, bottles of 'Red & white Champagne – Burgundy – two sorts of Claret – & lighter vintages'. He told Lady Melbourne smugly that 'Mine guest (late host) has just been congratulating himself on possessing a partner without *passion* – I don't know – & cannot yet speak with certainty – but I never yet saw more decisive preliminary symptoms.' In spite of her religious scruples Lady Frances had already managed to give Byron a note and to receive an answering letter and a ring from Byron before her husband's very eyes.

Later in October the whole house party from Aston, including Lady Frances' younger sister Catherine, reassembled at Newstead. Lady Frances had now demanded a lock of Byron's hair, eliciting his apologetic explanation: 'My proselyte is so young a beginner – that you must wonder at these exchanges & mummeries . . . she must at least be allowed an excellent taste!!' His proselyte was now beginning to show signs of lack of judgement, proposing she should share her apartments at Newstead with her sister not her husband. 'Bold' Webster indignantly asserted his marital rights.

Byron now found himself swept up in the drama, all the more convoluted because it was happening at his own ancestral seat. He and Lady Frances were keeping up their clandestine correspondence, sitting up all night scribbling to one another, coming down 'like Ghosts' to breakfast the next day. Lady Frances would pass over her epistles in a music book. He was now finding Frances 'very handsome – & very gentle though sometimes decisive – fearfully romantic – & singularly warm in her *affections*'. She was accomplished, clever, 'though her style a little *German* – no dashing nor desperate talker – but never – and I have watched in *mixed* conversation – saying a silly thing'. He judged her almost as good-tempered as Lady Oxford and, an added attraction, as jealous as himself, 'the ne plus ultra of green eyed Monstrosity'.

The affair approached its climax. 'We have progressively improved into a less spiritual species of tenderness – but the seal is not yet fixed though the wax is preparing for the impression', ran one of his now daily reports. Suspense was driving him insane. Distractedly, one midnight, Byron reached for the old skull cup which had featured in his revelries with Hobhouse, Matthews and Scrope Davies before he went abroad, and filled it to the brim with claret. The cup held a whole bottle. Byron quaffed this 'at *one draught*'. Fletcher, taking him to bed, reported that he had first gone into convulsions and then become so motionless his valet imagined he must be dead. A day or two later, when he and Frances were left alone together at the Abbey, she at last succumbed, telling him, 'I am entirely at your *mercy* – I own it – I give myself up to you.' She offered him the choice of seducing her or not. At this point Byron 'spared' her, checking back with Lady Melbourne, 'Was I wrong?'

Why did Byron 'spare' the woman he had chased with such assiduity? Partly because he liked her, and believed her when she told him she would not be able to bear the guilt of a clandestine affair or, as Byron had proposed, of running away with him. He did not want to risk a duel with Webster, who for all his idiocies was an old friend. Most of all, perhaps, the explanation lies in Byron's physical evasiveness where women were concerned. What had absorbed him was the uncertainty, the tension, the problematic interplay of personalities: as he put it to his mentor Lady Melbourne, 'there is no comedy after all like real life.' Now Lady Frances had capitulated he was not so interested in a consummation. This was a man who admitted that his most pleasurable moments in lovemaking came at the final stages, 'when there is nothing more to be required'.

Their parting was traumatic. These were Byron's words for it:

> 'When we two parted
> In silence and tears.'

However, as so often with his women, Lady Frances' passion, once aroused, long outlasted his. She sent him tearful, frantic letters, written in the soulful language he derided as that of a novel from the circulating library. For example: 'when the moment of torture arrived, when I felt my hand locked in yours for the *last time* – and stole a look at that *too* dearly cherished countenance – when necessity forbade me throwing my arms around and breathing out my *soul* in *sorrow* on your neck . . .' Maybe Byron's criticism of her prose was justified. She told him she was reading *The Giaour* again and again until it was printed on her heart. In November, before leaving for Scotland to stay with her husband's relations, she begged Byron for his picture. Enjoying the duplicity, he extracted from Lady Caroline Lamb the miniature by James Holmes that he had given her, telling her he needed it for a friend who was leaving England. Caroline was not deceived.

Even Lady Melbourne, to whom Byron was sending Lady Frances' letters for her comments, started to feel sorry for this wan, discarded lover who had, all too optimistically, entreated him to stay faithful for a year. Byron was now belittling the affair, reducing it to a few meaningless kisses, blaming himself for having been the dupe of 'her whimsical romance'. Vindictively he began talking about marriage to Frances' sister, Lady Catherine Annesley, whom he described as 'very pretty, but fearfully young – and I think a *fool*'. This was his revenge for the way Frances had held out on him. She was made the butt of his wounded vanity.

On 8 November 1813 Byron was writing to his 'dearest Augusta' with excuses for his 'present & long silence' which had been 'occasioned by a thousand things'. Perhaps she could guess what they were. If only she had been with him to prevent them. In his 1813 will Byron left her half his property. At the end of November he wrote to Lady Melbourne: 'I am much afraid that that perverse passion was my deepest after all.'

Self-absorption, the recasting of his personal and often painful history, was the mainspring of much of Byron's work. 'He was himself the beginning, the middle, and end of all his own poetry – the hero of every tale – the chief object of every landscape', so Macaulay summed up the creative use he made of his peculiar personality, the art feeding on the life, the life generating art. Byron's violent emotional turmoils of the summer and autumn of 1813 are reflected in the second of his Turkish tales, *The Bride of Abydos*. He claimed to have written the 1,200-line poem in four nights in mid-November. Even allowing for the fact that he later said it had taken him a week and taking into account his usual numerous revisions to the proofs, this was still an impressive feat of composition. 'Bold' Webster, himself a plodding writer, was convinced that Byron 'must write by steam'.

The Bride of Abydos, the story of Zuleika and her tragic love for her cousin Selim, the exotic pirate chief, takes place beside the Hellespont. Even here there is an autobiographical connection: in a note to the poem Byron informs his readers that he once 'amused himself' in swimming the Hellespont, and may well repeat the feat. For *The Bride of Abydos* Byron abandoned the fragmentary structure he had used for *The Giaour*, reverting to a more straightforward narrative. The valiant Zuleika was the first female protagonist of any Byron poem; indeed, the work was originally named *Zuleika*. His ambition was to depict a convincingly sexual woman. He had wanted 'to preserve her purity without impairing the ardour of her attachment'. But some contemporary critics were to find Zuleika's erotic outpourings to Selim disconcertingly indecorous.

When the poem was published in December 1813 Lady Frances Webster was the first of many female readers to identify herself with Zuleika. She wrote to Byron from 'the foot of the Grampians', quoting back to him his own line, 'That oath tho' sworn by one hath bound us both'. Pathetically hopeful, she asks him, 'Dearest Byron, art thou still my Selim?' There are indeed some traces of Lady Frances in demure, intense Zuleika with her fiery bursts of passion. But there are many more reminders of Augusta. In Byron's original version of the poem the lovers Zuleika and Selim were sister and brother. He transformed them into cousins, feeling himself '*two centuries* at least too late for the subject'. A subject openly confronted by the English dramatist John Ford in his rich and solemn tragedy *'Tis Pity She's a Whore*, in 1633, was now no longer viable. In early nineteenth-century England incest had become a taboo.

In his hectic composition of *The Bride of Abydos* we see Byron trying to write himself out of the crisis with Augusta. 'I believe the composition of it kept me alive', he confessed the day after he finished it, 'for it was written to drive my thoughts from the recollection of – "Dear sacred name, rest ever unreveal'd".' The quotation is Byron's version of Pope, substituting 'sacred name' for 'fatal name'. He explained, more circumspectly, to William Gifford that *The Bride* had been written in a state of mind 'that rendered it necessary for me to apply my mind to something – anything but reality – and under this not very brilliant inspiration it was composed'. He told Lady Melbourne that 'it will for some *reasons interest you* more than anyone'. His covert references to Augusta and to Frances would be all too clear to her.

A few days later Augusta sent her brother a lock of her hair with the Zuleika-like message:

'Partager tous vos sentiments
ne voir que par vos yeux
n'agir que par vos conseils, ne

vivre que pour vous, voila mes
voeux, mes projets, & le seul
destin qui peut me rendre
heureuse.'

Byron added this to his by now substantial collection of the hair of women to whom he had been attached, labelling Augusta's 'La Chevelure of the *one* whom I most *loved*'. He marked it with their love symbol, the cross.

At Christmas they were together at Six Mile Bottom. Byron, perhaps buying his brother-in-law's complicity, was magnanimously offering to help extricate Colonel Leigh from his debts. From mid-January 1814 he and Augusta were at Newstead, conveniently snowed up. Byron wrote to John Murray on his birthday, 22 January, in the bliss of isolation:

'The roads are impassable – and return impossible – for ye present – which I do not regret as I am much at my ease and *six* and *twenty* complete this day – a very pretty age if it would always last. – Our coals are excellent – our fire places large – my cellar full – and my head empty – and I have not yet recovered [from] my joy at leaving London – if any unexpected turn occurred with my purchaser – I believe I should hardly quit the place at all – but shut my doors & let my beard grow.'

Relations between Byron and John Murray were easing their way beyond the strict concerns of business. His publisher had become his confidant.

This was Augusta's first visit to Newstead. She was moved by the shared family associations, and soon accustomed to the romantic dilapidation of the house. Byron's responses, mingled as they were with recent memories of Lady Frances, were more complex. A possible reunion with Mary Chaworth Musters, his 'old love of all loves', lent further poignancy. Mary had suddenly started corresponding with him again. Her marriage to Jack Musters had been a disaster. He had been 'playing the Devil – with all kinds of *vulgar* mistresses', and had been violently cruel to his wife. In throwing herself on the mercy of Byron, begging him to meet her after all these years, Mary showed many of the signs of female fandom which Byron's public persona now evoked, upbraiding him coyly for his reputation as a ladykiller, insisting he should correspond with her in secret. Remembering their childhood history Byron was initially sympathetic and intrigued.

But once at Newstead he became less enthusiastic. Augusta did her best to dissuade him from a visit to his one-time flame: 'for if you go', she warned him, 'you will fall in love again, and then there will be a scene; one step will lead to another, *et cela fera un éclat*.' Byron in confidence to Lady Melbourne, to whom he had been forwarding Mary's imploring letters, offered his own reason for wanting to avoid a merely sentimental meeting: 'the kind of feeling which has lately absorbed me has a mixture of the *terrible* which renders all other – even passion (pour les autres) insipid to a degree.' After incest, conventional flirtations seemed pointless. He postponed the reunion, using the snow as an excuse.

One of the reasons for Byron and his sister's delay in leaving Newstead was that Augusta was, once again, 'in ye family way'. Her pregnancy made it doubly unwise to travel until the roads were safe. The question of whose child she was carrying has never been resolved. Was it her husband's, or could it have been Byron's? Augusta's third daughter was born on 15 April 1814, nine months after she and Byron had met again in London. In May she was christened Elizabeth Medora, with Byron as her godfather. But the fact that Medora herself, in later life and encouraged by a bitterly resentful Lady Byron, came to think of herself as Byron's daughter certainly does not amount to proof. Nor can any definite conclusion be drawn from the fact that Medora is the name given to Byron's heroine in *The Corsair*, the poem he was composing during Augusta's pregnancy. One of the Duke of Rutland's racehorses was also called Medora. The Duchess of Rutland was one of the other sponsors of the child.

The main argument for the case that Elizabeth Medora Leigh was Byron's daughter has been a letter he wrote to Lady Melbourne ten days after the baby's birth in which he tells her, 'it is not an "Ape" and if it is – that must be my fault.' This seems less a straightforward confession referring to the medieval superstition that children conceived incestuously would be born as monsters than an ambiguous joke of the kind Byron and Lady Melbourne loved to share. He could equally well be suggesting that forbidden intercourse between him and his sister might have malformed a child generated by George Leigh.

Two further episodes relating to Medora need to be considered, neither totally convincing. In her evidence gathered for the separation case Lady Byron recalled a scene at Six Mile Bottom, where they stayed with Augusta in 1815, soon after their marriage: 'I said I should like to have him painted when he was looking at Medora (A's youngest child) – the tenderness of expression at those moments I had thought quite lovely. This affected him incomprehensibly to me at that time. I don't remember what was his remark to her about it, but a mystery was implied.' This can be interpreted as an incident made more sinister by hindsight, as is frequently the case with Lady Byron's separation Narratives and Statements, rather than one providing any positive proof.

In support of her belief that Medora was Byron's daughter, Lady Byron also quoted Lady Caroline Lamb in whom Byron had apparently confided: '"Oh I never knew what it was to love before – there is a woman I love so passionately – she is with child by me, and if a daughter it shall be called *Medora*."' (Lady Caroline is said to have riposted, 'I could believe it of *you* – but not of *her*.') Again we are in the realms of probable misstatement – the product of Lady Byron's vindictiveness, Lady Caroline's malice and/or Byron's own characteristically wilful claims.

The case against Byron's paternity of Medora rests on his own attitude towards her. Byron was inordinately if fitfully possessive of his offspring. But he showed no signs of paternal pride in Elizabeth Medora such as he evinced for Ada, his legitimate daughter by Lady Byron, or Allegra, his illegitimate daughter by Claire Clairmont. Of Augusta's female children his favourite was always apparently the eldest, Georgiana, 'my Georgiana' as he called her, to whom he sent presents and about whom he often enquired caressingly. His lack of any special interest in Medora suggests that Byron was never convinced she was his child.

The Corsair, the poem Byron had written '*con amore* and much from *existence*' that midwinter, was published on 1 February 1814. *The Bride of Abydos* had sold remarkably well: 6,000 copies in the first month. But 10,000 copies of *The Corsair* were sold on the day of publication and a jubilant John Murray was soon writing to tell Byron: 'I believe I have now sold 13,000 Copies a thing perfectly unprecedented & the more grateful to me too as every buyer returns with looks of satisfaction & expressions of delight.' One of the earliest and most delighted readers was Princess Charlotte, the Prince Regent's daughter, who claimed to have had the first copy issued '& devoured it twice in the course of the day . . . there are passages that would admit of being written in gold'. Murray maintained that its fame spread far beyond royal circles: 'You can not meet a man in the Street who has not read or heard read the Corsair.'

Over the next four years the poem went into seven editions, with as many as 25,000 copies sold. The total rises to at least 100,000 when you count copies circulating through the libraries and being passed from hand to hand. Byron, holding to his amateur status and no doubt remembering the scorn he had poured on money-grubbing authors in *English Bards and Scotch Reviewers*, was still refusing direct payment for his work. To Murray's irritation, his 500 guinea payment for the copyright of *The Corsair* was handed on to Dallas. Byron maintained airily that rhyming came so easily he deserved no remuneration.

Why was *The Corsair* so popular? Basically because it was an enthralling yarn of the rescue from death of Gulnare, chief slave in the Pacha's harem, after her murder of the Pacha, by Conrad the pirate chief. When he and Gulnare reach his pirate island Conrad's first love Medora has died from grief, imagining that he is dead. The pirate then mysteriously disappears. Byron's poem provides another dashing, haunting, enigmatic hero, the Corsair whose name is 'Linked with one virtue, and a thousand crimes', and it introduces another controversial female portrait in Gulnare. Her determined role in releasing Conrad from the Pacha's prison reflects Byron's own awareness, his half-horrified half-fascinated interest, in the vocal, freedom-seeking women amongst his own contemporaries, the liberated Lady Oxford being a case in point.

Above all, *The Corsair* was attractive to its readers in giving far-off places a new immediacy. It made the legendary live again. This was armchair travel at the highest level. As Francis Jeffrey commented in the *Edinburgh Review*:

'Lord Byron, we think, is the only modern poet who has set before our eyes a visible picture of the present aspect of scenes so famous in story; and, instead of feeding us with the unsubstantial food of historical associations, has spread around us the blue waters and dazzling skies – the ruined temples and dusky olives – the desolated cities, and turbaned population, of modern Attica.'

Speculation continued about how far Byron's heroes had been drawn from real life. The poet jeered at public rumours 'that *I* am the actual Conrad, the veritable Corsair, and that part of my travels are supposed to have passed in piracy'. At the same time he encouraged them, not least in commissioning the painter Thomas Phillips to portray him in what was virtually a Corsair costume for the picture exhibited in 1814 as *Portrait of a Nobleman in the Dress of an Albanian*, for which Byron wore one of the 'magnifique' Albanian dresses he had purchased on his travels. The showy theatricality of Phillips' portrait suggested to the twentieth-century art expert David Piper that this was Lord Byron as played by the swashbuckling American film star Errol Flynn.

While Phillips was working in his studio on the portrait of Byron in Arnaout dress he was painting a second portrait, now almost as famous, showing Byron in more poetic pose, his midnight blue cloak flung nonchalantly over his open-neck white shirt. The head in the two portraits is almost identical, give or take Byron's Albanian moustache. Here Byron again exerted some control over his image, asking Phillips to retouch the nose which both he and Hobhouse felt was too turned up. The paintings were shown side by side in the Royal Academy exhibition in London in summer 1814 and they express remarkably the two faces of Byron, man of action, man of vision, secret ruminator, public exhibitionist, aspects of his personality that frequently collide.

Another portrait then in Phillips' studio, displayed alongside Byron, was of Lady Caroline Lamb in her page's costume proffering a plate of fruit. She put the anxious question to John Murray, by this time something of a father figure to her, 'Do you not think my Picture as a Page standing by Lord B. will have a bad effect.' Someone had already interpreted her portrait 'as a Page Holding a plate of Fruit to Lord Byron as a friar!' The sexual messages were too explicit. She asked Murray to tell Phillips to put her picture out of sight.

The summer of 1814 was 'the summer of the sovereigns'. The previous October Wellington's army had entered France and Napoleon had been defeated in 'the Battle of the Nations' at Leipzig. Prussia, Russia and Austria were now united against France. In March 1814, at the battle of Laon, the combined allied army had forced Napoleon to withdraw. A fortnight later the allies triumphantly took Paris and in April Napoleon abdicated unconditionally and was banished to Elba. With the war on the continent apparently over and Napoleon vanquished, important foreign allies arrived in England to celebrate their victories. The incursions into London of the Tsar of Russia, the King of Prussia, Prince Metternich, Marshal von Blücher and their entourages confirmed Byron in his view of the vanity of human power.

This was also the summer of masquerades in London. Byron gave the Albanian costume in which he had posed to Thomas Phillips to his friend Margaret Mercer Elphinstone, suggesting that if she were to wear it at a ball she might prefer to shorten his ankle-length Camesa or kilt. He assured her: 'It is put off & on in a few minutes – if you like the dress – keep it – I shall be very glad to get rid of it – as it reminds me of one or two things I don't wish to remember.' His Eastern promiscuities still reverberated in his mind.

It was John Cam Hobhouse who donned Albanian dress for the great masquerade held in honour of Wellington by Watier's Club at Burlington House on 1 July 1814. At this spectacular event, with 1,700 people sitting down to supper, Byron dressed as a monk in a dark brown flowing robe: 'His whole countenance so bright, severe and beautiful, that I should have been afraid to have loved him,' admitted Harriette Wilson, the celebrated courtesan. Once again Lady Caroline, masked and dominoed, was on her worst behaviour. 'Lady C. Lamb', complained Hobhouse, 'played off the most extraordinary tricks – made Skeffington pull off his red guard's coat – walked up into the private rooms.' In spite of the fact that Byron 'scolded like her grandfather', she insisted on periodically revealing 'her green *pantaloons*'.

Byron had now left his rooms in Bennet Street and moved across Piccadilly into grander and more comfortable lodgings in Albany with all his books and sabres. 'This night got into my new apartments, rented of Lord Althorpe, on a lease of seven years,' he wrote in his journal on 28 March. Lord Althorp, later 3rd Earl Spencer, had departed to be married. Byron revelled in the luxury of so much extra space.

Albany, originally Melbourne House, had been built by Lord Melbourne in the 1770s. The Melbournes had then exchanged their house on Piccadilly with King George III's second son, the Duke of York and Albany, themselves moving to the mansion in Whitehall where, in 1812, Byron had been a scandalous habitué. Now the Duke of York himself had moved on and the house had been reconstructed and expanded by a consortium of trustees to provide 'elegant and convenient sets of independent Apartments of Chambers' for resident bachelors. These were planned by the architect Henry Holland in two long apartment blocks running the full length of the garden linked by a canopied walkway.

The old Melbourne House itself had been divided into twelve apartments, and Byron had now moved into one of these, No. 2 chambers, on the left of the main entrance. His bow-windowed drawing room had been carved out of what was once the magnificent Melbourne library. He wrote to Lady M: 'I am in *my* and *your* Albany rooms – I think you should have been included in the lease.'

Byron's valet Fletcher moved with him to Albany, presumably occupying one of the 'garrets', rooms provided for servants in the attics of the building. To the surprise of his male friends, Byron also took with him Mrs Mule, the 'witch-like' housemaid who had worked for him at Bennet Street, showing the same dependence on continuity he had shown in his long patronage of Old Joe Murray. Besides, he admitted in his journal, 'There is something to me very softening in the presence of a woman – some strange influence, even if one is not in love with them, – which I cannot at all account for, having no very high opinion of the sex.' Somehow, he always felt in a better humour if there was 'a woman within ken'. Even Mrs Mule his firelighter, 'the most ancient and withered of her kind', grumpy with everyone but Byron, touched him with her faithfulness and could always make him laugh. The final creature comfort Byron brought to Albany, more entertaining to him than most of his contemporaries, was a talkative macaw.

Its architecture gave Albany a pleasantly collegiate atmosphere. In this environment of bachelor bonhomie Byron might almost have been back at Trinity. The other residents were drawn from an elite and slightly raffish social clique of aristocrats, landed gentry, politicians, interrelated and often intermarried. The Earl of Desart occupied the rooms opposite Byron's. Many of the residents were known to him already. They included the middle-aged writer and rich plantation owner Matthew 'Monk' Lewis, about whom Byron had mixed feelings: 'It is a good and good-humoured man, but pestilently prolix and para-doxical and *personal*.' Because Lewis was cultivating him Byron had gone back and reread 'the worst parts' of Lewis's precocious horror novel *The Monk*, *succès de scandale* of 1796. He was not impressed. 'These descriptions', wrote Byron in his journal, 'ought to have been written by Tiberius at Caprea – they are forced – the *philtred* ideas of a jaded voluptuary. It is to me inconceivable how they could have been composed by a man of only twenty – his age when he wrote them.' Byron was shaking off the excessive enthusiasms of his youth.

At Albany Byron fell into a dandyish routine: rising late, sparring with Jackson and practising the broadsword with Henry Angelo, who visited Byron's cham-bers at midday. Byron preferred the broadsword to the foil not only because of its Scottish origins but also because, being heavier, it made a more effective reducer of his weight. Before fighting he would strip, put on a thick flannel jacket and over this a pelisse lined with fur, tied around with a Turkish shawl. After exercise he would either sweat it out under a pile of blankets or get Fletcher to rub him down. The more violent the fatigue, the better Byron's spirits. By the evening he could, with luck, achieve the mood of 'calm languor' he liked most.

At this period we catch convivial glimpses of Byron and his friends out drinking at the Cocoa Tree Club in St James's Street from six in the evening until five in the morning:

'We clareted and champagned till two – then supped, and finished with a kind of regency punch composed of madeira, brandy, and *green* tea, no *real* water being admitted therein. There was a night for you!'

He frequented the theatre, often with Tom Moore. He had immediately recog-nised the abilities of 'a new Actor named Kean – he is a wonder'. He responded to Edmund Kean's stance as the radical outsider, admiring his emotionally expressive performances as Shakespeare's self-mocking villain-heroes Richard III and Shylock as well as sympathising with Kean's confrontational politics and recklessly dissipated style of life. After seeing Kean's bravura performance as Sir Giles Overreach in Massinger's *A New Way to Pay Old Debts*, Byron gave him a magnificent Turkish sword with a Damascus blade and donated £50 to the fund for the penurious Kean's benefit.

Literary composition now took place in the night hours. In the early summer Byron was writing *Lara*, the fourth and final of his Turkish tales. He later told John Murray that he wrote it 'while undressing after coming home from balls and masquerades in the year of revelry *1814*'.

Byron is rightly seen as one of the great love poets in the English language. One of his most transparent lyrics emanates from Albany:

'She walks in beauty, like the night
  Of cloudless climes and starry skies;
And all that's best of dark and bright
  Meet in her aspect and her eyes:
Thus mellow'd to that tender light
  Which heaven to gaudy day denies.'

This was in fact a morning-after poem, written after Byron had seen Mrs Anne Wilmot, wife of his cousin Robert John Wilmot, at a party given by Lady Sitwell in Seymour Place. The beautiful Mrs Wilmot, then in mourning, had appeared with dark spangles on her dress. On returning to Albany with 'Bold' Webster he had ordered Fletcher to bring him a tumbler of brandy, in which he drank Mrs Wilmot's health and retired to bed much the worse for wear. When he woke the next day he wrote the three-verse poem.

What few of its admirers realise is that this tranquil hymn of adoration to a lovely woman was written at a time of intense unhappiness and instability so great that Byron's condition came close to schizophrenia. Byron the adorer could easily turn into Byron the tormentor of women. Witness his treatment of one of his young fans, the persistent Swiss girl Henrietta d'Ussières who had been writing to him since the spring of 1814 with a poignant innocence. 'Do not I wish to be your sister? And then Thyrza whom I love and regret.'

Eventually, receiving some encouragement from Byron, she had penetrated Albany. At first he had received her courteously. She admired Byron's writing desk, the parrot, the crucifix that hung on his drawing-room wall. She and Byron exchanged small talk for half an hour. Then he suddenly and crudely made her a proposition. She lamented in her next letter to Byron: 'for the remainder of the evening it was no longer Lord Byron – indeed it was not.' But Henrietta was not totally deterred. She returned another day, ringing at Albany's back entrance. Fletcher informed her that his master could not see her as he was entertaining male company. Henrietta persuaded Fletcher to allow her to wait. She stole into 'a sort of *Pantry* . . . a Pantry flanked with mops and brooms!' Byron did not come to rescue her. He did not reply to any further letters. For him, the episode was over. It shows his sadistic streak.

It sometimes seems that Albany was thronging with distraught women seeking Byron. Lady Caroline Lamb was invading his rooms too, watching for the moment when entry would be feasible. He complained to Lady Melbourne in growing desperation: 'You talked to me – about keeping her out – it is impossible – she comes at all times – at any time – & the moment the door is open in she walks – I can't throw her out of the window.' Caroline reverted to a pathetic version of their old games of cross-dressing, disguising herself in a delivery man's coat. This may have made it easier for her to reach Byron's apartment through the subterranean passage used by tradesmen, giving access to the servants' quarters below stairs.

The last of their many so-called final parting scenes took place in Albany. According to her version, Byron showed her letters which altered her whole view of him and revealed things so shocking that all her old attachment went. We can only surmise that these were the letters and confessions that confirmed her suspicions of his incest with Augusta and perhaps elaborated on what he had told her previously of his sodomy with boys. 'The last time we parted for ever, as he pressed his lips on mine . . . he said "poor Caro, if every one hates me, you, I see, will never change – No, not with ill usage!" & I said "yes, I *am* changed, & shall come near you no more".' She could not have written it better in a novel. It had needed ruthlessness to dispose of Caroline.

In summer 1814, in a letter to Tom Moore, Byron writes of the 'indifference' which has 'frozen over the "Black Sea"' of almost all his passions. It is a bleak and horrifying image. For all his intermittent playfulness and grace, he had arrived at a state of despair. His apathy was not just a question of his personal emotions, the impasse he had reached in relations with Augusta, wanting to be with her but aware that this could only bring about her social ruin. His journal entries at this period show his bitterness as wider and deeper rooted, stemming from his disgust with society and the corruption that sustained it.

The previous year he had quipped to Lady Melbourne:

> ''Tis said – *Indifference* marks the present time
> Then hear the reason – though 'tis told in rhyme –
> A King who *can't* – a Prince of Wales who *don't* –
> Patriots who *shan't* – Ministers who *won't* –
> What matters who are *in* or *out* of place
> The *Mad* – the *Bad* – the *Useless* or the *Base*?'

In his identification with Napoleon Byron had been challenging this scene of inertia and folly. He had seen Napoleon's meteoric progress as proof of an alternative to mediocrity. The Emperor stood for the supremacy of the individual will. By 1814, after Napoleon's defeats, Byron's disillusionment extended far beyond impatience with the British monarchy and Parliament. He was now in a condition of total pessimism, seeing disadvantages in all political regimes:

'As for me, by the blessing of indifference, I have simplified my politics into an utter detestation of all existing governments; and as it is the shortest and most agreeable and summary feeling imaginable, the first moment of an universal republic would convert me into an advocate for single and uncontradicted despotism. The fact is, riches are power, and poverty is slavery all over the earth, and one sort of establishment is no better, nor worse, for a *people* than another.'

With the world immobilised by the inertia and cynicism of its institutions, he was reaching a position in which the freedom of the individual was the only valid cause.

Byron's maverick opinions were making him unpopular. His blatant sympathy for Napoleon was suspect. There had been attacks on him in the Tory press when his anti-monarchical squib 'Lines to a Lady Weeping', previously published anonymously, was published under Byron's own name in the second edition of *The Corsair*. He wrote excitedly if nervously to tell Tom Moore that a long poem, 'an "Anti-Byron"', would soon be coming out, aiming to show that he had 'formed a conspiracy to overthrow, by *rhyme*, all religion and government . . . [I] have already made great progress!' He began, he said, to feel like a miniature Voltaire. Inevitably, a backlash started to build up against him. Celebrity had its cycles, even in the early nineteenth century.

In early July Byron had been at Six Mile Bottom with Augusta. Later in the month they were at Hastings in Sussex, 'in a county of downs – and a town of fishery'. Byron had asked his clergyman friend Francis Hodgson, already staying in Hastings, to look out for a house capable of housing Mrs Leigh, her four children and three maids as well as himself, Fletcher and a footman. He asked Hodgson to make sure that his own bedroom was remote from the nursery and that the maid-servants' rooms should be 'near together – and as far from me as possible'. As long as the Leighs were comfortable he did not much care about the price.

The closest Hodgson could come to this specification was Hastings House, a large and once imposing cupolaed building set up high on the cliffs to the east side of the town. The house, which had been Wellington's official residence when he commanded the garrison at Hastings, had now gone rather to seed. But it was discreetly placed for a secret summer idyll, close to the woods and glades of Sussex downland, with an immense sea view. Byron was soon back in his old mood of holiday exuberance:

'I have been swimming and eating turbot, and smuggling neat brandies and silk handkerchiefs, – and listening to my friend Hodgson's raptures about a pretty wife-elect of his, – and walking on cliffs, and tumbling down hills, and making the most of the "dolce-far-niente".'

Even after drinking two bottles of claret he had managed to hobble two miles *up* hill.

Hastings' popularity as a resort was only just beginning. Byron chose it in preference to its neighbour Brighton because it was not 'a *regular* fashashash-ionable watering place'. However, even here the fans attacked him. A pious young woman who had watched her idol climbing the rocks wrote to tell him that she had offered up a prayer to God to awaken him to the sense of his own danger. He had had great difficulty in deflecting a visit from Mary Chaworth Musters who was now writing to him almost daily. She moved into Hastings House when Byron and Augusta left it, and here began evincing the first signs of mental illness that prostrated her in the autumn of that year.

The snatched seaside holiday had elements of melancholy. Worse news came from Hanson about the '*non* – and never likely to be – performance' of the purchase of Newstead by Mr Claughton 'of *im*pecuniary memory'. By the first week in August it was fairly clear that the sale had fallen through and Claughton finally forfeited £25,000 of his £28,000 deposit. The prospect of Newstead now reverting to him concentrated Byron's mind. On 10 August he wrote to Annabella Milbanke, telling her he loved her. On 9 September, by which time he was himself back at Newstead with Augusta, he sent her a pro-posal, with Augusta's connivance. By 18 September he was engaged to the woman he had described three months earlier as 'the most prudish & correct person I know'.

At the end of September Byron's skull was examined by the fashionable German phrenologist Johann Christoph Spurzheim. After passing his hand over Byron's head he pronounced his verdict that Byron's faculties and dispositions were unusually antithetical. All his characteristics were balanced by their opposite, in a manner so strongly developed that good and evil were at perpetual war in him. 'Pray heaven', said Byron, 'the last don't come off victorious.'

15

Seaham

1814–1815

Byron's poem *Lara* was published anonymously in August 1814 in a joint edition with Samuel Rogers' *Jacqueline*. Byron called the duo 'Jacky and Larry'. Lady Caroline Lamb upbraided John Murray for publishing the two poems together: 'if you did it to make Jacqueline sell – it was in bad taste.'

Lara, immediately recognisable as Byron's, was advertised as a sequel to *The Corsair*, with similarities in 'the hero's character, the turn of his adventures, and the general outline and colouring of the story'. The pirate king Conrad lives again in the mysteriously brooding hero Lara, returned home after a long absence with his devoted page Kaled who is his love, the slave Gulnare, in disguise. The work that Byron claimed to have thrown off during the intervals of summer revelry in London turned out to be the darkest and most austere of his Turkish tales. Lara had come back to a great welcome: like Byron himself, 'He mingled with the Magnates of his land'. But he was unable to feel the pleasure of it, paralysed in his emotions, alienated from the acclaim of society by the guilty secret '*that* must not be known'.

Byron was more explicit in a 24-line prefix which he wrote for *Lara*, linking the hero's hidden anguish to his own doomed devotion to Augusta:

> 'When she is gone – the loved – the lost – the one
> Whose smile hath gladdened though perchance undone –
> Whose name too dearly cherished to impart
> Dies on the lip but trembles in the heart.'

These lines were not published for another seventy years.

Lara sold more than adequately: in 1814 there were three combined editions of around 7,000 copies followed by a fourth of about 3,000 of *Lara* alone, now under Byron's name. But, to Byron's disappointment as well as to John Murray's, the poem did not enjoy the runaway success of *Childe Harold* or *The*

Corsair, a falling off that Byron attributed to its lack of narrative excitement. The poem was 'too metaphysical to please the greater number of readers'. It had little of *Childe Harold*'s easy glamour. Byron's future wife Annabella Milbanke registered the poem's relative solemnity when she referred to it as on a par with Shakespeare 'diving into the great deep of the human heart'.

In the months leading up to his engagement Byron's forebodings about marriage had intensified. This was not simply the result of his turbulent feelings for Augusta, but of an antipathy rooted far back in his past. Childhood memories of a lurid story about marriage read in a Roman history book erupted into his mind. At the time he had wanted his mother to explain to him why he should not marry. The disastrous Roman marriage and the turmoils of his parents seem to have united in his early consciousness. When Augusta later wrote to Francis Hodgson of 'recollections' in her brother's mind 'fatal to his peace', which jeopardised his prospects of happiness in marriage, Byron's Cambridge friend would easily have made the connection to Byron's love for Edleston and other teenage boys.

But Byron was always susceptible to influence. With an almost apathetic submission to his fate, he gave in to pressure: pressure from Lady Melbourne, still viewing Byron's marriage as the safer alternative to incest with Augusta as well as a refuge from Lady Caroline Lamb; and, even more persuasively, pressure from Augusta herself, confused as she was about their intense relationship, its practical effects upon her family life, its potential danger to her social position and that of her husband, Colonel Leigh. She saw Byron's marriage, however risky, as the only possible way out of the impasse both for her and for him. He wrote to Lady Melbourne:

'she wished me much to marry – because it was the only chance of redemption for *two* persons – and was sure if *I* did not that I should only step from one scrape into another – particularly if I went abroad.'

Byron's approach to marriage was a characteristic blend of fatalism and panic. In a show of cynicism he had decided that all prospective wives would be much the same: he had no heart to spare, and would expect none in return. Through 1813 and 1814 Miss Milbanke had merely been one of many options. Just before his liaison with Augusta had begun he had been seriously considering Lady Adelaide Forbes, daughter of the 6th Earl of Granard, a young woman whose resemblance to the Apollo Belvedere was to strike Byron forcibly when he was in Rome. They met frequently at London parties but the relationship had not progressed beyond 'the every-day flirtation of every-day people' over a light supper accompanied by spirited social discussion of the merits of white soup and plovers' eggs.

Immediately before his engagement to Annabella, Byron's sights had been set on an alternative candidate, Lady Charlotte Leveson-Gower, eldest daughter of the Marquis of Stafford, and Augusta's friend and favourite. 'Whatever she loves I can't help liking,' wrote Byron in his journal, pleased to see that Lady Charlotte had 'an air of *soul* about her – and her colour changes – and there is that shyness of the antelope (which I delight in) in her manner'. Her aunt was married to Lord Carlisle and, because of Byron's problematic relations with his guardian, Augusta was negotiating with Lady Charlotte on her brother's behalf.

She seemed to be making good progress, but suddenly, early in September 1814, while Augusta was at Newstead, a flustered and apologetic letter came with news that Lady Charlotte's favoured suitor, Henry Charles Howard, soon to be Earl of Surrey and later 13th Duke of Norfolk, was arriving to make his official proposal for her hand. Lady Charlotte's withdrawal was the somewhat arbitrary catalyst for Byron's own return to the pursuit of Annabella Milbanke. Moore remembered enough of the account that Byron gave of this farcical episode in his memoirs before they were destroyed to quote Byron as saying to Augusta as they sat together at Newstead on the morning of Lady Charlotte's withdrawal: 'You see that, after all, Miss Milbanke is to be the person; – I will write to her.'

He had been corresponding at great length with Annabella, with her parents' approval, since the beginning of the year. The letter of proposal he wrote at Newstead Abbey on 9 September was tentative in phrasing:

'Are the "objections" – to which you alluded – insuperable? – or is there any line or change of conduct which could possibly remove them? – I am well aware that all such changes are more easy in theory than practice – but at the same time there are few things I would not attempt to obtain your good opinion – at all events I would willingly know the worst – still I neither wish you to promise or pledge yourself to anything, but merely to learn a *possibility* which would not leave you the less a free agent.'

It is a self-consciously charming, deferential, reasonable letter, read over and approved by Augusta before he sent it. Byron knew by now he was not risking a rebuff. Annabella's fixation on Byron was as evident to him as to her mother, Lady Milbanke, who maintained that she had '*always* thought Lord Byron was the only Man who ever interested her'.

Though the intellectual Annabella considered herself to be in a very different category from the multitude of female fans that flocked around Byron, she was in fact equally susceptible to his incandescent beauty and extraordinary fame. As Byron diagnosed it later, 'I was the fashion when she first came out; I had the character of being a great rake, and was a great dandy – both of which young ladies like.' She shared with many others of his devotees the conviction that she, and she only, could save him from his rakish past and the religious scepticism which he had already admitted in his letters:

'I thank you very much for your suggestions on Religion – but I must tell you at the hazard of losing whatever good opinion your gentleness may have bestowed upon me – that it is a source from which I never did – & I believe never can derive comfort . . . why I came here – I know not – where I shall go it is useless to enquire – in the midst of myriads of the living & the dead worlds – stars – systems – infinity – why should I be anxious about an atom?'

The pious and self-confident young woman felt wonderfully challenged by this nihilism. 'She married me from vanity, and the hope of reforming and fixing me': Byron's analysis was cruel but tragically correct.

Annabella, taking no chances, sent him her immediate acceptance not once but twice: one letter to Albany, another to Newstead which arrived when he and Augusta were at dinner. He handed the letter to her across the table, almost fainting with agitation, saying, 'It never rains but it pours.' With his obsessive interest in portents Byron later made much of the coincidence that his mother's wedding ring, lost for many years, had suddenly turned up and was brought in by a servant while they were still sitting in the dining room, and indeed that relic, which Byron was soon to bestow on Annabella, was not the ideal harbinger of married bliss.

'Lord Byron is going to be married as I learn to Miss Milbank,' wrote Hobhouse in his diary on 30 September 1814. There is a certain bleakness in the comment, registering the loss of his old and close companion, whom Hobhouse admitted only a few months earlier he had come to 'love more and more every day'. The fact of his engagement brought Byron's past back to him. He was soon in correspondence with John Cowell, the endearing boy who had played with Byron's dogs on the Brighton seafront, over a bet made amongst his friends that Byron would never marry. The odds against were calculated at a hundred to one, back in that hazy summer of 1808.

In the flurry of responses to the news about his marriage Byron most dreaded the reaction of Lady Caroline Lamb. She had already threatened, if Byron ever married, to go out and buy a pistol at Manton's 'and stand before the Giaour and his Legal Wife & shoot myself'. Byron now decided that she was the likely source of the mysterious rebuttal in the London *Morning Chronicle* of the announcement of the engagement in the local Durham paper. He complained to Lady Melbourne: 'C I suspect has been at her cursed tricks again – the D[urham] paragraph is *contradicted* in the M[orning] Chronicle . . . it could only be *her* – no one else has the motive or the malignity to be so *petty*.' He took the matter up with James Perry, the editor of the *Morning Chronicle*. 'Nobody hates hustle so much as I do; but there seems a fatality over every scene of my drama, always a row of some sort or other,' wrote Byron *faux-*naively to Tom Moore. But Caroline, at least in public, was relatively docile, sending him generous congratulations, enclosing some heartsease from the Holy Well, telling him cryptically she loved and honoured him as a friend would love him or 'as a sister feels – as your Augusta feels for you'. She sent an emotional letter to John Murray, telling him to keep the little page who brought it 'as a bond & pledge' of her future good conduct and to burn and put out of his mind all her earlier confidences about his best-selling author. These instructions were ignored.

The family home of Sir Ralph and Lady Milbanke was at Seaham, on the north-east coast near Durham. Annabella, an adored only child, born when her mother was forty, after fifteen years of marriage, had been brought up at Seaham where the expectations of Sir Ralph, the 6th Baronet, ebbed and flowed according to the fluctuating fortunes of the local collieries. He had at one point had grandiose visions of creating a harbour, to be named Port Milbanke, on the seafront at Dalden Ness but settled for the less extravagant alternative of using Stephenson's locomotives to transport coal from his collieries at Hetton to the northerly port of Sunderland.

Seaham itself, as described in 1808 in *Memoirs of a Highland Lady*, 'was the most primitive hamlet ever met with – a dozen or so of cottages, no trade, no manufacture, no business doing that we could see; the owners were mostly servants of Sir Ralph Milbanke's'. It was a poor and inbred community. Seaham Hall, originally a small and unpretentious seaside residence, had been greatly expanded by the Milbankes in the 1790s, stuccoed and relandscaped. But it was in a remote position, standing exposed high up on the cliffs. Since resuming correspondence with Annabella in late summer 1813, Byron had received several pressing invitations to visit Seaham. But he had never gone.

The engagement increased the Milbankes' hopes of Byron's visit. But he found multiple reasons for delay. First he lingered at Newstead with Augusta. Before leaving on 20 September 1814 he carved their joint names into the bark of an unusual double elm tree in the so-called Devil's Wood. He next decided that before leaving for Seaham he must settle 'some business' with John Hanson in London and equip himself with a new blue coat.

By 1 October Lady Milbanke was imagining he would be in Seaham 'in the course of the week'. However, a fortnight later, Byron was still in London, dining with Edmund Kean and other theatrical cronies, and he was still at leisure to receive a visit to his chambers in Albany on 24 October from Eliza Francis, an impecunious poet who arrived in search of patronage. She was twenty-five but Byron assured her she looked sixteen or seventeen at most. He promised to read her poems in manuscript and he handed her a £50 cheque as a subscription for their publication.

On 29 October he finally set off for Seaham, spending that first night at Six Mile Bottom with Augusta, the next night at the same inn at Wansford where Lady Rosebery had recently dined after eloping with her brother-in-law Sir Henry Mildmay, a coincidence he reported with delight to Lady Melbourne, his mind still on Augusta:

'Don't you think they are not much better than some people you may have heard of who had half a mind to *anticipate* their example – & don't yet know whether to be glad or sorry they have not!'

Byron's painfully slow progress can be explained by his usual shyness at meeting with strange people. Even his fiancée was to some extent a stranger: they had corresponded voluminously but had not met for almost a year. Added to this was Byron's terror at his altered state, his gloom at the prospect of surrendering his freedom of manoeuvre, taking on the booby's role in a comedy of manners. 'I confess that the character of wooer in this regular way does not sit easy upon me,' he told Hobhouse, in a poignantly affectionate letter. It would be a comfort if Hobhouse too could find himself a wife and they could then be coupled together 'like people electrified in company through the same chain'.

Annabella was waiting for him when he reached Seaham in the evening of 1 November 1814. Two years later she was able to remember every detail:

'He had been expected for the two preceding days. My Mother was impatient & dissatisfied at the delay. I remained calm, with that perfect self-possession which had not suffered any interruption since the time that I accepted the offer of marriage. I was sitting in my own room reading, when I heard the Carriage. I put out the Candles, deliberated what should be done, resolved to meet him first alone. It was so arranged. He was in the drawing room standing by the side of the Chimney-piece. He did not move forwards as I approached towards him, but took my extended hand & kissed it. I stood on the opposite side of the fireplace. There was a silence. He broke it. "It is a long time since we have met" – in an undertone. My reply was hardly articulate.'

As Byron himself described it to Lady Melbourne: 'A's meeting & mine made a kind of scene – though there was no acting nor even speaking – but the pantomime was very expressive.' It is striking that what Annabella tells with deadly accuracy Byron recounts in terms of theatre. He reports to Lady Melbourne that her niece, now his fiancée, 'seems to have more feeling than we imagined – but is the most *silent* woman I ever encountered – which perplexes me extremely – I like them to talk – because then they *think* less – much cogitation will not be in my favour.'

His nervousness of commitment to a marriage for which he knew he was unsuited tempted him at this stage to withdraw from the engagement. 'However the die is cast –' he wrote on 4 November, 'neither party can recede – the lawyers are here – mine & all – & I presume the parchment once scribbled I shall become Lord Annabella – I can't yet tell whether we are to be happy or not – I have every disposition to do her all possible justice.' But he feared the worst.

Byron's lawyer John Hanson had been, as usual, dilatory, making the excuse of a violent bilious attack at Ilfracombe en route. But he arrived at Seaham a few days after Byron to finalise the marriage settlement, proposing on Byron's behalf a settlement of £60,000, raised by a loan secured on a still anticipated sale of Newstead, which would yield £3,000 a year to provide for any future children and to fund a jointure if Annabella lived longer than her husband. In the circumstances it was a generous settlement. Hanson had at first suggested £50,000. But Byron considered 'it was best to do things handsomely'.

Annabella herself had considerable prospects. On marriage £16,000 was due to be raised for her from her father's estates at Halnaby in Yorkshire. She was heir to Sir Ralph's estates at Seaham and eventually, through her mother, to the Noel family estates at Kirkby Mallory in Leicestershire. These were the estates of Annabella's uncle Lord Wentworth, settled on his eldest sister Lady Milbanke and estimated at about £5,000 a year. There was, as Byron knew, an element of chance in this. Sir Ralph might remarry and produce a second family, jeopardising Annabella's inheritance; Lord Wentworth might decide to leave his property elsewhere. But, relying as Byron still was on a regular income after the sale of Newstead and his properties at Rochdale, the financial underpinnings of the marriage at this juncture seemed reasonably sound.

However, the tensions between Byron and his wife-to-be were evident to John Hanson, who had known Byron since he was a child. When Hanson first reached Seaham he felt impelled to provide some explanation for Byron's delay in arriving in the north. Annabella replied graciously, 'Mr Hanson where there is no intention of offence there can be no wrong', while Byron fidgeted sulkily in the background. Hanson heard him muttering, 'Damn oh damn. I beg you will be seated.' Later, finding Hanson alone in his room, Byron poured out his discontents: 'There, I told you Hanson how prudish and quaint in her sayings. I never liked Prudes so stiff but she is very clever & knows Greek and Latin.'

Hanson was under no illusions about Byron ever being in love with Annabella. In his view they were a mismatch from the start. 'Lord B. disliked a short thick or dumpy woman. He says somewhere "I hate a dumpy woman". The Lady was remarkably dumpy.' Hanson's misgivings about the bride's physique were echoed maliciously by Lady Caroline Lamb: Byron would 'never be able to pull with a woman who went to church punctually, understood statistics and had a bad figure'. In contrast Annabella's professionally idealised portraits show her as somewhat busty but slim waisted and prettily petite.

Byron was at Seaham for a miserable fortnight. Before he even arrived he had 'imbibed a mortal aversion' to Lady Milbanke. He found her overbearing and gushing: how he wished he could exchange his future mother-in-law for 'la tante'. He got on more easily with the bluff raconteur Sir Ralph Milbanke, named 'Old twaddle Ralph' by the Duchess of Devonshire, lover of all things English, detester of the French. But he found it a relief when Sir Ralph, a home musician, got out his instrument and conversation ceased. Though even the cello was an object of suspicion. According to Hanson, Byron read the worst into Sir Ralph's lavish affection for his only daughter: he had heard 'ante vel post conjugium ut Curata Cello erat Pater felice et Curata Cello performed those operations which it was supposed nature had inhibited to Sir RM'. The code resorted to by Hanson may be garbled, but Byron's imputation of incest is clear.

He and Annabella walked along the breezy clifftops. Sometimes their relations were cheerful and confiding. But Byron, obsessive about his own health, was disconcerted by what he saw as Annabella's signs of hypochondria. She was being taken ill 'once every 3 days with I know not what'. He was irritated by her inability to take anything he said at face value: 'the least word – or alteration of tone – has some inference drawn from it'. The final straw had been the '*scene*', which recalled to Byron the worst days of his relationship with Lady Caroline, in which Annabella, alarmed by Byron's dark hints about his transgressions in the past, attempted to break off the engagement. He 'became quite livid', staggered and fell back fainting on the sofa. It was a premonition of the larger dramas to come.

Byron tried to overcome Annabella's silence by methods in which he was well practised. He told Lady Melbourne that he had discovered 'her *passions* stronger than we supposed'. Byron had 'had recourse to the eloquence of *action*'. He found that kisses and embraces succeeded very well and soothed her, giving him 'some hopes of the efficiency of the "calming process" so renowned in "*our* philosophy". – In fact and entre nous, it is really amusing – she is like a child in that respect – and quite *caressable* into kindness and good humour.' But Byron's caresses soon frightened Annabella. She did not want to be seduced before her marriage. Her fiancé's intemperate behaviour upset her and she suggested he should now return to London. Byron wrote to her rather testily from Boroughbridge where he spent the night on his journey south: 'If it will give you any satisfaction – I am as comfortless as a pilgrim with peas in his shoes – and as cold as Charity – Chastity or any other virtue.' He made for Newstead and then for Six Mile Bottom. It was now Byron's turn to try to break off the engagement. He wrote a parting letter which Augusta persuaded him not to send. He was later to reproach her for this, telling her that his unfortunate marriage had been her fault.

Before returning to London Byron made two visits to Cambridge, that place of deeply ambivalent emotions. Here he went to the Senate House to vote for Dr William Clark, who was standing for the Professorship of Anatomy. Clark, a Fellow of Trinity, had been lined up to accompany Byron as his physician on the journey to the Levant planned and then cancelled in 1813. Hobhouse too had come to Cambridge to cast his vote for Clark and was amused to watch the candidate himself and William Lort Mansel, Master of Trinity and Bishop of Bristol, vying for the honour of accompanying Byron: 'this is well for a Bishop to attend upon a poet who has the reputation of an atheist and has done something to deserve it.' Byron's visit to Cambridge as a fully-fledged celebrity assumed something of the aspect of the return of the prodigal son. The students clapped him from the crowded upper gallery when he arrived in the Senate House and again when he left after voting. Hobhouse was assured that this ovation was unprecedented. He noted in his diary that Byron 'looked red as fire'.

Arrangements for the wedding went on inexorably. Safely away from her, Byron wrote to Annabella amiably:

'Don't scold *yourself* any more – I told you before there was no occasion – you have not offended me – I am as happy as Hope can make me – and as gay as Love will allow me to be till we meet and ever my Heart – thine B.'

What was lethal in Byron was his emotional duplicity. The language of love came all too easily to the great amatory poet, and indeed he seems to have been writing himself into a temporary belief in his own sincerity. Love *in absentia* was one thing. It was the reality of love with a complicated, well-bred, intellectual female, the face-to-face demands, the challenges, the suffocating cosiness, that Byron could not bear.

Through late November and December Annabella sent a stream of impatient, loving letters. The worldly-wise Lady Melbourne had given her niece instructions to avoid any further delays: people were already gossiping and speculating about why Byron was in London. Annabella told him that preparatory wedding bells were ringing, sent him bulletins about the making of the cake, to which Byron replied jovially: ' "*The* Cake" dearest – I am in such agitation about it – if it should be spoiled or mouldy – or – don't let them put too many eggs & butter in it – or it will certainly circulate an indigestion amongst all our acquaintance.'

Meanwhile Eliza Francis, another of Byron's adoring young women with her own ambitions as a writer, was paying further visits to his rooms at Albany. He was back at playing cat and mouse with his female admirers, one day warm and welcoming, the next day chilling in his manner, telling her he could not help her because he was engaged. Eliza was later to give an excitable account of what she evidently saw as the central episode of her life: 'as I stood with my head bent down, he lightly put aside some little curls which had escaped from under my cap behind and kissed my neck – this completely roused me and I struggled to free my hand, but he then clasped me to his bosom with an ardour which terrified me.' He threw himself into an armchair: 'he had drawn me down upon his knee, his arms were round my waist, and I could not escape.' He was about to kiss her lips when Eliza, who kept up a veneer of respectability, made a final valiant effort and tore herself away from 'the truly noble Lord Byron'.

A previously unidentified letter in the Murray archive reveals Byron in just this shilly-shallying state.

'My dear Eliza,

I shall probably be occupied a good deal for some days on business – and unable to call upon you as I intended before they are expired. – Under present circumstances this absence may perhaps be agreeable – at any rate of no consequence to yourself – & having already urged all I can upon the subject of your determination I shall for the future trouble you upon that topic no further – When we next meet you will find me less importunate – but always very truly yrs.'

He signed the letter with mysterious initials. Engagement had not diminished his need for surreptitious emotional entanglements.

One of the anxieties which kept Byron in London in the weeks before his marriage, in ironic counterpoint to his own preparations, was the burgeoning scandal of what he called 'Ld. Portsmouth's lunatic business'. The previous March Byron had been prevailed upon by Hanson to give away his eldest daughter Mary Ann, then twenty-four, to the Earl of Portsmouth, who was in his middle forties and mentally unstable. This union had in effect given Hanson control of Portsmouth's property. The validity of the hastily arranged and secret marriage was now being challenged by Portsmouth's younger brother, the Hon. Newton Fellowes, on grounds of the Earl's insanity. Byron's soberly worded defence of his own role in this marriage, drawn up for the court and no doubt drafted by Hanson, influenced the dismissal of the charges, though the case was to be resurrected nine years later in a much more lurid form.

His own earlier, private recollections of the ceremony, and the evidence of the Hanson family, argue his much greater complicity in a scene of horrifying social cynicism, of the kind he was to satirise so brilliantly in *Don Juan*. It is clear that Hanson sought the public support of Byron in a transaction he knew to be highly dubious. According to her brother Newton, Mary Ann had been courted by Byron himself for three or four years, and he had promised, 'tho' I can't make you a lady of Title you shall be a Countess nevertheless.' Byron later joked about how he had reminded Mary Ann of his seduction of her as he led her up the aisle of St George's Church in Bloomsbury. He had been up late at two balls the night before. 'Made one blunder', he noted in his journal for that day, 'when I joined the hands of the happy – rammed their left hands, by mistake into one another. Corrected it – bustled back to the altar-rail, and said "Amen".' He had concluded: 'Queer ceremony that same of marriage.' Hanson's son Newton maintained that his mother, who died a month after the ceremony, had actually died of shame.

Besides the Portsmouth marriage problems Byron had been detained in London by further agitations over the sale of Newstead. The defaulting Claughton had resurfaced with fresh proposals, for a time taken seriously by John Hanson. But when he saw that these involved a reduction of the purchase price and further delays in payment, Byron was decisive, telling Annabella on 8 December: 'I have ordered the flattest of all possible negatives in reply and there's an end.' He asked her and her parents to decide 'how far this may – will – or ought' to result in the marriage being at least postponed. The immediate financial prospects now looked much less promising. Byron was honest in telling Annabella of his worries not only about their lack of income until

Newstead could be sold but also on account of his mass of unpaid debts. Annabella was unruffled. But the possibility of putting off the marriage now becomes a constant theme in Byron's letters, right up to the day of setting off for Seaham. The marriage took place in an atmosphere of not only emotional but also financial doubt.

On 16 December Byron made a personal application to the Archbishop of Canterbury for a special licence which would enable them to be married in a room in Seaham Hall 'without fuss or publicity' rather than in church, showing the almost pathological desire for privacy that alternated with his craving for exposure and fame. He and Hanson went to the Doctors' Commons chambers for the issue of the licence. Byron asked the Doctor of the Commons gravely: 'Pray, sir, what is the proportion of those who come here first to make marriages, and then afterwards to unmake them?' The licence was in Byron's portfolio when he and Hobhouse, appointed to be best man at the marriage, left London for Seaham on 24 December 1814.

Once again it was slow progress, Byron nervous and procrastinating. Hobhouse stayed in Cambridge while Byron broke the journey at Six Mile Bottom. It was chilly weather, as he wrote to his bride on Christmas Day: 'Dearest A – I am thus far on my way and as warm as Love can make one with the thermometer below God knows what.' He reported that Colonel Leigh was seated opposite him, complaining of illnesses and clamouring for medicine. Augusta, however, was 'looking very well – and just as usual – in every respect – so that better can't be in my estimation.' With a sublime tactlessness he wished Annabella 'much merriment and minced pye'.

On Boxing Day he and Hobhouse set off north again together. 'Never', noted Hobhouse, 'was a lover in less haste.' Next day they got as far as Newark, through the snow and rain, 'the bridegroom more and more *less* impatient', the best man enjoying John Murray's new edition of Gibbon's complete works. Two days later, when they arrived at Thirsk, Byron was evincing 'indifference almost aversion'.

At 8 o'clock in the evening of Friday 30 December Byron and Hobhouse reached Seaham Hall at last. Lady Milbanke was so put out by their lateness that she had retired to her room. Annabella received Hobhouse alone in the library, taking his hand 'with great frankness' straightaway, and 'presently in tottered her father'. Hobhouse cast an appraising eye over Miss Milbanke: 'rather dowdy looking & wears a long & high dress (as B had observed) though she has excellent feet & ancles – the lower part of her face is bad, the upper expressive but not handsome – yet she gains by inspection.' When she heard

Byron emerging from his room Annabella ran to meet him, out of sight of the others. She threw her arms round his neck and burst into tears. To Hobhouse she seemed 'doatingly fond' of Byron, 'gazing with delight on his bold and animated bust', whilst he saw, from signs he knew so well, that Byron was now physically drawn to his affianced, at least while she was within his sight.

The next day was fine and sunny. Hobhouse walked along the seashore. Byron wrote to John Murray to insist upon his cancelling plans to illustrate the forthcoming collected edition of Byron's poetry with an engraving taken from a version of Phillips' 'cloak' portrait, of which Byron disapproved: 'do *do* it – that is burn the plate – and employ a new *etcher* from the other picture – this is stupid & sulky.' It tells us much about Byron's preoccupation with his image that he should send this letter two days before his marriage. In the evening there was a rumbustious mock marriage with Hobhouse taking the part of Annabella and the Milbankes' lawyer William Hoar as best man. The clergyman who would be officiating at the wedding, the Reverend Thomas Noel, illegitimate son of Lord Wentworth, Annabella's uncle, took the opportunity of rehearsing his own role.

It appears that, in those last few days at Seaham, a final attempt was made to extricate Byron from the marriage. Thomas Noel was approached by Hobhouse, who tried to persuade him to break off the match on grounds 'that those persons were much to blame who trusted their child with such a man, speaking particularly of his *violence* as being *unsafe*'. These words are Annabella's, in a letter to her legal adviser in the heated correspondence of the separation crisis over a year later. The reported accusation may not be entirely accurate. But the evidence points to a conversation having taken place on Hobhouse's own initiative or, more likely, at Byron's request, giving Noel confidential reasons for cancelling the marriage. The clergyman said it was too late and refused to intervene. Dinner at Seaham Hall on the night before the wedding was relatively muted. Byron reminded Hobhouse: 'this is our last night tomorrow I shall be Annabella's.'

On 2 January 1815, a Monday, they were married in the drawing room at Seaham Hall, a fine room on the first floor looking out over the sea. Byron was twenty-six and his bride was twenty-two. Lady Milbanke's hand had been so shaky with emotion she had been unable to make the tea at breakfast before the morning ceremony. The bridegroom and best man walked upstairs to the drawing room a little after half past ten. Church kneelers had been laid out for the service. Byron later complained about the hardness of these cushions 'which were stuffed with Peach-stones I believe'. Thomas Noel and the Vicar of Seaham, dressed formally in their canonicals, stood waiting with the

Milbankes. The bride entered attended by her retired nurse and governess, Mrs Clermont, now treated by the Milbankes as a family friend. Mrs Clermont, like Annabella's mother, was visibly affected by the scene.

The bride wore a muslin gown trimmed with lace around the hem and a white muslin jacket. She had no headdress. Hobhouse described the ensemble, a little disapprovingly, as 'very plain indeed'. When the Vicar of Seaham read the responses Annabella 'was as firm as a rock'. All through the ceremony she gazed steadily at Byron, repeating the marriage promises 'audibly and well'. Byron was not so confident, hesitating at first when he said, 'I George Gordon.' When he came to the vow, 'With all my worldly goods I thee endow', he looked round at Hobhouse with a small grimace. By eleven they were married. Hobhouse shook Annabella by the hand after the parson had done so, and embraced Byron. Lady Milbanke kissed her new son-in-law. Annabella left the room but soon returned to sign the register. She was by now becoming tearful, conscious that she was leaving her father and mother for an uncertain future. She changed into her travelling dress of slate-coloured satin trimmed with white fur and sat down quietly in the drawing room. Hobhouse felt he had 'buried a friend'.

Just before midday Hobhouse led the bride downstairs to join Byron in the carriage that would take them on their honeymoon. His wedding gift for Annabella was already in the carriage: the complete collection of Byron's poems, a whole emotional history bound in orange morocco. When Hobhouse wished her happiness she said, 'if I am not happy it will be my own fault.' Byron clutched his friend's hand through the carriage window and was holding on to it as the carriage drove off.

Seaham was still a primitive community where old ceremonies lingered. Before the wedding guests left they were entertained outside the hall by the sword dance of the colliers, a traditional New Year ritual involving ten local miners 'fantastically dressed'. Hobhouse described in his journal how the colliers danced in a slow circular procession dominated by the characters of pantaloon and fool, the fool being finally beheaded. The entertainment was as mythical and in its way as exotic as any of the dances Byron and Hobhouse had witnessed in the East. The little bells of the Saxon church at Seaham began to peal after the wedding, and six men fired off muskets in front of the house.

The honeymoon, or 'treacle moon' as Byron whimsically called it, took place at another of the Milbanke mansions, Halnaby Hall at Croft near Darlington. Byron had originally planned to take Annabella to John Hanson's country house, Farleigh in Hampshire, but the crisis over the Portsmouth marriage had prevented this. The bulletins sent out by Byron were optimistic. 'I don't dislike this place –' he told Lady Melbourne, 'it is just the spot for a Moon.' His main complaint was the lack of a library and the fact that, to start with, the bridegroom had a cold.

But later evidence suggests that the Halnaby honeymoon was not so tranquil. However wary one must be about accepting at face value Lady Byron's accounts of her mistreatment and humiliation by her husband there is a ring of authenticity in her picture of Byron's strange and gloomy mood as they travelled in the carriage through Durham into Yorkshire. 'He began singing in a wild manner', a signal of growing desperation, and attacked her for having kept him waiting for so long before consenting to marry him. There is an echo in this of the vindictiveness with which he had turned on Lady Frances Webster, lending conviction to Lady Byron's accusation that he married her partly out of a spirit of revenge.

Byron '*had* Lady Byron on the sofa before dinner on the day of their marriage'. This was what Moore recollected from his reading of Byron's destroyed memoirs. Samuel Rogers remembered another passage:

'on his marriage-night, Byron suddenly started out of his first sleep; a taper, which burned in the room, was casting a ruddy glare through the crimson curtains of the bed; and he could not help exclaiming, in a voice so loud that he wakened Lady B. "Good God, I am surely in hell!"'

The American writer Washington Irving, another of the readers of Byron's lost memoirs, had also been struck by this incident, though remembering it slightly differently: in his account Byron woke up early in the morning, Lady Byron beside him, imagining he was Orpheus in hell with Proserpine. Byron, who had always resisted sharing his bed with a woman, made it clear that the marriage bed was no delight to him. He told Annabella that 'one animal of the kind was as good to him as another', provided she was young.

At Halnaby Byron was feeling trapped and showing it, telling Annabella horror stories of his murderous, fire-raising, suicidal ancestors, hinting at his own 'atrocious crimes'. He informed her that he was 'more accursed in marriage than any other act of his life', maintaining that Hobhouse could corroborate his villainy. He dropped hints, inexplicable to Annabella, about his past history of sodomy and other sins from which she could have saved him if she had accepted his proposal two years earlier. He assured her that no good woman could ever comprehend his evils of excess.

Some of these outbursts sound like genuine remorse for the impossible marriage they were both now engaged in. Some of it was play-acting – Byron's habit of half-joking exaggeration or 'bamming' so familiar to his male friends but incomprehensible to his decorous new wife. He was later to explain to Lady Blessington:

'This extraordinary degree of self-command in Lady Byron produced an opposite effect on me. When I have broken out, on slight provocations, into one of my ungovernable fits of rage, her calmness piqued and seemed to reproach me; it gave her an air of superiority that vexed, and increased my *mauvaise humeur.*'

When Byron was bad Annabella made him worse.

With hindsight Annabella claimed that during these early days of their marriage it began to dawn on her that Byron's relations with his sister were unnatural; she noted his excitement on receiving a letter from Augusta at Halnaby and his rage and terror when she mentioned an incestuous union between a sister and brother who did not realise they were related. Annabella had been reading *Don Sebastian* by Dryden. Whether this is true or a false trail of memory created by subsequent events, she wrote to Augusta suggesting that she should join them on the honeymoon. Augusta pleaded 'MY YOUNG FAMILY' as an excuse.

At Halnaby Byron was at work on *Hebrew Melodies*. He had yielded to persuasion from Douglas Kinnaird to provide the words for a collection of mainly holy songs for the Jewish composer Isaac Nathan. Nathan is important as the first composer to recognise the innate musicality of Byron's poetry, the quality to be exploited by later nineteenth-century Romantic composers, especially Mendelssohn. Byron's songs for Nathan were to be sung by the well-known tenor John Braham, also a Jew. As Byron wrote to Annabella when the project was first mooted, 'it is odd enough that this should fall to my lot – who have been abused as an "infidel" – Augusta says they will call me a *Jew* next.' This episode shows that Byron was quite capable of joining in his friends' anti-Semitism, joking to Tom Moore about Nathan's 'vile Ebrew nasalities'. But to Nathan himself he showed the sympathy easily aroused in him by peoples who had been reviled and dispossessed in history. Nathan sensed that he 'exhibited a peculiar feeling of commiseration towards the Jews', as indeed he did towards the Irish. His sympathy for victim nations was augmented by his sense of outcast self.

It is strangely apposite that Byron, at Halnaby, should have been composing the biblical lamentations 'Herod's Lament for Mariamne' and 'On the Day of the Destruction of Jerusalem by Titus'. He loved these Hebrew songs for their depths of ancient sadness, evocations of exile. Annabella spent many hours of her honeymoon providing fair copies of these poems, among them the plangent 'By the Rivers of Babylon We Sat Down and Wept'.

The treaclemoon couple were back at Seaham Hall by 22 January, Byron's twenty-seventh birthday. Seaham's isolation was worse than he remembered. He complained to Tom Moore:

'Upon this dreary coast, we have nothing but county meetings and shipwrecks; and I have this day dined upon fish, which probably dined upon the crews of several colliers lost in the late gales. But I saw the sea once more in all the glories of surf and foam, – almost equal to the Bay of Biscay, and the interesting white squalls and short seas of Archipelago memory.'

He was not used to English country life as lived by the Milbankes with their deadly routines of tea drinking, card playing, passing of the port. He was drawn into their private pantomimes, one evening disguising himself in Lady Milbanke's wig, which he had playfully snatched from her head, while Annabella dressed up in Byron's long coat and travelling cap, adding whiskers and moustachios. Sir Ralph Milbanke had recently retired after twenty-two years of undistinguished Whiggery in Parliament. Compared with the radical ardours of Eywood the politics of Seaham were provincial indeed and the 'mysterious necessity of his return to the East', threatened on Byron's honeymoon, seemed ever more attractive. He also mooted to Tom Moore a visit to Italy, with or without their wives.

At Seaham he continued with the *Hebrew Melodies*. Byron's draft of 'The Destruction of Semnacherib' is dated 19 February 1815, and again Annabella wrote out a fair copy which Byron then corrected.

> 'The Assyrian came down like the wolf on the fold,
> And his cohorts were gleaming in purple and gold;
> And the sheen of their spears was like stars on the sea,
> When the blue wave rolls nightly on deep Galilee.'

This is the most anthologised of Byron's poems, familiar to those who know no other poetry of his. Based as it is on the second Book of Kings and the Book of Isaiah the poem shows how deeply the language of the Bible was implanted in his mind, and how from this material Byron makes a highly coloured picture which has much of the immediacy of a stained glass window. Here the aristocrat arrives at a powerfully moving and democratic art.

'And there lay the steed with his nostril all wide,
But through it there roll'd out the breath of his pride:
And the foam of his gasping lay white on the turf,
And cold as the spray of the rock-beating surf.

And there lay the rider distorted and pale,
With the dew on his brow, and the rust on his mail;
And the tents were all silent, the banners alone,
The lances unlifted, the trumpet unblown.'

This vivid image of the unhorsed rider had contemporary connotations. Byron's poem was a jeremiad for the Emperor Napoleon, so recently and cruelly flung from his great charger; it can be read, too, as a lament for the poet himself, facing his own destruction, his own tragi-comic hubris, as he moped along the shore.

The saddest thing about the Byrons' marriage is that there were intervals of happiness. Sometimes Byron would be the 'wild mirthful boy' again, clambering up the rugged rocks as he used to do in Scotland. He would be loving and wheedling with his wife, calling her 'Bell' and 'Pip' or 'Pippin', in deference to her rosy apple cheeks. In a good mood he allowed her to breach the worst taboo and would refer in baby language to his 'little foot'. One night he said, 'I think I love you – better even than Thyrza.' Annabella assumed that Thyrza was a woman, and Byron encouraged this misapprehension over the next weeks and months, delving into the large collection of hair shorn from his lovers and showing her a little girlish lock of Edleston's.

But there were more black days than good days while Byron was at Seaham. Though they had not yet met, Annabella and Augusta were already in close and frequent correspondence, locked into a curious interdependence that would endure for another forty years. Augusta gave sisterly advice on how to deal with Byron's cycles of depression, assuring Annabella that it was 'a family failing in ye Bs to have *uneven* spirits', though conceding that the 6th Lord's were among the worst. She tried to convince Annabella that Byron's melodramas, coyly referred to as his '*comical proceedings*', should not be treated solemnly. He could be laughed out of them. She made nudging references to Annabella's sex life surviving menstruation: 'I am glad B's spirits do not decrease with THE Moon. I rather suspect he rejoices at the discovery of your "ruling passion for mischief in private".' Surely the main motivation for Augusta's bracing tastelessness was that she was anxious for the marriage to succeed.

Byron was never at his best in carriages. Locomotion in an enclosed space with Annabella increased his sense of panic. In March 1815, on their three-day journey from Seaham to Six Mile Bottom to stay with Augusta he showed the same violent aggressiveness with which he had treated her on the way to their honeymoon at Halnaby. This time Annabella, assuming a false gaiety, managed to calm her husband down and by the time they reached Wansford on the night before arrival he was all affection, asking: 'You married me to make me happy, didn't you?' When she told him that she had, he said joyfully: 'Well then, you *do* make me happy.' But nearing Six Mile Bottom his mood altered yet again and he pronounced gloomily: 'I feel as if I was just going to be married.' He then began caressing Annabella, wanting her to kiss him, perhaps to allay the suspicions of the maid who was also in the carriage and could have overheard.

He had planned that Annabella should remain in the carriage while he went in alone to warn Augusta. But she was not downstairs, so he fetched Annabella and they entered together, Byron seeming desperately nervous. Augusta soon appeared. She shook hands with Annabella: Byron reproached her later, in the tormenting mood which quickly came upon him at Six Mile Bottom, for not having greeted his wife with a kiss.

Imagining ingenuously that Byron and Augusta would have much to talk about Annabella left them together for some time. When she returned Byron suggested she should go to bed early, showing 'undisguised preference' for his sister's company. This happened every night they stayed at Six Mile Bottom. Byron would dismiss her with the comment, 'We can amuse ourselves without you, my dear', or, with his lethal sarcasm, 'my *charmer*'. He drank far too much brandy. When he finally arrived in Annabella's room on their first night in the house he was in a state of frenzy, saying, 'Now I have *her*, you will find I can do without *you*.' He had originally tried to dissuade Annabella from coming to Six Mile Bottom with him, and he reminded her: 'I told you you had better not come here, and you will find it so.' Our understanding of the sequence of events of that fortnight's *ménage à trois* at Six Mile Bottom is, again, dependent upon Lady Byron's recollections and statements to her lawyers. But even considering her capacity for overliteral interpretation, and the bitterness with which she by then viewed her marriage, her detailed account still seems persuasive.

It was here, in that household of cruel hints, that Annabella became more convinced of what had up to then been a mere suspicion of incest between Byron and Augusta. A day or two after they arrived, a parcel from a London jeweller was delivered containing two gold brooches, one with an A, one with a B, mounted with hair from each of them and marked with the cross symbol of their illicit love. Byron said to Augusta, jeering at his wife, 'if she knew what these meant.'

It appears that now, after Byron's marriage, Augusta refused to resume sexual relations. His anger and frustration at this may well have goaded him into attacks so crude that Annabella could not bring herself to record them without recourse to code in the statement to her lawyers. 'Some of his expressions convey too *indelicate a sense* to offend the eye of the reader, yet I fear it may be necessary to preserve what will give an idea of my trials . . . I shall use Beeby's short-hand, without abbreviations.' These cryptic shorthand entries were finally elucidated by the 2nd Earl of Lovelace, grandson of the Byrons, who worked on Lady Byron's papers at the end of the nineteenth century. The previously garbled words in square brackets are his transcriptions.

'[He would draw personal comparisons] between [us, in the most vicious manner.] And he has said twice (perhaps oftener) once at S.M.B. and once in London [speaking of women's dress], "A *I know* [you wear drawers]" or to me, "*I know* A [wears them]", with an *emphasis* perfectly unequivocal . . . His [personal intercourse with me was less at] S.M.B. than [ever before, but] towards [the end of our visit there it was renewed], yet without any appearance of affection for me, and he signified some reason which did not make the alteration very flattering to me during those three or four days. [I heard from] A herself [that she was in a particular way during those days.] He said once, I *think* oftener, to her in the morning alluding, apparently to the night before – "So you wouldn't Guss" – mischievously. His insinuations of the passion he felt for her were continual – I never would appear to understand them.'

Nothing was straightforward in that Cambridge country household, crowded out with children, including the baby 'Mignonne' or Medora, Byron's goddaughter, and possibly his daughter, a relationship he played on, saying nonchalantly, 'You know that is my child!' Did Augusta's older children get any sense, one wonders, of the complicated games the three adults were involved in: Annabella disguising her suspicions as innocence; Augusta attempting to keep up the appearance of light-hearted hostess; Byron performing his dual role of pantomime king and devotee of the Marquis de Sade.

He invented tripartite sex games: according to Annabella his delight was '*to work us both well*'. She added in her confessional shorthand: 'He kept her in a state of misery beyond mine I thought.' He forced them into humiliating collusion, lying down on the sofa and instructing his wife and his sister to take it in turns to kiss him. Annabella was 'sensible that he was more warm' towards Augusta than he was to her. Byron asked Augusta to give an account to Annabella of his 'conduct relating to amours before marriage'. This was a task that Augusta, unsurprisingly, chose not to carry out.

They departed on 28 March, Annabella desperate to leave 'the scene of such deep horrors', Byron notably reluctant. As they drove away from Six Mile Bottom he waved his handkerchief to Augusta 'in the most passionate manner' and continued to 'after-eye' her until she receded in the distance. He turned to Annabella to ask for her opinion of his sister. She replied diplomatically and possibly truly that she thought Augusta cleverer than he had described her. He appeared delighted to hear this, congratulating himself on having made Annabella and Augusta friends.

When asked later why she had not confronted Byron with her suspicions at this juncture, and why she had continued her friendship with Augusta, Annabella maintained that she had no real proof of their criminality. She did not want to risk alienating her husband, forcing him into still greater crimes against herself. She did not want to ruin Augusta and her children. Augusta's reputation was especially vulnerable, since she had just been appointed a Woman of the Bedchamber in Queen Charlotte's household, with a much-needed stipend of £300 a year.

Annabella however appointed herself the future moral keeper of Augusta and her brother:

'It was hopeless then to keep them apart – it was not hopeless, in my opinion, to keep them innocent. My Duty allowed me no resource but to constitute myself the Guardian of these two beings, who seemed indeed on "the brink of a precipice".'

This was the sanctimonious reason. But it is possible also that Annabella had been fascinated into a reluctant complicity.

While Byron was at Six Mile Bottom there had been momentous events in Europe. Napoleon had escaped from exile on Elba and landed in France with only seven hundred men. The soldiers sent out to oppose him acclaimed him as their leader and Louis XVIII was forced to flee. Napoleon entered Paris on 20 March 1815. 'Buonaparte!!!' wrote Byron to Hobhouse, his fellow enthusiast, 'I marvel what next.' He was so exhilarated by this coup that he felt able to forgive the Emperor for 'utterly falsifying every line' of the Ode of dismay and derision Byron had addressed to him only the year before. If Byron had been bitterly, and personally, affronted by Napoleon's abdication he was now lifted out of his depression by the news of this startling recovery which was already affecting British politics. There were mobs in London, there were even riots in Sunderland. Byron was more than ever transfixed by Napoleon's luck and bravery and staying power: 'It is impossible not to be dazzled and over-whelmed by his character and career.'

16

Piccadilly Terrace
1815–1816

In *Don Juan* Byron provides a cynical exposé of married life in London:

> 'A young unmarried man, with a good name
>   And fortune, has an awkward part to play;
> For good society is but a game,
>   "The royal game of Goose", as I may say,
> Where every body has some separate aim,
>   An end to answer, or a plan to lay –
> The single ladies wishing to be double,
> The married ones to save the virgins trouble.'

The game of Goose was a board game recently imported from the continent, a test of plotting and criss-crossing in which the devious win.

At the end of March 1815 Lord and Lady Byron established themselves in 13 Piccadilly Terrace, a substantial building at the Hyde Park Corner end of Piccadilly, facing towards Green Park. This grandiose town house had been taken for them by Lady Melbourne: 'As Ld B wants Space', she wrote, 'I hope it will suit him.' It belonged to the Duchess of Devonshire, formerly Lady Elizabeth Foster, who was travelling abroad, and the negotiated rent was £700 a year. Hobhouse had been sent to vet the building and Byron told him to pay particular attention to 'those *essentials* to happiness', the number and position of the wcs.

This was the first time Byron and Annabella had been on their own territory since the wedding three months earlier. Indeed it was Byron's first experience of living in permanent proximity with another woman since his mother died. When he first contemplated marriage Byron had envisaged a more remote relationship. He had seen the draughty expanses of Newstead as ideal for contentment: 'my wife & I shall be so happy, – one in each Wing.' No. 13 Piccadilly

Terrace, although big by London standards, imposed a different, more personally demanding way of living. There were so many formal spaces, so few bolt-holes. Piccadilly Terrace soon induced the claustrophobia to which Byron was so prone. Of the many tensions that arose in Byron's marriage all were exacerbated by the social demands made on a man whose psychological and creative imperatives gave him a sometimes desperate need to be alone.

Callers began coming. A fortnight after the Byrons were installed Augusta Leigh arrived accompanied by her friend Lady Shelley who recorded the disconcerting visit in her diary:

'We mounted the stairs, and were about to be ushered into the drawing-room, when the door suddenly opened, and Lord Byron stood before us. I was, for the moment, taken aback at his sudden appearance; but I contrived to utter a few words, by way of congratulations. Lord Byron did not seem to think that the matter was adapted to good wishes; and looked as though he resented my intrusion into the house. At least I thought so, as he received my congratulations so coldly, and the expression on his face was almost demoniacal.'

A still more problematic party assembled in Piccadilly Terrace soon after the Byrons' marriage when, apparently at Byron's own request, Lady Melbourne brought her daughter-in-law Lady Caroline Lamb to see her cousin by marriage, Annabella. Besides these three women, strangely linked in their claims on Byron's loyalty, Augusta Leigh and Annabella's mother were also in the room. The nuances were suffocating, and for Caro the encounter was an agony: 'I never looked up. Annabella was very cold to me. Lord Byron came in & seemed agitated – his hand was cold, but he seemed kind.' The battle of Waterloo was fought a few weeks later. Caro's brother Frederick Ponsonby was wounded, and she left for Brussels and then Paris. This was the last time that she and Byron met.

Even in those early weeks there were signs that in moving into their impressive London mansion the Byrons had overstretched their resources. Augusta lamented: 'Could not B – content himself with a *small* house in Town. Oh no – I know his soaring spirit.' Niggling arguments about money soon began to surface and on Hobhouse's first visit to Piccadilly Terrace he was made anxious by the warning he was given by Byron not to marry, 'though he has the best of wives'.

The long-awaited death of Lady Milbanke's brother Viscount Wentworth, which took place on 17 April 1815, brought no immediate improvement to the Byrons' finances. The bulk of the property now passed to Lady Milbanke and she and her husband took the name of Noel according to the terms of the will. Annabella's inheritance still lay in the future. Byron had no means of settling his

Pen and ink sketch of the newly married Lord and
Lady Byron by Lady Caroline Lamb

debts, which he had recently computed at £30,000, and only the small income from the marriage settlement to sustain the considerable upkeep of the house with its retinue of servants besides a coach and coachman. His shame at these recurrent financial crises, sharpened by Annabella's lack of sympathy, encouraged Byron to seek his interests and amusements outside the married home.

Byron's friendship with his publisher John Murray had never been a conventional business relationship. Much more was expected, as indeed much more was given, in terms of practical support and human sympathy. While Byron was at Seaham Murray had been expected to act as caretaker of Byron's rooms in Albany: 'You will oblige me very much by making an occasional enquiry in Albany at my chambers – whether my books &c. are kept in tolerable order – and how far my old woman continues in health and industry as keeper of my late den.' When Byron moved to 13 Piccadilly Terrace, taking the ill-favoured Mrs Mule along with him, transformed in a splendiferous new wig, the friendship with Murray was further cemented and Byron began paying almost daily visits to 50 Albemarle Street, a few minutes' walk away.

Albemarle Street became a kind of home from home to him. The morning gatherings in Murray's first-floor drawing room attracted many of the leading literary figures of the day, and it was here, on 7 April 1815, in the company of Murray's adviser William Gifford, William Sotheby, and James Boswell, son of Johnson's biographer, that Byron first met Sir Walter Scott. Byron may have abused Scott in *English Bards and Scotch Reviewers* but by 1814 he was describing *Waverley* as 'the best & most interesting novel I have redde since – I don't know when'. It was a momentous meeting. Scott and Byron were locked in conversation for two hours. Though opposed politically, Scott being a staunch Tory, they were linked by their heightened sense of history, the thrill of narrative in their poetry and prose, and by a heroic ideal of manliness, a respect for the straightforward qualities of goodness which in the case of Byron coexisted with, and nurtured, paradoxical excesses. Scott made the perceptive comment about Byron that he was more likely to have turned Catholic than Methodist.

John Murray's young son, also John, was wide-eyed witness to more meetings between Scott and Byron over the spring and summer of 1815, Byron in his London morning wear of black dress coat and either grey or buff-coloured cotton trousers, rings massed on his fingers and a brooch clasped across his open-necked white shirt:

'Lord Byron's deformity in his foot was very evident, especially as he walked downstairs. He carried a stick. After Scott and he had ended their conversation in the drawing room, it was a curious sight to see the greatest poets of the age – both lame – stumping downstairs side by side.'

Amusing himself in his journal two years earlier Byron had drawn a pyramid of poets, putting Scott at the summit, Thomas Moore and Thomas Campbell on the second level, with Southey, Wordsworth and Coleridge bracketed together on level three. Of the three 'Lakers' whom Byron often ridiculed he was always less abusive of Coleridge than the others: 'Coleridge is the best of the trio', he had admitted to the poet James Hogg, the Ettrick Shepherd, '– but bad is the best.' He had in fact been instrumental in arranging the production of Coleridge's play *Osorio*, rewritten as *Remorse*, at Drury Lane Theatre in

January 1813. What he responded to in Coleridge was his wildness, his unpredictability, his visionary obliqueness, his touch of ancient magic: very different qualities from those that Byron admired in Walter Scott.

Now Coleridge, sensing Byron's goodwill, wrote to him at Murray's, maintaining in an anxiously self-conscious letter that he was addressing himself to Byron's own poetic genius rather than his rank. He wanted Byron to recommend a reputable publisher. Byron's response was immediate and practical, showing the alacrity with which he could rouse himself from his own troubles to interest himself in others' affairs. He used his influence with Murray, who published Coleridge's *Christabel*, a volume including 'Kubla Khan' and other poems, the following year. He encouraged Coleridge to set to work on a new tragedy: 'In Kean, there is an actor worthy of expressing the thoughts of the characters which you have every power of embodying.' Generously and endearingly he took back all his old insults, disclaiming what he said of Coleridge in *English Bards*: 'it was written when I was very young and very angry, and has been a thorn in my side ever since.'

Besides Albemarle Street Byron's main axis of activity in summer 1815 was the theatre at Drury Lane. In late May he was appointed to the Sub-Committee of Management, brought in by his talkative friend Douglas Kinnaird. William Lamb's brother George was another of the members. The Committee sat most afternoons, three members constituting a quorum, their lively but disorganised discussions often continuing till late. When Byron joined the Committee there was a backlog of about five hundred plays for consideration. He made sure that these were read, many by him personally. But all had to be rejected: 'There never were such things as most of them,' he said. He saw it as his role to recruit possible writers: encouraged by Scott, he made overtures to Charles Robert Maturin whose tragedy *Bertram* was produced successfully at Drury Lane Theatre in May 1816.

Byron loved the flurry of activity, the dramas within dramas, of his work as Drury Lane's chief literary adviser: 'the Scenes I had to go through! – the authors – and the authoresses – the Milliners – the wild Irishmen – the people from Brighton – from Blackwell – from Chatham – from Cheltenham – from Dublin – from Dundee – who came in upon me! – to all of whom it was proper to give a civil answer – and a hearing – and a reading.' He was embroiled in the broader policy decisions of the theatre, such as whether it was feasible to raise seat prices without alienating the public and whether to make use of the latest technology and light Drury Lane with gas.

In contrast to the anxious formality of Piccadilly Terrace he enjoyed the Green Room camaraderie and gossip. His chameleon-like personality allowed him to be on easy social terms at all levels of society and he made particular friends with the stage manager, George Raymond, who had played the Ghost in *Hamlet* when Drury Lane reopened: 'We are old fellow-travellers', wrote Byron, 'and, with all his eccentricities, he has much strong sense, experience of the world.' Byron sometimes involved himself in the details of production, as when he defended the actress Miss Smith, who reminded him heart-rendingly of Lady Jane Harley, in a row about her dance steps with the obstinate ballet master, Oscar Byrne.

In the 1815 Drury Lane pantomime he appeared on stage himself, putting on a mask and joining Douglas Kinnaird and one or two other gentlemanly amateurs in the professional chorus of *figuranti*. The divertissement was a re-enactment of the masquerade held in Wellington's honour in 1814. This was the masquerade that both Kinnaird and Byron, in his monk's robe, had attended at the time. 'It was odd enough that D.K. & I should have been both at the *real* Masquerade – & afterwards in the Mimic one of the same – on the stage of D.L. Theatre.' Such mingling of the real and imaginary fascinated him. One of the things he most enjoyed about performing was the vista outwards from the vast stage into the encircling auditorium. He found this 'very grand'.

Three years later John Keats put forward a theory that there were 'two distinct tempers of mind in which we judge of things – the worldly, theatrical and pantomimical; and the unearthly, spiritual and ethereal'. In the first category, the theatrical, he places Byron and Napoleon Buonaparte.

The public face of Byron's marriage was still inviolable as he and Annabella were seen around London at dinners and the theatre. He was observed at parties 'hanging over the back of her chair, scarcely talking to anybody else, eagerly introducing his friends to her'. To some of his former critics he seemed improved by marriage, gentler and less affected. To Leigh Hunt, now released from prison, Byron seemed to have filled out with contentment. 'His appearance at that time was the finest I ever *saw* it.' Hunt had just glimpsed Lady Byron waiting in her carriage with her 'pretty earnest look' and her healthy pippin face.

One of the things that had most attracted Byron into marriage, besides the dubious freedom of 'kissing one's wife's maid', had been the prospect of his first-born child, the promulgation of the hereditary principle. There is a genuine delight in the announcement Byron made to Francis Hodgson on 29 April 1815, in the postscript to a letter written by Augusta, that Lady Byron 'is in the Family Way'. When George Ticknor, a young American in London, visited the Byrons at Piccadilly Terrace he was impressed by the tenderness between them: 'She was dressed to go and drive, and, after stopping a few minutes, went to her carriage. Lord Byron's manner to her was affectionate; he followed her to the door, and shook hands with her, as if he were not to see her for a month.' This scene was repeated when he called a few days later. Byron was treating Annabella with what seems proprietorial concern.

But there were mounting pressures within the Byron household. Augusta had been in residence since the second week in April. Her duties as Queen Charlotte's Woman of the Bedchamber, involving her attendance on the Queen when she was in London, brought with them an apartment in St James's Palace. But this was not yet ready. Annabella's invitation to Augusta to stay nearby at 13 Piccadilly Terrace was in one sense a family obligation. It was also a facet of the curious alliance that had now arisen between the two women. Although Byron himself had at one point asked his sister to come and stay with them in London he had since then become totally opposed to the idea. He 'told me *I was a fool for letting her come & I should find it so – that it would make a great difference to me in ALL ways*', Annabella recorded in one of her long statements. He was out of the house when Augusta arrived, bringing her daughter Georgiana with her. When Byron came back he was in a black mood, with the 'lowering looks of disgust and hatred' with which he had greeted Augusta at Six Mile Bottom a few weeks earlier.

Augusta was with the Byrons until the end of June. Inevitably the strains and emotional struggles of the stay at Six Mile Bottom were recreated, adult turmoils being given an extra twist by the presence of seven-year-old Georgiana, Byron's favourite of Augusta's children. Annabella, who describes herself as being at the time in a mood of 'romantic forgiveness' towards the sister-in-law she strongly suspected of incest with her husband, made an effort to make friends with Georgiana, plotting 'to touch her Mother's heart by having her picture taken, & giving it to her'.

As at Six Mile Bottom, Byron's initial fury soon turned to a blatant and, to Annabella, an insultingly amorous fondness for Augusta. Again he sat up at night, chattering and joking, while Annabella went to bed alone. Her pregnancy was making her excessively sensitive. She lay awake listening for Byron's footsteps on the stairs, not knowing whether she would hear 'the stride of passion', signifying Byron storming up alone, or 'the irregular pace of animal spirits, rousing up "flashes of merriment"' as he and Augusta came up together. A recurring memory in Annabella's records of that cruel summer is of Byron and his sister coming laughing up the stairs.

Sexual relations between husband and wife were suspended. When Byron did spend half an hour in Annabella's room he talked obsessively about *The German's Tale*, Harriet Lee's popular novella, forcing her to read it and comparing the bad character of the central figure, another Conrad, to his own.

The German's Tale, or *Kruitzner*, was the basis for Byron's drama *Werner*, a tragedy begun in 1815 but interrupted by what he described as 'Lady Byron's farce', the commotion surrounding the breakdown of his marriage. *Werner* was not resumed until late in 1821.

Byron revived his sly innuendoes about incest, which had caused Annabella so much anguish in the spring. Annabella recorded a complex scene between the three of them, with Byron tormenting her by teasing his half-sister:

'He said to her "Ly M[elbourne] does not like you Guss". She expressed something to this effect – that she was ignorant of any offence she had committed against her. He replied very significantly he would tell her why, and went up to whisper something, after which she looked embarrassed. He would sometimes threaten her – half jesting, half serious – "I'll tell, Augusta" – to which she one day replied (desperately I thought) "I don't care". He said "Well if I ever heard any thing like the impudence of the woman".'

Annabella's indignation sometimes led her to inaccuracy, but taunts like this have the convincing ring of Byron's voice. What seems less convincing is the story spread much later by Annabella's friend, Sophia De Morgan, that at 13 Piccadilly Terrace Annabella had been driven to accuse her husband and Augusta of incest to their faces. Recollections and correspondence of that period bear witness to the greater torture of things half-understood but never said.

Perhaps cruellest of all was the way in which Byron removed his pregnant wife from her friends and from her family, forcing her to collude with his anti-social moods. Over that summer their social life dwindled to almost nothing, as Augusta told Hobhouse with concern: 'They go out but little, I think (or Lady B. thinks) almost *too* little, but you know B. can't do any[thing] moderately.' He did his best to remove her from her parents' influence. He never called upon the Noels, although they were in London for the summer, and systematically refused their invitations, so Annabella claimed.

Augusta now found herself in the unexpected position of Annabella's supporter and protector. She threatened to leave the house when, for no obvious reason, Byron had refused to speak to Annabella for four days, demonstrating 'the most violent aversion' for his wife. Annabella always expressed gratitude for Augusta's kindness. But her presence in Piccadilly Terrace induced hatreds which could, at their worst, become murderous. One evening Annabella's tears and agitation disturbed Byron and Augusta, who were conversing downstairs. Augusta was sent upstairs to investigate. Annabella confirmed later: 'The thought of his dagger lying in the next room, for I was in the adjoining room (then the library), crossed my mind – I wished it in her heart.'

In the end it was Annabella who suggested that Augusta and her daughter should return to Six Mile Bottom. She reasoned it was her duty to her husband 'to remove a guest who whatever the cause might be, seemed to increase his ill dispositions'. A few days after Augusta's departure she was filled with remorse again. What were Augusta's own feelings on dismissal? Her attitude is always difficult to gauge, so adept was she at smoothing over difficulties, showing the devoted mother's determination to keep the household afloat. Her treatment of Byron himself was often that of the hopeful parent of a wayward child. Soon after she left she sent Hobhouse news of Byron: 'What a blessing it is that he has such a Lady B! for indeed I do think her the most perfect person I ever saw, heard of, or read of.' Augusta's practised diplomacy excelled itself.

Hobhouse, abroad again from April 1815, had been a witness to the triumphant celebrations that followed Napoleon's return in March, sending detailed reports of their idol back to Byron. He had been present at the glorious parade in the Tuileries on 16 April when Napoleon, in his hat with small tricoloured cockade, inspected 30,000 troops of the French National Guard. For a moment the Emperor's eye met Hobhouse's. He was still in France on 18 June when Napoleon was finally defeated by the British and Prussian allies at Waterloo, and wrote bitterly to Byron of 'the mass of misery accumulated in the most wicked cause for which brave men have ever died'. Hobhouse's brother Benjamin was killed at Quatre Bras early in July.

As Napoleon abdicated for the second time and Louis XVIII returned to the Tuileries Byron kept aloof from the victory celebrations, the bonfires, the illuminations, the self-congratulatory euphoria of the British, viewing the defeat of Napoleon as another tragic episode in the triumph of corrupt and reactionary regimes. In July 1815, while Napoleon was being held aboard the British warship *Bellerophon* at Torbay, awaiting his exile to St Helena, Byron wrote the poem 'Napoleon's Farewell', which purported to be a translation from the French:

> 'Farewell to the Land, where the gloom of my Glory
> Arose and o'ershadowed the earth with her name –
> She abandons me now, – but the page of her story,
> The brightest or blackest, is filled with my fame.
> I have warred with a world which vanquished me only
> When the meteor of Conquest allured me too far;
> I have coped with the nations which dread me thus lonely,
> The last single Captive to millions in war!'

Here, even after Waterloo, Byron is still in blatant sympathy with England's vanquished enemy, the Emperor Napoleon, speaking for an increasingly unpopular minority. When the poem was published in the *Examiner* it was prefaced by the note: 'We need scarcely remind our readers that there are points in the following spirited lines, with which our opinions do not accord.'

After Wellington's victory many leading members of London society gravitated towards Paris. Lady Caroline Lamb, staying there with her husband, hoped that Byron would arrive in Paris too. She heard rumours at a dinner party given by Lord Holland that he was on his way. The following day had been fixed for their departure. Lady Caroline insisted on prolonging her stay. Later that night, back at the Hôtel Meurice, she first pleaded with William, kneeling at his feet, then proceeded to wreck the suite in which they were staying, hurling cups, saucers, vases, candlesticks and furniture around the room. The curtains had been left open, room lights blazing. The scene was watched with amazement across the hotel courtyard by their fellow residents. But Byron never came.

Lady Caroline had meanwhile consoled herself in Paris with a flirtation with the Duke of Wellington, new hero of the hour. Byron's violent animosity to Wellington was not just a question of hatred of his ultra-Tory cast of mind. There was also a personal jealousy as women flocked around the victorious general. Among these was Lady Frances Wedderburn Webster, Byron's pale Genevra, whose relations with Wellington became the subject of scandal in summer 1815. When the gossip reached Byron in London his pique surfaced, and he penned 'When We Two Parted', verses addressed to Lady Frances, with a penultimate stanza so insulting it was censored from the published version of the poem:

> 'Then fare thee well, Fanny,
>   Now doubly undone,
> To prove false unto many
>   As faithless to one.
> Thou art past all recalling
>   Even would I recall,
> For the woman once falling
>   Forever must fall.'

Byron's bitterness was no doubt increased by the reflection that Wellington had succeeded where his own attempt had failed.

The lines hark back to a poem he had once written to Caroline:

> 'For the first step of Error none e'er could recall,
> And the woman once fallen forever must fall;

Pursue to the last the career she begun,
And be *false* unto *many* as *faithless* to *one*.'

He was endlessly replaying his own insecurities, and when James Wedderburn Webster, now so publicly cuckolded, himself began pursuing Lady Caroline in Paris, Byron issued a comradely warning: 'she is most *dangerous* when *humblest* – like a Centipede she *crawls & stings*.'

Hobhouse was back in England at the end of July 1815, disappointed to find 'Byron is not more happy than before marriage'. On 28 July they went together to Garraway's auction rooms where the Newstead and Rochdale estates, put up for sale in desperation, failed to reach their reserve, Newstead being bought in at 95,000 guineas and Rochdale at £16,000. On 8 August Hobhouse attended a bachelor dinner at which Byron, Kinnaird, Francis Burdett and Henry Gally Knight 'all grumbled at life'. At the end of the month Byron left London to join Augusta again at Six Mile Bottom. He had now made a new will providing for Augusta and her children, which Annabella had rather ostentatiously approved.

In the days immediately prior to his departure Byron and his wife had been on bad terms, but Byron did his best to make amends en route, writing from Epping on his way to Newmarket to ask her to send on to him '*two phials labelled "drops"*', containing a white, clear liquid needed for his medication which 'the learned' Fletcher had left out of the luggage. He signed the letter 'ever most lovingly thine B (not *Frac*.)', by which he meant no longer fractious and unpleasant. She wrote to him in similarly fond and frisky mood, addressing him as 'Darling duck', quoting the old proverb 'When the Cat's away, the Mice will play' and adding, '*They* shall have their holiday, but I can't fancy it mine. Indeed, indeed *nau* B – is a thousand times better than *no* B': '*nau* B' was 'naughty Byron' in their nursery-like code.

Byron sent amusing bulletins from Six Mile Bottom, reporting that he had nearly lost a toe from being caught in a mousetrap: 'All the children here look shockingly – quite *green* – & Goose being as *red* as ever you have no idea what a piece of patchwork might be made of the family faces.' He joked about the billet-doux which had arrived from Annabella's maid, Ann Rood, to his valet William Fletcher, now a widower: their relationship advanced as their employers' deteriorated, and they were married the following year. But Byron's five-day stay at Six Mile Bottom was by no means wholly happy. Augusta admitted that they had 'a little *Sparring* about *Brandy*', and it was clear once he returned to London that Byron was offended with his sister, probably because she was persisting with the ban on lovemaking. He was bracketing her with Annabella as his adversaries, making grim threats to Annabella in their carriage: 'I shall break your heart & A's after all.'

Drury Lane became a new bone of contention between the Byrons. In theory Annabella shared Byron's interest in the theatre. Her parents' admiration for Mrs Siddons, the greatest tragic actress of the day, had developed into personal friendship. Mrs Siddons had been invited to stay at Halnaby and had written an enthusiastic letter of congratulation to Annabella on her engagement, drawing the comment from Byron: 'her style to be sure is vastly poetical – and her epithets would be no worse for weeding than her periods for pruning – but then with her dramatic habits all this is but natural and you ought to be very thankful it was not in blank verse.' In summer 1815 there had been family outings to the theatre. The American George Ticknor, invited to watch a performance by Kean from Byron's private box at Drury Lane, found Annabella and her parents there, 'a very pleasant party'. They talked throughout the afterpiece, *Charles the Bold*, 'a genuine melodrama, full of drums and trumpets, and murder and music'. 'Monk' Lewis was in the adjoining box.

But by the autumn Annabella had become less approving of Byron's connections with the theatre, and criticised his involvement with Drury Lane and its business. She complained to her father: 'Lady Hardwicke told me it was only fit for *a six and eight penny man*, and it seems to involve a species of business & attendance which I did not at all foresee. In short it is the vocation of an *Acting* Manager – to superintend candlesnuffers, lecture the performers, &c. &c.' She had asked Lady Melbourne to accompany her to see William Dowton as Shylock because, she explained bitterly, 'the Manager is always trotting about behind the Scenes'.

What Annabella resented more and more about the theatre was the use Byron made of it to subvert the values of their marriage. His love of the theatre reflected his delight in subterfuge and fantasy on both sides of the footlights, a displaced morality in which conventional standards of behaviour lapsed into pleasurable anarchy. From his box at Drury Lane or Covent Garden this deliciously false world spread out before him, with leading London ladies of society, carefully concealing their immorality, seated alongside well-known courtesans.

One night at Covent Garden even Byron had been momentarily shocked at seeing, in the box opposite, a high-class courtesan, educated for her profession, sitting with her mother, an outrageous army prostitute. But when he looked around the theatre he burst out laughing, realising that this pair were no worse than all the rest:

'What an assemblage to *me*, who know all their histories. It was as if the house had been divided between your public and your *understood* courtesans; – but the Intriguantes much outnumbered the regular mercenaries. On the other side were only Pauline and *her* mother, and, next box to her, three of inferior note. Now, where lay the difference between *her* and *Mamma*, and Lady — and her daughter? Except that the two last may enter Carleton and any *other house*, and the two first are limited to the opera and the b— house. How do I delight in observing life as it really is! – and myself, after all, the worst of any?'

In this world of professional illusion Byron could both lose and accept himself.

In his half-joking moods Byron tormented Annabella with the likelihood that he would find himself an actress, telling her, 'I am looking out to see who will suit me best.' There was a close precedent in that Douglas Kinnaird, his fellow Committee member, had been living for some years with Maria Keppel, a singer, referred to by Byron as Kinnaird's 'Piece': 'she is pretty . . . perhaps only prettyish.' Kinnaird was generally supposed to have had a son with her. The child's paternity, however, later became a matter for dispute.

London gossips would soon be linking Byron's name with that of Mrs Charlotte Mardyn, the Irish actress who had made her reputation in Dublin and appeared for the first time in London in September 1815, starring in *Lovers' Vows*, the popular play by Mrs Inchbald, at Drury Lane. Byron is shown, eyeing her lasciviously, in I.R. Cruikshank's cartoon *The Lobby Loungers (taken from the Salon of Drury Lane Theatre)*. But when Byron came to select his own actress it was a lesser performer, Susan Boyce, who attracted his attention. Susan Boyce was a minor member of the Drury Lane company, perhaps one of the chorus of *figuranti*. Their affair was certainly in progress by November, as is charted by her many letters. These have an artless energy, a naive directness, reminiscent of her earlier namesake, Susan Vaughan. She wrote to Byron: 'you are a most *uncommon* character, and I myself being a *bit of an oddity* the instant and almost instantaneous regard I felt towards you is perhaps the *natural* consequence of *two rather extra-ordinary beings* meeting on the terms we did.'

To make herself more easily available Susan left the lodgings she had lived in with her sister and, with her small son Frederick, moved into a room in New Ormond Street in Bloomsbury, not far from the theatre. One evening Samuel Rogers, who had been invited to Drury Lane by Byron and imagined he was sitting in Byron's box alone, was surprised when his host and 'Miss Boyce (the actress) emerged from a dark corner'. On another night Susan sat patiently through the whole performance of Rowe's *Tamerlane* watching Byron in the box opposite, hoping he would see her. She sent a note to him: 'I shall be in the Prompter's place in the green-room: if you will condescend to speak to me for a minute, pray do so, or I shall be wretched.' Annabella was right to have been suspicious of Drury Lane affairs.

Susan Boyce was not discreet. She left her brooch in Byron's carriage, and wrote to warn him: 'If you receive this before anything is said about it you will then be on your guard and can say what you think proper. I am vexed a good deal about it – not for any particular value I put on the thing itself but I fear it may lead to something unpleasant.' She became hysterical when, following his usual pattern, his interest waned, alternating high-pitched pleadings with reproaches in her tear-stained letters to him: 'Oh my heart did ache when your carriage passed me on Saturday night but that's gone by, I was a fool.'

Their tragi-comedy, played out in the streets of early nineteenth-century London theatreland, has a peculiar vividness as Byron evaded and Susan Boyce pursued. Her affair with Byron alienated her from the other Drury Lane performers. She was attacked 'in a most cruel manner' by a certain Mrs Scott who, she told Byron, was '*much elevated* – I don't know whether it was the *smell* or *taste* of gin – one it was for certain. She was most disgusting in her manner.' Susan was humiliated by Byron's new attentiveness to the dancer Miss Smith in preference to her. Discarded by Byron she felt herself becoming 'the jest of the *dirt* and refuse of the theatre'. In a parting letter written the following April she wrote pathetically: 'if 'twill give you any satisfaction to know you *did wound* me in my tenderest part, rest satisfied, for you *did indeed*.'

Susan ended like other of Byron's short-lived mistresses 'in an *Attic* without a *Shilling in the World*', as she put it in a begging letter sent to Hobhouse. She had been dismissed from her job at Drury Lane. She managed to imply that her son Frederick was Byron's, although at the time of the liaison the boy was six years old. In 1821 Byron himself received a tale of woe from Susan, to which he responded unemotionally. He wrote from Ravenna to Douglas Kinnaird:

'she was a transient piece of mine – but I owe her little on that score – having been myself at the short period I knew her in such a state of mind & body – that all carnal connection was quite mechanical & almost as senseless to my senses as to my feelings or imagination. Advance the poor creature some money on my account.'

By now Kinnaird's Maria had also been disposed of. Actresses at that period were expendable.

Out with his male friends, through the autumn and winter of 1815–16, Byron was still brilliantly sociable. Taking an early dinner at Long's restaurant with Walter Scott, he was 'playful as a kitten'. Scott had never seen him 'so full of fun frolic wit and whim'. But the black moods at Piccadilly Terrace were becoming more frightening and Byron's cycles of depression more disabling. He was also drinking heavily, particularly brandy. In his drunken rages he would storm around the house, breaking and burning things. It seems likely he was in an almost incoherent state of drunkenness when he asked Annabella if the child in her womb was dead.

He boasted to her of his Drury Lane mistress, forcing the knowledge upon her in what Annabella called 'the grossest and most insulting manner', maintaining that he 'could not take the trouble of acting the Hypocrite'. Augusta returned to take up residence at Piccadilly Terrace on 15 November in the early stages of another pregnancy. This time there was no doubt that the father was George Leigh. Augusta was included in these crude and cruel revelations about his affair with Susan Boyce which Byron made a double game of, proclaiming his unfaithfulness to both of them, telling Augusta he no longer wanted her sexually as he had once done.

In a house now becoming stiflingly maternal, with two babies growing in two wombs, Annabella's obsessive speculation about her husband's incest with Augusta had been diverted into still more dangerous directions: 'I confess I had at that time so far lost the suspicions in which he was concerned from the apprehension of crimes on his part yet more dreadful.' Byron's drunken confessions evidently now included reckless references to sodomy.

Hobhouse was aware of a looming crisis when he called on Byron at Piccadilly Terrace on 25 November after a long absence in the country: 'in that quarter things do not go so well – strong advices against marriage – talking of going abroad.' He had noted with surprise that Byron and Annabella did not dine together. Byron's dislike of seeing women eating extended to his pregnant wife. He was showing signs of being driven mad by money worries. Hanson had not managed to avert a threatened execution on Byron's property and a bailiff had now moved into 13 Piccadilly Terrace. Although Byron, with his unbounded interest in human nature, soon established a rapport with the man whom Annabella had described as 'a sad brute', discovering that he had previously spent a year as bailiff in Sheridan's establishment, his chagrin at the situation was extreme. When his publisher John Murray heard that Byron had ordered the sale of the books from his library he tried to intervene, sending Byron a cheque for £1,500, offering to double it in a few weeks' time and to sell his copyrights on Byron's behalf. Byron was too proud to accept his generosity and wrote back: 'Your present offer is a favour which I would accept from you if I accepted such from any man.'

Byron had written very little since his marriage. One of his few specific complaints against his wife was that she interrupted him when writing, not respecting a writer's need for solitude. But by the end of November he had struggled to the end of *Parisina*, his beautiful and bitter narrative poem based on a fifteenth-century Italian tragedy of incest: the love of Parisina for Hugo, illegitimate son of her husband Azo, alias Niccolò III d'Este, ruler of Ferrara. Byron had been recasting and revising it for the last three years. Like *The Bride of Abydos* its sexual complexity was a painful echo of his own. *Parisina* also had contemporary political connotations. Niccolò III of Ferrara was notoriously profligate. Byron insinuates a parallel with the Prince Regent. The death sentence, demonstrably an unjust one, carried out on Parisina and her lover, implies a swingeing criticism of the double standards, the canting false morality of the British monarchy of his own time.

In her final weeks of pregnancy, Annabella made a fair copy of the poem. When the manuscript was delivered, Murray maintained he would not have dared to read it aloud to his wife had he not recognised Lady Byron's reassuring hand. Byron answered: 'I am very glad that the handwriting was a favourable omen of the morale of the piece – but you must not trust to that – for my copyist would write out anything I desired in all the ignorance of innocence.'

Byron had been desperate to ensure that the bailiffs would have left Piccadilly Terrace before Annabella gave birth. The complex legal negotiations to release some of the money still due from Sir Ralph Noel for Annabella's portion of the marriage settlement were not completed until 9 December, the very day that Annabella began her labour. Even allowing for the melodrama of Annabella's self-serving recollections of Byron's violence at the time of her confinement, it was a nightmare scene. Augusta was still at Piccadilly, providing a screen of protectiveness to Annabella and her unborn child. Mrs Clermont, her devoted former governess, was also in attendance, imported by Augusta who had told her that if Byron 'continues in this way God knows what he may do'. Byron's valet Fletcher kept a wary eye on Byron's pistols – which Byron kept beside him, loaded, in the bedroom – lest his master should be tempted to use them. As Annabella realised, poor Fletcher was in an altogether impossible position, 'being of a timid & simple disposition – much attached to his master, but interested also for me'.

When Annabella told Byron her labour was beginning he is said to have asked her peremptorily, 'with the strongest expression of aversion & disgust', whether she wanted to live with him any longer, reducing her to tears. He then went out to the theatre. She complained that, once he had returned, he spent the night downstairs hurling soda bottles at the ceiling to disturb her labour in the room above. Doubting this accusation Hobhouse later inspected the ceiling but found no mark of blows. He concluded that Byron's playful habit 'of knocking off the heads of the bottles with a poker sufficiently accounted for the noise'.

The child was born at 1 p.m. on Sunday 10 December. It was not the son and heir Byron had envisaged but a daughter to be named, with an intrepid tactlessness, Augusta Ada. After the birth Annabella recalled Byron speculating about where the baby was conceived: 'if it was at Newmarket, no wonder if it should be like A.' The baby's second name came from an Ada who had married into the Byron family in the reign of King John. Amongst the subsequent tales of Byron's infamy is an account of his exclamation on the first sight of his daughter lying on the bed beside her mother: 'Oh! what an implement of torture have I acquired in you!' This seems too pat to be quite credible. But certainly Augusta Ada was soon to become a pawn in the escalating war between the Byrons.

On their honeymoon, hinting to Annabella that he had been 'guilty of *some* heinous crime', he had told her that he would confess further when she had a child since 'any woman might be bound by that tie'. Ada's birth did indeed provoke Byron to fresh and more specific avowals of guilt. Soon after Annabella confided to Byron's doctor, Matthew Baillie: 'I have reason to think there is a person who possesses the key, & whose visits always *evidently* produced the diseased associations, till we seemed to notice them. Since then Lord B. has studiously disguised them, & appeared confused & guilty at the mention of that friend.' The friend is obviously Hobhouse, the one person who had intimate knowledge both of Byron's love for Edleston and of his sodomitical pursuits in Greece.

On 3 January 1816, a day on which Byron stormed around Annabella's room quarrelling and threatening 'to *do every thing wicked*', he returned to the subject: 'I have never done an act that would bring me under the Law – at least on this side of the Water.' He implies that his criminal activities had ceased in 1811, once he returned to England. This accords with the account he gave William Harness at that period of his determination to reform: 'The latter part of my life has been a perpetual struggle against affections which embittered the earlier portion.' The pressure of this constant battle with his instincts also probably accounts for his recurring longing to leave England for Greece and for the East where homosexual affections could be expressed freely. Annabella's understanding of the threats he began making in the days after the birth of their daughter was that Byron was proposing to revert to his homosexual practices.

It had been decided between Annabella and her mother that she should take the infant on a visit to the Noels at Kirkby Mallory. Three days after his ferocious verbal attack, Byron wrote a letter speeding his wife's departure:

'When you are disposed to leave London – it would be convenient that a day should be fixed – & (if possible) not a very remote one for that purpose. – Of my opinion upon that subject you are sufficiently in possession – & of the circumstances which have led to it – as also to my plans – or rather – intentions – for the future.'

What were these intentions? He was desperate to escape from married life.

Annabella was now half-convinced of his insanity. She rummaged through his trunks and letter cases searching for evidence, discovering a little bottle of laudanum and a secret copy of the Marquis de Sade's *Justine*, a book then not considered 'fit for an open library'. She confided her fears of Byron's alarming symptoms to a sceptical John Hanson, showing him her marked-up copy of the *Medical Journal*, indicating passages referring to insanity. Before she returned to her parents, Annabella set a medical investigation in train, bringing in the same Dr Baillie who had passed judgement over twenty years earlier on Byron's lame leg. She told Baillie of her husband's delusion of being 'a fallen angel, though she was half-ashamed of the idea'. She described his self-tormenting guilts: 'he dreams himself (as he has said) a villain for marrying me on account of former circumstances.' She asked for his moral views. 'Ought I to suffer him to fulfil his intention of going abroad to the spot with which I know his most maddening feelings to be connected, without restraint, if I can impose it?' Baillie proposed that Byron should be put under the discreet surveillance of Annabella's own physician, Francis Le Mann.

During the evening of 14 January, at Piccadilly Terrace with Annabella and Augusta, 'he said, very significantly – "When Shall we three meet again?"' to which his wife replied, '*In Heaven I hope*.' Early next morning she got ready to depart, taking the baby with her. The carriage was already at the door. On the way downstairs she passed Byron's bedroom: 'There was a large mat on which his Newfoundland dog used to lie. For a moment I was tempted to throw myself on it, and wait at all hazards, but it was only a moment – and I passed on.'

17

Piccadilly Terrace

1816

Annabella broke the journey at Woburn, where she wrote Byron an arch and prissy letter: 'I hope you are *good*, and remember my medical prayers & injunctions. Don't give yourself up to the abominable trade of versifying – nor to brandy – nor to any thing or any body that is not *lawful* & right.' The travellers arrived at Kirkby Mallory on 16 January and she wrote again the next day:

'Dearest Duck

We got here quite well last night, and were ushered into the kitchen instead of drawing-room, by a mistake that might have been agreeable enough to hungry people. Of this and other incidents Dad wants to write you a jocose account, & both he & Mam long to have the family party completed. Such a w c! and such a *sitting*-room or *sulking*-room all to yourself. If I were not always looking about for B, I should be a great deal better already for country air. *Miss* finds her provisions increased, & fattens thereon. It is a good thing she can't understand all the flattery bestowed upon her, "Little Angel". Love to the good goose, & every body's love to you both from hence.

Ever thy most loving
Pippin ... Pip – ip'

Byron, used to her tone of sugary domesticity, had no suspicion that she had been advised by the doctors to write 'a few lines in the usual form without any notice of serious subjects'. This letter shows a capacity for deviousness which Byron, the practised writer, could not have begun to emulate. Particularly masterly is Annabella's reference to the w c.

Augusta remained at Piccadilly Terrace. As a precaution against Byron's possible violence and suicidal impulses their cousin and Byron's heir, George Byron, a naval officer a year younger than Byron, was now staying in the house. Keeping a close watch on his patient, Dr Le Mann found no evidence of insanity, although he registered concern at Byron's level of alcohol consumption. His liver was very bad and Le Mann prescribed some camomile pills. The doctor suspected he had had a slight stroke on one side of his body which accounted for the fact that the lesser of his two uneven eyes was now looking 'so much smaller'. At this point it appears that Byron was still confident of his wife's imminent return.

On 2 February 1816, the week after his twenty-eighth birthday, Byron received a letter from Sir Ralph Noel asking him to agree to a separation. The original letter, posted to Piccadilly Terrace, was intercepted by Augusta and returned to Kirkby Mallory. She hoped to play for time. Sir Ralph circumvented this by bringing the letter to London himself. Drafted by Dr Stephen Lushington, his legal adviser, its message was as follows:

'*Very recently* Circumstances have Come to my knowledge which Convince me, that with your opinions it cannot tend to your happiness to continue to live with Lady Byron, and I am yet more forcibly convinced that her return to you after her dismissal from your house and the treatment she experienced whilst in it is not consistent either with her Comfort, or, I regret to add, personal safety.'

He suggested that Byron should appoint his own lawyer to meet Sir Ralph's in order to 'discuss and Settle such terms of Separation as may be mutually approved'.

What had happened in the intervening fortnight while Annabella had been in Leicestershire? Although she had confided to Mrs Clermont her grave doubts about the marriage in the weeks of upheaval before she left London, she was by no means resolved not to return. But, once away from Byron, there were many pressures on Annabella, who was in any case in that state of nervy edginess that often follows pregnancy. There were admonitions from her closest London friend Selina Doyle who wrote to Annabella at Kirkby urging her to consider seriously taking 'that *final step*' of separation from her husband. Selina, a confidante since childhood, had come to view Byron's marriage in almost de Sadeian terms: 'We have both (you & me) at times talked of his treatment of you as an experiment . . . Perhaps you are not the first on whom he may have tried his powers thus – but would he love you were he to conquer your strong sense of virtue?' Selina Doyle's analysis was shrewd.

Annabella was now also under pressure from her mother, whose response to the accounts of Byron's 'outrages' was one of horror. Only two days after reaching Kirkby Mallory Annabella prepared a statement, the first of many, which Lady Noel took with her to London in order to seek legal advice. Lady

Noel consulted Sir Samuel Romilly, the most respected legal arbitrator of the time, a great legal reformer but a sternly unimaginative moralist. She also met Samuel Heywood, Serjeant-at-law, and Colonel Francis Hastings Doyle, Selina's brother, who would play a key role in the separation and its aftermath. It was Heywood who arranged a private interview for Lady Noel with Stephen Lushington, the ambitious young barrister whose cool professional zeal in pursuing the case as the Noels' chief legal adviser was to have the effect of ruling out all prospect of reconciliation between Byron and his wife.

At Kirkby, all through January, Annabella was receiving Augusta's detailed bulletins from Piccadilly Terrace. Few of these were reassuring. For example, on 26 January,

'B. went *with Hobhouse* to the *Royal Society* & then to the Play, & came home soon after us in the worst of humours & more mad than I've seen him since you been gone. *Paris* is ye favourite theme . . . says he will go off with ye first woman who will go with him – & constant allusions to Ly F[rances Webster], to whom he has written a most improper answer . . . he has been FLIRTING if not worse at the Theatre tonight. To say the truth I think flirting is ye *worst* for everybody talks & stares of course.'

One late night Fletcher reported how his master had carelessly left the house door open at three o'clock in the morning. 'Lucky we had not all our throats cut!'

The still vacillating Annabella was affected by further bulletins from her governess, the professionally protective Mrs Clermont, who insisted that she should not live under Byron's roof again unless the situation changed radically. Most crucially of all, since Annabella had had moral and social scruples about abandoning a sick husband, Dr Le Mann's verdict pronouncing Byron sane propelled her towards a legal separation.

In writing to Byron, Sir Ralph Noel had assumed that the subject of his letter would come as no surprise. This was far from the case. It was a total shock. When Hobhouse called at Piccadilly Terrace on 5 February, three days after Byron had received the letter, he discovered him 'completely knocked up'. Byron had a mental capacity for obliteration amounting to amnesia. He had blocked out the rows and tears, hysterics and rampagings of the past few months, telling Hobhouse that he and Annabella had 'parted good friends' and that he had been thinking of joining her at Kirkby Mallory. Years later in Pisa, describing his married life to Thomas Medwin, he was still insisting that he only remembered ever saying one harsh thing to Lady Byron. This happened one evening at Piccadilly Terrace shortly before their parting: 'I was standing before the fire, ruminating upon the embarrassment of my affairs, and other annoyances, when Lady Byron came up to me and said, "Byron, am I in your way?" – to which I replied, "Damnably!"'

A horrified bemusement hangs over the letters Byron wrote in early February. He was feeling very ill, with the shiveriness and headache that had marked the beginning of his fevers in the East. He was taking laudanum: Fletcher attempted to water down the contents of the bottle but Byron had locked it up. He replied to Sir Ralph:

'I have received your letter. – To the vague & general charge contained in it I must naturally be at a loss how to answer. – Lady Byron received no "dismissal" from my house in the sense you have attached to the word – she left London by medical advice – she parted from me in apparent – and on my part – real harmony.'

He claimed to be 'ignorant of any particular ill treatment' which Annabella had encountered: 'she may have seen me gloomy – & at times violent – but she knows the causes too well to attribute such inequalities of disposition to herself – or even to me – if all things be fairly considered.' He wrote to Annabella begging her to reply to him directly: 'I am really ignorant to what part of Sir Ralph's letter alludes – will you explain? – To conclude – I shall eventually abide by your decision – but I request you most earnestly to weigh well the probable consequences – & to pause before you pronounce.'

Annabella had been instructed not to grant her husband an interview. Byron went on writing every few days, imploring her to see him, to return to him, at least to give him some explanation: 'Were you then *never* happy with me?' he asked her, 'did you never at any time or times express yourself so? – have no marks of affection – of the warmest & most reciprocal attachment passed between us? . . . had I not acknowledged to you all my faults & follies – assured you that some had not – & would not be repeated?' The sense that all hopes of married stability, conventional happiness, are shattered seems to have filled him with despair. On 12 February, as an astounded Hobhouse was hearing the true story of the Byrons' married life at Piccadilly Terrace from Augusta and George Leigh, Byron was reported to be 'crying bitterly' upstairs in his bedroom. 'Poor, poor fellow,' commented his friend. Yet behind all this grief lay the curious detachment of a man who had already suffered far beyond his years. Byron wrote to Tom Moore a few weeks later: 'If my heart could have been broken, it would have been so years ago, and by events more afflicting than these.'

Lady Melbourne, who had done so much to engineer the marriage, was distraught to hear the news of its impending dissolution. She was furious in her indignation against her sister-in-law Lady Noel when Hobhouse encountered her at Piccadilly Terrace on 12 February. Byron was preparing himself for accusations of cruelty, drunkenness and infidelity. But by now the ramifications were extending beyond even the worldly experience of 'la tante'. Lady Caroline Lamb had been spreading vicious rumours: 'accused B. of — poor fellow, the plot thickens against him.' The dash in Hobhouse's diary stands for sodomy. He brought starkly alarming news of what he had been hearing '*in the streets*' that day.

In the homophobic climate of the times the rumours of sodomy were deeply threatening to Byron. When he heard this news from Hobhouse, Byron was 'astounded indeed'. He became 'dreadfully agitated', saying he was ruined and threatening to blow out his brains. A few days later, Augusta wrote off to Annabella in a panic, telling her of 'reports abroad of a nature *too horrible to repeat* ... Every other sinks into nothing besides this MOST horrid one.' She repeated what Byron had said the previous night: 'Even to have such a thing *said* is utter destruction & ruin to a man from which he can never recover.' In a postscript to her sister-in-law Augusta added: 'I think you will not misunderstand to what I allude.'

As it happened, the week in which the fearful rumours surfaced was the week in which John Murray was publishing Byron's *The Siege of Corinth*, dedicated to Hobhouse, and *Parisina*, dedicated to Scrope Davies. Naturally he was anxious about the possible effects of all this bad publicity, fearing he might have printed too many copies of the poems.

Meanwhile Annabella brought suspicions of incest into the official arena by requesting her own interview with Dr Stephen Lushington. She had begun to fear that Byron might attempt to claim legal custody of Ada. She told Lushington: 'There are things which I, and I only, could explain to you in conversation that may be of great importance to the thorough understanding of the case.' At their meeting on 22 February she went over the allegations against Byron and Augusta. Although Lady Byron's evidence, as spouse, would not be admitted in a court of law, and a charge of incest not legally upheld, Lushington accepted that Byron's cruelty in flaunting the relationship would contribute to the evidence of 'brutally indecent conduct and language' with which he could convincingly be charged. By the end of February gossip relating to Byron and his sister, first whispered in the summer of 1813, was circulating more openly and in cruder form.

There was also a suggestion of marital sodomy. Against the somewhat glib explanation given in Moore's *Life* that Annabella's reason for the separation was 'nothing more, after all' than 'some dimly hinted confession of undefined horrors' from her husband, Hobhouse pencilled in the margin: 'Something of this sort certainly unless, as Lord Holland told me, he tried to — her.' The possibility of anal intercourse between Byron and his wife was to paralyse some of Byron's best-known twentieth-century biographers. 'I fear that I cannot complete that sentence,' wrote Harold Nicolson in 1924, unmanned by Hobhouse's evasive dash, while Doris Langley Moore, in 1974, ridiculed the notion that Annabella could at any time have submitted 'responsively to a perversion that was then a felony – and which would still, I fancy, repel any woman of delicacy'.

In a sexually less squeamish age we can confront the subject more honestly. As is obvious from Annabella's letters and her later reconstructions of their married life, the sexual bond between the Byrons was a complex one, stimulated by the almost constant presence of Augusta, complicated by Byron's oblique references to sexual practices in the East. She was made very aware of the attractions of perversity and had expressed to Selina Doyle her fear of being drawn into Byron's unconventional scenarios.

Her own emotions at the parting were confused to the point of hysteria. Her maid, now Mrs Fletcher, found her at Kirkby Mallory 'rolling on the floor in an agony of regret at having *promised* to separate & being *forced* to separate'. Annabella was showing withdrawal symptoms of an acute kind. Mrs Clermont, who knew her charge well, was terrified that she would weaken if she once saw her husband: 'you might have a return of Love.' In Tom Moore's journal there is a suggestive reference to Annabella's later account to a close friend of 'attempts to corrupt her morals by things not to be uttered and which without having heard them one would not even have imagined'. Moore took this to refer to 'certain beastly proposals'. Although there is no proof of anal sex between the Byrons it is not so unlikely as has been supposed.

Hobhouse was all too aware of how the two most dramatic accusations against Byron, those of sodomy and incest, 'struck at the very existence of Lord Byron as a member of society'. He had spent much of his adult life shielding Byron from just this disastrous denouement. He went into action in his friend's defence. 'I am decided for going to work openly to disprove everything,' he declares in his diary for 16 February, and on 7 March he drafted a declaration, intended as a preamble to any separation agreement, in which Lady Byron 'disavowed cruelty, systematic unremitted neglect, gross and repeated infidelities, incest and — ' A more watered-down version was finally agreed by Annabella and her legal advisers, declaring that no rumours injurious to Byron had been disseminated by her family and that 'the two reports' – of sodomy and incest – 'do not form any part of the charges which, in the event of a separation by agreement not taking place, she should have been compelled to make against Lord Byron'. Hobhouse and Byron, in accepting this statement, were apparently unaware that Annabella had not actually denied the charges but merely undertook not to introduce them in court. She had in any case been advised by Lushington that they would not be upheld.

In these protracted negotiations Byron's cousin, Robert Wilmot, acted as a somewhat shifty mediator between Byron and his wife. Annabella maintained her stance of undeviating rectitude, but her mother and her friends recognised that she was almost at breaking point. Augusta too was badly shaken. For some weeks she remained at Piccadilly Terrace with her brother, unwilling to fuel the London gossip by too hasty a removal, but on 16 March she retreated to her apartment at St James's Palace.

Byron's first instinct had been to take the case to court, maintaining '*that nothing could or would be proved by anybody against him, and that he was prepared for anything that could be said in any court*'. But, with such damaging rumours proliferating, his loyal patron Lord Holland as well as Robert Wilmot advised avoidance of public exposure because of the possibility of 'something horrid' being proved against him. The Noels had always wanted a private settlement, and the basis of a separation contract was agreed on 17 March. It came too late to prevent the blackening of Byron's reputation.

Once Byron had accepted that all hope of reconciliation with his wife was over, the tone of his letters to her changed from wounded badinage to grim reproach. He wrote on 25 March:

'my name has been as completely blasted as if it were branded on my forehead: – this may appear to you exaggeration – it is not so – there are reports which once circulated not even falsehood – or their most admitted & acknowledged falsehood – can neutralize – which no contradiction can obliterate – nor conduct cancel: – such have since your separation been busy with my name – you are understood to say – "that you are not responsible for these – that they existed previous to my marriage – and at most were only *revived* by our differences" – Lady Byron, they did not exist – but even if they had – does their *revival* give you no feeling? – are you calm in the contemplation of having (however undesignedly) raised up that which you can never allay? – & which but for you might never have arisen? – is it with perfect apathy you quietly look upon this resurrection of Infamy?'

Two days after Byron wrote this letter Lady Caroline, creating a bizarre alliance, called on Annabella at the house of her sister-in-law, the other Caroline, married to George Lamb. She was in a new mood of feminine solidarity, blaming herself for not having warned Annabella about Byron: 'think of my situation when I saw you an innocent unsuspicious sacrifice to his selfish and cruel vanity.' She now promised Annabella '*that which if you surely menace him with the knowledge shall make him tremble*', ammunition that would assist her if Byron attempted to claim their child.

Having offered to arrive 'any Evening after dark', Lady Caroline gave Annabella a scandalised account of Byron's incestuous relations with Augusta, producing examples of incriminating letters, maintaining he had boasted of 'the ease of his conquest'. She raised the old ghosts of Byron's page Robert Rushton and the three Harrow schoolfellows Byron had perverted; she told tales of unrestricted criminal activities in Turkey, the confession of which had made him turn 'quite faint and sick'. The name not mentioned, perhaps because Byron had not divulged that secret to Caroline, was John Edleston's.

Annabella was now able to report to Dr Lushington that her 'strong suspicions' of Byron's incest and sodomy had been transformed into '*absolute certainty*'. He sent unctuous congratulations on her 'final escape from all proximity to or intercourse with such contamination'.

Climatically the winter of 1815–16 was an erratic one. A series of cataclysmic eruptions from 1812 onwards had affected the world's weather. There was a small earthquake at Newstead in March. Byron's moods ebbed and flowed, following their own rhythms of paralysis and exuberance: 'it is odd, but agitation or contest of any kind gives a rebound to my spirits and sets me up for the time,' he told Tom Moore. In one of his interludes of charm and helpfulness, during the weeks before he finally left England, Byron met Samuel Taylor Coleridge, receiving him at 13 Piccadilly Terrace on 10 April, encouraging him to pursue the publication of his still uncompleted mystic poem *Christabel*, which Byron admired as 'the wildest & finest I ever heard in that kind of composition'. A few weeks earlier he had sent Coleridge a cheque for £100. He was moved by the predicament of a poet of such 'wonderful talent' being so unappreciated, and convinced that Coleridge only needed 'a pioneer and a sparkle or two to explode most gloriously'.

On that visit, Byron persuaded Coleridge to recite his as yet unpublished poem 'Kubla Khan' in the drawing room at Piccadilly Terrace. Leigh Hunt overheard the recitation while waiting for Byron in an adjoining room. Byron was overcome with admiration for the poem and by Coleridge's marvellous flow of conversation. Coleridge reciprocated with the most sympathetic and alluring portrait we have of Byron at this period, capturing his peculiar mobility:

'If you had seen Lord Byron, you could scarcely disbelieve him – so beautiful a countenance I scarcely ever saw – his teeth so many stationary smiles – his

eyes the open portals of the sun – things of light, and for light – and his forehead so ample, and yet so flexible, passing from marble smoothness into a
hundred wreathes and lines and dimples correspondent to the feelings and
sentiments he is uttering.'

Byron's 'wild originality' of countenance was corroborated by a less immediately welcome visitor to Piccadilly Terrace in April 1816. 'Having been once
seen you are not to be forgotten,' wrote Claire Clairmont, the last and most persistent of his London female fans. Claire, born Clara Mary Jane, was the daughter of Mary Jane, known as Mrs Clairmont, although at that time she was
probably not married. In 1801 'Mrs Clairmont' became the second wife of
William Godwin, the novelist and radical political theorist. The child was
brought up in London, in an intellectual and iconoclastic household, crowded
with other children of varied parentage. Godwin's first wife, Mary
Wollstonecraft, had written the controversial *A Vindication of the Rights of
Women*. Claire's mother set up a publishing house, producing children's books
and school texts, distributed from a shop on the ground floor of the family
home near the Old Bailey. Claire Clairmont had been nurtured in the families
of women of opinion and enterprise.

Eighteen months before she met Byron, Claire had been a co-conspirator in
the elopement of Godwin's daughter Mary with the young, and already
married, poet Percy Bysshe Shelley. She had travelled round France with them
in the summer of 1814 in an exhilarating and disreputable convoy often
assumed to be a sexual *ménage à trois*. After they returned to London in the
autumn, Mary showed signs of finding her stepsister's constant presence
irksome. They had temporarily parted company. Claire had set off alone to
Lynmouth in Devon; she had paid a visit to her brother in Ireland, and, by the
time Claire first wrote to Byron, she seems to have been living in lodgings in
London, eager to embark on a liaison with a poet of her own.

Byron was an obvious choice for her, not just because of his sexual charisma
and the radical tenor of his poetry, but because of his reputation within the
Godwin household as an admirer and supporter of her stepfather. Earlier in
1816 Byron had attempted to divert to William Godwin £600 of John Murray's
proposed payment for *The Siege of Corinth* and *Parisina*. There had been a
row between them when Murray objected strongly to this quixotic act.

'An utter stranger takes the liberty of addressing you.' The determined and
self-confident Claire approached Byron frankly. As she later explained to him
her lack of inhibition, 'I who was educated by Godwin however erroneous my
creed have the highest adoration for truth.' She threw herself upon Byron's

THE MAKING OF A LEGEND

mercy, confessing the love she had borne him for 'many years'. She asked him to receive her 'alone & with the utmost privacy' at seven o'clock, or indeed any other hour he cared to mention. Her adoration for truth was only slightly eroded by the fact that in these early approaches Claire used a variety of pseudonyms.

She made valiant attempts to elicit Byron's interest, begging him for advice on a theatrical career, asking for his judgement of a half-completed novel, making the most of her connection with Shelley who, two years earlier, had sent Byron a copy of his iconoclastic poem *Queen Mab*. The unresponsive Byron had gradually weakened: 'Ld. B is not aware of any "importance" which can be attached by any person to an interview with him – & more particularly by one with whom it does not appear that he has the honour of being acquainted. – He will however be at home at the hour mentioned.' 'God bless you – I *never* was so happy!' she scribbled triumphantly on one of Byron's more forthcoming notes. On one of her visits to Piccadilly Terrace she brought Mary Godwin with her as a decoy, asking Byron to make certain of preparing his servants for the visit 'for she is accustomed to be surrounded by her own circle who treat her with the greatest politeness. I say this because on Thursday evening I waited nearly a quarter of an hour in your hall, which though I may overlook the disagreeableness – she, who is not in love, would not.'

It was Claire who took the sexual initiative, proposing to Byron they should travel out of London for ten or twelve miles, taking the stage or mail coach: 'there we shall be free & unknown; we can return early the following morning.' Byron made an alternative plan for the assignation to take place in a discreet house in town on Saturday 20 April. Perhaps the appointment was postponed or possibly an actual consummation was not achieved until a later meeting since on 21 April Claire was writing, 'tomorrow will inform me whether I should be able to offer you *that* which it has long been the passionate wish of my heart to offer you.' She begged for more meetings before Byron left England for the continent and, to his displeasure, threatened a reunion in Switzerland.

Claire Clairmont, with her high colour and dark hair, her challenging expression and gypsy look, did not appeal to Byron physically. He described her to Kinnaird as 'that odd-headed girl'. Lady Frances Webster, with a certain bias, went so far as to say 'the woman was hideous'. Because of her upbringing Claire lacked the polish of the society women Byron mixed with. He seems to have acquiesced through lassitude: 'I never loved nor pretended to love her – but a man is a man – & if a girl of eighteen comes prancing to you at all hours – there is but one way.' Claire in fact was seventeen at the time of the liaison, and it left her pregnant with Byron's child.

Byron later assumed vagueness about whether the child had been conceived in London or in Geneva, where he and Claire resumed relations. But this was not before June 1816. Allegra, born the following January, certainly originated in the confused days before Byron's departure from England in the spring. This second child, like Ada, was to prove an 'instrument of torture' to its parents, to be loved and squabbled over. Her mother was to write:

'I am unhappily the victim of a *happy passion*; I had one like all things perfect in its kind, it was fleeting and mine lasted ten minutes but these ten minutes have discomposed the rest of my life.'

Opinion in England had hardened against Byron. The hostility was all the more intense because of his former fame. Walter Scott viewed him at the time of the separation crisis as a bull at a bullfight, arrogant and angry at the squibs, darts and insults of 'the unworthy crowds'. The disillusionment that spread through London society is summed up in a letter to Tom Moore from his friend Mary Godfrey in February 1816:

'The world are loud against him, and vote him a worthless profligate . . . He is completely lost in the opinion of the world; and I fear he is the sort of character never to make an effort to recover it. So I look on him as given up to every worthless excess for the rest of his life.'

Augustus Foster, another of Annabella's unsuccessful suitors, gave his laconic judgement on the parting in a letter to his mother Elizabeth, Duchess of Devonshire: 'They were certainly two very opposite people to come together, but she *would* marry a poet and *reform* a rake. As to him, he has at length proved himself a true Childe Harold.' The Duchess wrote: 'Lady Byron's fate is the most melancholy I ever heard, and he must be mad or a Caligula.'

Byron aggravated public feeling against him by allowing John Murray to print for private circulation fifty copies of two poems written in March 1816. The first of these was 'Fare Thee Well!', addressed to and sent to Annabella a few days after the signing of the preliminary separation papers:

'Fare thee well! and if for ever –
   Still for ever, fare *thee well* –
Even though unforgiving, never
   'Gainst thee shall my heart rebel. –
Would that breast were bared before thee
   Where thy head so oft hath lain,
While that placid sleep came o'er thee
   Which thou ne'er can'st know again.'

It is a many-layered poem, superficially sad and sentimental, regretting their solitary futures, tender to their orphan child:

> 'When our child's first accents flow –
> Wilt thou teach her to say – "Father!"
>   Though his care she must forego?
> When her little hands shall press thee –
>   When her lip to thine is prest –
> Think of him whose prayer shall bless thee –
>   Think of him thy love had bless'd.'

'Fare Thee Well!' made Byron's royal admirer Princess Charlotte cry 'like a *fool*'. But looked at more closely it can be seen to be a poem of deep and terrible resentment, woundingly sardonic in its underlying thrust. It is a prime example of Byron's irresistible urge to make the private public, to justify himself in a reckless flow of words, and he defended the poem as an act of primal utterance when he wrote to Annabella: 'This at such a moment may look like affectation, but it is not so. The language of all nations nearest to a state of nature is said to be Poetry. I know not how this may be; but this I know.'

The second of the poems, 'A Sketch from Private Life', is more blatantly aggressive, a cruelly snobbish attack on Mary Anne Clermont, the skivvy raised to a governess, whom Byron believed to have been responsible, in collusion with Annabella's mother, for engineering the separation.

> 'Born in the garret, in the kitchen bred,
> Promoted thence to deck her mistress' head:
> Next – for some gracious service unexprest,
> And from its wages only to be guess'd –
> Rais'd from the toilet to the table, – where
> Her wondering betters wait behind her chair,
> With eye unmoved, and forehead unabash'd,
> She dines from off the plate she lately wash'd.
> Quick with the tale, and ready with the lie –
> The genial confidante, and general spy –
> Who could, ye gods! her next employment guess –
> An only infant's earliest governess!'

The gleeful ease of this invective shows how far he had perfected the satiric technique he first launched on his headmaster back at Harrow. Gifford compared its savagery to the Italian painter Caravaggio's: 'can any human being deserve such a delineation? I keep my old opinion of Lord Byron – he may be what he will – why will he not *will* himself to be the first of poets and of men? I lament bitterly to see a great mind run to seed, & waste itself in such growth.'

Even Caroline Lamb, to whom Murray indiscreetly showed the poems, was adamant they should not be published. But Murray went ahead with the private edition and, through the malevolent intervention of Henry Brougham, the powerful Scottish lawyer believed to be a non-partisan adviser of both Byrons but in fact a strong supporter of Lady Byron's side, the poems were reprinted in the *Champion* newspaper on 14 April, under the heading 'Lord Byron's Poems On His Own Domestic Circumstances'. They were supported by an editorial censuring Byron's political ambivalence vis-à-vis the French.

The poems subsequently appeared in other newspapers and pirated editions and 'A Sketch' in particular, seen as an unforgivable attack on a social inferior, was instrumental in swaying public opinion still further against Byron. For instance, on 26 April, at a small family dinner party given in London by the artist Richard Westmacott, 'Lord Byron's conduct was spoken of, & His verses addressed to Lady Byron and Her Late Governess were reprobated'. 'Fare Thee Well!' became the subject of a magnificently scurrilous, if inaccurate cartoon by George Cruikshank, published in the month of Byron's departure from England, showing him, in the arms of the actress Mrs Mardyn, being rowed across the sea.

Was Byron in fact forced to leave the country? Hobhouse, disguising the truth even from himself, made a note in Moore's *Life*: 'There was not the slightest necessity even in appearance for his going abroad.' But Moore himself is more convincing when he says that Byron's exile 'had not even the dignity of appearing voluntary, as the excommunicating voice of society left him no other resource'. Had the scandal been only that of the breakdown of his marriage Byron might, if he had chosen to do so, have ridden out the storm. It was the additional element of incest, and more critically sodomy, that made his departure unavoidable: as he wrote to Scrope Davies two years later: 'You can hardly have forgotten the circumstances under which I quitted England, nor the rumours of which I was the Subject – if *they were true* I was unfit for England, if *false* England is unfit for me.'

Byron was already being treated as an outcast. On 8 April he appeared with Augusta, to general consternation, at a party given by Lady Jersey where they were cut by some of the guests, including Mrs George Lamb and Henry Brougham; the spirited Margaret Mercer Elphinstone went out of her way to talk to Byron, reputedly telling him, 'You had better have married *me*.' Byron's own account of this dramatic scene was lost when his memoirs were destroyed in 1824. But, in *Don Juan*, he paid a poignant tribute to female loyalty:

> 'I've also seen some female *friends* ('tis odd,
>   But true – as, if expedient, I could prove)
> That faithful were through thick and thin, abroad,
>   At home, far more than ever yet was Love –
> Who did not quit me when Oppression trod
>   Upon me; whom no scandal could remove;
> Who fought, and fight, in absence too, my battles,
> Despite the snake Society's loud rattles.'

Much of the public abuse was crude and repetitious. Byron once made a list from contemporary journals of 'the different worthies, ancient and modern' to whom he was compared, amongst them Henry VIII, George III, Heliogabalus, Caligula, Epicurus, Apicius and Nero: at least three of these were well-known homosexuals.

More wounding than these direct attacks was the insidious innuendo building up around him: 'the atrocious caprice – the unsupported – almost unasserted – the kind of *hinted* persecution – and *shrugging* Conspiracy – of which I was attempted to be made the victim'. In Dante's *Inferno* Jacopo Rusticucci is sent to take eternal punishment in the third ring of the seventh circle, the area for sodomites. Byron later wrote to Hobhouse: 'they tried to expose me upon earth to the same stigma, which the said Jacopo is saddled with in hell.'

Homophobic mob violence became a threat to Byron. He was haunted by the memory for years, recording in 1819 in an unpublished answer to an attack on him in *Blackwood's Edinburgh Magazine*:

'I was advised not to go to the theatres, lest I should be hissed, nor to my duty in parliament, lest I should be insulted by the way; even on the day of my departure my most intimate friend told me afterwards, that he was under apprehension of violence from the people who might be assembled at the door of the carriage.'

Hobhouse might deny it later, but at the time, as Byron claims, 'even Hobhouse thought the tide so strong against me – that he imagined I should be *assassinated*'. The opprobrium was so great that the Drury Lane actress Mrs Mardyn, Byron's reputed mistress, was sent anonymous letters threatening to drive her from the stage. The violence of reaction against Byron is a foretaste of the hatred that, at the end of the century, followed the sentencing of Oscar Wilde.

*

Early in April Byron's precious library, apart from the volumes he picked out to take abroad with him, went under the hammer at R.H. Evans of Pall Mall, fetching £723 12s 6d. Hobhouse spent £34 and John Murray's purchases amounted to much more. They included the splendid decorated screen with the portraits of famous pugilists and actors which Byron and Henry Angelo, his fencing master, had made for Byron's rooms in Albany.

On 14 April, he said goodbye to Augusta, now installed in her official apartments at St James's Palace. She was heavily pregnant with her fifth child, Frederick, and was due to return to Six Mile Bottom the next day. It was a doom-laden parting: 'we shall not meet again for some time, at all events – if ever,' wrote Byron, excusing himself from going out to dinner that evening with Samuel Rogers and Sheridan. On that Easter Sunday Augusta presented him with the Bible he still had with him at Missolonghi. There was no escape from God.

He wrote to Annabella with excruciating bitterness: 'I have just parted from Augusta – almost the last being you had left me to part with – & the only unshattered tie of my existence.' He admonished Annabella to be kind to his sister, 'for never has she acted or spoken otherwise towards you – she has ever been your friend'. In its strange way, this was true. He asked her to transmit news of their daughter through Augusta, and he enclosed a ring 'of no lapidary value – but it contains the hair of a king and an ancestor – which I should wish to preserve to Miss Byron'. His pride of aristocracy remained.

In those painful days of severance he wrote the poem 'To Augusta':

> 'When all around grew drear and dark,
>   And reason half withheld her ray –
> And hope but shed a dying spark
>   Which more misled my lonely way;
>
> In that deep midnight of the mind,
>   And that internal strife of heart,
> When dreading to be deemed too kind,
>   The weak despair – the cold depart;
>
> When fortune changed – and love fled far,
>   And hatred's shafts flew thick and fast,
> Thou wert the solitary star
>   Which rose and set not to the last.'

He had given the poem to John Murray, who could not resist letting Lady Caroline Lamb read it. In her schizophrenic state, appalled to see the disastrous repercussions of the scandal she had helped to create, she wrote impulsively: 'judge Byron what my feelings must be at Murray's showing me some beautiful verses of yours – I do implore you for God sake not to publish them . . . I will say I think they will prove your ruin.' Byron issued another furious reprimand to Murray: 'I wished to have seen you to *scold you* – really you must not send anything of mine to Lady C L – I have often sufficiently warned you on this topic – you do not know what mischief you do by this.' However, he gave specific instructions that the stanzas to Augusta should not be circulated before he went abroad.

On 21 April Byron signed the final deed of separation. Married women at this period had scant rights of property, and the freehold of the Noel property at Kirkby Mallory would normally have reverted to Byron, as Annabella's husband, on Lady Noel's death. Annabella's lawyers had pressed for the property to be divided in half. When Byron's side resisted, the case went for arbitration to the Solicitor-General, Sir Samuel Shepherd, who unusually came down in favour of the woman and adjudged Annabella entitled to half the inheritance. Byron's ability to combat this decision was hampered by the scandal now surrounding him. He agreed, by the terms of the settlement, to increase Annabella's personal spending money from £300 to £500 per annum, secured from the interest on her marriage property. The signing of the deed was witnessed by John Hanson and by Hobhouse, a witness of the marriage sixteen months earlier. Byron expostulated: 'I deliver this as Mrs Clermont's act and deed.'

By the evening of 22 April everything was in train for Byron's departure. His documents and letters were left with Hanson. Some of his correspondents, notably Lady Melbourne, were already showing signs of alarm at the thought of what indiscretions might escape. Douglas Kinnaird and his opera-singer mistress arrived at Piccadilly Terrace with the present of a cake and two bottles of champagne. The Jewish composer Isaac Nathan also brought a gift for him: 'the unleavened bread', Byron promised gratefully, 'shall certainly accompany me in my pilgrimage.'

He set off from London in his new Napoleonic coach accompanied by Scrope Davies. Hobhouse and the young doctor, John Polidori, recruited for Byron's travels on the continent, went on ahead in Scrope Davies's chaise. A threatening crowd was at the door of 13 Piccadilly Terrace and, losing sight of Byron's carriage in the road behind them, Hobhouse imagined 'all sorts of accidents'. The coach, however, caught up with them, Fletcher and Robert Rushton in attendance. Rushton was now back in Byron's service. However extreme Byron's vicissitudes the faithful inner circle of his entourage remained.

Within minutes of the coach's departure the bailiffs had returned to Piccadilly Terrace, seizing Byron's property in lieu of rents still due to the Duchess of Devonshire. They took the servants' possessions, including those of Fletcher and his wife, as well as Byron's parrots and his squirrel. That evening, when the party reached Dover, Hobhouse was careful to have the coach put safely on board ship in case the bailiffs travelled south to claim that too.

They all dined at the Ship Inn, drinking 'light French wines', in a sad parody of the send-off that had preceded Byron and Hobhouse's departure for the East. The curiosity surrounding Byron was so great that some ladies apparently disguised themselves as chambermaids to get a closer view of him. Byron and his party had to spend another night in Dover since sailing was delayed by a strong contrary wind. Whiling away the time, Hobhouse and Davies walked over the white cliffs remembering the scene of the king's madness in Shakespeare's *King Lear*. That evening, after dinner, Byron took a stroll to the church with his two oldest and most devoted friends. In the churchyard they paid homage at the tomb of the eighteenth-century satirist Charles Churchill whose work had delighted Byron when he discovered it as a boy at Dr Glennie's Academy. The old sexton pointed out 'a green sod with a common head gravestone' inscribed with a quotation from Churchill's *The Candidate*:

'Life to the last enjoy'd, *here* Churchill lies.'

Impulsively Byron lay down on Churchill's grave and gave the sexton a crown to renovate the turf.

On 25 April Byron got up so late he almost missed the sailing. The passengers were all on board and the captain getting impatient by the time Byron emerged from the hotel, taking Hobhouse's arm to walk down to the quay. The Swiss guide Berger, another new employee, had got up even later. The commotion of departure 'kept B. in spirits – but he looked affected when the packet glided off'. Hobhouse ran to the end of the wooden pier as the ship sailed alongside it through the rough sea: 'the dear fellow pulled off his cap & wav'd it to me – I gazed until I could not distinguish him any longer – God bless him for a gallant spirit – and a kind one.' Scrope Davies echoed this.

'Farewell to the Land, where the gloom of my Glory
Arose and o'ershadowed the earth with her name –
She abandons me now.'

These lines written the previous July at the point of Napoleon's exile to St Helena now had added resonance. Now more than ever, disgraced by his own recklessness, Byron identified himself with the anti-hero of the age Napoleon, the eagle who flew too near the sun. He left a trail of domestic devastation behind him. 'Poor Lady Byron's fate is enough to alarm all parents. She is wretched, ill, and persecuted by him,' wrote Elizabeth, Duchess of Devonshire in April. When John Hanson went to see Lady Byron on official business the day before Byron's departure she was dignified, but he told Hobhouse she was 'torn "here" putting his hand to his breastbone for the place of his heart'. After the separation Lady Byron's personality became more muted, her once piquant features appearing to have deadened. She was soon reported to be living on a milk diet and seeming older than her years. She still clung to the illusion that Byron would return to her and implore her forgiveness, as in the verses 'By thee Forsaken' which she composed in reply to her husband's 'Fare Thee Well!':

> 'But it must come – thine hour of tears,
>   When self-adoring pride shall bow –
> And thou shalt own my "blighted years",
>   The fate that thou inflictest – *thou*!
>
> *Thy* virtue – but from ruin still
>   Shall rise a wan and drooping peace,
> With pardon for unmeasured ill,
>   And Pity's tears – if Love's must cease!'

But Byron was never to see his wife, or their child, again.

In October 1816, at Weimar, the elderly Johann Wolfgang von Goethe, a recent convert to Byron's poetry, was also evincing fascination with the mysterious circumstances 'of his late separation from his wife'. He found the story of the Byrons 'so poetical that if Lord Byron had invented it he would hardly have had a more fortunate subject for his genius'. There were other painful breakdowns of marriage in the early nineteenth century. But Goethe grasped the extent of convoluted strangeness that gave the Byrons' marriage, for its own and for future generations, a sense of almost cosmic drama, of human culpability writ large.

CELEBRITY IN EXILE

18

Geneva

1816

'I recollect Great Britain's coast looks white,
But almost every other country's blue.'

On 25 April 1816 Byron watched the Dover cliffs receding. His departure from England was noted in the *Morning Chronicle*. The crossing to Ostend was choppy and Byron was slightly seasick when 'a damned "Merchant of Bruges" capsized his breakfast' alongside him; but he recovered enough to draft the first three stanzas of Canto III of *Childe Harold* on board ship.

It is doubtful if Byron was in any sense aware of what lay ahead. After so many months of domestic upheaval and public harrying he was still in a condition of wounded bemusement: 'Exiled from my country by a species of ostracism – the most humiliating to a proud mind'. In his bewildered fury Byron seems not to have seen his exile as permanent: he writes of returning to England the next spring. Even the possibility of a reconciliation with Lady Byron was not ruled out for at least another year.

Byron's crossing of the English Channel in 1816 was, however, a symbolic and irrevocable move. The next eight years, as he lived and travelled in Switzerland, Italy and Greece, saw him established as a European. With his empathy, his capacity for quick assimilation, he adopted continental ways in his style of life, his attitude to human relations, his solemn sense of history and mode of thought. Towards the end of this long sojourn abroad he was even conscious of losing his old fluency in the English tongue.

In the years of his exile Byron's writing changed and deepened. Tom Moore was to see the rush of eloquence in Byron's poems of summer 1816 – the third canto of *Childe Harold*, *The Prisoner of Chillon*, 'The Dream', 'Darkness' – as a defiant reaction to his recent struggles, the effect on his mind of these conflicts 'in stirring up all its resources and energies'. But from 1816 there are also the first signs of a new sensibility, a grandiloquence that finds its full expression in the famous lines from *Manfred*:

> 'Sorrow is knowledge: they who know the most
> Must mourn the deepest o'er the fatal truth,
> The Tree of Knowledge is not that of Life.'

Out of England, determined to kick the dust of this now hated country from his feet, Byron finally renounced all traces of the provincialism of his early poems. Many of his European readers were to respond to Byron's mature poetic conception of himself as a man grandly and fatally flawed, who had lived so intensely and sinned so outrageously that he, and he alone, was doomed to suffer the retribution of the gods. After incest, after accusations of sodomy, his sense of himself as outlaw was now boundless. He had come a long way since *Hours of Idleness*.

Byron and his small entourage spent their first night at Ostend which he found 'a very tolerable town', better than Dover, with its heavily ornate Flemish architecture, the women and girls in tall headdresses and clogs. The customs officials had been polite. He wrote a high-spirited letter to Hobhouse, who was expected shortly to join him in Geneva, giving peremptory instructions: 'Don't forget the Cundums – and will you tell Manton that he has put a very bad brush into the pistol case – & to send me *two* good new ones by your servant (when you come) for cleaning the *locks* of my pistols.' His mood of joyful relief at being away from England recalls his skittishness on board the Lisbon packet. When he reached his room in the Cour Impériale hotel (the '*Cure* imperial' as William Fletcher called it) Byron 'fell like a thunderbolt upon the chamber maid'.

In the party at Ostend there were the two survivors of Byron's previous travels. Robert Rushton, once Byron's henchman page, was now a young man in his twenties. Byron's strong attachment to him seems to have receded now the boy had matured. William Fletcher, recently married to Ann Rood, known as 'Roody', Lady Byron's maid, bore the scars of the Byrons' complex marital wranglings. She had been used as a go-between, delivering confidential correspondence from Byron to his wife, and she had been persuaded to make a deposition in support of Byron, if the case came to court, denouncing Mrs Clermont for malicious misstatement. Mrs Fletcher was to be denied a reference by Lady Byron because of her refusal to testify to Byron's ill-treatment of his wife. While Fletcher was reinstated by his master in the familiar role of buffoon servant and complaining expatriate, Mrs Fletcher was left behind in London to bring up the two sons of his previous marriage. Inevitably their finances were precarious but Byron, at Fletcher's request, wrote to Augusta to request her to intercede with Lord William Cavendish Bentinck, one of the governors, to find a place for one of Fletcher's boys at the charitable Bluecoat School.

Of the party travelling with Byron his physician, Dr John Polidori, was an unknown quantity. A member of a distinguished London family of political refugees, he was the son of Gaetano Polidori, a Tuscan man of letters who had been secretary to the dramatist and revolutionary Alfieri and was now a teacher of Italian in London. Of the next generation the poet and painter Dante Gabriel Rossetti would have been Polidori's nephew, had the doctor not died young, and the poet Christina Rossetti his niece. The handsomely saturnine young doctor had recently graduated from the Edinburgh Royal College of Physicians, having presented a dissertation on sleepwalking. He was still only twenty when taken on by Byron for his medical knowledge and presumed linguistic skills. John Murray had made a deal of £500 with Polidori for the rights to the diary he would keep en route with Byron. The pretentious and neurotic 'Dr Dori', whom Byron alternately patronised and ridiculed, had his own literary ambitions. A reading from one of the three tragedies he had already written, given in the inn at Dover on the night before departure, had Byron and Hobhouse in fits.

Byron and his companions had arrived in a new Europe. It was almost the first time within a generation that the war-torn continent had been open to tourists. Political alignments had altered in the aftermath of the Napoleonic wars and England had emerged as the wealthiest of the nations in the West. Byron, bitterly opposed to the unenlightened Tory government and monarchy and smarting from his personal humiliation, refused to associate himself with Britain's triumph. His Napoleonic coach was as blatant a political statement as his Cambridge bear. The route he chose through Europe, reaching Switzerland via the Low Countries and the Rhine, consciously avoided Bourbon France. He had no wish to see 'a degraded country – & oppressed people'. Byron's resentment at his own unjust banishment now made him more acutely sympathetic to any loss of freedom, whether in the form of restrictions on domicile, censorship of thought and language, or persecution on account of race. 'I sometimes wish that I was the Owner of Africa – to do at once – what Wilberforce will do in time – viz. sweep slavery from her deserts – and look upon the first dance of their freedom,' Byron was soon to write.

The coach set off from Ostend at three in the afternoon of 26 April. It was driven by a glowering postillion wearing thighboots, a blue and red coat and a leather hat with a broad brim. This coachman was a 'dreadful smacker of his whip' and drove the four horses hard as they travelled through the flat, highly cultivated country towards Bruges. They had hired a smaller carriage to accommodate the luggage. Byron disliked the monotony of the landscape. As he wrote in an early letter to Augusta, 'level roads don't suit me – as thou knowest – it must be up hill or down– & then I am more au fait.' But he was delighted by the beauty of the towns of the Low Countries: first Bruges, then Ghent, where they got a good view by climbing the 450 steps of a steeple, Byron valiantly dragging himself up. Finally, in Antwerp, after viewing the harbour built for Napoleon's navy, they went to see the pictures in the museum and Byron's worst impressions of Rubens were confirmed:

'he seems to me (who by the way know nothing of the matter) the most glaring – flaring – staring – harlotry imposter that ever passed a trick upon the senses of mankind – it is not nature – it is not art – with the exception of some linen (which hangs over the cross in one of his pictures) which to do it justice looked like a very handsome tablecloth – I never saw such an assemblage of florid night-mares as his canvas contains – his portraits seem clothed in pulpit cushions.'

Byron, evidently horrified by Rubens' fleshy females, responded more enthusiastically to the aristocratic portraiture of Van Dyck.

After the coach had broken down three times the travellers were diverted to Brussels for repairs. Byron sent an abusive message back to England to Baxter the coachmaker, demanding a reduction of the bill to take account of the faulty wheels and springs. In Brussels he was greeted by Pryse Lockhart Gordon, a family connection of his mother's who had not seen Byron since he was at Harrow and found him surprisingly unchanged: 'a beautiful, wild, and intelligent eye, fringed with long and dark lashes; an expansive and noble forehead, over which hung in thick clusters his rich dark natural curls'. We do not know whether he told Byron that his facial expression had become just like his mother's. They exchanged reminiscences of childhood in Banff and Aberdeen and later, when they were teenagers, of racing their ponies in Hyde Park.

Brussels, less than a year after Waterloo, was thronged with soldiers and with English sightseers. Gordon offered his services as guide when Byron and Polidori visited the battlefield on 4 May. They set out early. It was a fine day, but as they drove through the dank forest of Soignies, Byron became noticeably silent and depressed. They first went to Mont Saint-Jean to view the monuments, fending off small boys trying to sell them souvenirs of battle, 'the glitter of buttons in their hands'. Byron then borrowed a Cossack horse and took a gallop over the battlefield. He was shown the exact spot of the attack upon the

French by the heroic Scots Greys, whose discipline and courage had so impressed Napoleon. He stopped at the chapel of the Château de Hougoumont, assembly point for the many British wounded, and he and Polidori wrote their names in the visitors' book.

Byron was by now such a connoisseur of battlefields that he was not easy to impress, telling Hobhouse, 'The Plain at Waterloo is a fine one – but not much after Marathon & Troy – Cheronea – & Platea.' His view of Waterloo was darkened by his hatred of the politics behind the battle: he detested 'the cause & the victors – & the victory – including Blucher & the Bourbons'. Byron's vision of post-Napoleonic Europe was one of inevitable doom. However, at Hougoumont he could not resist acquiring his own battle souvenirs, despatching back to England to his publisher John Murray:

> 'One packet of Eagles tricolours
> 1 brass Cuirass (breast & back)
> 1 brass helmet with plume
> 1 sword.'

As they cantered off the battlefield Byron was heard singing a Turkish song.

Back in Brussels, Byron declined an invitation to dine with the Gordons, but came in after dinner when he was persuaded to accept an ice. He was conversational, affable, and stayed till 2 a.m. When Mrs Gordon brought in her scrapbook, proudly displaying the Waterloo stanzas Walter Scott had written for her a few months earlier and asking for a contribution from Byron, he agreed to take the scrapbook away to his hotel and compose a few verses before he went to sleep. He came back the next morning with two stanzas which appeared, only slightly amended, in *Childe Harold*: 'Stop, for thy tread is on an Empire's dust'. They are grandly sardonic verses in which Byron's picture of the overweening vanity of war is overlaid by regrets at his own susceptibility to the mischievous flattery of fame.

If the first two cantos of *Childe Harold* show clear signs of having been written in transit, Canto III is still more evidently international travelogue. The manuscript now in the possession of John Murray, a patchwork of multiple scraps of paper, written at different times, in different locations, shows how much Byron's poem was day-to-day reportage of his own response to a Europe redefined by Waterloo. He seizes the moment, and the poem draws its immediacy from having been written on the wing. The Waterloo stanzas in particular give an effect of present passion as they mix the elegiac and the venomous: 'How that red rain hath made the harvest grow!' He moves masterfully from the glamour of the ball in Brussels on the eve of battle to the scene of carnage, with fifteen thousand English corpses on the battlefield, to make the point that victory contains within itself a terrible ambiguity: beauty and horror, triumph and loss.

Amongst those dead was Byron's own relation, the Hon. Frederick Howard, third son of his guardian, the Earl of Carlisle. On his tour of the battlefield he had asked to be shown the place where Howard had fallen while attacking a company of enemy infantry. The little hollow in the ground made by the corpse of the young man had already been ploughed over, and a new crop of grain had been sown. Byron wrote a memorial for Howard in *Childe Harold*:

> 'There have been tears and breaking hearts for thee,
> And mine were nothing, had I such to give;
> But when I stood beneath the fresh green tree,
> Which living waves where thou didst cease to live,
> And saw around me the wide field revive
> With fruits and fertile promise, and the Spring
> Come forth her work of gladness to contrive,
> With all her reckless birds upon the wing,
>   I turn'd from all she brought to those she could not bring.'

It is possible to accuse Byron of shallowness in writing so feelingly of a distant kinsman with whose father he had feuded bitterly. He may have written the stanzas partly to placate Augusta. This is by the way. What made him so reson-ant a poet at a period when few families were unafflicted by grief was his courage in interpreting national catastrophe in such deeply personal terms.

Byron's coach left Brussels on 6 May. The cavalcade now travelled south towards the Rhine, the Napoleonic carriage 'jolting, rolling, knocking' along the worst-made road that he had ever encountered. At Cologne Byron had 'a ludicrous adventure': the owner of his hotel mistook the German chamber-maid, whose red cheeks and white teeth had tempted Byron to 'venture upon her carnally', for his wife and stood at the door swearing at the two of them 'like a squadron of cavalry' until his wife emerged blamelessly from her own room.

The next morning Byron, the aficionado of skulls, was shown around the macabre museum of the church of St Ursula in Cologne. He and Polidori examined the bones and skulls of the eleven thousand martyred virgins, arranged in immaculate order, some of them gilded: 'A whole room bedecked with them'. On 10 May, they proceeded on to Bonn, with its hills, steeples and turrets, and on 11 May they passed through Drachenfels. The ruined castle on the summit of one of the highest pinnacles appears in the poem Byron wrote later that same day and sent to Augusta. These verses too were material for *Childe Harold*:

> 'The castled crag of Drachenfels
> Frowns o'er the wide and winding Rhine.'

At Coblenz they crossed the river, passing the joint tomb of two famous French warriors, General Marceau, killed at Altenkirchen fighting the Archduke Charles of Austria in 1796, and General Hoche, who defeated the Austrians at Neuwied in 1797 and who was intended leader of the abortive French invasion of Ireland in 1798. Byron mourned both valiant men. He then scrambled energetically up the ancient battered fortress of Ehrenbreitsen which Marceau had besieged. The sublime mountain scenery reminded Byron of Cintra, and he and Fletcher compared their progress south through Germany to the rugged routes they had taken in Albania, travelling from Delvinaki to Tepeleni. So far Fletcher much preferred this European journey to their travels in the East.

The Rhine country was becoming precipitous and forested. On 13 May, leaving St Goar, they noticed men hacking at vines, wearing cocked hats with great buckles. They travelled along the south side of the river, passing Bingen and crossing the Rhine again at Mannheim on a bridge of boats. As they travelled, Byron's state of health had been improving; it was the doctor who was taken ill, suffering from headache, vertigo and faintness. Polidori dosed himself with magnesia, lemon acid and stewed apples, but still felt weak when, on 19 May, they set out from Offenbach, travelling over hills, through misty woods, until they could see the distant Alps and Jura mountains. On the road near Berne they entertained themselves debating whether the clouds were mountains, or the mountains clouds.

Byron's was not an incognito exile. By the time he left England his self-conscious, softly disdainful face was instantly recognisable. Of the forty or so portraits of Byron still extant the majority were made during his years of fame in London, reproduced in engravings, widely distributed in popular social and fashion magazines. Before he departed, Byron's aristocratic features had been imprinted in the minds and the imaginations of the public. His questionable private life had much increased his fame.

As he travelled through Europe notoriety preceded him. Polidori was impressed that their arrival had been announced by the *Ghent Gazette* and the pattern was repeated in each town where they stopped. Byron was now the object of mixed alarm and fascination to English residents and visitors abroad. 'We know no spectacle so ridiculous as the British public in one of its periodical fits of morality': Lord Macaulay's retrospective comment, made in 1831 in the *Edinburgh Review*, emphasises the violence with which the public mood had swung from adulation to disgust. The sanctimonious baiting of Byron had not ended at the Channel. It continued through the years of his exile. Byron came to see it in histrionic terms, as a martyrdom:

'I withdrew – But this was not enough – In other countries – in Switzerland – in the shadow of the Alps – and by the blue depths of the Lakes I was pursued and breathed upon by the same blight. – I crossed the Mountains – but it was the same – so I went – a little farther, and settled myself by the waves of the Adriatic, – like the Stag at bay who betakes him to the waters.'

To a man of such sensitivity this pursuit through Europe – the nudges, whispers, gossip – was an ordeal that confirmed him in his detestation of England and the English. Only in England, he argued, did pre-eminence so inevitably and cruelly give way to 'envy, jealousy, and all uncharitableness'. From the time of his exile his writing became implacably and recklessly opposed to the English ruling class.

At the same time Byron could not totally relinquish the need for exposure which was, to a great degree, his lifeblood. He veered from a paranoid insistence on his privacy to moods in which he courted public recognition, as if wanting to make certain it was there. Byron wrote morosely in the 'Epistle to Augusta', a poem of that summer:

> 'With false Ambition what had I to do?
> Little with love, and least of all with fame!
> And yet they came unsought and with me grew,
> And made me all which they can make – a Name.'

He saw fame in all its fatuity and its destructiveness but, as he recognised so painfully, he was now public property. This was the price he paid.

They arrived at the Hôtel d'Angleterre in Sécheron near Geneva on 25 May 1816, having added to their luggage a collection of old bones of Burgundian soldiers slaughtered by the Swiss on the fifteenth-century battlefield of Morat. 'From Morat', Byron wrote to Hobhouse, 'I brought away the leg and wing of a Burgundian: – the descendants of the vanquished – when last here in the service of France – buried or carried away the greater part of the heap – except what the Swiss had made into *knife-handles* – but there are still a few left.' In the hotel register Byron entered his age as a hundred, mystifying the proprietor. Getting up the next morning he and Polidori found a boat in the garden and, on the spur of the moment, set out for a row on Lac Leman, followed by a bathe. On 27 May Polidori makes a mention in his diary of their new companion at dinner at the d'Angleterre, a man he describes uneasily as Percy Shelley, author of *Queen Mab*: 'bashful, shy, consumptive; twenty-six; separated from his wife; keeps the two daughters of Godwin, who practise his theories; one L B's.' Godwin's theories were those of sexual freedom. At the time Shelley was not twenty-six but twenty-three.

Percy Bysshe Shelley, Mary, their four-month-old son William and the pregnant Claire Clairmont had been at Sécheron for the last ten days. Shelley had planned to go to Italy but Claire had managed to divert them to Geneva to await Byron's arrival. Byron had come upon the three of them on the hotel jetty. Glad of the diversion he greeted them warmly, with a smile, and they spent the next three months very much together in a tense and stimulating atmosphere of personal and literary entanglement.

Meeting Shelley at this juncture was more important to Byron than he ever admitted. Sir Timothy, Shelley's father, was a baronet and wealthy Sussex landowner. Both poets came from a similarly privileged background, but Shelley was by far the more iconoclastic. The younger man's purity of attitude, his radical idealism, sustained a solemn belief in the intrinsic value of poetry and in Byron's responsibility to himself and to others as one of poetry's supreme practitioners. Affectionately, Byron was to name Shelley 'Shiloh' after the imagined child in the womb of the Methodist prophet Joanna Southcott who, in 1813, announced the impending birth of Shiloh, the new Messiah, and whose prophecies then attracted a great following. Though Byron considered Shelley too farouche and other-worldly to be listed amongst his intimates, he appreciated his directness, seeing Shelley as a genuinely good man. To some degree at least it was Shelley's strong belief in him that helped to restore his shattered confidence.

Shelley and Mary, known as Mrs Shelley in a practical compromise with the conventions, soon moved out of the Hôtel d'Angleterre. This may partly have been out of fear of compromising Claire. They rented the Maison Chappuis, a small but comfortable house with its own little harbour on the opposite side of the lake at Montalègre. Byron would row over every evening to visit them and one of Mary Shelley's enduring memories of that summer, her *Frankenstein* summer, was of Byron rowing back again to Sécheron on the dark waters late at night. As she later told Tom Moore: 'the wind from far across, bore us his voice, singing your Tyrolese Song of Liberty, which I then first heard and which is to me inextricably linked with his remembrance.' Mary was susceptible to Byron too.

On 10 June Byron had moved into his own larger and grander house, the

Villa Diodati at Cologny, high on the sloping river bank above the Shelleys, with expansive views over lake, city and the Jura mountains from the wrought-iron balcony that ran around the upper floor. The Diodati had its own literary antecedents. John Milton had stayed there with his friend Charles Diodati in 1639. Here Byron quickly fell into a domestic routine of breakfast, followed by a visit to the Maison Chappuis and an excursion in the sailing boat. He would dine at five, usually by himself, then if the weather was fine he and Shelley would go out again.

But the weather that summer was unusually tempestuous. The climate in Europe was still being affected by a sequence of global disturbances, culminating in an immense eruption of the Tambora volcano on the island of Sumbawa in Indonesia. In a letter from Geneva Byron complains of mists, fogs, rains and 'perpetual density'. In his poem 'Darkness' he describes an eerie deadness:

> 'The bright sun was extinguish'd, and the stars
> Did wander darkling in the eternal space,
> Rayless, and pathless, and the icy earth
> Swung blind and blackening in the moonless air.'

Most of their evenings were spent ensconced at Villa Diodati where, in mid-June, the home-grown entertainment took the form of a reading of German ghost stories from the *Fantasmagoriana*, translated into French. Byron then suggested that the four of them – Claire not being included – should themselves compose ghost stories. '*Have you thought of a story?*' Byron asked Mary Shelley every morning. For a long time she had not.

Genial in his own villa, intrigued by his new companions, Byron was the ringleader in this enterprise. The high-pitched mood of it, not far removed from spookery at Newstead, is clear from Polidori's diary:

'Began my ghost story after tea. Twelve o'clock, really began to talk ghostly. L.B. repeated some verses of Coleridge's *Christabel*, of the witch's breast; when silence ensued, Shelley suddenly shrieking and putting his hands to his head, ran out of the room with a candle. He was looking at Mrs S, and suddenly thought of a woman he had heard of who had eyes instead of nipples, which, taking hold of his mind, horrified him.'

Of the four ghost stories two failed to develop further. Mary Shelley recalled that 'Poor Polidori had some terrible ideas about a skull-headed lady, who was so punished for peeping through a key-hole – what to see I forget – something very shocking and wrong of course.' Polidori's tragic heroine ended in the tomb of the Capulets, 'the only place for which she was fitted'. Shelley soon got bored with his story based on the experiences of his early life. It was only Mary Shelley's and, indirectly, Byron's which achieved a lasting significance.

The tale that eighteen-year-old Mary eventually arrived at, to be published two years later as *Frankenstein, or The Modern Prometheus*, was the fruit of that competitive gathering, product of an intense meeting of brilliant young minds. Encouraged by Byron '*to think of a story*' she had lain awake at night, her imagination working, evolving a narrative 'which would speak to the mysterious fears of our nature, and awaken thrilling horror – one to make the reader dread to look round, to curdle the blood, and quicken the beatings of the heart'.

Her Gothick tale of Frankenstein, the German student of natural philosophy who discovers the scientific secret of bringing inanimate matter to life, creating a terrifying, tragic human monster, drew upon the many excited speculative conversations of that summer. She had listened avidly to Byron and Shelley's philosophical discussions on the nature and principle of life, their fascinated references to the experiments of Erasmus Darwin 'who preserved a piece of vermicelli in a glass case, till by some extraordinary means it began to move with voluntary motion'. Polidori, the medical graduate, made his own contribution to these debates, drawing on his special study of dreams, nightmares and somnambulism and his interest in the possibility of life after death.

The moral crux of *Frankenstein*, in which the Promethean figure challenges the dividing line between men and gods, has its parallels in Byron's writings of this period: the character of Bonivard in Byron's poem *The Prisoner of Chillon*, his Manfred, his own version of Prometheus. There is a remarkable match between Frankenstein's monster and Byron's consciousness of himself as deformed, rejected and fatally destructive. As the monster recognises his isolation, 'the fallen angel becomes a malignant devil. Yet even that enemy of God and man had friends and associates in his desolation; I am alone.'

The ghost story Byron composed at Villa Diodati was the fragment of a novel, later published with *Mazeppa*, on the subject of the vampyric aristocrat Augustus Darvell. He started writing in an old account book of Annabella's, hoarded because it contained 'the word "*Household*" written by her twice on the inside blank page of the Covers': the only specimen Byron still had of his wife's writing, other than her signature on the separation deed. After page eight of this manuscript Byron had abandoned the attempt.

It was left to Polidori to take up Byron's theme in his story *The Vampyre*, written in two lazy mornings at Geneva. As Tom Moore put it, he had 'vamped up' Byron's vampire. Polidori's version, much to Byron's fury, was published in England in 1819 under Byron's name. In fact it was Polidori's sub-Byronic

Vampyre, in its many subsequent editions and translations, that established the cult of vampirism in England and the continent, a mania which culminated in the publication of Bram Stoker's *Dracula* in 1897.

Was Polidori blameworthy or innocent? His *Vampyre* manuscript reached England without his knowledge, by a circuitous route. He bore no responsibility for publishing the work. But not only had he purloined Byron's original idea, he had used it as the basis for a none-too-subtle attack on his travelling companion. Relations between them had deteriorated badly since they left Ostend. His status as Byron's personal physician was uncertain: with Lord Byron equality tended to be relative. Polidori, himself vain, felt himself constantly upstaged by his patron: he was merely an invisible star 'in the halo of the moon'. He lacked judgement and was physically clumsy. Polidori's succession of accidents and scrapes brought out Byron's streak of sadism: 'he was exactly the kind of person to whom, if he fell overboard, one would hold out a straw to know if the adage be true, that drowning men catch at straws.' At Diodati 'Dr Pollydolly' bore the brunt of Byron's cruel badinage. Once, out on the lake, they had quarrelled and, accidentally on purpose, Polidori struck Byron on the knee with an oar.

It can hardly have been coincidence that Polidori transformed Byron's Augustus Darvell into his own deeply sinister Lord Ruthven, the vampyre with the deathly pallor and basilisk grey eye. The allusion is a coded one. Clarence de Ruthven, Lord Glenarvon, is the Byron figure in *Glenarvon*, Caroline Lamb's novel of revenge published in May of that same year. Byron as horror villain, as predator, as bloodsucker? Polidori's story, much like Lady Caroline's, is a fictional table-turning, an imaginary come-uppance, with the added irony that its readers thought Byron had written it himself.

Switzerland was not to rate as one of Byron's favourite places. He later called it 'a curst selfish, swinish country of brutes, placed in the most romantic region of the world. I never could bear the inhabitants, and still less their English visitors.' At the time of Byron's visit the canton of Geneva, which had become part of the Swiss Confederation after Napoleon's defeats in 1814, was being rediscovered by the English. A stop to see the natural wonders of the region – the waterfalls and mountains, the glaciers of Chamonix, the vistas round the lake – was now *de rigueur* for travellers on their way to Venice or Rome. Byron complained of the tight-fistedness and even the deceitfulness of the Swiss in their exploitation of tourism. His own and Shelley's presence in Geneva during that famous summer of 1816 increased Switzerland's allure as a tourist destination, and indeed still does.

The city of Geneva, with its well-known expertise in watchmaking, was self-contained, self-regulated, described by a contemporary English visitor as a 'Lilliput republic', smugly oblivious to the poverty in the countryside around it. The doors of the city were locked every night at ten. The conscientious local police were on the alert for signs of misbehaviour by their controversial visitors. Polidori, in his diary, notes that he was stopped and questioned in the city. When he attacked a local apothecary, shattering his spectacles and pulling off his hat, on the grounds that he had supplied substandard drugs, presumably for use by Byron, a warrant was put out for Polidori's arrest. Police records show that Byron noisily, but wrongly, accused some local residents of stealing an anchor and ship's fittings from the harbour at Maison Chappuis. There was a report also of a breaking-and-entering attempt on the Villa Diodati. Geneva was proving a far from tranquil retreat.

Hardest to bear for Byron was his ordeal at the hands of other English visitors to Switzerland. Gossips, he recollected bitterly, made his stay a nightmare:

'there is no story so absurd that they did not invent it at my cost. I was watched by glasses on the opposite side of the Lake, and by glasses too that must have had very distorted optics. I was waylaid in my evening drives – I was accused of corrupting all the *grisettes* in the Rue Basse. I believe that they looked upon me as a man-monster, worse than the *picqueur*.'

The glasses Byron refers to were telescopes hired out by the proprietor of the Hôtel d'Angleterre, Monsieur Jacques Dejean, to give his guests a better view of scandalous events at the Villa Diodati directly across the lake. It was rumoured that they were able to make out 'certain robes and flounces on his Lordship's balcony', thought to be the discarded petticoats of Byron's harem. More likely this was just the household linen drying in the breeze.

Byron's liaison with Shelley, self-declared atheist, proponent of free love, brought a new element to his reputation, gaining him a double notoriety. That Byron was the permitted lover of both Mary and Claire Clairmont, believed erroneously to be Mary's sister when she was not a blood relation but a step-sister, was the substance of the current '*chronique scandaleuse*'. The damaging gossip was seized on and repeated, especially by those already hostile to Lord Byron.

Byron's old antagonist, the lawyer Henry Brougham, who had leaked the poem 'Fare Thee Well!' to the *Champion*, was amongst the thousand or so English visitors in and around Geneva by midsummer 1816. Since the separation he had kept up his barrage of hostile innuendo around the London clubs, publicising the fact that Byron had never paid the rent to the Duchess of Devonshire for 13 Piccadilly Terrace, stoking up the sexual allegations against him, maligning Byron even for his physical deformity. Now Brougham made the most of the rumour that Lord Byron was living near Geneva 'with Percy Shelley, or rather, with his wife's sister'. So sharp were Byron's sensitivities that when, four years later, in Ravenna, he learned of Brougham's long vendetta, he issued a formal challenge, accusing him of going about 'shrugging & whispering & malignantly countenancing every report to my disadvantage . . . you have proclaimed yourself my personal enemy & I treat you accordingly.' Whether Brougham ever received Byron's challenge is uncertain. Byron did not return to England. The duel was never fought.

In a similar episode in 1817, the poet Robert Southey, smarting from Byron's earlier insults, returned to London from Switzerland with scurrilous stories that Byron and Shelley 'had formed a League of Incest'. When Byron eventually discovered this betrayal, his minor sallies against Southey escalated into open war.

A glimpse of the way in which Byronic scandal burgeoned, becoming embellished and distorted in the process, is given by Lord Glenbervie, a former host of Byron's in London. He reported in his Swiss travel diary that Byron was being '*cut*' by everyone:

'They tell a strange adventure of his, at Déjean's Inn. He is now living at a villa on the Savoy side of the lake with that woman, who it seems proves to be a Mrs Shelley, wife to the man who keeps the Mount Coffee-house'.

Lord Glenbervie had confused Mary Godwin with Shelley's estranged wife, formerly Harriet Westbrook. It was Harriet's father, John Westbrook, who kept the fashionable Mount Coffee House. In any case Byron was always to deny that there had been 'promiscuous intercourse' within the party at Maison Chappuis and Villa Diodati, 'my commerce being limited to the carnal knowledge of the Miss C', as he assured Hobhouse. The burden of being a legend in his lifetime was this gross accumulation of inaccurate report.

Over the years Claire Clairmont has been denigrated, even by female biographers of Byron, as uncouth, if not brazen, in her pursuit of him. Perhaps it is only at a period in which women feel more confident in their own destinies that we can view Claire's honesty more sympathetically. She was not simply a maladroit young girl. She had already lived and travelled on her own. Her unusual intellectual upbringing had given her a rare degree of curiosity and independence. When Thomas Medwin met her in Florence six years later he noted that her eyes 'flashed with the fire of intelligence . . . Though not strictly handsome, she was animated and attractive, and possessed an *esprit de société* rare among our countrywomen.'

Unusually among his female correspondents, she spoke her mind to Byron. Her letters express a candid view of him, acknowledging his kindness and charm to his dependants, his gentleness with children, his indulgence to his dogs, but reproaching him for his inability to cope with competition: 'let any one more on a par with your self enter the room you begin to suspect & be cautious & are consequently very cruel.' She offered Byron unconditional love, and if he could not see it this was the worse for him.

Claire was not unrealistic. Her grasp of his exploitative attitude to women had prompted her to tell him, 'I had ten times rather be your male friend than your mistress.' Had she sensed, or heard rumours of, his homosexuality? On the way to Switzerland she wrote to him from Paris: 'I cannot call you friend for though I love you yet you do not feel even interest for me; fate has ordained that the slightest accident that should befall you should be agony to me; but were I to float by your window drowned all you would say would be "Ah voila!"' Once arrived in Geneva it was Claire again who forced the pace, importuning Byron, staying late or overnight at the Villa Diodati, where a surprised gardener found her slipper in the vineyard that sloped down to Maison Chappuis. Byron explained his acquiescence to Augusta: 'I could not exactly play the Stoic with a woman – who had scrambled eight hundred miles to unphilosophize me.' He made pointed excuses about his recent suffering from sexual deprivation. Besides, Claire proved to have her uses as his scribe, providing fair copies from his draft manuscripts.

When told that Claire was pregnant he went at once on the defensive. 'Is the brat *mine*?' he asked in a notably ungallant letter to Douglas Kinnaird:

'I have reason to think so – for I know as much as one can know such a thing – that she had *not lived* with S[helley] during the time of our acquaintance – & that she had a good deal of that same with me. – This comes of "putting it about" (as Jackson calls it) & be damned to it – and thus people come into the world.'

Byron implies that Shelley and Claire Clairmont had previously been lovers, but he was always eager to spread the worst calumnies about the Shelleys' mores, in some ways more extreme and more courageous than his own, partly to deflect attention from his reputed scandals and also because he found their sexual openness genuinely shocking. However, despite their close interdependence there is no evidence of a sexual bond between Shelley and Claire. Indeed Claire seems to imply that she was a virgin at the time she and

Byron started their affair. Byron's hard-hearted response contains an element of posturing. He proved a fond, possessive if quixotic father when Claire's daughter Allegra was eventually born.

For Byron and Shelley the region round Geneva was hallowed literary ground. It was the country of Rousseau, Voltaire and the historian Edward Gibbon. Byron celebrated the two latter in *Childe Harold*:

> 'Lausanne! and Ferney! ye have been the abodes
> Of names which unto you bequeath'd a name;
> Mortals, who sought and found, by dangerous roads,
> A path to perpetuity of fame:
> They were gigantic minds, and their steep aim
> Was, Titan-like, on daring doubts to pile
> Thoughts which should call down thunder, and the flame
> Of Heaven, again assail'd, if Heaven the while
> On man and man's research could deign do more than smile.'

On 23 June, when Shelley and Byron set off together for a week's excursion round Lac Leman in the new English-built boat Byron had now acquired, they took with them an English translation of Jean-Jacques Rousseau's novel *Julie, ou La Nouvelle Héloïse* which Shelley read out loud to his companion as they sailed.

Shelley looked back on that expedition with unalloyed pleasure. Polidori, to his chagrin, had been left behind at the Villa Diodati. He had broken his ankle, having been encouraged by Byron to jump down from the balcony to offer Mary his arm. Apart from the Swiss boatman Maurice and his crew, the two poets were on their own for the first time and Byron's close society caused Shelley to remember the voyage in 'the light of an enchantment which can never be dissolved'. The differences between them were more potent than their shared interests – the still dandyish Byron, aged by experience: the blazing, beardless Shelley, gawky in his innocence, 'habited like a boy, in a black jacket and trousers, which he seemed to have outgrown'; Byron's effeminate drawl: Shelley's 'cracked soprano'. They fascinated, maddened one another. Intellectually compatible they were yet poles apart, Byron upholding the traditional and factual bases of philosophical argument, Shelley pursuing the further reaches of the experimental and visionary. Gradually, half unconsciously, Shelley edged him into what Tom Moore called 'more abstract and untrodden ways of thought'.

They sailed round the lake anti-clockwise, spending the first night at the little village of Nernier where they walked by the lakeside, watching the fish darting, and were taken aback by the deformed children, almost all suffering from goitrous enlargement of the throat, who were playing a game resembling ninepins. The poverty of the area encouraged malnutrition and disease. Byron gave some coins to one small crooked boy of otherwise angelic aspect. Shelley watched as he took Byron's donation 'without speaking, with a sweet smile of easy thankfulness, and then with an unembarrassed air turned to his play'. The austerity of their lodgings in Nernier reminded Byron of his travels in Greece: he said it was five years since he had slept in beds like these.

Next day they came to Evian, town of the mineral waters known locally as *eaux savonneuses*. The scenery had now got wilder, with the Savoy mountains' mingled ice and snow, jagged rocks and deep green pine trees. Thousands of *besolets*, purple-backed water birds like small seagulls, gathered where the River Drance flowed into the great lake. Evian at the time was Savoy territory, in the hands of the King of Sardinia, the same 'Cagliari Majesty' whom Byron recollected having seen 'at his own Opera – in his own city – in 1809'. Shelley castigated the 'wretched' town of Evian as evidence of the 'blighting mischiefs of despotism' in contrast to the adjoining independent Swiss republics. In fact Byron's fleeting contact with its ruler turned out to have its uses. Challenged for their passports, which they had thoughtlessly left behind in Geneva, Byron pulled his rank and connections. The passport official respectfully withdrew.

On 25 June they were at Meillerie, revisiting the scenes of *La Nouvelle Héloïse*, retracing the steps of the tutor Saint-Preux and his passionately adoring pupil Julie through the pine, chestnut and walnut groves and meadows aromatic with thyme. Like Rousseau's characters, their dinner that night included honey, judged by Shelley to be the best he ever ate. Rousseau, like Napolean, was one of Byron's alter egos, his flawed heroes. Stanzas he had recently written for *Childe Harold* on 'the self-torturing sophist, wild Rousseau' show how far he identified with the ruined genius, from whose frenzied iconoclasm the French Revolution had risen as 'a fearful monument!'

The weather had now worsened, whipping up into a storm after the boat left Meillerie. As huge waves flooded the deck the crew panicked, the rudder was broken and the boat lurched out of control. Byron took off his coat, expecting to have to swim for it. Shelley, who could not swim, was fatalistic about drowning, sitting down quietly on one of the ship's lockers, grasping the metal rings and resisting Byron's determination to save him. Shelley later explained: 'I was overcome with humiliation, when I thought his life might have been risked to preserve mine.' When the battered vessel finally put in at St Gingoux, a small crowd had assembled, exchanging looks of wonder, as if witnesses to some medieval miracle.

Byron and Shelley's pilgrimage continued with the Château de Chillon, a massive turreted stone castle built out into the lake. From the sixteenth century the dungeons, excavated below the water, had been used for political and religious prisoners, many of whose names were inscribed on the stone columns. Byron's signature was probably a later nineteenth-century addition to the scene. Beyond the dungeons was a secret execution chamber of which Shelley wrote: 'I never saw a monument more terrible of that cold and inhuman tyranny, which it has been the delight of man to exercise over man.'

After visiting Chillon, Byron became obsessed by the story of François Bonivard, the libertarian Prior of St Victor's Monastery, imprisoned in the castle in 1530 by the Duke of Savoy. Bonivard was reputed to have been chained to a pillar, gruesomely connected to his two imprisoned brothers. Of the three, he alone had stayed alive. Over the next few days, staying in the Hôtel de l'Ancre at Ouchy, Room 18, Byron wrote the poem *The Prisoner of Chillon*, exploring deeply felt, self-referential themes of the nature of freedom and the inertia that can accompany survival:

> 'My very chains and I grew friends,
> So much a long communion tends
> To make up what we are: – even I
> Regain'd my freedom with a sigh.'

He had also been adding new stanzas to *Childe Harold*, while Shelley was embarking on his 'Hymn to Intellectual Beauty'. It was a remarkably productive week.

Before they left Ouchy, Byron had written to his publisher, 'the superb Murray', the first of many revealing letters he would send to him from exile, enclosing a sprig of acacia plucked from the terrace of Edward Gibbon's house near Lausanne where they had been shown the decayed summerhouse in which Gibbon had completed his *Decline and Fall of the Roman Empire* with a great onrush of joy nearly thirty years earlier. They were back in Montalègre on 30 June, Shelley having reached the conclusion that 'Lord Byron is an exceedingly interesting person, and as such is it not to be regretted that he is a slave to the vilest and most vulgar prejudices, and as mad as the winds.'

Byron was far from sociable in Geneva. He particularly dreaded encountering his countrymen. Invited to dine at their villa by Sir Hew Dalrymple-Hamilton and his wife Jane, daughter of Viscount Duncan, he arrived at the entrance, saw the room full of people, lost his nerve and drove off again, leaving Polidori to enter on his own. But one of the grand houses for which he made an exception was the Château de Coppet on the north shore of Lac Leman. Coppet, formerly the residence of Jacques Necker, pre-revolutionary French minister of finance, was now home to his daughter, Baronne Germaine de Staël-Holstein, the intrepid intellectual known as Madame de Staël.

When he had met her in London three years earlier Byron had ridiculed the middle-aged woman he named 'Mrs Corinne', after her famous novel *Corinne* published in 1807, or 'Mrs *Stale*', the ageing beldame in a comedy of manners. He described her briskly to Lady Melbourne as 'a very plain woman forcing one to listen & look at her with her pen behind her ear and her mouth full of *ink* – so much for her'. He disapproved of Madame de Staël's changeability, the way she switched when it suited her from revolutionary politics to those of the establishment. But even then the spoiled young man was delighted by her writer's fluency and her intellectual vigour, and he welcomed her unashamed flattery. Now in Switzerland, exiled and himself victimised, he was even more disposed to make the most of her ready sympathy.

Madame de Staël operated Coppet as a recondite residential salon: 'she has made Coppet as agreeable as society and talent can make any place on earth,' Byron told John Murray. On his visits there in July and August 1816 Byron encountered some formidable figures of intellectual Europe: August Wilhelm von Schlegel, Madame de Staël's long-term protégé, once tutor to her children; Charles Victor de Bonstetten, Swiss literary veteran who Byron was fascinated to discover had corresponded with the poet Thomas Gray; the Abbé de Brême, Italian libertarian, friend of the poet-patriot Ugo Foscolo. In this cosmopolitan society Byron's outlook broadened, his sympathies expanded. In particular his interest in the Italian revolutionary movement was awakened by this early encounter with de Brême. Madame de Staël's daughter, the Duchesse de Broglie, watched Byron at a dinner party at the Château: 'In all his movements there is the grace of a cat (I hope you find small cats graceful).' Like others at Coppet she was charmed by him.

But even at Coppet there were constant reminders of past scandal. He was visibly shaken when, arriving one evening for dinner, he found the room full of strangers who had come to stare at him 'as at some outlandish beast in a raree-show'. Among them he recognised Mrs Elizabeth Hervey, William Beckford's half-sister, herself a writer and sentimental novelist whose works were satirised by Beckford, and a close friend of the Noels. At the sight of Byron, Mrs Hervey fainted and had to be taken outside to recover. The Duchesse de Broglie was sarcastic: 'This is *too much* – at Sixty five years of age!'

Byron was also embroiled unwillingly in discussions of *Glenarvon*, Lady Caroline Lamb's novel, about which Madame de Staël had told him 'marvellous & grievous things'. After Byron's departure Caroline had gone completely off the rails. There had been an embarrassing assault on one of her own boy employees. The page, 'a little *Espiègle*', had enraged her with his habit of throwing explosive missiles into the fireplace at Melbourne House. He had thrown a squib and Lady Caroline, intercepting it, had flung it back, hitting the page on the temple. Bleeding badly, he cried out, 'Oh, my Lady, you have killed me!' Lady Caroline had rushed into the hall, astonishing the other servants and even alerting passers-by in Whitehall, as she exclaimed: 'Oh God, I have murdered the page!' William Lamb was driven to the limits of his patience, and arrangements for a separation were set in motion. This was the point at which Caroline had resumed work on *Glenarvon*, the novel of revenge she had been writing intermittently since her affair with Byron ended. She described how she had written this flamboyant tale of enchantment and possession secretly at night, composing in a flood of fury, dressed in her page's clothes.

With its cast of recognisable socialites, *Glenarvon* had been the talk of London through the summer of 1816. At a crowded dinner table at the Château de Coppet Byron was now asked by Madame de Staël whether he was not himself the original of Lord Glenarvon, the death-loving and death-giving anti-hero of the book. He answered diplomatically, 'C'est possible, Madame, mais je n'ai jamais posé.' At this point he had not read *Glenarvon*. A few weeks later Madame de Staël lent him her copy. His response was succinct:

> 'I read "Glenarvon", too, by Caro. Lamb,
> *God damn!*'

Lady Caroline had scored her point.

Madame de Staël did not believe in taboos. She insisted that Byron unburden himself on the subject of his separation, levering herself into the position of chief confidante formerly enjoyed by Lady Melbourne, and, in late August, she attempted to engineer a reconciliation between the poet and Lady Byron. He responded to this suggestion with a letter written in his best manner of wounded sincerity.

'The separation may have been *my* fault – but it was *her* choice – I tried all means to prevent – and would do as much & more to end it, – a word would do so – but it does not rest with me to pronounce it. – You asked me if I thought that Lady B. was attached to me – to that I can only answer that I love her.'

Madame de Staël's hope that Lady Romilly, a friend of both the Byrons, would intervene between them on the basis of this letter was sabotaged by Henry Brougham, who continued to be Byron's determined enemy.

Byron's claim that he loved Lady Byron and would welcome her return to him was far from the whole truth. The story of bewildered innocence was one that he continued to promote throughout his years abroad, and in certain moods he may himself have believed it. But his festering bitterness towards his estranged wife emerges in a poem written in Geneva in September, 'Lines On Hearing that Lady Byron was Ill'. He was by now increasingly distraught by his enforced separation from Ada, the daughter whose absence he lamented in the opening stanzas of *Childe Harold*. He had become half-conscious of Augusta's gradual emotional withdrawal, cowed and bewildered as she was by the bullying vendetta that had been launched by Annabella and Augusta's former friend Theresa Villiers as they pressed her to confess and make atonement for her sins. Annabella insisted that Augusta should send on her brother's letters for inspection and attempted to control the tenor of the letters that Augusta wrote to him, specifically warning her to avoid 'all phrases or *marks*' (she meant the coded crosses) 'which may recall wrong ideas to his mind'.

In his poem, written after he had read a newspaper report that Lady Byron was unwell, Byron turned upon his wife in renewed hatred and defiance. She is here his unmistakable opponent:

> 'A moral Clytemnestra of thy lord,
> And hew'd down, with an unsuspected sword,
> Fame, peace, and hope – and all the better life
> Which, but for this cold treason of thy heart,
> Might still have risen from out the grave of strife,
> And found a nobler duty than to part.'

He told Augusta in a letter written at this period that he felt as if an elephant had trodden on his heart.

19

The Swiss Alps

1816

'Could I remount the river of my years . . .' The shorter, personal poems Byron wrote in 1816 in Switzerland reflect the bleakness and despair that followed his banishment, winding in and out of his past amatory history – the Seaham marriage ceremony, Mary Chaworth's madness – as if in a haze of hurt and puzzlement. This unburdening of his private emotions in poems finally intended for the public was an essential part of the phenomenon which Matthew Arnold called 'the pageant of his bleeding heart'.

The most deeply imagined of these poems, 'Darkness', projects domestic grief into the cosmic, with its strange apocalyptic vision of a world laid waste after a sudden, total loss of light and the gradual death of an entire population.

> 'The world was void,
> The populous and the powerful – was a lump,
> Seasonless, herbless, treeless, manless, lifeless –
> A lump of death – a chaos of hard clay.
> The rivers, lakes, and ocean all stood still,
> And nothing stirred within their silent depths;
> Ships sailorless lay rotting on the sea,
> And their masts fell down piecemeal; as they dropp'd
> They slept on the abyss without a surge –
> The waves were dead; the tides were in their grave,
> The moon their mistress had expired before;
> The winds were withered in the stagnant air,
> And the clouds perish'd; Darkness had no need
> Of aid from them – She was the universe.'

This grand and terrifying poem shows the persistent influence of Byron's childhood reading of the Bible, especially the Book of Revelation. Its eerie evocation of the aftermath of terrestrial catastrophe reminds us of how thoroughly the scientific theories of the Enlightenment had been absorbed into his poetic imagination. Inevitably a reader of Byron's generation would construe the poem as a picture of a Europe left desolate by war, a ravaged Romantic landscape in the manner of Henry Fuseli or John Martin. 'Darkness' shows how conscious Byron was of the landscape now around him: the uncompromising scenery of Switzerland itself. The poem takes up the theme of last survivors as one by one men die, leaving only the dogs to eat their masters' corpses. Thomas Campbell, whose own poem 'The Last Man' was to be published in 1823, accused Byron of plagiarism, claiming to have divulged the idea in conversation with Byron before he left England. The theme may well have been Campbell's suggestion, but it is likely that the main influence was local: phantasmagoric conversations at the Villa Diodati and Byron's growing interest in epic and visionary themes which Shelley had helped to stimulate.

There was renewed interest in the ghostly and macabre once Byron's fond but tedious friend 'Monk' Lewis had arrived at the Villa Diodati in mid-August. Finding himself stranded in a sweltering Geneva without accommodation, Lewis had sent Byron a mock-medieval letter: 'Be it known to you that I arrived in your neighbourhood this day, and hear, that you are the Lord of a Castle, which (I hope) is haunted.' Not having seen Byron since the separation crisis he was careful to make clear the side that he had taken: 'you will find my good-will towards you undiminished.' Byron could always be touched by loyalty.

Lewis had recently returned from a visit to the sugar plantations he had inherited in Jamaica. His whole economy was bound up in his Negro labourers. Byron subversively 'set him by the ears with Madame de Staël about the slave trade' to which she was vociferously opposed. While at Villa Diodati, Lewis signed a codicil to his will providing for the future improvement of conditions for his slaves, and promising liberty for some of them. Byron, Shelley and Polidori were the witnesses to the codicil, which can perhaps be seen as a concession to both Byron and Madame de Staël. While at Diodati, Lewis went with Byron to Voltaire's old house at Ferney, a visit which inspired Byron to equip himself, once he got to Venice, with the ninety-two volumes of Voltaire's complete works.

On 26 August, after many delays, two more eagerly expected visitors from England, Hobhouse and Scrope Davies, reached Geneva. They had travelled via Calais where they visited another legendary exile, Scrope Davies's old gambling confederate 'Beau' Brummell, whose £50,000 debts at Watier's Club had forced him to flee England. 'I could hardly believe my eyes,' wrote Hobhouse, 'seeing Brummell in a greatcoat drinking punch in a little room with us.' After Calais they had followed Byron's own route from Brussels to Cologne and down the Rhine. They took a boat over Lac Leman to the harbour below the Villa Diodati. Hobhouse recorded in his diary: 'went up & found Byron – in a delightful house and spot.'

The mood at Villa Diodati was to change with the departure of Shelley, with Mary and Claire Clairmont, on 29 August. Before they left there had been discussions between Shelley, Claire and Byron on the future of Claire's child. Byron had proposed that Augusta Leigh should raise it, a suggestion which Claire strongly opposed. It was finally agreed, reluctantly by Byron, that the child would live with one or other of its parents. Byron did not say goodbye to Claire; there were no kisses or embraces. Claire was one of Lady Caroline's readers who recognised Byron instantly in the fictional character of Lord Glenarvon: in particular, 'the very impertinent way of looking in a person's face who loves you & telling them you are very tired & wish they'd go'. She persisted in hoping that Byron would write to her. 'My dreadful fear', she told him, 'is lest you quite forget me. I shall pine through all the wretched winter months while you I hope may never have one uneasy thought. One thing I do entreat you to remember & beware of any excess in wine; my dearest dear friend pray take care of yourself.'

As well as Byron's daughter in Claire's womb, Shelley and his party transported back to England the manuscript of Canto III of *Childe Harold* to deliver to John Murray. This and the accompanying manuscript of *The Prisoner of Chillon* were the fair copies that Claire had written out. The day after he received them Murray wrote:

'My Lord, I have rarely addressed you with more pleasure than upon the present occasion – I was thrilled with delight yesterday by the announcement of Mr Shelley with the MSS of Childe Harold – I had no sooner got the quiet possession of it, than trembling with auspicious hope about it, I carried it direct to Mr Gifford, who has been exceedingly ill with a Jaundice, unable to write or do anything.'

The sight of Byron's manuscript temporarily revived him. Gifford could not put it down until he had read it through, pronouncing it not only 'most splendid original & interesting' but also 'the most finished' of Byron's poetry. Byron had suggested that Shelley should supervise progress and correct the proofs of *Childe Harold* but Murray, who saw Shelley as unreliably extreme, made certain that Gifford took this responsibility.

On 29 August, as Shelley and his party left Geneva, Hobhouse, Davies and

Byron, with Polidori and three servants and guides, set off in two carriages on an expedition to Chamonix and Mont Blanc. This was Byron's first experience of the high Swiss mountain regions, his exhilaration at the grandeur of the scene being only slightly marred by the presence of so many English tourists. Hobhouse recognised Thomas Hope, classicist, orientalist and arbiter of taste, dining en plein air with his wife in the orchard of a small inn at Servoz. Byron jeered at an Englishwoman, in the shadow of Mont Blanc, whom he overheard asking the members of her party whether they had ever seen anything so rural, as if it were Highgate, Hampstead, Brompton or Hayes.

In the afternoon of 30 August, driving precipitously up the zigzag paths, they caught sight of their first avalanche descending from the mountain top; soon after, they reached the glacier of Bossons, described by Hobhouse as 'immense durated masses of blue ice'. Their guides took them up the right side of the glacier through the pine woods: 'rather a painful ascent'. They came out on to the plain, crossing the deep broad crevasses across the glacier, hearing the ice springs roaring below. Byron had managed to keep up with the party until they began on a perilous descent of the left side of the glacier. He now slid uncomfortably down an ice-ridge but did himself no harm.

That night they stayed at one of the many Hôtels d'Angleterre along their route, this one just across the Savoy border at Chamonix. Shelley had travelled this route before and at another mountain inn Byron had found Shelley's name in the visitors' book, the self-description 'atheist & philanthropist' written in Greek. 'Do you not think I shall do Shelley a service by scratching this out?' Byron asked Hobhouse, erasing the entry with great care. As the story was retold unjustly, it was Byron who inscribed 'Atheist' after his own name.

On 5 September Scrope Davies left for England, bearing Byron's packages of Swiss souvenirs for Augusta and her children: 'seals – necklaces – balls &c. – & I know not what – formed of Chrystals – Agates – and other stones – *all of & from Mont Blanc* bought & brought by me on & from the spot'. Ada had a special present of a soft granite ball 'wherewithall to roll & play – when she is old enough – and mischievous enough – and moreover a Chrystal necklace – and anything else you may like to add for her – the Love!' Scrope Davies also took a second manuscript copy of *Childe Harold*, Byron's original fair copy, which then disappeared until 1976, when it was discovered in the depths of Davies's long forgotten trunk.

Robert Rushton travelled back to England with Scrope Davies. Byron was not to see his handsome page again. Rushton married a local Nottinghamshire girl in 1827, and kept a school with his wife before taking over a farm on the Newstead estate; he was to die soon afterwards, leaving his widow with three children. Byron gave Polidori notice in September in what was a painful if inevitable parting of the ways. One final error had been Polidori's failure to meet the boat bringing a visitor to dine at Diodati, which put Byron in a fury. 'He does not answer to Madame de Staël's definition of a happy man, whose capacities are squared with his inclinations,' judged Hobhouse, who helped Polidori to settle his 'involved accounts' with Byron before he took his leave.

Before they too left Switzerland Byron and Hobhouse made a longer and more ambitious mountain journey, visiting the Bernese Oberland. On 17 September they set off at seven in the morning, taking the Swiss guide Berger. Fletcher was left in charge of the Villa Diodati: Byron was still agitated about possible intruders. Their first night was spent at Ouchy, where Byron had stayed with Shelley in late June. Byron and Hobhouse stopped to visit the castle of Chillon and Rousseau's 'bosquet de Julie' at Clarens before crossing the mountains to Montbovon on horseback and mules.

Fond though they still were of one another, the easy camaraderie of their early journeys through Albania had disappeared. The traumatic events of the past year had left Hobhouse nervously protective of his friend; he wrote from Geneva to reassure Lady Melbourne, herself now out of touch with Byron, that allegations about 'Leagues of Incest' had been much exaggerated: 'Whatever has passed everything has been conducted with the utmost decency and you may safely contradict, if worth while, every story told of the irregularities said to be imported from Piccadilly amongst the Naiads of this Lake.' Though in this same letter Hobhouse described Shelley genially as a 'goodnatured strange being, the son of one Sir Timothy Shelley', he realised that Byron's new alliance with Shelley had subtly undermined their own relationship. His response to the third canto of *Childe Harold*, which Byron gave him to read in manuscript, had been uncertain: though he found it 'very fine in parts' he had complained of 'an air of mystery & metaphysics about it'. His jealousy of Shelley's personal and literary influence on Byron is palpable.

However, as they travelled further into the mountains, they fell back into an approximation of old juvenile routines, Byron pelting Hobhouse with snowballs, both of them laughing and tumbling as they struggled up and down the icy slopes. They were once again beset by minor accidents of travel: the baggage strapped to one of the horses worked itself loose and fell into a ravine where its descent was fortunately halted by a large tree. He and Hobhouse were overwhelmed by this new scenery, by the stupendous Alpine sights they saw together, delineated by Byron with a lovely fluency in the travel journal he was writing for Augusta and recorded more laboriously by Hobhouse in his diary.

From the highest point of the route to Montbovon they could see the great expanse of Lac Leman and the whole canton of Vaud spread out before them like a map. The scene gave Byron intimations of primitive magic amongst the stolid Swiss:

'The music of the Cows' bells (for their wealth like the Patriarchs is cattle) in the pastures (which reach to a height far above any mountains in Britain –) and the Shepherds' shouting to us from crag to crag & playing on their reeds where the steeps appeared almost inaccessible, with the surrounding scenery – realized all that I have ever heard or imagined of a pastoral existence . . . this was pure and unmixed – solitary – savage and patriarchal – the effect I cannot describe – as they went they played the "Ranz des Vaches" and other airs by way of farewell. – I have lately repeopled my mind with Nature.'

It has been said that Byron's poetry of this period is imitative of Wordsworth. William Wordsworth himself was to tell Tom Moore of his disgust that the whole of the third canto of *Childe Harold* was 'founded on his style & sentiments – the feeling of natural objects, which is there expressed not caught by B. from Nature herself, but from him', from *Tintern Abbey* in particular. Certainly, having been persuaded by Shelley at the Villa Diodati to take Wordsworth's work more seriously, Byron was becoming more susceptible to pantheistic modes of thought. But the Alpine Diary shows Byron as more than capable of communing with nature on his own.

The most impressive section of the journey began on 22 September, when Byron and Hobhouse passed through Interlaken and arrived at the foot of the Jungfrau. They were now in German-speaking Switzerland, in the canton of Berne, 'the district famous for Cheese – liberty – property – & no taxes'. On the way Byron met a pretty, blonde-haired young Swiss girl who reminded him of Lady Frances Webster: he bought some pears from her and patted her upon the cheek. He noticed a rock with an inscription commemorating two brothers, one of whom had murdered the other; 'just the place for it,' he thought.

As they explored the Lauterbrunnen valley they heard an avalanche fall with colossal reverberations. Now a majestic storm began: 'thunder – lightning – hail – all in perfection – and beautiful'. Byron was on horseback. Seeing that he was struggling, one of the guides offered to carry his cane. On the point of handing it over Byron recollected it was a swordstick. Afraid that the metal might act as a lightning conductor, he kept the stick himself although 'a good deal encumbered' with it and with his heavy cloak. Once they reached Lauterbrunnen they recovered, changed and dined in the comfortable guest house run by the local pastor, which Byron judged much better than most English vicarages.

The next morning they went to inspect at closer quarters the great Lauterbrunnen waterfall, the Staubbach Falls, descending just opposite the pastor's house. The sun shining on the lower portion made a rainbow 'of all colours – but principally purple and gold – the bow moving as you move'. This was a new phenomenon to Byron. They now mounted their horses and rode up the Wengen Alp. Nearing the summit, 7,000 feet above sea level, Byron took off his coat and they completed the ascent on foot. The view before them was of the Jungfrau with her glaciers, the Dent d'Argent, 'shining like truth', then the twin peaks of the Kleiner Eiger and the Grosser Eiger mountains, and 'last not least' the Wetterhorn. When they looked back the other way they could see the clouds rising from the opposite valley, 'curling up perpendicular precipices – like the foam of an Ocean of Hell during a Springtide – it was white & sulphery – and immeasurably deep in appearance'.

Lying down for a few minutes to contemplate these wonders, Hobhouse and Byron were irritated by the sudden appearance of two or three female tourists on horseback when they had imagined they had the mountain to themselves. They wrote their names on a piece of paper which they hid under a small stone near a blue flower. As they travelled on to Grindelwald they passed whole woods of pines, '*all withered* – trunks stripped & barkless – branches lifeless – done by a single winter'. Byron claimed, with a black humour that would not have been lost upon Augusta, that 'their appearance reminded me of me & my family'.

On 24 September they left Grindelwald for Scheidegg, the scenery almost obscured in a cold mist. They passed the Rose Glacier, 'suspended like a sea at a vast height', and halted to rest the horses by the Reichenbach waterfall. It was raining heavily by the time they reached Brienz. That night in the Hotel Weisses Kreuz, where Goethe too had stayed in 1779, what seemed like the entire population of the town had gathered for music and dancing. Four Swiss peasant girls from Oberhasli sang their country songs: 'they sing that *Tyrolese air* & song which you love – Augusta – because I love it – and I love because you love it – they are still singing.' Byron's Alpine Journal was his love letter as well. He and Hobhouse were amused to see Joseph, the hired guide, 'capering an *Allemand* with shoes & stockings off, greatly to his own delight & really well', while their own 'more gentlemanly' Berger was persuaded to join in the waltzing later. Byron could countenance waltzing in a mountain inn in Switzerland: 'the English can't Waltz – never could – nor ever will.'

They had now left the mountain regions, heading back towards Geneva. The next morning, 25 September, they were rowed across the lake from Brienz to Interlaken. Byron was surprised and intrigued to find that the rowing boats were '*manned by* women': 'one very young and very pretty – seated myself by her – & began to row also.' They got to Thun that evening, went on to Berne and Fribourg, where Byron bought a fierce and ugly dog with a foreshortened tail named Mutz. Byron became devoted to Mutz, like all his dogs, although this distant relation of a sheepdog did not prove as ferocious as he looked.

In Aubonne, on 29 September, with the Villa Diodati now only hours away, Byron wrote the final entry in his journal for Augusta. In theory, the Alpine tour had brought him great delight:

'I was disposed to be pleased – I am a lover of Nature – and an Admirer of Beauty – I can bear fatigue – & welcome privation – and have seen some of the noblest views in the world. – But in all this – the recollections of bitterness – & more especially of recent & more home desolation – which must accompany me through life – have preyed upon me here – and neither the music of the Shepherd – the crashing of the Avalanche – nor the torrent – the mountain – the Glacier – the Forest – nor the Cloud – have for one moment – lightened the weight upon my heart – nor enabled me to lose my own wretched identity in the majesty & the power and the Glory – around – above – & beneath me.'

The following evening, as he was sailing out on the lake with Hobhouse, the pole holding the mainsail slipped in tacking, hitting Byron violently on his bad leg. He fainted: 'a sort of gray giddiness first – then nothingness – and a total loss of memory on beginning to recover'. He began to complain of giddiness and further feelings of faintness after this.

The lasting legacy of Byron's journey into the Alps is his dramatic poem *Manfred*, the three-act tragedy he described as being 'of a very wild, metaphysical, and inexplicable kind'. This is Byron's temptation drama, focused on the reclusive magician figure, 'half dust, half deity', living alone in his mountain eyrie, tormented by guilt for his mysterious sins. He evokes the spirits of the universe who offer him anything except the self-obliteration he craves.

The Faustian overtones are obvious, and indeed a starting point for Byron was Goethe's *Faust*, translated 'extemporaneously' from the German by 'Monk' Lewis at Villa Diodati earlier that summer. Byron agreed that he had been 'naturally much struck' with Goethe's drama but insisted, in a letter to John Murray, that 'it was the *Staubach* & the *Jungfrau* – and something else – much more than Faustus' that caused him to write *Manfred*. The scenic splendour of the Bernese Oberland which he saw with Hobhouse pervades the austerely tragic drama; exact images and phrases used by Byron in the Alpine Journal are recycled in the poem. The 'something else', Byron's own private griefs and his still anguished sense of guilt towards Augusta, are manifested in the character of Manfred's beloved Astarte, named after an incestuous pagan goddess:

> 'Thou lovedst me
> Too much, as I loved thee: we were not made
> To torture thus each other, though it were
> The deadliest sin to love as we have loved.'

Goethe himself was overcome with admiration at the strength of imagination with which Byron had recast the Faust legend for his own purposes and in his own self-tormenting image. *Manfred* illustrates his growing preoccupation with the concept of supermen, Titanic figures midway between the mortals and the gods. Byron's Manfred on the Jungfrau became a motif for the Romantic movement: the solitary hero hopelessly pitched against the power of the elements.

On 5 October, Byron, Hobhouse and the servants, now including a cook Stevens recruited in Switzerland, left Geneva for Milan. The Napoleonic coach travelled over the Simplon Pass, completed nine years earlier by Napoleon's engineers. Byron judged the Pass 'magnificent in its nature and its art – both God & Man have done wonders – to say nothing of the Devil – who must certainly have had a hand (or hoof) in some of the rocks & ravines through & over which the works are carried'. Such early nineteenth-century engineering feats thrilled the scientist in Byron.

When the travelling cavalcade reached Ornavasso in northern Italy they began to take precautions against the robbers known to be active in that area. They slept at the hotel with loaded pistols in their rooms, dogs chained under the chairs, while Berger was left on guard in Byron's coach. Setting off the next morning they had four braces of pistols in the coach, two swords and two swordsticks as well as Byron's dagger. Byron's two carbines were in the second carriage. The hired coachman, Angelo Springhetti, was armed. Nearing Lake Maggiore they were alarmed to see five or six men running after the last carriage. They stopped and challenged them only to find that the supposed robbers were boatmen offering to take the travellers across the lake to the Borromean Isles.

In the boat on the way to Isola Madre they passed the town of Pallanza where Napoleon had kept his state prisoners. The white painted villas, deep green groves and clear blue water made the scene already look quite Mediterranean. Landing on the island they walked over the terraces, oranges and lemons growing along the walls, and wandered round the gardens of fine cypresses. On

Isola Bella, a ghost island of colonnades and porticoes and laurel trees, they were shown the very room where Napoleon had slept.

After these excursions, they arrived in Milan on 12 October. Byron stayed in Milan for the next three weeks, describing it as a striking city with a superb cathedral, only a little inferior to Seville. He viewed the Italian paintings in the Brera with more enthusiasm than he had regarded those of the Flemish school. In the Ambrosiana Library he lingered over the original letters and verses that had passed between Lucretia Borgia and Cardinal Bembo. He called these 'the prettiest love letters in the world', reminding Augusta about the old rumours of Lucretia Borgia's incest with her brother, Cesare Borgia, and her father Pope Alexander VI, and remarking that Lucretia too had signed her letters with a +.

Milan was now under Austrian control. Byron's and Hobhouse's main contacts were with the liberal writers and the ex-Napoleonists. One of these was the Abbé de Brême, one of Napoleon's almoners for the Kingdom of Italy, whom Byron had met at Coppet. De Brême had now returned to Italy. Henri Beyle, the French novelist who took the pseudonym Stendhal and who had once been one of Napoleon's secretaries, watched one evening at La Scala as 'a stranger made his appearance in Monsignor de Brême's box. He was young, of middling stature, and with remarkably fine eyes. As he advanced, we noticed that he limped a little. "Gentlemen," said Monsignor de Brême, "this is Lord Byron."' Stendhal noticed how, watching the opera, Byron gradually lost his self-consciousness, succumbing to the action and his emotions as if he came from the southern Mediterranean himself.

In the society of the Milanese intelligentsia Byron was a name to conjure with. Hobhouse makes a slightly plaintive comment in his diary about the extraordinary friendliness and interest with which his 'poetical friend' was received. Through the Abbé de Brême, Byron was now introduced to Vicenzo Monti who was, he told Augusta, 'the most famous Italian poet now living'. Though aged, opinionated and very deaf, Monti sat down quietly with Byron after dinner, discussing Milton and the origins of *Paradise Lost*.

Monti later called on Byron, bringing with him the young poet and Italian patriot Silvio Pellico, author of the tragedy *Francesca da Rimini* which Byron and Hobhouse jointly set about translating. This translation, at least partly completed by Hobhouse, never found a publisher. But Byron returned to the subject of 'Fanny of Rimini', who fell fatally in love with her husband's younger brother, translating the episode from Dante's *Inferno* once he reached Ravenna, where Francesca had lived.

Byron was already an enthusiast for the romantic-fantastical element in Italian literature. In Geneva he had read the *Novelle amorose* of Giambattista

Casti, which Pryse Gordon had sent him from Brussels, so avidly he almost knew it by heart, liking it even better than Casti's *Animali parlanti*, his high-spirited political fable of the court and parliament of the animals. During these few weeks in Milan, watching the street scenes, going to the theatre, where people meet 'as at a rout – but in very small circles', Byron quickly became attuned to the Italian view of life itself as a performance. His own sense of comedy became more Italianised, with the movement, vivacity, delight in grotesque detail he would soon be pouring into *Beppo* and *Don Juan*. He particularly loved the sexual nonchalance he found there: 'the state of morals in these parts is in some sort lax. A mother and son were pointed out at the theatre, as being pronounced by the Milanese world to be of the Theban dynasty – but this was all,' he reported to Tom Moore.

One night he went to see the famous *improvvisatore* Tommaso Sgricci who recited with a manic fluency long poems composed on the spot. Surprise subjects had been written on little scraps of paper extracted from a vase by a little boy 'holding up his hand like the blue coats at the lottery'. Sgricci, with his wild black hair, blue waistcoat, white pantaloons and yellow Turkish slippers, was also, according to Byron, a 'celebrated Sodomite'. Though his verbal contortionist act had its detractors, Byron explained to Hobhouse that Sgricci's sexual tastes were not an issue: 'they laugh, instead of burning – and the Women talk of it as a pity in a man of talent.' The Italian attitude towards homosexuality was surprisingly, and refreshingly, relaxed.

A slight cloud on the horizon was the reappearance, in Milan, of Dr Polidori who, after his dismissal from the Villa Diodati, claimed to have walked across the Alps. Polidori was still causing commotion. One night when Byron was 'quietly staring at the Ballet', sitting at La Scala in di Brême's box, he was sent for urgently. He found Polidori in the guardroom, having been arrested by the Austrian police after an altercation which he was alleged to have started. 'There was much swearing in several languages'; the guard were threatening to hold him for the night. When Byron gave his own name and vouched for Polidori they released him, but next day he was expelled at twenty-four hours' notice. Five years later Polidori was found dead in his father's house in London, having almost certainly committed suicide by swallowing prussic acid. Having never found his métier he had become deranged. Should we consider Polidori a sad casualty of the Diodati summer? We cannot ignore the possible effect on an already unstable young man of the combined derision of Byron and Shelley, who told him his literary work was worthless.

Byron and Hobhouse departed from Milan on 3 November, making their way to Venice via Verona where they visited the amphitheatre, which in

Byron's view beat even those of Greece, and found the 'plain, open, and partly decayed sarcophagus' in an unkempt convent garden which purported to be the tomb of Juliet. In Vicenza, a beautiful dilapidated town, they were charmed by Palladio's fantastically ornate theatre, the Teatro Olimpico, where Byron stood on the stage and recited the speech of Turnus from Virgil's *Aeneid*, Book XI, and the chorus from Euripides' *Phoenissae*, Hobhouse providing his sole audience.

Byron was now suffering sharp jabs of rheumatism, brought on by the autumn rains of Lombardy, and although still only twenty-eight was feeling 'ancient'. His teeth too were loosening. But he had a little talisman. Before he left Milan he had purloined, from the Ambrosiana Library, a single strand of Lucretia Borgia's bright yellow hair.

20

Venice: Frezzeria and La Mira
1816–1817

On Sunday 10 November 1816, after eating an inferior dinner at Mestre, Byron embarked in his first gondola, the lugubrious high-prowed vessel that was always to delight him:

> 'It glides along the water looking blackly,
> Just like a coffin clapt in a canoe,
> Where none can make out what you say or do.'

Rowed by the gondoliers, he and Hobhouse had travelled in the dark for an hour and a half; passing between embankments, cutting round corners and between tall water stakes, when they were suddenly conscious of the lights of Venice. Peering out through the windows of the little inner cabin, they saw that they were now gliding past high houses and stone piers. Then they realised from the echo of the oars that they were under a bridge: the boatman yelled out, 'The Rialto!' Soon after, they reached the landing stage of the Hôtel de la Grande-Bretagne on the Grand Canal where they were escorted up 'a magnificent flight of stairs into rooms whose gilding & painted silks showed they belonged to better people in better times'. The proprietor conversed with them in English and, before retiring early, they drank tea.

In Milan Byron had felt under constant observation: the stultifying formal social life reminded him of 'a ship under quarantine'. Arriving in Venice, the city that soon became almost synonymous with his name, he experienced an immediate and a marvellous relief. He felt he knew Venice already, before he had even seen it: like the East, it had pre-existed in his inner consciousness, 'the greenest island of my imagination'.

All his descriptions emphasise this dreamlike quality of a city that was actually the sum of seventy small islands, a mysterious, ineffably comic waterland, that made Hobhouse immediately think of Cadiz flooded. 'Everything about

Venice is, or was, extraordinary,' wrote Byron in his preface to *Marino Faliero*, his play about the Doges. There were canals where you expected pavements; shops and workshops, the greengrocers and butchers, poulterers and iron-workers, the commerce of the town, were stranded along little narrow alleys. This topsy-turviness, the sense of dislocation, enchanted him. He loved to tell the tale of how the Hapsburg government had issued a directive from Vienna for a coach and four horses to take part in the procession carrying the new patriarch of Venice to St Mark's. Byron wrote to John Murray: 'you have only to imagine our Parliament commanding the Archbishop of Canterbury to proceed from Hyde Park Corner to St Paul's Cathedral in the Lord Mayor's Barge.'

After so many months of tribulation the 'marine melancholy' of Venice suited Byron. He was more than ever responsive to the sublime sadness of the sea, and he felt a personal involvement in the pathos of a once powerful civil-isation now in visible decline. Politically, Venice had had a chequered history since the fall of the Venetian Republic in 1797. First the Austrians had domi-nated Venice, then Napoleon had ruled it as the 'second city' of his Kingdom of Italy. Since 1814 the new Hapsburg government had been in control of a resentful Venice whose heyday was over. The population had declined from 150,000 in 1778 to a bare 100,000 by the time Byron arrived there. Mary Shelley's near-contemporary view was of a dismally decaying city full of dirt and squalor. Byron saw beyond the filth to enjoy the spectacle of crumbling grandeur. 'I have been familiar with ruins too long to dislike desolation,' he told Tom Moore, throwing himself into his favourite role of ruin amongst ruins. Byron played up to Venice. The city exaggerated, and to some extent exoner-ated, the painful consciousness of his own fall from grace.

Crippled by extortionate levels of taxation, the population of Venice was rotting like its buildings. The spectacle of city beggars, which had shocked Byron and Hobhouse in Vicenza, was worse in Venice where even patricians begged. Byron and Hobhouse, with their guide, were followed into St Mark's Square by an impoverished nobleman, hat in outstretched hand. Hobhouse, disconcerted, told him brusquely to put it on again. Byron, however, gave the nobleman two francs which he had impulsively extracted from the guide.

Besides its long and plangent history one of the great attractions of Venice was, for Byron, its richness of literary associations. This was the very setting of Shakespeare's *Merchant of Venice* and *Othello*: Byron was able to hear Rossini's operatic version of *Othello* in Venice in 1818, judging it inferior to the original. He meandered around Venice re-imagining the scenes of Thomas Otway's seventeenth-century verse tragedy *Venice Preserv'd*, a play he had often seen in

London. Belvidera had been one of Mrs Siddons' starring roles. Entering St Mark's by moonlight Byron was always conscious of a sinister novel by Schiller, *Geisterseher*, translated as *The Armenian, or The Ghost-seer*, to which he had been addicted as a boy. But perhaps the most alluring of all literary Venices was Mrs Radcliffe's Venice, an eerie Gothick backdrop to *The Mysteries of Udolpho*. When he wrote to Augusta, 'I am going out this evening – in my *cloak & Gondola* – there are two nice Mrs Radcliffe words for you', he had become a Radcliffean character himself.

Byron did not at first see himself as settling in Venice. In early letters of the winter of 1816–17 he wrote of returning to England in the spring. But in fact he became acclimatised and lingered for the next three years. The relative remoteness of Venice at that period offered a perfect refuge for a celebrity of damaged reputation. Compared with Geneva, English tourists were few and those who came did not stay long but hurried on to Florence and Naples, 'their Margate and Ramsgate' as Byron put it with aristocratic disdain. The innate foreignness of Venice made it an exile's paradise, a place where you could lose yourself to discover yourself in another guise. The role of the vivacious but always secret city in giving its American and English visitors a new sense of life's emotional possibilities would be explored by many writers after Byron, most notably by Henry James.

For Byron himself the city acted as a catalyst, Venice the 'sea Cybele' becoming the subject of some of his most memorable work. Not just the opening stanzas of Canto IV of *Childe Harold*, with the pilgrim posed self-consciously on the Bridge of Sighs, but Byron's hilarious Italian comic poem *Beppo* and his verse dramas *Marino Faliero* and *The Two Foscari* show how deeply the city of shimmering ambivalence was to enter his creative imagination.

> 'Oh Venice! Venice! when thy marble walls
> Are level with the waters, there shall be
> A cry of nations o'er thy sunken halls,
> A loud lament along the sweeping sea!'

In 'Venice. An Ode' he confronts the tragic inertia of the Venetians in failing to resist their Austrian oppressors, and unconsciously predicts another sort of death for Venice: death by mass tourism and gradual subsidence.

In the winter of 1816 Byron immersed himself to the full in Venetian life. He had introductions from Lady Holland, still his supporter, to the highest social echelons. The Governor, the Austrian Count Goetz, received Byron and Hobhouse, and they were indoctrinated into the arcane rituals of the Venetian salons or *conversazioni*, gatherings ruled by local hostesses, held in their palazzi late at night after the theatre. *Conversazioni*, Byron informed Moore, 'are like our routs, or rather worse, for the women sit in a semicircle by the lady of the mansion, and the men stand about the room. To be sure, there is one improvement upon ours – instead of lemonade with their ices, they hand about stiff *rum-punch* – *punch*, by my palate, and this they think *English*.' Against his better judgement Byron became within his first few weeks a regular attender at the *conversazioni* of Countess Isabella Teotochi Albrizzi.

The Countess was renowned as the Madame de Staël of Italy: 'a very poor copy indeed', wrote Hobhouse tartly, 'though she seems a very good natured woman'. The Countess was a friend of many writers, including Alfieri and Ugo Foscolo, and was herself a writer and art connoisseur. She had published an authoritative study of the sculpture of Canova whose carving of Helen, a gift from the sculptor, provided a centrepiece for her Venetian soirées. Byron wrote a poem 'On the Bust of Helen by Canova':

> 'In this beloved marble view
>> Above the works and thoughts of Man –
> What Nature *could* – but *would not* do –
>> And Beauty and Canova *can*!
> Beyond Imagination's power –
>> Beyond the Bard's defeated art,
> With Immortality her dower –
>> Behold the *Helen* of the *heart*!'

Hobhouse observed that the last four lines were unmistakably 'Byronean'.

Countess Albrizzi was of Greek extraction, often speaking Greek herself, and for Byron part of the attraction of her salon was the presence of her Greek compatriots. She was a widow, then in her mid-fifties, an age to which Byron was particularly susceptible, and she too became a devotee, penning a portrait which, for all its excesses, sees to the heart of Byron's character, detecting beneath the self-protective mask of arrogance his 'constant, and almost infantine timidity'.

Byron had now moved out of the Grande-Bretagne and was lodging in the Frezzeria, one of the little narrow streets leading out of St Mark's Square to the north-west. Here his landlord was a draper, a genuine Merchant of Venice, Pietro Segati. The name above his shop, Il Cervo, the stag, was converted by the local gossips into 'Al Corno Inglese', the house of the Englishman's cuckold, as Byron quickly formed a liaison with the draper's wife. Marianna Segati was twenty-two and another of Byron's antelope women, shy and graceful with 'large, black, oriental eyes'. In a letter announcing his new passion to Tom Moore Byron itemised her regular, rather aquiline features, her small mouth, her clear, soft skin 'with a kind of hectic colour'. Her dark, glossy, wavy hair reminded him of Lady Jersey's. Her figure was 'light and pretty'. Marianna was a semi-professional songstress. In the free and easy society of Venice she was sometimes received at *conversazioni* because she was attached to one of the Venetian musical academies.

Impressed by Byron's generosity and rank, Pietro Segati proved a complaisant husband, accustomed to the Venetian habit of turning a blind eye to adultery, if not confronted with the actuality. Nonetheless there was a certain element of risk – that sense of danger that Byron relied on to sustain him through so many of his love affairs with women – in seducing his landlord's wife in their own house. The suspense was redoubled one evening when Byron, who imagined that his *amorosa* and her husband were both out at a *conversazione*, was paid a visit by a 'well-looking and (for an Italian) *bionda* girl of about nineteen' who announced that she was Marianna's sister-in-law and 'wished to have some conversation with Lord Byron'. Within a few minutes Marianna herself suddenly returned, having been alerted by the sight of her sister-in-law's gondolier lurking on the stairs. Marianna, 'after making polite courtesy to her sister-in-law and to me, without a single word seizes her said sister-in-law by the hair, and bestows upon her some sixteen slaps, which would have made your ear ache only to hear their echo'. In his account of it Byron clearly relishes the Venetian theatricality of the scene.

The sister-in-law fled. Marianna 'fairly went into fits' in Byron's arms and 'in spite of reasoning, eau de Cologne, vinegar, half a pint of water, and God knows what other waters beside, continued so till past midnight'. When her husband arrived an hour later she was lying dishevelled, pale and apparently unconscious on Byron's sofa. 'His first question was, "What is all this?"' Marianna was unable to reply, so Byron did his best: 'I told him the explanation was the easiest thing in the world; but in the mean time it would be as well to recover his wife – at least, her senses.' It was a near thing. Byron believed that the draper, although having his suspicions, had not realised how far the liaison had developed. However, Marianna must have used her ingenuity to placate her husband. By next morning the situation was resolved.

The liaison with Marianna Segati was to be one of Byron's longest, enduring for the next fifteen or sixteen months. There was an easiness, almost a domesticity, between the merchant's wife and the man she addressed as her 'Caro Giorgio'. He told Augusta that this adventure – 'very tranquil, very loving' – had come at the right moment, partly obliterating the tortures of the past two years, in particular his anguished memories of 'that virtuous monster Miss Milbanke'. He appreciated Marianna's sexual forthcomingness, boasting that there was 'never a twenty-four hours without giving and receiving from one to three (and occasional an extra or so) pretty unequivocal proofs of mutual good contentment'. Marianna's seductive presence in those first few months in Venice provides much of the immediacy and drama of Byron's letters to London:

'here is Signora Marianna just come in and seated at my elbow . . . I really cannot go on. There is a pair of great black eyes looking over my shoulder, like the angel leaning over St Matthew's, in the old frontispieces to the Evangelists – so that I must turn and answer them instead of you.'

In the John Murray archive there is a small thick book bound in light brown leather with gold tooling. It is an Armenian–Italian dictionary, inscribed and dated by Byron 30 November 1816, the day he began the study of the Armenian language with Father Paschal Aucher at the monastery of San Lazzaro. This monastery was on an island in the Venetian lagoon, formerly the site of a leper colony. A community of Armenian Mechitarist monks had been established there since 1717. By the time of Byron's visits the church and monastery held seventy monks, 'very learned and accomplished'. Like Byron they were exiles. The monks were proselytisers for Armenia and the Armenian language, and there was a printing press attached to the monastery.

For his first few months in Venice, Byron rowed over in his gondola from the mainland to the Isola San Lazzaro almost every day. His choice of Armenian as a subject of study was characteristically perverse. He had found that his mind 'wanted something craggy to break upon'. The difficulty of Armenian, with its 'Waterloo of an alphabet', was notorious. To add to the complexity he studied the language in two versions: modern-colloquial and ancient liturgical Armenian. As an antidote to Venice's lazy sensualities this was the hardest task he could devise.

Byron's daily expeditions to the monastery satisfied his intermittent yearning for the religious life. As Hobhouse noted, his deep instinctive sense of a divinity, though he was unable to account for it, was as certain a proof to him that there was a cause for it as the influence upon the compass was a sign that there was some cause for the attraction of the magnetic needle to the pole. Byron promised himself that he would turn devout when he turned thirty, admitting that his faith was encouraged by the weather: 'I am always most religious upon a sunshiny day.' In the wintry sunshine of Venice the Isola San Lazzaro worked its charm. Byron admired the Superior of the Friars, a bishop and 'a fine old fellow, with the beard of a meteor'. His own spiritual preceptor Father Paschal was 'a learned and pious soul' who had spent two years in England. Byron was delighted by the curious manuscripts in the monastery library: translations from lost Greek originals and from the Persian and Syriac, besides Armenian works.

As well as pursuing his Armenian studies he was helping Father Paschal to put together an Armenian–English grammar. He did his best to interest John Murray in the commercial possibilities of this, asking him to investigate whether there were any Armenian types or letterpress available in Oxford or Cambridge. He began to see the San Lazzaro island settlement as near perfect, uniting 'all the advantages of the monastic institution, without any of its vices'. He pointed to the decorum, gentleness, unostentatious faith, and the intellectual and practical accomplishments of the brethren, qualities 'well fitted to strike the man of the world with the conviction that "there is another and a better" even in this life'. Sometimes Byron would sit out in the monastery garden, indulging in spiritual reveries.

Armenia became another of Byron's adopted countries. As he grappled with the language, he came to identify with the beleaguered Armenians themselves. Theirs was, after all, the country defined by the Scriptures as the original site of Paradise: 'It was in Armenia that the flood first abated, and the dove alighted.' For centuries the victim of its geographical position, hemmed in by both the ruling satraps of Persia and the pashas of Turkey, the relatively small country of Armenia was all too clearly a paradise lost. It was now being encroached upon by Russia, which had annexed most of the Caucasus and was extending its authority over other parts of Armenia. Byron's championing of the alphabet and writings of 'an oppressed and noble nation', victim of an expanding international 'House of Bondage', was a bid to draw public attention to the cause of Armenia, as he was later to do much more convincingly for Greece.

By the end of February 1817 Byron's Armenian studies had evidently lapsed and he looked back wryly on his hopes for his own earthly paradise on San Lazzaro: 'I went seeking it – God knows where – did I find it? – Umph!' The long, uproarious Venice Carnival had intervened. He deserted San Lazzaro, saying he would return when his head ached a little less. It seems he never did.

While he was in Venice Byron's main point of contact with England was his publisher John Murray whom he envisaged 'enjoying inglorious ease at his green table – & wishing for someone to keep him in hot water'. Byron wrote to Murray frequently, partly on literary business, partly to make peremptory requests for books, magnesia, soda powders, his special brand of red tooth powder unobtainable abroad, tincture of myrrh and even English bulldogs. A

'Capital Bull Dog' obtained for him by Murray was returned four months later to the man who had sold it, when Byron seemed to have lost interest in bull-dogs. Murray concluded he had meant it as a joke.

The real *raison d'être* of Byron's letters was their sparkling narrative of his Venetian life, portraying its hectic glamour, playing up the lewd. His tendency to treat correspondence as performance was now boosted by Byron's conscious-ness that Murray would be reading out his letters proprietorially to the gathering of literary cronies beneath Thomas Phillips' portrait of Byron in the Albemarle Street drawing room. The letters from Venice were an act of defiance, ebullient proof for himself as well as others of Byron's ability to rise above disgrace.

His account of his first Carnival in Venice, held in the early weeks of 1817, is a particularly vivid one, conveying his excitement at the masking, humming, fifing, drumming, guitaring, strumming confusion of the scene. He was there for the preliminaries, at the Feast of St Stephen on 27 December, when 'every mouth was put in motion – there was nothing but fiddling and playing on the virginals – and all kinds of conceits and divertisements on every canal of this aquatic city'. He took a box for the opera at La Fenice, open only for the six weeks of the Carnival, attended the Ridotto, the late-night Venetian musical assemblies, made incognito assignations.

He remained at the Carnival until the bitter end, staying up all night for the masked ball at the Fenice when the theatre was illuminated and the whole population of Venice was on the streets buffooning. After this he admitted he was quite worn out and had succumbed to 'a sort of lowish fever', a recurrence of the tertian fever he had suffered from in Patras, the result of what his pugi-listic mentor 'Gentleman' Jackson would have called 'taking too much out of oneself'. In this state of sexual exhaustion Byron wrote the poignant verses:

> 'So, we'll go no more a roving
>   So late into the night,
> Though the heart be still as loving,
>   And the moon be still as bright.
>
> For the sword outwears its sheath,
>   And the soul wears out the breast,
> And the heart must pause to breathe,
>   And love itself have rest.
>
> Though the night was made for loving,
>   And the day returns too soon,
> Yet we'll go no more a roving
>   By the light of the moon.'

Even now, after so many setbacks and humiliations, Byron had not lost his grand ambition to do great things. If he lived ten years longer he foresaw that he would startle the world with something that 'like the cosmogony, or creation of the world, will puzzle the philosophers of all ages'. He had an extraordinary resilience of spirit. But just then, in Venice in 1817, he doubted if his constitution would hold out.

Amidst all the new activity of Venice some of Byron's memories of England started blurring. Hodgson's ponderous letters from the vicarage in Bakewell, where the Duke of Rutland had given him a living, seemed like missives from another world. Byron's desperate need for Augusta lessened as he became impatient with her confusion of remorse. Only his infant daughter Ada was still of urgent concern to him as he responded to reports that Lady Byron was planning to take or send their daughter to the continent, out of reach of possible abduction by her father. The information reached him indirectly via Lady Melbourne. He instructed Hanson to take preventative measures, if necessary legal action: '*let it be immediately settled & understood that in no case is my daughter to leave the country.*' It was another painful episode in the power struggle between the Byrons, but one can also see it as a realistic concern on his small daughter's behalf: 'in the present state of the Continent', he argued, 'I would not have my child rambling over it for millions.' A few weeks later he expressed his delight when Murray told him that the precocious one-year-old Ada was already making great progress with her speech.

Byron's other absent daughter, his child by Claire Clairmont, was born in Bath on 12 January 1817. He had written coyly to Augusta to tell her that 'the *Demoiselle* – who returned to England from Geneva – went there to produce a new baby B.' Since Claire had travelled back from Geneva with Shelley and with Mary there had been a succession of family disasters. First, in October, Fanny Imlay Godwin, the daughter of Godwin's first wife Mary Wollstonecraft by the American adventurer Gilbert Imlay, committed suicide in Swansea at the age of twenty-two. Only a few weeks later, on 10 December, the body of Shelley's deserted young wife Harriet was discovered. She had drowned herself in the Serpentine. At the end of December Shelley and Mary married and were reconciled with the Godwins. In this unsettling atmosphere Claire awaited the birth of her baby. She was now in independent lodgings in New Bond Street in Bath, attended by the Shelleys' Swiss nursemaid Elise Duvillard. Shelley was anxious that people should not assume that he was the father of Claire's child.

Although she still wrote to him at length and with passion, Byron refused to communicate with Claire directly. Shelley acted as the go-between, sending news to Byron on 23 April about 'a little being whom we – in the absence of all right to bestow a *Christian* designation – call Alba, or the Dawn'. Albe had been the Shelleys' pet name for Byron. 'She is very beautiful, and though her frame is of somewhat a delicate texture, enjoys excellent health. Her eyes are the most intelligent I ever saw in so young an infant. Her hair is black, her eyes deeply blue, and her mouth exquisitely shaped.' The Shelleys had now moved to a house at Marlow in Buckinghamshire, and Shelley explained to Byron that the baby 'passes here for the child of a friend in London, sent into the country for her health, while Claire has reassumed her maiden character'.

Shelley wanted to know what Byron's plans were for his daughter. His attitude was indolent. He confessed to Augusta: 'I am a little puzzled how to dispose of this new production . . . but shall probably send for & place it in a Venetian convent – to become a good Catholic – & (it may be) a *Nun* – being a character somewhat wanted in our family.' With all the uncertainties surrounding Ada he seems to have regarded this new infant as a potential substitute, a kind of reserve daughter: 'I must love something in my old age.'

It took him another year to send for her. He informed his friend and agent Douglas Kinnaird on 13 January 1818 that he had finally decided to 'acknowledge & breed her myself – giving her the name of *Biron* (to distinguish her from little Legitimacy)'. He would christen her Allegra, 'which is a Venetian name'.

Hobhouse had left Venice early in December. He took leave of his friend casually with the left hand, in the hope that they would soon meet again in Rome. Having seen Constantinople, Byron was anxious to view 't'other fellow'. He had plans to see the Pope, to tell him 'I vote for the Catholics and no Veto'. On 17 April 1817, once he had recovered from his fever, Byron set off south.

He had resisted the entreaties of Marianna Segati that she should travel with him. He had to some extent detached himself from Marianna during the sexual free-for-all of the Venice Carnival. It was probably at this stage that he took his own casino, a small rented apartment for private entertainment in one of the waterside campos near St Mark's, giving him a place of assignation independent of the draper's house. If Marianna left her husband to travel with Byron she would be flouting the conventions of adultery in Italy, licensed only in so far as it was discreet. Though still attracted by her, Byron was not prepared to take sole responsibility for Marianna, who already had a child. He had troubles enough with other mothers and their children, writing to Hobhouse: 'How could you suppose that I should bring any (carnal) baggage with me? do you suppose me quite out of my senses? – I had enough of that in Switzerland.'

Byron broke his journey at Ferrara on purpose to visit the cell in the Hospital of Sant' Anna where one of his heroes, the sixteenth-century poet Torquato Tasso, had been imprisoned for seven years by Alphonso II, Marchese d'Este. That night, in Bologna, he wrote his own long poem *The Lament of Tasso*, developing the theme initiated in *The Prisoner of Chillon*, of the effect of long incarceration upon the human spirit. In a powerful study of neurotic creativity, the tragic figure of Tasso himself, the traduced genius driven by his suffering to the verge of madness, is less Tasso than Byron, the poet made articulate by his own despair.

In Bologna, the town 'celebrated for the production of Poets – Cardinals – painters – & sausages', Byron was fascinated by the waxworks on display in the Anatomical Gallery of the university. These were of private parts 'made & moulded by a *female* Professor'. He was unimpressed by her models of male organs, 'being considerably under our Northern notions of things – & standard of dimensions in such matters', he reported to John Murray, 'more particularly as the feminine display was a little in the other extreme'.

He hurried on to Florence, rising at 4 a.m. to see as many of the sights as he was able in one day. Though ready to denigrate the English tourists, Byron too could be energetic in his sightseeing. He saw the two art galleries, the Medici and the Pitti Palace, 'from which one returns drunk with beauty'. He admired particularly Raphael's and Titian's portraits, Canova's sculpture of Venus, Michelangelo's *Parcae*. At last, he said, he was beginning to understand the connoisseurs' 'entusimusy' for the visual arts.

In Florence he visited the Medici Chapel, 'fine frippery in great slabs of various expensive stones – to commemorate fifty rotten & forgotten carcasses', and saw more tombs of famous men, Machiavelli, Michelangelo, Alfieri, Galileo, in the church of Santa Croce, Florence's equivalent of Westminster Abbey: 'all of them seem to me to be overloaded – what is necessary but a bust & a name? – and perhaps a date? – the last for the unchronological – of whom I am one.' What moved Byron more was his encounter in the mountains near Florence with a crying child chewing a piece of bread bulked out with grass. Byron took the bread as a memento and gave the child some money. He had not lost his passion for human incident.

Away from Venice Byron was more vulnerable to the English visitors who regarded their still glamorous but raddled exiled peer as one of the most compelling sights of Italy. His scandalous reputation now had a new dimension, coloured by lurid rumours of his Venetian orgies, some of which had originated in the risqué letters he was sending to John Murray in Albemarle Street. In Florence, at a dinner where the hostess was an aristocratic Englishwoman,

Byron was visibly annoyed by 'the excess of attention lavished upon him by all the ladies'; one especially plain woman was almost on her knees.

Byron arrived in Rome on 29 April and was once again the centre of speculation. He avoided the winter, prime time for English tourists, that 'parcel of staring boobies, who go about gaping and wishing to be at once cheap and magnificent'. But there were still many aristocratic residents and English members of the flourishing artistic colony in Rome. Lady Liddell told her daughter to avert her eyes from Byron – 'Don't look at him, he is dangerous to look at' – when they encountered him at St Peter's, perambulating with other sightseers high up on the roof. His widespread notoriety was agony, yet at the same time irresistible to Byron. With his taste for the theatrical, he adored its absurdity, observing to Augusta: 'Heaven knows why, but I seem destined to set people by the ears.'

Byron was in Rome for three weeks. New evidence in the Murray archive has confirmed that he stayed in rooms at 66 Piazza di Spagna, where he was spotted standing on the balcony. He had brought his saddle horses with him, and maintained that most of his time was spent out riding, exploring 'Rome – the wonderful'. Rome, both ancient and modern, thrilled him more than anywhere he had been since Athens and Constantinople.

Besides St Peter's, Byron saw the Colosseum, the Pantheon, the Vatican, the Palatine. He lingered at the ancient Roman tomb of Cecilia Metella on the Appian Way, speculating on her history as if he had been an intimate of hers. Byron 'excursed and skirred the country round to Alba – Tivoli – Frascati – Licenza – &c. &c.', visiting the Falls of Terni twice. On his way back to Rome from Terni, near the temple by the banks of the River Clitumnus, 'the prettiest little stream in all poesy', he helped himself to some of that river's famous trout.

He saw so much on that brief visit that at first the individual scenes merged together in his mind. He explained to John Murray: 'my first impressions are always strong and confused – & my Memory *selects* & reduces them to order – like distance in a landscape – & blends them better – although they may be less distinct.' This was essentially a poet's way of seeing; stocking the mind with images on which to draw later on.

While in Rome, Byron sat for his bust to Bertel Thorwaldsen, the Danish sculptor then working in the city. The devoted Hobhouse had commissioned the bust from an artist who was then at the height of his fame, considered on a par with Canova, '& by some preferred to him'. It was not an altogether comfortable sitting. Byron had misgivings about being memorialised in marble, as if he were already dead. He had to contend with Hobhouse's desire to have the bust surmounted by a laurel wreath. Laurels reminded him all too forcibly of Southey, his detested Poet Laureate: 'I won't have my head garnished like a Xmas pie with Holly – or a Cod's head and Fennel – or whatever the damned weed is they strew round it. – I wonder you should want me to be such a mountebank.'

Hobhouse had evidently failed to prepare Thorwaldsen for Byron's arrival. He arrived at the atelier unannounced, wrapped up in his cloak, and was guided by an attendant through a mass of other works in progress. These included the *Dancer*, one of Thorwaldsen's important carvings of that date. The sculptor himself left an account of Byron's sitting:

'He posed for me, but at once started to put up quite another face than his usual one; "Now won't you sit quiet", I said, "You must not make those faces." "That is my expression!" said Byron. "Indeed", said I, and then I did him as I wanted to, and everybody said when it was finished that it was like him; but when Byron saw it: "It is not a bit like me", he said, "I look more unhappy!"'

It took another four years for the first marble copy of Thorwaldsen's original model to reach England. When it finally arrived John Murray wrongly assumed it was for him. After an embarrassing exchange of correspondence Byron eventually saved the day by suggesting that Murray should commission a second marble copy from Thorwaldsen. This is still at 50 Albemarle Street, while the first, having been bequeathed to King George V by Lady Dorchester, Hobhouse's daughter, is now in the collection of the Queen.

On his final day in Rome, Byron watched the execution of three robbers in what is now the Piazza del Popolo. He was still in search of the sensational, watching the proceedings through his opera glasses, 'determined to see – as one should see every thing once – with attention'. He relished the sombre theatricality of masked priests, half-naked executioners, condemned men with bandages around their eyes, the effigy of the black Christ with his banner carried before them, the scaffold, the soldiery, 'the slow procession – & the quick rattle and heavy fall of the axe – the splash of the blood – & the ghastliness of the exposed heads'. The first of the criminals had had to be forced to lie down at the guillotine. Then it seemed that his neck was too large for the hole and the priest had tried to drown out the prisoner's loud cries with religious exhortations before the head was eventually cut off close to the ears. The tension of all this turned Byron 'quite hot and cold'; he shook so badly he could hardly hold the opera glass. But by the second and third deaths he was, he admitted, completely unaffected: 'how dreadfully soon things become indifferent.'

He left Rome on 20 May, resisting the temptation to accompany Hobhouse further south to Naples. He could not face the risk of encountering more

English tourists. Having seen Constantinople and Lisbon, the first and third best of the western world's sea views, he felt justified in dispensing with the second best. Besides, he was missing Marianna. He was back in Venice on 28 May. A few weeks later he had begun Canto IV of *Childe Harold*, 'working up', as he put it, his impressions of his journeys through Italy. He dedicated this Italian canto to Hobhouse, his long-time travelling companion, 'a friend often tried and never found wanting', a compliment Hobhouse certainly deserved.

Byron's literary rhythms ebbed and flowed. During the first few months of 1817 he had been unproductive, his energies absorbed in the pleasures of the Carnival. 'As for poesy', he wrote in explanation to Murray, 'mine is the *dream* of my sleeping Passions – when they are awake – I cannot speak their language – only in their Somnambulation – & Just now they are dormant.' By June he was back in the full flood of creativity. He had now abandoned the more metaphysical tenor of the third canto of *Childe Harold* to revisit northern Italy hero by hero, place by place, travelling from Venice to Petrarch's Arqua; Tasso and Ariosto's Ferrara; Dante and Boccaccio's Florence. This is travelogue on a grand scale in which Byron recklessly combines historical résumé, lyrical description, topographic disquisition, sarcasm, jeremiad for a post-Napoleonic Italy still beautiful but morally as well as physically threatened. The most impassioned of his stanzas are those on Rome, the ultimate city of flawed magnificence.

> 'Oh Rome! my country! city of the soul!
> The orphans of the heart must turn to thee,
> Lone mother of dead empires! and controul
> In their shut breasts their petty misery.
> What are our woes and sufferance? Come and see
> The cypress, hear the owl, and plod your way
> O'er steps of broken thrones and temples, Ye!
> Whose agonies are evils of a day –
> A world is at our feet as fragile as our clay.'

Byron's attitude to Italy has become possessive. Unlike the writings of his contemporary English traveller in Italy Lady Shelley these are not the neat impressions of the passer-by. Byron's vistas of Rome have more to do with Goethe's *Italian Journey* and the rhetorical, ornate background of Madame de Staël's Roman novel *Corinne*. In Canto IV Byron is overwriting unashamedly.

'I am just returned from a gallop along the banks of the Brenta – time – Sunset,' Byron informed Murray on 18 June with his talent for precipitating his correspondents into the detail of his current scene. After spending only a few hot days in Venice he had taken a summer villa near the village of La Mira fourteen miles outside the city, on the bank of the Brenta Canal. The Villa Foscarini was one of the large white colonnaded houses, many of them shabby or abandoned, which Hobhouse and Byron had noticed in passing as they travelled into Venice the previous year. Byron was apologetic about the Foscarini, which had few of the advantages of Villa Diodati: 'more space than splendour – & not much of that'. The smells rising from the Brenta Canal were sometimes noxious. The house was also very near the road.

But Byron settled contentedly into his rural retreat. Marianna was installed at La Mira. 'I am just come out from an hour's swim in the Adriatic; and I write to you with a black-eyed Venetian girl before, reading Boccacio.' In its published version this letter, to Tom Moore, receives another run of Moore's censorious asterisks. Signor Segati was occasionally present, but he had a Venetian mistress of his own.

With his taste for human oddities Byron was greatly pleased with his ill-assorted neighbours in the village of La Mira: the ninety-year-old Spanish Marquis who lived opposite and the Frenchman whose *casino* was beside the Marquis's. 'We are exactly one of Goldoni's comedies,' he told John Murray, referring to *La vedova scaltra*, where a Spaniard, Don Alvaro di Castiglia, a Frenchman, Monsieur le Blau, and the English Milord Runebif are introduced. 'We are all very good neighbours, Venetians, etc., etc., etc.,' Byron claimed. Local *conversazioni* at La Mira, besides visits to a physician and his wife with four unmarried daughters all under eighteen, friends of Marianna's, provided Byron with an undemanding summer social life.

'Monk' Lewis came to visit him, followed a few weeks later by Hobhouse, who found lodgings in a house nearby. Out of curiosity the three of them went to watch the circumcision of a Jewish child, 'a sucking Shylock' as Byron described the infant, adding: 'I have seen three men's heads & a child's foreskin cut off in Italy. – The ceremonies are very moving.'

Another visitor to Villa Foscarini was George Ticknor, the young American writer, who had not seen Byron since he and Annabella were London newlyweds in the summer of 1815. Although Byron's appearance seemed to him unchanged Ticknor was conscious of an altered conversational style: 'he was more lively and various, and came nearer to what a stranger might expect from him.' He was less dependent on esoteric Piccadilly gossip, more willing to embark on intellectual and political argument. His talk was becoming more Europeanised.

Much of their conversation was on the subject of the United States since Hobhouse and Byron had been planning a joint visit to the land of another of

Byron's heroes, George Washington. While he had been in Europe, pondering Napoleon's dubious legacy, Byron's mind had been focusing upon America as the real and future nation of the free. Ticknor saw them as unlikely travelling companions; soberly professional Hobhouse and romantic, politically volatile Lord Byron:

'Hobhouse, who is a true politician, talked only of seeing a people whose character and institutions are still in the freshness of youth; while Lord Byron, who had nothing of this but the prejudices and passions of a partisan, was evidently thinking only of seeing our Indians and our forests; of standing in the spray of Niagara; even of climbing the Andes, and ascending the Orinoco.'

When Byron parted from Ticknor at the Villa gate he promised to meet him in America in a couple of years.

Byron could still be ferociously irascible, his pugnacious Harrow schoolboy self. Near La Mira he had 'a small row in the road'. He was on horseback, overtaking a party of people in a hired carriage, when one of the passengers stuck his head out of the window and apparently insulted Byron, who retaliated by giving him a violent slap in the face. He got off his horse, opened the door of the carriage and ordered his insulter to get out, threatening another blow. There was much mutual swearing, during which Byron announced his name and residence. His opponent, uncowed, went off to the police to report Byron for an unprovoked attack. Byron called in witnesses and the complaint was dismissed.

But this was an isolated incident. Byron described his life just then as 'quiet & healthy'. The unassuming country routine of the 'villegiatura' was suiting him. Hobhouse was relieved to see that at La Mira Byron was 'well, and merry and happy, more charming every day'. He seemed to be recovering his equilibrium. One reason may have been that the situation vis-à-vis Lady Byron had clarified itself. The recent tense and anxious months of altercation, during which Byron was combating Sir Ralph Noel's bill in Chancery which aimed to deprive him of his paternal rights, had put an end to any lingering hopes of future reconciliation. After they had spent an evening at La Mira talking over Byron's family affairs, Hobhouse noted in his diary, 'He does not care about his wife now – that is certain.' Though Byron was always to retain a strange ability to correspond with Lady Byron as if they were still on terms of unchanged intimacy, he made clear to his confidential friends the hatred he now felt for her. Their relationship was one of settled enmity.

Like his own Prisoner of Chillon, Byron was discovering a feasible modus vivendi in adversity. In August at La Mira he was diverted from memories of

Lady Byron, as indeed from thoughts of Marianna Segati, by two unusually pretty Venetian girls he and Hobhouse had encountered among a group of peasants as they were 'sauntering on horseback along the Brenta one evening'. The girls were cousins. The smaller of the two, who was unmarried, took fright when Hobhouse made advances 'for here no woman will do anything under adultery'. The other taller, more experienced girl, Margherita Cogni, wife of a baker, was a great deal more receptive towards Byron. Byron described Margherita as having 'the strength of an Amazon'. According to his later account, 'in a few evenings we arranged our affairs – and for two years – in the course of which I had more women than I can count or recount – she was the only one who preserved over me an ascendancy – which was often disputed & never impaired.'

Like Marianna Segati, Margherita was twenty-two when Byron met her. But she was lower in the Venetian social scale, a working woman referred to jokingly as 'La Fornarina', probably a reference to the portrait of Raphael's mistress of the same name which Byron had noticed in the gallery at Florence. Moore describes Margherita disdainfully as a woman whom Byron had 'picked up in rags & who was nothing better than what is in vulgar slang called a blowing'. Her husband Andrea Magnarotto was consumptive. Her initial approach on the banks of the Brenta had indeed been more or less that of a beggar. Margherita had apparently called out to the English lord well known for his considerable if erratic generosity, 'Why do not you who relieve others – think of us also?'

The reasons for Margherita's ascent into Byron's affections, and her eventual supplanting of Marianna as his chief Venetian mistress, were succinctly outlined by her lover in one of his famous letters to John Murray: 'firstly – her person – very dark – tall – the Venetian face – very fine black eyes – and certain other qualities which need not be mentioned.' The drawing of 'La Fornarina' made in Venice by George Henry Harlow suggests she had a softer side as well. Because she had not had children she 'had not spoilt her figure – nor *anything else* – which is I assure you – a great desideratum in a hot climate where they grow relaxed and doughy and *flumpity* in a short time after breeding'. She could not read or write, which he seized on as a bonus since it meant she could not plague him with letters. But he appreciated her usage of the spoken word, seeing her as 'a thorough Venetian in her dialect – in her thoughts – in her countenance – in every thing – with all their naïveté and Pantaloon humour'.

He admired the headstrong energy with which Margherita gave as good as she got, recounting her confrontation with 'La Signora Segati' who, urged on by some of her female friends, was rash enough to threaten her one evening near La Mira:

'Margerita threw back her veil (fazziolo) and replied in very explicit Venetian – "*You* are *not* his wife: I am *not* his *wife* – *you* are his Donna – and *I* am his *donna* – *your* husband is a cuckold – and mine is another; – for the rest, what *right* have you to reproach me? – if he prefers what is mine – to what is yours – is it my fault?" '

What Byron loved in Margherita was her entertainment value, her sense of the primitive logic which was an essential component of Italian comedy.

There is much of the spirit of Margherita in the poem *Beppo*, Byron's portrait of Venice 'as the seat of dissoluteness', written in the early autumn of 1817. The comedy of the middle-aged lady of Venice, installed with her long-term lover, taken aback by the sudden reappearance of the husband who was assumed to have been lost many years before at sea, was based on a story told around the dinner table in that summer at La Mira by Marianna's husband, Signor Segati. When he got to the end Marianna made the comment, fixing Byron in her gaze, 'I'm sure I would not leave my amoroso for any husband.' Hobhouse, much embarrassed, wrote in his diary: 'This is too gross even for me.'

Byron wrote the poem fast. He later claimed to have composed it in two days at the Villa Foscarini, though as usual there were many additions and revisions. It was in a new style, colloquial and racy, with an inner core of sadness. Since being in Italy, Byron was feeling more than ever disenchanted with the direction being taken by poetry in England, writing of Tom Moore, whose oriental poem *Lalla Rookh* had just been published, 'I am convinced the more I think of it – that he and *all* of us – Scott – Southey – Wordsworth – Moore – Campbell – I – are all in the wrong – one as much as another – that we are upon the wrong revolutionary poetical system – or systems – not worth a damn in itself.' With *Beppo* he was evolving a manner of expression that was both intrinsically English and ebulliently Italianate.

Byron formally acknowledged the influence on *Beppo* of 'William and Robert Whistlecraft', double pseudonym for John Hookham Frere, whose mock-epic poem *Prospectus and Specimen of an Intended National Work* introduced the Italian *ottava rima* to the English reader. But, already familiar with the works of Casti, Luigi Pulci and the Venetian satirist Buratti in the original, Byron now invested the *ottava rima* with a vitality and freedom of his own.

> 'I love the language, that soft bastard Latin,
>   Which melts like kisses from a female mouth,

And sounds as if it should be writ on satin,
   With syllables which breathe of the sweet South,
And gentle liquids gliding all so pat in,
   That not a single accent seems uncouth,
Like our harsh northern whistling, grunting guttural,
Which we're oblig'd to hiss, and spit, and sputter all.'

In *Beppo* he starts experimenting with the daring elisions and outrageous rhymes which became so much a part of his stylistic vocabulary.

Above all *Beppo* shows Byron in a new mood as the amorous Venetian comedy of 'Vile assignations, and adulterous beds,/ Elopements, broken vows, and hearts and heads' leads on to something much more serious and savage, with a foretaste of the flexibility of writing he perfected in *Don Juan*. It satirises English literature, social life and culture. For its period the sexual politics are lethal, with a dangerous undercurrent attacking his own marriage. Byron was right in maintaining that *Beppo* 'has politics and ferocity'.

A few years later, in Pisa, Shelley was heard 'spouting some lines out of Beppo', while they were playing billiards at the Palazzo Lanfranchi. 'What stuff is that?' enquired Lord Byron. 'Some of your stuff,' said Shelley, '& some of the best you ever wrote.'

By 13 November the lease of Villa Foscarini was expiring. Byron returned to Venice. He was soon arranging to lodge his horses at the Lido, the narrow island strip directly opposite the city. Byron adopted a new routine of rowing over in his gondola and taking 'a spanking gallop of some miles daily along a firm and solitary beach', from the fortress on the Lido to Malamocco, almost at the long island's southern tip. It was while riding along the beach with Hobhouse that he met a German banker who handed on the news of the death in childbirth of Princess Charlotte, subject of Byron's once controversial 'Lines to a Lady Weeping'. The sudden announcement brought back memories for both of them. Wrote Hobhouse: 'We were really affected by this news, and went home conjecturing.'

News came too of the sale, at last, of Newstead Abbey. The purchaser, Byron's Harrow contemporary Thomas Wildman, had had a successful military career, serving in the Peninsular War and acting as Lord Uxbridge's aide-de-camp at Waterloo. His buying of Newstead may have been in part hero-worship, an attempt to associate himself with his celebrated schoolfellow. On completion, Wildman asked Byron for his portrait. Tom Moore later noted Wildman's 'zeal in everything relating to Byron' who, for his part, felt contented that the purchaser was someone connected through the past. The £94,500 paid by Wildman for the house and the estate, together with the substantial fees he was now accepting from John Murray, eased Byron's financial worries. He could pay off most of his debts, starting with the Jewish moneylenders. He urged Kinnaird, having successfully negotiated Newstead, to put renewed efforts into getting rid of Rochdale: 'I should be then quite clear.'

When Hobhouse left Venice for England on 8 January 1818 he carried in his luggage the manuscript of Canto IV of *Childe Harold*. Byron appended a letter in verse:

> 'My dear Mr Murray,
> You're in a damned hurry
> To set up this ultimate Canto,
> But (if they don't rob us)
> You'll see Mr Hobhouse
> Will bring it safe in his portmanteau ...
>
> Now, I'll put out my taper
> (I've finished my paper
> For these stanzas you see on the *brink* stand)
> There's a whore on my right
> For I rhyme best at Night
> When a C—t is tied close to *my Inkstand*.'

Another year, another Carnival. With Hobhouse gone Byron had 'taken again to the Natives': Countess Albrizzi's evenings, the Ridotto, balls and operas, Haydn and Handel oratorios at the San Benedetto theatre. After meeting her at the Masque, he was 'in the estrum & agonies of a new intrigue' with a fair-haired blue-eyed girl 'insatiate of love'. He had been infected with the clap, the first gonorrhoea he had not actually paid for, by a 'Gentil Donna', Elena da Mosta. If he had to die young, then he preferred to expire '*standing*'. The political inertia of Venice depressed him. But the social life of the city was *mouvementé* and familiar. And, so Byron told Samuel Rogers, he was now preferring it to any other place in Italy: 'here I have pitched my staff – & here I propose to reside for the remainder of my life.' Venice had become a kind of home.

21

Venice: Palazzo Mocenigo

1818

'Good night – or, rather, morning. It is four and the dawn gleams over the Grand Canal, and unshadows the Rialto. I must to bed.'

Byron was adept at composing his own legend and nowhere more successfully than in the Palazzo Mocenigo, his Venetian residence from May 1818 to the end of the next year. The image of the poet in his palace, lounging on his velvet sofa, lost in reverie, as depicted in W.L. Price's mid-nineteenth-century watercolour *Byron in Palazzo Mocenigo*, became for many people the quintessential Byron, fixing his personality for posterity.

It may have been the break in his relations with Marianna Segati that prompted him to move from his lodgings in the Frezzeria. The sale of Newstead Abbey could also have encouraged him to find a place in Venice more fitted to his station and with a better view. He had first begun negotiating with Count Gritti for a lease on the Gritti Palace not far from St Mark's Square. But he finally settled for one of the four Mocenigo palazzi further down the Grand Canal, where it takes a sharp bend and then runs on to the Rialto. Lady Mary Wortley Montagu had once resided there. He took the palace for three years, at an annual rent of £200.

Byron left his indelible mark on the great palace, forming what was almost an emotional bond with it, investing it with his own hopes and fears for Venice. He occupied the second of the four palazzi, as approached from St Mark's Square. Since the two central palazzi were once interconnected he may have spread over to the third. His main apartments appear to have been on the second floor, the *piano nobile*, with its balcony overlooking the Grand Canal. Newton Hanson, visiting the Mocenigo with his father in 1818, gave an account of their complicated route 'up a flight of massive marble staircases, through a lofty billiard room, and then through a bedroom, to an apartment' where Byron was waiting at the door to greet them.

As was usual in Venice the palazzo had two entrances: one connecting to the city, on dry land, while the other, the water entrance, gave access to the Grand Canal. It was here, on the ground floor, that Byron kept, in their individual cages, his fast-increasing menagerie of dogs, birds, two 'charming' monkeys, a fox and a wolf. He would stop to play with them or sometimes feed them as he passed through on his way to his gondola. Running the gauntlet of Byron's animals could be frightening to visitors as they made their way across the sub-terranean hall with the master's admonitions, 'Keep clear of the dog' and 'Take care, or that monkey will fly at you', ringing in their ears.

Byron's household was large and not totally controllable. At one point, once his daughter Allegra had arrived, he refers to 'my ragamuffins – Gondoliers, Nurses – cook – footmen &c.' His complement of servants at the Palazzo Mocenigo was around fourteen. Besides Stevens the cook and his valet William Fletcher, Byron's staffing had been strengthened by a local recruit, Giovanni Battista Falcieri, known as 'Tita', from a celebrated family of gondoliers whose father and brothers had served the Mocenigos. Byron had paid to have him released from conscription. When Shelley met him in Ravenna he described the outsize Tita as 'a fine fellow with a prodigious black beard, who has stabbed two or three people, & is the most goodnatured looking fellow I ever saw'. Tita became the exotic counterpart to Fletcher in the inner circle of Byron's entourage, with a love of his employer that rivalled Fletcher's own.

It was not in Byron's nature to discipline his servants. The British Consul in Venice thought him 'culpably lenient' towards his obstreperous adopted family: 'he rather bantered with them than spoke seriously to them' even when they cheated him or blatantly neglected their duties. His own increasingly chaotic amours raised the temperature in the Palazzo Mocenigo. The maidservants shrieked and squabbled and told tales. One of these was Fletcher's volatile mistress Marietta, known ironically by Byron as 'the Countess'. Much as he hated dismissing any servant she eventually wore out even Byron's patience and Marietta flounced out of the palazzo, leaving Stevens the cook 'to get drunk alone'.

Marietta reappears in a hilarious letter written by Byron from Venice in June 1818. Purporting to be from Fletcher, the letter informs Hobhouse of his late dear master's sad demise at ten o'clock that morning, a sudden death 'caused by anxiety – sea-bathing – women & riding in the Sun' although his valet had strongly advised him to be cautious. The letter climaxes in a crescendo of Fletcherian self-justification:

'if I did keep the Countess (she is or ought to be a Countess although she is upon the town) Marietta – Monetta – Piretta – after passing my word to you and my Lord that I would not never no more – still he was an indulgent master – & only said I was a damned fool – & swore & forgot it again. – What Could I do – she said as how she should die – or kill herself if I did not go with her – & so I did – & kept her out of my Lord's washing & ironing – & nobody can deny that although the charge was high – the linen was well got up.'

Did Fletcher ever see this letter, in which Byron recaptures so exactly his blend of innocence and calculation and his still near native Nottinghamshire idiom? Byron's zest in finding materials for human comedy all around him was undiminished.

One essential component of the legendary decor of the Palazzo Mocenigo was the flashing-eyed, raven-haired La Fornarina, Byron's untameable 'fine animal', a woman 'fit to breed gladiators from'. When he left La Mira for Venice in the winter of 1817 Margherita had followed him. She made the most of Signora Segati's fall from favour, one reason for which seems to be that Marianna had sold on the diamonds Byron had bought her. When he found them at a jeweller's he repurchased them and confronted Marianna with her ingratitude.

Margherita herself had behaved badly at the Cavalchina, the masked ball held on the last night of the Carnival, snatching the mask from the face of the Italian noblewoman, Madame Contarini, who was then on Byron's arm and riposting when rebuked for insulting her social superior: 'If she is a lady – I am a Venetian.' Later versions of this story, embellished in retelling, have Margherita unmasking Byron himself. La Fornarina was determined to infiltrate the palazzo and by midsummer 1818 she was living there as Byron's dictatorial housekeeper, reputed to be frightening 'the learned Fletcher out of his remnant of wits'. The baker Magnarotto complained to the police of the forcible abduction of his wife by two of Byron's gondoliers, said to have seized her by the hips before her husband's very eyes and taken her to the palace, 'place of a forbidden, shameful cohabitation'. But these accusations ceased once Byron bought him off.

At the Mocenigo, Margherita Cogni's natural vanity flourished. When Countess Benzoni, Countess Albrizzi's rival as leader of the Venetian social scene, began taking notice of her, Margherita began to show delusions of grandeur. She discarded the veil worn by women of the Venetian working classes and to Byron's dismay trumped herself up in hat and feathers. He threw these in the fire. She immediately bought more and stalked around the palace in pseudo-aristocratic gowns with trains.

But he was touched by her wild passions, her operatic frenzies, the way she crossed herself in the midst of making love when a distant prayer bell rang. With her grand airs and penchant for drama Margherita Cogni provides a perfect subject for set-piece descriptions in Byron's letters to Albemarle Street:

'In the autumn one day going to the Lido with my Gondoliers – we were over-taken by a heavy Squall and the Gondola put in peril – hats blown away – boat filling – oar lost – tumbling sea – thunder – rain in torrents – night coming – & wind increasing. – On our return – after a tight struggle: I found her on the open steps of the Mocenigo palace on the Grand Canal – with her great black eyes flashing through her tears and the long dark hair which was streaming drenched with rain over her brows & breast; – she was perfectly exposed to the storm – and the wind blowing her hair & dress about her tall thin figure – and the lightning flashing round her – with the waves rolling at her feet – made her look like Medea alighted from her chariot – or the Sibyl of the tempest that was rolling around her.'

As Byron describes the furious Fornarina, a Venetian Medea, he could be delin-eating a Veronese painting. Significantly, Medea was an image Byron also applied to his vengeful English wife.

Simultaneously with Margherita Cogni, Byron was involved with another, more professional scenemaker. Arpalice Taruscelli was an opera singer. She already had a complicated entourage of lovers, ex-lovers and an official *cava-liere servente*, a colonel in the occupying Austrian army. As Byron makes clear in a letter to Hobhouse it was never a formalised affair: 'She is the prettiest Bacchanti in the world – & a piece to perish *in* ... recollect there is no *liaison* only *fuff-fuff* and passades – & fair fucking.' This intermittently strenuous rela-tionship, which lasted through the summer of 1818 and on into the following year, was sustained by the intermediary of gondoliers and maids, midnight assignations, a succession of jealous rows and tearful reconciliations. Arpalice Taruscelli had the mania for drama of an Italian Caroline Lamb.

Byron's policy towards his old mistresses was generous. He was never a dog in the manger, he boasted: 'I am not like those Venetian fellows who – when their ambitions are over with a piece – would prevent all others from partaking of the public property.' Once their affair was finished, Marianna Segati moved on to an Austrian officer, who was said to have ruined himself trying to be as generous to her as Byron had been. After a double suicide attempt, first with a knife, then by immersion in the Grand Canal, Margherita Cogni was handed over to Byron's crony Alexander Scott, who offered her to Thomas Moore when he arrived in Venice. When Arpalice Taruscelli came to London on a professional visit in 1821, in company with the famous Italian tenor Alberico Curioni who was making his Covent Garden debut, she bore Byron's strongest recommendation.

He encouraged his publisher John Murray to receive 'a Venetian lady of great beauty and celebrity and a particular friend of mine – your natural gallantry will I am sure induce you to pay her proper attention.' He suggested that another of Murray's authors, Isaac D'Israeli, might succeed in getting some literary anecdotes from Taruscelli: 'I presume that he speaks Italian.'

The introduction to Douglas Kinnaird was more specific: '*Try her* – you will find her a good one to go – and she is – or was uncommonly *firm* of *flesh* – a *rarity* in Italian & Southern women after twenty – She is also sufficiently expert in all the motions – like the rest of her country-women – and though a little too full in her person – is certainly a desirable woman.'

Just how many mistresses did Byron have in Venice? In a letter written jointly to Hobhouse and Kinnaird he names a whole string of them, in the manner of the conquests itemised by the servant Leporello in Mozart's opera *Don Giovanni*:

'the Tarruscelli – the Da Mosti – the Spineda – the Lotti – the Rizzato – the Eleanora – the Carlotta – the Giulietta – the Alvisi – the Zambieri – The Eleanora da Bezzi – (who was the King of Naples's Gioaschino's mistress – at least one of them) the Theresina of Mazzurati – the Glettenheimer – & her Sister – the Luiga & her mother – the Fornaretta – the Santa – the Caligari – the Portiera – the Bolognese figurante – the Tentora and her sister – cum multis aliis? – some of them are Countesses – & some of them Cobblers wives – some noble – some middling – some low – & all whores.'

We know the poignant reality of some of these liaisons from the letters to Byron from Taruscelli and Segati, and the cries for attention which the illiterate Margherita Cogni dictated to a Venetian scribe – emotional outpourings now collected together in the distant and rarefied environment of the Carl H. Pforzheimer Library, New York.

Early in 1819 Byron claimed to have made love to all these women '& thrice as many to boot' in the last two years. At other times he put the overall figure of his Venetian conquests at around two hundred. This seems a somewhat arbitrary figure, the sort of grand total Byron easily reached for. It was also the number of 'pl & opt Cs' he recollected achieving at the Athens monastery in 1810.

Certainly Byron's life in Venice was promiscuous. The interesting question is whether he confined himself to women. From Geneva he had written to Augusta reassuringly: 'As to "pages" – there be none such – nor any body else.' But once arrived in Venice, where sex was so easily available, had he reverted to his homosexual past? There is something suspiciously insistent about the bravado of Byron's narratives of his encounters with women in letters back to England, which in effect were public bulletins. Shelley probably brings us closer to the truth in his alarmed report, in the winter of 1818, of Byron's moral and physical disintegration. Besides countesses reeking horribly of garlic 'he associates with wretches who seem almost to have lost the gait & phisiognimy of man, & who do not scruple to avow practices which are not only not named but I believe seldom even conceived in England'. Mary Shelley too was depressed by his connections: 'What a miserable thing it is that he should be lost as he is among the worst inhabitants of Venice.'

Byron himself called Venice a 'sea-Sodom'. It seems likely that his Venetian sexual exploits were a good deal more varied than he claimed.

Between April 1817 and autumn 1818 Byron was working intermittently on *Mazeppa*, a strange and haunting story based on an incident from Voltaire's *Histoire de Charles XII*. The poem is a nightmare of perpetual motion, the tale of a young man, found to be the lover of the young wife of an old husband, who is punished by being bound naked to the back of a Tartar steed and sent off to what seems certain death – Byron's Corsair enchained. This poem, with its macabre eroticism, its uncertain balance between tragedy and farce, was to appeal strongly to French Romantic painters of the early nineteenth century.

Mazeppa can be seen to originate in Byron's almost frenzied, often ill-assorted sexual couplings in Venice at that time. It carries echoes, too, of his own habitual daily riding at the Lido, Adriatic seaspray rising as he pounded along the sands. As Byron aged he still depended upon physical exertion as a relief from tension, from writing and from thinking, and for the reassurance it gave him of his physical stamina.

Once Hobhouse had left Venice, Byron's regular companion on these rides was the British Consul, Richard Belgrave Hoppner. Though Byron claimed to have gone native in Italy, and to some extent he did, he always managed to recruit an admiring local Englishman to act as his intermediary, his fixer. The careful, conventional Richard Hoppner left affectionate accounts of their rides together, their gentleman-to-gentleman relations: 'Nothing could exceed the vivacity and variety of his conversation, or the cheerfulness of his manner. His remarks on the surrounding objects were always original.' Hoppner, son of the artist John Hoppner, had himself trained as a painter and so was aware of how Lord Byron was 'feelingly alive to the beauty of nature', responsive to Hoppner's comments on the effects of light and shadow and, especially evident in Venice, 'the changes produced in the colour of objects by every variation in the atmosphere'.

The disadvantage of their rides was the way that it exposed Byron to English sightseers who thronged to his known point of disembarkation at the Lido, a place that had once been a Jewish cemetery and where the broken tombstones still littered the ground. Hoppner found it 'amusing in the extreme to witness the excessive coolness with which ladies, as well as gentlemen, would advance within a very few paces of him, eyeing him, some with their glasses, as they would have done a statue in a museum, or the wild beasts at Exeter 'Change'. Byron was usually able to bear all this with patience, though Hoppner could clearly see he was annoyed. But one day, when two or three men began running down the opposite shore of the Lido, hoping to reach the gondola before him, the extent of Byron's paranoia showed. He threw himself down from his horse, leapt into the gondola and closed the curtains of the cabin, cowering in a corner out of sight.

The most triumphant of Byron's swims took place in Venice. In June 1818 he and Hoppner took part in what was a trial run, a swim from the Lido to a gunship anchored on the quayside, near the Piazzetta. The other swimmers were Byron's and Hoppner's young friend Alexander Scott, a wealthy Scottish traveller resident in Venice, and the Cavalier Angelo Mengaldo, bombastic former officer in Napoleon's army. Though Mengaldo had a reputation as a swimmer, having swum across the Danube in Napoleon's campaigns and crossed the Beresina during the retreat from Moscow, Byron claimed that he himself swam twice the distance of the others, commenting disdainfully that Hoppner and Mengaldo both spewed up when they got out of the sea.

The real test took place a few days later. This time Hoppner was not a contestant but the timekeeper as Byron, Scott and Mengaldo swam off from the Lido and past San Giorgio Maggiore to the entrance of the Grand Canal. According to Byron's account he and Scott were well clear of Mengaldo, who was picked up by a gondola, although Mengaldo maintains in his diary that it was Scott who had been left behind. Byron, now on his own in the water, swam on down the whole length of the Grand Canal, from the Rialto bridge to Santa Chiara, getting out of the water at the point where the canal opened out to the lagoon again. He had been in the water for four and a quarter hours and reckoned he could have carried on for longer, in spite of the encumbrance of the trousers he was wearing. 'I could not be much fatigued', he remarked to Hobhouse, 'having had a *piece* in the forenoon – & taking another in the evening at ten of the Clock.'

On the subject of Byron's remarkable amphibiousness another of his swimming companions made the comment that, while obviously handicapped in riding, boxing, fencing and even walking, 'in the water a fin is better than a foot, and in that element he did well; he was built for floating – with a flexible body, open chest, broad beam, and round limbs.' Another reason for Byron's success of course was will-power: in competitive swims he had a driving need to win.

Through 1817 Allegra and her mother had been living with the Shelleys at Albion House, Great Marlow. On Allegra's first birthday, 12 January 1818, Claire Clairmont wrote Byron a long letter telling him about his daughter, whom she described as having 'pretty eyes of a deep dazzling blue more like the colours of the waters of Lake Geneva under a summer sky than anything else I ever saw, rosy projecting lips & a little square chin divided in the middle exactly like your own'. How she wished Byron could see the infant: 'she is just now so very interesting'. Enclosed in a little piece of silver paper she sent him a lock of Allegra's hair which had now turned from dark to blonde. Clearly, by sending news of the infant, Claire wished to maintain her connection with Byron. But at the same time she was anxious to discourage him from taking Allegra from her, preferring to bring up their daughter on her own.

Though she could see the material advantages in her daughter being brought up by Byron, all Claire's instincts were against it. Her own physical bond with the child was such a close one, she told Byron: 'We sleep together and if you knew the extreme happiness I feel when she nestles close to me, when in listening to our regular breathing together, I could tear my flesh in twenty thousand different directions to ensure her good.' The baby, she pleaded, was 'peculiarly delicate' with digestive problems that needed a mother's sensitive surveillance. She expressed her dread 'lest I should behold her sickly & wasted with improper management lest I should live to hear that *you* neglected her'. The 'various and ceaseless misgivings' Claire admitted about Byron's suitability to care for a small child were shared by Mary Shelley who understood his capacity for boredom, his fundamental unreliability: 'promises with Albe! the first object that engaged his attention would put them all out of his head.'

Like all Claire's other letters, Byron left this one unanswered. He was still only negotiating with her via Shelley. But he was intent on having at least one of his daughters to live with him in Italy. 'Ah Coquin! Vare is my Shild?' he joked to Hobhouse, imitating Shylock in search of his lost Jessica. Hobhouse was instructed to approach Shelley, to see if he could arrange to send 'the illegitimate one' out to Venice with a nurse that spring.

As far as Claire was concerned, Shelley's deteriorating health was an unfortunate coincidence. In early 1818 his physicians, alarmed by the signs of consumption he was showing, encouraged him to move to Italy himself where the climate would be of benefit to him. On 11 March when he and Mary left England, taking with them two-year-old William and their new baby Clara, who was just six months old, Claire Clairmont and Allegra accompanied them. The Swiss nurse Elise Duvillard was also in the party: she too was the mother of an illegitimate daughter, left in Switzerland. Two days before their departure William, Clara and Allegra were baptised at the London church of St Giles-in-the-Fields. Allegra's name was entered as Clara Allegra Byron, born of 'Rt. Hon. George Gordon Lord Byron ye reputed Father by Clara Mary Jane Clairmont'. No attempt was made to gloss the matter. The father's address was given as 'No fixed residence. Travelling on the Continent.'

An increasingly despondent Claire journeyed with the Shelleys to Milan. Rejecting Shelley's suggestion that he join them at Lake Como, Byron sent a somewhat disreputable messenger, Francis Merryweather, who kept a produce store on the bridge of the Bereteri, to collect Allegra and Elise, who had been deputed to accompany the child. There were wrenches at the parting: Shelley wrote to Byron of his daughter, 'I think she is the most lovely and engaging child I ever beheld'; Mary, he said, had been accustomed to regard Allegra 'almost as one of her own children'. Claire begged Byron to send her some of his own hair so that she could wear it with Allegra's in a locket. It seems that when she first reached Venice, Allegra and her nurse were lodged with Richard Hoppner and his wife, but by June they were living with Byron at the Palazzo Mocenigo.

In her letter of January 1818 Claire had jealously pictured to herself Allegra's life with Byron:

'You will have a little darling to crawl to your knees & pull you till you take her up – then she will sit on the crook of your arm & you will give her raisins out of your own plate & a little drop of wine from your own glass & she will think herself a little Queen in Creation. When she shall be older she will run about your house like a Lapwing . . .'

Their life at the palazzo was much as Claire predicted. Byron loved and spoilt his daughter, treating her as an endearing addition to his menagerie. In August 1818 he reported to Augusta that blue-eyed, fair-haired Allegra was 'very pretty – remarkably intelligent – and a great favourite with everybody'. She had a self-possession that reminded him peculiarly of Lady Byron's, but also 'a devil of a Spirit', which was surely her Papa's.

The commotion of Palazzo Mocenigo, with Margherita Cogni's tantrums, cannot have been good for a child of eighteen months. Mrs Hoppner, a Swiss woman who had strict standards and who saw that Elise was too inexperienced to cope with that strange ménage, offered to take Allegra in on a more permanent basis. The child was with the Hoppners in late August when Claire and Shelley arrived in Venice from Bagni di Lucca, where they had spent the summer. Shelley saw an alteration in Allegra: 'she is pale & has lost a good deal of her liveliness, but is as beautiful as ever though more mild.'

Not wanting to announce Claire's presence, Shelley made his way alone to the Palazzo Mocenigo, arriving at three in the afternoon of 23 August. Byron greeted him enthusiastically, taking him off to the Lido in his gondola. They talked vociferously as they rode along the shore, Byron indulging in histories of his wounded feelings, asking questions about Shelley's own affairs and making great professions of friendship and regard for Shelley. He recited some stanzas from the new fourth canto of *Childe Harold*. Their reunion gave Shelley the basis for his poetic dialogue *Julian and Maddalo: A Conversation*, with himself as an approximation of Julian, 'an Englishman of good family, passionately attached to those philosophical notions which assert the power of man over his own mind', and Byron as the charming, spellbinding Count Maddalo, rich Venetian nobleman of ancient family.

Maddalo is 'a person of the most consummate genius', as Shelley explains in the Preface to the poem,

'capable, if he would direct his energies to such an end, of becoming the redeemer of his degraded country. But it is his weakness to be proud: he derives, from a comparison of his own extraordinary mind with the dwarfish intellects that surround him, an intense apprehension of the nothingness of human life.'

Shelley had come to see Byron much more clearly since they had first met in Geneva two years earlier. He viewed Byron's life in Venice as wasteful, self-destructive, reporting to his friend Thomas Love Peacock:

'He is not yet an Italian & is heartily & deeply discontented with himself & contemplating in the distorted mirror of his own thoughts, the nature & the destiny of man, what can he behold but objects of contempt & despair? But that he is a great poet, I think the address to Ocean [Byron's final stanzas of *Childe Harold*] proves. And he has a certain degree of candour while you talk to him but unfortunately it does not outlast your departure.'

There is a profound sadness in Shelley's perception of Byron at this point.

As Shelley had feared, Byron was indeed horrified when he discovered that Claire had come to Venice. 'Allegra is well', he told Augusta in September, 'but her mother (whom the Devil confound) came prancing the other day over the

Appenines – to see her *shild* – which threw my Venetian loves (who are none of the quietest) into great combustion – and I was in a pucker till I got her to the Euganean hills where she & the child now are.' He had declined to see her, he added, 'for fear that the consequence might be an addition to the family'.

He had already offered the Shelley family the loan of his house, I Capuccini, in the hills at Este, a house which he had arranged to lease from Richard Hoppner the previous winter but had not yet occupied. Here he allowed Allegra to join her mother. In this villa, built on the site of a Capuchin convent overlooking the ruins of the massive castle of Este, haunt of owls and bats, Shelley composed 'Lines written among the Euganean Hills' and began *Prometheus Unbound*.

At Este there occurred another of the tragedies that dogged the Shelleys' lives. Their infant daughter Clara, who had been ill since leaving Bagni di Lucca, became suddenly much worse, with convulsive movements of the mouth and eyes. Shelley and Mary took the baby to Venice to find a physician. Little Clara died 'silently, without pain', at an inn en route. The ever-receptive Hoppners took the shocked and grieving parents in.

In November the Shelleys and Claire Clairmont departed for Rome and Naples. Allegra was back with her father when John Hanson and his youngest son arrived in Venice that month with the Newstead documents of sale. They went out in Byron's gondola, Byron and his lawyer engaged in conversation while Newton Hanson 'played with and amused' Allegra, who prattled to him in Venetian. Byron told them he had taught her to swim by throwing her out of the gondola into the Adriatic, 'to the horror of her Nurse'.

Byron had been characteristically casual about the details of his meeting with the Hansons and Colonel Wildman's representative, a Mr Townsend. They had expected to meet him at Dejean's Hotel in Sécheron, but found only a letter telling them he could not possibly cross the Simplon at that time of year and instructing them to travel on to Venice. One reason he was anxious to avoid Geneva may have been the memory of Monsieur Dejean's telescopes.

Byron sent his gondola to fetch them from the Hôtel de la Grande-Bretagne. When he met them at the Palazzo Mocenigo, Newton was aware of 'a nervous sensitiveness in his Lordship, which produced a silence for some minutes'. Byron said jocularly, 'Well, Hanson! I never thought you would have ventured so far.' His eyes were filled with tears. He had few illusions about Hanson whom he referred to as 'Spooney' or 'Parchment' and knew to be both dilatory and a rogue. But this was a man he had known for twenty years, since he first acceded to his title. John Hanson was the most enduring link with his lost past.

Newton was alarmed by his childhood friend's appearance. Byron was only thirty, but 'he looked 40. His face had become pale, bloated, and sallow. He had grown very fat, his shoulders broad and round, and the knuckles of his hands were lost in fat.' Loose living in Venice had evidently undermined Byron's determination to keep down his weight. The young man's conversation had become that of the roué. Newton noted Byron's irritability of temper. He had asked John Hanson to bring him three large packages from John Murray. The fact that Hanson had brought only one, a package that contained not the books he was expecting but merely toothbrushes, toothpowder and kaleidoscopes, London's latest fashionable toys which Murray had hoped would entertain Venetian ladies, put him in a rage which lasted for some hours. Newton noticed that Lord Byron was still biting his nails.

What surprised the visitors was that Byron, once so lavish, was now showing signs of extreme parsimony. Stinginess, he said gleefully, had become his latest vice. Fletcher grumbled to the Hansons that Byron had become 'so very economical it was quite disagreeable'. The servants could not comprehend this change of heart and complained that they were always hungry. Byron seemed to take great pleasure at this period in driving hard financial bargains with John Murray, as if compensating for his earlier amateurism over fees.

John Hanson was anxious to assess the real situation vis-à-vis Lady Byron. He tried several times to raise the question of a possible reconciliation. He was foiled when, three days after their arrival, Byron received a letter from John Murray telling him about the suicide of Sir Samuel Romilly, apparently the result of his extreme grief at the death of his wife. Byron went down in his gondola to the Grande-Bretagne to pass the news on to the Hansons, remarking, 'How strange it is that one man will die for the loss of his partner, while another would die if they were compelled to live together.' John Hanson dropped the subject of reconciliation.

Soon the Englishmen's visit appeared to lose its charm for him. Byron's feelings about England were now painfully ambivalent. Perhaps the contrast was too stark between Venice's easygoing habits and these representatives of English formal life. He may also have been influenced by the fact that Hanson presented a bill for fees totalling £9,000, of which Byron reckoned only £5,000 was due. After a week he intimated, via Fletcher, that he was 'becoming fidgetty' for their departure. Obediently the lawyers packed and left Venice the next day.

Byron's *Beppo* had been published anonymously at the end of February 1818. Though the sales were well below what Murray had achieved in the halcyon days of *The Corsair* he told Byron in June that 3,000 had been sold even before its authorship was generally known. Critically *Beppo* had been well received: John Hookham Frere saw 'the protean talent of Shakespeare' in the poem. Murray was anxious for a sequel. On 19 September Byron wrote from Venice to Tom Moore:

'I have finished the First Canto (a long one, of about 180 octaves) of a poem in the style and manner of "Beppo", encouraged by the good success of the same. It is called "Don Juan", and is meant to be a little quietly facetious upon everything.'

He sent Moore a small sample:

> 'My poem's Epic, and is meant to be
>   Divided in twelve books, each book containing,
> With love and war, a heavy gale at sea –
>   A list of ships, and captains, and kings reigning –
> New characters, &c. &c.'

Don Juan was to occupy Byron for the next five years. Like *Beppo*, the poem is ostensibly a rollicking amatory narrative, again written in *ottava rima*. But *Don Juan* is altogether grander, more ambitious. When Byron first read Canto I aloud to him in Venice, Shelley instantly recognised that this new poem was 'infinitely better' than *Beppo*. This was in fact the epic he had for so long been encouraging Byron to write, an energetic work of serious critical engagement with the events and morals of Byron's own age. Shelley was to remain *Don Juan*'s staunchest admirer. 'Nothing has ever been written like it in English – nor if I may venture to prophesy, will there be.'

Byron was always conscious that *Don Juan* would mean trouble. 'I doubt whether it is not – at least, as far as it has yet gone – too free for these very modest days,' he wrote in September 1818. The first canto of the poem, the tale of the seduction of the young Juan by the forward Spanish married lady Donna Julia, was doing the rounds of his friends in England in the last week of the year. *Don Juan* was discussed anxiously by Hobhouse, Kinnaird, Scrope Davies, Frere and Moore, forming what Byron saw indignantly as a 'Committee' of censorship.

At breakfast on 27 December, Scrope Davies and Hobhouse read the poem together. Hobhouse wrote in that day's diary: 'I have my doubts about Don Juan – blasphemy & bawdry & the domestic facta overpower even the great genius it displays.' Two days later Kinnaird communicated his misgivings direct: 'I have read your poems – Don Juan is exquisite – it must be *cut* for syphilis.' Tom Moore summarised the general view of Byron's friends that although the poem was 'full of talent and singularity' it was unpublishable. Augusta Leigh wrote nervously to Francis Hodgson: 'This new Poem, if persisted in, will be the ruin of him, from what I can learn.' Lady Caroline Lamb gave John Murray her opinion that the poem was 'neither witty nor in very good taste ... though to strangers it must appear incoherent nonsense, to those who penetrate it further it will excite contempt and disgust.' This did not prevent her from appearing as Don Giovanni at a masquerade at Almack's in July 1820, with 'a whole legion' of devils surrounding her.

The problems in *Don Juan* that most exercised his friends were, first and foremost, Byron's portrait of Juan's mother, the bluestocking Donna Inez, all too easily recognisable as Lady Byron in her prim dimity dresses: 'dimity rhyming very comically to sublimity', as Tom Moore pointed out. The conclusion of one stanza, 'I hate a dumpy woman', seemed particularly cruel. They were concerned about Byron's attacks on religion and his abuse of contemporary writers. The poem was dedicated to the Poet Laureate Robert Southey, Byron's *bête noire*, savagely attacking his political affiliations. To add insult to injury Byron nicknamed Southey 'dry Bob' in a lewd slang reference to copulation without emission.

In April 1819 the second canto of *Don Juan* reached John Murray. This was the canto of the shipwreck, containing scenes of gleeful serio-comic cannibalism, and Don Juan's rescue and revival by the pirate's daughter Haidée. The new episode did nothing to assuage the fears of Byron's friends. They were conscious of a wilful pursuit of the voluptuous in Byron's descriptions of the erotic courtship of Juan and Haidée. They accused him of 'a systematized profligacy'. In Moore's view Byron had been too long away from England to know what was feasible in terms of public taste.

Murray was bullied by Hobhouse to take action on *Don Juan*. Murray had his own reasons for wanting to avoid a public scandal or, still worse, a prosecution. He was a family man, as he reminded Byron, 'with very near Six Children'. As publisher of the *Quarterly Review* and publisher to the Admiralty, he had important contacts within the establishment: in bad moods, Byron would call John Murray 'a damned Tory'. With his copyright investments and plans for new collected editions of Lord Byron's works Murray had an obvious commercial interest in his author's continuing popularity. 'As to poor me', he wrote to Byron, 'though the most minute particle of the Comets Tale – yet I rise and fall with it – & my interest in your soaring above the other Stars – & continuing to create wonder even in your aberrations – is past calculation.'

In spite of, and because of, the separation scandal, Byron's star was still in the ascendant throughout England: 'Believe me there is no Character talked of

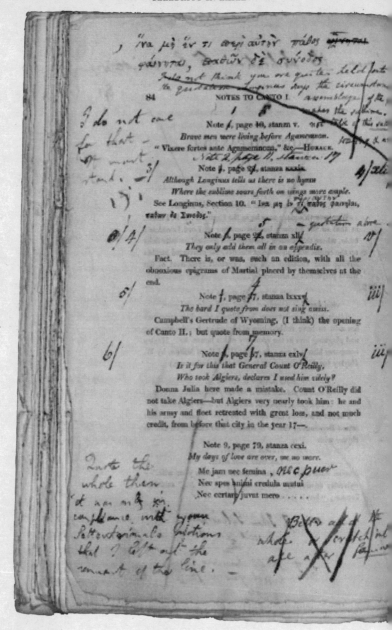

Byron's many instructions and amendments on page proofs of *Don Juan*, Cantos I and II.

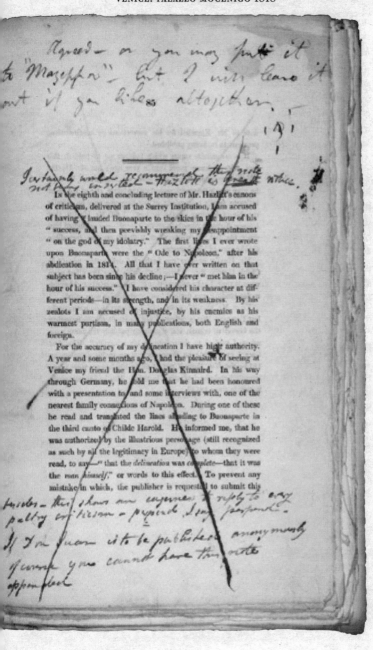

Agreed — or you may put it to "Mazeppa" — but I will leave it out if you like altogether. —

I certainly would recommend the note not being inserted — Hazlitt is beneath notice.

In the eighth and concluding lecture of Mr. Hazlitt's canons of criticism, delivered at the Surrey Institution, I am accused of having "lauded Buonaparte to the skies in the hour of his "success, and then peevishly wreaking my disappointment "on the god of my idolatry." The first lines I ever wrote upon Buonaparte were the "Ode to Napoleon," after his abdication in 1814. All that I have ever written on that subject has been since his decline;—I never "met him in the hour of his success." I have considered his character at different periods—in its strength, and in its weakness. By his zealots I am accused of injustice, by his enemies as his warmest partisan, in many publications, both English and foreign.

For the accuracy of my delineation I have high authority. A year and some months ago, I had the pleasure of seeing at Venice my friend the Hon. Douglas Kinnaird. In his way through Germany, he told me that he had been honoured with a presentation to, and some interviews with, one of the nearest family connections of Napoleon. During one of these he read and translated the lines alluding to Buonaparte in the third canto of Childe Harold. He informed me, that he was authorized by the illustrious personage (still recognized as such by all the legitimacy in Europe) to whom they were read, to say—"that the *delineation* was *complete*—that it was the *man himself*," or words to this effect. To prevent any mistake in which, the publisher is requested to submit this

besides — they shew an eagerness to reply to any paltry criticism — prepared, I say prepared. —

If you mean it to be published anonymously of course you cannot have this note appended.

in this Country as yours is – it is the constant theme of all classes & your portrait is engraved & painted & sold in every town throughout the Kingdom.' Murray was intent on preserving his most famous author's reputation. Through the spring and summer of 1819 he wrote to Byron frequently on the subject of *Don Juan*, praising the poem highly but suggesting excisions, entreating him to use his 'most tasteful discretion and wrap up or leave out certain approximations to indelicacy', passing on such unwelcome messages from Gifford as 'I read again this morning the Second Canto of Don Juan & lost all patience at seeing so much beauty, so wantonly & perversely disfigured. A little care & a little wish to do right would have made this a superlative thing.'

Byron's proneness to irritation with John Murray had increased since he had been abroad. Postal delays created misunderstandings. Byron was swift to invent imagined insults and assume neglect. The previous summer he had threatened to move his publications to Longman. There had been a few rumblings over *Beppo*, which Byron had told Murray must not be '*garbled* or *mutilated*'. But these differences paled beside Byron's now furious defence of the integrity of *Don Juan*. There was nothing in the poem, he maintained, as shocking as what was already in the public domain in the books of Ariosto or Chaucer, Fielding or Voltaire. His own adventures, so he claimed, had been a great deal more erotic and extraordinary than his hero's. The charge of immorality was breathtakingly irrelevant when the poem was itself a highly moral protest against hypocrisy.

'Donny Jonny', Byron insisted, should not be interfered with. His poem should be 'an entire horse or none'. The few changes he agreed to were relatively minor. He reserved his author's right to use his chosen words to show things as they were. 'I will not give way to all the Cant of Christendom,' he wrote defiantly, 'I have been cloyed with applause & sickened with abuse.' The row over Cantos I and II of *Don Juan* revealed a fundamental disagreement between Byron and his publisher that was to worsen painfully in the coming years.

22

Venice and Ravenna

1819

In January 1819 Byron declared he had 'quite given up Concubinage'; he was sick of promiscuity. In late March or early April he met 'a pretty fair-haired girl', a Romagnola countess who still showed the influence of her convent in Ravenna. He had already encountered Teresa Guiccioli fleetingly the year before at one of Countess Albrizzi's *conversazioni* when he had led her in to view Canova's famous sculpture of *Helen* on display in the Countess's private gallery. Then Teresa had been newly married and preoccupied. As he commented to Hobhouse, 'They always wait a year.'

Now Byron had transferred his allegiance from the bluestocking Albrizzi to the more easygoing and, to Byron, more congenial gatherings of her rival, Countess Marina Querini Benzoni. A spirited and generous woman, in her youth at the time of the French occupation of Venice, she had danced around the Tree of Liberty in St Mark's Square with the poet Ugo Foscolo, dressed in a revealing Grecian tunic. Out in her gondola the Countess had developed the Venetian knack of keeping a slab of polenta warm between her breasts in case she felt a sudden pang of hunger. As this slightly smouldering apparition passed, the gondoliers cried out, '*el fumeto!*' It was she who inspired the lilting love song 'La biondina in gondoleta'. At a *conversazione* at the Palazzo Benzoni Byron and Teresa Guiccioli met again.

Teresa outlived Byron by almost fifty years and her memories, glamorised by distance, retained a fervent impression of their meeting. It was nearly midnight. Byron was sitting on the sofa in the salon with Alexander Scott when the door opened and the young Countess entered with her much older husband, Count Alessandro Guiccioli, who despite the hour had persuaded her to come on with him from the theatre. She was tired and still emotionally drained, having given birth in November to a son who had died four days later. But 'as she entered the drawing room her eyes met those of the young lord, seated opposite the entrance door – and the effect of that meeting sealed the destiny of their hearts'.

Byron too was a reluctant recruit to the liaison he would later call 'a finisher'. When Countess Benzoni suggested introducing him he said to her, 'You know very well that I don't want new lady acquaintances; if they are ugly, because they are ugly – and if they are pretty, because they are pretty.' However, she insisted, Scott encouraged and Byron finally gave in. Countess Benzoni presented him to Teresa as an English peer and England's greatest poet, an accolade that apparently brought to Byron's lips one of what Coleridge called his 'gate of heaven' smiles.

What did Teresa look like? Her portraits show a young woman of great charm and demure self-confidence. In their early days Byron described her unoriginally as 'fair as Sunrise – and warm as Noon'. He was especially intrigued by her blondness, in contrast to so many of his swarthy Venetian lovers. The particular red-goldness of her hair reminded him of Scandinavian women more than English. He judged Teresa's bust as 'uncommonly good'. But not everyone who saw her was equally admiring. To a disappointed Englishman meeting her in Genoa 'her graces did not rank above mediocrity. They were youth, plumpness, and good-nature.' Leigh Hunt was still more caustic about 'Madame Guiccioli with her sleek tresses', viewing her as 'a kind of buxom parlour-boarder, composing herself artificially into dignity and elegance'. He perceived her as top-heavy: Teresa's head and bust were 'hardly sustained by limbs of sufficient length'.

The first assignation took place the day after Countess Benzoni's *conversazione*. She and Byron arranged to meet in the evening at Byron's casino in Santa Maria Zobenigo at the time Count Guiccioli usually took his rest. She was transported there in Byron's gondola. She wrote: 'I was strong enough to resist at that first encounter, but was so imprudent as to repeat it the next day, when my strength gave way – for B. was not a man to confine himself to sentiment.' The only source for this narrative is a little dubious, a so-called 'Confession' of Teresa to her husband. But Teresa's relatively easy acquiescence tallies with the memory of a later lover, Henry Fox: 'I was not prepared for the extreme facility of the conquest, which (such is the perverseness of one's nature) scarcely gave me pleasure . . . She is a woman of very strong passions.' Byron's own recollection was that the '*Essential* part of the business' occupied him and Teresa for '*four* continuous days'.

Teresa's role in sentimental biographies of Byron, and indeed in her own retelling of her story, is of an ultimate love who brought him peace and happiness, the woman he had searched for unavailingly till then. Tom Moore refers to Teresa Guiccioli as 'this last, and (with one signal exception) only *real* love of his whole life'. In mentioning the one signal exception Moore holds firm to the old Mary Chaworth legend, disregarding Augusta and omitting Byron's boys.

When Moore, carried away, writes of a 'final amour' with Teresa Guiccioli 'deep-rooted enough to endure to the close' of Byron's days, Hobhouse scrawled another of his disbelieving comments in the margins of Moore's *Life*: 'mistake – he told me quite the contrary'. Certainly, even in the weeks immediately following his meeting with Teresa, Byron was by no means single-minded. He had, for example, made an assignation with Angelina, a well-born young Venetian girl, which was interrupted when his foot slipped in getting into his gondola 'owing to the cursed slippery steps of their palaces'. Byron had tumbled into the Grand Canal, 'flounced like a Carp' and gone 'dripping like a Triton' to his sea-nymph. He could never break the habit of flirtation. All the same, with Teresa, he found an unaccustomed level of contentment, almost of domestic repose. There is a sense in which Moore's depiction of an enduring love between Byron and La Guiccioli is correct.

What held him to Teresa in his closest approximation to a happy marriage for the next four years? Byron thrived on difficulty and the problems in extracting Teresa from her husband provided him with challenges beside which his hair's-breadth exploits with drapers' and bakers' wives paled. Count Alessandro Guiccioli was a powerful and deeply equivocal figure. 'Sixty years old – and not pleasant' is how Byron described him in a letter to Augusta; the Count, actually in his late fifties, 'had had two wives already – & a little suspected of having poisoned the first'. Teresa's predecessor, Angelica Galliani, was a maid he had seduced who bore him six illegitimate children before he had managed to dispose of his first wife and marry her. Angelica had died in 1817.

The Count's public persona was as ruthless as his private one. His family had been rich landowners in Imola and Ravenna since the twelfth century. His pedigree was arguably more awesome than Byron's. The Guiccioli dynasty was politically high-powered and cynically manipulative. The Count, who had switched sides for and against Napoleon, was reputed to have been involved in at least two political assassinations. But the man of violent action was also a man of culture. Alessandro Guiccioli was a devotee of the theatre. The theatre at Ravenna was restored at his expense. He had been a friend of Alfieri's and had even acted in his plays. In many respects, as he confronted Count Guiccioli, Byron had met his match. The liaison with Teresa was conducted in an atmosphere of stealth and potential skulduggery. The lovers' go-between, Fanny Silvestrini, had for some time been a versatile employee in the Guiccioli household. She had acted as governess to the Count's children. In Venice she was Teresa's close companion, with whom Teresa ostensibly practised the French language. Fanny, herself the mistress of Lega Zambelli, the Count's steward, by whom she was to have two children, was sympathetic to her mistress's romance, providing alibis for their meetings and carrying letters between Byron and Teresa. Like Byron's hated Mrs Clermont, Fanny Silvestrini proved herself a devious ex-governess.

If treated circumspectly Byron was domestically pliable. William Fletcher made the comment that anyone could manage Byron except for Lady Byron. Over the years Teresa developed the management of Byron into a great skill. Teresa was no fool, 'although she looks so', said one of her ex-lovers. She had been well-educated at the Santa Chiara convent, where she had acquired the love of literature that Byron found endearing, and in common with all Italian girls of her class she had been trained to please. At the time she met Byron, Teresa was already displaying a certain native cunning. She had deceived her husband at least once, having had a brief affair in autumn 1818. Though she seems to have told Byron she was nineteen, the register in the Battistero di San Giovanni in Fonte in Ravenna reveals that she was twenty. Already, so young, she had falsified her age.

'Exigeante' was the word her lovers used about Teresa. She employed temperamental scenes as a method of control: whims, accusations, tantrums, followed by conciliatory sex. Byron was clear-headed about Teresa's faults, seeing her as 'a great Coquette – extremely vain – excessively affected – clever enough – without the smallest principle – with a good deal of imagination and some passion'. He was aware that she had carried him off partly out of vanity: he was after all the greatest trophy of the age.

But he valued Teresa for her fierce loyalty and her originality, seeing her as an 'odd' woman, appreciating the unusual directness he had first loved in Lady Caroline Lamb. He admired, while being very much embarrassed by, the tactlessness with which she answered back, in her Romagnola accent, on social occasions when she should have been discreet. She had horrified the guests at a *conversazione* at Countess Benzoni's by calling out 'Mio Byron' in ringing tones. Byron found that he could relax with her and laugh with her. He told Augusta, 'She has a good deal of *us* too – I mean that turn for ridicule like Aunt Sophy and you and I & all the B's.'

He began to sign his letters to Teresa, written in Italian, with the sign of the cross which had once been the sacred sign between him and his half-sister. 'Scrivimi nel più bel stile di Santa Chiara. Pessimo O +++++++': 'write to me in the finest style of Santa Chiara. Very naughty O.'

Ten days after the meeting between Byron and Teresa she left Venice with her husband for their home town of Ravenna. Anguished correspondence passed between the lovers, facilitated by the eager Fanny Silvestrini who assured her mistress, not entirely accurately, of Byron's continued faithfulness. On 1 June 1819 Byron himself set off to visit the Countess and her husband, alarmed by reports of Teresa's serious illness. She had already been pregnant when in Venice and had begun to miscarry while on the journey to Ravenna. Teresa suggested, with some reason, that the termination had been caused by their energetic sexual activity.

> 'River! that rollest by the antient walls
>   Where dwells the Lady of my Love, when she
> Walks by thy brink and there perchance recalls
>   A faint and fleeting memory of me,
> What if thy deep and ample stream should be
>   A mirror of my heart, where she may read
> A thousand thoughts I now betray to thee
>   Wild as thy wave and headlong as thy speed?'

Byron's stanzas 'To the Po' were written as he travelled along the same route south that Teresa had taken with the Count a few weeks earlier. He was making a journey into a remote area of eastern Italy, pursuing a dangerous relationship of which the consequences were unpredictable. There was a symbolism in the crossing of the Po.

He wrote some of his most 'lemancholy' letters as he journeyed on his way 'to cuckold a Papal Count in his own house'. It was scorchingly hot. He smoked in the dust of Padua, then was threatened with broiling 'like a Sausage' in Bologna. Wandering in the Ferrara cemetery, he came upon two epitaphs: 'Martini Luigi *Implora pace*' and 'Lucrezia Picini "Implora eterna quiete"'. They moved him deeply: 'it appears to me that these two and three words comprize and compress all that can be said on the subject – and then in Italian they are absolute Music – They contain doubt – hope – and humility.' He noticed the quantities of roses and rose petals scattered over the gravestones at Ferrara, pleased to recognise that the Italians, like the Greeks, strewed flowers on their tombs.

Arriving in Ravenna on 10 June, in the midst of Corpus Domini celebrations, Byron stopped at the Albergo Imperiale in the Via di Porta Sisi. He had an introduction to Count Giuseppe Alborghetti, Secretary-General to the Papal Legate governing Ravenna, and that evening joined Alborghetti in his box at the theatre. The theatre enthusiast Count Guiccioli was also present and made friendly overtures. Byron went to visit Teresa the next day at the Palazzo Guiccioli. She was still frail, coughing and spitting blood, but she rallied when she saw him. Teresa was nothing if not resilient.

Byron's two-month stay in Ravenna developed its own pattern. The Count was ostentatiously hospitable, taking Byron on drives around the town and countryside in 'a coach and *six* horses' as if he were Dick Whittington become Lord Mayor of London. The deceived husband is already one of Byron's comic characters. Teresa and her lover read Dante together. This was the convent girl who 'could almost repeat any part of the Divine Comedy'. It was at her suggestion that Byron began writing the poem *The Prophecy of Dante*, based on Dante's exile and death in Ravenna, dedicating it to her. As Teresa's health improved they went out riding in the pine forests that stretched from Ravenna to the sea. She was not the natural rider well-bred Englishwomen were, and Byron lamented to Augusta that Teresa was 'a bore in her rides – for she can't guide her horse – and he runs after mine – and tries to bite him – and then she begins screaming in a high hat and sky-blue habit – making a most absurd figure – and embarrassing me and both our grooms'.

As she strengthened, their sexual relations were resumed in, *faute de mieux*, the great salon of the Guiccioli palace during the Count's siesta. These assignations depended on a complex network of messengers and spies: a priest, a chambermaid, a young Negro page, and one of Teresa's ubiquitous female friends. The doors had no locks. The risks of discovery increased the excitement. He wrote to Teresa:

'*Think*, my love of *those* moments – delicious – dangerous – but – *happy*, in every sense – not only for the pleasure, more than ecstatic, that you gave me, but for the danger (to which you were exposed) that we fortunately escaped. The Hall! Those rooms! The open doors! The servants so curious and so near – Ferdinando – the visitors! how many obstacles! But all overcome – it has been the real triumph of Love.'

For Byron, there was an extra frisson in the expectation of the Count's favourite method of retaliation: 'a Stiletto' in his gizzard 'some fine afternoon'.

But eagerly as he entered into the suspense, he also felt himself at an unaccustomed disadvantage in Ravenna, uncertain of the Count's ambivalent responses, uncertain of Teresa who, as she recovered, showed signs of the resumption of her innate flirtatiousness. Byron too began flirting with her black-eyed best friend, a young married woman, Geltrude Vicari. Teresa detected them in thigh pinching and hand holding and Geltrude was despatched to Bologna by Byron's 'own dear precious *Amica* – who hates all flirting but her own'.

Byron's sequence of agitated letters of this period, written to the woman he claims to be his final passion, 'l'ultima mia Passione', are still in Ravenna, in the

Classense Library, and they are curiously touching documents which show Byron in a state of relative defencelessness. He had the hazards of an unfamiliar language to contend with: as he tells Teresa, 'I have to overcome the double difficulty of expressing an unbearable suffering in a language foreign to me.' His Italian, though brave, is ungrammatical and, writing in a foreign tongue, Byron loses his asperity, wallows in a world of unhappy lovers' clichés: 'I am writing to you in tears – and I am not a man who cries easily. When I cry my tears come from the heart, and are of blood.' This is not a Byron Lady Melbourne would have recognised.

Throughout the summer saga of plottings and unmaskings, botched arrangements, recriminations, panics, passionate forgiveness scenes, there is always a sense of Byron writing his own melodrama, always a prospect of some horrible fatality on the horizon. In the sultry city of Ravenna on the Italian coast, we see Byron more than ever in the grip of his superstitious conviction that he brought death and disaster to those in his vicinity: John Edleston, Augusta, his animals, his godchildren. And surely now Teresa? He wrote to Richard Hoppner in July: 'I greatly fear that the Guiccioli is going into a consumption – to which her constitution tends; – thus it is with every thing and every body for whom I feel anything like a real attachment – "War – death – or discord doth lay siege to them" – I never even could keep alive a dog that I liked or that liked me.' His attachment had always turned out to be a curse to creatures he loved. However a week later Byron reported to Alexander Scott: 'our amatory business goes on *well* and *daily* – not at all interrupted by extraneous matters or the threatened consumption.'

The affair had been attracting attention in the city. Ravenna, ostensibly ruled over by the Papacy, was effectively, like Venice, under Austrian control. The police spies were busy with their ploddingly inaccurate reports on the love-life of a man seen as a potentially dangerous political subversive. Ballads of the cuckolding of Count Guiccioli were sung in the Ravenna streets. Though the Count showed no signs of anger, this may have been the reason for his sudden decision, on 9 August, to travel north with Teresa to his palace in Bologna. Byron followed the next day, taking his own apartment in the eighteenth-century Palazzo Merendoni in Via Galliera but soon, at the invitation of the strangely accommodating Count, moving into rooms on the ground floor of the nearby Palazzo Savioli, where Teresa and her husband were now living.

It was not long after his arrival in Bologna that Byron went into convulsions at the theatre, towards the end of a performance of Alfieri's tragedy of incest *Mirra*, crying, sobbing, almost fainting. Teresa attributed the fit to his admiration of the powerful performance by Madame Pelzet, the Mrs Siddons of

Bologna. But it seems more likely to have been a reaction to a summer of considerable emotional strain.

The Count once again removed Teresa from her lover, taking her on an extended tour of his country estates at Molinella, on the south side of the Po between Bologna and Ferrara. Left in Bologna, Byron moped around the inner garden of the Palazzo Savioli, with its central fountain, and managed to gain entrance to Teresa's own apartments on the second floor where he amused himself looking through her books and inscribing messages in them. One of these, another relic of Byron's *ultima passione* in the Biblioteca Classense in Ravenna, was written in her copy of the Italian edition of Madame de Staël's *Corinne, or Italy*, the complex psychological novel about a young Scottish peer, Lord Nelvil, and his agonised love for Corinne, a beautiful female poet, the personification of Italy.

For Byron and Teresa, this was of course their story. Byron wrote to his Corinne: 'I have read this book in your garden; – my Love – you were absent – or I could not have read it – It is a favourite book of yours – and the writer was a friend of mine.' This time Byron wrote in English, so that no one else would understand his message. It bore an extra poignancy in that Madame de Staël had died in 1817. Though Byron felt she had often been wrong-headed, he acknowledged that she was 'almost always true' in her delineation of the heart.

During Byron's intense preoccupation with Teresa, Allegra in Venice had been half-forgotten. Passed from family to family she and the nurse Elise, by early 1819, were back living with the Hoppners. All the upheavals were making her more fractious. 'She was not by any means an amiable child', wrote Richard Hoppner, 'nor was Mrs Hoppner or I particularly fond of her.' They had taken her in as a duty, almost an extension of Hoppner's consular responsibilities. Isabelle Hoppner sent a letter of lament to Mary Shelley about Allegra's backwardness, her lack of animation: she was 'tranquille et sérieuse', like a little old woman. The Venice winter did not suit her: her feet were always like blocks of ice. The child was regularly wetting her bed.

The Hoppners suggested that she should be brought up in Switzerland, Isabelle Hoppner's country, where the climate was much healthier and education better. A wealthy English widow, Mrs Vavassour, perhaps a fan of Byron's, took a fancy to Allegra at the Hoppners' and offered to adopt her. Byron offhandedly rejected these ideas. By the middle of the summer, when Allegra was reported to be suffering from a violent cough, probably whooping cough, the Hoppners had made plans to leave Venice for Switzerland themselves. Byron was surprised to discover that Allegra's nurse Elise had now been given notice.

Mrs Hoppner informed him that they were leaving Allegra in the care of the wife of their servant Antonio, 'for whose good manners and honesty', she wrote reassuringly, 'I can vouch'. The child stayed for a while with Antonio's family where the four young Italian girls fussed over her. She was then transferred to the care of Mrs Martens, wife of the Danish Consul. Henry Dorville, Hoppner's vice-consul in Venice, was in nominal control of the abandoned child.

In August, in Teresa's absence, Byron sent for two-year-old Allegra to join him in Bologna. 'I wish to see my child – and have her with *me*,' he instructed Alexander Scott, who did his best to dissuade Byron from the scheme. Both he and Hoppner felt that Byron's liaison with La Guiccioli was unworthy of him: this was a peer of England making himself ridiculous. Nor did they trust the Count's intentions. Once the child was in Ravenna she would become a hostage for Byron's future conduct. If Allegra were put into a convent 'it would be no easy matter to get her out again'. Scott asked Byron if the Count had any male children, and whether he had already raised the question of a dowry. Sinister financial machinations were predicted. One of the fears underlying all these arguments was that, having extracted Allegra, Byron would not be returning to Venice again. They would miss his company and no doubt dreaded unravelling his complicated household affairs and his accumulated debts.

But Byron was adamant. Allegra was brought to Bologna in late August by Richard Edgecombe, the British consular clerk who was acting as Byron's Venice factotum. Edgecombe was soon to be accused of 'imputed peculation and irregular accounts'. His account books, later investigated at Byron's instigation by Lega Zambelli, Count Guiccioli's steward, revealed many discrepancies. In September Byron wrote to tell Augusta that Allegra was now with him, speaking nothing but Venetian and greeting her father in the morning, 'Bon *di* papa.' He reported that the child was 'very droll – and has a good deal of the Byron – can't articulate the letter *r* at all – frowns and pouts quite in our way – blue eyes – light hair growing *darker* daily – and a dimple in the chin – a scowl on the brow – white skin – sweet voice – and a particular liking of Music – and of her own way in everything'. Though Byron did not mention it, her mother Claire Clairmont was remarkably musical. The reunion with her father seems to have brought back some of Allegra's old vivacity.

The Count returned to Bologna. There was more trouble. Guiccioli, trading favours for his tacit acceptance of Byron's relations with his wife, had already asked Byron to procure for him the honorary post of British Vice-Consul at Ravenna: he wanted British protection in order to strengthen his precarious position with the Papal government. Byron obligingly wrote to his publisher to ask him to intervene through his 'many splendid Government Connections' to have Guiccioli made a Consul; alternatively, Murray could arrange for Byron to be made the British Consul at Ravenna 'that I may make him my Vice'.

Now Count Guiccioli started making new demands. He had lost a lawsuit in Brescia and asked Byron for money to help cover his liabilities. In one of Teresa's later accounts of this episode he asked for only a small sum of money, which Byron paid without demur. In another of Teresa's versions it was 'a very large sum of money' which Byron, warned by his own banker in Italy, refused Count Guiccioli. Whatever the truth, Guiccioli's request for money brought latent tensions out into the open. The Count turned upon Teresa. She reverted to illness, claiming a threatened prolapse of the womb, saying she must go to Venice to consult Byron's physician, Dr Aglietti, who had come to Ravenna to attend her earlier. The Count found an urgent reason for returning from Bologna to Ravenna. He left them to travel north together, Byron in his Napoleonic carriage, from which the green paint was now visibly flaking, Teresa with her maid and manservant in the lord mayoral coach-and-six.

On the way, there was an idyllic stop at Arqua in the Euganean hills. 'It was one of those Italian days – all serenity, sweetness, and splendour', as Teresa recollected in her most romantic vein. They climbed the hill to Petrarch's house, through pomegranate trees and vines heavy with grapes, 'wrapped in an atmosphere as caressing' as that of Dante's earthly paradise. The house at Arqua was something of a tourist shrine. They examined the worm-eaten chair in which Petrarch was reputed to have died, and Byron was entranced to see Petrarch's very cat, which had been embalmed and was displayed in a nook above a doorway with its own inscription. Byron had already written his name in the visitors' book on a visit to Arqua two years earlier, at the time he took the house at Este which he later lent the Shelleys. Now he could not resist reinscribing his name in the book in conjunction with Teresa's. 'She signed her name with feeling, then handed the pen to Lord Byron, who wrote his name beside it while uttering the wish that those two names might never be parted again.'

They spent that night at Padua, having been received by an innkeeper tearful with gratitude to Byron who, in one of his fits of generosity, had apparently rescued him from penury and set him up again in business. The innkeeper provided a banquet and night music which made Byron tearful too. But there was a growing sense of complication the nearer to Venice the travellers came. Next morning Byron received an unwelcome visitation from Countess Benzoni and her long-established *cavaliere servente* Count Giuseppe Rangone, who had arrived by chance at the same inn the night before.

'They had an embarrassed and comical look about them,' Byron told Teresa. 'They seemed to be wondering whether I deserved their blame or their protection.' The Countess Benzoni showed signs of great anxiety at the dramatic results of her own introduction of Byron to Teresa. It may partly have been jealousy: the gossip in Venice was that she too had had her eye on Byron; at sixty she was at the same dangerous age as Lady Melbourne. But her disapproval also stemmed from the fact that her own liaison with the Count Rangone, who was himself now seventy or so, had lasted thirty years, abiding by the *cavaliere servente* protocol. Lovers were tolerated, even encouraged, so long as they did not disrupt the domestic status quo. Countess Benzoni had the expertise to know that by extracting Teresa from her husband's household, and travelling through Italy with her, staying at the same hotels, Byron had embarked on a serious flouting of the rules. Meeting them unexpectedly put her in a quandary, unwilling as she was to be seen to countenance a liaison of which, according to Italian convention, she could not approve.

The challenge for the Countess could have been still greater. What she did not realise was that, while at Padua, Byron and Teresa had been on the brink of an elopement, tempted to escape further off together, to France and South America. Teresa was prime mover in this reckless scheme. Byron, older, more world-weary, ultimately self-defensive, had persuaded her to think again.

Leaving Padua, they stopped briefly at La Mira, where Byron was again leasing the Villa Foscarini. From there they took gondolas to Venice with the servants and the luggage. Byron returned to the Palazzo Mocenigo where he was reunited with the remnants of his ragamuffin crew. Count Guiccioli's steward, Lega Zambelli, had been instructed to prepare independent lodgings for Teresa in the Palazzo Malipiero. Antonio Lega Zambelli, a defrocked priest who, as the Archbishop of Ravenna complained, had abandoned his ecclesiastical robes, 'forgetting his priestly character entirely', would be gradually absorbed into Byron's own household as his Maestro di Casa, guarding his treasure, Byron liked to think, 'like the Dragon watching the golden fruit in the garden of the Hesperides'. Teresa rejected Palazzo Malipiero, telling her husband that Dr Aglietti strongly disapproved on his patient's behalf of 'the unsavoury inhalations' rising from the narrow canal on which the Malipiero palace was built. She was soon installed in an apartment in the more salubrious Palazzo Mocenigo, and she and Byron left for La Mira within the next few days.

In the country, at the Villa Foscarini, they were able to spend quiet days in one another's company, walking in the 'giardino all'inglese', Teresa listening while Byron read aloud. He was translating Pulci's *Morgante Maggiore* and writing the third canto of *Don Juan*. But there was an uneasiness in their tranquillity. Teresa's father, Count Ruggero Gamba Ghiselli, an upright Ravenna nobleman, showed growing signs of alarm at his daughter's indiscretion. He appears not to have registered the fact that she and Byron were already lovers but wrote to warn her of the dangers of exposing herself to public scrutiny in company with 'this most seductive young man'. More warnings came from Teresa's younger brother, Count Pietro Gamba, who passed on malicious stories he had heard at school in Rome. These focused on Byron's ill-treatment of his wife, said to have been kept incarcerated in his castle, in the mode of Dante's Pia de Tolomei in the *Purgatory*, daughter of a Siena nobleman whose husband had brought her to live in the Maremma and had either poisoned her or killed her by exposing her to lethal air. Byron now had to suffer cross-examination from Teresa on his problematic past.

He and Teresa, under pressure, had abandoned plans to travel on to Lake Como and the Alps. As in his affair with Lady Oxford, Byron's old restlessness was returning. Stranded at La Mira, where Teresa now had piles, he seems to have become conscious of the full indignity, and the potential monotony, of the *cavaliere servente* role. Unconscious of his unease, Fanny Silvestrini wrote to Teresa of La Mira as 'the enchanted abode of Armida'.

Byron's irritation at finding himself on the brink of a condition of dependence he had been resisting all his life is evident in the letters he was writing to Hobhouse in the autumn of 1819. He felt bitterly that a self-respecting man, still less an English peer, 'should not consume his life at the side and on the bosom – of a woman – and a stranger', however great the recompense. And he was evolving a possible escape route. He would emigrate, without Teresa, to America – not North America, where the inhabitants were 'a little too coarse' and the climate too cold, but South America, preferably Venezuela, where two years earlier Simón Bolívar had established a rebel government independent of Spain. Bolívar was Byron's latest hero. The revolutionary leader's style of benevolent dictatorship appealed to him. When asked who he thought the world's greatest man, Byron smiled and said he used to think it was Jackson the pugilist but had now decided it was Simón Bolívar.

He envisaged his new life in Venezuela as an active life, a man's life: 'Better be an unskilful planter – an awkward settler – better be a hunter – or anything than a flatterer of fiddlers – and a fan-carrier of a woman.' He could soon learn Spanish. He would take Allegra with him. If he could once sell Rochdale he could buy land and establish himself as a bona fide citizen, under the new Patriotic Government. 'Advantageous offers' were being made to prospective settlers in Venezuela.

Hobhouse poured scorn on the project, dismissing it to Murray as 'this mad scheme . . . our poet is too good for a planter – too good to sit down before a fire made of mare's legs; to a dinner of beef without salt and bread'. He would be prone to plague and Yellow Jack fever and starvation, deprived of tooth-brushes, corn-rubbers and the *Quarterly Review*: 'in short, plenty of all he abominates, and nothing of all he loves'. No doubt Hobhouse was right. But Byron's enduring dream of South America was only finally abandoned in 1823, when he sailed for Greece.

The first two cantos of *Don Juan* were published on 15 July 1819, without the name of the author or the publisher, though as usual the poem's authorship was well known. John Murray wrote to Byron from the safe haven of his house on Wimbledon Common: '*La Sort est jetté* – Don Juan was published yesterday, and having fired the Bomb – here I am out of the way of the explosion.' The mood throughout the country was nervy and unsettled. A month later at least ten demonstrators for reform of the franchise were killed and hundreds injured in the so-called 'Peterloo massacre' on St Peter's Field in Manchester when local magistrates ordered the cavalry of the Manchester yeomanry to arrest Henry Hunt, the popular radical orator. It was not a propitious moment to be publishing a controversial poem by an already scandal-ridden author who unequivocally called a pox a pox.

In fact the sales of *Don Juan* were perfectly respectable: by 3 September only 300 copies remained of the original quarto edition of 1,500. In explaining why sales were not even better, Murray pointed out that the poem had been published too late in the season to make the most of its potential. But whatever gloss he put on it *Don Juan* fell far short of Byron's earlier commercial success.

One problem was the poem's sexual effrontery. This lost him much of the faithful female readership which, often to Byron's chagrin, had been a mainstay of his popularity. In the course of the outcry which followed publication of the poem John Murray complained: 'its sale would have been universal if some 20 stanzas had been altered & wch by preventing the book from being shown at a Lady's work table – have cut up my Sale.' In respectable households, particu-larly those with unmarried daughters, *Don Juan* was regarded as subversive, 'a sealed book for virgins under parental care', read if read at all by adults cam-ouflaged between plain covers. Even the celebrated courtesan Harriette Wilson wrote to Byron from Paris, where she had found a copy in Galignani's book-shop, upbraiding him for lewdness: 'Dear *Adorable* Lord Byron, *don't* make a mere *coarse* old libertine of yourself.'

It was not just a matter of sexually risqué scenes and taboo language. The basis of the scandal attaching to *Don Juan* then and later was the way Byron depicted women as taking the sexual initiative. 'That women did not like it he was not surprised; he knew they could not bear it because it *took off the veil*; it showed that all their d—d sentiment was only an excuse to cover passions of grosser nature.' Byron analysed women's responses to *Don Juan* as part of a conspiracy, a grand hypocrisy, which denied that a woman could be sexually demanding, still less sexually predatory. Yet from his own experience, right back to his Scottish nurse May Gray, he knew this to be untrue.

Byron was confident that he had never written better. He was as sure of this, he said, 'as the Archbishop of Grenada'. He responded to what he saw as puny criticisms with a flood of invective, the extraordinary imaginative vigour that rose to the surface when he was opposed. To charges that the style of *Don Juan* was uneven, lurching uneasily from grave to crudely comic, Byron answered his critic Francis Palgrave with an elaborate 'scorching and drenching' questionnaire:

'Did he never play at Cricket or walk a mile in hot weather – did he never spill a dish of tea over his testicles in handing the cup to his charmer to the great shame of his nankeen breeches? – did he never swim in the sea at Noonday with the Sun in his eyes and on his head – which all the foam of the ocean could not cool? did he never draw his foot out of a tub of too hot water damning his eyes & his valet's? did he never inject for a Gonorrhea? – or make water through an ulcerated Urethra? was he ever in a Turkish bath – that marble paradise of sherbet and sodomy? – was he ever in a cauldron of boiling oil like St John . . .'

A man who could not be scorched, then drenched, and who saw no point in such extremes of experience, was missing out on life.

Byron's view of poetry was that it was necessary to have known strong passions in order to depict them. This was behind his condemnation of John Keats' writing as 'a sort of mental masturbation – he is always f—gg—g his *Imagination*'. Byron's spirited defence of *Don Juan* sprang from his view of himself as a man of prodigious experience of the world. He teasingly urged Kinnaird to admit that his poem rated as 'the sublime of *that there* sort of writing – it may be bawdy – but is it not English? – it may be profligate? – but is it not *life*, is it not *the thing*? – Could any man have written it – who has not lived in the world? – and tooled in a post-chaise? in a hackney coach? in a Gondola? against a wall? in a court carriage? in a vis a vis? – on a table or under it?' But there was an anxiety behind the bravado. Byron confessed that the outcry against *Don Juan* had frightened him. He was aware that nowadays in England '*Cant* is so much stronger than *Cunt*'.

The attack that affected him most strongly, returning him to the state of paranoia that had followed the separation crisis, was the review published in *Blackwood's Edinburgh Magazine* for August 1819. In this review, apparently written on the instructions of the editor William Blackwood, probably either by John Wilson, the author identified by Byron, or by John Gibson Lockhart, *Don Juan* was condemned as a 'filthy and impious poem' in which the elaborate satire on his wife revealed its author as 'an unrepenting, unsoftened, smiling, sarcastic, joyous sinner'. The reviewer soon departed from any pretence at literary criticism to embark on a diatribe of personal abuse. Byron retaliated in December in a letter to John Murray: 'Your Blackwood accuses me of treating women harshly – it may be so – but I have been their martyr – My whole life has been sacrificed *to* them & *by* them.'

He brooded on the article depicting him so mercilessly as 'one of the most remarkable men' to whom England 'had had the honour and the disgrace of giving birth'. A few months later, in a long open letter, 'Some Observations upon an Article in Blackwood's Magazine', Byron launched into a counter-attack, defending himself with all the power of invective and verbal ingenuity at his command to annihilate his enemies. It is here Byron provides his most profound and bleak analysis of the events surrounding his exile from England in 1816, reliving the circumstances of his 'Ostracism', rerunning the whispered accusations of sodomy and incest, recreating the opprobrium that pursued him around Europe, with a mixture of self-justification and self-pity, social censure and personal grief, that gives a premonition of Oscar Wilde's *De Profundis*.

Byron sent 'Some Observations' to John Murray, intending him to publish it. Murray responded nervously: 'The letter on Blackwood's Magazine is very curious & interesting – & must make a noise – I am sorry however that you touch upon the idle talk about Incest – and it is not well to let the world know – as a quoteable thing – your having had both those Ladies.' John Murray believed the worst of Southey's 'League of Incest' rumours about the goings-on at the Villa Diodati. 'Some Observations' remained unpublished at the time of Byron's death.

The article in *Blackwood's Magazine* turned Byron irrevocably against England and marked another phase in his quarrels with John Murray who was still, apart from Kinnaird, Byron's main contact in London. Murray's constant reminders of the limits of middle-class morality made him seem almost a spokesman for the aspects of his country that Byron most despised. The new contretemps with England encouraged his emotional identification with Italy. The review had described Venice as 'the lurking place' of Byron's 'selfish and polluted exile'. 'By my troth these be bitter words!' expostulated Byron:

'How far the capital city of a Government which survived the vicissitudes of thirteen hundred years, and might still have existed but for the treachery of Buonaparte and the iniquity of his imitators, – a City which was the Emporium of Europe when London and Edinburgh were dens of barbarians – may be termed a "lurking place" I leave to those who have seen – or heard of Venice to decide.'

Byron was at La Mira with Teresa when Tom Moore arrived on a visit in early October 1819. He reached the Villa Foscarini at two in the afternoon to find that Byron, only just up, was in his bath. But he soon appeared, greeting Moore delightedly with 'the frank outbreak of cordiality and gaiety' that had always endeared Byron to his close male friends. He and Moore had not seen each other for five years. Byron's instant impression was that Moore looked 'quite fresh and poetical'. Though nine years older than Byron he seemed younger: Byron attributed this to a contented marriage and the uneventfulness of English country life.

Moore, like the Hansons, found Byron greatly changed, much fatter in figure and puffier in face. He had lost 'some of that refined and spiritualized look' of the era of *Childe Harold* and his hair was now quite grey: Moore was disconcerted by the whiskers he was growing, by the long hair straggling down over his collar. He disliked also the rather outré style of dress Byron had taken to: gold chains worn high and tight around his neck, one of them descending to his waistcoat pocket, frogged greatcoat and 'a curious foreign cap', presumably the peaked foraging cap that Byron is seen wearing in several later portraits in Italy and Greece. Byron was still dandified but no longer in the English style. Moore detected what to him were suspect signs of European decadence.

Byron took his late breakfast standing: one or two raw eggs, a cup of tea with no milk or sugar, a dry biscuit – he was still following his abstemious diet at La Mira. Before he hurried Tom Moore away to Venice, Byron introduced him to Teresa. In his later *Life* of Byron, Moore refers back unctuously to the impression of 'intelligence and amiableness' the Countess gave him. But in his journal for that day he makes the comment that it would have been safer for Byron 'to stick to his Fornarinas'.

He and Byron crossed the lagoon to Venice in the evening, just as the sun was setting. Moore, with his nose for fame, was impressed to be approaching the city of the Bridge of Sighs with the poet 'who had lately given a new life to its glories'. Byron, in a mood of high merriment, was more intent on reminiscing of their bad mad days in London: their 'joint adventures with the Bores and Blues', their 'joyous nights together' at Watier's and Kinnaird's. He was now looking back on the wild exploits of his youth with something of an old man's sentimentality.

For these few brief days in Venice, Byron clutched at the pleasures of his past relationship with Moore: their verbal rapport, their poet's eye for human detail, the shared delight in wit and whimsy that had been, for Hobhouse, such a source of jealousy. At one time Tom Moore had ordered a twin coat in green like Byron's. They were brothers united in amusement at the world. Though Moore would have preferred the Hôtel de la Grande-Bretagne, Byron persuaded him to use his own empty apartments at the Palazzo Mocenigo. On Moore's first evening in Venice they stood out on the Mocenigo balcony above the Grand Canal watching two gentlemen, evidently English, being rowed past in their gondola. As Moore described the scene, 'observing them to look our way, Lord Byron, putting his arms a-kimbo, said with a sort of comic swagger, "Ah, if you, John Bulls, knew who we two fellows are, now standing up here, I think you *would* stare!"' This was something Byron had been missing: automatic complicity in his jokes.

In the daytime Moore was guided round the sights of Venice by Alexander Scott, both of them indulging in a little disloyal dismantling of the legend of Lord Byron as promulgated in his letters. For example, Moore noted in his journal: 'The Angelina (of whom B. wrote such a romantic story to Murray – the daughter of a nobleman, to whom he said he climbed up a high balcony every night) is an ugly ill-made girl & the balcony is a portal window at the side of the hall-door.' Each evening Byron came over from La Mira and they dined at Palazzo Mocenigo, eating food brought in from a local trattoria, or went out to a restaurant. They talked away and got pleasantly drunk.

On Moore's final evening in Venice Byron read him as much as he had then written of the third canto of *Don Juan*. Determined to make a night of it, and having been given permission by Teresa, they dined at the Pellegrino with Scott, went on to the opera and then, at twelve o'clock, arrived in a 'sort of public house' in St Mark's Square to drink hot punch. At two in the morning Byron took Moore and Scott home in his gondola by moonlight, instructing the gondoliers to travel slowly so that Moore could appreciate Venice at its stillest and its grandest, with the palaces reflected in the water. Byron handed Moore a white leather bag containing what he called 'My Life and Adventures' when they said a last goodbye at La Mira the next day.

Byron had been considering the writing of his memoirs since he first arrived in Italy. In April 1817, just before he left for Rome, he had told John Murray temptingly: 'I won't be posthumous yet if I can help it – notwithstanding – only think

– what a "Life & adventures" – when I am in full scandal – would be worth.' He was evidently working on an 'autobiographical Essay' through the following summer at Palazzo Mocenigo, reporting in late August that he had completed more than forty sheets of 'very large long paper'. When he gave it to Tom Moore the manuscript had grown to seventy-eight folio sheets.

There had been a precedent for Byron's consignment of his memoirs to Tom Moore. He had already given Moore the journal he had kept in London in the winter of 1813–14, not for publication but as a mark of friendship and token of respect. How did this new manuscript differ from the journal? It was clearly more of a consecutive narrative than a sequence of day-to-day reflections; Byron calls it a '*Memoranda* – and not *Confessions*'. He admitted to some frustration with it: 'I have left out all my *loves* (except in a general way) and many other of the most important things – (because I must not compromise other people).' This threatened to make it a little like Shakespeare's play of Hamlet without the Prince.

Reading between the lines, it is clear that Byron's self-censorship extended to his loves for boys. But he maintained that the manuscript contained 'a detailed account' of his marriage and its consequences. Indeed this appears to have been its *raison d'être*, part of the process of self-justification Byron now had in train. It was written for eventual publication, but not until after his own death. He told Tom Moore that he was free to circulate it amongst any of his friends whom Moore 'considered worthy of it'. Later in the month he wrote to Murray giving him permission to read the memoirs when they arrived in England and to show them to anyone he liked. Murray always denied that he had read the memoirs. Considering his sharp publisher's instincts, it is difficult to believe that he did not.

Byron expressed the hope too that Lady Byron would read the memoir, so that she could check it for accuracy, marking 'anything mistaken or misstated'. He was still in intermittent correspondence with his wife, usually on the subject of Ada. On 31 December 1819, anniversary of the date on which, as he reminded her, he was on his way to their 'funeral marriage', he wrote to offer her a preview of the manuscript. 'You will find nothing to flatter you – nothing to lead you to the most remote supposition that we could ever have been – or be happy together.' When Lady Byron rejected the offer he could not have been surprised. The whole of Byron's memoir project – its limited circulation, its posthumous publication – already had the elements of a surreal joke.

In late autumn Byron had returned to the Palazzo Mocenigo from La Mira with the adoring and possessive Teresa, resigned to his new life of 'the strictest adultery'. In a letter to Hoppner, with a little shudder of apprehension, he had raised the question of how married people passed their evenings. Back in Venice he succumbed to a bout of tertian fever, caught after getting drenched when out in the countryside on horseback. He tossed and turned, disturbed by nightmares about Lady Byron's mother. One night he surfaced to find Fletcher sobbing on one side of the bed, 'la Contessa G' weeping on the other, like mourning angels in an Italian cemetery.

Byron's recovery was not accelerated by Count Guiccioli's arrival at the palazzo with one of his sons. Count Gamba had been recalling Guiccioli to his duty, entreating his elderly son-in-law to save his daughter's honour. Temporary residence in Byron's palace was seen as the best way to deflect Venetian gossip. The devious Guiccioli had now decided to confront the situation and arrived with a lengthy code of future conduct for his wife. Over this they 'quarrelled *violently*' and, according to Byron, the Count then delivered the ultimatum, '*him* – or *me*'. She of course chose Byron. But Byron persuaded her to go back to Ravenna with the Count. He felt gratified to have done his duty. But with Teresa's peremptory departure, he told Kinnaird, Italy had suddenly 'become sad' to him. For the first time since his exile he was overcome by a sense of isolation.

Byron now made impetuous plans to leave himself. He would take Allegra and return to England after all, probably as a first stage towards Venezuela. He gave instructions for the closing down of the Palazzo Mocenigo, the dispersal of 'Chairs – tables – dog – monkeys – and fox – old woman &c.', the selling of his water-posts and gondola. He arranged to pay some, though by no means all, his bills. But his departure was delayed by the multiple dramas and excuses that attended all Byron's plans for a change of domicile. He had another attack of tertian fever. His little Allegrina fell seriously ill with *doppia terzana*, an extreme form of malaria. Eventually, as witnessed by Fanny Silvestrini:

'He was ready dressed for the journey, his gloves and cap on, and even his little cane in his hand. Nothing was now waited for but his coming downstairs – his boxes being already on board the gondola. At this moment, my Lord, by way of pretext, declares that if it would strike one o'clock before every thing was in order (his arms being the only thing not yet quite ready), he would not go that day. The hour strikes and he remains!'

Byron was superstitious but not quite so superstitious. His final decision to cancel the journey and return to Ravenna was the result of news that Teresa was ill again, so seriously ill that her husband and her father had agreed that Byron should be summoned to her bedside. Byron wrote to

Teresa with an edge of irony: 'La Fanni ti avrà detta colla sua *solita sublimatà* – che l'Amor ha vinto.' 'Fanny will have told you, with her *usual sublimity*, that Love has won.'

In the last weeks before he left Venice Byron received another visitor from the past, his old Trinity confederate William Bankes who had since made his name as an explorer. Byron now admired him as 'Bankes the Nubian Discoverer'. Of all Byron's contemporaries it was probably Bankes's exploits which he would have most liked to emulate. Bankes had travelled widely in Egypt, sailing up the Nile. At Giza he had fainted in the sarcophagus chamber of the Great Pyramid while exploring the interior by torchlight. Bankes, like Byron, was accustomed to living off his nerves. On the sacred island of Philae in the Nile he had made a first attempt to remove and transport home to England a great granite obelisk of the fourteenth century B C, an ambition he eventually achieved. He had made further explorations in Syria and Palestine. Bankes was said to have been the first Englishman to visit the holy city of Mecca, disguising himself as a half-witted beggar. Byron was bowled over by his stamina and flair.

As an explorer Byron put his old friend Bankes on a level with von Humboldt. He was not just an adventurer but a dedicated recorder, taking meticulous notes in the Egyptian chamber-tombs, making thousands of accurate drawings of monuments and temples, copying hieroglyphics and ancient wall-paintings. 'Bankes *has* done *miracles* of research and enterprise,' wrote Byron to John Murray. As he travelled, Bankes amassed paintings, carvings and antiquities, the basis of the collection now at Kingston Lacy: he was also a scholar and a considerable connoisseur. When Byron compared his own career to that of Bankes he found himself distinctly wanting: 'It is now seven years since you and I met; – which time you have employed better for others & more honourably for yourself than I have done.'

Bankes arrived in Venice en route home from Egypt. He had just emerged from quarantine in Trieste. In Byron's grand and gloomy palace on the Grand Canal they had an extended reunion, discussing the strange turns in events that had transformed their old Cambridge contemporaries into Lords of the Treasury, Lords of the Admiralty, reformers and orators, going through the roll-call of the recently deceased: Sheridan and Lady Melbourne and 'Monk' Lewis who had died of yellow fever after what proved the ultimate visit to his slave plantations in Jamaica. He had died calmly, after asking his servant to turn his hat over to make a table on which he wrote his will.

As 1819 ended these two gossipy, erudite and sodomitical Englishmen made the voyage back into their shared history. They were among the most talented of their generation: Bankes the prodigious traveller and archaeologist, Byron the foremost poet of the age. Both were exiles and wanderers, washed up temporarily in that painful, beautiful city of decay. For Byron Venice had become an 'empty Oyster-Shell'. It would be the disgraced Bankes's eventual place of death.

23

Ravenna

1820–1821

'To be the first man – not the Dictator – not the Sylla, but the Washington or the Aristides – the leader in talent and truth – is next to the Divinity! Franklin, Penn, and next to those, either Brutus or Cassius – even Mirabeau – or St Just.'

Right back into his childhood Byron had respected men of action and political imperatives. He felt the intoxication of the fight for the just cause. But in winter 1813, when he wrote those words in London, at the height of his literary celebrity, he did not see himself as a political activist: 'I shall never be any thing, or rather always be nothing. The most I can hope is, that some will say, "He might, perhaps, if he would".'

The experience of exile altered him. His resentment at what he saw as the injustices against him sharpened his moral outrage against cruelty in general. The casual dissoluteness of his Venice years propelled him towards activity and purposefulness, almost as an act of expiation, undertaken as an antidote to his role as *cavaliere servente*. Perhaps there was desperation in the eagerness with which he took to the insurgent politics of Ravenna: a culminating episode in Byron's long-running drama of the death wish. He was always conscious of not having much time left.

The Napoleonic regime in the Romagna had ended only five years before Byron's arrival in the city. After the end of the Napoleonic wars control of Italy rested with three authorities: the Pope and the Catholic church; the Austrians under Metternich; and King Ferdinand of Naples whose territory included both Naples and Sicily. The Papal Legate who, in theory, governed Ravenna was subservient to the Austrians. But there were already signs of the revolution in Naples which broke out in the summer of 1820, and the local resistance movement in the Romagna had hopes of breaking free from the Austrian regime.

In Ravenna, Byron took to the liberation of Italy as if it was a cause ready waiting to embrace him: 'It is a grand object,' he wrote in his journal, 'the very *poetry* of politics. Only think – a free Italy!!!' From now on, although he still wrote magnificently, poetry became subordinated to politics as Byron threw himself into the fight for freedom with childlike zest and the convert's solemnity. He spent close on two years in Ravenna, embarking on a new phase of serious political involvement that only ended at Missolonghi in 1824.

On Christmas Eve 1819 Byron arrived in Ravenna from Venice claiming to feel like a Triton coming ashore. On the way, at Bologna, he had had his hair cut, sending 'all the *long hair*', to which Augusta had objected in the drawing made by Harlow, back to her in England. He went back temporarily to the distinctly unimperial Hotel Imperiale. The snow was a foot deep. The Carnival would begin in mid-January. Meanwhile there was theatre and opera: Rossini's *Barber of Seville*. Byron was welcomed as if he had never been away, invited to attend a reception for two or three hundred people given by the Marquis Cavalli, Teresa Guiccioli's uncle, where he was impressed by the high proportion of youth, beauty and diamonds among the women. Byron found a freshness in the women of Ravenna that had gone from the Venetians long ago. He was accepted automatically as Teresa's *cavaliere servente*, a fate he joked about to Hoppner: 'I am drilling very hard to learn how to double a Shawl, and should succeed to admiration – if I did not always double it the wrong side out.'

Carnival in Ravenna was less boisterous than in Venice but just as entertaining. Allegra was taken under Teresa's wing to join the cavalcade through the Corso in Count Guiccioli's coach-and-six. William Bankes arrived too, at Byron's pressing invitation: 'Tita's heart yearns for you, and mayhap for your broad silver pieces; and your playfellow, the monkey, is alone and inconsolable.' Is the implication that Tita was for sale? Bankes and Byron went masquerading, two buffooning Englishmen, one tall and sinewy with travelling, the other shorter, flabbier, running a little to seed.

Byron ordered carnival masks for himself and for Teresa from Giovanni Ghinaglia, a Ravenna mask-maker who delivered Byron's mask in conditions of 'the utmost secrecy', as he was later to attest. He was paid a louis d'or in the presence of Lega Zambelli, now Byron's official 'Secretario' and paymaster. The wax mask, according to its maker, 'shows the face of a very serious and thoughtful man between forty-five and fifty years of age'. Originally it had realistic hair and a thick beard. This macabre reminder of how much one of Europe's most instantly recognisable men delighted in his subterfuges and disguises is now in the collection of the Keats–Shelley House in Rome.

The tenor of Ravenna life appealed to Byron greatly. He approved of a place that did not disband the Carnival just because the ruling Cardinal had died. For Byron, the capital of Romagna had an elegant small-town quality, a social coherence not unlike the Nottingham of his childhood. He discovered an educated and liberal outlook amongst the upper classes, whilst the Romagnola peasantry, he claimed, were 'the best people in the world'. He saw it as a city in a time warp, where the citizens preserved the old Italian manners: 'it is out of the way of travellers and armies – and thus they have retained more of their originality. They make love a good deal – and assassinate a little,' he informed Lady Byron in another of his curiously amiable, discursive letters. She may or may not have been impressed.

Certainly, the few English visitors who did arrive there were conscious of Ravenna's outlandishness. Sir Humphry Davy, the chemical scientist, passing through Ravenna on one of his many visits to Vesuvius, noted 'the *primitive Italian* character of the peoples'. Shelley found it 'a miserable place: the people are barbarous & wild, & their language the most infernal patois you can imagine'. For Byron this foreignness became a virtue, a badge of his one-upmanship: he was proud of living 'among the natives' in a part of Italy where no Englishman had resided before. When a young Italian count maintained that in Ravenna society no one would take Byron for an Englishman because 'his manners were so different', Byron took this as a tremendous compliment.

As always when he travelled, literary associations engulfed Byron. Ravenna was 'poetical ground'. Dante's monument and tomb, close to Byron's Hotel Imperiale, is itself memorialised in Canto IV of *Don Juan*:

> 'I pass each day where Dante's bones are laid:
>   A little cupola, more neat than solemn,
> Protects his dust.'

When Byron was in the pine forest east of the city he was reminded endlessly of Boccaccio's *Decameron* and Dryden's English version of Boccaccio's love story, 'Theodore and Honoria', set in Ravenna:

> 'Sweet hour of twilight! – in the solitude
>   Of the pine forest, and the silent shore
> Which bounds Ravenna's immemorial wood,
>   Rooted where once the Adrian wave flow'd o'er,
> To where the last Cesarean fortress stood,
>   Evergreen forest! which Boccaccio's lore
> And Dryden's lay made haunted ground to me,
> How have I loved the twilight hour and thee!'

Ravenna was his favourite of all Italian cities, the place where he said he could have settled contentedly had other events not intervened. As with Venice, Byron's presence there has made its contribution to the image of the city, providing a focus for the later development of its tourist trade. There is now, of course, a Hotel Byron in Ravenna.

On 29 January 1820, a week after Byron's thirty-second birthday, King George III died after many years of incapacity. Hobhouse had expected him to laugh at the news, but both Byron and Fletcher were affected by it: 'one can't help being sorry,' Byron wrote to Murray, 'though blindness – and age and insanity are supposed to be drawbacks – on human felicity – but I am not at all sure that the latter at least – might not render him happier than any of his subjects.'

Byron, as a peer, had the right to attend the coronation of George IV, but he was not inclined to return to England. He wanted to avoid a ceremonial appearance with Lady Byron; 'I shall let *"dearest Duck"* waddle alone at the Coronation,' he told Hobhouse. Nor was he in the mood for confronting his enemies in England: 'How could I stand the sight of certain persons – colleagues even, whom I now know to have contributed to spreading abominable lies – odious slanders against me – without demanding satisfaction from them?' 'Certain persons' included Henry Brougham and Robert Southey whose libellous attacks could not be overlooked. 'The mere word London made the Countess shudder,' Teresa admitted in her life of Byron. She was clearly applying pressure to keep him at her side.

In any case the scene in London had changed greatly in what was now almost four years since Byron's departure. He suspected he would find it as unfamiliar as Peking. Political allegiances had shifted, even amongst his closest friends. To Byron's disapproval, since he had been in Italy, the Liberal Whig Hobhouse had 'foamed into a reformer'. Though Byron himself had always, as he claimed, been 'a friend to and a Voter for reform' he distrusted the reformers with whom Hobhouse was connected in the public mind, populist radicals such as William Cobbett and Henry 'Orator' Hunt. Byron had no sympathy with the democratic or the demagogic. 'If we must have a tyrant – let him at least be a gentleman who has been bred to the business, and let us fall by the axe and not by the butcher's cleaver.' He believed in leadership from above.

In early 1820 Hobhouse was in prison. An inflammatory pamphlet he had written on behalf of the Radicals, in defiance of the Whigs, was voted a breach of parliamentary privilege and he was committed to Newgate Gaol. Hobhouse's imprisonment led Byron to compose a gratuitously cruel little ballad to the tune of 'Where hae ye been a'day, My boy Tammy O?'

'How came you in Hob's pound to cool
My boy Hobbie O?
Because I bade the people pull
The House into the Lobby O.'

The lines were included in a letter to John Murray who allowed the poem to be circulated in London. A garbled version appeared in the *Morning Post*. Even in his diary Hobhouse could hardly bring himself to write down his true feelings at such a betrayal by his friend: 'to give way to such a mere pruriency & itch of writing against one who has stood by him in all his battles & never refused a single friendly office – is a melancholy proof of want of feeling & I fear of principle.' Hobhouse now realised that even he was not immune to the creative ruthlessness with which Byron pursued his literary targets oblivious of the hurt he would be causing. Though the quarrel was patched up when Byron more or less apologised, their friendship would never be quite the same again.

There was another absence that may well have contributed to Byron's reluctance to return to England for King George IV's coronation. Early in January, Scrope Davies had fled to the continent to escape his gambling debts. He had never recovered from a disastrous phase in 1815–16 when he had lost around £17,000 playing mainly hazard in the London gaming clubs. By 1820 he was down to his last £130, finally as Byron put it 'dished, diddled, and done up'. Elegant, laconic, undemanding, loyal Scrope: Byron saw his loss as irreparable and, in a sorrowful letter sent to Hobhouse in Newgate, linked Scrope Davies to a long line of now departed friends and heroes: 'Brummell – at *Calais* – Scrope at Bruges – Buonaparte at St Helena – you in – your new apartments – and I at Ravenna – only think so many great men!'

But perhaps most of all Byron's unwillingness to travel simply shows a return of his habitual indolence as Teresa's charms and smiles were reasserted and Byron was drawn more closely into the rituals of the city's inner life. On 25 February they had been gathering violets by the roadside. Ravenna was becoming difficult to leave.

The tittle-tattlers had caught up with Byron at his new location. 'I hear Lord Byron is at Ravenna, deeply in love with the fairest and wealthiest sposa in the place. Is it so?' wrote Augustus Foster from Copenhagen to his mother Elizabeth, Duchess of Devonshire. 'Bold' Webster addressed Byron with the jovial question: 'How is the young Countess G. at Ravenna? If ye sex were admitted into ye church I should not despair of seeing you with a Cardinal's hat.'

But however fantastical the visions of the gossips, the reality of the situation was still stranger. Within his first few months back in Ravenna, Byron had moved out of the Hotel Imperiale and into the Palazzo Guiccioli where he leased the second floor, the *piano nobile*, from Count Guiccioli who occupied the lower apartments with his wife. What were the Count's motives in allowing such proximity? Byron still found Guiccioli's complicity mysterious. One reason for it was probably financial. The Count had been pressing Byron for further loans while he and Teresa were at La Mira in the autumn. Perhaps he was still hopeful. As it was, the rent for the apartment was offset against the total of the Count's previous debt.

The Count had many commitments, social, cultural, political. There was an element of convenience in having Teresa's accredited *cavaliere servente* near at hand, available to escort her to the theatre and to parties. He liked and admired Byron: at one revealing moment he admitted to imagining that Byron was more interested in him than in his wife. The Count was an inherently devious and sexually complicated man and there are signs that he took a sadistic pleasure in the *ménage à trois* of himself, Byron and his wife.

The Count's continuing demands on his wife caused Byron anguish. He tormented himself by imagining Guiccioli's 'dotardly caresses': 'how to make him forget to come to you,' he wrote. Sometimes he was driven to reproaching her directly for leading the Count on: 'this evening when you thought I was reading the manuscript that A[lessandro] put into my hands, I observed, by the fire certain things that do not suit me. You will know well enough what I mean, without my saying any more.' The Count's ongoing affair with yet another of his maidservants, also called Teresa, turned the Ravenna *ménage à trois* into an implausible *ménage à quatre*.

Byron moved his furniture from Bologna and from Venice into the Count's palazzo. The bills of lading relating to the shipment of Byron's possessions from Venice were discovered in a sort-out of the British Foreign Office archives in 1932. The list has the transitory, random quality of a household permanently on the move. The shipment included chairs, a sofa, four mattresses, two small wooden dog kennels, four boxes of books, a bath tub, four commodes packed in matting, and a small bed described as being that of a 'putello', Venetian dialect for child.

The first few months in the palazzo were relatively tranquil as Byron settled in with Allegra, the servants, the monkeys, birds and dogs. To some extent it was much like the previous summer, with Byron and Teresa engineering their secret trysts. There was more clandestine coming and going up and down the wide palazzo stairs as notes to Byron were delivered by Teresa's messengers, either her maid or her East African page. Count Guiccioli also had a Negro page, counterpart of Teresa's, a boy who came from the coast of Guinea. The rival pages wore ornate oriental costume, with pistols and daggers in their belts.

There was a return to the routine of jealous tiffs between Byron and Teresa. Byron hotly denied gossip that linked his name to that of the visiting prima donna Madame Pasta. The question of his obvious interest in Teresa's friend Geltrude Vicari arose again. Such recriminations had become almost a way of life to them. Back in what was now a familiar environment, where even the altercations were stimulating, Byron was in a phase of energetic literary productivity. Early in 1820 he completed his translation of Pulci's *Morgante Maggiore*, wrote the poem 'Francesca of Rimini', and started the tragedy *Marino Faliero, Doge of Venice*. Of *Faliero* he told Murray: 'I never wrote or copied *an entire Scene of that play* – without being obliged to *break* off – to *break* a commandment; – to obey a woman's, and to forget God's.'

The mood at Palazzo Guiccioli changed alarmingly after Byron and the Countess were, as Byron expressed it, 'taken together quasi in the fact'. In April the Count had forced open Teresa's writing desk, which was kept locked with a skeleton key, and found incriminating evidence. Unfortunately Teresa's manuscript account of this episode is not completely legible, having suffered the depredations of mice. But we do have her fuller description of the scene, a few weeks later, when the Count, returning home from an evening out to find Byron and Teresa together, *in flagrante* or close to it, announced that the visits he had once permitted must immediately cease. Byron listened fairly calmly, and returning the sly comment that he would defer to his host's age, made a dignified exit to his own apartment on the upper floor.

It is unlikely that this scene had been spontaneous. The Count had already been piling up the evidence from the eighteen servants and tradesmen whom he also used as spies. A blacksmith, for example, testified that he was ordered by the Countess to remove the lock from the room leading into Byron's bedroom. Count Guiccioli, returning to the palace, had then ordered the smith to replace the lock. 'At the sound of the hammering, Lord Byron and Countess Teresa appeared on the other side of the door.' All these witnesses' accounts come very close to farce. In his new, and more formalised, antagonism towards Byron, Count Guiccioli may well have been urged on by the governing church faction in Ravenna who were already hostile to the English lord of known liberal sympathies. According to Byron there was little local sympathy for Count Guiccioli's stance. After all, he had tolerated the liaison for the past year. The law was against him, because he had persisted in sleeping with his wife even after her confession of misconduct. Byron told John Murray that all Teresa's relatives 'who are numerous, high in rank & powerful' were furiously indignant not with her but with her husband. The Count was merely making himself ridiculous by 'not wishing to be cuckolded at *three* score' when other Italian noblemen resigned themselves to being cuckolded at twenty. Teresa's father Count Ruggero Gamba now petitioned Pope Pius VII for a decree of separation between his daughter and Count Guiccioli.

What are we to make of this reversal of policy by Count Gamba, previously so anxious to preserve his daughter's marriage? In the petition he claimed that it had now become impossible for her to live any longer with so demanding a husband. On 23 June Count Gamba sent a letter to Cardinal Rusconi, newly appointed Papal Legate in Ravenna, accusing Count Guiccioli 'for vile financial considerations', of prostituting, selling and disgracing his daughter. He next challenged Count Guiccioli to a duel. Though the Count did not go into further details, his disgust and indignation suggests he had discovered facts that changed his attitude entirely. There is a curious parallel with Sir Ralph Noel's response to the revelations of ill-treatment of Lady Byron by his son-in-law.

And what of Teresa? Surely Byron was right to suspect her, during those tense and anxious summer months, of continuing to fraternise with a husband who still exerted a mysterious sexual hold on her. On 6 July the Pope issued the decree granting their separation. But in 1826, after Byron's death, she and Count Guiccioli were temporarily reconciled.

The terms of Teresa's separation put her under the protection of her father. She returned with him to the Gamba family home in the country at Filetto, fifteen miles south-west of Ravenna. Byron remained in the palazzo, in uneasy proximity to his landlord. He did not see Teresa for almost two months, but knew now that he was more than ever committed to her. In his mind he had become Teresa's quasi-husband. 'I only meant to be a Cavalier Servente', he told Moore, 'and had no idea it would turn out a romance, in the Anglo fashion.' He was amused to see himself behaving like a perfect English gentleman.

The highly strung Allegra fell ill again and Byron took a country house, the Villa Bacinetti, for her and the nurse who had replaced Elise. From here Filetto was more accessible and the ban on his visits to Teresa was gradually dropped. The Gambas lived an easy and hospitable life in their rambling late seventeenth-century house. Used mainly as a summer house it had an enormous open saloon on the first floor with bedrooms above, leading out on to a gallery. The doors of these rooms would be left open on hot nights so that conversation wafted across from bed to bed. The convivial Gambas, according to Lord Malmesbury, a later lover of Teresa, 'might well have been called the Osbaldistones of Italy. They were all sportsmen according to their knowledge, which consisted of hunting a slow pointer, who stood woodcock and partridge equally well, through the forests and vineyards.' Since the episode of the wounded eaglet at Vostizza, Byron took no part in shooting birds. Nor did he like fishing. But he joined the Gambas in their games of bowls.

Byron now met Teresa's brother Pietro, who had returned from his school in Rome. 'I like your little brother very much – he shows character and talent.' He was taken with Pietro's big eyebrows and long legs. How little in fact was Pietro? By then he was nineteen or twenty, good-looking and impetuous. He and Byron formed an alliance that lasted for their two foreshortened lives. Byron also got to know Teresa's younger sisters 'on whom he lavished his caresses'. This was not the only echo at Filetto of his former days at Eywood with the Oxfords. Once again it was as if he were adopted by relations. Accepted by the Gambas, he felt fully integrated with Italy itself: 'Now, I have lived in the hearts of their houses, in parts of Italy freshest and least influenced by strangers, – have seen and become (*pars magna fui*) a portion of their hopes, and fears, and passions, and am almost inoculated into a family. This is to see men and things as they are.'

One evening in September Byron was invited by Teresa to Filetto to watch an eclipse of the sun. When he reached the house she and her guests were already in the garden, 'armed with optical instruments and smoked (or tinted) glasses', watching the beginning of the eclipse. Byron sat down in their midst, not wanting to disturb them, and was rapidly engrossed in the great spectacle. Scrutinising him possessively Teresa thought she saw 'the noble thoughts' soon to be expressed in the religious dramas then taking shape in his imagination.

Through the spring and summer of 1820 anxieties over *Don Juan* continued. Byron had suffered a loss of confidence over public reactions to the first two cantos. He had even offered to refund John Murray's payment for the copyright. When Bankes, on his Venice visit, tactlessly repeated the comment of a resident Englishman that '*Don Juan* was all Grub Street', Byron was so upset that he did not touch the poem again for several weeks. However, in February, he had sent Murray Cantos III and IV, the episodes in which the lovers on the island are surprised by the return of Haidée's father Lambro, the mild-mannered pirate – Byron's Ali Pasha figure – and Don Juan is despatched in a pirate ship to be sold in the slave market at Constantinople. These two cantos had originally been a single long one, but in making the fair copy Byron had split them in two. The tale went that he had done this to extract a double payment. But it is clear from Byron's correspondence that the decision was an artistic not a mercenary one.

Byron's despatch of the manuscript was followed by the silence from Albemarle Street that always disconcerted him. By April he was thundering to Murray: 'You are not expected to write frequent or long letters – as your time is much occupied – but when parcels that have cost some pains in the composition, & great trouble in the copying are sent to you I should at least be put out of Suspense by the immediate acknowledgement per return of post addressed *directly* to *Ravenna*.' In fact Murray had punctiliously acknowledged the receipt of *Don Juan* on 7 March, half an hour after he received the manuscript, promising: 'these Cantos I shall announce instantly & publish fearlessly.'

But two months later, after worried discussions with Hobhouse and Kinnaird, Murray had changed his mind and wrote Byron a letter that radiates embarrassment: 'Upon my soul I never felt more at a loss to express myself – We all think Canto III by no means equal to the two first.' Nor was 'the Committee' enthusiastic about Byron's Pulci translation, his long essay in defence of Pope or even *The Prophecy of Dante* which, 'though very good', was felt to be too lightweight to justify publication on its own. Murray judged it wisest to delay all publication until Byron sent him some new writing more certain to produce 'that sensation which has hitherto attended the publication of your works'.

Byron half-agreed with Murray's strictures on *Don Juan*. He admitted to Kinnaird that 'the trash is not very brilliant this time', and certainly Canto III, being more reflectively ironic in tone, lacks the narrative flash and flourish of its predecessors. But, although Byron agreed to delete six abusive stanzas on 'those two impostors Southey and Wordsworth', he was adamant in his refusal to tinker with the whole.

Over the months, Murray went on pleading: 'If you would but yield to our united wishes about the Don Juans I would sell millions of them – & you would have the full enjoyment of fame arising from One of the finest poems in any language.' Byron went on resisting Murray's demands for a 'retouching' of the poem, arguing that he was temperamentally unable to amend: 'I am like the tyger (in poesy) if I miss my first Spring – I go growling back to my Jungle.' Murray had no need to pay him: he would rather give his works away than 'hack & hew them'. Murray had no obligation to publish him. At a peak of indignation over Murray's shilly-shallying he asserted his right to preferential treatment: 'You must not treat a blood horse as you do your hacks otherwise he'll bolt out of the course.'

Through all these bitter arguments and threats, he still continued to bombard John Murray with requests for such domestic necessities as soda powders and new novels by Walter Scott. 'What is *Ivanhoe*?' he asked. He wanted Murray to send on a portrait of his daughter Ada which Byron had negotiated with Lady Byron. He was still depending on his publisher as confidential go-between.

Writing in 1820, in a mood of self-analysis, Byron gave Augusta a review of his character at the time:

'a temper not softened by what it has seen and undergone, a mind grown indifferent to pursuits and results, but capable of effort and of strength under oppression or stimulus, but without ambition, because it looks upon all human attempts as conducting to no rational or practicable advantage'.

He saw his own ruthlessness, a steeliness of soul, that would make him, once forced by circumstances into action, 'about as dangerous an animal as ever joined in ravage'. This energy was now focused upon the liberation of the Romagna from Papal-Austrian domination. In July or August 1820 he joined the clandestine revolutionary society of the Carbonari, the 'charcoal-burners'. After years of vacillation Byron had found a role.

He had been intensely interested in the local political scene since returning to Ravenna. Besides the natural division in the city between the Jacobins, the old Napoleonic liberals, and the clerical party dominated by the Austrians, there was a third element, the secret freedom fighters, dedicated to the liberation of Italy. Revolution had been fomenting in Ravenna in the spring. On 30 April Byron was reporting to England, 'We expect a rising.' The children in the streets started chanting revolutionary slogans. The rebels had been writing slogans such as 'up with the Republic' and 'death to the Pope' on the city walls and the walls of the palaces. Palazzo Guiccioli was plastered with graffiti. As Byron commented, this would not have counted for much in London, where the walls of Hyde Park were often defaced by obscenities and death threats to the royal family. But Ravenna was unused to fierce political inscriptions: 'the police is all on the alert, and the Cardinal glares pale through his purple.'

Initially Byron's position had been that of the sympathetic spectator, one who felt he was in the right place at the right time: 'I shall think it by far the most interesting spectacle and moment in existence – to see the Italians send the Barbarians of all nations back to their own dens.' But he was by now too closely identified with Italy, 'inoculated among the people', not to be drawn in. In particular Byron's attachment not just to Teresa but to her extended family, the Gamba clan, made his eventual involvement in the uprising almost inevitable. The middle-aged Count Ruggero was an experienced revolutionary who had already been temporarily exiled from the Romagna by the Papal-

Austrian occupying forces, after the departure of the Napoleonists in 1814. His son, the young Count Pietro, was identified by Byron as a fine brave fellow who was 'wild about liberty'. Count Gamba's nephew, Antonio Cavalli, was another moving spirit in the Romagna Carbonari. Byron had been the proud member of many clubs in London where the secret and competitive rules of membership satisfied his innate longing for acceptance: the Alfred, the Cocoa Tree, Watier's, the Union, the Pugilistic, the Owls or 'Fly-by-Night', the Hampden. To this list of clubs which had elected him a member he now added, 'though last, *not least*', the Italian Carbonari.

The atmosphere was rather different from Watier's. The Ravenna Carbonari was one of a network of insurrectionist groups active in the Italian papal states. Their historic links with Freemasonry were evident in the obsessive secrecy with which they operated, the stress on ritual and high spiritual values. These were conspirators for virtue, with membership drawn from across the social classes: disaffected merchants, working-class Republicans, with the usual admixture of professional adventurers, semi-criminals and malcontents.

A good impression of the complex rituals within the Ravenna lodge of the Carbonari is given by a closely written confidential document amongst Lega Zambelli's papers now in the British Library. It seems likely that Byron's steward was a co-conspirator. Did Byron undergo the full initiation ceremony as an Apprentice: the blindfold interrogation by the Grand Master; the ceremonial *voyage*, with the candidate still blindfold, round the chamber of the lodge; the purification by water; the taking of the oath, followed by the handing on of the secret signs, the handshake and passwords of the lodge? Certainly Byron was later to tell Hobhouse that while the objects of the Carbonari were pure, their ceremonies were ridiculous.

Byron was particularly useful to the movement because of his friendship with the genially irresponsible Count Alborghetti who, as Secretary-General of the local Papal Legation, was able to pass Byron information from official documents relating to the Austrian enemy. He was soon appointed a captain in the third and popular section of the Ravenna Carbonari, known as 'la turba' or 'the mob'. He controlled his own troop, the *Cacciatori Americani* – originally a band of hunters in the forest – whose uniform was a red cap, red shirt and red and white striped trousers. In writing to John Murray Byron proudly told him that his troop comprised 'some thousands, etc.' – he could not be more precise for fear of police interceptors of his post. It has been estimated that in summer 1820 more than 15,000 freedom fighters were enrolled in the Romagna branches of the Carbonari. In 1822 Byron gives the figure of 800,000 members in the whole of Austrian-occupied Italy.

Local meetings were held in Ravenna, at Filetto, in the camouflage of the pine forest. It is obvious that Byron enjoyed the cloak-and-dagger aspects of the movement. But he was also realistic about the shortcomings of the Italian revolutionary forces: 'they want Union – and they want principle – and I doubt their success.' Teresa tells us that he was apt to be bad-tempered at the heated and long-winded meetings in the forest, urging a more coherent plan of action. Already we see Byron pragmatic, dedicated to a cause of which the outcome was extremely problematic, with the austerity of purpose he was to show in Greece.

Early in July 1820 the expected revolt against the Austrians by the Carbonari and other secret societies had broken out in Naples and King Ferdinand of Naples was dethroned. There was an expectation that this would spark off full-scale revolution further north. Byron was now describing the situation in Ravenna as being 'like the middle ages – Grand Uncertainty'. There had been a number of political assassinations. On 12 August he reported: 'Italy's primed and loaded – and many a finger itching for the trigger.' A fortnight later the 'Italian vespers' were said to be fixed for 10 September. But, to Byron's chagrin, the uprising by the joint forces of the Carbonari was abandoned when the rebels from the city of Bologna withdrew their support.

Through the autumn the dangerous situation simmered. A large Austrian army was now marching south to quell the insurrection at Naples. Byron described the position in September: 'the Huns are on the Po – but if once they pass it on their march to Naples all Italy will rise behind them – the Dogs – the Wolves – may they perish like the Host of Sennacherib!' He wrote to Lady Byron to warn her to take measures to protect the family investments in the economic chaos that would follow the Austrian crossing of the Po: 'I request you to consider how far a foreign war is likely to affect your own funds – and to permit my trustees to place the remaining fortunes of my family upon a securer tenure than the Bank Bubble – even at the expence of some present loss.' He wrote to Kinnaird too, urging him to impress on Lady Byron the urgent necessity of removing the investments from the settled Noel property at Kirkby Mallory from government funds. 'If she don't', Byron threatened, 'I will come over – be a radical – & take possession of the Kirkby estate – before Lady Noel is in Hell – no long time.' He was especially anxious to protect the money that would eventually revert to Augusta and her children from his own expected inheritance after the death of Annabella's mother, Lady Noel.

In Ravenna wild plans were made to attack the Hapsburg forces as they passed through the Romagna. Byron now came under more rigorous surveillance, constantly harassed by the police who picked quarrels with his servants.

In one episode the police complained that Byron's household liveries too closely resembled their own. 'Yesterday they sent to know why I had such a quantity of Cartridges,' he told Kinnaird indignantly: 'The fact is that as you know pistol and rifle shooting has been always rather a pastime of mine – and I have hitherto indulged it – without rendering accounts to the Commander in Chief.' Teresa had now returned to Ravenna, where she was living in her father's city palace, and she too was targeted. Probably with Count Guiccioli's connivance, there were threats from the security forces to incarcerate her in a convent, an attempt to intimidate Byron as well as the Gamba family.

Byron was made more than ever aware of the ironic fortunes of war when, a fortnight before Christmas, the Military Commander of Ravenna, Captain Luigi Dal Pinto, was shot dead in the street two hundred paces from the entrance to the Palazzo Guiccioli. It was just eight in the evening. Byron had been putting on his greatcoat to visit Teresa at the Palazzo Gamba when he heard the shot. Going into the hall he found the servants collected on the balcony exclaiming that a man had been murdered. Byron extracted Tita, the bravest of his servants, to follow him downstairs. They found the Commandant lying on his back, 'almost, if not quite dead', with a wound in the heart, two in the stomach, one in the finger, another in the arm. He was surrounded by his adjutant, Diego, who was crying like a child, a surgeon, who seemed to be paralysed with terror, and a priest who was 'sobbing a frightened prayer'.

Though the dying man was in theory his enemy Byron took charge of the situation, sending two soldiers off to inform the guard, despatching Diego to the Cardinal, and ordering Tita with two men from the crowd to carry the Commandant up to his own apartment. But he was dead by the time they laid him on William Fletcher's bed.

Byron had the body stripped. He and the surgeon carried out a post-mortem, presumably partly to furnish evidence for an official report if required but also, it appears from Byron's letters, in a spirit of scientific enquiry. Investigating intrepidly, Byron felt one of the bullets which had gone right through Dal Pinto's body, almost to the skin. The gun with which the shots were fired had been found on the pavement, near to the scene of the murder. It was an old gun, half filed down. The Commandant left a wife and children, 'quite destitute' as Byron described them pityingly. Cardinal Rusconi issued an official decree announcing the homicide and offering a reward for the capture of the murderer. It does not appear that Dal Pinto's assassin was tracked down.

The incident made a strong impression upon Byron. He gives detailed accounts, with much the same phraseology, in letters to Thomas Moore, John

Murray and even Lady Byron. He reuses the material in Canto V of *Don Juan*, which he was composing that winter in Ravenna:

> 'The other evening ('twas on Friday last) –
>   This is a fact and no poetic fable –
> Just as my great coat was about me cast,
>   My hat and gloves still lying on the table,
> I heard a shot – 'twas eight o'clock scarce past –
>   And running out as fast as I was able,
> I found the military commandant
> Stretch'd in the street, and able scarce to pant.'

The episode is full of fascinating mysteries. Had the murder been carried out by the Carbonari? Or, as Byron was later to suggest, was the Commandant a double agent, himself a Carbonaro? Had the assassination close to Byron's residence been selected by the police in an attempt to incriminate Byron? Police laxity in pursuit of the assassin was itself suspicious. The death of Dal Pinto was followed by an assassination attempt on Byron himself, perhaps at the instigation of Count Guiccioli: 'I had my foot in the stirrup', he recollected vividly, 'at my usual hour of exercise, when my horse started at the report of a gun. On looking up I perceived a man throw down a carbine and run away at full speed.'

But what interested Byron most about the murder was not the local politics but the underlying strangeness, what it said about the human condition. What was the dividing line between a life and death, he wondered as he sat beside the oddly tranquil body of the physically courageous but unpopular Dal Pinto, a man he had met often at Ravenna *conversazioni*? He noted how the lieutenant on duty by the corpse was smoking his pipe 'with great composure. – A queer people this.'

In Ravenna in the winter of 1820–1, still only in his early thirties, Byron entered a new and intense phase of reminiscence. He had added more instalments to his memoirs and on 9 December sent Thomas Moore three packets containing eighteen further sheets. Knowing Moore to be in acute financial trouble Byron suggested he should sell them to Longman or John Murray. He was still insisting that the memoirs should not be published until after his own death, 'for a man always *looks dead* after his life has appeared'. This was the basis of the agreement made between Moore and John Murray the following November. Murray paid £2,000 for the right to posthumous publication, an arrangement which both Kinnaird and Hobhouse greeted with fury and alarm.

Hobhouse, taking it as a personal affront, burst out in his diary against the vulgar instincts of Moore, Murray and Byron himself:

'The truth is that my friend Byron has a most extraordinary anxiety that every, even the smallest traits, of his conduct, and all the accidents of his life, as well as the train of his thoughts should be in some shape or other before the world.'

At the start of the new year Byron took up the journal that had lapsed since he left Switzerland in 1816. This diary, kept intermittently through 1821, gives us a vivid impression of how he spent his days. For example, on 5 January:

'Rose late – dull and drooping – the weather dripping and dense. Snow on the ground, and sirocco above in the sky, like yesterday. Roads up to the horse's belly, so that riding (at least for pleasure) is not very feasible. Added a postscript to my letter to Murray. Read the conclusion, for the fiftieth time (I have read all W. Scott's novels at least fifty times) of the third series of "Tales of my Landlord", – grand work – Scotch Fielding, as well as great English poet – wonderful man! I long to get drunk with him.

Dined versus six o'the clock. Forgot that there was a plum-pudding, (I have added, lately, *eating* to my "family of vices",) and had dined before I knew it. Drank half a bottle of some sort of spirits – probably spirits of wine; for what they call brandy, rum &c. &c., here is nothing but spirits of wine, coloured accordingly. Did *not* eat two apples, which were placed by way of dessert. Fed the two cats, the hawk, and the tame (but *not tamed*) crow. Read Mitford's History of Greece – Xenophon's Retreat of the Ten Thousand. Up to this present moment writing, 6 minutes before eight o'the clock – French hours, not Italian.

Hear the carriage – order pistols and great coat, as usual – necessary articles. Weather cold – carriage open, and inhabitants somewhat savage – rather treacherous and highly inflamed by politics. Fine fellows, though – good materials for a nation. Out of chaos God made a world, and out of high passions comes a people.

Clock strikes – going out to make love. Somewhat perilous – but not disagreeable. Memorandum – a new screen put up today. It is rather antique, but will do with a little repair.'

What makes Byron's journal remarkable is not just the accretion of immediate detail, but the mingling of the inconsequential and reflective, the sense of inner harmonies, that brings the writer and the revolutionary in his labyrinth so thoroughly to life. There is a strong sense, too, of the containment of the present in the past as old scenes of Aberdeen and Harrow, Trinity and high society in London, duels, speeches, ancient jokes, parties at the Jerseys', forgotten confrontations in the House of Lords, are recalled with a sadness that is almost tangible.

So much of that familiar landscape had now changed. Old Joe Murray had died the previous October. Byron felt 'the very Ghosts' had died with him: 'Newstead and he almost went together.' His London dentist Waite and barber Blake were also dead, a sudden shock to Byron who had left them both apparently 'in the most robust health' five years before. His depression, so hard to keep at bay, descended at the thought of the wastage of the years gone by. On his thirty-third birthday he surveyed himself with horror, writing his own epitaph, lamenting

> 'the Thirty-Third Year
> of an ill-spent Life,
> Which, after
> a lingering disease of many months
> sunk into a lethargy
> and expired,
> January 22[d], 1821, A.D.'

On 1 March 1821, a Thursday, four-year-old Allegra was sent to the convent school of San Giovanni Battista at Bagnacavallo, a little town that had originated as a Roman fortress, on the marshy plains twelve miles west of Ravenna. Since rejoining her father Allegra had been wilful. Byron was soon describing the small girl as 'obstinate as a Mule – and as ravenous as a Vulture . . . temper tolerable – but for vanity and pertinacity. She thinks herself handsome – and will do as she pleases.' She was especially spoilt, amongst the sallow Italian children, because of the fairness of her skin.

Teresa, ambivalent towards the illegitimate daughter of her *cavaliere servente*, alternately petted and complained about Allegra. There is a note of anxiety in Byron's confession to Teresa: 'Allegrina has already spoiled your present – breaking one of the little carriages.' Teresa describes her at the Villa Bacinetti singing popular Italian songs and mimicking the servants. Byron, playing the dutiful father, deprecated Allegra's 'tendency to mockery', a habit which 'sooner or later brings trouble to those who practice it' as Byron, of all people, had cause to know.

Her natural mother had been asking for her back. Claire Clairmont, then living at Pisa with the Shelleys, had written to Byron in March 1820 saying, 'It is now almost a year and a half that I have not seen Allegra', and entreating a visit from her in the summer. But Byron was adamant in withholding Allegra from what he saw as the contamination of the Shelley household. He wrote to Hoppner: 'About Allegra – I can only say to Claire – that I so totally disapprove of the mode of children's treatment in their family – that I should look upon the Child as going into a hospital – Is it not so? Have they *reared* one?' His cruel reference is to a further disaster for the Shelleys: the death of three-year-old William in Rome in June 1819. With all the venom of a conventional pater-familias Byron hit out against the Shelleys' vegetarian and atheistic regime: 'the Child shall not quit me again – to perish of Starvation, and green fruit – or be taught to believe that there is no Deity.' Claire Clairmont's eyes were by now opened. When Mrs Hoppner sent her a copy of the letter she exploded in her journal: 'I spend the day in cogitation and I write to *my damn'd Brute*.'

The idea of a convent education for Allegra had been in Byron's mind for many months before her eventual departure. He had a natural bias towards Roman Catholicism as 'assuredly the eldest of the various branches of Christianity': after all, he had spoken in the House of Lords in favour of the Catholic Emancipation Bill. His sceptical temperament made him the more susceptible to a religion of moral dogmatism. In this respect Catholicism was the equivalent of the Calvinism of his boyhood. His emotionalism and theatricality responded to Catholicism's outward show: 'What with incense, pictures, statues, altars, shrines, relics, and the real presence, confession, absolution, – there is something sensible to grasp at.' He liked Catholicism's excess. Byron felt that if people had any religion at all then they could not have enough.

As far as Allegra's future was concerned, he saw a convent education as probably more practical than the alternative of returning her to England. Whereas in England illegitimacy would be a hazard to her marriage prospects this was much less so in Italy, where a reasonable dowry counted most. Byron had already settled £5,000 on Allegra in a codicil to his will. His consciousness that Allegra now needed to be educated was no doubt sharpened by reports he was receiving of the advanced attainments of his highly intelligent other daughter Ada. Teresa, so unobtrusively well read, appreciative, admiring, was a constant reminder of what could be achieved by an Italian convent education.

It is likely that Byron's decision was affected by stories circulating in autumn 1820 that gave rise to the so-called 'Hoppner scandal'. These rumours originated with the Shelleys' Swiss nurse Elise who had looked after Allegra while she was in Venice. She had found new employment with an English lady and, passing through Venice in summer 1820, had regaled Hoppner with the scurrilous story that a baby born on 27 December 1818 in Naples where the Shelleys had been staying for the winter, and baptised Elena Adelaide Shelley two months later, had in fact been Claire Clairmont's child by Shelley. Hoppner relayed the information to Byron in a letter dated 16 September 1820:

'I therefore proceed to divulge to you, what indeed on Allegra's account it is necessary that you should know, as it will fortify you in the good resolution you have already taken never to trust her again to her mother's care. You must know then that at the time the Shelleys were here Clara was with child by Shelley: you may remember to have heard that she was constantly unwell, & the quantity of medicine she then took was not for the mere purpose of restoring her health. I perceive too why she preferred remaining alone at Este, notwithstanding her fear of ghosts and robbers, to being here with the Shelleys.

Be this as it may, they proceeded from here to Naples; where one night Shelley was called up to see Clara who was very ill. His wife naturally thought it very strange that he should be sent for; but although she was not aware of the nature of the connection between them she had had sufficient proof of Shelley's indifference & of Clara's hatred for her; besides as Shelley desired her to remain quiet she dared not interfere. A Mid wife was sent for, & this worthy pair who had made no preparation for the reception of the unfortunate being she was bringing into the world bribed the woman to carry it to the Pietà, where the child was taken ½ an hour after its birth being obliged likewise to purchase the physician's silence with a considerable sum.'

According to Elise, Mary had remained unaware of the squalid outcome of 'their adventure at Naples'. The infant had subsequently died. The truth behind the story is still a mystery. What is clear is that Byron was convinced by, or found it convenient to believe, a scandal that gave him leverage when it came to insisting on removing Allegra from her mother's sphere of influence.

By 10 February 1821 her father was telling Hoppner that Allegra's behaviour was becoming insupportable: 'Allegra is well – but not well disposed – her disposition is perverse to a degree.' She was so obstreperous the servants could not control her. Byron's further comment that 'it was not fit that she should remain with them longer in any case' was corroborated by Shelley's view, on his August visit to Ravenna, that the household at Palazzo Guiccioli was 'composed entirely of dissolute men servants who will do her nothing but mischief'. It occurred to Claire that Allegra could be in danger from Byron himself.

When she left Ravenna for the convent it was represented to the Shelleys and to Hoppner as a temporary measure. Allegra was by far the youngest pupil in the school recently established by the Capuchin nuns. She arrived with her own bed, washstand, chest of drawers, two chairs, eighteen chemises and a black woollen cloth dress. She also brought her dolls, so exquisitely dressed that the wife of the convent carpenter later used their clothes as garments for her own small children. Byron donated his own Peer's robes to the convent, delivering them via Teresa's major-domo, with instructions that a dress for Allegra should be made from them. The robes were later turned into a curtain for the convent church.

On the day of her arrival, on which Allegra gave a ceremonial dinner for the nuns, the brother of one of them wrote to tell Lord Byron:

'I think it my duty to send you a report at once about your child Allegrina – a well-chosen name which suits her happy nature. As soon as she arrived she went off to play with several other little girls. Last night she slept quietly, and this morning I have found her more cheerful and lively than ever. She has already chosen her favourite playmate, among the many who are here.'

The Mother Superior was watching over her. As soon as she heard what had happened to her daughter, Claire wrote Byron a letter castigating him for the way he had condemned Allegra 'to a life of ignorance and degradation'.

A few weeks after Allegra's departure Byron wrote to ask John Murray to arrange to commission the miniaturist James Holmes to come out to Italy at his expense to paint Allegra's portrait and at the same time to paint the Countess Guiccioli 'and the head of a peasant Girl – which latter would make a study for Raphael. – It is a complete *peasant* face – but an *Italian* peasant's – and quite in the Raphael Fornarina style – Her figure is tall, but rather large – and not at all comparable to her face – which is really superb – she is not seventeen and I am anxious to have her likeness while it lasts.' He urged Murray: 'It must be *Holmes* – I like him because he takes such inveterate likenesses.' He was irritated to hear that Holmes was unable to accept the commission, being preoccupied with painting the man he still thought of as Prince Regent. '"*Painting the King*" as you call it!' Byron expostulated to John Murray in a note only recently discovered in the archive. 'Painting a sepulchre . . . why don't he *whitewash* him – he wants it.' He was even more scornful of the British monarchy because the new king, George IV, was over sixty years of age.

'The king-times are fast finishing. There will be blood shed like water, and tears like mist; but the peoples will conquer in the end. I shall not live to see it, but I foresee it.'

From his position as analyst and poet of historic evolution Byron was now personally involved in the making of history, a part of the republican processes set in train by the American War of Independence and the French Revolution. Popular revolutions had already taken place in South America, liberating country after country from Spanish and Portuguese domination. Byron believed that revolutions were imminent in Portugal and Spain themselves. He told Hobhouse: 'I certainly lean towards a republic – all history – and experience is in its favour even the French – for though they butchered thousands of Citizens at first, yet *more* were killed in any one of the great battles than ever perished by a democratical proscription – America is a Model of force and freedom & moderation – with all the coarseness and rudeness of its people.' It was with some misgivings that he foresaw a republic even in England: 'it may not be in ten or twenty years but it is inevitable.'

Meanwhile the revolution on his doorstep in Ravenna was claiming his energy. As the Austrians showed signs of striking camp to head south through the Romagna, the Ravenna military government tightened its security. Byron made plans to shelter beleaguered patriots in his, or rather the Count's, house if necessary. He would arm his servants to defend them. He calculated that with twenty men the palazzo could hold out for twenty-four hours against any besieging force.

Byron's close involvement in the Carbonari plots had been another reason for sending Allegra to Bagnacavallo. He did not want her with him 'in the seat of war'. Count Gamba had had a consignment of arms delivered to the palazzo without warning Byron, which had alarmed him since, of his servants, only Lega Zambelli, Tita and Fletcher were known to be loyal to the partisans. By 18 February 1821 Byron describes the basement of the palace as 'full of their bayonets, fusils, cartridges, and what not. I suppose that they consider me as a depôt, to be sacrificed in case of accidents.' He was philosophic. 'It is no great matter, supposing that Italy could be liberated, who or what is sacrificed.'

Byron was quickly disillusioned by the realities of revolution. At the end of January, just when a concentrated attack on the Austrian army seemed feasible, some leaders of the Ravenna Carbonari, including Pietro Gamba and a colleague, went off on a shooting party lasting several days. It was not even a bona fide hunting expedition but 'nothing more or less than a real snivelling, popping, small-shot, water-hen waste of powder, ammunition and shot, for their own special amusement', Byron wrote indignantly.

The Carbonari passwords had begun to lose their magic. Byron was even more depressed by late February when the Neapolitan rebel army caved in, reneging on their alliance with the Carbonari of the northern states. 'The *plan* has missed,' wrote Byron dejectedly, 'the Chiefs are betrayed, military, as well as civil.' He diagnosed this as a fundamental problem: national lack of unity and weakness of motivation. When a young Ravenna woman, sitting tearful at her harpsichord, suggested to Byron that the Italians would now have to go back to making operas, he was tempted to agree.

In the military clampdown in Ravenna in summer 1821 many of the Carbonari were arrested. The all too visible Tita Falcieri was apprehended after a quarrel with a lieutenant in the street. The officer claimed that Tita had attacked him with a knife without provocation. The Cardinal, through his intermediary Alborghetti, ordered Byron to dismiss his servant who would inevitably be expelled from the state. Byron sent back a firm letter, refusing to be bullied, demanding that Tita should be given an open trial according to due process of law, at the same time objecting to the harassments he himself had received, including the public posters in Ravenna putting a price upon his head. Apparently ashamed, the authorities climbed down. Tita was given a mere three days' imprisonment and told to make a public apology.

But there was worse to come. On 10 July, Pietro Gamba was arrested by the police as he was leaving the theatre and exiled from Romagna. The next day the Palazzo Gamba was searched and Count Ruggero Gamba too was ordered to leave Ravenna within twenty-four hours. Making use of all possible contacts Byron wrote to Elizabeth, Duchess of Devonshire, who was then living in Rome on terms of close friendship with Cardinal Consalvi, the Papal Secretary of State. He wanted her to intervene through her allies within the Vatican for the repeal of sentence on one, if not both, of the Counts Gamba. With a reminder of old intimacies, Byron trusted she would be able to decipher his scrawl 'from a long acquaintanceship with the hand-writing of Lady Bessborough'. He forbore to remind her that she had been his landlady at 13 Piccadilly Terrace. In any case, the dowager Duchess was away from Rome and her eventual reply reached him too late.

On 25 July, following renewed threats from the state authorities to place her in a convent, Teresa went to join her father and brother in Florence. Byron remained in Ravenna alone and morose.

Through July 1821 Byron was writing *The Two Foscari*, his third tragedy in twelve months. This was part of a cycle which had begun the previous April with *Marino Faliero, Doge of Venice* and continued with *Sardanapalus*, written in Ravenna between January and May 1821. What Byron was attempting was a new species of drama in English, convinced as he was that the heavily plotted blank verse tragedies of action by Shakespeare and his followers were now a worn-out genre. In his view great tragedy was 'not to be done by following the old dramatists – who are full of gross faults – pardoned only for the beauty of their language – but by writing naturally and *regularly* – & producing *regular* tragedies like the *Greeks*'. Structurally, he was intent on following the classical unities. Byron's other models were the French seventeenth-century dramatists Corneille and Racine and the eighteenth-century Italian tragedian Alfieri.

His own experiences at Drury Lane had proved the limitations of theatrical performance. Byron's plays were not intended to be acted. They were written for the '*mental theatre*' of the reader; there was no love interest, no melodrama, no mistaken identities, no 'outrageous ranting villains'. As he told John Murray, whose heart must have sunk when he received the letter, he was not aiming at popularity but at inventing a new form of drama 'simple and severe'.

It was an extraordinary project to embark on in a remote and incendiarist city in the Romagna in the early 1820s. Local Italian power struggles are writ large in Byron's austere and often splendid tragedies which focus on the moral responsibilities and capacity for suffering of the individual. *Marino Faliero* is a five-act tragedy based on historical fact: the conspiracy by the Venetian Doge Marin Falier against the corrupt rulers of the city in 1355. In the succession of portraits of past Doges on exhibition in the council chamber of the Ducal Palace the discredited Marin Falier is represented not by his head but by a curious rectangle of black cloth inscribed with the grim words: 'HIC EST LOCUS MARIN FALIERI DECAPITATI PRO CRIMINIBUS'. It was this public slur on Falier's memory, the attempt to obliterate his physical reality, that first interested Byron while he was in Venice:

'The black veil which is painted over the place of Marino Faliero amongst the doges, and the Giant's Staircase where he was crowned, and discrowned, and decapitated, struck forcibly upon my imagination, as did his fiery character and strange story.'

The story of Falier, the Venetian Doge's courage in defence of his beliefs, his isolation, betrayal and execution, had contemporary connotations both in regard to Italy and to England. 'It is full of republicanism', maintained Byron, 'so will find no favour in *Albemarle* Street.' *Marino Faliero* caused a further, different kind of trouble to John Murray after it was published in April 1821. In spite of Byron's stipulations and Murray's attempts to obtain a preventative injunction from the Lord Chamberlain, a cut version of the play was given seven performances at Drury Lane. Though not an outright failure, it was not a great success.

For his next drama Byron took another subject which had been lingering in his mind. This new tragedy, 'ycleped "Sardanapalus"' and written according to the rules of Aristotle minus the chorus, which Byron could not stomach, was taken principally from the second book of Diodorus Siculus' *Bibliothecae*

Historicae and William Mitford's *History of Greece* of 1818. It told the story of the effete but courageous Sardanapalus, last king of Assyria.

Byron did his best to reassure Murray that his play was not a satire on contemporary monarchy 'as you may tremulously imagine'. In fact it is something much more personal and complex. In Sardanapalus, Byron creates a pleasure-loving ruler who is also 'brave' and 'amiable'. His pacifism is depicted not as dissolute inertia but as the expression of subtle intelligence and human sympathy. Referring to the scene in which the king 'calls for a *mirror* to look at himself in his armour' Byron half-apologises for what might look like the use of a cliché: 'the trait is perhaps too familiar – but it is historical – & natural in an effeminate character.' Tom Moore was delighted by the originality of Byron's character of Sardanapalus with his 'sly, insinuated sarcasms'. Moore must have recognised these as close to Byron's own.

Indeed the whole description of the self indulgent monarch hardened by impending crisis in his kingdom into a brave, self-sacrificing military leader is both comical and challenging. It is not simply a recapitulation of Byron's own transformation from Venetian layabout into Carbonari mainstay. The play makes a broader, more interesting argument for a Byronic versatility of temperament. In *Sardanapalus* the king prejudged as an effeminate voluptuary moves to take an active and virile role at the head of his troops. He dies a hero, even in defeat.

For the romance of Sardanapalus' tragic end, immolated on a funeral pyre with Myrrha, his favourite Greek slave, we should probably blame Teresa Guiccioli. Byron had eschewed love interest in his classical tragedies; Teresa's plea, with all 'the eloquence of St Chiara', persuaded him to add a little in.

With *The Two Foscari* Byron returned to Venice and the story of Jacopo, son of another Foscari doge, Francesco. Jacopo has been recalled from exile on treason charges. The play opens with his interrogation on the rack. In this strong and simple tragedy of divided loyalties, in which the father signs a new warrant of exile for his son, Byron drew on his recent experience of revolutionary Ravenna. He completed it rapidly, in under a month.

Byron was irritated when John Murray offered only 2,000 guineas for *Sardanapalus*, *The Two Foscari* and Cantos III, IV and V of *Don Juan*. Murray had received Canto V early in 1821. It now seemed that he was paying less to his most famous author than Byron's work would be worth on the open market, and that other Murray writers were being offered more than him. Citing Horace Walpole, Earl of Orford's *Memoirs of the reign of George the Second* and James, Earl Waldegrave's *Memoirs*, Byron vented his indignation in rude verses:

'For Orford and for Waldegrave
You give much more than me you *gave*,
Which is not fairly to behave
                              My Murray!

Because if a live dog, 'tis said,
Be worth a Lion fairly sped,
A *live lord* must be worth *two dead*,
                              My Murray! –

And if, as the Opinion goes,
Verse hath a better sale than prose –
Certes, I should have more than those,
                              My Murray!

But now – this sheet is nearly crammed,
So – if *you will* – *I* shan't be shammed,
And if you *wont* – *you* may be damned,
                              My Murray!'

A few weeks later Byron sent Murray a new drama, *Cain, A Mystery*, and was further outraged when Murray now proposed to pay 2,500 guineas for the lot. He complained to Kinnaird that '*three thousand*' guineas for the three plays and the three *Don Juan* cantos would have been a fairer price. After all, Murray's offer of 2,500 guineas was 'nearly the same as for the 4th Canto of C[hild]e H[arol]d which is inferior in quality'. So the once warmly creative literary partnership began to descend into acrimonious haggling over price.

There seemed to be a brief return to the glory days when Cantos III, IV and V of *Don Juan* were published, at last, in August 1821. Samuel Smiles, Murray's official memorialist, records how 'The booksellers' messengers filled the street in front of the house in Albemarle Street, and the parcels of books were given out of the window in answer to their obstreperous demands.' More detached publishing historians have suggested that this description may be exaggerated.

Don Juan had its passionate adherents. But the numbers printed were still small in relation to the early cantos of *Childe Harold* and Byron's Eastern tales. In 1821 1,500 copies were printed in octavo. Murray also published a smaller, cheaper edition, hoping to forestall the piracies which had followed publication of the earlier cantos of *Don Juan*. During his years of exile, as Byron's traditional readership diminished, it was in the cheap editions and indeed the piracies that his future influence predominantly lay.

Shelley never swerved in his admiration of *Don Juan*. He came to Ravenna on 6 August 1821 and, in their first few days together, Byron read him Canto V, the narrative of Juan in Constantinople. Shelley wrote to tell Mary that the poem was 'astonishingly fine'. He elaborated:

'It sets him not above but far above all the poets of the day: every word has the stamp of immortality. – I despair of rivalling Lord Byron, as well I may: and there is no other with whom it is worth contending. This canto is in style, but totally, & sustained with incredible ease & power, like the end of the second canto: there is not a word which the most rigid assertor of the dignity of human nature could desire to be cancelled: it fulfills in a certain degree what I have long preached of producing something wholly new & relative to the age – and yet surpassingly beautiful. It may be vanity, but I think I see the trace of my earnest exhortations to him to create something wholly new.'

Seeing Byron for the first time since he had left Venice, Shelley was pleasantly surprised. Then he had seemed on a self-destructive course. Now he seemed transformed in both health and outlook: 'He has got rid of all those melancholy and degrading habits which he indulged at Venice.' Shelley attributed the change to Byron's settled domesticity with 'one woman, a lady of rank' here in Ravenna. He was living within his income, devoting a quarter of his total of about £4,000 a year to charity: 'he is becoming what he should be, a virtuous man.' Shelley noticed that away from the dissolute atmosphere of Venice, William Fletcher too had recovered his good looks and was sprouting 'a fresh harvest of flaxen locks' in the midst of his premature grey hairs.

Shelley's enthusiasm over Byron's reformed nature may have been somewhat ingenuous, but he provides the most convincing picture that we have of Byron's way of life in those last few months in Ravenna, stranded in Count Guiccioli's palace. He was getting up at two in the afternoon, breakfasting late, after which he and Shelley sat talking until early evening. From six to eight they took a gallop through the pine forests, practising pistol shooting with a pumpkin for the target. They returned to the palazzo to dine and gossip on through the night till 6 a.m. The servants, the eight enormous dogs, three monkeys, five cats, the eagle, crow and falcon that Shelley counted, all stalked around Byron's apartment 'as if they were the masters of it'. Every now and then the building resounded with their quarrels. Shelley's vision of Byron is that of an eccentric and benevolent magician, ruler of a 'Circean Palace' in an obscure city. In a postscript to a letter to Thomas Love Peacock he lists additional members of Byron's menagerie: 'I have just met on the grand staircase five peacocks, two guinea hens, and an Egyptian crane. I wonder who those animals were before they changed into these shapes.'

Shelley's main motive in coming to Ravenna had been to review the situation of Allegra, whom he still regarded as part of his own family. He rode out to see her at Bagnacavallo – something her father had apparently not done – and stayed with her at the convent for three hours or so. He told Mary that the child had 'grown tall & slight for her age'. Her features had become more delicate and she was paler, 'probably from the effect of improper food'. Her hair, still very fair, hung in big curls down her back. She was dressed prettily in white muslin and 'an apron of black silk with trousers'. Allegra's 'light & airy figure & her graceful motions were a striking contrast to the other children there – she seemed a thing of finer race & a higher order.' She was already much affected by the convent discipline. Shelley was aware of a new submissiveness in her.

At first she was shy with him. But Shelley won her over with caresses and the gift of a gold chain from Ravenna, and she was soon leading him all over the garden and the convent rooms, running and skipping, showing off her little bed and the chair she used at dinner and the toy carriage she played in with her favourite companion. Shelley had brought her a basket of sweetmeats, and before helping herself she offered them to her small friend and all the nuns: 'that is not much like the old Allegra,' he observed. When Shelley asked what message he should take back to her father she demanded he should come and bring '*la mammina*' with him: Shelley took this to mean Claire, but it is surely more likely that Allegra was referring to Teresa. Shelley's account gives the impression that the child was suffering acute confusion of loyalties. He was confirmed in his opinion that Allegra should be removed from Bagnacavallo as soon as possible and given a liberal English education: 'the idea of bringing up so sweet a creature in the midst of such trash till sixteen!'

Shelley's fortnight in Ravenna was overcast by a new episode of the 'Hoppner scandal'. Hoppner had urged Byron to be discreet about it, both for Mary Shelley's sake and because the Hoppners did not want it known that they had passed on a story told to them in confidence. But Byron could not resist divulging information likely to cause trouble. According to Leigh Hunt, he 'had an incontinence, I believe unique, in talking of his affairs, and showing you other people's letters. He would even make you presents of them; and I have accepted one or two that they might go no further.' Another friend made the comment that Byron had a footman's penchant for the breaking of bad news. At the same time he was probably anxious to deflect any likelihood of Shelley attempting to persuade him to return Allegra to her mother. On Shelley's first night at the palace Byron showed him the letter that Hoppner had sent the previous September, detailing the nurse Elise's accusations that the mysterious baby born in Naples had been Shelley's and Claire's, that Shelley had obtained for Claire 'the most violent medicines to procure abortion' and when these had failed to take effect had removed the child and sent it to a foundling hospital. The horror in the letter Shelley now wrote to Mary suggests that he had known nothing of these rumours up to then. He urged Mary to reply to the Hoppners refuting 'a charge which you only can effectually rebut'.

On 10 August 1821 Mary, in Pisa, wrote a long, careful and indignant letter to Isabella Hoppner, maintaining that Elise's story was malicious and false and that she had been put up to it by her lover, now her husband, Paolo Foggi, an ex-servant of the Shelleys who was attempting blackmail. Mary sent the letter, as instructed, to Shelley at Ravenna so that he could forward it to the Hoppners. She was also anxious for Byron to read it, although imagining 'he gave no credit to the tale'. In fact, of course, Byron had been eager to believe it, commenting high-handedly to Hoppner, 'it is just like them.' It is doubtful if Mary's letter reached its destination. It was discovered among Byron's papers after his death. Was this simple negligence or, perhaps more likely, had Byron decided it suited him better for this slur on Claire's reputation to remain?

By the time Shelley left Ravenna a decision on Byron's future destination had been made. Reminded of the aggravations of the summer of 1816, he was easily dissuaded from his plans to settle in Geneva with the Gambas. Instead Shelley talked him into the advantages of Pisa. On 11 August he was writing to Mary to ask her to find Albe 'a large & magnificent house'. Part of the inducement was the plan for Byron and Shelley to inaugurate a literary review in Pisa. Leigh Hunt would be invited out to join this enterprise. The idea of a new review attracted Byron greatly. This was something he had previously discussed, abortively, with Moore.

On his way back to Pisa, Shelley stopped in Florence to see Teresa, Count Gamba and Pietro, to propose this new scheme to them. Teresa took the opportunity to scrutinise him closely on this, their first meeting. Although Byron's description had prepared her for a remarkable man the reality surpassed her expectations. 'Shelley was not a man like any other', so she described him in her memoir of Byron. She judged him as by no means so conventionally handsome as her own lover was. His smile was bad, his teeth misshapen and irregular, his skin covered with freckles, his unkempt hair already threaded through with premature silver. 'He was very tall, but stooped so much that he seemed to be of ordinary height; and although his whole frame was very slight, his bones and knuckles were prominent and even knobbly.' But Shelley still had a kind of beauty, 'an expression that could almost be described as godly and austere'. Teresa was reminded of 'those ethereal, innocent faces from primitive Italian schools of painting'. Shelley radiated fervour, enthusiasm and intelligence.

On 26 August Byron wrote to Shelley from Ravenna telling him that he and the servants were already 'in all the agonies of packing'. He was sending the furniture ahead before setting out himself for Pisa. But he delayed and Lega Zambelli bumbled. The usual psychological barriers descended, and it took him a further two months to depart.

In those weeks he wrote three substantial poems: *The Irish Avatar or Messiah*, a furious, reckless anti-monarchical commentary on King George IV's post-coronation visit to Ireland in August and September 1821; the first act of *Heaven and Earth, A Mystery*, 'a little lyrical drama' on the Old Testament subject of the Deluge; and *The Vision of Judgement*, the most brilliantly lethal of his satires, Byron's response to Southey's own *Vision of Judgement*, the Laureate's effusive eulogy to his deceased monarch George III. All these works were sent to Murray but he was never to publish them.

Byron busied himself in Tom Moore's project for the memoirs, suggesting that with assistance from John Murray Moore should now round up as much as possible of Byron's correspondence for future use by himself as Byron's editor and by Byron's executors. He alerted Murray to the large collection of letters kept since he had been a boy of sixteen, which had been left in England in Hobhouse's care, and to the ever-swelling hoard of correspondence, at least doubling the total, 'all received since my last Ostracism'. Byron wanted Moore to have access to these letters '*not*', he said, 'for the purpose – of *abusing confidences* – nor of *hurting* the feelings of correspondents living – or the memories of the dead', but to provide the evidence for what would be, as far as possible, a definitive account. But how definitive was definitive? Byron was aware of whole areas of secrecy, conscious that the task would 'require delicacy'.

Of all his past correspondence he was particularly anxious for the return of the letters he had written to Lady Melbourne: 'They are very numerous & ought to have been restored long ago.' These were the letters, he told Murray, which would provide the evidence of his 'real views and feelings' on the subject of his marriage. '*If* by yr. own management you can extract any of my epistles from Ly. Caroline Lamb (mind she don't give you *forgeries* in my *hand*; she has done as much you *know* before now) they might be of use in yr. collection.'

From the safety of Ravenna Byron compiled lists of those who would probably have preserved his correspondence: Lady Oxford; Lady Frances Webster;

Miss Elizabeth Pigot of Southwell; possibly even Mary Chaworth, though 'these latter are probably destroyed or inaccessible'. He reminded Murray that all the letters he had ever written to Lady Byron, both before and since their marriage, were still in her possession. He suggested, however, that these letters were too much to his credit for her to return them: 'never mind . . . we can do without them.' There is a palpable sense of Byron's enjoyment at venturing into this emotional minefield, as if he were aware of laying up a joke for posterity.

In his now furnitureless rooms in the Palazzo Guiccioli he began writing an ever more discursive version of his journal:

'Man is born *passionate* of body – but with an innate though secret tendency to the love of Good in his Main-spring of Mind – But God help us all! – It is at present a sand jar of atoms.'

Rain descended for five days running in October. Byron was back in the grip of a terrible depression. One of the books he asked Murray to send him was Burton's *Anatomy of Melancholy*. He complained that Lega was like a tortoise in his preparations. In desperation Byron went out for a walk with a Signora of Ravenna under the thin crescent of a very young moon. It was 'a *new* woman, (that is, new to me)' who evidently expected to be made love to. But Byron merely made 'a few common-place speeches'. Even the once automatic sexual responses were now failing him.

At last, on 29 October, after sitting up all night 'to be sure of rising', Byron left Ravenna. He abandoned the most decrepit of the animals: the goat with the broken leg, the far from handsome mongrel, the species of heron who would eat only fish, the badger on a chain and the two ugly old monkeys. He also deserted Allegra in her convent. It had been Byron's instinct to take his daughter with him. But Teresa insisted she was better where she was.

Shortly before he left there had been a message from Allegra, written painstakingly in Italian on the back of a letter to Byron from the Prioress, begging him to come and see her. She told him the fair would soon be on, there were many things she wanted him to buy her: 'will you not please your Allegrina who loves you so?' His response to this plea was cynical: 'Sincere enough but not very flattering – for she wants to see me because it "is the fair" to get some paternal Gingerbread – I suppose.' One of Byron's last letters from Ravenna mentions having 'to settle some arrangements about my daughter', but there is no suggestion he went to visit her.

The Earl of Clare had recently been much in Byron's mind, recommended to John Murray as a 'very voluminous' correspondent of the Harrow period. On the road between Imola and Bologna suddenly, quite unexpectedly, their coaches crossed. They got out and greeted one another. As Byron described the encounter, 'It was a new and inexplicable feeling like rising from the grave to me', as if he and Clare had never been apart. 'Clare too was much agitated – more – in *appearance* – than even myself – for I could feel his heart beat to the fingers' ends – unless indeed – it was the pulse of my own which made me think so.' The account in Byron's journal, written a few days later, mobile, blotchy, heavily underlined, still conveys the strange emotionalism of the scene.

He and Clare were together for only five minutes, and in the public road 'but', wrote Byron, 'I hardly recollect an hour of my existence which could be weighed against them'. When they parted – Clare to travel south to Rome and Byron north to Pisa – they agreed to meet again in the spring.

24

Pisa

1821–1822

> 'Much had passed
> Since last we parted; and those five short years –
> Much had they told! His clustering locks were turned
> Grey; nor did aught recall the Youth that swam
> From Sestos to Abydos. Yet his voice,
> Still it was sweet; still from his eye the thought
> Flashed lightning-like, nor lingered on the way,
> Waiting for words. Far, far into the night
> We sat, conversing – no unwelcome hour,
> The hour we met; and, when Aurora rose,
> Rising, we climbed the rugged Apennine.'

As Byron travelled through Tuscany to Pisa in late October 1821 there had been another reunion, this time a planned one, with the now elderly Samuel Rogers who recorded his impressions in his poem *Italy*. Rogers' lines show that Byron still had his capacity for instant empathy.

He met Rogers at Bologna and they travelled on together to Florence, chattering and gossiping in the post-chaise, excoriating their mutual acquaintances. They stopped to pass the time of day with Byron's friend the sexton in the cemetery at Certosa, who cast acquisitive eyes on Rogers' skull–like head. In company with such a professional connoisseur Byron returned to the art galleries in Florence he had enjoyed in 1817, but complained that there were too many visitors crammed in to allow him 'to *feel* anything properly'. He shuddered to hear 'one bold Briton' announcing to the woman on his arm as they looked at Titian's Venus, '"well now – this is very fine indeed . . ."'

Byron and Rogers parted company at Florence. Nearing Pisa, just past Empoli, there was another criss-crossing on the road as Claire Clairmont, leaving Pisa in the public coach on purpose to avoid his arrival, coincided briefly with 'Lord B – and his travelling train'.

The official spies were vigilant. Cavaliere Luigi Torelli, 'la spia delle spie', entered a report in his confidential journal *Arcana politicae anticarbonariae*: 'The famous poet, Lord Byron, who, if he had not the reputation of being mad, ought to be watched by the whole police of Europe, has taken the Palazzo Lanfranchi for a year, at a rent of 200 zecchini paying six months in advance.' He had come with a large train of attendants, all of them from Bologna or the Romagna, except one English servant and a groom. He brought with him fourteen horses, all his carriages bearing his arms and the motto 'Crede Byron'. In the turbid world of Tuscan politics even Byron's motto struck a note of dread.

Byron arrived in a Pisa that was beautiful and melancholy with its nearly deserted monuments and strangely leaning tower. Shelley had described it when he first arrived there as 'a large disagreeable city almost without inhabitants'. Apart from its ancient university, Pisa seemed like a city with little *raison d'être*. The house that had been found for Byron by the Shelleys, the Palazzo Lanfranchi, was a mid-Renaissance building on the slow bend of the Arno opposite the Chiesa di San Sepolcro. He described it, with some hyperbole, to Murray as 'a famous old feudal palazzo on the Arno – large enough for a garrison – with dungeons below – and cells in the walls – and so full of *Ghosts* that the learned Fletcher (my Valet) has begged leave to change his room – and then refused to occupy his *new* room – because there were more Ghosts there than in the other'. Byron liked to think the staircase had been built by Michelangelo, but there is no evidence for this.

Like the city itself the Palazzo Lanfranchi had a certain grimness. Thomas Medwin remembered it as 'large, gloomy, and uncomfortable'. To Shelley the entrance hall 'seemed built for giants'. The original owners of the palace were of the same noble family as the Lanfranchi who appears in Dante's *Inferno* as one of Count Ugolino's tormentors. A picture of Ugolino and his sons, together with a miniature of Ada, hung in Byron's vast apartment on the *piano nobile*. Moretto, the bulldog who had been pupped in Venice, was kept chained outside the door on the first-floor landing to discourage unwanted visitors. Years later, when Newton Hanson visited the palace, he was shown an inscription in pencil on the side of the door frame marking a man's height. He remembered the wording only vaguely: 'a Man can no more add one minute to his existence or life (I forget which) than he can add one cubit to his Stature.' But Hanson was confident the handwriting was Byron's, a forlorn attempt to personalise the place.

Byron's life in Pisa was secluded. He avoided the university professors with an arrogance that made him unpopular with local intellectuals. He had nothing to do with the little flurry of social activity around the Court of Tuscany which migrated to Pisa for the winter season and the Carnival. Byron had had enough of masquerades and indeed of grand duchesses. 'I have most of my Italian relations near me,' he told Douglas Kinnaird. The Gambas were living nearby at Palazzo Parra on the Lungarno. Byron's loyalties were now, so late in life, quasi-familial.

He gravitated to the Shelleys and the group of literary, military expatriates around them. The Shelleys too were neighbours, having furnished what Mary called 'very nice apartments' at the top of the Tre Palazzi di Chiesa on the south side of the Arno, opposite Byron's palazzo. 'So Pisa you see has become a little nest of singing birds,' she told her friend Maria Gisborne. She described Teresa Guiccioli charitably as 'a nice pretty girl, without pretensions, good hearted and amiable – her relations were banished Romagna for Carbonarism'.

Four days after Byron reached Pisa, Shelley introduced him to a new friend, Edward Williams, a young officer recently returned from India, whose conversation was still full of boastful references to lion and tiger hunting. Williams had left in a cloud of scandal, having run away with the wife of a brother officer; the two now lived in Italy as Edward and Jane Williams. Shelley appreciated them as 'nice, good natured people; very soft society after authors & pretenders to philosophy'. He was, inevitably, to develop an extreme tendresse towards Jane. Edward, whose literary interests were stronger than Shelley suggests, was immediately won over by Byron's open friendliness, writing in his journal for Monday 5 November:

'Shelley read me some passages of his Hellas, which are very fine, and his translation of the only Greek farce which has been handed down to us [Euripides' *Cyclops*]. In the evening S. introduced me to Lord Byron, on whom we called. So far from his having haughtiness of manners, they are those of the most unaffected and gentlemanly ease; and so far from being (as is generally supposed) wrapt in melancholy and gloom, he is all sunshine and good humour. On our taking leave, he took up a book from the table, saying, "I will lend you others tomorrow; in the meantime you will find something in the *Annuaire Historique Universel* to amuse you, besides the general matter it contains, for at the end it takes infinite pains to prove that I am the devil".'

Williams's sweet-natured and conscientious journal gives a revealing account of Byron's day-to-day life in Pisa.

Another member of the Shelley circle was John Taaffe, eldest son of a leading Catholic family in Louth, a would-be intellectual whom Byron sarcastically called 'an Irish genius'. Taaffe too was escaping a disreputable past, a scandalous liaison in Edinburgh, and was now 'sentimentally attached' to Madame Artemisia Castellini Regny, a Frenchwoman with impressive contacts within the Tuscan nobility. As a translator of Dante, Taaffe was 'as impassioned as he was ponderous', in Teresa Guiccioli's expert view. Byron judged his poetry to be very good Irish and out of loyalty and mischief urged John Murray to publish Taaffe's *Comment on the Divine Comedy of Dante*. 'He will die, – if he is *not* published – he will be damned if he *is* – but that *he* don't mind. We must publish him.' Murray resisted Byron's blandishments.

From the middle of November the group was reinforced by the arrival of Shelley's second cousin, Captain Thomas Medwin. He, like Williams, had been an Indian army officer and was now retired on half-pay on grounds of ill health. He had become a professional wanderer and occasional writer, spending a year in Geneva where he rented a house with his ex-army colleague Edward Williams. Shelley had then invited him to Pisa. He travelled on to Florence, Rome and Venice and was back in Geneva when Shelley wrote to tell him of Byron's imminent arrival. He returned to Pisa quickly. Medwin was a man for the main chance, and he cast himself in the role of Byron's Boswell, the avid though none too reliable recorder of the poet's accumulated memories.

In those first few weeks in Pisa, Byron and Shelley were constant companions, whilst around them circulated Williams, Taaffe and Medwin, riding, shooting, playing billiards, reading poetry. Mary Shelley and Teresa were thrown very much together, in an unexpected and incongruous alliance. The men fell into an evening routine of riding together beyond the city gates of Pisa to a farmhouse where they practised pistol firing, the target a bull's eye or a half crown piece. This was a favourite amusement of Byron's. He was a good shot, much improved since his London days at Manton's, but his hand still shook with nerves when he took aim. When Rogers later came to Pisa and joined the shooting party he observed that the farmer's very pretty daughter Francesca had her arms covered with bracelets which Byron made clear had been gifts to her from him.

When Byron had arrived in Pisa in November the weather was still summery. He had plucked the oranges in his palace garden with so much enthusiasm that they had given him diarrhoea. But as Christmas approached the weather worsened with mists and squalls over the Arno. Byron began laying in 'some English household comforts' from Leghorn (now Livorno). English mustard and choice clarets were amongst the luxuries he ordered from his agents, the Leghorn merchant Henry Dunn. While living in Ravenna his strict vegetable and fish diet had been modified: 'Ay! and you will find me eating flesh, too, like yourself or any cannibal, except it be upon Fridays,' he had informed William Bankes. Consciousness of his stomach disorders had receded with the excitements of Romagna politics. In Pisa he responded eagerly to the gift of a wild boar from the Maremma sent by Captain John Hay, the Scots friend of Byron's youth who was now travelling in Italy.

At the Palazzo Lanfranchi he established a tradition of male dinners, held on Wednesday nights. These gatherings became known as Lord Byron's Pistol Club. Shelley reported primly: 'Lord Byron visits us at a weekly dinner where my nerves are generally shaken to pieces by sitting up, contemplating the rest making themselves vats of claret &c. till 3. o'Clock in the morning.' Byron led the conversation, happy, charming, recreating the easy cronyism of his Piccadilly days.

At one of the dinners, as Byron reminisced about the theatrical triumphs of his younger days, a plan was mooted for amateur dramatics at the Palazzo Lanfranchi. After all, as Teresa put it pointedly, 'the actors were all to hand'. A precedent had been set by Alfieri, who had formed his own dramatic society in Pisa. The first production would be Shakespeare's *Othello*, with Byron as Iago, a part in which he often admired Edmund Kean. They got as far as the first run-through which persuaded Thomas Medwin that Byron could have been one of the world's great actors. 'His voice had a flexibility, a variety in its tones, a power and pathos beyond any I ever heard; and his countenance was capable of expressing the tenderest as well as the strongest emotions. I shall never forget his reading Iago's part in the handkerchief scene.' It was said that Byron even looked like Iago. But Teresa became jealous of the prospective Desdemona, John Taaffe's companion Madame Regny, whom she judged to be now in determined pursuit of Byron, and she vetoed the performance. Williams's diary records sadly: 'Othello that was talked of laid aside.'

From New Year 1822 there was a new recruit at Byron's table, the most actorly of all. The six-foot, raven-haired, swarthy-complexioned adventurer Edward John Trelawny arrived in Pisa on 14 January, encouraged by Edward Williams whom he had known in Geneva. Trelawny was a Cornishman from the minor landed gentry whose career in the navy had been mysteriously cut short. Drawn to Pisa because Byron and Shelley were both living there, he was received by Byron at the Palazzo Lanfranchi the following day. In some alarm Byron recognised his literary progeny, telling Teresa he had just met an Englishman who, ever since he was a boy, had intended to put the life of Byron's own Corsair into practice: 'He keeps the poem under his pillow.' His lurid adventures in India were said to have been influenced by Byron. Trelawny was living proof of the Byron effect.

He had his own dark glamour. Mary Shelley described Trelawny as 'extravagant – un giovane Stravagante – partly natural, & partly perhaps put on – but it suits him well'. As they met daily in Pisa, riding and shooting, exchanging competitively dramatic stories of their lives, Byron found himself half touched and half repelled by the wild brusque handsome man who was in many ways his counterpart. There was always a deep ambivalence in their relationship. What bound them together, through their many reciprocal irritations, was their shared sense of identity as tale-tellers and seafarers. Trelawny, like Byron, was addicted to the sea. He had already commissioned the building of an open boat for Shelley, Williams and himself in the naval dockyard at Genoa under the supervision of an English naval officer Captain Daniel Roberts. Byron, not to be outdone, now asked Trelawny to organise the construction of a schooner, again by Captain Roberts. Trelawny's specification for the schooner for Byron was luxurious: 'She is to have *Iron Keel*, copper *fastenings* and *bottom* – the cabin to be as *high* and *roomy* as possible, no *expence* to be *spared* to make her a complete B E A U T Y ! We should like to have four guns, one on each bow and one on each quarter, as *large* as you think *safe* – to make a devil of a noise!' In the end two guns were fitted. The boat was to be called the *Countess Guiccioli*, but was later renamed – just as indiscreetly – the *Bolivar*.

In this atmosphere of male rivalries and fantasies Medwin's project as Byron's memorialist flourished. Late at night, at the end of the long convivial dinners at the Palazzo Lanfranchi, Medwin seized his chance to cross-examine Byron, egging him on with a journalist's complicity into a series of rambles round the past. These interviews, after Byron's death, were to be published as Medwin's *Journal of the Conversations of Lord Byron at Pisa*. Their detractors insisted that Medwin had merely cobbled them together after the event. William Fletcher was a particularly stern critic, writing to Augusta after publication of the book: 'any one must say why this must be onley a Mass of falsehoods Gleaned from one or a Nother, And No Conversation's of my Lord's.' Indeed there are many factual inaccuracies in Medwin's reportage. But the immediacy of recall and the closeness to the tone of voice in Byron's correspondence suggest that Medwin took at least some verbatim notes. It gives the best impression we have of Byron's postprandial conversation man to man, its buttonholing confidentiality, its raciness, its blatant and brilliant exaggeration as Byron fights to keep Pisan boredom at bay. Byron's friends would claim that Medwin had exploited him. But it was Byron in a way who was making use of Medwin, entertaining himself by rewriting his own legend. When Lady

Blessington later made the comment that Byron was well aware that Medwin 'meant to print what he said, and purposely *hummed* him', she was certainly correct.

Byron's circumstances changed substantially with the death of Lady Noel. Over the years his relations with Annabella had reached a kind of accommodation. He continued to correspond with her over Ada and, interestingly, seems to have assumed that Lady Byron would be sympathetic to the cause of Italian liberation. But his hatred of Lady Noel, whom he still held largely responsible for the separation, had remained implacable. At Christmas 1821, when Byron and his friends assembled at the Palazzo Lanfranchi for a celebratory feast, he had made a heartless bet of £1,000 with Shelley that Lady Noel would outlive Shelley's father Sir Timothy. 'That old Serpent the She Noel' struck him as the sort of woman who would live for ever. But Lady Noel died on 28 January 1822. When he heard the news just over two weeks later, Byron had the grace to forgive her memory, reacting with an unexpected surge of feeling, as so often, to the fact of death.

By the terms of the separation settlement, the income from the Wentworth estates was due to be divided between the two parties. From the death of his mother-in-law he gained about £2,500 a year. His total income, excluding his earnings from John Murray, now amounted to at least £6,000, more than he needed to sustain his comparatively frugal life abroad. He quickly took out a £10,000 insurance on Lady Byron's life since, once she died, the Wentworth income would be redistributed and he would be the loser. He wrote to John Hanson asking him to send over 'a Seal with the new arms', plus a smaller one embellished with the coronet and the new initials *NB*. Byron signed himself Noel Byron from now on.

The sudden warmth of his feelings for his deceased mother-in-law diminished when he heard of the directive in her will that the Thomas Phillips portrait of Byron in Albanian dress, which she had bought in 1815, was to be enclosed in a box and kept at the family house at Kirkby Mallory. Ada was not to be shown it until she was twenty-one, and then only with her mother's consent. Byron resented bitterly what he called 'this portrait whim of Lady Noel's', interpreting it, rightly, as an attempt to bring Ada up in a state of suspicion and ignorance of him.

Early in 1822 Edward Williams called on Byron and found him 'sitting for his bust to Bartolini'. The following week he called again and saw the artist at work on 'a fine bust'. Lorenzo Bartolini was then a fashionable sculptor in Florence, not in the Thorwaldsen league but with a following among the English. He was an ardent Napoleonist, a pupil of David and friend of Ingres, and had created a large-scale bronze bust of the Emperor in 1805. It was no doubt this connection that drew him towards Byron: he had proposed the work himself. Byron had been reluctant, as he had been with Thorwaldsen: he disliked the idea of a monument in marble. But he agreed on condition that Bartolini made a bust of Teresa Guiccioli too.

Byron had intended to send the pair of busts as a present to John Murray, to make amends for the earlier misunderstanding over the bust by Thorwaldsen. But the commission soon ran into problems. When she saw the plaster mould Teresa was dismayed by her own depiction, complaining somewhat unjustly of its compressed lips, over-prominent cheekbones and the 'peculiar arrangement of her hair'. Afraid that no sculptor on earth could capture a beauty 'wellnigh superhuman in its manifestation' she had gone to great lengths in helping to pose Byron, imploring him to tuck his hair behind his ears so that Bartolini could appreciate 'the full span of his godlike countenance'. But Byron's portrait was a still greater disappointment than hers had been. When he first saw Raphael Morghen's engraving of the bust Byron exclaimed that it 'exactly resembles a superannuated Jesuit', making him look over seventy. It showed only too clearly the ravages of time.

In May 1822, when John Murray enquired about progress on the busts, Byron warned him that the transition from the model to the marble was likely to be lengthy: 'Bartolini is famous for his delays, something like yourself.' The following October he wrote backhandedly to tell him: 'The busts are finished – are you worthy of them?' Bartolini's busts had by now become the pawns in Byron's altercations with his publisher and never found their way to Albemarle Street.

Byron's anger at John Murray's treatment of *Don Juan* was still smouldering. He accused Murray of 'playing the Stepmother' to the poem, ashamed or afraid of putting his name to it. He saw this as being 'sad half and half dealing – for you will be a long time before you publish a better poem'. He kept up a barrage of complaints about the misprints with which Murray's printer had defaced *Don Juan*. But the reason why he had now discontinued work on the project originally conceived as almost boundless, with Don Juan taking an extended tour of Byron's Europe, ending as a Prussian baron caught up in the revolution in France, was not Byron's disillusionment with Murray but rather a domestic embargo.

Teresa Guiccioli had read the first two cantos of *Don Juan* in its French translation and was 'greatly disquieted' not just by the content but by her now clearer understanding of the dangers of Byron's sexual and political involvements. An attack on Byron's morals in the *Milan Gazette* had especially alarmed her. She was no doubt anxious that further cantos in the same contro-versial vein could rebound on her own family. Byron's reading of the situation was that Teresa, even more than other women, had disliked his unsentimental rendering of women's sexuality: her objection, he said, 'arises from the wish of all women to exalt the *sentiment* of the passions – & to keep up the illusion which is their empire'. When Teresa wrote to thank her lover for the sacrifice he had agreed to make on her behalf she added the postscript: 'I am only sorry that Don Juan was not left in the infernal regions.'

For want of other occupation in the winter of 1821–2 Byron returned to the Germanic tragedy of *Werner, or The Inheritance*, started just before his mar-riage and interrupted by the separation crisis. He asked Hobhouse to 'rummage out' the original draft from his papers left in London and post it on to Pisa. But he seems to have restarted the tragedy without it. Medwin tells us that the five-act play was completed in twenty-eight days, with one entire act being written at a sitting. Even allowing for Medwin's exaggeration it is clear that he worked on it concentratedly. Byron's interpretation of *The German's Tale, or Kruitzner*, the tragedy which had haunted him as a boy, has now been overlaid by his own history of anguish, his exile and his travels. It exudes a kind of emptiness of spirit and explores the possibilities of endurance in situations from which all real hope has fled.

Though the guilt-ridden Werner, abandoned by his God, is in some ways the standard Byronic character, and the central theme of flawed inheritance takes us back to the vicissitudes of 'Mad Jack', Byron's father, the autobio-graphical elements in the play have taken on a new and interesting slant. Werner's love Josephine is an affectionate version of Teresa:

> 'an Italian girl,
> The daughter of a banish'd man, who lives
> On love and poverty with this same Werner'.

Werner's son Ulric is a brigand who is also a political partisan, a terrorist who evolves into a freedom fighter at the head of a bona fide military force. There is a significant parallel with Byron's own shift from sulky rebelliousness to close political involvement: the pursuit of constructive leadership that started with his joining of the Romagna Carbonari and ended with the campaign for inde-pendence in Greece.

Since Byron was now seeking alternatives to Murray he sent the fair copy of *Werner*, written out by Mary Shelley, to Tom Moore in Paris. He was hopeful that Galignani, the French publishers, would publish it there.

Meanwhile, in London, on 19 December 1821, John Murray had brought out

Byron's *Cain* in a volume also containing *Sardanapalus* and *The Two Foscari*. In a letter to Byron, Murray refers fleetingly to 'humbug Row over Cain'. It was a good deal more serious than that. Byron's dramatic poem, based on the account of the fall and Abel's murder by his brother given in the Book of Genesis, generated the greatest outcry yet against the poet and his work, with accusations of wilful, dangerous iconoclasm that reverberated for the remainder of the nineteenth century.

The biblical story had already been given epic treatment in English by John Milton in *Paradise Lost*. Byron's defence, and that of his supporters, was that he went no further than Milton in questioning the existence of the godhead: if people condemn *Cain* 'then they must condemn the *Paradise Lost*, if they have a mind to be consistent', argued Walter Scott, accepting Byron's dedication of the poem to him. But there was of course a difference between Byron and Milton. Byron's poem shows how far he had absorbed the Voltairean spirit of religious scepticism, expressing the dilemma of faith in his own quintessentially personal terms. He defends the right to question. Byron's Cain says of his Maker:

> 'I have look'd out
> In the vast desolate night in search of him; ...
> I watch'd for what I thought his coming; for
> With fear rose longing in my heart to know
> What 'twas which shook us all – but nothing came.'

The dangers in publishing *Cain*, a work he privately considered 'inconceivably ridiculous & dull', had been predicted by Hobhouse, who could see that Byron laid himself open to charges of blasphemy. When he wrote to remonstrate, Byron answered airily, 'I dare say your opinion about "Cain" is the right one', but as there were opposite views, Moore for example finding the poem 'wonderful – terrible – never to be forgotten', he would leave it to the public to find out.

When John Murray wrote to ask him to tone down some of Satan's speeches he refused: 'The two passages cannot be altered without making Lucifer talk like the Bishop of Lincoln – which would not be in the character of the former.' Byron went on maintaining, wittily and obstinately, that this was a play, an argument, an entertainment. An author could not be held responsible for views expressed by characters he had created. Anyway, '*who* was ever altered by a poem?' He accused John Murray of self-serving cant.

Soon after *Cain* was published, clergymen began denouncing it in pulpits round the country as 'a book calculated to spread infidelity'. The attacks on its author were hysterical and personal. The Reverend John Styles, for example, preached a sermon in Holland Chapel, Kennington, in which he denounced

Byron as 'a denaturalised being, who, having exhausted every species of sensual gratification, and drained the cup of sin to its bitterest dregs, is resolved to show that he is no longer human, even in his frailties, but a cool, unconcerned fiend'. The accusations of sodomy are not far from the surface.

Bishop Heber's review of *Cain* in the *Quarterly Review*, published by Murray, brings the attack still closer to home. Heber analyses the insidious cleverness that made Byron so dangerous an influence:

'Even the mystery of *Cain*, wicked as it may be, is the work of a nobler and more daring wickedness than that which delights in insulting the miseries, and stimulating the evil passions, and casting a cold-blooded ridicule over the lofty and generous feelings of our nature; and it is better that Lord Byron should be a manichee, or a deist, – nay, we would almost say, if the thing were possible, it is better that he should be a moral and argumentative atheist, than the professed and systematic poet of seduction, adultery and incest.'

The great danger of Lord Byron is the glamour, the attractiveness. Again, the basis of the Bishop's attack is Byron's sexual deviation.

Murray himself, as *Cain*'s publisher, came under fire. Early in 1822 an anonymous pamphlet appeared, signed 'Oxoniensis' and entitled *A Remonstrance to Mr. John Murray, Respecting a Recent Publication*. Because of the controversial content of the poem the Lord Chancellor, Lord Eldon, refused to issue Murray with an injunction to prevent pirated editions. When it looked as if a prosecution might ensue, Byron characteristically sprang to the defence of his now beleaguered publisher. He wrote to tell John Murray that any proceedings against *Cain* must be transferred to him – 'who am willing & *ought* to endure them'. If Murray had lost money, he would refund the copyright. If Murray was prosecuted he would return to England. He even instructed Moore in Paris to forward the manuscript of *Werner* to John Murray: 'I neither can nor ought to leave him.' All his affection and gratitude returned.

From Pisa in mid-February 1822 Byron sent Murray a conciliatory letter:

'I write to you about all this row of bad passions – and absurdities – with the *Summer* Moon (for here our Winter is clearer than your Dog days) lighting the winding Arno with all her buildings and bridges – so quiet & still – what nothings we are! before the least of these Stars!'

This sweetly philosophical mood was not to last.

In the spring of 1822 the Tuscan police reports grew longer and more excitable as a result of the episode known as 'the Pisa Affray'. This began on Sunday 24

March, in the early evening, when Byron, Shelley, Trelawny, Pietro Gamba and Captain John Hay, who was visiting Pisa, were returning from their pistol practice in the countryside. Byron's courier Giuseppe Strauss was in attendance. Mary Shelley and Teresa Guiccioli were following behind them in Teresa's carriage, driven by Byron's coachman Vincenzo Papi with Teresa's servant Antonio Maluchielli. The literary Irishman John Taaffe rode up to join the party as it was approaching the city's eastern gate.

This cavalcade was disturbed by another horseman rushing through aggressively from behind, causing Taaffe's horse to rear and jostle against Byron's. Byron angrily rode after the rider, accompanied by Shelley and Trelawny. Heated words were exchanged and Byron, registering the man's impressive epauletted uniform and good horse, took him to be an army officer and issued a challenge. This turned out to be an embarrassing breach of etiquette since Stefani Masi was not, as Byron put it, 'an officer or a Gentleman', merely a Sergeant-Major of the Tuscan Royal Light Horse.

There was a violent scene. Pietro Gamba struck the Sergeant-Major in the chest with his riding whip, calling him 'Ignorante'. Masi roared out to the guards at the town gate to arrest the 'maledetti Inglesi'. Byron, followed by Pietro, rode on through the gate. Shelley, Trelawny, Hay and Giuseppe Strauss, the courier, were caught up in the fight during which Shelley was knocked unconscious by the hilt of Masi's sabre, Hay's face was badly slashed and Strauss received sword-wounds in his chest which resulted in a haemorrhage of the lungs.

Byron returned with Gamba to the Palazzo Lanfranchi for arms and reinforcements. He sent Lega Zambelli to inform the police of the affray at the town gates and set out again along the Lungarno towards the eastern gate. It was now getting dark. Here he again met Masi who rode up, still belligerent, saying, 'Are you content now that I have beaten you all?' Byron had equipped himself with a swordstick which he half-drew to show Masi he was armed. Tita Falcieri emerged from the palazzo brandishing two sabres and seized the bridle of the Sergeant's horse. Byron ordered him to let Masi go and the Sergeant started to ride off.

What Byron did not know at the time was that another servant, the coachman Vincenzo Papi, had intercepted the departing Masi and speared him with an implement said to be a pitchfork. In the confusion of the Sunday night crowd of passers-by, the Sergeant had staggered down the street into a café, badly wounded in the abdomen, and was taken to the hospital of Santa Chiara where he was not expected to survive the night.

The immediate panic of the situation is made clear in Williams's diary. The scene at the Shelleys' house that evening was dramatic: 'Lord B. came in, the Countess fainting on his arm, S. sick from the blow, Lord B. and the young Count foaming with rage, Mrs S. looking philosophically upon this interesting scene, and Jane and I wondering what the devil was to come next.' Wild rumours were already circulating in Pisa that Byron had been leading an insurrection of peasants who had made an attack upon the guard, 'that the guard maintained their ground manfully against an awful number of the armed insurgents, that they were at length defeated – one Englishman, whose name was Trelawny, left dead at the gate, and Lord B. mortally wounded, who is now telling me the tale – and I drinking brandy and water by his side'.

Sergeant Masi recovered. He was treated in hospital by the eminent surgeon Professor Vaccà at Byron's expense. The coachman Vincenzo Papi, who had now confessed to Byron that he had been the perpetrator of the attack, was arrested but released the next day after Byron's grooms had falsely testified that he had driven the Countess's carriage to the stables after the fracas and remained there at work. Byron was determined to protect his servant though Teresa, alarmed that the affair might escalate with probable repercussions for her family, argued that Papi ought to be dismissed. The possibility that Papi may have been an agent provocateur, planted by the Tuscan authorities to discredit Byron and his household, cannot be ruled out.

Tita Falcieri, who was also arrested, was held in prison. His association with the Carbonari was no doubt held against him, as well as his evident loyalty to Byron, who lamented the loss of his 'best servant' and made repeated interventions to obtain his release. Byron paid a fine to free Tita from punishment and detention for carrying arms, and financed the celebratory feast which Tita gave to a dozen fellow prisoners. But Tita was only given freedom to mix with other prisoners for a day before being returned to solitary confinement. In April he was sentenced to be exiled. In prison in Florence his great beard – the beard that caused him to be known as 'Il Barbone' – was removed. The spy Torelli noted: 'when told to shave it off with a razor, he imagined his beard was to be given to his master, Lord Byron; but on being told this was not the case, he wrapped it up most carefully in a piece of paper.' An emasculated Tita was then taken to the Tuscan frontier in an act of vindictiveness against Byron himself.

A further cruel twist was the imprisonment of Teresa's footman, Antonio Maluchielli, although there was no evidence against him. The aim clearly was to harass Byron and the Gambas. Byron's position was weakened when John Taaffe prevaricated over giving evidence in the affair, nervous about stating that he had been the rider who was first jostled by Masi. The disillusioned Pisa

417

circle started calling Taaffe 'Falstaffe'. The Masi affair created disruption and farce.

In February 1822 Claire Clairmont, despairing of her life in Italy, was planning a move from Florence to Vienna where her brother Charles was living. She wrote a letter to Byron, of which only a draft copy still exists, declaring: 'I cannot go without having first seen and embraced Allegra.' She entreated him to change his policy of keeping her apart from their daughter: 'My dear Friend, I conjure you do not make the world dark to me, as if my Allegra were dead.'

In fact Claire did not go to Vienna. Encouraged by Mary Shelley, she travelled to Pisa to discuss the situation and then returned to Florence after all. Over the next weeks it seems that her anxieties about Allegra worsened. On 19 March she attempted to enlist the Shelleys' support for a scheme to kidnap Allegra from the convent. Whilst advancing a number of practical arguments against so reckless an endeavour Mary assured her, 'No one can more entirely agree with you than I in thinking that as soon as possible A. ought to be taken out of the hands of one as remorseless as he is unprincipled.'

On 9 April Claire wrote to Mary again saying, 'I am truly uneasy for it seems to me some time since I have heard any news from Allegra. I fear she is sick.' This was a kind of maternal second sight, for Allegra was indeed ailing during April. On 13 April Byron's banker in Ravenna, Pellegrino Ghigi, passed on a message to Lega Zambelli at Pisa from the Reverend Mother at the convent at Bagnacavallo. She reported that Allegra, who had recovered from a fever some months earlier, had had a recurrence. Dr Rasi, a physician from Ravenna, had been sent for. At this point the fever fits, almost certainly typhus fever then raging in the Romagna, were said to be 'light and slow'.

The message reached Pisa on 17 April. Presumably Lega gave the news to Byron, preoccupied as he then was with the complex dramas of the 'Pisa affray' and an imminent visit from Samuel Rogers. On 19 April further bulletins arrived from the Abbess and from Ghigi. The fever had now attacked Allegra's chest and Dr Rasi, in consultation with the convent doctor, had decided that the child should be bled. There was still no sense of emergency; Allegra was said to be improving. But if the situation suddenly deteriorated Ghigi would send word to Pisa by express post. No further warning reached Byron until the announcement of Allegra's death arrived by express messenger on 22 April. Byron wrote to Shelley: 'The blow was stunning and unexpected, for I thought the danger over, by the long interval between her stated amelioration and the arrival of the express.'

Allegra's death had been announced to Byron by Teresa. She describes his reaction in her life of Byron: 'A mortal paleness spread itself over his face, his strength failed him, and he sunk into a seat . . . He remained immovable in the same attitude for an hour, and no consolation seemed to reach his ears, far less his heart.' How genuine was Byron's grief for the daughter he had not seen for over a year, whom he had failed to visit at the convent in spite of her entreaties? We underestimate his strange capacity for sudden surges of powerful emotion if we refuse to see him as desperately moved. For all her reservations about Byron, Mary Shelley realised that 'he felt the loss, at first, bitterly – he also felt remorse.'

Though Byron did not realise it Claire herself came to Pisa on 15 April to spend the summer with the Shelleys and was in Pisa on the day Allegra died. She had not heard the news when she left for the Gulf of Spezia with Edward and Jane Williams to look for a house by the sea for the summer. They found a house, the Casa Magni at Lerici, and returned to Pisa. Shelley, playing for time, did not tell her of Allegra's death until they had all travelled back to Casa Magni, the bleak house on the seashore, taking their goods and chattels. The news was broken to her there.

Mary Shelley was surprised to see that, after her first outburst, Claire was 'tranquil – more tranquil than, when prophesying her disaster, she was forever forming plans for getting her child from a place she judged, but too truly, would be fatal for her'. In a way the loss of Allegra, and her consequent distancing from Byron, helped to settle her mind. But she went on grieving silently. A few months later, when Claire finally set off for Vienna to seek work as a governess, she told a friend: 'I tried the whole journey to follow your advice and admire the scenery – dearest Lady it was all in vain – I only saw my lost darling.'

Byron decided to send the corpse to England. The little body was embalmed and consigned to Leghorn in a lead coffin. Byron contested the apothecary's bill for embalming spices, arguing that he had been charged enough for the embalming of a full-grown person and asking for the bill to be reduced by two-thirds. When they came to him in Pisa to report the coffin's safe delivery to Leghorn, Byron refused to receive the two messengers, one a priest, who had accompanied it, either from inertia or because he could not bear to. Allegra's corpse was being forwarded to London to John Murray. In the most bizarre of all commissions given to his publisher, Byron asked him to arrange for Allegra's burial in Harrow Church, where Byron had once hoped to lay his own remains. He wished the funeral to be 'very private' and hoped that his old Harrow tutor Henry Drury would read the burial service.

Few arrangements connected with Byron remained private. Accounts relating to John Murray's outlay for the transport of Allegra's body from

London Wharf to Harrow suggest a quite elaborate procession. There are payments for a hearse and a mourning coach, each with four horses with feathered plumes and velvet coverings, two porters, four hearse bearers, two coach pages with wands, a mourning scarf, hatband and silk gloves for Henry Drury, funeral garments for the clerk, the sexton and the beadle. Controversy had already been raging at the church where the Rector, the Reverend John William Cunningham, urged on by the churchwardens, was reluctant to agree to the church burial of a child who was illegitimate. Cunningham refused to erect the inscriptional tablet specified by Byron, which made a formal avowal of Allegra as the daughter of 'G.G. Lord Byron', giving her age and date of death, and quoting the words from the second Book of Samuel: 'I shall go to her, but she shall not return to me.' The Rector told Murray that he felt 'constrained to say that the inscription he proposed will be felt by every man of refined taste, to say nothing of sound morals, to be an offence against taste and propriety'. After diplomatic negotiation the best Murray had been able to achieve was permission for Allegra to be buried just inside the church building, probably in the south aisle to the right of the south porch, with no inscription registering her name.

Gossip proliferated. It was reported in the *Morning Herald* that 'a package, containing a "*pledge of love*", was lately received in London, by a person whose name is familiar to the public, from an eccentric but distinguished genius, who for some time since has not resided on this side of the Alps'. It was said that Allegra's body had been consigned in two packages to disguise the contents. In fact the child's organs and heart had been placed in two lead vases within the outer coffin. It was further rumoured that Byron had selected Harrow Church as the place of burial because he knew that Lady Byron worshipped there and had asked for the inscription to be placed on a wall immediately opposite Lady Byron's pew. 'God help me!' exploded Byron, 'I did not know that Lady B had ever been in Harrow Church and should have thought it the very last place she would have chosen.' The position he had wanted for Allegra's memorial had appealed to him simply because it was close to a church monument he had gazed at as a boy.

This episode created a new wave of self-pity. He lamented to Augusta, 'it has been my lot through life to be *never pardoned and almost always misunderstood.*' The story of Allegra's burial seemed 'the epitome or miniature of the Story of my life'.

Allegra's death is a constant theme in Byron's letters of that summer. It caused him to speak of his other daughter Ada with greater anxiety and prompted him to search for substitutes for the child he had lost. In May 1822, he entered into negotiations with Henry Dunn, the Leghorn merchant, to buy the liberation of a sixteen-year-old Turkish girl whom Byron believed to have been captured by a Greek sea captain with whom she was now living as his slave. This scheme collapsed when it emerged that the girl was happy with her captor, who was not a roving Greek but a respectable resident in Leghorn who was protecting her from 'the insults of her own People'. She had no wish to return to her own land.

There is another reminder of Allegra in Canto X of *Don Juan*, in the touching figure of ten-year-old Leila, the gentle, serious Turkish orphan adopted by Don Juan who travels around Europe with wide oriental eyes:

> 'He *naturally* loved what he protected:
> And thus they formed a rather curious pair;
> A guardian green in years, a ward connected
> In neither clime, time, blood, with her defender;
> And yet this want of ties made their's more tender.'

For Byron the sheer oddness of the bonding was attractive. Natural love occurred in many permutations. He deliberately courted ambiguity.

Teresa had now lifted her ban on *Don Juan*, after persuasion from Mary Shelley who deplored the cessation of a poem that set Byron 'not only above, but far above the poets of the day'. He had promised Teresa, his 'female Censor Morum', that from now on *Don Juan* would be irreproachable. There is a marvellous new energy in the cantos Byron was writing through the late spring and summer of 1822: the farcical-magical narrative of Don Juan's adventures in the harem in female disguise; the episode of the sacking of the Turkish fortress of Ismail in which Byron vented his bitterest sarcasm against 'those butchers in large business', the mercenary soldiery.

It was an unusually sultry summer. In mid-May, while the repercussions of the Masi affair continued, Byron moved his household out of Pisa in search of fresher air and sea bathing, which had been recommended to Teresa by the physician Dr Vaccà to improve her nerves. He took the Villa Dupuy at Montenero on the coast a few miles south of Leghorn. The pretty, rather sprawling country house was painted pink and was known locally as the Villa Rossa. Byron's local factotum Henry Dunn recommended it as 'decidedly the best house in Monte Nero'. Its spectacular situation, on a high slope looking down over the port of Leghorn, was vividly described by Byron to Isaac D'Israeli, his fellow Murray author who had recently sent him a present of the new edition of *The Literary Character*, a study of the creative temperament to which Byron had contributed:

'I write to you from the Villa Dupuy, near Leghorn, with the islands of Elba and Corsica visible from my balcony, and my old friend the Mediterranean rolling blue at my feet. As long as I retain my feeling and my passion for Nature, I can partly soften or subdue my other passions and resist or endure those of others.'

May and June at Montenero gave him a brief, hot lull. He wrote through the night, went to bed at daybreak, got up late and swam, spent the evenings sitting with Teresa on the terrace underneath the awning. Scents of Spanish jasmine, heliotropes and roses reached them from the garden. Sometimes they played draughts, with Byron breaking all the rules. To counteract the sultry heat Byron liked to order 'an avalanche of sherbets' which were handed round the household, including all the servants. One night, beneath the canopy, Byron and Teresa watched, from that great distance, the spectacle of the Pisa Luminara, a festival held every five years. The shooting stars and rockets from the city 'rose up on the horizon like the Northern Lights'.

The Mediterranean squadron was then at anchor at Leghorn. With his natural affinity for the heirs of Washington, and a sense of being more *persona grata* in America than he was in England, Byron accepted an invitation from the Commodore to visit the frigate *Constitution*. He told Douglas Kinnaird he had been received with 'the greatest Kindness and *rather too much ceremony*'.

A young American student, George Bancroft, later a well-known historian, left a record of this visit, describing how Byron, accompanied by Lega Zambelli, had mounted the gangway at about noon. He seemed nervous, probably because of his embarrassment at the ungainliness of the ascent as well as his continuing shyness amongst strangers. But finding himself surrounded by genial Americans 'his manner became easy, frank and cheerful'. Every single officer and guest on board was introduced to him. Byron was assailed by an American fan, an officer's wife, Mrs Catherine Potter Stith, who begged him for the rose he was wearing in his buttonhole so that she could carry it back to America. He was shown a baby boy, son of a sailor, born recently on board the *Constitution*. To Byron's approval the child had been christened 'Constitution Jones'.

On his tour of another frigate, the *Ontario*, Byron was especially delighted to discover a New York edition of his poems in the junior officers' quarters. He was also gratified by the news he heard from Bancroft, who had been studying in Germany, of his developing reputation there. Though Byron was always irritated by the literary shortcomings in translations of his work, he enjoyed the idea of translation: the spread of his opinions and the international status it gave him. 'All this', he told Murray, 'is some compensation for your English native brutality so fully displayed this year.' Bancroft had visited Goethe at Weimar and at Jena. Byron could not resist passing on to Murray his report that 'Goethe and the Germans are particularly fond of Don Juan – which they judge of as a work of Art.' Since, to his annoyance, Murray had apparently ignored Byron's instructions to dedicate *Sardanapalus* to Goethe, Byron, feeling the glow of Goethe's approbation, asked him to dedicate *Werner* to Goethe instead.

A visiting American businessman, George H. Bruen of New York, now commissioned a portrait of Byron from William Edward West, a painter from Philadelphia studying in Italy. Byron's delighted acceptance of what he would surely once have spurned as a humdrum proposition is probably as much a reflection of his current pro-American sentiments as of an increasing vulnerability. He crowed to Murray: 'It is singular that in the same year that Lady Noel leaves by will an interdiction for my daughter to see her father's portrait for many years – the individuals of a nation not remarkable for their liking to the English in particular – nor for flattering men in general, request me to sit for my "portraicture" – as Baron Bradwardine calls it.' The jocular reference is to Scott's *Waverley*.

The sittings took place at the Villa Rossa. West, like Holmes and Thorwaldsen before him, found Byron an unsatisfactory model, restless and over-talkative or silent and self-conscious, in which mode 'he assumed a countenance that did not belong to him, as though he were thinking of a frontispiece for Childe Harold'. He only relaxed when Teresa appeared at the window and was invited in. The 'playful manner' he adopted with Teresa made him a better sitter. Byron himself commissioned a portrait of Teresa and they sat jointly from then on. Sadly, West's Montenero portrait of Byron, now in the Scottish National Portrait Gallery, a pseudo-Romantic derivation of Phillips' 'cloak portrait', is one of the weakest of all extant Byron portraits, giving no impression of his trickiness and wit.

In June 1822 Lord Clare paid Byron a brief visit. He came down from Genoa, just before going back to England. Byron was particularly joyful while his one-time Harrow idol was at Montenero with him, so Teresa noted, but she saw his eyes filling with tears as Clare departed, as if he already knew the parting would be final. Byron wrote to Hobhouse: 'These transient glimpses of old friends are very painful – as I found out the other day after Lord Clare was gone again.' They reminded him of 'a dose of Laudanum – and its subsequent languor'. Clare took with him Byron's journal notebook of 'Detached Thoughts' written in Ravenna, with a few entries from Pisa, to deliver to John Murray at Albemarle Street.

Byron's beautiful new boat, the *Bolivar*, 'a little thing of about 22 tons', reached Leghorn on 18 June. Trelawny, with a crew, had sailed the schooner down from

Genoa. But once the *Bolivar* arrived the Tuscan authorities, suspicious that Byron might use the warlike boat with its provocative revolutionary name for embarking and disembarking political incendiarists along the Tuscan coast, issued an order forbidding it to cruise within sight of the port. They forbade Byron even to row a boat out to undress in when he went to take a swim in the deep water which he much preferred to shallow sea-bathing from the beach.

The embargo on the *Bolivar* was just one episode in a new accumulation of frustrations and anxieties at Montenero towards the end of June. The Gambas, father and son, had been at Florence, awaiting the final verdict on the Masi affair. The Austrian and ecclesiastical authorities put pressure on the Tuscan courts to expel the Gambas, and their enforced exile from Tuscany to another Italian state now seemed likely. On 29 June Pietro arrived in Montenero bearing the unwelcome news.

The summer heat was stultifying. The window recesses at the Villa Rossa were packed with greenery which was kept sprayed in an attempt to cool the atmosphere. Though Byron had specified a house with a good, pure water supply this proved quite inadequate: his legal dispute on this subject with the landlord Francesco Dupuy was still in progress when Byron was in Greece. As the tanks ran dry the only source of water was a mountain spring a mile away. Barrels for the household were filled there and transported down to the house on the back of mules. In charge of this arduous daily expedition was Byron's coachman Vincenzo Papi, still in Byron's household after his arrest in Pisa and becoming an increasing liability. It appears to have been Papi who provoked a violent quarrel between the servants by refusing to set out for the spring, 'railing at the rich and the nobility, and talking of equality and fraternity'. Again, his stance seems that of agent provocateur, turning Byron's language of the Romagna uprising back upon itself.

Teresa's sitting to the painter Edward West was interrupted by a manservant rushing in pale with terror crying out that Papi, who had snatched up a knife, was threatening to kill him. Byron and Pietro Gamba were also in the room and Pietro went out to investigate. A woman screamed. They all hurried into the hall to find Pietro standing with a pistol in each hand. Papi had slashed out at Pietro, whose face was now covered with blood. He had also been wounded in the arm. Teresa became hysterical, imagining they were all going to be murdered. Byron too had armed himself with a pistol and they now collected together all the firearms in the house which, according to West, 'were not a few'. They barred the doors and sent William Fletcher off to Leghorn to notify the police.

This was the scene that met the amazed gaze of Leigh Hunt who arrived at Montenero that same day:

'The day was very hot; the road to Monte-Nero was very hot, through dusty suburbs; and when I got there, I found the hottest-looking house I ever saw. Not content with having a red wash over it, the red was the most unseasonable of all reds, a salmon colour.

But the greatest of all the heats was within.'

It was now almost a year since Hunt had responded to the idea of joining Shelley and Byron in Pisa and four and a half months since Byron, not so eagerly, had contributed £250 to the travelling expenses of Hunt, his wife and children. Hunt had landed at Leghorn only two days earlier. Tuscany was still a strange land to him and the mood at Villa Rossa alarmingly outlandish:

'Everything was new, foreign and violent. There was the lady, flushed and dishevelled, exclaiming against the "*scelerato*"; the young Count wounded and threatening; the assassin, waiting for us with his knife; and last, not least, in the novelty, my English friend, metamorphosed, round-looking, and jacketed, trying to damp all this fire with his cool tones, and an air of voluptuous indolence.'

Not least of the surprises for Hunt was that Byron had become almost unrecognisably plump.

After the latest outburst of violence, and probably at Teresa's insistence, Vincenzo Papi was at last dismissed. Hunt's English susceptibilities were stretched to the utmost when the men left the house to take the usual evening ride and were confronted by the outstretched figure of a frenziedly repentant Papi on a bench by the front door. He was weeping and wailing, asking Byron's pardon, 'and to crown all, he requested Lord Byron to kiss him'. Byron said that he forgave Papi but that the decision must stand. However, the coachman reinstated himself in Byron's service at Genoa and was in the entourage that sailed to Cephalonia in 1823.

On 2 July both the Counts Gamba were called to a tribunal at Leghorn which confirmed their banishment from Tuscany. The upheavals at the Villa Rossa had probably made this outcome yet more certain. They were given four days to leave. Byron's courier Giuseppe Strauss was also exiled in a move to isolate Byron and persuade him to leave Tuscany himself without openly expelling him. 'Of course this is virtually my own exile,' wrote Byron when he heard of the dismissal of the Gambas, 'for where they go – I am no less bound by honour than by feeling to follow.' The Gambas found temporary asylum in Lucca. Byron returned to Pisa and Teresa and her servants now moved into the Lanfranchi with him. They had no reason not to since Count Guiccioli had already made a successful application to the Pope to suspend his wife's allowance on the grounds of her cohabitation with Byron in the Villa Rossa at Montenero.

'Every body is in despair & every thing in confusion,' wrote Shelley to Mary at Lerici on 4 July. Byron was already planning departure, contemplating Genoa, reconsidering America. Leigh Hunt could not have chosen a worse time to arrive.

Shelley met Leigh Hunt at Leghorn and went on with him to Pisa. Byron followed a day later. As arranged, the Hunts and their large family moved into rooms on the ground floor of the Palazzo Lanfranchi, which Mary Shelley had prepared for them. Byron had contributed £50 for furniture. When Byron returned to Pisa a welcome scene was staged for him at the palazzo. A young male servant came in smilingly, followed by his sister, a handsome brunette dressed in country-style bodice and sleeves, with flowing hair. She presented Byron with a basket of flowers, took his hand and kissed it. She turned to Leigh Hunt and kissed his hand as well. It appears that this was Francesca, the girl Byron called on during their shooting practice outside the city gates.

Though the original plan had almost been forgotten in the rush of events, Hunt had come to Italy on purpose to inaugurate with Byron the new literary periodical that eventually became *The Liberal*. That title, Byron's own suggestion, was more politically pugnacious than it now appears. For Byron the initial attraction of the project was to give himself an independent mouthpiece. Leigh Hunt and his older brother John, who would be publishing the new periodical, had a long and, to Byron, admirable record of political intransigence and journalistic courage with their reformist weekly *The Examiner*.

At this stage Byron particularly welcomed literary associates at the opposite end of the spectrum from John Murray. The Hunts' natural allies had been Lamb, Hazlitt and Keats, lower-middle-class writers of the so-called London 'Cockney School', rather than Murray's Tory grandees exemplified by Sir Walter Scott. Byron's donation, in Hunt's first few days in Italy, of the copyright of his dangerous *jeu d'esprit*, *The Vision of Judgement*, for publication in *The Liberal* was partly an attempt to compensate poor Hunt for the scenes of disarray that greeted his arrival and Byron's new uncertainty about his future plans. But Byron had his own agenda in procuring publication of this and other works which John Murray had been sitting on and in delivering what was offered, and received, as a considerable snub.

There were fundamental difficulties in the new alliance between Byron and Leigh Hunt, not least the difference in status of the peer of England, the most celebrated poet of his generation, and the son of a poor clergyman, educated charitably at Christ's Hospital, a literary struggler with an embittered sense of his own worth. Moore, who had his own reasons, poured scorn on the idea of a creative partnership between Byron, Shelley and Hunt: '*Alone* you may do any thing,' he adjured Byron, 'but partnerships in fame, like those in trade, make the strongest party answerable for the deficiencies of the rest, and I tremble even for you with such a bankrupt *Co*.' Shelley too, who had brokered the arrangement, was beginning to see it as problematic: 'how long the alliance between the wren & the eagle may continue I will not prophesy.' Byron himself now had grave doubts about the enterprise, writing to Thomas Moore ten days after Hunt's arrival: 'He seems sanguine about the matter, but (entre nous) I am not. I don't, however, like to put him out of spirits by saying so, for he is bilious and unwell.'

Byron evidently did his best. In Hunt's later, and on the whole vitriolic, memoir *Lord Byron and Some of his Contemporaries*, those early days in Pisa stand out as a period of harmony and hope. Byron disarmingly called Leigh Hunt 'Leontius', the name Shelley had suggested as a way of overcoming the Italians' difficulty with 'Leigh Hunt'. There was a lot of gentle joking. Byron 'breakfasted: read: lounged about, singing an air, generally out of Rossini, and in a swaggering style, though in a voice at once small and veiled; then took a bath, and was dressed; and coming down-stairs, was heard, still singing, in the courtyard, out of which the garden ascended at the back of the house'. Aware

Lord Byron as he appeared after his daily ride at Pisa and Genoa. Samuel Freeman's engraved version of Marianne Hunt's original cut paper silhouette

427

of Leigh Hunt writing in his study, a small room in a corner of the courtyard, 'with an orange tree peeping in at the window', Byron would stumble over and start an amiable conversation.

If Shelley had not died could the situation have been rescued? Would Shelley have managed to keep a truce between them? Could *The Liberal* have lasted longer than it did? This is one of the great literary might-have-beens. On 8 July, after depositing Hunt at the Lanfranchi, Shelley and Williams returned to Leghorn to board their own new boat, which was originally intended to be called the *Don Juan*. Though Shelley later changed his mind, preferring the name *Ariel*, the name *Don Juan* had been painted on the mainsail, on Byron's instructions, when the boat was delivered two months earlier. Shelley and Captain Roberts had removed the lettering, cutting out the piece of canvas bearing the inscription. But the boat continued to be known as the *Don Juan*. Shelley and Williams now sailed north in it from Leghorn towards the Casa Magni at Lerici. Off the coast of Viareggio they ran into a squall. The exact circumstances of the disaster are uncertain. There is a possibility that the boat was rammed and sunk by a marauding vessel. Whatever happened, Shelley, Williams and their English boy sailor, Charles Vivian, were drowned.

In the week of suspense between the *Don Juan*'s disappearance and the recovery of the bodies, Byron was drawn into a terrible sequence of events. On 11 July Trelawny brought the news to him at Pisa, later describing how 'When I told him, his lip quivered, and his voice faltered as he questioned me.' The next day Mary Shelley, still frail after a miscarriage, arrived at the Lanfranchi from Lerici with Jane Williams, desperately seeking news. They arrived at midnight and were taken in by Byron and Teresa, who commented that Mary was looking like a ghost.

By 13 July Trelawny, with Captain Roberts, had initiated a search along the coast for signs of survivors. Byron offered the use of the *Bolivar* to cruise the waters. But too late: on 16 July the first two bodies were reported to have been washed ashore three or four miles north of Viareggio. Byron and Leigh Hunt made two journeys to the spot, to the mouths of the rivers Arno and Serchio, but found that because of health office regulations the bodies had already been buried in the sand. Two days later a third body was washed up, nearer to Viareggio itself. This was the corpse of Shelley, by now so badly decomposed that Trelawny was able to identify it only by the copy of Keats's poems that had been in Shelley's jacket pocket when he drowned.

Coming so soon after the death of Allegra, Shelley's death was an almost insuperable blow. Byron's shock and grief was sharpened by the knowledge that, although he had lent Shelley £50 on his departure for Leghorn, their recent relations had been strained. Living in such close proximity at Pisa Shelley had found himself resenting Byron's dominating talent: 'I do not write,' he confessed earlier that year, 'I have lived too long near Lord Byron & the sun has extinguished the glow worm.' The painful history of Allegra had further damaged their relationship. Oscar Wilde put forward the theory that the friendship between Byron and Shelley ended when Byron attempted to make love to Shelley and Shelley resisted the overtures, an explanation which if not convincing in its detail recognises the complex emotional dependencies between them. Byron certainly saw Shelley as a brother outcast: 'There is thus another man gone, about whom the world was ill-naturedly, and ignorantly, and brutally mistaken. It will, perhaps, do him justice *now*, when he can be no better for it,' he wrote to Moore indignantly.

He attended two macabre ceremonies on the shore, the cremation of Edward Williams's body on 15 August and that of Shelley the next day. Permission had been given to exhume the bodies from their burial places in the sand, where they had been interred in quicklime. Trelawny had ordered a special metal frame from an ironmonger, a bed-like structure about four and a half feet long and eighteen inches wide with a three- or four-inch rim, supported by four iron legs. He had gathered firewood. Byron brought the necessary spices, sugar, salt, wine, oil and incense in his carriage. 'You can have no idea', he told Tom Moore, 'what an extraordinary effect such a funeral pile has on a desolate shore, with mountains in the back-ground and the sea before, and the singular appearance the salt and frankincense gave to the flame.'

There was little left of Edward Williams's body. Byron, the expert on such matters, was able to identify him by his teeth. Williams's boot was found to tally with the boot that had been brought from Pisa for purposes of comparison. Looking at the lurid mass of shapeless flesh Byron said, 'are we to resemble that? – why it might be the carcase of a sheep for all I can see.' He noticed that the black silk handkerchief round Williams's neck was still intact and reflected that the products of the silkworm lasted longer than 'the matter of which man is made!' Byron travelled back to Pisa with the urn containing Williams's ashes in his carriage, to be given to Jane. He was so exhausted that Teresa tried to dissuade him from returning to the seashore for the cremation of Shelley the next day.

Shelley's body had been buried a mile or so south of Williams's on the beach near Massa. The markings were unclear, and it took about an hour to locate it, by which time Byron and Leigh Hunt had arrived from Pisa, accompanied by two mounted dragoons and four foot soldiers to keep prospective sightseers at bay. The corpse was by then putrid and stinking. Shelley's outer garments and linen were now black. His flesh was of a dingy blue. Trelawny started the fire under Shelley's body and, carried away by the grandeur of the scene, offered up his own incantations. 'I restore to nature through fire the elements of which this man was composed, earth, air, water; everything is changed, but not annihilated; he is now a portion of that which he worshipped.' Byron, standing beside him, said: 'I knew you were a Pagan, not that you were a Pagan Priest; you do it very well.'

Byron requested that Trelawny should keep Shelley's skull for him, as a memento. Trelawny, remembering that Byron had had a Newstead skull transformed into a drinking cup, had apparently been anxious that Shelley's skull 'should not be so profaned'. In fact the skull disintegrated as Trelawny attempted to remove it from the pyre: 'it broke to pieces – it was unusually thin and strikingly small.'

There was further controversy over Shelley's heart, which again was particularly small and, in Byron's words, 'would not take the flame'. Trelawny's recollections of the scene provide more details: the heart 'although bedded in fire – would not burn'. They waited an hour, continually adding fuel, until 'it becoming late we gave over by mutual conviction of its being unavailing – all exclaiming it will not burn – there was a bright flame round it occasioned by the moisture still flowing from it – and on removing the furnace nearer to the sea to immerse the iron I took the heart in my hand to examine it – after sprinkling it with water: yet it was still so hot as to burn my hand badly and a quantity of this oily fluid still flowed from it.'

Byron's presence at this agonising scene, which soon came to be regarded as a key moment in Romanticism, has been assumed. In Louis-Edouard Fournier's mid-nineteenth-century oil painting *The Cremation of Shelley's Body*, Byron is in the forefront of the mourners as a fully clothed, immaculately visaged Shelley is laid out on a bier of firewood on the beach. In the popular print *Retrieval of the Corpse of Shelley from the Sea at Viareggio*, Byron is the central figure, his tartan cape swirling around him in the gale. But in fact during the later stages of the funeral, while the heart of Shelley failed to conflagrate, Byron was almost certainly absent, swimming far out to sea as he had done at the cremation of Edward Williams the day before.

While Byron was out of sight, swimming off towards the *Bolivar* which lay at anchor in the bay, Leigh Hunt had begged from Trelawny Shelley's by now heat-blackened heart. Byron decided, after his return, that Shelley's heart by rights belonged to Mary. Hunt, the next day, wrote indignantly to her: 'With regard to Ld B. he has no right to bestow the heart, & I am sure pretends to none. If he told you that you should have it, it could only have been from his thinking I could more easily part with it than I can.' However Hunt was finally shamed into giving it to Mary. When she died, the heart, by then dry and shrunken, was found in a copy of *Adonais*.

Byron's three-mile swim out to the *Bolivar* and back on the day of Shelley's funeral had ill effects. Another fever now attacked him. The joint action of the sea and blazing midday sun burned and blistered the skin on his arms and back. Two days later it began to peel painfully. Teresa saved and kept a little piece of Byron's blistered skin. She claimed his striking loss of weight from then on started with this episode: 'his health received a sharp shock that day.'

With the death of Shelley the 'nest of singing birds' in Pisa effectively broke up. The incompatibility of Byron and the Hunts was painfully confirmed. 'There was a sense of mistake on both sides', as Leigh Hunt put it. In London physical distance between them made things feasible. In Pisa, with Hunt so edgily dependent, their relationship, already delicate, was doomed.

When Byron first moved into the Palazzo Lanfranchi he had made expansive offers to Augusta that she should come and join him with her children and her 'drone of a husband'. Living in close proximity with a large lower-middle-class London family was altogether different. The painter Benjamin Robert Haydon put the problem bluntly: 'How could Byron sympathise with the mawkish, unmanly namby pamby effeminacy of Leigh Hunt; one who could neither ride, swim, shoot, drink – and who though he would sophisticate in favour of adultery, yet shrank from timidity at committing it – A cockney to the bone!' Byron found Hunt's constant want of money deeply irritating, feeling that supporting him was like pulling a drowning man out of the river only to find him flinging himself back again.

His antipathy to Hunt's wife Marianne was even more pronounced. She was ill when she arrived, believed by Vaccà to be dying. Byron had hardly deigned to greet her. He detested her self-pity, her suspicion of Italians, her undisguised disapproval of his ménage, and her middle-class knowingness. It was Mrs Hunt who, viewing an engraving of Harlow's much reproduced Byron portrait of 1815, said that it 'resembled a great school-boy, who had a plain bun given him, instead of a plum one'. Byron dismissed Marianne as no great thing.

Living on the ground floor of the palazzo were also Thornton, John, Mary Florimel, Swinburne, Henry Sylvan and Percy Bysshe Shelley Leigh Hunt. The six children were aged from thirteen downwards, anathema to Byron as they swarmed around the building. He wrote warning Mary Shelley: 'I have a particular dislike to any things of S[helley]'s being within the same walls with Mr Hunt's children. – They are dirtier and more mischievous than Yahoos.' What they could not destroy with their filth they would attack with their fingers. The Hunt children put Byron in his most tyrannical mood.

Why did Byron continue in a situation he found intolerable? Why did he not withdraw from *The Liberal*, a venture he already felt was far from certain to succeed? Natural inertia. A strain of masochism. A sense of gratitude and loyalty to Hunt who had stuck by him 'through thick & thin – when all shook, and some shuffled in 1816'. He did not feel he could renege on *The Liberal* once his support had been promised: for all his prevarication Byron remained a man of his word. Nor could he leave the Hunts stranded in Italy. In spite of his pretensions to hard-heartedness he saw and sympathised with the real human situation. Leigh Hunt was no better than a child in worldly matters. 'The death of Shelley left them totally aground.'

Through the summer's many vicissitudes and tragedies, Allegra's death, the Gambas' exile, Shelley's drowning, Byron continued with the writing of *Don Juan*. On 24 July he told Douglas Kinnaird: 'To occupy my mind – (which had need of it – & in such a way as to distract it from present things) I have nearly completed three more Cantos.' This brought him close to the end of Canto VIII. Hunt, in his memoir, records how Byron wrote through the night at Pisa, imbibing gin and water. By 24 August, in an extraordinary outburst of resilience, Byron was finishing Canto IX, in which Juan reaches St Petersburg, to find himself embroiled in the embraces of the Empress of Russia, the lascivious and fickle Catherine the Great. This canto has a wonderful spring to it as Byron alternates the light and dark, the acceptable and shocking, picturesque travelogue and bitter sexual satire. He leaps from contemporary comment to scientific futurism as, pursuing the theories of Georges Cuvier on the cycles of the world's destruction and recreation, he makes an excursion into the realms of geophysical speculation:

> 'it will one day be found
>   With other relics of "a former world",
> When this world shall be *former*, underground,
>   Thrown topsy-turvy, twisted, crisped, and curled,
> Baked, fried, or burnt, turned inside-out, or drowned,
>   Like all the worlds before, which have been hurled
> First out of and then back again to Chaos,
> The Superstratum which will overlay us.
>
> So Cuvier says; – and then shall come again
>   Unto the new Creation, rising out
> From our old crash, some mystic, ancient strain
>   Of things destroyed and left in airy doubt:

Like to the notions *we* now entertain
    Of Titans, Giants, fellows of about
Some hundred feet in height, *not* to say *miles*,
And Mammoths, and your winged Crocodiles.'

During August, Byron had been fascinated by the news from London of the arrest of Percy Jocelyn, Bishop of Clogher, apprehended with a guardsman named Moverley in the White Lion Tavern near the Haymarket, a well-known meeting place for sodomists. The Bishop was said to have put up so much resistance that, had his breeches not been down, it was thought he would probably have got away. The usual dangerously threatening crowd assembled. When the Bishop was released on bail he fled from England. 'What do you think of your Irish bishop?' Byron asked Tom Moore. 'Do you remember Swift's line, "Let me have a *barrack* – a fig for the *clergy*"? This seems to have been his reverence's motto.' He wrote more, but in Moore's *Life* Byron's letter at this point peters out in another maddening succession of censoring asterisks.

With his delighted sense of topicality Byron inserted a passing reference to Clogher in the eighth canto of *Don Juan*, in the stanza referring to a group of Cossack soldiers left stranded in the battle of Ismael:

'Then being taken by the tail – a taking
    Fatal to bishops as to soldiers – these
Cossacques were all cut off as day was breaking.'

It was a double entendre that would have been appreciated by Charles Skinner Matthews, Byron's one-time Cambridge friend.

Byron's own immediate destination was now settled. When Hobhouse arrived in Pisa on 15 September 1822 he found Byron packing for Genoa. It seemed to Hobhouse that Byron was much changed, with a new, rather injured expression on his face. Hobhouse was disconcerted by Countess Guiccioli, 'a liberally good looking young woman', and by the openness of their liaison. He was still more disapproving of Byron's literary liaison with Leigh Hunt and tried to talk him out of proceeding with *The Liberal*. Hobhouse was even worried by the Lanfranchi dungeons. It took two days for these friends, once so inseparable, to get back to anything approaching their old terms.

Hobhouse, now a Radical MP for Westminster, still resented Byron's gibes at his imprisonment; Byron had not forgiven Hobhouse's attack on *Cain*. In Pisa, Byron read aloud to him the sequence of exuberantly insulting epigrams he had written to the memory of Lord Castlereagh, the British foreign minister who had recently committed suicide, probably as a result of homosexual blackmail. One of these reads cruelly:

> 'So Castlereagh has cut his throat; – The worst
> Of this is, – that his own was not the first.'

Another sums up Byron's long opposition to Castlereagh's policies:

> 'So *He* has cut his throat at last! – He? Who?
> The man who cut his country's long ago.'

Hobhouse, fearful that these attacks, if published, would rebound on Byron, strongly advised caution. But, as he wrote in his diary, Byron 'did not quite agree with me'.

Distantly fond but disappointed, they said farewell to one another on 20 September. Hobhouse delivered the tactless parting salvo that Byron 'should write less and not think the world loved so very much about his writing or himself'. A week later Byron was on the road to Genoa, travelling in the Napoleonic coach accompanied by two carriages. Another carriage brought the Hunts. The servants and heavy luggage had been despatched to Leghorn to embark on the felucca that would take them north by sea. At Lucca, Count Gamba and Pietro joined Byron's cavalcade. Additional passengers were three large geese being fattened up to be eaten on Michaelmas Day, 29 September. Byron believed superstitiously that bad luck would descend on those who failed to eat goose at Michaelmas. The geese travelled in a cage which swung from the back end of the coach.

Byron regarded Genoa as a temporary refuge. At Lord Clare's instigation, the British Minister to the Kingdom of Sardinia, William Noel Hill, had offered protection to the Gambas and to Byron, who had taken a house, the Casa Saluzzo at Albaro, for one year. He was still considering the idea of emigrating from what he saw as a 'worn out Europe', toying with both South and North America and 'even Van Dieman's Land – of which I hear much as a good place to settle in': Tasmania, at that period, was in its early stages of colonial development. But the Greek War of Independence had effectively begun in 1821 with a revolt in Moldavia, after an earlier outbreak in Wallachia, against the Ottoman Turks' oppressive rule. Ideas of emigration further afield faded as Byron became preoccupied with Greece.

25

Genoa

1822–1823

One of Byron's last and strangest poems is *The Deformed Transformed*, begun in 1822 but never finished. It is a drama of shape-changing, part pantomime, part Faustian moral confrontation, in which the hunchback Arnold, derided and taunted by his mother, is transformed into the warlike figure of Achilles. An underlying theme is that deformity itself has its own special power:

> 'Deformity is daring.
> It is its essence to o'ertake mankind
> By heart and soul, and make itself the equal –
> Aye, the superior of the rest.'

Genoa was, more than anywhere, Byron's own place of transformation.

Here in the 'Superb City', his last stopping place in Italy, he altered physically, becoming more slender and apparently much taller, the elongated figure of his final portraits. His personality changed too. He drew in upon himself. His social life was more muted, his letters less entertaining and more functional. The greatest change of all from the Byron who arrived in Venice four years earlier was his sense of higher purpose. Teresa noted his anxiety to counter rumours that he was 'lost in the flabbiness of an enervating climate'. Feeling aged, alienated from the things he had most cared for, he was becoming increasingly concerned with his lasting reputation. To Douglas Kinnaird he confided his anxiety to leave something to his relatives 'more than a mere name; and besides that to be able to do good to others to a greater extent'. He added: 'If nothing else – will do – I must try bread & water – which by the way – are very nourishing – and sufficient – if good of their kind.'

In deciding to invest his reputation in the cause of Greek independence Byron was now more than ever the author of his legend, choosing himself a future more public, more demanding than his association with the Romagna insurrection. But it would be wrong to see the choice of Greece as calculating. As always Byron was driven by feelings, secret loyalties, chance connections. Greece was an essential component of his history, stretching back to Harrow and his reading of the classics, Athens and his travels in the summer of 1810. Nostalgia was a powerful motive force. He saw Greece as 'the only place I ever was contented in'. He had a powerful attachment to the idea of liberation for the country in which he had felt briefly so sexually and spiritually free.

In 1821 and early 1822, news of the progress of the Greek revolution had percolated through to Pisa. On 13 January 1822 a national assembly of Greek patriotic leaders had adopted the liberal republican Constitution of Epidaurus; on 27 January Greek independence from the Turks was formally proclaimed and foreign volunteers had begun arriving to fight alongside the Greeks. A passionate enthusiasm for the uprising had been a bond between Byron and Shelley, whose poem *Hellas* of 1821 was dedicated to the cause of freedom. Prince Alexandros Mavrocordatos had been at the centre of a group of Greek exiles in Pisa where he had known the Shelleys well, giving Mary Shelley lessons in Greek in return for tuition in English. Mavrocordatos left Pisa for Greece in June 1821, shortly before Byron himself arrived, but while at Pisa Byron had made contact with Mavrocordatos's cousin Prince Argiropoli, a first-hand source of information on Greek revolutionary politics.

Byron's involvement in the Greek cause was urged by Pietro Gamba, the 'thorough Liberty boy' who, now that the Romagna insurrection had failed, was eager to join a revolution wherever he could find one. Other ex-Carbonarists were already gravitating towards Greece. Byron, indulgent to Pietro, loved the young man's ardour. At this period, according to Trelawny, the 'under-current of his mind' could be seen to be drifting irrevocably eastward, concentrated hopefully if guiltily on 'his early love, the Isles of Greece'.

Byron, with Teresa and the Gambas, reached Genoa at the beginning of October 1822. Byron had been extremely ill en route. The party had decided to avoid the perils of the mountain roads and proceed by sea from Lerici to Sestri. At Lerici, Byron collapsed. Trelawny had brought the *Bolivar* to meet them there and Byron had taken another unwise swim. He spent the next four days in bed in 'the worst inn's worst room' with rheumatic attacks, biliousness and constipation. An incompetent young doctor administered an anal enema, an indignity which made Byron question the justice of the case against Bishop Jocelyn and the soldier with whom he had been caught *in flagrante* 'since if the episcopal instrument at all resembled the damp squirt of the Ligurian apothecary – the crime will have carried its own chastisement along with it'. In desperation he had treated himself out of Thompson's book of prescriptions, a medical manual with which John Murray had provided him. He revived on the sea voyage to Sestri enough to share the sailors' meal of cold fish and to drink 'a Gallon of country wine'. But an evening cough continued once he got to Genoa. Teresa reported him to be still bilious, cross and sleepy. Over the nine months that Byron was in Genoa he was never to be completely well.

Genoa was a place of extraordinary beauty, the Mediterranean seaport and citadel poised on the expanse of its great bay. The richness of its history, its natural exuberance, were expressed in its architectural marvels, whole streets of Renaissance marble palaces, memorials to the Dorias, the Durazzi, the Brignoli, and its collection of great works of art. Up to the eighteenth century Genoa had been a powerful republic. But since the Congress of Vienna in 1815 Genoa had been annexed to Piedmont, historically its rival, and was now suffering political repression by a regime dominated by the clergy under the King of Sardinia's nominal control. The once muscular and aristocratic merchant city had now become another Byronic place of compromised privilege.

Byron's house, the Casa Saluzzo, was a large palace which he rented for £24 a year, considered a bargain even at the time. It stood in a good position on a hill at Albaro, two miles east of the city, then a semi-rural area of vineyards and olive trees in between stone alleyways; a place of bees and butterflies, fireflies and lizards. The entrance was down a narrow lane, through tall iron gates leading into a courtyard with yew trees cut into grotesque shapes. Though picturesque, the Saluzzo was far from comfortable, especially in winter, with only one chimney to heat an estimated fifty or sixty rooms. Visitors' accounts describe negotiating an enormous hall equipped with a billiard table and progressing on through numerous desolate apartments before arriving at Byron's private rooms with their cheerful English furnishings and books.

It had been the advice of William Hill, the British Minister, that it would be safer for Teresa, her father and brother to be lodged in Byron's house since they would then be considered part of his suite. Such official protection as Byron enjoyed would automatically be extended to them. The Gambas had their own apartment in the Casa Saluzzo, Teresa and Byron taking their meals apart. Fletcher was still attending Byron and approaching his seventh year away from England and his wife. The exiled Tita Falcieri had now found his way back to Byron's household, and his beard had regrown. A visiting clergyman described with some alarm being received at Albaro by 'a man of almost gigantic stature, who wore a beard hanging down his breast to a formidable length'. At the Casa Saluzzo, Byron's menagerie of dogs, monkeys, rabbits and assorted birds was augmented by the geese brought with him from Pisa which, after all, he had not had the heart to eat on Michaelmas Day.

The Hunts and their 'six little blackguards' were no longer lodged with Byron but now shared a house with Mary Shelley. The large, bare Casa Negroto was also in Albaro, a mile further down the hill. Marianne was again pregnant and the Hunts' seventh child, Vincent Leigh, was born in Genoa in June 1823. Byron was surrounded by an agonising circle of dependants, financial, literary and emotional. The awkwardness of the situation fuelled the malice of Leigh Hunt's later memoir in which he depicts Byron in Genoa as cruelly high-handed, 'joking away the consciousness of our position', and only tolerable at night when he was drunk and lachrymose.

Relations with Mary Shelley were still more problematic. Byron had been named in Shelley's will as his executor, a responsibility he accepted to the extent of writing to inform Shelley's father, Sir Timothy, of the destitute state of Mary and her small son Percy Florence, stranded in Italy with no means of returning to England. The relationship between Byron and Mary was now fraught with complications: she on her side outraged at his treatment of Claire Clairmont and Allegra; Byron, sensitive as he was to the nuances of love, aware of her own attraction towards him and consequently evasive. After Shelley's death her emotions were still raw and Byron's unnerving presence intensified her grief for her lost husband. As she wrote in her journal, 'when in company with Albe, I can never cease for a second to have him [Shelley] in my heart & brain with a clearness that mocks reality, interfering even by its force with the functions of life.'

At Genoa, as at Pisa, Byron found himself yearning for the amiable, familial laughter of Augusta. Why could she not come and live near him at Nice? He would pay travelling expenses for the whole family. He told her that life for the children would be better, and cheaper, abroad. 'You would also be *near* me if that would be an allurement.' It is unlikely that Augusta gave the proposal serious thought.

In late September 1822 John Murray returned from Allegra's funeral at Harrow – the funeral Byron had asked him to arrange – to find two letters from Byron waiting for him. They were quickly followed by a third. These letters, written as Byron was leaving Pisa, are not to be found in the records at John Murray. Maybe Murray found them too painful to preserve. The surrounding evidence suggests that these were letters of violent complaint on the subject of lines omitted from *Cain* without Byron's approval and on Murray's continuing vacillation over *Don Juan*. Byron was just then in the process of despatching Cantos VI, VII and VIII, sending them via Kinnaird with a note of defiance in advance. He was by now almost assuming that Murray would attempt to censor him: 'I won't be dictated to by *John Murray Esqre.*'

On 25 September Murray sent Byron a wounded but dignified letter:

'If you are so kind so nobly generous as to allow me the honour of continuing to be the publisher of such of your writings as are of your former glorious class – I shall feel more than ever grateful – But, I beg leave to repeat, that no adverse determination of yours can diminish – at any time – my sense of obligation to you, nor of the most sincere personal attachment – and as you have avowed that, when an occasion offered you did not find me mercenary or indisposed to practical gratitude I trust that our mutual feelings will be such as to leave the door open to a speedy renewal of the most delightful connexion which I ever formed in my life.'

Byron replied to him on 9 October, maintaining that he did not object to cuts *per se* but he objected to omissions made secretly and to Murray's lack of courage in defence of Byron's work: 'I have no wish to break off our connection – but if you are to be blown about with every wind – what can I do?' The rift with John Murray, as it developed through the autumn, was aggravated by Byron's own sense of his authorial dignity. 'I cannot', he told Murray, 'alter my convictions.' He was not prepared to compromise the march of his own mind.

Two external factors precipitated the crisis. Crucial to the breakdown of relations between Byron and his publisher was the role of Byron's business manager Douglas Kinnaird. The outspoken and abrasive Kinnaird paid scant respect to Murray, who found him almost impossible to deal with. 'Murray is really a sad old man of business,' Kinnaird reported to Byron in the autumn of 1822. The idea of pricking the pomposity of a publisher so much at the heart of Tory England appealed to the iconoclastic Kinnaird, who threw himself into the challenge of finding an alternative publisher for *Don Juan*. When *Heaven and Earth* was eventually published in *The Liberal*, Kinnaird seems to have viewed this as a personal triumph: 'What will John Murray Esqre say? Surely he will bite his fingers off.'

Even harder for Murray to bear than Kinnaird's arrogance was the arrival on the scene of Byron's rival publisher John Hunt, a man from the opposite pole of London social and literary life. Murray's outrage is clear in the account he gave to Byron of Hunt's arrival at Albemarle Street to collect the manuscripts to be published in *The Liberal*:

'With regard to my reception of Mr John Hunt whom I was not aware that your Lordship had ever seen, he sent up word that "a Gentleman" wished to deliver into my hands a Letter from Lord Byron, &, with instantaneous joy, I went down to receive him – there I found Mr Hunt & a person obviously brought there as a *witness*. – He delivered the letter in the most tipstave formal manner to me staring me, fully & closely in the face as if having administered a dose of Arsnick he wished to see its minute operations – & to all that I civilly & simply replied – with the same assassin look, he ever repeated "are those your words Sir" – "is that your answer Sir" – "am I to write these words to Lord Byron" – in fact if you knew the insulting behaviour of this man – you would I am sure excuse me for having directed my confidential Clerk to tell him when he called again that, he might be assured that whatever papers Lord Byron directed Mr Murray to send him would be carefully and, as speedily as possible delivered at his house – but that personal intercourse was not agreeable & could not be necessary. A friend of yours!!!'

Byron responded airily from Genoa: 'With regard to Mr J. Hunt how could I tell that he insulted you? of course if he did – show him the door – or the window – he had no warrant from me but the letter you received.'

On 11 October Murray sent Byron another distraught letter: 'I entreat you as a most particular favour that you will not place me in personal intercourse with Mr John Hunt – for I have invicible [*sic*] reasons for not wishing to know him – As to giving myself airs in the matter – I can assure you that no one can charge me with any alteration in this respect since I had first the good fortune of seeing you – and as to my going about talking of my losses – it is utterly destitute of all foundation.' He refuted Byron's accusations that he was spreading word that his once best-selling author had become unprofitable. 'I beseach you not to set me down for such an incurable Blockhead as not to thing [*sic*] of you with every body around me as far superior as a Man of Genius to any man breathing.' Murray's letters become incoherent with emotion. Referring to Thomas Phillips' 'cloak' portrait in the Albemarle Street drawing room he adds a desperate postscript: '*Every day of my life* I sit opposite to your Lordships Portrait.'

On 15 October the first number of *The Liberal* was published, containing Byron's political satire *The Vision of Judgement*, King George III's 'Apotheosis in a Whig point of view', which Murray had been too nervous to publish. Byron was provoked to a fresh assault on Murray when he realised that the poem had been published by John Hunt without its prose preface and that his final proof corrections had not been implemented. He suspected Murray of withholding this material in an attempt to sabotage the work.

Murray's response was now almost one of heartbreak. On 29 October he wrote to inform Byron of 'the universal disappointment and condemnation which has followed publication of the "Liberal" . . . really Lord Byron it is dreadful to think upon your association with such outcasts from Society, it is impossible, I am sure, that you can conceive any thing like the horrid sensation created in the mind of the public by this connexion, unless you were here to feel it.' When John Hunt was indicted for libel at the December Sessions of the Grand Jury for Middlesex, charged as publisher of Byron's *The Vision of Judgement* with defaming the characters of George III and George IV and with bringing the monarchy into disrepute, Murray's worst fears were realised.

In what was in effect a farewell letter to the poet whose fame he had facilitated Murray gave his frank opinion of the new cantos of *Don Juan*, which Kinnaird had read aloud to him:

'I declare to you, these were so outrageously shocking that I would not publish them – if you would give me your estate – Title – & Genius – For heavens sake revise them, they are equal in talent to any thing you have written, & it is therefore well worth while to extract what would shock the feeling of every man in the Country – & do your name everlasting injury.

My Company used to be courted for the pleasure of talking about you – it is totally the reverse now – &c, by a re-action, even your former works are considerably deteriorated in Sale.'

Murray implored Byron to be cautious both for his own sake, since his name was intimately connected with Byron's reputation, and also for Augusta's sake. They were in a state of constant alarm in case his sister should be deprived of her place at Court. He ended:

'Do let us have your good humour again & put Juan in the tone of Beppo . . . I entreat you to believe that nothing but the most devoted regard could have induced me to write this Letter & that I ever WILL remain
> your Lordships
> devoted Friend
> Jno. Murray.'

Murray's letter crossed in the post with instructions from Byron, dated 31 October 1822, that all compositions at present in his possession should be delivered to Douglas Kinnaird, including the six new cantos of *Don Juan*, but excluding the memoirs for which Murray had already paid Tom Moore. From now on Byron's main publisher was to be John Hunt. Relations with John Murray were not broken off completely. In November 1822 Murray published *Werner*. Around Christmas Byron dangled the possibility of a journey to Naples to generate material for a further two cantos of *Childe Harold*. But the day-to-day friendship between them was over. Murray was now at the receiving end of Byron's bitter sarcasm: 'You seem to forget that whether as a tradesman or as a gentleman you are bound to be decent and courteous in your inter-course with all classes.' The chasm of class difference opened between them, and this was what must have grieved John Murray most.

In choosing Genoa as a temporary haven Byron had imagined he would be safe from English visitors. But Genoa was a thoroughfare compared with Pisa. Though Byron himself was intent on new beginnings, former friends and acquaintances caught up with him at Genoa, bringing him a forcible recon-nection with the past. One of these was James Wedderburn Webster, about whom Byron had always had mixed feelings. When he arrived in Genoa in October, Byron had not seen Webster for almost a decade, since they were men about town together. He was alarmed to find that Webster had now taken to wearing a black wig. He reported to Kinnaird: 'I found him increased rather – but not much; – looking redder – but tolerably fresh – and no wiser than here to fore. He talked a great deal of shimble shamble stuff.'

'Bold' Webster was now transformed into Sir James, having been knighted, much to Byron's disgust, for taking the King's part in the 'trial' of Queen Caroline in 1820. Byron soon reverted to his old sport of taunting his friend. Finding the entry Webster had made in the register of the Croce di Malta hotel, in which he described himself as 'Baronet' and entered his age as thirty-two, Byron took a pen and altered it to '*Knight* – aged 40'. He had not forgiven Webster for failing to repay the £1,000 he had lent him before he left England, with all the interest now accrued.

Webster had now parted from his wife although while in Genoa he tried to enlist Byron to make peace between them. Byron still referred to Lady Frances as 'the best of them', sign of his preference for an unconsummated affair. Webster was now in pursuit of Lady Hardy, widow of Sir Thomas Masterman Hardy who had been on the *Victory* when Nelson was fatally wounded and had been the recipient of the famous last words 'Kiss me, Hardy'. Anne Louisa Emily Hardy, still in her early thirties, now travelling in Italy, was less than enthusiastic about Webster's suit. Distantly related to Byron through his Berkeley great-grandmother, wife of the 4th Lord Byron, Lady Hardy had met Byron fleetingly in London at 'some Masquerade or party' in 1814. The family connection prompted him to respond warmly when she wrote to him in Genoa: 'My dear Cousin – For I believe we are cousins are we not? – I am very glad to hear from you – and should be no less so to see you – if you can make it con-venient.' His general rule to avoid fashionable English visitors, the residents of 'Welbeck Street and Devonshire Place broke loose', did not apply to her.

Byron and Lady Hardy met in Genoa in early November 1822 and their correspondence continued over the next year. Byron claimed to be too old and disillusioned for love but this was a kind of love affair on paper, all the more piquant because its limits were defined in advance. He wrote to Lady Hardy, in the person of the amiable cynic:

'Now – as *my* Love perils are – I believe pretty well over – and yours by all accounts are never to begin; – we shall be the best friends imaginable – as far as both are concerned – and with this advantage – that we may both fall to loving right and left through all our acquaintance.'

She replied in like kind:

'I quite agree that *friendship* when it is honestly nothing more is far more to be relied on as well as more agreeable between Man & Woman than two of either of the same sex, and as I clearly understand you never will nor expect you ever will be in love with me I think we are *friends for life*.'

Their intimacy was based, like Byron's with Augusta, on a shared background: they knew each other's reflexes. With Lady Hardy he returned to domestic interchange, the cosiness of well-bred England from which Byron had been estranged for many years. They exchanged news of Lady Hardy's three children, who were travelling with her, and of Byron's Ada. He had just received a new picture of his daughter, he told her: 'I have never seen the original since she was a month old.'

Byron's friendship with Lady Hardy gave scope to his irresistible habit of betraying those near and dear to him. He ridiculed and vilified her suitor 'Chevalier' Webster who, he told her, had 'persisted in declaring himself an ill-used Gentleman – and describing you – as a kind of cold Calypso – who lead astray people of amatory disposition – without giving them any sort of compensation'. In his frank and flirtatious correspondence with a sophisticated, sympathetic Englishwoman Teresa too was inevitably betrayed. He is all too clearly thinking of Teresa when he analyses sexual love as an essentially selfish relationship: 'Indeed I rather look upon Love altogether as a sort of hostile transaction – very necessary to make – or to break – matches and keep the world a-going – but by no means a sinecure to the parties concerned.'

The episode with Lady Hardy shows how Byron, middle-aged in Genoa, hair greying and teeth loose, retained his attractiveness to women, a devotion that derived from his particular gift for empathy. Lady Hardy was clearly less resigned to mere friendship with Lord Byron than she had pretended. She continued to write to him in Cephalonia, wondering when they would ever meet again.

Meanwhile Byron was still attracting worship from afar. A well-educated English girl Isabella Harvey, taking the pseudonym of Zorina Stanley, wrote to him in Genoa, pouring our her heart:

'I well remember at school how intimately I connected the author and his works. This was natural, but how happens it that the author is now more to me than his writings, that he is the food of my thoughts, the impulse of my life – my imagination has perhaps dressed you in attributes that do not really belong to you – but such as I imagine you, you are the bright dream of my existence.'

She asked him to reply c/o The Post Office, Fitzroy Square. He wrote back and for a few months the correspondence flourished, Byron addressing Isabella as 'my child' while she reciprocated with 'My dear Papa'.

On 22 January 1823 Byron was thirty-five. He was in a state of severe depression from the beginning of that year, veering from deep gloom to manic exuberance then lapsing into sadness. As he described it to Hoppner, 'all my *humours* are topsy turvy – and playing the devil – now here now there.' After his illness on the way to Genoa he had returned to his abstemious regime and was once more as thin as a skeleton. Teresa would press her finger to her cheek to demonstrate how hollow Byron's face had become.

His parsimony too was now a ruling passion. He had saved £3,300 out of his previous year's income, in spite of spending £1,000 on the *Bolivar* and donating over £300 to Leigh Hunt. He had had the schooner laid up for the winter in the Genoa Arsenal and rather ruthlessly dismissed the crew. He had sold five of his horses and given notice to the more superfluous of his servants. Now Byron personally took over the supervision of his household accounts from Lega Zambelli, settling the payments daily: 'and you cannot imagine the difference', he wrote smugly to Kinnaird. Though the problems of Rochdale were still unresolved, and a good many old English debts remained outstanding, the money from his Noel inheritance was beginning to come in. With his imminent departure in prospect Byron was anxious to have funds to provide, if necessary, for Augusta and her children and there was a new motivation for economy: he was stacking up money to assist the Greek cause.

Money is a major theme of the poem that preoccupied Byron in the first weeks of 1823. *The Age of Bronze* is a complicated satire, a review of politics and contemporary life in what Byron calls his 'early English Bards style'. It focuses on the Congress of Verona, the summit meeting of late 1822 called to settle the affairs of post-Napoleonic Europe. With ironical, savage wit Byron brings out the vested interests of the leaders taking part, pointing to the cynical economic considerations that underlay their policies. The poem shows him in opposition to international hypocrisy and cant, hoping to influence public opinion by revealing the iniquitous realities of political brokering. When John Hunt published the poem on 1 April the first edition of 2,000 copies sold out in a week.

A day or two after *The Age of Bronze* was finished Byron began another poem in a very different style. *The Island*, which turned out to be his last complete long poem, is romantic narrative and Utopian dream in the lush, exotic setting of the South Sea islands. Byron's two main sources are John Martin's account of the peoples and culture of the Tonga Islands and the true story of the mutiny on the *Bounty* in 1789 when Captain Bligh was ejected by a rebellious crew and despatched on to the ocean in an open boat. Byron takes the leader of the rebels, Fletcher Christian, as the model for the last Byronic hero, tormented and tormenting:

> 'But Christian, of an higher order, stood
> Like an extinct volcano in his mood;
> Silent, and sad, and savage, – with the trace
> Of passion reeking from his clouded face.'

When Christian, reproached by Bligh for his ingratitude, exclaims, 'I am in Hell! In Hell!' he echoes the words cried out so loud by Byron he awakened Annabella on their unsuccessful wedding night at Halnaby Hall.

At the centre of the poem is the Polynesian idyll between the uninhibited native girl Neuha and the Highland boy Torquil, 'the blue-eyed Northern child'. As so often in Byron's love-narratives it is she who indoctrinates him. The exotic wish-fulfilment of *The Island* relates as clearly to Byron's own experiences with Lady Oxford in the enchanted climes of Eywood as it does to the love scenes between Haidée and Don Juan. The poem shows also his fascination with ideas of noble savagery: what is truly natural and what the result of social indoctrination? In those final months in Genoa the prospects of idyllic wildernesses were impinging on his mind. If Greece fell through, he planned to buy his own small South Sea island to which he might retire for the remainder of his life.

He was writing as if he now had little time left. From the South Seas the scene moved back to the British Isles. Through February, March and April he was working on the English cantos of *Don Juan* in which the hero is precipitated into a bewildering social whirl of balls and house parties, shoots and fox hunts, the combination of grand spectacle and dull domestic ritual that gave a special flavour to county society. As Byron freely admitted, all the characters – hostesses, ingénues, complaisant husbands, the connoisseur, the architect, the over-jovial parson – were based on people he had known. These are fiercely moralistic cantos in which Byron exposes the hypocrisy and double-thinking underpinning the whole structure of English public life. In *Don Juan* Byron was taking his revenge on the society which had first adulated and then excluded him. But these cantos also constitute a love-poem to England, glowing with the detail of a way of life which, much as he suspected and derided it, Byron was well placed to understand:

> 'There was a goodly "soupe à la *bonne femme*",
>> Though God knows whence it came from; there was too
> A turbot for relief of those who cram,
>> Relieved with dindon a la Périgueux;
> There also was – the sinner that I am!
>> How shall I get this gourmand stanza through? –
> Soupe à la Beauveau, whose relief was Dory,
> Relieved itself by pork, for greater glory . . .
>
> Fowls à la Condé, slices eke of salmon,
>> With sauces Genevoises, and haunch of venison;
> Wines too which might again have slain young Ammon –
>> A man like whom I hope we shan't see many soon;
> They also set a glazed Westphalian ham on,
>> Whereon Apicius could bestow his benison;
> And then there was Champagne with foaming whirls,
> As white as Cleopatra's melted pearls.'

Byron grasped the moral significance of the trivial with a conviction not seen before or since.

Don Juan was never finished. It breaks off with a cliff-hanger at the end of Canto XVI as the sexually voracious Duchess of Fitz-Fulke enters Juan's bedroom concealed in a friar's cowl. The first fourteen stanzas of a further canto were in Byron's baggage when he left for Greece.

News reached Byron in Genoa of the resurrection of the Portsmouth scandal, an echo from the disreputable past, recalling the morning in March 1814 when Byron had laughingly led John Hanson's daughter up the aisle of St George's, Bloomsbury, to give her in marriage to the mentally unstable Earl of Portsmouth. Though the earlier attempts made by the Earl's brother, the Hon. Newton Fellowes, to invalidate the marriage on the grounds of the Earl's insanity had been dismissed, he had now gathered a formidable amount of new evidence and a second trial was held in February 1823.

Byron was riveted by the squalid detail as new episodes of this melodrama were reported in the English and continental newspapers. The Earl's erratic mental state often erupted into violence. He pinched and beat his servants, flogged and bled his animals sadistically, drove his cattle to the slaughterhouse himself where, axing them to death, he would cry out triumphantly, 'That serves them right, ambitious toads.' Lord Portsmouth had a mania for attending funerals, which he called 'black jobs', and would stage home-made funerals, forcing his servants to bear great logs on their shoulders pretending they were coffins.

His young wife Mary Ann had attempted to introduce some sanity, dismissing the most compliant of Portsmouth's servants. But she had soon been drawn into the cycle of violence herself. The new evidence showed that by 1815 she had begun horsewhipping the Earl when he was naked. With William Alder, her barrister lover and father of her children, she introduced a reign of counter-terror, assaulting and knocking the Earl down in his own house, treating him like a vicious animal. The other Hanson daughters had also been involved. Hobhouse wrote to Byron in Genoa: 'You recollect what a pretty smock faced girl Laura Hanson was in our time, who looked as if butter would not melt in her mouth. Well, it turns out that she used to beat and whip and spit upon this poor crazy creature and joined in all the cruelties against him.' The jury at the Portsmouth trial unanimously returned a verdict declaring that the Earl had been a lunatic since 1809 and the marriage was annulled.

Byron resented the way in which this new wave of publicity sensationalised his own role in the affair. As before, he went on pleading ignorance of the sordid implications of the Portsmouth marriage, expostulating to Hobhouse that he could not have foreseen a scenario of horsewhipping and 'black jobs', still less the possibility that the Earl was impotent:

'It struck me as so little an entrapment for Ld. P that I used to wonder whether the *Girl* would have him – and not whether *he* would take the Girl. – I knew nothing of his ignorance of "fuff – fuff – fuff" – as Cheeks Chester called it – but as he was of a robustous figure – though not a Solomon – naturally imagined he was not less competent than other people.'

Referring to the Earl's esoteric theory that bloodletting with a lancet gave women sexual thrills Byron made the comment:

'We owe to him however the greatest discovery about the blood since Dr Harvey's; – I wonder if it really hath such an effect – I was never bled in my life – but by leeches – and I thought the leeches d—d bad pieces – but perhaps the tape and lancet theory may be better – I shall try on some great emergency.'

The verdict on the Portsmouth marriage had the effect of transforming the Countess back into Miss Hanson. A pleading letter from her brother to the third John Murray shows that by 1858 she was destitute in Berwick-on-Tweed.

In the spring of 1823 Byron had succumbed to a local epidemic which took the form of a painful inflammation of the face. He had made this worse by walking home to Albaro uphill in a bleak wind when his carriage broke down after dinner with Hill, the British Minister. He was still embarrassed by his unsightliness when two sets of English visitors arrived in Genoa: Henry Fox, the young son of Lord Holland, a boy to whom Byron had been devoted and who still seemed 'the ne plus Ultra of the Amiable'; and Lord and Lady Blessington.

Was Byron pleased or irritated as these final months in Italy brought so many remembrances of his old life? He was certainly glad to re-encounter Fox, whose lameness in the old days had made such a bond between them, and he rose to the occasion with Lady Blessington, reporting to their mutual friend Tom Moore: 'Miladi seems highly literary . . . She is also very pretty, even in a morning, – a species of beauty on which the sun of Italy does not shine so frequently as the chandelier. Certainly, Englishwomen wear better than their continental neighbours of the same sex.'

Marguerite, Countess of Blessington, 'the most gorgeous' Lady Blessington as her admirers called her, was a clever Irishwoman of doubtful reputation who was herself a writer of travel books. She was the daughter of a minor landowner in Co. Waterford. Her father had apparently forced her into marriage at the age of fifteen with the violent Captain Maurice St Leger Farmer of the 47th Regiment of Foot. The marriage had not lasted and she had lived the life of an adventuress, first under the protection of a Captain Jenkins, then progressing to Lord Mountjoy who, in 1816, became the 1st Earl of Blessington. Her husband Captain Farmer having conveniently died from a fall out of a window in the King's Bench prison, she had married the Earl in 1818.

At their London house, 11 St James's Square, the vivacious Lady Blessington gathered many admiring men around her: prominent politicians, lawyers, artists, actors, even clergymen. She was cold-shouldered by most women whose attitude was summed up in a letter sent to Byron by his new friend Lady Hardy when she heard that Lady Blessington was in Italy: 'I have seen Lady Blessington in the Park and I thought her very handsome but am surprised to hear she is a literary lady as I believe her first rudiments of learning were learned at the Lakes in Tipperary . . . when Women take to write there is no saying where they will stop.'

The Blessingtons had left London the previous autumn on a continental tour. In France they were joined by the famously beautiful Count Alfred D'Orsay, twenty-two- year-old son of Count Albert D'Orsay, who had been one of Napoleon's generals. D'Orsay was a young man of great artistic talent and considerable sexual ambiguity. Byron describes the arrival in Genoa on 31 March of this intriguing trio:

'Milor B and *epouse*, travelling with a very handsome companion, in the shape of a "French Count" (to use Farquhar's phrase in the Beaux Stratagem), who has all the air of a *Cupidon déchainé*, and is one of the few specimens I have seen of our ideal of a Frenchman *before* the Revolution – an old friend with a new face, upon whose like I never thought that we should look again.'

Lady Blessington was a celebrity hunter: 'And am I indeed in the same town with Byron!' she had exclaimed on reaching Genoa. She had never before felt such a longing to see in the flesh someone she had previously known only by his works. Her great worry was that Byron would be fat, as Moore had described him and indeed as he had been when Leigh Hunt encountered him: 'for a fat poet is an anomaly in my opinion'. Byron was no longer fat. But when the Blessingtons first met him at the Casa Saluzzo she was disappointed by his flippancy of manner and 'a want of the self-possession and dignity' that should characterise a man of his high birth and reputation.

Over the next ten weeks, while the Blessingtons remained in Genoa, staying in style at the Albergo della Villa, a close friendship developed between Lady Blessington and Byron. It was not one of his older woman friendships since she and Byron were almost identical in age. But it resembled his relationship with Lady Melbourne in the sense of shared worldliness that lay at its heart: they met as men and women of experience, exchanging views on life and love as they rode in the countryside around Genoa. Teresa's jealousy was not without cause. Byron wrote poems to Lady Blessington which were, to all intents and purposes, amatory. One of these was his flirtatious support for her idea of taking a villa in Genoa named 'Il Paradiso':

> 'Beneath Blessington's eyes
> The reclaimed Paradise
> Should be free as the former from Evil.
> But if the new Eve
> For an Apple should grieve –
> What Mortal would not play the Devil? –'

Lady Blessington kept a record of Byron's conversations. Her lack of inhibition made her an expert interviewer. Indeed in 1846, having once again fallen on hard times after her husband's death, she joined the staff of the newly founded *Daily News*. As she questioned and gently interrogated Byron, playing upon his easy confidentiality, she too contributed to the growing cache of information and impressions that went to form the Byron legend. Lady Blessington's *Conversations of Lord Byron* first appeared in instalments in the *New Monthly Magazine* in 1832 and 1833 before being published in book form by Henry Colburn in 1834. Compared with Medwin's *Conversations* hers are more astute, more nimble. Lady Blessington, herself a parvenu, has a greater grasp of Byron's own vulgarity, exemplified by the flamboyant use he made of his family motto 'Crede Byron'. From her own worldly experience of sexual difference she had a surer sympathy with Byron's effeminacy, the mannered exaggeration of his style.

If the relationship with Lady Blessington is interesting, that with Count Alfred D'Orsay is even more so. The Parisian dandy, toweringly handsome at six foot three, oiled and scented, always beautifully dressed, was considered the handsomest young man of his period and, like Byron, was enormously attractive to both sexes. If Lady Blessington adored her temperamental 'Parisian Paladin', Lord Blessington was enraptured by him too, telling Byron that he loved D'Orsay as if he had been his own son or brother, affirming that he had 'a heart more valuable & more pure than gold. When he travelled with us first we called him Le Jeune Lion.' Blessington was later to negotiate the marriage of D'Orsay to his fifteen-year-old daughter Lady Harriet Gardiner. But the marriage soon broke down, having evidently been a *mariage blanc*.

In observing the man described by Carlyle as 'the Phoebus Apollo of dandyism', a person of manly pursuits but as careful of his beauty as a woman would have been, Byron was conscious of the parallels with his own past. D'Orsay allowed him to read a copy of the journal he had written when he had been in London living at the heart of fashionable society in 1821 and 1822. It was almost as if Byron had been born again. Byron was impressed at the way in which D'Orsay had penetrated '*not* the *fact* – but the *mystery* of the English Ennui at two and twenty', mirroring Byron's similar discovery in the same social circles at almost the same age.

Byron encouraged D'Orsay to draw his portrait at Genoa. There are four of these pencil drawings still extant, two full length showing the slim figure leaning on his cane on a Mediterranean seafront promenade, trousers cut wide to conceal his foot. Two others are head and shoulder portraits, one depicting Byron with receding hair above a high sloped forehead, the other in a frogged jacket and a peaked cap. This was presumably the portrait made by D'Orsay in response to Byron's letter, 'I have a request to make to my friend Alfred –

(since he has not disclaimed the title –) viz. – that he would condescend to add a cap to the Gentleman in the Jacket – it would complete his costume – and smoothe his brow – which is somewhat too inveterate a likeness of the original, – God help me!'

Before Count D'Orsay left Genoa, Byron presented him, via Lady Blessington, with an outsize ring formed out of lava, 'so far adapted to the fire of his years and character'. Half jealous, half admiring, Byron recognised D'Orsay's eruptive quality.

In the afternoon of 5 April Byron was visited at the Casa Saluzzo by Edward Blaquière and Andreas Louriotis. Captain Blaquière was a naval officer and political propagandist, one of the founders of the London Greek Committee. Louriotis had been sent to London by the Greek government to seek British support for the revolution against Turkish rule. They were now returning together to Greece on a fact-finding mission. For Byron the meeting was decisive. He wrote to Hobhouse two days later:

'I saw Capt. Blaquiere and the Greek Companion of his mission on Saturday. – Of course I entered very sincerely into the object of their journey – and have even offered to go up to the Levant in July – if the Greek provisional Government think that I could be of any use. – It is not that I could pretend to anything in a military capacity – I have not the presumption of the philosopher of Ephesus – who lectured before Hannibal on the art of war – nor is it much that an individual foreigner can do in any other way – but perhaps as a reporter of the actual state of things there – or in carrying on any correspondence between them and their western friends – I might be of use – at any rate I would try.'

Practical, realistic, a little tentative: there is a new tone of serious undertaking as Byron identifies himself with the Greek cause.

Compared with its progress in other parts of Europe, particularly Germany, Switzerland and France, support for the Greek revolution in England had been sluggish. But the outrages of the massacre of Khios in spring 1822, in which at least 25,000 Greeks out of a total population of 100,000 had been slaughtered by the Turks and the whole island ravaged, had helped to galvanise sympathy. The London Greek Committee was formed in January 1823 and its first meeting was held at the Crown and Anchor tavern in the Strand on 28 February. The Tory government was disinclined to support the revolution, afraid the way would be open, if the Turks were defeated, for the Russians to dominate Greece, endangering the European balance of power. Support for the

Greek cause was largely a preserve of the reformist wing of the Whig Opposition, and the London Greek Committee was dominated by many of Byron's former London cronies, acquaintances and rivals, including Sir Francis Burdett, Henry Brougham, Jeremy Bentham the great liberal utilitarian, John Cam Hobhouse and the Hon. Douglas Kinnaird.

There had been earlier overtures to Byron on behalf of the Committee. William Smith had written from the Crown and Anchor tavern on 8 March to inform him that several friends of the Greeks had met together 'to give action and effect to the sympathy' for the Greek cause 'which they have reason to believe is very widely diffused over the Country'. He asked Byron to allow his name to be added to the Committee. The Hon. Secretary, John Bowring, wrote to Byron a week later, with Hobhouse's encouragement, saying: 'as you, more than any living being have been instrumental in awakening that sympathy which I hope will now become an *effective* sympathy we trust you will lend us your talents & your influence to give our exertions more certain success.'

Blaquière had also had an intimation from Trelawny in Italy that Byron would be likely to offer his support. His potential usefulness was obvious to a propaganda campaign which, while sensationalising the plight of the Greek people as victims of the infidel Turk, also made a subtler, more intellectual link between ancient Hellenic cultural values and the civilised Great Britain of the nineteenth century. Byron was a poet, *the* poet, of liberty; a poet already identified in the public consciousness with Greece. The more doubtful connotations of Byron's reputation were forgotten in the Committee's eagerness to enlist him in the Greek revolutionary cause.

When Blaquière arrived in Genoa he confirmed that Byron's election as a member of the Greek Committee had been unanimous. He brought Byron's official credentials and a mass of supporting papers, assuring him that at the Crown and Anchor his name was already 'a tower of strength'. Here was a new club for him to belong to. If Byron's support for the Greek revolution was useful to the London Greek Committee it also met his own need for rehabilitation, acceptance and gratitude amongst his peers. Trelawny commented that 'the propositions of the Committee came at the right moment; the Pilgrim was dissatisfied with himself and his position. Greece and its memories warmed him, a new career opened before him.' This analysis is partly true. The ever-astute Lady Blessington agreed that Byron's decision to go to Greece resulted from his 'need to prove in his own person that a poet may be a soldier'. She knew that the experience would be hard for him.

In approaching Byron, the London Greek Committee had had little idea of how much they could expect from him: perhaps simply his name and some financial aid. When it emerged that he might be willing to go to Greece in person, Blaquière was overjoyed. Three weeks later, himself en route to Greece, he wrote to Byron from Zante urging him to make the journey as soon as possible: 'your presence will operate as a talisman, & the field is too glorious, – too closely associated with all you hold dear, to be any longer abandoned.' He told Byron, with a somewhat exaggerated optimism, 'The Cause is in a most flourishing state.' In the Ionian Isles, the effects of his mentioning the news of Byron's planned arrival on the scene had been 'quite electric'. Blaquière ended his letter: 'Anxious to see your Lordship in the land of heroes, I remain, most truly & devotedly yours –'

Byron was thinking himself into the role of leader. On 12 May he wrote formally to Bowring on the subject of his election to the London Greek Committee: 'I have great pleasure in acknowledging your letter and the honour which the Committee have done me. – I shall endeavour to deserve their confidence by every means in my power.' He gave his practical assessment of the priorities: 'the principal material wanted by the Greeks appears to be – 1st. a pack of field Artillery – light – and fit for Mountain service – 2dly. Gunpowder – 3dly. hospital or Medical Stores.' He himself, so he announced to Bowring, would be sending an initial consignment of gunpowder and medical supplies to Greece. He was also seeking inside information on the progress of the war from Nikolaos Karvellas, a Greek now studying at Pisa. In this Byron's judgement appears to have been faulty since Karvellas provided no useful information but demanded a loan on his own account from Byron. Hobhouse denounced Karvellas's reports as trash.

In this first official letter Byron gave Bowring his views on the best way of approaching military intervention in the Greek War. 'Raw British soldiers', Byron felt, would prove 'unruly and not very serviceable – in irregular warfare – by the side of foreigners.' Byron's instinct was to rely on elite leadership, and rather than recruiting a brigade of soldiery he urged the Committee to concentrate on selecting a small body of '*Officers* of experience', especially artillery officers and engineers. Preference should be given to those who spoke Italian, which was widely understood in Greece, and those who had served in the Mediterranean. Warming to his theme Byron continued:

'It would also be as well that they should be aware – that they are not going "to rough it on a beef steak – and bottle of Port" – but that Greece – never of late years – very plentifully stocked for a *Mess* – is at present the country of all kinds of *privations*, – this remark may seem superfluous – but I have been led to it – by observing that many *foreign* Officers – Italian – French and even German –

(but *fewer* of the latter) have returned in disgust – imagining either that they were going to make up a party of pleasure – or to enjoy full pay – speedy promotion and a very moderate degree of duty; – they complain too of having been ill received by the Government or inhabitants, but numbers of these complainants – were mere adventurers – attracted by a hope of command and plunder, – and disappointed of both.'

Byron's comments were pertinent. In the Greek War of Independence the wastage level was high amongst the foreign volunteers now to be seen straggling back through Europe to their native lands. Two bedraggled and destitute Germans found their way to the Casa Saluzzo in May, where Byron talked to them and Pietro Gamba gave them breakfast. But such clear-eyed observations were not to be voiced. Hobhouse rebuked Byron for the satiric comments that crept into his official communications with the London Greek Committee: 'You must not be so waggish as you have been in your two last folios: which I had some doubt whether I should send to the committee fearing these grave gentlemen would think you not in earnest.' His London Greek Committee letters had to be censored to make them fit for publication.

As far back as the young Byron's debut speech in the House of Lords, his instinct was always to report the truth. He could not be bland, and this had set his limits as a statesman. Now as always, even in his formal statements, the trenchant humorist broke out.

Even while he was corresponding in such detail with the London Greek Committee, Byron was still vacillating about leaving. Teresa was the sticking point. How to reconcile love with glory, a theme he had addressed so often in his poetry, was almost impossible for Byron to resolve in practice. Outside observers were aware that he was finding Teresa's possessiveness irksome. Their liaison was well over the three-year limit Byron himself had allowed for the duration of a love affair. His capacity for feeling, so he confided in Lady Blessington, was exhausted. He was more like a man of sixty than one in his mid-thirties, 'less capable than ever of those nameless attentions that all women, above all, Italian women require'. He had not encouraged Lady Hardy's proposition that Teresa should accompany him in male disguise. 'Were I in her place', she had written, 'I should try to see if I could not realise Lara's page. Would not that be heroic & troublesome to the last degree?'

Byron never envisaged taking Teresa with him. But a definite break was almost more than he could manage. He was still bound to Teresa and the Gambas by numerous ties of obligation, familiarity, shared memories, affection.

He was terrified of her capacity for scenes, her tales of 'ill usage and abandonment – and Lady Carolining – and Lady Byroning – and Glenarvoning – all cut and dry'. 'There never was a man', Byron lamented, 'who gave up so much to women – and all I have gained by it – has been the character of treating them harshly.' This was likely to be a new, and worse, version of the same theme.

Byron's dilemma was finally resolved when it was announced that Count Gamba was permitted to return to Ravenna from his banishment on condition he brought Teresa with him. Pressure had been exerted by the old Count Guiccioli. Byron still did not dare to tell her himself that he planned to leave for Greece. The task was delegated to Pietro. But of course Teresa, such a creature of suspicions, had noticed the 'unusual abstractedness and sometimes great sadness in his features, which disturbed her'. She was aware of the fact that Byron's poetry was not enough for him, that 'writing, even with genius, did not appear to him to fulfil a great man's duty: it had to be linked with action.' The news was not a shock to her. In a sense Teresa had known it all along.

That hurdle over, Byron began to concentrate his mind on departure. He would sit locked in discussion with Pietro every evening, out on the terrace of the palace at Albaro, the town and the blue Mediterranean stretched beneath them. When Colonel Stietz, a Westphalian officer who had been fighting in the Greek war, came to call he found Byron sitting at a table heaped with books and papers, studying a map of Greece. Byron's letters of late May and June 1823 are full of the minutiae of preparation. He had received a £4,000 letter of credit from Kinnaird to be added to the £2,000 he had already saved. He began selling his furniture, books, snuffboxes and watches, anything of value he could lay his hands on to benefit the war effort. His acquisitive instincts were now redeployed in the ordering of military equipment. Through James Alexander, English doctor in Genoa, he spent £70 on enough medical supplies to last a thousand men for two years.

The Blessingtons and Count D'Orsay left Genoa on 2 June. For Byron this was another wrench, a last farewell to that stimulating world of cosmopolitan gossip and flirtation. Lady Blessington remembered how one night just before their departure Byron, lying on the sofa while they were at dinner, 'burst out a-crying'. Teresa, in her memoirs, insisted that the crying was done by Lady Blessington. Before they departed, Byron bought Lady Blessington's superb Arab charger Mameluke to take to Greece with him: she was annoyed that he beat her down on price. Meanwhile Lord Blessington entered into protracted and, in the end, acrimonious negotiations with Byron, through his English banker in Genoa Charles Barry, to purchase his schooner the *Bolivar*. Byron asked to retain the cannon he had installed plus some American flags and two chairs which bore the Byron coronet, assuming that all these would be of less use to Lord Blessington than to him.

At the beginning Byron's intention had been to take only a supporting role in the Greek war. 'If I could do any good in any way – I should be happy to contribute thereto – and without *eclât*,' he had told Lord Blessington, 'I have seen enough of that in my time – to rate it at its value.' But his sense of theatre took over as the plans progressed. Through Barry, he chartered an English brig, the *Hercules*, to take him and his entourage as far as the Ionian Isles. He ordered scarlet and gold military uniforms to be made in Genoa, ready for a Greek landing. He commissioned three helmets of classical proportions from Giacomo Aspe, a skilled decorative metalworker. The least ostentatious of the three, intended for Pietro Gamba, was of deep green cloth on a brass and black leather base. One of the huge gilt helmets was ordered for Trelawny. Another, the most splendid, with his coat of arms beneath the plume and the motto 'Crede Byron', was Byron's own. 'Have you seen my three helmets?' he was tactless enough to ask a determinedly unimpressed Leigh Hunt.

Trelawny was part of the *mise en scène*. Byron had recalled him from Florence where he had been staying after superintending the reburial of Shelley's ashes in the New Protestant Cemetery in Rome. 'My dear T,' Byron wrote cajolingly, 'You must have heard that I am going to Greece. Why do you not come to me? I want your aid, and am exceedingly anxious to see you.' This was not an invitation the adventurous Trelawny could refuse. More puzzling is why Byron was so anxious to secure the services of this would-be Corsair whom he knew to be bombastic and unreliable. The answer must lie in his preference for the familiar, though problematic, as against the threateningly unknown.

In these last weeks in Genoa Byron extricated himself not entirely gracefully from his complicated web of obligations. He had gradually pulled out of the critical and financial disaster of *The Liberal*, persuading himself that the involvement in the enterprise of 'the most unpopular man in England' did little good either to the Hunts or to him. Byron's *Heaven and Earth* was included in the second issue on 1 January 1823; *The Blues*, his satire on female intellectual salons, in the third, published on 24 April; and his translation of Pulci finally appeared in the fourth issue on 30 July, after which *The Liberal* folded. Byron undertook to pay John Hunt's legal charges for the prosecution over *The Vision of Judgement*, which was still in train. He maintained that he was willing to pay the expenses for Leigh Hunt and his family to return to England, and in fact gave him money to travel on from Genoa to Florence. But Hunt was not assuaged.

At Casa Negroto resentment against Byron flourished as his preparations for Greece accelerated. Mary Shelley felt herself isolated and abandoned. In February Byron had parried Mary's urgent request that he should send some money to Claire Clairmont, said to be dangerously ill in Vienna, suggesting that Mary herself should send the money and he would then repay her: he still could not contemplate direct contact with Claire. Now, in the last rushed days before Byron's departure, acrimony grew over the money Byron had promised Mary, to finance her return to England. On 28 June he wrote impatiently to Hunt: 'I have received a note from Mrs S. with a fifth or sixth change of plans – viz. – not to make her journey at all – at least through my assistance on account of what she is pleased to call "estrangement &c." – On this I have little to say.'

He proposed to advance her the money through Hunt without her knowing, 'thus she will be spared any fancied humiliation'. Byron now declined to continue to act as Shelley's executor and refused Shelley's legacy of £2,000. Hunt passed the message on, intent on troublemaking and reminding Mary that, since Lady Noel had predeceased Sir Timothy, Byron still owed the £1,000 he had bet Shelley at Pisa on Christmas Day 1821. Gratuitously Hunt told Mary that Byron disliked her and was bored by her, that although he was willing to pay for her voyage he did not want to see her again. It was true that at this juncture Shelley's widow was not the foremost of Byron's priorities.

His hardest task was to divest himself of Teresa. Partly prepared though she had been for his departure, when the time came she could not relinquish him easily. Over those weeks, she wept and she entreated. She wrote frantic little letters to him during her sleepless nights. Most of these she would tear up, but as Teresa recollected in her memoirs: 'one day Lord Byron had arrived in Madame Guiccioli's sitting room when she was out, and he found one of these fragments addressed to him. He read it, and kept it; and it was found again among the letters which he preserved religiously, and were brought back from Greece to England.' When Byron told Teresa he had given instructions to Charles Barry to draft a new will she became hysterical. Byron, to placate her, promised not to complete it. He had wanted to transfer to Teresa the £5,000 he had previously left to Allegra, but she refused to accept any legacy. Soon after, he came into her apartment carrying a large packet of manuscripts. 'These are a few of my scribblings,' he told her, suggesting she should keep them in her family archive, unless she felt like burning them. 'It's possible that they'll be sought after, one day.'

In the desperation of the time, other arrangements for Teresa's immediate future were considered: should she enter the Convent of the Sisters of the Visitation in Nice? Should she remain in the protection of a respectable gentlewoman in Genoa? The idea of the convent foundered when Teresa discovered that the strictly enclosed order would not allow sea-bathing. So soon after the death of Allegra in the convent at Bagnacavallo, Byron was relieved. No respectable lady was forthcoming in Genoa. So it was decided that Teresa would accompany her father Count Ruggero to Ravenna, as previously planned. Byron tried to calm her down, assuring her that he would be returning. But Teresa felt an 'incomprehensible foreboding, not formulated, not avowed, almost in a dormant state, but a very real presentiment'.

He was due to leave Albaro in the early evening of 13 July 1823 in order to spend that first night on board the *Hercules*. He stayed by Teresa's side from three o'clock till five. He had arranged for Mary Shelley to be there to comfort her when the moment of his departure came. Teresa's half-mad jottings over the next few days have a terrible pathos: 'I have promised more than I can perform, and you have asked of me what is beyond my strength . . . My God, help me! Come and fetch me, Byron, if you still want to see me alive, or let me run away and join you, at any cost.'

Byron was now taking a long farewell of Italy. He left his banker Charles Barry in charge of closing down the Casa Saluzzo at Albaro. The devoted Barry gave orders for all Byron's books to be locked up in the room in which he used to sit, where Barry planned to 'take the liberty' of reading them himself; Trelawny had already been detected in helping himself from Byron's library. Barry also shouldered responsibility for Byron's Napoleonic coach and two smaller carriages, and another abandoned menagerie. His wife took to riding the old grey horse which was not easily saleable. He puzzled over what to do with the reprieved Michaelmas geese.

As well as Italy, Byron took his final leave of England. He asked Lady Blessington, on her return home, to obtain for him a copy of the miniature of Lady Byron he remembered as once belonging to her mother. He said he had no picture 'nor indeed memorial of any kind of Ly. B.' He was coming to accept her as part of his history, the mother of his daughter. A few months earlier he had mentioned that he could no longer remember what she looked like, it was so long since they had met.

In reporting Lord Byron's departure from Genoa for Greece, *The Times* newspaper asserted that he had taken on board his own vessel 'warlike accoutrements equal to the equipment of fifteen hundred men. Many English officers, on half pay, then resident in Italy, are said to have accompanied him.' This shows how wildly the Byron legends were proliferating. In fact Byron boarded the *Hercules* on 13 July with Trelawny, Pietro Gamba and the young

Drawing of Byron at Genoa, based on a miniature by Isola, probably the last portrait of
Byron made before he left for Greece

Italian doctor Francesco Bruno who had been recommended by James
Alexander, the English doctor in Genoa. There were eight servants, including
Lega Zambelli, William Fletcher, Tita Falcieri, the reinstated coachman
Vincenzo Papi and Benjamin Lewis, an American Negro previously employed
by Trelawny and now taken on by Byron. Lewis spoke some French and
Italian; cookery and horses were his special areas of expertise. Byron had given
a passage on the ship to a Greek from Constantinople, Prince Schilizzi. Five
horses went with them, one of which was Lady Blessington's Mameluke. Also
on board was the fierce bulldog Moretto and a majestic Newfoundland dog
Lyon given to Byron by an admirer, an ex-naval officer Edward Le Mesurier, a
few weeks before he sailed.

At ten the next morning all was ready for the sailing. But there was no wind.

He thought of returning to the Casa Saluzzo but when he heard that Teresa had already left at dawn he, Barry, Trelawny and Pietro made for the beautiful Villa Lomellina on the shore about six miles west of the city, where Byron had liked to ride with Lady Blessington. They picnicked there under a tree, on cheese and fruit. 'It was a most memorable day,' wrote Barry, 'which will never vanish from my recollection.'

They slept aboard and the *Hercules* set off again at sunrise the next morning, 15 July. They remained close to the harbour all day, still in sight of Genoa. It was fine Mediterranean weather, scorching sun and a light wind. Towards midnight a strong westerly wind arose. At first they made some headway but the captain was forced to steer back towards Genoa as a violent storm arose, pitching and tossing the ship Trelawny had described disparagingly as 'a collier-built tub of 120 tons, round-bottomed, and bluff-bowed'. The horses, terrified and in makeshift stalls, started careering about and doing damage. Byron, trying his best to control them, spent almost the entire night on deck. The sight of the great storm thrilled him, as it always did, encouraging a surge of reflections on the sublimity of nature. Though most of his fellow passengers were seasick Byron did not succumb until they were sailing back into the port of Genoa at 6 a.m.

That day, 16 July, had to be spent repairing damage to the *Hercules*. Byron now made a melancholy expedition, with Pietro and Barry, to the deserted Casa Saluzzo. 'Where shall we be in a year?' he asked Pietro on the way. In fact one year later to the day he would be buried in the ancestral vault at Hucknall Torkard. Once they reached the palace he was prostrated by depression, spending three or four hours in gloomy contemplation in his inner sanctum and dining alone on more cheese and figs. Over those two days, while still stranded in Genoa, Barry was aware of a conflict in Byron. At this last moment he was tempted to give up the whole journey. Barry later told Tom Moore: 'That he had not fixed to go to England, in preference, seemed one of his deep regrets; and so hopeless were the views he expressed of the whole enterprise before him, that, as it appeared to Mr Barry, nothing but a devoted sense of duty and honour could have determined him to persist in it.' Another thing that held him to his intention was the prospect of the ridicule he would incur from Hobhouse and his London friends if he reneged.

In the evening of 16 July they were ready to set off again. The banker Barry, close to tears, took a boat to the end of the pierhead to catch a last glimpse of his departing client. The *Hercules* reached Leghorn in five days. Here Byron took the opportunity to write effusively to Goethe, 'undisputed Sovereign of European Literature', thanking him for the verses he had written when he heard of Byron's heroic enterprise. From Leghorn, Byron also added a hasty postscript to Pietro's farewell letter to Teresa:

'My dearest Teresa – I have but a few moments to say that we are all well – and thus far on our way to the Levant – believe that I always *love* you – and that a thousand words could only express the same idea.

ever dearest yrs. NB'

From now on all his letters to Teresa would be similarly brisk.

The *Hercules* stayed in harbour for two days, loading on board supplies of gunpowder and stocks of English goods from Henry Dunn. Byron's arrival was greeted with excitement by the many Greeks resident in Leghorn. He was given letters of introduction from the patriotic Greek Bishop Ignatios of Arta, then residing at Pisa, to his contacts among the Greek revolutionary chiefs, in particular Prince Mavrocordatos and Markos Botsaris, leader of the Greek forces in Akarnania. Botsaris and his soldiers were now confronting the Turkish army north of Missolonghi. Two more passengers boarded the *Hercules* at Leghorn: James Hamilton Browne, a young Scots Philhellene who was intending to join the revolutionary forces, and a somewhat dubious Greek, Captain Georgios Vitalis, whom Byron had promised a passage home.

Browne left a revealing account of shipboard life on the ten-day voyage to the Ionian Isles and of Byron himself in his informal but fastidious nautical dress of nankeen embroidered jacket, white Marseilles vest buttoned 'a very little way up', fine linen shirt with the collar 'thrown over in such a way as almost to uncover his neck', short buff laced boots sometimes worn with gaiters and his boyish Tuscan straw hat. Browne observed him on deck boxing with Trelawny, fencing with Pietro. Sometimes, although Byron disliked shooting at birds, he and Trelawny would procure the food for dinner by firing at a duck suspended in a wicker basket from the mainyard of the mast. It seems that Byron himself did not join the feast. His usual dinner, eaten on deck alone, was 'a considerable quantity of decayed Cheshire cheese, with pickled cucumbers or red cabbage', washed down with a bottle of cider or the Burton ale they had procured en route.

As they sailed down the west coast of Italy they saw Elba and Corsica. Byron had just been reading the first volume of the Comte de Las Cases' memoir of St Helena: the conversation on board became fixed upon Napoleon and Byron's mingled admiration and disgust for the great European Emperor. On a clear night, the *Hercules* passed Stromboli. Byron was disappointed that the volcano was not active: he had never seen a volcano erupt. But when they got to Sicily they were met by the magnificent sight of Mount Etna enveloped in a thick cloud of its own smoke.

On board Byron was playful, talkative, responsive. Browne was surprised, and perhaps a little repelled, by his 'fascinating and insinuating mode of address'. When the Greek Prince Schilizzi used to flatter him by telling him that his pro-monarchical countrymen would probably ask Byron to become their king, it seemed to Browne that 'this idea did not displease his Lordship, who said he would perhaps not decline the offer, if made, adding, "but we shall retain our own monies; and then if our appetite disagrees with kingly authority, we shall, like Sancho, have the alternative of abdicating".' Monarchy was acceptable, but only on his own terms.

When he took against the other Greek passenger, Captain Vitalis, Byron became embroiled in a characteristically sadistic joke, telling the conventionally homophobic English captain of the *Hercules*, Captain Scott, that Vitalis was 'addicted to certain horrible propensities, too common in the Levant'. Scott was horror-struck, 'wondering how such a scoundrel could dare to look any honest man in the face'. The Greek was mystified by Captain Scott's hostility. When Vitalis was spied by the Captain through a skylight lying asleep on the cabin table clad only in his drawers, Scott could not resist emptying a bucket of dirty water over him. 'Lord Byron at these scenes was absolutely convulsed with laughter.' Another grotesque joke on board the *Hercules* was at Captain Scott's expense. As recounted by Trelawny:

'On great occasions when our captain wished to be grand he wore a bright scarlet waistcoat; as he was very corpulent, Byron wished to see if this vest would not button round us both. The captain was taking his siesta one day when he persuaded the boy to bring up the waistcoat.

"Now", said Byron, standing on the gangway, with one arm in the red waistcoat, "put your arm in, Tre, we will jump overboard to take the shine out of it." So we did.'

There were times on that journey when Byron's moods changed quickly. He could be seen to be abstracted and distressed. Browne observed how 'in the midst of the greatest hilarity and enjoyment', as the company assembled on deck after the siesta for wines and other drinks, Byron's tragic mask descended: 'A cloud would instantaneously come over him, as if arising from some painful and appalling recollection; the tears would bedew his eyes, when he would arise and quit the company, averting his face, in order to conceal his emotion.'

How far was Byron conscious that he was on a voyage that would end in death? Perhaps not totally. But he realised the dangers inherent in his mission, and in fact he made that mission more militaristic than anyone else expected of him. Byron was in search of glory. When he talked of the possibility of dying in Greece, 'I hope it may be in action,' he remarked, 'for that would be a good finish to a very *triste* existence.' The *Hercules* brought him to Argostoli on Cephalonia on 3 August 1823.

26

Cephalonia

1823

On board the *Hercules*, Byron's spirits lifted as the islands of Cephalonia and Zante came into sight and beyond them the distant coastline of mainland Greece. Irresistibly reminded of his early travels and his first hopeful sight of Ancient Greece, glimpsed through that same channel between Cephalonia and Zante, he remarked to Trelawny: 'I don't know why it is, but I feel as if the eleven long years of bitterness I have passed through since I was here, were taken off my shoulders, and I was scudding through the Greek Archipelago with old Bathurst, in his frigate.' He was now to spend five months on Cephalonia, from early August to late December 1823.

The island, ruled by Venice for four centuries, had been annexed by revolutionary France in 1797. Over the next decade it was disputed territory, as it was to be again in the Second World War. In 1809 the island was taken by the British from the imperial French. By 1823 Cephalonia was one of the seven Ionian Isles then under a British protectorate, administered by a High Commission in Corfu – under 'the not very Tolerant Thomas Maitland', as Byron described this formidable character – and officially neutral in the struggle between the Greeks and Turks.

Here on the edge of the war zone Byron found the predictable hierarchies of British Resident and Deputy; General, officers and soldiers of the garrison; engineers, health officers, clergymen and wives, clerks, servants and hangers-on, playing out the rituals of an early nineteenth-century colonial administration. Byron was wary of this transplanted British way of life but he allowed himself to be drawn into it, aware of the dignity, glamour and kind-heartedness in the midst of the absurdity. It was a world he had understood since childhood, the ambience of his father and of many of his Harrow friends. One day Lieutenant-Colonel John Duffie, second-in-command of the 8th Regiment (King's) of Foot which was stationed in Cephalonia, met Byron out riding and led him down the line of the whole regiment. He was impressed and moved. 'After all there are not finer looking soldiers in the world than the English,' Byron said.

The Governor and Military Resident of Cephalonia was Lieutenant-Colonel Charles James Napier, later to be renowned as the conqueror of Sind. In 1823 Napier's military reputation was already legendary. Byron knew him as 'one of Sir John Moore's "Well done my Majors!"' At the battle of Corunna in the Peninsular War Napier's bravery had been conspicuous: he had been wounded five times during the retreat leading his battalion in Lord William Bentinck's brigade. After Byron's usual initial suspicion of strangers, especially distinguished ones, he and Napier settled to friendship and great mutual respect. There were many points of similarity. They shared an aristocratic background: Charles Napier's grandfather was the 6th Lord Napier and his mother Lady Sarah Lennox one of the four beautiful and spirited daughters of the 2nd Duke of Richmond. Napier like Byron was a strikingly attractive figure, though scarred and disabled by his Corunna injuries as well as by a leg badly broken in his youth. He too was open to the unconventional liaison, fathering two daughters by a young Cephalonian woman, Anastasia.

If Byron was a would-be soldier, Napier was a writer manqué. Besides his disquisitions on colonial practice and his detailed memoir on the rebuilding of the Cephalonian roads, Napier was the author of essays, translations, even *William the Conqueror: a Historical Romance*, of which the chief protagonist was another Harold, twin to Byron's Childe. In outlook an imaginative liberal, Napier was in method an autocrat: here too there are parallels with Byron. Both combined a real humanitarianism with the respect for high courage and glory in battle that was typical of their times. The strangest coincidence is that they should have met at all at this juncture on the rocky island of Cephalonia. For here were two of the most able Britons of the post-Napoleonic generation, still searching for a role. Byron at thirty-five, Napier at forty-one, were both deeply disillusioned at the loss of the many great causes of their youth.

It was Napier's discreet sympathy for the Greek revolution that had brought Byron to Cephalonia rather than to Zante, the original destination of the *Hercules*. James Hamilton Browne, through his former military service in the Ionian Isles, was aware of Napier's enlightened attitudes. According to Trelawny, 'From what we learnt of him we altered our plan, and instead of Zante decided on going to Cephalonia, as Sir C.J. Napier was in command there, and the only man in office favourably disposed to the Greeks and their cause.' In 1821 Napier had written an anonymous pamphlet 'War in Greece', a copy of which he later gave to Byron. In their attitude to Greek independence neither was a romantic Philhellene: both were men of pragmatism. In Napier's later view, of all the many foreigners who came to help the Greeks only Byron and Thomas Gordon, the one experienced military member of the London Greek Committee, managed to achieve a balanced view of the Greek war.

'All came expecting to find the Peloponnesus filled with Plutarch's men, and all returned thinking the inhabitants of Newgate were moral. Lord Byron judged them fairly; he knew that half-civilised men are full of vices, and that great allowance must be made for emancipated slaves. He, therefore, proceeded, bridle in hand, not thinking them good, but hoping to make them better.'

Behind the nineteenth-century colonialist language is a true appreciation of Byron's patient objectivity in the conduct of the war.

Byron arrived in Cephalonia to face the first of many disappointments of the next few months. 'Dear Sir, – Here am I – but where are *you*?' he demanded in a letter to Edward Blaquière on his first night on the island, writing by lantern light with a squall blowing. He was still on board ship. Byron had expected Blaquière, his chief contact with the London Greek Committee, to be there to meet him and give him a briefing on the state of things in Greece. Blaquière, however, was already at Corfu on his return journey to England, intent on writing a quick self-promotional account of his own Greek exploits. Byron was insulted and incensed. He had reached Cephalonia with the equivalent of around £9,000 in Spanish dollars, some in cash, most in bills of credit. With no instructions from the Committee on priorities, Byron was now left to make his own decisions. Besides, as he pointed out indignantly to Blaquière, who had earlier given him an over-hopeful picture, 'the Greek news is here anything but Good'.

The war had reached a stage of bewildering complexity. Initially the Greeks had met with a good deal of military success. In taking the Peloponnese from the Turks they had been able to set up the Greek provisional government and, in theory at least, had laid the foundations of the nation state. By 1823, two years into the war, the Turkish fleet still held superiority at sea and blockades were in place along the western coast of Greece. On the mainland the Greeks had made no further progress, partly because of disorganisation and apathy and also because of the serious dissensions which had broken out amongst the Greeks themselves.

By the time Byron arrived in the Ionian Isles, the Greek war had entered a new phase, an internal power struggle between the three main rival factions: the Greek primates, local territorial leaders whose authority went back to the

466

Turkish occupation; the captains or warlords maintaining their own armies; and the westernised Greeks, many of whom had returned from exile to claim their own role in the resurgence of their nation. Underlying these disputes were sharply conflicting concepts of what the Greek future should be. The primates and the warlords, with their vested interests, backed a structure of semi-independent principalities: much the same as before, but without the Turks. The Europeanists, including Mavrocordatos and Andreas Londos, whom Byron had met as a young man in 1809, envisaged the new Greece with a Western-style constitution administered by a central government.

Though the Europeanists had at first been in the ascendant, the military party, led by Theodoros Koloktronis, Prince Alexandros Ypsilantes and Odysseus Androutsos (also known as Ulysses), had been gathering strength. Mavrocordatos, the first Greek president proclaimed by the new constitution of 1822 and in some ways Byron's natural ally, had been edged out by the military leaders and was now in exile on the island of Hydra. Byron had been aware of these difficulties. He had noted while at Leghorn that the Greeks were 'somewhat divided amongst themselves', though united in their calls for 'Money – Money – Money'. Arriving in Cephalonia he soon realised that the situation was more intractable than he had imagined and that his intervention in the war as envoy of the London Greek Committee was a mission that verged on the impossible.

Byron has often been criticised for remaining in the Ionian Isles rather than proceeding straight to mainland Greece. That would have been the more dramatic course of action. In fact Byron's decision to pause and weigh things up, discuss the possibilities and gather information, shows the quiet purposefulness with which he approached his task. In those first few weeks, Byron contacted Konstantinos Metaxas, Governor of Missolonghi, and Markos Botsaris, the Suliote commander of the Greek forces in Akarnania in Western Greece. He sent letters to the government in Tripolitza in the Peloponnese, trying to position himself to the best advantage and allot his financial resources where these would be of most practical use. He wrote to Hobhouse in September: 'I have not yet gone to the Main – because to say the truth – it does not appear that I could avoid being considered as a favourer of one party or another – but the moment I can be of real service I am willing to go amongst them.' Byron at last seems to have discarded all frivolity in setting his mind to the task ahead.

He spent his first few weeks in Argostoli still on board the *Hercules* in the beautiful small harbour that must have reminded him vividly of Venice. The Cephalonian merchants' houses were built in elegant Venetian architectural style, reflecting the modest prosperity of the local trade in grapes, oil, cotton and silk. A former commandant of the island, Major Charles-Philippe de Bosset, had built a bridge and causeway across the harbour, part of the ambitious network of new roads which Colonel Napier was to continue. A celebratory stone pyramid had been erected 'To the glory of the British Nation 1813'. A clergyman visiting Argostoli a few years after Byron found 'a little Naples with all the cleanliness of an English watering place'.

In spite of their official neutrality, Byron had been given a warm welcome by the British. Captain John Pitt Kennedy, Secretary to the Resident, had come aboard the *Hercules* to welcome Byron on behalf of Napier who happened to be temporarily away. When, on his return, Napier invited him to move into the Residency Byron resisted, ostensibly because he did not want to be a liability, but more probably out of shyness and because he preferred to guard his privacy. But within his first few days he accepted invitations to dinner, putting up with the Cephalonian wine which Napier diplomatically served instead of claret. 'Lord Byron is here', wrote Napier privately a few days after his arrival, 'and I like him very much.'

The official reports on Byron's movements that Napier, as Resident, was compelled to send to the British High Commission in Corfu play down Byron's potential military involvement in Greece, while accentuating his charm and generosity. On 10 August, Napier wrote to the Deputy High Commissioner, Sir Frederick Adam: 'Lord Byron tells me he only wants to look about him in Greece as a sort of Agent for the London Greek Committee, and while he remains here only wishes to avoid giving any offence to the Ionian Government. Like all men of real talent he is without humbug and is fair and open – he means to assist the Greeks with what money he can afford.'

The appearance of the notorious Lord Byron in person on the island of Cephalonia caused intense speculation amongst the small, close-knit and often under-occcupied expatriate community. As was his usual practice he fuelled the interest and then resisted it. Byron took to riding out from the *Hercules* along the Marina and on to the point opposite Guardini (now Vardiani) island dressed up like the warrior-figure of a Tartar 'with his high feather and his silver epaulets'. He had taken into his pay on Cephalonia a band of Albanian Suliote warriors, exiles for whom Napier had provided a safe haven, and a Suliote attendant in tribal dress as dramatic as his master's often rode out with him. Inevitably the British residents and the islanders craned to get a glimpse of him on these expeditions. To their disappointment Byron put the spurs to his horse and rode off rapidly whenever a group of ladies appeared.

In his reaction there was a genuine diffidence at the prospect of resuming relations with the countrymen he had not met en masse for many years and whom, in the years after the separation, Byron had demonised in his imagination. When, soon after his arrival, Colonel Duffie was reported to be on the point of inviting him to dine at the mess of the 8th King's Regiment, he was evidently nervous, deliberating with Trelawny and Browne over whether he ought to accept the invitation, if in fact it ever reached him. In his mind he felt sure it would never materialise.

However, the affable Colonel and his Adjutant persuaded him to go, and the evening was a considerable success. Byron joked with the initially overawed young officers. He replied emotionally to the toast proposed by Duffie at the end of the dinner, a toast to Byron's health (an ironic toast indeed) and success to the glorious cause on which he had embarked. Revealingly Byron asked Duffie anxiously after he had spoken if he had acquitted himself adequately, explaining that he was unused to public speaking and rusty in expressing himself in his own language. According to Browne, Byron 'frequently reverted to his cordial reception as one of the brightest days in the tablet of a chequered life, saying, that the real truth had never flashed on his mind till that moment, and that he had much, very much, to thank his countrymen for'. The claim may be exaggerated, but these weeks in Cephalonia mark a clear advance in Byron's sense of his rehabilitation.

His mood at this period, high-spirited, tractable, good-humoured, as if on an unexpected holiday, emerges in his curious friendship with James Kennedy, British Army staff surgeon and Christian evangelist whose *Conversations on Religion with Lord Byron* were published in 1830. Kennedy, an earnest Scot five years Byron's junior, had first encountered Byron at Colonel Duffie's regimental dinner when they had discussed such mutually interesting topics as miracles, the Apocalypse, the literal fulfilment of prophecies and the character of Pope Pius VII. 'I like his holiness very much,' Byron had commented, 'particularly since an order, which I understand he has lately given, that no more miracles shall be performed.'

The missionary Kennedy was planning a series of classes for four sceptical army officers, all Scotsmen, hoping to convert them to the true religion. These Sunday meetings were to be held at the house of Dr Henry Muir, the Officer of Health at Argostoli. When he heard of this scheme Byron suggested that he should be included: 'You know I am reckoned a black sheep; yet after all, not so black as the world believes me.' At Kennedy's first meeting the attendance was swollen not just by Byron but by Pietro Gamba, James Hamilton Browne and Colonel Napier. Byron sat on the sofa, the Colonel in a chair beside him and the others took their places in a semi-circle around Kennedy, who sat at the table opposite. Byron had promised that he would sit through the twelve hours that

Kennedy had allotted for the meeting without interrupting him. He was docile to begin with, but the performer in Byron soon broke out and he set up a dialogue with Kennedy, throwing in his own snatches of autobiography, recalling that when he was young he went to church regularly and read theological works, denying that he was an infidel: 'on the contrary, he was very desirous to believe'. But he maintained, as he always had, that the hypocrisy he saw in so many avowed Christians alienated him from formal religion. He told Dr Kennedy: 'Prayer does not consist in the act of kneeling, nor in repeating certain words in a solemn manner. Devotion is the affection of the heart, and this I feel.'

It is an irresistible scene: Byron the renowned poet of ungodliness, denounced for *Cain* from pulpits throughout England, locked in gentle, bantering argument with an evangelical preacher on a Sunday afternoon in Cephalonia. Rather to Kennedy's relief, since he distracted the other participants, Lord Byron was not present at any further meetings at Muir's house, but their discussions continued in private. What Kennedy discerned, and Byron appreciated, was that although by no means a conventional believer Byron came closer to Christianity than his detractors would have suspected. The zealous Dr Kennedy had realised that Byron was 'so nearly a tolerable Christian that he is trying to make me a whole one', as Byron told Charles Barry. He enjoyed being on the edge of a conversion as he had once loved to be on the edge of a seduction, cherishing the interval of suspense.

Watching and waiting through the last weeks of the summer Byron explored the rocky Cephalonian countryside, informing Hobhouse that he had taken 'a tour over the hills here in our old style'. In the middle of August, with Pietro, Trelawny, Browne, Dr Bruno and the servants, he made a six-day expedition to Ithaca, the island he had contemplated purchasing in 1810. Before embarking at St Euphemia (Ayia Evfimia), he wrote to Teresa. She had never reached Ravenna. Count Ruggero, in spite of his permit to travel issued by the Papal Consul in Genoa, had been stopped at the frontier by the police and despatched to Ferrara where he spent several years imprisoned in the fortress. Teresa had taken refuge in Bologna, living quietly in the house of her old tutor in literature, the liberal Paolo Costa. From the seashore, writing in English, Byron sent her a slightly longer and more loving letter than his norm:

'When we meet again (if it pleases God) I hope to tell you several things that will make you smile – I kiss your Eyes (*occhi*) and am ever most affectly.

a. a. in e. ++++

NB'

Following old habits he signed himself 'amico ed amante in eterno', friend and lover for ever, followed by the cross signs of their amatory code.

Byron was particularly anxious to see Ithaca, Ulysses' legendary island, as the counterpart to Troy. It was early evening on 11 August when they made the crossing of the channel between the islands, a stretch of water some nine or ten miles wide. There was no sign of life when they landed, not a house in sight. Byron suggested spending the night in one of the many caves along the coast. But Browne and the protective Gamba, who was nervous about exposing Byron to the night air, set off up the hill in search of lodgings while Byron and the others took a swim. They found a small cottage where the host, a local antiquarian and fierce Greek patriot, made them pay in advance for their accommodation by forcing them to listen to his long historical dissertations. Byron made his escape with Pietro, walking out through the vineyards and over the steep hills reminiscing happily about his earlier Greek travels. The whole party spent the night crammed into the cottage's one room, still in their cloaks.

At daybreak Browne hurried off to Vathy, the main town of Ithaca, to alert the British Resident, Captain Wright Knox, of Byron's arrival. The government boat was instantly sent out to fetch him from the point where the party had landed the evening before. By this time Byron had wandered away from the cottage to find a steep rock face covered in ivy and climbing plants which was said to be the Castle of Ulysses. Discovered near the top fast asleep under a wild fig tree at the entrance to a cavern, Byron was annoyed to be woken by Gamba since he had been having a beatific dream. It puzzled the athletic Gamba that Byron had managed to climb so far up a rock face that even he had found a struggle. But when he offered his assistance in descending, Byron 'rather summarily dismissed him' and, out of sight of the rest of the party, made his own way down.

They reached Vathy in the afternoon and Byron was once again embraced by the expatriate community, the initial consternation at his arrival being followed by surprise that he should be so affable and human. Captain Knox and his wife dedicated themselves to Byron's entertainment for the next few days. First came a picnic at a local landmark, the fountain and grotto of Arethusa, all travelling by mule through the olive groves and over wooded clifftops in heat that Byron's Negro servant Benjamin maintained was as great as that of the West Indies. Under the trees in front of the grotto, which was in fact a giant cavern, the servants spread out the tablecloths and the Resident's party ate and drank beside the natural spring which cascaded down the ravine to the sea. In the cavern they discovered two Albanian goatherds who obligingly entertained the English with what seemed a discordant music on their pipes. The view across the sea stretched to the entrance of the Gulf of Corinth and the fort of Lepanto, with the mountains of Epirus and Aetolia purple in the distance. Browne noted that Byron's spirits were 'buoyant and elastic; as usual, on such occasions, he overflowed with an inexhaustible fund of anecdote.'

The next day Captain Knox's plans for them included the inspection of one of the new Macadamised roads that were such a feature of the British admin-istration in the Ionian Isles. On the third day of their visit they were taken to the north side of the island to view the ruins known as the School of Homer. Travelling in an elegant Ithacan rowing boat with four oarsmen, Trelawny took the tiller while Byron sat in the centre seat facing the stern, under the awning. Calling to Tita to bring out a two-gallon stone jar of English gin, Byron mixed it with water, dispensing glasses of an intoxicating gin-swizzle to the other passengers. Near the Homeric stones, they met an old Greek bishop with a bristly beard, smelling violently of garlic, who recognised Byron from his visit to Ali Pasha's Janina in 1809. For Byron, as indeed for Ulysses, the island of Ithaca provided a strange homecoming, an emotional reconnection with lost pasts.

With his capacity for spontaneous intimacy Byron established an immedi-ate rapport with the Knoxes and their multitude of children. In those few days on Ithaca the Knoxes became another of Byron's adopted families. As Browne later analysed it, truly if simplistically, Byron contrasted 'the quiet, domestic life of the Resident's family with his own stormy restless career'. With Knox he talked politics, questioning the Resident's automatic denigration of the Greeks, urging him to be more flexible: 'You must be inspired with Classical feelings of what they were and restore them to their former selves and they will be great and Heroic again.'

With Mrs Knox, whose maiden name was Gordon, he applied the technique that had always been the foundation of his success with women: allowing her to feel that she alone could bring him out. He appeared 'Pale, bloated and Careworn' when she met him, obviously in a nervous state, 'very quiet & sudden'. But after a few days on Ithaca, she recollected, Byron was a changed person, evincing such 'a playfulness and fondness for the Children' that Captain Knox invited him to become the godfather of the child his wife was then expecting. He refused on the grounds of his superstitious fear that he brought death to anything he fathered or adopted. The child in any case died suddenly at the age of eight.

While he was in Ithaca, Byron's heart was wrung by the plight of the many Greek refugees from the fighting on the mainland, from Khios and Patras and other parts of Greece in Turkish control. He handed over to Knox the generous sum of two hundred and fifty Spanish dollars for the refugees' immediate relief and also arranged weekly allowances for some of the poor widows and orphans on Ithaca. He transported a once prosperous, now destitute family from Patras back to Cephalonia with him, the living memento of his island tour. The Chalandritsanos (or Khalandritsanos) family, particularly recommended by the Knoxes as worthy recipients of Byron's charity, consisted of an invalid mother and her three young daughters. Byron housed them and supported them in Argostoli. A fifteen-year-old son of the family named Loukhas was still in the Peloponnese, in the service of the warrior chieftain Koloktronis. Hearing of the family's reversal of fortune he and his brother joined them in Cephalonia where the handsome wilful Lukas, as Byron now rechristened him, became Byron's last but by no means most devoted page.

Byron and his party left Ithaca regretfully on 16 August. The Waverley novels of Walter Scott – 'Watty' as Byron called him – were the chief topic of conversation in the boat on the return journey to Cephalonia. The travellers dined at St Euphemia and were then escorted further across the bay to the monastery of Theotokos Agrilion, dedicated to the Virgin Mary, on the hill above Sami where lodgings had been arranged for the party for the night. At first Byron was in high spirits, clambering into one of the open sarcophagi outside the walls of the monastery and lying there on his back, quoting lines from the skull scene in *Hamlet*. But once he reached the monastery his behaviour changed alarmingly. Browne and the other members of the party watched with horror as 'he gradually locked himself into one of those furious and ungovernable torrents of rage, to which at times he was liable'. The Abbot had been waiting to greet him with a benediction, flanked by all the monks in their canonicals, but his prepared speech of welcome stopped short as Byron became violently abusive. Seizing a lamp and crying out, 'My head is burning; will no one relieve me from the presence of this pestilential madman?' Byron seemed on the verge of an apoplectic attack.

He rushed from the assembly hall, calling for Fletcher to go with him. The braver members of the party ventured one by one towards the room into which Byron had now barricaded himself with a table and chairs. He was still shouting curses, saying he was in hell. The inexperienced Dr Bruno was paralysed with fright. It was Browne who gave Byron the pills that eventually calmed him down. He subsided into childish drivel and slept through the night. The next morning he was sheepish, tacitly apologetic, and as they rode back over the Black Mountain to Argostoli he revived, singing popular street songs and Moore's melodies at the top of his voice.

What had caused Byron's paroxysm? Three days earlier, on the way to the spring of Arethusa, Byron had been struck on the head by a branch with a violence that had temporarily stunned him. He could have been suffering delayed concussion. On the day of departure from Ithaca, waiting impatiently for the boat to collect them, he had taken yet another unwisely prolonged swim in the midday sun. The fit could have been brought on by sunstroke. Or, like earlier illnesses, it could have been a sign of endemic weakness, a combination of mental and physical exhaustion caused by a life of extraordinary stresses, many of them self-induced.

Of the various tribal factions involved in the Greek War of Independence, Byron's strongest attachment was to the Suliotes, the military caste of orthodox Christian Albanians some still exiled from their country, whom he regarded, in his more romantic moments, as the Eastern equivalent of a Scottish clan. He had fond memories, sentimentalised by distance, of the faithful Albanian followers of his early travels, the servants who had been at his side through threatened shipwreck, who had been his 'kind though rough *nurses*' in illness. One of these Albanian servants, Demetrius Zograffo, who had returned with Byron to Newstead, had become a leader of the Athenian insurgents, a promotion that came as some surprise to Byron: 'He was a clever but not an enterprising man – but circumstances make men.'

When Byron had first arrived in Argostoli and a crowd of desperate Suliote soldiers swarmed on to the *Hercules* to find him, he had greeted them as long-lost friends. As Browne described the scene: 'He bounded on deck, evidently very much affected, his expressive countenance radiant with gladness to welcome them.' He immediately took on some of the Suliotes to form his personal bodyguard, promising to employ more of them in the future. He was only slightly disillusioned when they asked for more money than he had offered, also demanding payment in advance. By the time he returned from Ithaca Byron was employing forty Suliote soldiers and they were causing constant trouble, squabbling, cheating and extorting. Captain Scott of the *Hercules* strongly disapproved of these disruptive foreigners, calling them 'the damned Zodiacs'. But as with his own servants, Byron remained patient: these were his people, to be protected and if necessary indulged. His feelings for them were embodied in the vigorous war song he wrote for them:

> 'Up to battle! Sons of Suli –
> Up, and do your duty duly –
> There the wall – and there the Moat is
> Bourrah! Bourrah! Suliotes!

> There is booty, there is Beauty –
> Up my boys and do your duty. –
>
> By the sally and the rally
> Which defied the arms of Ali –
> By your own dear native Highlands
> By your children in the Islands –
> Up – and charge – my Stratiotes –
> Bourrah! – Bourrah! – Suliotes!'

Byron also had great hopes of Markos Botsaris, the Suliote chief who was then endeavouring to check a Turkish advance on Anatolikon, to the north of Missolonghi. Botsaris had responded warmly to the letter Byron had written him in early August – a letter delivered by a small boat which had run the Turkish blockade around the coast of Western Greece. The news had already spread that Byron had arrived with great quantities of money, which the Greek fighting forces conspicuously lacked. Botsaris would have been aware of this when on 18 August he replied to Byron that his letter had filled him with joy: 'Your Excellency is exactly the person of whom we stand in need.' Though on the point of going into battle, he intended within the next few days to set out 'with a few chosen companions' to meet Byron, hoping to persuade him to come over at once to Greece. On 21 August, however, Botsaris died a hero's death at Karpenisi, leading only a few hundred Suliote troops in what was in effect a suicide raid against a Turkish force estimated at between 15,000 and 20,000. His letter of encouragement arrived too late.

Byron, mourning him, said that Botsaris died 'with the character of a good Soldier – and an honourable man – which are not always found together nor indeed separately'. Botsaris's death, added to Mavrocordatos's exile, left him yet more undecided as to what action to take. Had Markos Botsaris not died so suddenly Byron's own history might have followed a very different course.

At the beginning of September 1823 Captain Scott's *Hercules* departed for England weighed down with a freight of Cephalonian currants. Trelawny and Browne also left the island, travelling in the opposite direction, making for the action in the Peloponnese. Trelawny was bored with what he saw as Byron's dawdling. 'The Noble Poet', he wrote to Mary Shelley, 'has been seized with a fit of his usual indecision when just on the brink – and when I would have him without talking, leap.' Though Byron initially resisted Trelawny's desertion he finally gave in, sending him with letters to the government at Tripolitza.

Trading on the prestige of his connection with Byron Trelawny found a welcome amongst the more colourful faction of the Greek warlords and joined the party of Odysseus Androutsos, the most charismatic leader in Eastern Greece, second only to Koloktronis in military might. The impressionable Trelawny viewed Odysseus as 'a really *great man* – a Grecian Bolivar', infinitely superior to Mavrocordatos whom he despised as 'a perfect *Constantinople* Greek'. Trelawny was eventually to marry Odysseus's thirteen-year-old half-sister. He took to wearing Suliote costume which, according to Browne, 'wonderfully became him', with his tall commanding figure and his Cornishman's dark skin. He soon wrote encouraging Byron to join him:

'they have given us rooms – & post horses – every one very civil – & open – provisions in great abundance & excepionly cheap – one piaster & a half we pay for dinner for ourselves and two servants – and good grubbing too – grub for horses cheap – maidenheads as plentiful as blackberries – there is good marketing in that way.'

Resisting these temptations Byron meanwhile moved to a small villa at Metaxata, south-east of Argostoli just inland from the coast. Here among the aromatic orchards he felt sufficiently at peace to begin another journal.

'Standing at the window of my apartment in this beautiful village, the calm though cool serenity of a beautiful and transparent Moonlight, showing the Islands, the Mountains, the Sea, with a distant outline of the Morea traced between the double Azure of the waves and skies, has quieted me enough to be able to write.'

From brief entries in the Cephalonian journal we can gain an insight into Byron's frame of mind in these few months of suspended animation before he left for Greece. The London Greek Committee had now asked him to act as their official representative with the Greek government at the seat of war, and entrusted him with the allotment of stores and ammunition which, together with the 'fire-master' William Parry, his mechanics and equipment for installing a war laboratory, were now on their way from England on the ship, the *Ann*.

Determined to act wisely in a situation of great diplomatic risk, he made the reluctant decision to pay off his unruly Suliote bodyguard and, furnishing them with arms, to send them to join the Suliote forces on the mainland. Byron's soldiers agreed, however, only after they had extracted extra severance pay in addition to the price of their passage: they drove a hard bargain to the last.

At Metaxata Byron was more than ever conscious of the need for coolness in fending off the many Greek contenders for his favours, all of them approaching him 'under the pretext that *they* are "the real Simon Pure"'. Pleas came from the Suliotes in Western Greece, the adherents of the dead Markos Botsaris. The Governor of Missolonghi, Count Metaxas, pressed his claims. From his island exile Prince Mavrocordatos wrote in conjunction with the Primate of Hydra inviting Byron to meet them there. Koloktronis urged him, and almost succeeded in persuading him, to leave for the Peloponnese. Numerous beseeching letters in Greek, which later found their way back to the Murray archive, show Byron at this period under great pressure from personal as well as political supplicants. He drew on resources of patience he had not displayed before, writing in his journal: 'As I did not come here to join a faction but a nation – and to deal with honest men and not with speculators or peculators – (charges bandied about daily by the Greeks of each other) it will require much circumspection to avoid the character of a partizan.'

Byron, of all people, could recognise a flatterer. He was under no illusions about the Greek capacity for self-serving and tortuous behaviour. 'The worst of them is – that (to use a coarse but the only expression that will not fall short of the truth) they are such d—d liars; – there was never such an incapacity for veracity shown since Eve lived in Paradise.' But his years of independent living abroad in largely foreign households had given him great tolerance. He viewed the Greek character philosophically. His own love of verbal ingenuity allowed him to appreciate the Greeks' great elasticity with words:

'One of them found fault the other day with the English language – because it had so few shades of a Negative – whereas a Greek can so modify a No – to a yes – and vice versa – by the slippery qualities of his language – that prevarication may be carried to any extent and still leave a loop-hole through which perjury may slip without being perceived.'

Compared with the professional administrators – Captain Knox on Ithaca and the unusually enlightened Napier – who tended to regard the Greeks as wayward children, Byron was able to accept them as they were and even to rejoice in their difference.

Through the autumn of 1823, even in the remoteness of Metaxata, Byron was besieged by visitors. 'Here are arrived – English – Germans – Greeks – all kinds of people in short – proceeding to or coming from Greece – and all with something to say to me,' he told Teresa, making yet more excuses for the brevity of his communications. One of these visitors was Byron's distant family connection Lord Sydney Osborne, son of the 5th Duke of Leeds, who had surfaced from a scandal in England to become Secretary to the British protectorate in the Ionian Isles. Byron judged him 'in good preservation – and as Clever and insouciant as ever', and suggested he would make a prime subject for conversion by Dr Kennedy.

Another eager visitor to Byron was the young George Finlay, then in his mid-twenties. Finlay exemplified a new phenomenon amongst the Philhellenes, those drawn to the Greek cause by Byron's own involvement in it. He was an avid reader of Byron's poetry, identifying with its libertarian themes, and was flattered that Byron, on first seeing him, thought he was the ghost of Shelley. He was not disappointed by meeting his literary hero face to face. Finlay, the future historian, was already a perceptive observer, noting the 'unemphatical, and rather affectedly monotonous tone' adopted by Byron when he embarked on any topic of conversation which might have appeared pretentious: 'Whenever he commenced a sentence which showed that the subject had engaged his mind, and that his thoughts were sublime, he checked himself, and finished a broken sentence, either with an indifferent smile, or with this annoying tone.' Finlay correctly surmised that he adopted it to conceal his real feelings 'when he feared to trust his tongue with the sentiments of his heart'.

Finlay was later to join Byron in Missolonghi. In that autumn at Metaxata there began assembling many of the people of the little inner circle which would surround Byron in his final months in Greece. In November arrived Colonel Leicester Stanhope, another leading light of the London Greek Committee and a dogmatic Benthamite. Stanhope too was on his way to Missolonghi where he and the much more pragmatic Byron would often be at odds. Another November visitor was Dr Julius Millingen, a young surgeon sent by the London Greek Committee to offer his services as a doctor in the war. Millingen left for Missolonghi in December. Their accounts, and the memoirs of Pietro Gamba, furnish an intimate picture of Byron's life in Metaxata.

The house on the hill shared by Byron, Gamba, Dr Bruno, Zambelli and the three servants, Fletcher, Falcieri and Benjamin Lewis, was a modest one, with two rooms for Lord Byron and two for all the others. The single public room was scantily furnished. One table was used for dining; another table, and the chair beside it, were both strewn with books. Other books, including most of Scott's novels, Mitford's *History of Greece* and Sismondi's *Italian Republics*, were ranged in order on the floor. It was an austere setting when compared with the comforts of Byron's Italian palazzi.

His everyday routine had altered too. He now rose as early as nine and worked with Pietro, answering letters and discussing Greek affairs. At eleven he had breakfast, which consisted of a cup of tea. At around noon he went out riding until mid-afternoon. Byron, Gamba and Bruno took their meals together, Byron eating only cheese and vegetables, though he allowed himself meat or poultry once a month. After dinner they sometimes practised firing with a pistol. They sat round talking till midnight or so. Dr Kennedy was apparently a welcome visitor. Byron still teased him, telling him that he had given some of his tracts to his valet William Fletcher 'who is a good sort of man, but still wants, like myself, some reformation'. According to Gamba the religious arguments between Kennedy and Byron sometimes lasted for five or six hours.

Byron appears from these accounts to have been in a state of muted happiness in Cephalonia. In a throwback to his childhood he had taken in recent months to wearing the tartan, and Millingen describes him standing on the balcony of the house in Metaxata 'wrapt in his Stewart tartan cloak, with a cap on his head, which he affected to wear as the Scotch bonnet, attentively contemplating the extensive and variegated view before him terminated by the blue mountains of Aetolia, Acarnania, and Achaia'.

At the same time Millingen was professionally aware of the great tensions building up in Byron. He was drinking heavily each evening and taking too much weight-reducing medication: pills composed of extract of colocynth, gamboge and scammony – commonly used purgatives – often supplemented by a large dose of Epsom salts. Byron confessed: 'I especially dread, in this world, two things, to which I have reason to believe I am equally predisposed – growing fat and growing mad; and it would be difficult for me to decide, were I forced to make a choice, which of these conditions I would choose in preference.' He was suffering from insomnia, pacing his room till three or four each morning. His mood swings were worsening and when the effects of alcohol wore off Byron would be plummeted into 'a condition often bordering on despair'.

His anxieties were deepened by news from England of the illness of his daughter Ada – news which affected him so badly that he was unable to continue his journal. Ada, now almost eight, was suffering from debilitating headaches which were affecting her eyesight. Lady Byron's rigorous education schedules for her little daughter were probably too much for her. Byron felt himself as guilty, replying to Augusta: 'I have been subject to the same complaint but not at so early an age – nor in so great a degree. – Besides it never affected my eyes – but rather my hearing.' A routine of bathing his head in cold water every morning had cured him, he said.

He speculated as to whether Ada would recover automatically with the onset of menstruation:

'Perhaps she will get quite well – when she arrives at womanhood – but that is some time to look forward to, though if she is of so sanguine a habit – it is probable that she may attain to that period earlier than is usual in our colder climate; – in Italy and the East – it sometimes occurs at twelve or even earlier – I knew an instance in an Italian house – at ten – but this was considered uncommon.'

Byron had not lost his interest in the physicality of little girls.

This sudden fit of anxiety for Ada made him conscious of how little he knew about his daughter. The last miniature he had of her was painted four years before. He deluged Augusta with questions about Ada's temperament, habits and moral tendencies. 'Is the Girl imaginative?' he asked, recalling that at her age he had had many feelings and notions which people would not credit were he to describe them now. 'Is she social or solitary – taciturn or talkative – fond of reading or otherwise?' he wondered. 'And what is her *tic*? – I mean her foible – is she passionate? – I hope that the Gods have made her any thing save *poetical* – it is enough to have one such fool in a family.' In writing about Ada his old feelings for Augusta, intimate, confiding, joyfully self-deprecating, were momentarily revived.

Through October there were earthquakes in Cephalonia. Byron was intrigued by the report that the whole line of Colonel Duffie's soldiers on parade had been lifted up 'as a boat is by the tide'. One of the shocks was so prolonged that the house in Metaxata had to be evacuated. By the time that Byron made his necessarily slow descent of the stairs he found that the others were already in the courtyard, having presumably jumped out of the windows. After this they decided to endure the tremors quietly in their beds, being persuaded that if the house were to fall it would collapse long before they got to safety. Byron's house at Metaxata endured until the great Cephalonian earthquake of 1953.

Worse reports were reaching Byron of confusion on the mainland, where the internal dissensions were approaching civil war. His chief informant among the Greeks on Cephalonia was Count Demetrius Delladecima, described by Millingen as 'a Cephaloniot nobleman of considerable shrewdness, sound judgement, and deep acquaintance with the Greek character'. Byron chose to call him '*Ultima Analise*' because of the Count's habit of using the phrase 'in ultima analise' to punctuate his conversations. Delladecima cast doubts on both the effectiveness and probity of the Greek provisional government.

Byron also received two very disconcerting letters and a long memorandum from Frank Abney Hastings, a young British Philhellene whose statue now stands alongside Byron's in the Missolonghi Garden of the Heroes. Hastings, a discharged British naval officer, had offered his services to the Greeks in 1822 and knew from bitter experience the incompetence of the so-called Greek navy, a motley gathering of ships commanded by merchant captains, as well as the Greeks' innate resistance to taking advice from foreigners.

Byron was impressed by Hastings' insistence on the urgent need for an armoured steamboat to be sent from England to give the Greeks superiority at sea. This was an idea that appealed to Byron greatly, in his desire for a more definite agenda and excited as he was by advanced technology. He passed on Hastings' recommendations to the London Greek Committee as 'on the whole faithful – intelligent and scientific. – Mr Hastings to the above qualities unites those of great courage and coolness as well as enterprise.' Although nothing was achieved until after Byron's death, Hastings' steamboat, the *Perseverance* or *Karteria*, played a significant part in later Greek operations against the Turks.

Byron's potential spending power in Greece increased with the sale of the Rochdale estates to James Dearden on 2 November 1823, after years of frustrating delays. The agreed price was £11,225. But even his resources brought with them their own problems. The Greek bankers in Cephalonia, Messrs Corgialegno, to whom he had been recommended by Charles Barry, claimed not to have sufficient funds available in Spanish dollars to meet Byron's bills of credit, and attempted to make charges so high that, complaining of 'this Hebrew proceeding of the Sieurs Corgialegno', Byron wrote them off.

He eventually found an English firm of merchants and bankers, Barff and Hancock, able and willing to take on his affairs. Samuel Barff, who had founded the firm in Zante, was a generous supporter of the many Greek refugees in the Ionian Isles and of the poverty-stricken and often wounded Philhellenes making the journey home. His younger partner Charles Hancock ran the branch of the bank in Argostoli. From an English Quaker background and likewise with strong Philhellenic sympathies, Hancock – 'Signor *'Ancock*' as Dr Bruno called him – very quickly fell under Byron's spell, entranced by his wit, sophistication and easiness of access, as Charles Barry of Genoa and Charles Hentsch, Byron's banker in Geneva, had been before.

Early in November, James Hamilton Browne returned to Metaxata from the seat of government. It was an official mission. With Browne were two Greek deputies, Ioannis Orlandos and Andreas Louriotis, who had first met Byron in Genoa with Blaquière. The Greeks were on their way to England hoping to negotiate a loan of £800,000 through the London Greek Committee to finance the next stage of the war. Meanwhile the Greek fleet had been languishing through the autumn in the port of Hydra on the island off the east coast of the Peloponnese. Orlandos and Louriotis had been authorised to ask Byron for an interim loan of £6,000 to pay the sailors and reactivate the fleet. Byron agreed to contribute £4,000, the equivalent of 20,000 Spanish dollars; but no more.

George Finlay was present at the official signing for this loan which took place on 13 November 1823 in the Argostoli health office, Byron separated by a railing from Browne and the Greek deputies who were in quarantine. Before Byron handed the signed bills to Browne, Finlay said to him: 'you may bid that money farewell, my Lord; you have taken the last look of it.' Byron shouted out, still grasping the bills, 'Not if I can help it. I shall this very day write to Douglas Kinnaird, and request him to make them pay me with the very proceeds of the loan, if they get one.' He did write to Kinnaird. But he knew very well it was unlikely that the loan would ever be repaid.

When the Greek deputies set off on the next stage of their journey Byron provided them with a thoughtful introduction to his old London patron Lord Holland, telling him:

'I think it probable that their acquaintance may be interesting to you – and am very sure that *Yours* will be useful to them and their Country – They will inform you of all that is worth knowing here – and (what is little worth knowing – unless you should enquire after a former acquaintance) of the "*whereabouts*" and *what*abouts of yrs. ever and truly Noel Byron.'

In principle Byron was in favour of the loan, realising that without financial investment from outside the Greek cause had no hope of a successful resolution. Using their need for the loan as the strongest argument against the escalation of a civil war, Byron wrote to the Greek government on 30 November:

'I must admit to you frankly that if some kind of order and union is not confirmed, all hopes for a loan will be lost, – any assistance that Greece might expect from abroad, which certainly would not be inconsiderable nor contemptible, will be suspended, and maybe even stopped, and what is worse is that the Great Powers of Europe, of which none was an enemy of Greece, and which seemed favourably inclined to agree with the establishment of an independent Greek state, will be persuaded that the Greeks are not capable of governing themselves and will arrange some means for putting an end to your disorder which will cut short all your most noble hopes, and all those of your friends.

Allow me to add this once and for always: I want what is good for Greece and nothing else: I will do everything in my power to insure this: But I do not

Byron in Venice, pencil sketch by G.H. Harlow made in 1818 when Byron's Venetian life was at its most [dissi]pated. English visitors were struck by his physical deterioration.

[P]alazzo Albrizzi, rear view from the canal. Byron was cultivated by the intellectual Countess Albrizzi and [atte]nded her *conversazioni*.

[P]alazzo Mocenigo on the Grand Canal. Byron leased the second of the four palazzi (in the centre of the [pict]ure), living there in ramshackle splendour from June 1818 to the end of the next year.

52 Marianna Segati, wife of the merchant who w[as]
Byron's landlord when he first arrived in Venice [in the]
winter 1816.

53 Margherita Cogni, known as 'La Fornarina', w[ho]
supplanted Marianna Segati as Byron's favourite
Venetian mistress. G.H. Harlow's drawing conve[ys]
little of her tempestuous personality.

54 Tita Falcieri, the Venetian gondolier who bec[ame]
Byron's devoted chief servant and was inherited [by]
Benjamin Disraeli. Drawing by Daniel Maclise.

Byron and his last, most enduring Italian mistress, Countess Teresa Guiccioli. In this portrait miniature
Girolamo Prepiani Teresa's face has been discreetly blocked out.

56 Palazzo Guiccioli, Ravenna. Byron lived here from early 1820 to late 1821 in an uneasy *ménage à trois*
Count Guiccioli and his wife.

57 Main staircase at Palazzo Guiccioli. Byron's apartments on the second floor, above the Count's.

58 The convent school at Bagnacavallo where Byron's daughter Allegra died of typhus fever in 1822.

59 Marble bust of Teresa Guiccioli made by Lorenzo Bartolini in 1822.

gione e della sua vita. Egli assistè in Roma alla
pompa funebre di Corinna. Si segregò da tutti
per lungo tempo in Tivoli, senza volere che ve
lo accompagnassero nè la sua moglie, nè la sua
figlia. Finalmente l'attaccamento e il dovere lo
ricondussero presso di loro. Eglino ritornarono
insieme in Inghilterra Lord Nelwil fu il modello
della vita domestica la più regolare e la più pu-
ra. Ma si perdonò egli la sua passata condotta?
Chi l'approvò, gli fu egli di consolazione? Si
contentò egli d'una sorte comune, dopo quanto
aveva perduto? Io non lo so, e non voglio su tal
proposito nè biasimarlo ne assolverlo.

Fine del lib. XX. e ultimo

*My dearest Teresa — I have read this
book in your garden; — my Love —
you were absent — or else I could
not have read it. — It is a fa=
=vourite book of yours — and the
writer was a friend of mine. —
You will not understand these English
words — and others will not understand
them — which is the reason I have
not scrawled them in Italian. —*

Byron's message to Teresa written in her copy of Madame de Staël's novel *Corinne* in the summer of 1819.

61 Palazzo Lanfranchi in Pisa which Byron described as 'a very good spacious house upon the Arno'. He l[ived] there for a year from 1821 to 1822.

62 Entrance hall to the Palazzo Lanfranchi. Leigh Hunt, his wife and six children, much to Byron's dismay, occupied the ground floor.

63 Leigh Hunt, pencil drawing by Thomas Charles Wageman. Byron collaborated with Leigh Hunt in the launch of the periodical *The Liberal* and his brother, John Hunt, succeeded John Murray as Byron's publish[er].

64 Edward John Trelawny, pen and ink portrait by Joseph Severn. The loquacious Cornish adventurer modelled his appearance on Byron's *Corsair*. He sailed to Greece with Byron in 1823.

Scene from *Don Juan*, one of a series of twenty-four illustrations for the poem made in 1820 by Richard
Westall. Byron admitted: 'Almost all Don Juan is *real* life – either my own – or from people I know.'

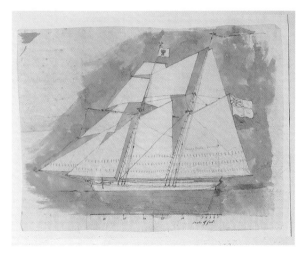

66 Byron in Genoa, sketch by Count Alfred D'Orsay showing Byron much slimmed down by dieting and illness in the months before he left for Greece.

67 The 'most gorgeous' Lady Blessington painted by Thomas Lawrence in 1822, the year before she met Byron in Genoa. Her *Conversations of Lord Byron* were published in 1832–3.

68 The *Bolivar*, the 'large & beautiful boat' Byron commissioned to be built for him at Genoa under the supervision of Captain Daniel Roberts, who also built Shelley's ill-fated *Don Juan*. The drawing of the 22-t schooner fitted with two cannon is Roberts's own.

Ruins of the Monastery of Theotokos Agrilion near Samos in Cephalonia where Byron suffered a
debilitating fit in the late summer of 1823.

Prince Alexander Mavrocordato, elected first President of Greece under the 1822 Constitution. The
Europeanised Mavrocordato was Byron's main personal contact among the Greek revolutionary leaders.

Site of Byron's modest house at Metaxata in the hills above the southern coast of Cephalonia. He lived
until he left for mainland Greece in December 1823. The house was destroyed in the earthquake of 1953.

72 Byron with his dog Lyon, watercolour by Robert Seymour based on a sketch of Byron made at Missolonghi by Major William Parry in the weeks before he died. The Newfoundland dog had been a gift him in Genoa. Byron's temperamental Suliote guards are in the background.

The house Byron used as his military headquarters in the marshy coastal town of Missolonghi, Western Greece. He and his entourage occupied the second floor, and it was here he died on 19 April 1824. Byron's death at the age of thirty-six sent shock waves through Europe. The neo-classical composition *Death of Byron* by Joseph-Denis von Odevaere, painted about two years later, shows the growing mortification of his memory.

75 *Liszt am Flügel* by Joseph Danhauser, 1840. L[iszt]
is at the piano in this group of worshippers of By[ron]
and Beethoven with, l. to r., Alexandre Dumas, [Hector?]
Berlioz, George Sand, Paganini, Rossini and Lisz[t's]
lover, Marie d'Agoult. The framed portrait of Byr[on]
on the wall is a version of G.H. Harlow's well-kn[own]
drawing; see no. 23.

76 Lady Byron photographed by Frederick Holl[?]
She devoted herself to self-justification and phila[n]
thropy and died in May 1860 at the age of sixty-s[even?]
after many years of precarious health.

Claire Clairmont, oil portrait by Amelia Curran. The self-willed stepdaughter of William Godwin propelled herself into a liaison with Byron just before he left England in 1816.

Allegra, Byron's daughter by Claire Clairmont, was born in January 1817. Byron later sent for her to live with him in Italy. The miniature shows her at eighteen months. She died aged five.

Ada, Byron's daughter by his wife. He referred to her as 'little Legitimacy'. He did not see Ada again after the separation but she was a constant preoccupation.

45 The radical poet Percy Bysshe Shelley was a friend and literary catalyst to Byron. They spent summer together in Geneva. Shelley's portrait by Amelia Curran was painted three years later.

46 The young Dr John William Polidori was Byron's physician on his continental travels in 1816.

47 Villa Diodati at Cologny, Geneva, the lakeside house taken by Byron after he left England. It was here, ing an exchange of ghost stories, that Mary Shelley formulated the idea for *Frankenstein*.

48 Madame de Staël painted by François Gérard. She was a loyal friend to the exiled Byron.

36 Annabella Milbanke, miniature by George
Hayter painted in 1812, the year she met Lord Byron.
He described her as 'piquant, and what we term
pretty'. They were married in 1815 and separated a
year later.

37 The Hon. Augusta Leigh, miniature by James
Holmes. Augusta was Byron's half-sister, daughter of
Captain John Byron by his first wife, Lady Amelia
D'Arcy, Baroness Conyers. Byron and Augusta's
incestuous affair, subject of scandalous rumour,
appears to have begun in summer 1813.

38 James Holmes's 1815 miniature was Byron's
preferred portrait of himself. This hand-coloured
engraved version was given to Byron's Italian mistress, Countess Teresa Guiccioli, by Augusta Leigh.

The Separation, a Sketch from the private life of Lord IRON who Panegyrized his Wife, but Satirized her Confidante!!

39 The first-floor drawing room at Seaham Hall, Co. Durham, scene of Byron's marriage to Annabella Milbanke on 2 January 1815, photographed under restoration in 2000.

40 The shore at Seaham, where Byron took desolate walks before and immediately after his marriage. 'Up this dreary coast, we have nothing but county meetings and shipwrecks,' he complained.

41 *The Separation, a Sketch from the private life of Lord Iron.* I.R. Cruikshank's cartoon shows Byron making off with the actress Mrs Mardyn, quoting his own poem 'Fare Thee Well!' to Lady Byron, the infant Ada and the detested Mrs Clermont, his wife's ex-governess.

consent, nor will I ever consent to permit the Public or private English citizens ever to be deluded about the true state of things in Greece. The rest depends on you, Gentlemen.'

The long letter is persuasively argued, statesmanlike, unshowy except for the culminating little flourish: it was his words, as well as his dollars, that Byron was contributing to the Greek cause.

In December events started to converge on Missolonghi. The Turkish sea blockade in the Gulf of Patras had been renewed and the town was under siege by an estimated 16,000 Turkish troops. The Greek fleet, galvanised by Byron's money, was now sailing from Hydra round the southern coast of the Peloponnese. Byron could see warships from his window in Metaxata without being certain which side they were on. Prince Mavrocordatos had decided to sail with the Greek fleet, arriving at Missolonghi on 11 December where he reassumed authority as Commander-in-chief and Governor of Western Greece. Byron now planned to join him there. In deciding, finally, for Mavrocordatos rather than the many other Greek contenders for his friendship and support, Byron took the pragmatic course, seeing Mavrocordatos as the most stable of the Greek leaders, the one whose qualities were potentially most statesmanlike. Judging national leaders as he did by the standards of George Washington, for Byron Mavrocordatos passed the Washington test. He was the leader most highly esteemed by the local people whose judgement Byron trusted: Count Delladecima and Colonel Napier. Byron felt that his determination to keep his independence until the situation resolved itself had now been justified.

On 6 December Stanhope set off for Missolonghi, followed two days later by Millingen. As soon as he arrived Stanhope wrote encouragingly to Byron enclosing a letter from Mavrocordatos: 'You will be received here as a saviour. Be assured, My Lord, that it depends only on yourself to secure the destiny of Greece.' This was an irresistible summons, even if Byron had too great a sense of irony to take it altogether seriously.

The London Greek Committee had not envisaged Byron in active service on the mainland. Hobhouse had simply suggested that he 'go to headquarters and look about you and come away again – A few days or weeks in the Morea would be quite sufficient.' But by the beginning of December Byron was clearly proposing to undertake an active military role, calculating in the journal he had now resumed that he would be able to maintain between five hundred and a thousand Suliote warriors for 'as long as necessary'. In his vision of himself at the head of a 'respectable clan or sect or tribe or horde' he demolished for ever the memory of the schoolboy cripple, as well as putting paid to rumours circulating in England that he had spent a languid autumn in a Greek island villa composing further cantos of *Don Juan*.

In the letters Byron wrote in the few days before departure there is a sense of barely suppressed triumph. While pretending that the possibility of power was of little interest to him, he boasted to Teresa that he and Mavrocordato had been mentioned jointly 'in some commission or other' by the Greek government in the Peloponnese. 'After all it is better playing at Nations than gaming at Almacks or Newmarket or in piecing or dinnering,' he assured Kinnaird.

Underlying his high spirits, as he prepared for the approaching journey to the scene of war, was a grim determination. In a letter to Tom Moore he lists the long line of poets and writers transformed into soldiers who had lost their lives in battle: Garcilaso de la Vega, prince of Spanish poets, who died from a wound after storming a fortress near Fréjus in 1536; Ewald Christian von Kleist, who lost a leg fighting against the Russians at Kunnersdorff in 1759 and subsequently died; Karl Theodor Körner, who was killed fighting the French near Schwerin in 1813, a few hours after he had written his *Schwert-lied*. Byron remembered the 'Russian Nightingale', Vasili Andreevitch Zhukovsky, who wrote the poem 'Minstrel in the Russian Camp' shortly before the battle on the Tarutino. He thought of Thersander, killed by Telephus in the Trojan wars and entreated Tom Moore that 'if anything by way of fever, fatigue, or otherwise should cut short the middle age of a brother warbler', Moore would remember Byron in his 'smiles and wine'.

Mavrocordatos had undertaken to send one of the best ships in the Greek squadron, such as it was, to transport Byron from Cephalonia. A Spetsiot brig, the *Leonidas*, put into the harbour at Argostoli pretending that the water supplies needed replenishing. The British authorities, preserving their neutrality, allowed the ship to remain only twenty-four hours and would not permit the crew any contact with the land. The *Leonidas* then moved further out to sea. Two days later, still at Metaxata, Byron watched another Greek brig sail in. This ship brought letters from Mavrocordatos and from Leicester Stanhope urging his departure: they were evidently frightened he had changed his mind. Mavrocordatos proposed that he should either travel back to Missolonghi in one of these brigs or return in convoy with it. Byron, still wary of allying himself formally with any Greek faction, preferred to make his own arrangements for the voyage.

He hired two boats to take the baggage and horses. The larger of these, a bombard, was allotted to Pietro, Lega Zambelli and the servants, with the bulkiest of the baggage and the multifarious supplies that Byron was transporting on behalf of the London Greek Committee, including the printing press that Colonel Stanhope had requested as essential to his strategy in spreading political enlightenment in Greece. In Byron's own vessel, a mistico – a lighter, faster-sailing long boat – he took his valet Fletcher, his doctor Francesco Bruno and his two new objects of extreme affection, the Newfoundland dog Lyon and Lukas Chalandritsanos, his Greek page.

By 27 December everything was loaded, but the weather was stormy and contrary winds kept the ships in port for another two days. Having abandoned the house at Metaxata, Byron lodged in Argostoli with his banker Charles Hancock who had just, coincidentally, received a copy of Scott's recently published novel *Quentin Durward*. Byron fell on this and took it away to his own room, refusing an invitation for a farewell dinner at the mess with the officers of the 8th Regiment, refusing even to join the Hancocks at their table. Hancock recalled how Byron 'merely came out once or twice to say how much he was entertained, returning to his chamber with a plate of figs in his hand'.

He went on reading *Quentin Durward* even when the wind had shifted and Gamba had already gone on board the bombard. James Kennedy found him alone and still immersed in it when he arrived at Hancock's house, hoping to catch Byron for a last goodbye. Kennedy undertook to send across to Missolonghi a consignment of religious literature which Byron said he would distribute, and it seems he kept his promise. Visitors to Byron's war headquarters were surprised to find a mountain of Kennedy's evangelical tracts.

Byron was 'gay and animated' when, in the early afternoon of 29 December, he set out in a little boat across the harbour towards the mistico. Muir, the health officer, and Hancock accompanied him on this first stage of his journey. He joked at Muir's despondent looks, jeered at Hancock's inexpert steering, exchanged comments in Italian with Francesco Bruno, telling the other passengers in English, which the doctor did not understand, 'he is the most sincere Italian I ever met with'. Fletcher, getting drenched by the spray that was breaking over the bows of the boat, was back in his old role as the butt of Byron's humour. They reached the mistico which was anchored, sheltered from the wind, in a little creek beneath the Convent of San Constantino. Here Muir and Hancock left him. 'We parted from him', wrote Hancock, 'to see him no more.'

> 'They only can feel freedom truly who
> Have worn long chains – the healthy feel not health
> In all its glow – in all its glory of

Full veins and flushing cheeks and bounding pulses,
Till they have known the interregnum of
Some malady that links them to their beds
In some wide – common – feverish hospital
Where all are tended – and none cared for, left
To public nurses, paid for pity, till
They die – or go forth cured, but without kindness.'

Byron's lines on freedom, written at Albaro earlier that summer, discovered in his rooms after his departure, remind us of how deeply his concept of liberty was rooted in his own peculiar sufferings. His deformity, his proneness to depression, his consciousness of his sexual apartness: all these gave Byron an extra degree of sensitivity. This breadth of sympathy, arising from his consciousness of his own malaise, differentiated him fundamentally from many well-born Englishmen of his generation – men like Byron's Cephalonian friend Colonel Charles Napier, who lived on to create Queen Victoria's empire.

When Byron and Napier converged for these brief months in Cephalonia it seemed they shared a vision for a free Greece which was still a young man's vision, based on optimism as well as realism. Byron spoke for both of them when he told John Bowring of the London Greek Committee: 'we must be permitted to view it with truth, with its defects as well as beauties, – more especially as success will remove the former *gradually*.' The plan under discussion between Byron and Napier, in their unofficial meetings in Byron's villa at Metaxata or in Argostoli in the autumn of 1823, was that Napier should leave his post in Cephalonia and, on behalf of the London Greek Committee, take command of the Suliote and the volunteer forces on the mainland of Greece. When Napier left for England in December to confer with the London Greek Committee he carried Byron's personal recommendation as the man most capable of forming a foreign corps in support of the Greeks.

Byron, once in Missolonghi, remained hopeful of Napier's return, expecting to cede military control to him. But negotiations foundered. Napier was unimpressed by the London Greek Committee and nervous of giving up his British Army commission and pay. Perhaps, when it came to it, prospects of his own freedom frightened Napier whilst they stimulated Byron. Though Napier's military career was to be crowned by his triumphs in Sind in the early 1840s – earning him his huge bronze statue in Trafalgar Square – Byron's future as he at last embarked for Missolonghi was more equivocal.

27

Missolonghi

1824

Once they left Cephalonia on 29 December 1823 the two boats – Byron's mistico and Gamba's larger vessel – sailed along together for the first few hours under a clear night sky. The passengers joined in the sailors' patriotic songs, monotonous rhythms wafting from boat to boat. All of them, but especially Byron, were in ebullient mood. As the mistico pulled ahead out of range of the other vessel, they signalled to one another by firing off pistols and carbines. 'Tomorrow we meet at Missolonghi – tomorrow.' This was an over-optimistic calculation.

It took Byron six more days to land in Missolonghi for the messiah's welcome that was predicted for him. On 30 December he put into Zante to replenish his money supplies from Barff and Hancock, collecting from them another 8,000 Spanish dollars. Sailing towards the Turkish blockade of the coast of Western Greece they were approaching the war zone, and early on 31 December Byron's mistico was intercepted and chased by a Turkish patrol boat. Although the mistico escaped, the bombard, with Gamba, the crew, horses, dogs, supplies and servants, was captured by the Turks and taken into custody.

The mistico continued to be harassed, 'chaced from Creek to Creek' as Byron put it in the account of his adventures which he sent a few days later to Lord Sydney Osborne in Corfu. Unable to land at Missolonghi, they sailed on and anchored in the shallow waters north of the town. Here Byron sent off messengers to ask for a military escort. Before it could arrive, Turkish boats forced Byron's mistico to sail as far as Dragomestre (now Astakos). Returning south they were driven twice on to the rocks by heavy storms, only narrowly escaping total shipwreck.

These dramas gave Byron a new surge of energy. He gave up his bunk below deck to William Fletcher, who was suffering doubly from seasickness and fear, and slept on deck himself. 'I never was better,' he told Osborne. 'So much so –

that being somewhat *obscured* by five days and nights without ablution or change of cloathes – I thought the shortest way to kill the fleas – was to strip and take a swim.' It was now the evening of 3 January, and the mistico had reached the relative safety of the Missolonghi lagoon.

Pietro's experiences had been even more traumatic. Once the Turks had taken the bombard, they had forced it to sail with them in convoy towards Patras. With some presence of mind Gamba had weighed down with lead shot the large packet of incriminating correspondence between Byron and the Greek chiefs which he had been transporting and threw it overboard. The Greek captain of the bombard was taken aboard the Turkish ship and threatened with instant execution. He was only reprieved when he reminded the Turkish captain that he was the very person who had once saved him, with his brother and eight other Turks, from shipwreck in the Black Sea – a recognition scene on a par with any of Byron's Eastern tales for suspense and high emotion.

After harmless interrogations in Patras, in which Gamba passed himself off as a traveller stumbling unwittingly into a foreign war, the bombard was released, arriving in Missolonghi the day before Byron finally came ashore on 5 January. Pietro's joy and relief at their reunion 'safe on the Grecian soil' after so many dangers was intense.

In Byron's accounts of the voyage from Cephalonia to Missolonghi there are several references to Lukas Chalandritsanos, thrown in with the compulsiveness with which the lover mentions the loved one's name even when the context does not strictly justify it. Lukas had been taken into Byron's service not long before departure. According to Gamba, Byron had told him frequently that he would be needing 'many young people' to serve him as pages when he arrived in Greece. The warlike chief surrounded by resplendent young followers was part of Byron's remembered picture of the East and indeed Dr Millingen describes the Greek chiefs in Missolonghi parading with their favourite companions, 'three or more lads handsomely dressed with their loose tresses floating over the shoulders, bearers of their master's silver-cup, pipe and tobacco-bag'.

Lukas was handsome and made the most of his attractions. Gamba portrays him as 'of a well-bred manner and person'. The English fire-master William Parry, when he met Lukas in Missolonghi, was to go still further, judging him as 'of a most prepossessing appearance'. He spoke Italian. Byron did not want to degrade a boy of education and some standing, whose family was already under Byron's protection, by treating him as a servant. Lukas was naturally fitted for the role of page.

During the alarms that punctuated Byron's sea journey, Lukas's safety was his main concern. On 31 December, the day on which the Turkish vessel had chased the mistico away from the approach to Missolonghi, Byron had written to Colonel Stanhope from the temporary refuge of a rocky cove on the Skrofes cape: 'I am uneasy at being here; not so much on my own account as on that of a Greek boy with me, for you know what his fate would be; and I would sooner cut him in pieces and myself too than have him taken out by those barbarians.' The inference is that if Lukas were captured he would be in danger not just of slaughter but also, still less bearable to Byron, of sexual assault.

When Byron sent his message to Missolonghi on 2 January, asking Stanhope for an escort, one of the two chosen messengers was Lukas. Byron had put his page ashore because, as he explained, 'Luke's life was in most danger'. (It is noticeable that he now uses Lukas's pet name.) The boy had rejoined the boat on 3 January when it made another attempt to get through to Missolonghi. This time it hit bad weather when circling the Skrofes rocks. With shipwreck threatening as the mistico struck the rocks Byron was obliged to concentrate his attention on saving the boy from drowning. This episode was related in a letter to Charles Hancock, which offers a revealing account of Byron's conversations with 'a Greek boy . . . telling him the fact that there was no danger for the passengers whatever there might be for the vessel – and assuring him that I could save both him and myself – without difficulty (though he can't swim) as the water though deep was not very rough'. Byron was preparing to take Lukas piggy-back and swim ashore with him, as he used to play with the little boys at Harrow by sitting them on his back and then diving in.

The sequence of events recurs in one of the very few poems Byron wrote in Missolonghi. It is a poem of direct but thwarted longing, a late flowering of his protective instincts:

> 'I watched thee when the foe was at our side –
>   Ready to strike at him, – or thee and me –
> Were safety hopeless – rather than divide
>   Aught with one loved – save love and liberty.
>
> I watched thee in the breakers – when the rock
>   Received our prow – and all was storm and fear,
> And bade thee cling to me through every shock –
>   This arm would be thy bark – or breast thy bier.'

In taking on this very public role in Greece Byron had been conscious of his sexual vulnerability. His susceptibility to women had up to now been easily exploitable. He confided to Charles Barry his fears that certain Greek factions might try to win an unfair influence: 'if these Gentlemen *have* any undue interest and discover my weak side – viz – a propensity to be governed – and were to set a pretty woman or a clever woman about me – with a turn for political or any other sort of intrigue – why – they would make a fool of me. But', he continued, 'if I can keep passion – at least that passion – out of the question – (which may be the more easy as I left my heart in Italy) they will not weather me with quite so much facility.'

What did Byron mean? As far as female passion is concerned he seems to imply his hope of staying loyal to Teresa Guiccioli, the most womanly of women. But he still leaves open the possible resurgence of another sort of passion, the old passion for the adolescent boy. In setting out for Greece was Byron consciously recreating the conditions in which his male passions had once flourished so disarmingly? And was Lukas an intrinsic part of this scheme? On the ship that took him from Genoa to Cephalonia Byron had been talking about Thyrza. This cannot have been a coincidence.

Byron's landing at Missolonghi on 5 January 1824 achieved an epic quality. Now that he was here at last Mavrocordatos orchestrated a hero's welcome for him. There were salvos of artillery and firings of muskets, to the accompaniment of wild music; a throng of soldiers and citizens of Missolonghi, merchants, priests, governing officers, old women, babes in arms, waiting on the shore as one of the boats of the Spetsiot squadron in the harbour brought Byron in. The gathering of local people was swelled by various visiting primates, warlords and their trains who had come to Missolonghi to attend a congress on the affairs of Western Greece. Among the crowd was Pietro Gamba, excitedly aware of how 'hope and content were pictured in every countenance'. Such was the scene that inspired Theodoros Vryzakis's monumental oil painting *Byron's Arrival at Missolonghi* of 1861, now in the National Gallery in Athens, embodying the moment for subsequent generations.

The arrival in Greece put Byron's understanding of the power of the image to its most important test. Mavrocordatos had told him that his presence would '*electrify* the troops'. Byron made certain that it did by wearing full military uniform for the landing, a splendid scarlet coat with gold epaulettes. This could have been the coat he had ordered to be made for him in Genoa or the uniform bequeathed to him by Colonel Duffie before Byron left Cephalonia, which Byron accepted 'in the mode of the ass in the lion's skin in the fable; or, rather in the hope which the Indians entertain when they wear the spoils of a redoubted enemy, viz – that his good qualities may be transferred to the new possessor with his habiliments'.

His appearance was not just magnificent theatre, though Byron certainly found his transformation into *deus ex machina* amusing: it was making an important connection in the public mind between Byron and military glory. As he once wrote to John Murray:

'Art is *not* inferior to nature for poetical purposes. What makes a regiment of soldiers a more noble object of view than the same mass of mob? Their arms, their dresses, their banners, and the *art* and artificial symmetry of their position and movements. A Highlander's plaid, a Mussulman's turban, and a Roman toga, are more poetical than the tattoed or untattoed buttocks of a New Sandwich savage.'

Byron, like Napoleon and indeed like Hitler, appreciated the use of the visual as a tool of political propaganda.

The Greek government wrote formally to welcome Byron, acclaiming his arrival as a favourable omen for Greece's independence. 'It warmly thanks him for his forethought for the sacred soil of Greece, praises his philanthropic sentiments and prays to the Heavenly Father that these qualities may persist.' As a recognition of his benevolence the Greeks intended to raise a statue 'in everlasting gratitude and remembrance'. When the Greeks acknowledged him as their delivering angel, their monetary expectations of Lord Byron were certainly high. But the many surviving Greek letters of this period, elaborately and effusively expressed, suggest there was also a real sense of wonder at the sudden apparition of the lame English lord allying himself so unequivocally with the Greek cause. Part of the wonder was that Byron was a poet, at the time the most famous of all European poets. As one of his grateful Greek correspondents wrote: 'There is no place on earth where his talent is not proclaimed. His brilliant poems will be preserved in immortality as are those of Homer and Virgil.' Perhaps he would write an epic for Greece.

The enigmatic Englishman in glorious red uniform disembarked. Byron was visibly moved by his reception. He was taken straight to the house which had been got ready for him, a few minutes' walk from the landing stage. Colonel Leicester Stanhope and Prince Mavrocordatos, with a large entourage of European and Greek officers, were waiting at the door.

Missolonghi was a town of some strategic importance standing on the southern coast of Western Greece, guarding the entrance to the Gulf of Corinth, directly overlooking one of the two possible military approaches to the Peloponnese. But its recent history had left it isolated. From Missolonghi in 1822 Mavrocordatos had initiated the campaign that ended in disaster for the Greeks at the battle of Peta in which the volunteer forces of the Philhellenes were more or less annihilated. After Peta, the Turks had reasserted their control over most of Western Greece, leaving Missolonghi struggling on alone, still in Greek hands. Byron arrived in a town combining the ordinary and extraordinary in almost equal measure. The historian in him recognised the archetypal tensions of the town under intermittent siege.

The town was built on a marshy plain beside a large shallow lagoon. Trelawny described it as 'a mud Istmus deservedly cut off from Greece', seeing it as a lunatic misjudgement that Byron chose to go there. Henry Fox, arriving in 1827, recorded in his journal: 'the stink, fog vapour, and bad air arising from it render this place pestilential.' Byron himself grumbled at the all-pervading water, telling Hancock, 'The Dykes of Holland when broken down are the Deserts of Arabia for dryness in comparison', and he predicted that 'if we are not taken off with the sword – we are like to march off with an ague in this mud-basket.' Missolonghi's mosquito-infested swamps spread malarial infections. He imagined he might die not '*mart*ially' but '*marsh*-ally'.

The great expanses of water around the town give the landscape a peculiar otherworldliness. Strung out towards the middle distance are the little, almost waterborne buildings raised on stilts. The quality of light obliterates all sharpness of vision. There is no real dividing line between the sea and sky. In Byron's time Missolonghi, perhaps more than any other Grecian town, was a place where human life had come to seem expendable. Only two years later, in the episode known as the Exodos, thousands of besieged citizens of Missolonghi made their desperate, heroic, ultimately suicidal mass exit from the town rather than capitulate to the Turks.

Byron's house at Missolonghi looked straight out over the lagoon. It was a rambling two-storey building on the seashore to the west of the town – contemporary prints show small boats beached almost up against the house. Byron and his servants occupied the top floor of the building. On the floor below was Leicester Stanhope, the 'typographical colonel' as Byron called him, the other official envoy of the London Greek Committee. On the ground floor were the quarters of the Suliote guard which quickly reassembled after Byron's arrival on the mainland. Soldiers and horses also occupied a number of ramshackle outhouses around the central courtyard. The Suliotes were drilled on the patch of ground behind. There was much coming and going, altercation and commotion. A surprised English visitor reported that there was 'often as little ceremony in the house, as if it had been an inn'.

Byron's own apartments were furnished in an ostentatiously military style. James Forrester, a British naval officer, paid Byron a surreptitious visit three weeks after his arrival. 'We found the mighty son of song in a room with Turkish sofas, and its walls hung round with arms of various descriptions, such as carbines, fowling-pieces, pistols, swords, sabres, a claymore.' The three Homeric helmets, which Byron had commissioned in Genoa, were also prominently displayed.

Byron's attendants added their own touch of the picturesque: the herculean Tita, his livery set off by two silver epaulettes; the 'honest-looking, though not remarkably elastic' William Fletcher, so strangely translated to the Missolonghi seashore; the 'young Greek, dressed as an Albanian or Mainote, with very handsomely chased arms in his girdle' – Byron was already lavishing presents on the decorative but sulky Lukas. But as usual it was Byron himself, the affable but endlessly unsettling presence, who stole the scene. As described by Forrester: 'He wore a dark green jacket with rough black cuffs and collar, and a profusion of black trimming, like the storm jackets of some of the cavalry regiments; a blue cap with a scarlet border, a black waistcoat, wide blue pantaloons with broad scarlet stripes, and boots.' Byron's hair was evidently going grey, though not in fact so grey as claimed in the writings in which he laments his ageing. Forrester was unimpressed by Byron's moustachios which were so pale as to be nearly white.

In this and the many other descriptions of Byron at Missolonghi the vestiges of his old self can still be seen: his glee at shooting off the ornaments on the turrets of the little house opposite his quarters, to the consternation of the Greek women living there; his playful conversations with the great dog Lyon. But even more apparent is the change that had overtaken him. When Hobhouse, at the receiving end of Byron's reports to the London Greek Committee, made the comment that in Byron's time in Greece he underwent an alteration of character, this was true of his domestic habits too. Byron had treasured his solitariness, ensuring that he could always shut himself away from the demands of other people. At Missolonghi he was constantly exposed. He had hardly had time to recover from the journey, so Gamba reported, before he was 'assailed by the tumultuous visits of the primates and chiefs', each with their suites of twenty, thirty or even fifty soldiers. Within the next few days he had to give his mind to the diplomatic problems caused by the Greek capture of an Ionian vessel, one of the many Greek infractions of British neutrality. He saw it as part of his duty to make himself endlessly available.

This is perhaps the real heroism of Byron's intervention in the Greek war. He, whose irritability was so intense, had to cope with the day-to-day friction of the varied military factions in Missolonghi, the constant sound of gunfire in the street. The writer disgusted by the brutal facts of war now had to endure the massacres and horrors of a primitive and savage confrontation in which prisoners were slaughtered without compunction: Byron's fears for Lukas were well based. His days of self-indulgent pleasure were over. He wrote to Teresa ruefully: 'Of course you may suppose that a country like this is not exactly the place to pass the Carnival in.'

The basic problem for an agent of the London Greek Committee arriving in the scene of confusion that was Western Greece in 1824 was to formulate any useful strategy. Between Byron and his colleague Colonel Leicester Stanhope there was a fundamental difference of view. Although they were of the same generation, Stanhope being five years Byron's elder, and although Stanhope too was an aristocrat, son of the 3rd Earl of Harrington whose title he was later to inherit, there was little of the easy rapport which had existed between Byron and Napier on Cephalonia.

In spite of his antecedents Byron found Stanhope prissy and suspected his dogmatic Benthamite belief that educating the Greeks in republican principles was the most constructive way to give them assistance. When Stanhope had recommended Jeremy Bentham's pamphlet *A Table of Springs of Action. Showing the Species of Pleasures and Pains of which Man's Nature is Susceptible*, Byron took one look at it and cried, 'Springs of Action! God Damn his Springs of Action.' 'What does the old fool know of springs of action?' he expostulated, claiming that his own instrument had more spring in it. Bentham, and by extension Stanhope, brought out Byron's old scurrility.

Stanhope's aim was to establish in Missolonghi the permanent substructure of a civilised republic. This entailed not only the formation of a disciplined military force but also the setting up of schools, dispensaries and hospitals, a press, a postal service, all of which would be left as a legacy once the Greeks had gained their independence. To Byron, sympathetic as he was to republican ideals as developed in America, such ideals in war-torn Greece seemed wholly unrealistic. He had reported to John Bowring of the London Greek Committee that Stanhope 'came up (as they all do who have not been in the country before) with some high-flown notions of the sixth form at Harrow or Eton, &c.' At the same time Byron complained to the Committee of the irrelevance of some of their supplies to current conditions in Greece:

'in the present state of Greece – for instance the Mathematical instruments are thrown away – none of the Greeks know a problem from a poker – we must conquer first – and plan afterwards. – The use of trumpets too may be doubted – unless Constantinople were Jericho – for the Hellenists have no ear for Bugles – and you must send us somebody to listen to them.'

Stanhope's efforts to found a free press in Missolonghi left Byron similarly doubtful, although he subscribed £50 to support it. He ridiculed the *Hellenica Chronica*, Stanhope's twice-weekly Greek newspaper which started publication on 14 January. This paper, intended to increase the spread of information, could have only a limited circulation since not many potentially interested foreigners could read Greek and few Greeks could read at all. The *Chronica*, the historian George Finlay complained, was written in an 'affected official law jargon' unintelligible to the common people even when read aloud to them.

Byron took a great dislike to the editor, Johann Jakob Meyer, a humourless Swiss accused by Byron of violating his own principles: 'Dr Meyer the Editor with his unrestrained freedom of the Press – takes the Freedom to exercise an unlimited discretion – not allowing any articles but his own and those like them to appear – and in declaiming against restrictions – cuts, carves, and restricts.' Byron then himself exerted censorship on an article attacking the monarchy in Austria which he considered to be inflammatory. He suppressed the whole issue. Now it was Stanhope's turn to accuse Byron of '*despotic* principles'.

When the *Hellenica Chronica* was followed by the *Telegrafo Greco*, an Italian-language newspaper printed in Missolonghi, Byron installed as co-editor his own nominee, the malleable Pietro Gamba, and directed that the editorial content should be confined to day-to-day reporting of the war rather than republican propaganda. His disagreements with Stanhope over the free press inevitably escalated into arguments about what was common sense and what were proper moral principles in the context of the war. They were bitter while they lasted, but Byron did not allow them to sour the relationship. His feuding times, like his whoring times, were finished. He did his best to work with Stanhope, making peace after their quarrels with an onrush of sweetness, saying to the Colonel: 'Give me your honest right hand.'

While Stanhope took the laborious long view, Byron was all for action. By mid-January at least ten Turkish warships could be seen cruising the waters in front of Missolonghi. Although he knew that no decisive military offensive would be possible before the arrival of the English loan, Byron was already planning a military expedition as a statement of intent, and also from his own point of view as an adventure after months of inactivity on Cephalonia. 'He was always for rushing into danger,' wrote Stanhope; 'would propose one day to go in a fireship; another time, to storm Lepanto; would, however, laugh at all this himself afterwards.' Pending Napier's arrival to lead the military operations Byron's vision of himself as active military commander sometimes struck him as too good to be true.

His most serious plan of operations at this juncture was the capture of Lepanto, now Navpaktos, a fortified town near the coast to the east of

Missolonghi which commanded navigation in and out of the Gulf of Corinth. The fortress of Lepanto was now in Turkish hands, but garrisoned by a small company of disgruntled Albanian troops who had been left without pay for many months and who had indicated that they might easily be bribed into surrender. Mavrocordatos gave Byron official approval for the operation on 25 January 1824, investing him with full military and civil powers, backed up by a military council led by the Suliote Notis Botsaris, uncle of the fallen Markos. To his delight Byron was titled 'Archistrategos' or Commander-in-Chief.

The choice of Lepanto as the object of Byron's first Greek military operation has curious reverberations. The 'bloody and considerable' battle that was fought there in 1571, in which the combined forces of Spain and Venice defeated the Turks, is mentioned in *Childe Harold*:

> 'Oft did he mark the scenes of vanish'd war,
> Actium, Lepanto, fatal Trafalgar;
> Mark them unmov'd, for he would not delight
> (Born beneath some remote inglorious star)
> In themes of bloody fray, or gallant fight,
> But loath'd the bravo's trade, and laughed at martial wight.'

Heroic and mock-heroic: the plan to storm the fortress of Lepanto represents the deep ambivalence of Byron's attitudes in those final months in Greece.

The lack of any proper military structure had been a source of amazement and dismay to many of the foreigners who went to fight in Greece. As one of these volunteers described the local forces to the London Greek Committee: 'they are in no way similar to the organised militias one finds in almost all other countries of Europe nor are they to be compared to the Spanish Guerillas, but only to the celebrated bands of Condottieri of Italy in times of old.'

Through January, as Byron made his preparations for the assault on Lepanto, he was reduced to forming what was in effect a private army. Fifteen hundred or so of the Suliote troops formerly commanded by Markos Botsaris were now in Missolonghi and Anatolikon, where they had been reinforcing local troops in the defence of these towns. But the Greek authorities were unable to pay them. The Suliotes and their families were destitute. Byron's feelings of affinity for the Suliotes, the ex-Albanians he still referred to as his people, had survived his experiences in Cephalonia. He agreed to take five hundred of them into his paid service, while suspecting that some of the candidates were not Suliotes at all. The Greek government agreed to subsidise a further hundred, so Byron immediately had six hundred soldiers under his command.

He regularly rode out with the fifty Suliotes of his bodyguard. The soldiers were on foot but still able to keep up with the horses at full speed. The captain of the guard, with some of his soldiers, preceded Byron, who generally rode accompanied on one side by his aide Pietro Gamba, on the other by his Greek interpreter. Behind Byron, on horseback, came two of his servants, usually Benjamin Lewis the black groom and the Venetian Tita, 'both dressed like the chasseurs usually seen behind the carriages of ambassadors, and another division of his bodyguard closed the cavalcade'.

Plans were also in train for the formation of an artillery corps of fifty men, to be financed jointly by Stanhope and Byron. This troop became known as 'Byron's Brigade'. Colonel Stanhope sent messages into the Peloponnese hoping to reassemble the remnants of the German Philhellenes at Missolonghi under Byron's banner. Other foreigners arrived eager to take advantage of Byron's offer to pay any officer willing to fight for independence for the Greeks. They came not only from other parts of mainland Greece, but from the Ionian Isles, from Western Europe, often drawn by Byron's personal charisma. A touching letter to the London Greek Committee from a Byron enthusiast in Kingston asks whether it is practicable to cross the Alps in winter. Another, dated January 1824, from a navy clerk, announces that the writer has secretly left home with only £9 in his pocket: 'I cannot speak the Greek language but can march, carry, load and fire a Gun and draw my sword in English.' At its maximum the corps seems to have totalled between a hundred and fifty and two hundred men, including nearly thirty officers. It was, Byron claimed, 'the only *regularly paid* corps in Greece'. He soon found himself paying the expenses of them all.

The small fighting force so randomly assembled had a polyglot quality that appealed to Byron. Its many hangers-on included the Italian wife of a Greek tailor who, with Byron's permission, recruited a group of 'unincumbered women, of almost all nations', some of them Negresses, 'to wash, sew, cook, and otherwise provide for the men'. They were given free quarters and rations but apparently rejected payment. 'Let me see', Byron said, 'my corps outdoes Falstaff's: there are English, Germans, French, Maltese, Ragusians, Italians, Neapolitans, Transylvanians, Russians, Suliotes, Moreotes, and Western Greeks, in front, and to bring up the rear, the tailor's wife and her troop. Glorious Apollo! no general had ever before such an army.'

Missolonghi's military resources were pitiful. The heavy cannon were in poor condition; supplies of gunpowder were almost at an end. In planning the Lepanto assault, Byron was desperate for the arrival of William Parry, the fire-master, with his laboratory of war which Byron expected to have the capability to 'construct ships of every type, cast cannons, mortars, bullets, and shrapnel bombs, construct carriers of every sort, make powder, Congreve rockets, and every sort of incendiary fire'. After many frustrating delays, Parry and the store ship *Ann* arrived in Missolonghi on 5 February. With him landed eight specialist English mechanics. 'Parry and his Men seemed a little disgusted with the appearance of Messolonghi,' Stanhope wrote sadly. 'Well they may.'

Byron watched the disembarking of the stores with great impatience. The Suliotes had been slow in completing preparations at the former seraglio in Missolonghi, the building now allotted to Stanhope's war laboratory. His fury increased when the Suliotes, taking advantage of one of Greece's many public holidays, left the precious chests of military equipment lying on the beach. Byron hurried to the shore himself and started the unloading. Gamba watched with alarm as he began grappling with the heavy packing cases. Finally the soldiers were shamed into co-operation.

There were several reasons for the abandonment of the plan to attack the fortress at Lepanto. The first setback was the discovery that Parry had brought no Congreve rockets, on which they had relied; it would take at least two months for him to manufacture them, and the expense would be prohibitive. The recruitment of officers capable of mounting an offensive had also proved a problem. There were far fewer Germans left in the Peloponnese than had been imagined. Where Byron had envisaged around two hundred, only twenty-six had been located, and of those some were ill and totally demoralised, some intent on returning home. Of those available to fight there were more infantry officers than the artillery officers Byron needed most. The Germans were particularly prickly about protocol and Byron, for instance, had to reprimand a high-born Prussian who resented serving under the practical but uncouth William Parry. It was almost impossible to arrive at a united fighting force. Even Pietro Gamba, Byron's chief lieutenant, given his own command of a corps of artillery, showed signs of getting out of hand, ordering material for uniforms, boots and spurs and horsewhips at what Byron considered exorbitant cost. 'But this comes of letting boys play the man,' he reflected; 'all his patriotism diminishes into the desire for a sky blue uniform.'

All these were contributory factors. The main cause for the cancellation of the raid was the obstructive behaviour of Byron's Suliotes. The Suliote chieftains were argumentative, divided amongst themselves. Fictitious soldiers were listed on the military records, pay claimed for them and pocketed by the chieftains. Demands were made for the appointment of a hundred and fifty Suliote officers, creating a top-heavy fighting force, at a much increased rate of pay. As Stanhope lamented to the London Greek Committee, 'There is no end to their avarice.' It was suspected that the Suliotes had been put up to these damaging tactics by Koloktronis, as a first stage in persuading them to leave Prince Mavrocordatos's Missolonghi faction and transfer to him.

Finally, and sadly, Byron had had enough. He had to own that as well as cheats the Suliotes had proved themselves cowards. He told Kinnaird: 'We were to have besieged Lepanto, but the Suliotes did not like the service "against Stone walls".' As a reminder to himself, he wrote an uncompromising note:

'Having tried in vain at every expence – considerable trouble – and some danger to unite the Suliotes for the good of Greece – and their own – I have come to the following resolution. – I will have nothing more to do with the Suliotes – they may go to the Turks or – the devil they may cut me into more pieces than they have dissensions among them, sooner than change my resolution.'

It was not naivety that had kept him faithful for so long to the devious Suliotes but his reluctance to deny the possibility that they could improve. The main force was now dismissed, 'boomed off', Byron retaining only the fifty or so members of his personal bodyguard.

On 22 January Byron was thirty-six. In the Murray archive are six lines in Greek by the nationalist poet Marmaroutis composed for Byron's birthday in 1810, praising the Briton who 'has blossomed phoenix-like in Greece'. Now, thirteen years later, Byron wrote his own commemorative poem, emerging from his bedroom into the public room where Stanhope and a few others had assembled and saying with a smile, 'You were complaining, the other day, that I never write any poetry now: – this is my birthday, and I have just finished something which, I think, is better than what I usually write.' He had written out the lines in his Cephalonia journal with the heading 'January 22nd 1824. Messalonghi. On this day I complete my thirty-sixth year.' It is a poem which makes plain the tensions between Byron's public life of politics and warmaking and the agonising sorrows of his unreciprocated love for Lukas Chalandritsanos:

> '"Tis time this heart should be unmoved
>   Since others it hath ceased to move,
> Yet though I cannot be beloved
>   Still let me love.
>
> My days are in the yellow leaf
>   The flowers and fruits of love are gone –
> The worm, the canker and the grief
>   Are mine alone.

The fire that on my bosom preys
  Is lone as some Volcanic Isle,
No torch is kindled at its blaze
  A funeral pile!

The hope, the fear, the jealous care
  The exalted portion of the pain
And power of Love I cannot share
  But wear the chain.

But 'tis not *thus* – and 'tis not *here*
  Such thoughts should shake my soul, nor *now*
Where glory decks the hero's bier
  Or binds his brow.

The Sword – the Banner – and the Field
  Glory and Greece around us see!
The Spartan borne upon his shield
  Was not more free!

Awake! (*not* Greece – She *is* awake!)
  Awake my spirit – think through *whom*
Thy Life blood tracks its parent lake
  And then strike home!

Tread those reviving passions down
  Unworthy Manhood; – unto thee
Indifferent should the smile or frown
  Of Beauty be.

If thou regret'st thy youth, why *live*?
  The Land of honourable Death
Is here – up to the Field! and give
  Away thy Breath.

Seek out – less often sought than found,
  A Soldier's Grave – for thee the best,
Then look around and choose thy ground
  And take thy Rest.'

Contemporary descriptions of Byron's birthday morning give no further details. Emerging from his bedroom, did Byron hand the poem over to the assembled company? Or was he more likely to have read it aloud? How aware was his audience of the underlying meaning? How did they interpret the phrase 'reviving passions'? It seems probable that Stanhope at least understood the nuances. After his return to England he confided in Hobhouse who noted in his journal: 'Stanhope told me one or two things too true I am sure about Byron's last career in Greece.' And Trelawny, in forwarding the manuscript to Hobhouse after Byron's death, was obviously aware of its potentially dangerous implications: 'this little song – & the last he composed – written on his birthday is one of his most feeling & beautiful productions and now affectingly so – I scarcely need point out that you and Mr D. Kinnaird had better look over his letters to distroy those which none but a friend's eye should see.'

Eliciting strong feelings had not been Byron's problem. It had been the opposite, both with the boys he had cultivated, Edleston and Cowell, Georgiou and Giraud, and with the army of his female fans. Lukas's evident disdain brought home to him the thing that he had fought off with a womanly persistence: the visible effects of ageing, the disintegration of his wonderful good looks. His frustration drove him into ridiculous excesses. Even the loyal Gamba was forced to admit that his attention to Lukas was so marked 'that one might call it a weakness'. In supporting Lukas's family in Cephalonia Byron had been generous but never over-lavish: at one point he suggested that the girls could enter service. For Lukas he provided large sums of spending money and magnificent clothes: a gold-embroidered jacket, a fine riding coat, an expensive 'fascia' or scarf, a saddle and saddlecloth with silk cording, pistols which were specially gilded for him. Lukas rode out at the head of his own contingent of thirty soldiers. Byron set aside half an hour each day for reading modern Greek with him, perhaps hoping to recreate the intimacy of his Italian lessons in Athens with Nicolo Giraud. The more Byron spoiled him the more unyieldingly arrogant the boy became.

On 1 February Byron made an expedition by flat-bottomed boat to Anatolikon, the town on the island in the middle of the marshes where only two months earlier a besieging Turkish force of twenty-four thousand soldiers, mainly cavalry, had been encamped. The Turks were now dislodged and this was a ceremonial visit, a gathering of local leaders. Byron was received with enthusiastic salvos of musketry and discharges of artillery and given a feast of fine fish, an English plum pudding and champagne. He was taken to the church of St Michael, claimed to be the site of a recent miracle. A shell from a mortar had fallen on the church at the beginning of the siege, killing the curate's mother but descending through the floor to open up the entrance to a hidden spring. The besieged were in desperate need of fresh water. Byron, so sceptical of miracles, may have found this narrative a little hard to take. As they walked around the town a large crowd followed the party, crying out ecstatically and playing raucous music. Women stood out on the balconies, dressed in their finest ceremonial costumes, doing obeisance to Byron as he passed.

But the day was spoiled by a deluge which descended on the party on the journey home. Gamba got soaked, becoming ill on his return with fever and colic. Lukas too succumbed, as Byron told Charles Hancock: 'Luke (not the Evangelist – but a disciple of mine) has been out of sorts.' Byron was so concerned that he gave up his own bed to his protégé. Cross-examined later by an anxious Hobhouse, once these sleeping arrangements had become the subject of malicious rumour, Gamba insisted that Byron had spent the next three or four nights on a Turkish divan in the bedroom shared by others of his suite. He pointed out that the gravity of Lukas's illness made a bed essential: Byron's was the only one available. He argued that Byron had offered *him* his bed in similar circumstances and cited as a further precedent Byron's sacrifice of his bunk to William Fletcher on the rough sailing from Cephalonia. Gamba concluded: 'Whatever suggestion was made to you that M[y Lord] could have slept in the same bed is absolutely false.'

On 15 February Byron had a fit. The warning signs were evident to Pietro Gamba who came into his room at seven in the evening to find him lying on the sofa. He called out, 'I am not asleep – come in – I am not well.' An hour later he was up and went downstairs to see Stanhope. The *Hellenica Chronica* was discussed more amiably than usual, with Byron agreeing to contribute some articles. When Gamba left he was laughing and joking with Stanhope and Parry and sharing the cider to which the fire-master was partial. A few minutes later his face changed. He complained of a pain in his knee. He attempted to stand up but was unable to walk. Almost fainting, he collapsed on Colonel Stanhope's bed. The two young doctors, Byron's own Dr Bruno and Julius Millingen, who was now in charge of the artillery corps clinic in Missolonghi, were called in.

Byron described this frightening episode in the last of the dated entries in his journal:

'I had a strong shock of a Convulsive description but whether Epileptic – Paralytic – or Apoplectic is not yet decided by the two medical men who attend me – or whether it be of some other nature (if such there be) it was very painful and had it lasted a moment longer must have extinguished my mortality – if I can judge by the sensations. – I was speechless with the features much distorted – but *not* foaming at the mouth – they say – and my struggles so violent that several persons – two of whom – Mr Parry the Engineer – and my Servant Tita the Chasseur are very strong men – could not hold me.'

According to the doctors the fit lasted two or three minutes but Byron reckoned it at ten.

Byron was carried to his own bed. He was weak but his features were no longer distorted and he had recovered his speech. The next day the two doctors prescribed bleeding, the fashionable remedy of the time, and eight leeches were applied to Byron's forehead. An unfortunate error was made in applying them too near the temporal artery, which caused excessive bleeding. It was, according to Stanhope, 'an extraordinary scene when the leeches had bit the temporal artery ... the two physicians squabbling over him, and he, weak as he was, joking at their expense'. There was a slight recurrence of the attack on 20 February, causing convulsions in Byron's deformed right leg. This was followed by sensations of vertigo, a dizziness reminding Byron of how he felt when drunk. Though he did not believe the condition was hereditary he was still alarmed enough to send a message via Augusta to Lady Byron in case Ada showed any similar symptoms.

What brought on the fit? Gamba blamed lack of exercise. Byron had been housebound by continuing rain. Stanhope blamed the Suliote rebellion, which had taken place on the day of Byron's fit, and the intemperate regime encouraged by Parry: an overdose of cider was central to the problem. Modern medical opinion views the illness as probably an epileptic episode, while Byron's subsequent attack of vertigo suggests anaemia, anxiety neurosis, or hypertension. The underlying emotional causes were obvious to Byron himself who admitted in his journal: 'I have been violently agitated with more than one passion recently – and a good deal occupied politically as well as privately ... I have also been in an anxious state with regard to things which may be only interesting to my own private feelings.' He was conscious that the many changes of place and passion in his previous thirty-six years, the turmoil of his personal history, had taken its toll of his physical strength.

On 21 February a violent earthquake shook Missolonghi. In obedience to Greek superstition answering muskets were fired throughout the town. Lukas's illness, Byron's fit, the terror of the earthquake: this succession of events, like Lukas's rescue from the shipwreck, is recorded in Byron's poem 'Love and Death'.

> 'I watched thee when the fever glazed thine eyes –
>   Yielding my couch – and stretched me on the ground –
> When overworn with watching – ne'er to rise
>   From thence – if thou an early grave hadst found.
>
> The Earthquake came and rocked the quivering wall –
>   And men and Nature reeled as if with wine –

> Whom did I seek around the tottering Hall –
>> For *thee* – whose safety first provide for – thine.
>
> And when convulsive throes denied my breath
>> The faintest utterance to my fading thought –
> To thee – to thee – even in the grasp of death
>> My Spirit turned – Ah! oftener than it ought.
>
> Thus much and more – and yet thou lov'st me not,
>> And never wilt – Love dwells not in our will –
> Nor can I blame thee – though it be my lot
>> To strongly – wrongly – vainly – love thee still. –'

Compared with the self-sacrificial tone of Byron's earlier birthday composition, his intention to renounce a forbidden love seems rather less secure.

'Love and Death' did not appear in print until 1887, in the second issue of *Murray's Magazine*, a publication initiated by John Murray III, the son of Byron's publisher. The lines were taken from a rough copy which had been returned from Greece with Byron's other papers in 1824. At that time Hobhouse had added the guarded explanation: 'A note attached to these verses by Lord Byron states they were addressed to nobody and were a mere poetical scherzo.' Whether Byron's own words or a gloss concocted by Hobhouse, the statement is evasive in a manner which reminds one of the sudden caution that followed the death of Edleston and the mystery surrounding the identity of Thyrza. Here again, faced with lines relating to Byron's love for Lukas, Hobhouse was intent on expunging any memory of Byron's homosexuality.

A second unknown poem by Byron, 'Last Words on Greece', appeared alongside 'Love and Death' in *Murray's Magazine*. Neither title was given by Byron: both have a late-Victorian grandiloquence.

> 'What are to me those honours or renown
>> Past or to come, a new-born people's cry
> Albeit for such I could despise a crown
>> Of aught save Laurel, or for such could die;
> I am the fool of passion – and a frown
>> Of thine to me is as an Adder's eye
> To the poor bird whose pinion fluttering down
>> Wafts unto death the breast it bore so high –
> Such is this maddening fascination grown –
>> So strong thy Magic – or so weak am I.'

The subject, once again, is obviously Lukas, the poet fixing his sardonic gaze upon his own emotional vulnerability. The fool of passion was after all the man who at that moment was the holder of the title of military Commander-in-Chief of Western Greece. The idea of erotic obsession, 'maddening fascination', became a central tenet of European Romanticism and the cult of decadence that followed. The quintessentially Byronic image of bird transfixed by serpent had been transformed, by the end of the nineteenth century, into the triumphant sinuosity of art nouveau.

Did Byron write further poems of hopeless passion in Missolonghi? The likelihood that Leicester Stanhope divulged to Hobhouse at least something of Byron's love for Lukas Chalandritsanos is reinforced by a short passage in Stanhope's 1825 memoir of Byron in Greece. Here Stanhope recollects how, after his return to England, he watched Hobhouse 'from motives of high honour destroy a beautiful poem of Lord Byron's, and, perhaps, the last he ever composed. The same reason that induced Mr H. to tear this fine manuscript will, of course, prevent him or me from ever divulging its contents.' This gentlemanly conspiracy suggests that Byron wrote at least one other Lukas poem.

As well as his infatuation with the boy Lukas, Byron developed an attachment to a Turkish child Hatadjé Aga, or Hato as he called her. This was a girl of eight or nine, victim of the terror of 1821 when Missolonghi had proclaimed itself a part of independent Greece and the resident Turkish males had all been massacred, their wives and daughters distributed as slaves to the Greek households of the town. Hatadjé's two brothers had been slaughtered: one had had his brains dashed out against the walls by Greek troops. She and her mother had fared better than most of their compatriots and were now residing with Dr Millingen, for whom her mother was working as an unpaid servant.

Here, early in February, Byron found Hatadjé. With his even-handed view of the virtues and defects of both Greeks and Turks he was already sympathetic to the plight of Turkish women left stranded in the town. He arranged to return twenty-four women and children to Prevesa, then a town under Turkish occupation, at his own expense. He was particularly vulnerable to Hatadjé, who was just at that age of pert pre-puberty he always found attractive in girls. As described by Millingen, 'He became so much struck by Hatadje's beauty, the naïveté of her answers, and the spiritedness of her observations on the murderers of her brethren, that he decided on adopting her.' He ordered elaborate and expensive dresses for the girl and her mother. He sent Hatadjé a sequin necklace and ordered Tita to go out and buy sweets for her, in the spirit of indulgence with which he had planned treats for his small cousin Eliza in the winter of 1813.

Millingen sent the child round twice a week to visit Byron. 'He would then take the little girl on his knees and caress her with all the fondness of a father.' For a time Hatadjé took the place of both his vanished daughters. She was more appreciative and more approachable than Lukas. A tender little poem, in Greek and Italian versions, presumably addressed to the adored child, came back to England in Byron's papers:

'I enter the garden, lovely Haïdi,
Where you were gathering roses and flowers every morning.'

Byron indulged in fantasies. He wrote to Teresa to tell her he had found a very pretty Turkish female infant 'whom I mean to send you by and bye – she is beautiful as the Sun – and very lively – you can educate her.' He wrote to Augusta singing the praises of the lively, quick child 'with great black Oriental eyes – and Asiatic features', proposing that Lady Byron could bring her up as a companion to Ada. It appears that Annabella, when told of this project, by no means condemned it out of hand.

As an interim measure Byron planned to send Hatadjé to Cephalonia, to be brought up in the Kennedys' formidably religious household. Hatadjé's mother wanted to go too, a prospect which would have overstretched their limited resources. 'But', said Mrs Kennedy, 'as Lord B. had put us to the test, as Christians opposed to Mahometans; although highly inconvenient, we consented to receive both.' However, all these schemes were abandoned after Byron's death, when Byron's maid of Missolonghi and her mother were reunited in Patras with Hatadjé's father. He exclaimed, when he saw them transformed by Byron's finery, 'I thought you were slaves and lo! you return to me decked out like brides.'

This tenderness towards Hatadjé can be seen as one of Byron's desperate responses to Lukas's indifference. At Missolonghi he indulged in some cruel sexual taunting which may also have been provoked by his frustration. A young Suliote soldier was dressed up as a woman to tempt the gullible Fletcher. When Fletcher fell for the disguise and took the boy-woman back to Byron's apartment another Suliote, pretending to be the woman's enraged husband, arrived on the scene with half a dozen of his comrades, 'whose presence and threats', according to William Parry, an amused spectator, 'terrified the poor lacquey almost out of his wits'.

The black groom Benjamin Lewis was another victim. He had befriended two Negresses, originally slaves to the Turks, who had been liberated when the Turks were ejected from the town but who were now left starving. He came formally to Byron to ask for them to be accommodated in the military headquarters. Byron pretended to reprove Lewis severely for his presumption. Again Parry was a witness:

'Blacky stuttered a thousand excuses, and was ready to do any thing to appease his master's anger. His great yellow eyes wide open, he trembling from head to foot, his wandering and stuttering excuses, his visible dread, all tended to provoke laughter, and Lord Byron, fearing his own dignity would be hove over-board, told him to hold in his tongue and listen to sentence.'

Parry was ordered to enter the sentence in his memorandum book. The terri-fied Lewis was relieved when Byron finally pronounced: 'My determination is that the children born of these black women, of which you may be the father, shall be my property, and I will maintain them.' To a present-day sensibility Byron's concept of liberty can seem a little crude.

In his mood of savage humour he could even turn on Parry who had now become his chief crony at Missolonghi, Parry's earthiness contrasting with his own effeteness in a way he found peculiarly satisfactory. Soon after the earth-quake they were having dinner when Parry, becoming aware of a thunderous noise in the room above, imagined it was a recurrence of the earthquake. But no; it was a practical joke devised by Byron: a contingent of Suliote soldiers had been instructed to hold on to the rafters and jump up and down on the floor with all their weight.

The week that followed Byron's fit on 15 February was an eventful one. As he recorded it:

'On Tuesday a Turkish brig of war ran on shore – on Wednesday – great prep-arations being made to attack her though protected by her Consorts – the Turks burned her and returned to Patras – on thursday a quarrel ensued between the Suliotes and the Frank Guard at the Arsenal – a Swedish Officer was killed – and a Suliote severely wounded – and a general fight expected – and with some difficulty prevented – on Friday the Officer buried – and Capt. Parry's English Artificers mutinied under pretence their lives were in danger and are for quitting the country – they may.'

As if that were not enough, news came on the Sunday that the Turkish army had reached Larissa, on the eastern side of Greece, with over a hundred thou-sand men.

Significantly this letter – one of the most vivid Byron wrote from Missolonghi – was addressed to John Murray. As if no rift had occurred between them, Byron was back in the mode of free and easy communication.

Notable, too, is Byron's energy of tone, the exhilaration of activity. Though opinion has had it that in the weeks succeeding his fit Byron was totally demoralised – an impression spread by accounts written after Byron's death by survivors from Missolonghi such as Stanhope, Parry and Millingen, all concerned to defend their own role in events – Byron's own letters, and Pietro Gamba's less self-serving diary, an intimate record of day-to-day events, show a very different Byron: still involved, responsive, excited, resilient. He was making an extraordinary effort to rise above his illness, to surmount his heartache. At Missolonghi, as never before in his existence, we see detailed commitment to the responsibilities he had taken on.

'My office here is no sinecure,' he told John Murray. This was an understatement. One of the episodes mentioned in Byron's letter, the vicious murder of the Swedish volunteer officer, Lieutenant Sass, by a Suliote soldier in a quarrel at the Arsenal, shows just how inflammatory the situation was, with so many troops of different nationalities and faiths cooped up together in a small coastal town. It was March before the dismissed Suliotes finally departed. Having paid them up to the point of their dismissal, Byron had to advance more money, which they claimed as arrears of pay, to get rid of them. Meanwhile they continued to represent a destabilising force.

Fear of the swaggering Suliote soldiers lay behind the threats of six of Parry's artificers, his skilled craftsmen, to leave Greece altogether. After Sass's violent death in their own workplace, the artificers downed tools, maintaining that they had never bargained for employment in a war zone. Byron tried to persuade them that Sass's death had been an accident, that the Suliotes would soon be leaving anyway, that his own presence in Missolonghi proved there was no danger. But his arguments were useless: 'they said they had heard balls whistle over their heads whilst at work, and that they should be murdered – they would go.'

Beyond these local disputes Byron was more acutely conscious of the need, pending the English loan, to keep the peace between the Greek leaders. He explained to Barff the banker: 'Almost every thing depends upon the arrival – and the speedy arrival of a portion of the loan – to keep peace amongst themselves – if they can but have sense to do this – I think that they will be a match and better for any force that can be brought against them for the present. – We are all doing as well as we can.'

Byron's policy was to keep talking, to keep options open. The enemy of trimming had schooled himself to be diplomatic. It has sometimes been claimed that Byron fell out with Mavrocordatos in the months at Missolonghi. Although to some extent the scales fell from his eyes and he realised that

Mavrocordatos could match the other Greek leaders for deviousness, Gamba's diaries show the frequency and the genuine friendliness of their communications. Byron treated him with respect and generosity, even subsidising his 'private pecuniary wants'. He sympathised with Mavrocordatos's own pressures, telling Murray: 'Prince Mavrocordato is an excellent person and does all in his power – but his situation is perplexing in the extreme.'

When overtures began to reach him from Odysseus Androutsos, alias Ulysses, Byron was cautious. The charming and treacherous Odysseus was almost a reincarnation of Ali Pasha, whose court attendant he had been as a young man. The very flamboyance that had attracted Trelawny, now acting as a kind of factotum to Odysseus in Athens, aroused Byron's suspicions: he had become immune to the romance of the East. He could see that Odysseus's aim was to detach him from his close alliance with Mavrocordatos, Odysseus's rival as Greek leader. Odysseus may well have been the source of rumours that the government aimed, through Mavrocordatos, to sell the nation to the English.

Byron was also well aware that Odysseus coveted his money and material supplies. Within the first few days of his arrival in Greece, Odysseus, via Trelawny, had demanded a share-out of the London Greek Committee's expected military equipment: bombshells and rockets, gunpowder and guns. The loan of £800,000 sought by the Greek deputies Orlandos and Louriotis had been signed in London, on 21 February 1824. This loan was in the name of the London Greek Committee, who designated Byron, with Stanhope and Napier, as one of the commissioners. Odysseus was obviously eager to stake his claim to the influx of funds for the Greek war.

Odysseus invited Byron, with Mavrocordatos, to attend a congress he was planning at Salona (now Amfissa) in Eastern Greece, a congress represented as an attempt to unite the eastern and western Greek leaders, and to reconcile militarists and constitutionalists. Byron at first prevaricated, unconvinced of the wisdom of venturing into an area in which the Turkish forces were now much in evidence. But he was unwilling to refuse outright any meeting that could conceivably be useful: 'if my presence can really be of any help at all in reconciling two or more parties, I am ready to go anywhere, either as a mediator, or, if necessary, as a hostage.' Byron had reached a point of practical humility.

Leicester Stanhope had now been won over by Odysseus – the Benthamite republican moved by the military commander who ruled by treachery and instinct: the Greek War of Independence was full of such compelling ironies. Stanhope left Missolonghi on 21 February and joined Odysseus in Athens, which became his new base of operations. Trelawny and Stanhope now approached Byron jointly, singing Odysseus's praises in their attempt to persuade him to attend the congress at Salona. Finally, George Finlay, Byron's young admirer, who was also in Athens, was sent to Missolonghi as a personal envoy to persuade Byron that his attendance was essential.

Byron eventually gave in. He wrote to Samuel Barff on 22 March:

'In a few days P. Mavrocordato and myself, with a considerable escort, intend to proceed to Salona at the request of Ulysses (Odysseus) and the Chiefs of Eastern Greece, to concert, if possible, a plan of union, between Western and Eastern Greece, and to take measures, offensive and defensive, for the ensuing campaign.'

Bandied around in the background were proposals that Mavrocordatos would be reinstated in the Greek government, either as leader or as co-leader with Byron, who would otherwise be given command of Western Greece supported by a council which included his old associate Andreas Londos. These proposals of high office may simply have been the inducements of the moment. But Hobhouse was convinced from his many discussions with the Greek deputies while they were in London that, had Byron lived, by 1825 'he would have been at the head of Greece'. The prospect of Byron as King of Greece is not impossible. In 1825 the failing Greek government petitioned Britain to take Greece under its protection, and it was a foreigner, Otho, a son of King Ludwig of Bavaria, who became King Otho I when Greece finally achieved independence in 1832.

Byron never got to Salona. Day after day the rains came down on Missolonghi. The roads out of the town became impassable, so miry that, as Byron lamented, 'every hundred yards brings you to a brook or ditch – of whose depth – width – colour – and contents – both my horses and their riders have brought away many tokens'. Through late March and early April they were unable to leave while Byron's attention was occupied from day to day with the usual onrush of local crises and administrative decision-making.

He received a request to provide four cannon for the Greek siege on the fortress of Patras, a strategic stronghold on the north coast of the Peloponnese still in Turkish hands. He replied sympathetically but firmly in a previously unpublished letter to Georgios Sisinis in Gastouni dated 25 March. The original is in Greek.

'You ask me for guns for the siege of Old Patras. You know, I imagine, Sir, that both the guns and all the other equipment which came from England were sent by the Greek Committee in London. They have charged me to take delivery of them and hold them pending the instructions of the government which I await.

And I am certain that you will excuse me if I am unable to oblige you even in this. You will find me willing to assist in whatever else you judge me competent to do.'

On 28 March his intervention was required in a dispute over the sentence given to an Italian soldier of the Byron Brigade convicted of robbing a poor peasant in the market place. The argument was not over the crime, which was admitted, but the punishment. The German officers who court-martialled the man condemned him to be bastinadoed, an Eastern form of punishment involving ferocious beating on the soles of the feet. The bastinado infringed the French military code adopted by the Greeks in the conduct of the war, and Byron, who did all in his power to reduce the level of atrocity on both sides, opposed the sentence on humanitarian grounds, proposing instead that the culprit should be stripped of his uniform and marched through the town with a label on his back, describing in Greek and Italian the crime of which he had been guilty. According to Gamba, 'it required not only all Lord Byron's eloquence, but his authority' to prevail upon the Germans to agree to this.

On 30 March Byron was given the freedom of the city of Missolonghi, an honour that was quickly followed by more requests for money. The town had already accumulated debts to him. On 1 April he was preoccupied with a Prussian officer who had run amok in his lodgings: to the disgust of his fellow Germans Byron had him put under arrest 'according to the Code', maintaining firmly that 'those who do not choose to be amenable to the laws of the Country and service – may retire – but that in all that I have to do – I will see them obeyed by foreigner or native'. A few days later he successfully quelled a minor uprising provoked when the nephew of Georgios Karaïskasis, a Greek chieftain at Anatolikon, was injured in a quarrel at Missolonghi and Karaiskasis's followers, seeking revenge, occupied the island fortress of Vasiladi in the Missolonghi lagoon. Byron was far from unmotivated, listless. Records show that on the contrary he was at his most resourceful in what was to prove his final week of active life.

Through all these events the details of his youthful life still stayed with him. When Finlay had visited him a few weeks earlier he had eagerly conversed about Cambridge, Brighton, London, conjuring up precisely the scenes of almost twenty years before, resurrecting anecdotes about Hobhouse and Scrope Davies. His memory strayed even further back, to Aberdeen and Newstead, still showing his peculiar exactness of recall. Finlay had been to Newstead, which was already becoming a place of pilgrimage for Byronists, and mentioned Boatswain and his tomb. Byron said that Newfoundland dogs had twice saved his life and that he could not do without one. Presumably at this point he looked across to Lyon.

Encouraged by Finlay's receptiveness his schooldays were included in this spate of reminiscence. When Finlay, reading an English newspaper which had just arrived, mentioned the name of Sir Aubrey de Vere Hunt, Byron sprang to life: 'Sir Aubrey was at Harrow, I remember, but he was younger than me. He was an excellent swimmer, and once saved a boy's life.' It may have been the recollection of Sir Aubrey, who after these exploits went on to serve in India, that prompted Byron to send a letter from Missolonghi to the Earl of Clare.

Byron and Lord Clare had been in touch again since they had last met in Italy. On hearing that Byron was about to join the Greeks, Clare had tried to dissuade him: 'pray don't,' he had written the previous August, 'surely they are only a shade better than their Turkish master and except for the sake of their ancestors not worth a thought . . . but wherever you go remember my dear Byron I shall never forget you.' He held out the hope that one day Byron would visit the Clare estates in Ireland, 'this land of potatoes'. Byron wrote back to Clare on 31 March, just as the Turkish fleet was bearing down upon Missolonghi harbour in a new blockade: 'I hope that you do not forget that I always regard you as my dearest friend – and love you as when we were Harrow boys together – and if I do not repeat this as often as I ought – it is that I may not tire you with what you so well know.'

After his fit in mid-February Byron had been complaining of violent headaches. These may have been exacerbated by his excessive blood loss when the leeches came too close to the temporal artery. He was thin and on edge, feeling a kind of generalised dread for no apparent reason. Byron's superstitious instincts, always present, were now heightened: when a letter came on 9 April from Augusta telling him that she had been ill at the same time as his fit he seized upon this as an extreme coincidence.

The bad weather, which had been keeping him indoors, had made him claustrophobic. On 4 April, a better day, he had ridden out with Pietro. Then the rains again descended. On 9 April, after dealing with his administrative tasks, writing letters to his bankers Barff in Zante and Barry in Genoa, he was so desperate for exercise that, although the skies were threatening, he insisted on riding out again: three or four miles outside the town he and Pietro were caught in a downpour. Because of the difficulties of access on horseback through the quagmire of Missolonghi, it was their usual practice to dismount at the town walls and take a boat round to the house. As this was an emergency, with Byron wet through and violently perspiring, Pietro urged him to take the town route. Byron refused, hating to give in, and they made the half-hour journey back across the lagoon exposed to the weather in an open boat.

Two hours after returning to the house Byron was shivering all over. He had a slight fever and rheumatic pains, his usual reaction after a bad soaking. The same thing had happened in Cephalonia. But this attack showed signs of being worse. At eight that evening, when Pietro came into his room, Byron was lying on a sofa, very restless. 'I am in great pain,' he said. 'I should not care for dying, but I cannot bear these pains.' During the evening he reverted time and again to the prediction made to him as a boy by the well-known soothsayer consulted by his mother that he should beware his thirty-seventh year.

Byron's own doctor, Francesco Bruno, saw him later that night. The other doctor, Julius Millingen, arrived at Byron's house apparently by chance. It is impossible not to feel sorry for these two young doctors, the diminutive, excitable, emotional Italian, just out of Genoa University, and the gangling, introspective Julius Millingen, educated in England although of Dutch extraction, recent graduate of the Edinburgh Royal College of Physicians, neither communicating easily with the other. They were precipitated into a crisis with which they were ill equipped to deal. Their own accounts of Byron's illness vary from Pietro Gamba's and indeed from one another's. But for the agonising sequence of Byron's final days the more reliable are those of Bruno and Gamba, who were keeping more or less contemporary diaries, rather than Millingen whose records were compiled with hindsight and whose tendency for self-serving makes him a less reliable witness.

So what exactly happened on the night of 9 April, after Byron's collapse on the sofa? Although Millingen was later to deny that he was professionally consulted at this juncture, Gamba is categoric that both physicians recommended bleeding and that Byron was adamant in his refusal, saying, 'Have you no other remedy than bleeding? – there are many more die of the lancet than the lance.' Gamba insisted that it was Millingen who then 'complied too much with his prejudice against bleeding, and told him there was no necessity for it'. This was to become a key issue. The failure to begin bleeding Byron sooner was to be seen by his contemporaries, though not by modern medical opinion, as the prime cause of his death.

The next day, 10 April, the shivering continued. Dr Bruno gave him a hot bath and a dose of castor oil which, according to the doctor's diary, 'produced three evacuations'. He still resisted bleeding. Byron managed to attend to urgent business but did not go outside. On 11 April he decided to go out riding an hour earlier than usual, hoping to cheat the onset of the rain. He and Gamba took a long ride in the olive woods, accompanied by Lambros, one of the remaining Suliote officers, and the usual cavalcade of Byron's bodyguard. Byron was talkative and seemed in a good mood. He returned to a domestic drama in the evening when the police reported that a Turkish spy, a relation of his Greek landlord, Apostolis Kapsalis, had taken refuge in Byron's house. Byron immediately gave orders for the man's arrest.

On 12 April Byron was worse. He had been eating very little: he had taken only three or four spoonfuls of the arrowroot with which Fletcher tried to tempt him, and symptoms of rheumatic fever were more pronounced. He was complaining of pain in his head and in his rectum. Lewis the groom was blamed for not changing Byron's saddle, which was still soaked through when he took his second ride. The next day, although the fever appeared to have diminished, the headache and the pains in his bones continued. He was irritable, suffering the effects of lack of sleep. Plans were now being made to take Byron and his servants to Zante where he already knew the English doctor, Dr Thomas, a friend of Samuel Barff. A few weeks earlier he had ordered Dr Thomas to send him some supplies of 'good *English* Calcined Magnesia'. But the stormy weather made Byron's embarkation to Zante an impossibility.

On 14 April he got up and proposed to go out riding. But the skies looked ominous and he was dissuaded. He was by now becoming delirious. No one was allowed to see him but the doctors, Pietro Gamba, the servants Fletcher and Tita, and the fire-master Parry, the 'rough burly fellow' with his fund of pot-house stories, whom Byron, in his perverse way, clung to in his illness in spite of the physicians' disapproval. As described by Parry, Byron's sickroom was chaotic:

'As there was nobody invested with any authority over his household, after he fell sick, there was neither method, order, nor quiet in his apartments ... There was also a want of many comforts which, to the sick, may indeed be called necessaries, and there was a dreadful confusion of tongues. In his agitation Dr Bruno's English, and he spoke but imperfectly, was unintelligible; Fletcher's Italian was equally bad. I speak nothing but English; Tita then spoke nothing but Italian; and the ordinary Greek domestics were incomprehensible to us all. In all the attendants there was the officiousness of zeal; but owing to their ignorance of each other's language, their zeal only added to the confusion.'

There is no mention of Zambelli, Byron's steward, and it seems that Lukas Chalandritsanos, probably on Byron's instructions, was excluded from the scene.

On 15 April there were some little signs of rallying. Byron still talked of going riding. He was pleased by the arrival of a letter from the Turkish governor of the Castle of the Morea, the modern Rio, thanking him for the release of four Turkish prisoners, delivered 'safe and sound'. But as the day progressed it was becoming clear that Byron was now very seriously ill. Pietro, charged by Teresa with looking after Byron, was distraught. So was Dr Bruno, overawed by the weight of his responsibility. Though it is clear that Millingen was present earlier, this is the date given by Millingen himself as the one on which he was officially called in for joint consultation with Byron's own physician. They both wanted to bleed Byron. But he still refused in what Millingen described as 'a manner excessively peevish', finding every possible reason for resisting: he maintained that 'of all his prejudices' the strongest was against bloodletting; he cited the promise his mother had extracted from him on her deathbed that he would never consent to be bled. Unless Millingen's report is itself a fabrication, Byron was lying: his mother was speechless long before he reached her deathbed. It was late at night when, after a spasmodic bout of coughing which brought on vomiting, he finally agreed to bleeding the next day.

By the morning of 16 April, Byron had changed his mind. He had had a better night and would not be bled. Why was he so resistant to bleeding? Partly, perhaps, because he saw it as a quasi-sexual violation of the body, a final invasion of his deepest privacy. Millingen remonstrated with him solemnly, informing Byron that if he would not agree to being bled neither he nor Dr Bruno could answer for the consequences; the disease, Millingen added, might otherwise 'operate such disorganisation in his cerebral and nervous system as entirely to deprive him of his reason'. This, as Millingen knew, was a clinching argument to a man already conscious of his fragile mental state. Byron cast both doctors 'the fiercest glance of vexation, he threw out his arm, and said, in the most angry tone: "Come; you are, I see, a d—d set of butchers. Take away as much blood as you will; but have done with it."' They seized the opportunity to extract a full pound of blood and two hours later took another pound. The blood was now 'very thin in appearance'. After this Byron slept for a little, relatively peacefully.

But the bloodletting did not result in the improvement the doctors had expected. During the night Byron's fever became worse and his speech more incoherent. In his delirium, phrases in English and Italian alternated wildly. Early on the morning of the 17th, he was dosed again with purgatives and allowed the doctors to draw ten more ounces of blood. Later in the morning Pietro, who had himself been in bed with a sprained ankle, hobbled in to see him.

'His countenance at once awakened the most dreadful suspicions: he was very calm; he talked to me in the kindest manner about my accident, but in a hollow, sepulchral tone. "Take care of your foot," said he; "I know by experience how painful it must be." I could not stay near his bed: a flood of tears rushed into my eyes, and I was obliged to retire.'

At one o'clock he got up so that his bed could be made. Two of the servants supported him through to the next room. Bruno followed and, becoming tearful, implored Byron to give in and allow a fourth bleeding. But he said he did not want any more blood to be taken: 'if I am destined to die from this disease, I shall perish whether I am bled or whether I am left all my blood.' Soon afterwards he asked to be taken back to bed. Byron had become silent and sad.

As his condition worsened it began to seem essential that another opinion should be sought. William Fletcher had been entreating Byron to send to Zante for Dr Thomas, since it was impossible for Byron to get to Zante himself. Meanwhile Bruno and Millingen, now panic-stricken, sought the professional opinion of two local physicians. These were Dr Loukas Vayas, regarded as Missolonghi's leading doctor, once consultant to Ali Pasha and more recently physician to Mavrocordatos, and Millingen's own assistant, Dr Enrico Treiber, a German attached to the Byron Brigade. Bruno's account puts the date of the joint consultation as 17 April, though both Millingen and Gamba suggest it was the 18th. Quite possibly the doctors were called in to Byron twice. He had been reluctant to see them, agreeing only on condition that they made their diagnosis and said nothing. When, feeling his pulse, one of them attempted to address him, he said: 'Recollect your promise and go away.'

In any case the physicians' opinions were divided. Where Vayas, Treiber and Millingen, seeing how much Byron had been weakened by the bleeding, apparently argued for allowing the fever to run its course, Bruno held out for immediate and still more abundant bleeding, convinced that without it Byron would soon die. With Vayas's approval, Bruno now administered an anti-spasmodic potion, a strong infusion of laudanum with ether which Byron had great difficulty in swallowing. It was decided that blisters should be applied to both his thighs. As Millingen was about to put these in place Byron asked him if it was feasible to place both glass domes on the same leg. He did not want his deformed foot to be exposed. Millingen agreed to apply both blisters to Byron's left leg, above the knee.

On 18 April, after another terrifying night of spasms and involuntary twitchings of the tendons, Byron reluctantly consented to more bleeding. Twelve leeches at the temples extracted about two pounds of blood. But he soon asked the doctors to desist. When letters arrived Pietro thought it best to keep back the report from Bishop Ignatios that the Sultan had denounced Byron, in the formal meeting of the divan, as the enemy of the Turkish Porte. Byron was still sharp enough to ask Pietro for the letter he knew had just arrived from the Greek deputy Louriotis to Mavrocordatos reporting on the progress of the loan. He opened the letter himself and, finding it written partly in French and partly in Greek, translated the French into English and, brushing aside Gamba's suggestion of getting the Greek passages translated, managed to make out the gist of them. The letter confirmed that arrangements for the loan were concluded and that the first instalment was on its way to Greece. What the dying Byron fortunately did not know was that of the total £800,000, after discount and deductions, only £300,000 was available for Greece.

That day, 18 April, was Easter Sunday. Missolonghi was *en fête*. It was the Greek custom to fire cannon and muskets at midday. The decision was made to march the Byron Brigade outside the walls and start firing the guns there to draw the crowds away from the vicinity of Byron's house. Meanwhile the Governor ordered the town guard to patrol the streets of Missolonghi to keep the people quiet out of respect to 'their illustrious benefactor'. Mavrocordatos, on behalf of the General Directorate of Greece, had already written to Pietro Gamba asking him to consult with the government to take appropriate action to secure the safety of Byron's effects 'if the unthinkable should occur'.

At about three that afternoon Byron struggled out of bed and walked into the next room, leaning on the massive Tita. He asked for a particular book and Tita brought it to him. There is no record of what book this was. He read for a few minutes, then feeling faint again he took Tita's arm, tottered through to the next room and was put back to bed.

While Byron was dying the weather remained tempestuous. In Parry's words, 'The pestilent *sirocco* was blowing a hurricane, and the rain was falling with almost tropical violence. In our apartment was the calm of coming death, and outside, was the storm desolating the spot around us.' It seemed to Gamba that only now, in the late afternoon, had Byron become aware that the end was near. Millingen and the two servants Fletcher and Tita, whose lives had for so long been bound up with Byron's, were grouped around the bed. Millingen and Fletcher were soon to leave the room, unable to contain themselves. Tita could not go, since Byron had hold of his hand, but in the emotion of the moment he turned away his face. Byron looked at him, saying half-smilingly in Tita's own language, 'Oh "questa è una bella scena".' Byron's sense of himself at the centre of the drama had not deserted him.

Parry returned from the military parade to this scene of desperation. He tried to persuade Byron to take some of the bark the doctors had prescribed. 'My Lord,' he said, 'take the bark, it will do you good, it will recover your Lordship.' Byron took his hand and said, 'Give it me.' He was able to swallow only about four mouthfuls. He seemed in great pain, clenching his hands and from time to time crying out, 'Ah Christi!' Parry loosened the bandages holding the cold compresses in place on Byron's temples and Byron wept at the relief.

By early evening he was hardly recognising those around him. He slept from five to about five-thirty. Gamba could no longer bear to go in to him. Parry entered the room and Byron mumbled a few incoherent messages. The doctors had given him an enema of senna, Epsom salts and castor oil and Byron left his bed on a final journey to evacuate his bowels. At six he said he wanted to go to sleep again. The doctors put yet more leeches to his temples and blood continued to flow out copiously through the night.

He remained unconscious for the next twenty-four hours. From time to time he moaned a little. Breathing was difficult and he seemed as if he might be suffocating. The rattling and choking in his throat continued every half hour. Fletcher and Tita raised his head when the fit came on. At a quarter past six in the evening of 19 April Byron opened his eyes and shut them again. The doctors felt his pulse and found that he was dead. At the end he did not seem to have suffered any pain. Pietro wrote to Augusta: 'He died in a strange land, and amongst strangers, but more loved, more wept, he could not have been.'

Byron died in a thunderstorm. After he died Tita cut off a lock of hair and removed from his finger the cornelian ring John Edleston had given him. A large sum of money in Spanish doubloons and silver francesconi was discovered to be missing from Byron's apartment. The prime suspect was his page. The theft was not investigated. Gamba later told Hobhouse that, when questioned, Lukas maintained Byron had given him some doubloons to assist his family. 'We did not wish to press the matter, because to recover the money appeared hopeless, and after all it might have been the cause of gossip damaging to the reputation of our friend. Every friend of Byron must desire that this *mischievous topic* should be buried if possible.' Hobhouse would have certainly agreed.

What killed Lord Byron? In the cycle of blame and counter-blame that followed his death the easiest person to accuse was the dead man. If only he had listened to his doctors and allowed them to start the bloodletting sooner, they claimed, he need never have died. Millingen blamed Bruno, as Byron's personal physician, for failing to take control of the situation and for his lack of expertise. Millingen denied responsibility for the tincture of bark and draught of ether prescribed by Bruno which, he implied, had hastened Byron's end. Both doctors blamed Parry, unfairly, for encouraging Byron to drink and eat meat, in defiance of his diet.

Modern medical opinion attributes Byron's death to an infection, with massive over-bleeding as the immediate cause. Dr Raymond Mills, who has made a special study of Byron's last illness, views the fever which began on 9 April as a febrile illness not directly connected with the fit at the monastery two months before. He proposes Mediterranean tick fever, an infection spread by dog ticks, as more likely than the malaria most often assumed to have been the cause of Byron's death. If this is the case then Lyon the Newfoundland and Moretto the bulldog are new candidates for blame. Dr Mills has calculated Byron's total blood loss from both lances and leeches as at least 2.5 litres, 43 per cent of his blood volume, a loss in itself great enough to have killed him. He was further dehydrated by purgings and the blisters that were being applied.

The day after Byron's death an autopsy was carried out by Dr Bruno and Dr Millingen in the presence of Dr Meyer, the editor of Stanhope's *Hellenica Chronica*. Millingen records how before beginning 'we could not refrain from pausing, in silent contemplation, on the lifeless clay of one, who, but a few days before, was the hope of a whole nation and the admiration of the civilised world'. They admired the 'perfect symmetry' of Byron's naked body.

'His physiognomy had suffered little alteration; and still preserved the sarcastic haughty expression, which habitually characterised it. The chest was broad, high vaulted, the waist very small, the pelvis rather narrow; the muscular system well pronounced; especially that of the superior extremities; the habit of the body plump.'

It was now in the excitement of the moment that the doctor lost his professional accuracy, describing Byron's 'only blemish' as a deformity of the left leg, not the right.

The autopsy revealed a cranium which showed all the signs of 'a man much advanced in age'. The appearance of the heart too was singular, of greater size than normal but flaccid: its flabbiness again reminded Millingen of someone who had died of old age. Byron's liver was 'beginning to undergo the alterations observed in persons who have indulged in the abuse of alcoholic liquors': it was smaller, harder in texture and lighter in colour than a healthy liver would have been.

In 1820 Claire Clairmont, in a mood of rage against Byron, had written in her journal a satiric account of an autopsy on him:

'Caricatures for Albé . . . The last his Death. He dead extended on his bed, covered all but his breast, which many wigged doctors are cutting open to find out (as one may be saying) what was the extraordinary disease of which this great man died – His heart laid bare, they find an immense capital I grown on its surface – and which had begun to pierce the breast – They are all astonishment. One says "A new disease." Another "I never had a case of this kind before." A third "What medicines would have been proper" the fourth holding up his finger "A desert island".'

Her macabre predictions had not been far wrong.

As to his last words, few of these were comprehensible since, as William Parry pointed out in his account of Byron's death, 'he was frequently delirious, for the last few days of his existence'. But from the jumbled sequence of laments and instructions, some in English, some in Italian, those around him in the sickroom understood Byron to mention specific names and sums of money. He was anxious about his servants. Byron promised William Fletcher, 'You will be provided for', and told him to bear a message to Ada, bitterly regretting he had not returned to England before he sailed to Greece. 'Oh, my poor dear child! my dear Ada! my God, could I but have seen her! Give her my blessing, and my dear Sister Augusta and her children; and you will go to Lady Byron, and say – Tell her everything – you are friends with her.' According to Fletcher Byron also mentioned Hobhouse and Kinnaird during those final days.

Pietro Gamba recollected him as saying, in Italian, 'There are things which make the world dear to me (*Io lascio qualche cosa di caro nel mondo*): for the rest, I am content to die.' Gamba construed this as a final message for his sister Teresa from her lover. It is evident that these witnesses extracted and repeated the sentiments they most wanted to hear. Fletcher's later report to Mary Shelley, that Byron had mentioned Claire Clairmont on his deathbed, struck even Claire as unconvincing. Byron was more likely referring to the Earl of Clare, his Harrow protégé.

We can, however, be certain that the Greek boy Lukas Chalandritsanos was much on Byron's mind. According to the accounts of his last rambling conversations he returned several times to his intentions for his page. Besides the money to which Lukas was suspected of having helped himself, Byron left him a more official legacy, attempting to arrange that the debt of 2,600 Spanish dollars owed to Byron by the city of Missolonghi should be repaid to Lukas for the benefit of his family. It seems it never was.

Byron's agony for Greece was another constant theme. 'Poor Greece, poor people, my poor family,' Gamba recorded him as saying. 'I have given her my time, my money, and my health; what could I do more? Now I give her my life.' The one statement of Byron's on which all accounts agree are his exhausted words on the evening before his death on 19 April 1824: 'I must sleep now.'

If Byron had not died, what future could there have been for him? One of the more intriguing of his plans was that, if Greece achieved its independence, he might become a kind of roving ambassador, travelling on Greece's behalf to, say, America. As an alternative he contemplated settling down in a free Greece, perhaps in Attica with all its enticing memories of Byron's youth. But it is difficult to see him resigning himself to happy indolence, just as it takes a stretch of the imagination to envisage him in any of the official roles later filled by his contemporaries. Byron as eminent Victorian minister in the Melbourne and Russell governments like John Cam Hobhouse, later to be elevated to Baron Broughton de Gyfford? Byron as future Governor of Bombay, like the Earl of Clare? His sense of the ridiculous would surely have triumphed. Nor did he have the staying power. Ultimately George Finlay was right in his judgement that 'the Genius of Lord Byron would in all probability never have unfolded either political or military talent. He was not disposed to assume an active part in public affairs.'

We can certainly regret the loss of *Don Juan* of which Byron was still promising a further hundred cantos. But Lord Byron old, rheumatic, hair thinning, maybe toothless? He had lived exhaustively. Perhaps he died at the right time.

Five or six days after Byron's death a tall bedraggled figure came wading through the streets of Missolonghi, buffeted by wind and water, to Byron's former house. It was of course Trelawny, hero-worshipper and tale-bearer. He had been crossing the mountain passes on his way to Missolonghi from the congress at Salona, having heard of Byron's illness, when a messenger intercepted him with the shocking news that Byron was already dead. He hurried on and was in time to view another great Romantic corpse, which he described with the same aplomb with which he had recorded Shelley's cremation at Viareggio.

'For three months this house had been besieged, day and night, like a bank that has a run upon it. Now that death had closed the door, it was as silent as a cemetery. No one was within the house but Fletcher, of which I was glad. As if he knew my wishes, he led me up a narrow stair into a small room, with nothing in it but a coffin standing on trestles. No word was spoken by either of us; he withdrew the black pall and the white shroud, and there lay the embalmed body of the Pilgrim – more beautiful in death than in life.'

521

From now on Byron's reputation was to burgeon in new ways, with the surges of regret, the accretions of sanctity that follow unexpectedly early deaths. Indeed it soon seemed that Byron had been younger than a man who was, after all, approaching middle age. Over the next centuries his peculiar appeal was to be double-edged – a matter both of the words he wrote, his marvellous, challenging, insinuating poetry, and of the person he had been.

THE BYRON CULT

28

The Return of the Remains

Byron's arrival in Greece had been described as electric by Prince Mavrocordatos. This was also the image invoked by George Finlay in response to his death: 'Wherever the English Language was known, an electric shock was felt.' Striking was not just the extent but the intensity of grief. People reacted with a personal sense of loss.

'Oh dolore! oh dolore! La maraviglia dell' Europa, il vanto della Gran Bretagna, l'Idolo de' suoi Amici, il Salvatore della Grecia – Lord Byron non è più.'

So his death was announced in the *Telegrafo Greco* in a lament probably composed by Pietro Gamba. The shock waves were felt first of all in multilingual Missolonghi where even the poorest of the citizens had been following the course of Byron's illness with anxiety, stopping Gamba and the servants in the streets with their enquiries, 'How is my Lord?' On the day of his death, Mavrocordatos issued a proclamation, a black-bordered notice distributed throughout the town cancelling the Easter Week celebrations, ordering the closure of shops and public offices and proclaiming a general mourning for twenty-one days with prayers for Lord Byron offered up in all the churches. The following morning, at daybreak, thirty-seven guns were fired from the Grand Battery of the fortress, one for every year of Byron's life. For the next two days, a profound silence descended on Missolonghi. Gamba remembered this quiet as 'like that of the grave'.

It had been intended to hold Byron's funeral on 21 April, but torrential rains put paid even to this. Instead the funeral took place on 22 April 1824, in the church of Ayios Nikolaos in Missolonghi where Markos Botsaris had been buried only a few months earlier. Byron's coffin was carried on the shoulders of the officers of the Byron Brigade, attended by Byron's own soldiers, the local Greek troops and crowds of mourners from the town. It was in some ways a rudimentary

Proclamation of Byron's death on 19 April 1824 (7 April according to the Greek calendar) printed in Missolonghi by order of Prince Mavrocordatos on behalf of the Provisional Government of Greece funeral. The coffin was a plain wooden one, roughly knocked together. A black cloak was used to make a pall; surmounting it was the helmet and sword Byron had intended to use for the siege of Lepanto with, finally, a crown of laurel similar to the one Byron had resisted on his bust by Bertel Thorwaldsen.

Its makeshift quality rendered the funeral more moving. Pietro Gamba was a witness that 'no funeral pomp could have left the impression, nor spoken the feelings of this simple ceremony. The wretchedness and desolation of the place itself; the wild and half civilised warriors around us; their deep-felt, unaffected grief; the fond recollections; the anxieties and sad presentiments which might be read on every countenance.' A solemn liturgy was chanted. A lengthy funeral oration was given by Spyridon Tricoupis, an ambitious Missolonghi-born Greek educated in Europe who had returned to his home town just in time to carry out this melancholy task. Tricoupis was to be a leading figure in the next phase of the Greek armed struggle.

Tricoupis's oration was probably responsible for one of the many misapprehensions associated with the Byron legend: that his heart was left in Missolonghi. Tricoupis declaimed, addressing Greece, 'Oh Daughter, most dearly beloved by him, your arms will receive him, your tears will bathe the tomb which contains his body, and the tears of the Orphans of Greece will be shed over the urn containing his precious heart.' This was followed by a misleading report in the *Telegrafo Greco* that Byron's heart had been left in the care of the city of Missolonghi. It is true that the coffin, over which Tricoupis spoke so dramatically, contained the earthenware urn within which was Byron's heart, removed with other organs at the autopsy two days before. The heart, described by Gamba as 'the most precious portion of his honoured remains', had been a last-minute substitute for Byron's corpse after the fear was raised that the uneven pavements in Missolonghi might have caused the coffin to be accidentally dropped. The bier containing the heart remained in the middle of the church overnight, guarded by a detachment of soldiers from Byron's brigade. Heart and corpse were reunited when, in the evening of 23 April, the bier was carried back by Byron's officers to his residence. The Greeks would certainly have liked to be left with Byron's heart: indeed they put in a claim for his whole body to be buried in Missolonghi or in the Temple of Theseus in Athens. But in the end the heart went back to England and all that was deposited in the church of San Spiridon in Missolonghi, from where it was soon stolen, was the urn containing Byron's lungs and larynx. In the words of Petros Kapsalis, brother of Apostolis Kapsalis in whose house Byron had lodged, 'we wished to have his lungs and larynx because he had used his breath and voice for Greece.'

Byron as usual left mixed messages regarding his wishes for his ultimate destination. The day before he died he had apparently told Millingen: 'One request let me make to you. Let not my body be hacked, or be sent to England. Here let my bones moulder – Lay me in the first corner without pomp or nonsense.' The first part of this request, on the hacking of the body, had already been conspicuously disregarded. Byron had, however, also said to William Parry, when the fire-master asked him what should be done about disposal of the body should Byron 'kick the bucket' while he was in Greece, 'Do you see that my body is sent to England.' The connection with his ancestry lingered in his mind.

The idea that Byron's body should be returned to England was supported by Gamba on emotional grounds: 'the most becoming course was to convey him to his native country.' Stanhope, originally in favour of pleasing the Greeks by depositing Byron's ashes in Athens, was soon to change his mind, seeing the propaganda advantages of a full-blown public burial for Byron in London. Edward Blaquière, the London Greek Committee's agent, had coincidentally sailed into Zante from England only a few days after Byron's death. With him aboard the *Florida* was the first instalment of the Greek loan. The sensational news was announced by the Zante harbourmaster who had sailed out to greet the incoming English ship. Blaquière, shocked and alarmed by an event which had never entered into the London Greek Committee's calculations, was strongly in favour of bringing Byron's body home.

But there was a contrary view amongst the British in the Ionian Isles. Byron's remains attracted as much controversy as his living persona had done. The occupying British officials were nervous of appearing to sanction a hero's return for the peer whose intervention in the Greek war had been contrary to British foreign policy. There were arguments for keeping Byron's body in Greece. Lord Sydney Osborne came over from Corfu to discuss the situation urgently with Blaquière, who reported back to London: 'Lord S. O. is of opinion that the body ought to be burned in Zante!!!!!!' To Hobhouse, Blaquière complained: 'there is great mystery observed by those who wish to detain the body here, it will I fear be some days before anything positive is known on the subject.' Eventually, after delicate negotiations in which Samuel Barff the banker was involved as chief 'go-between fixer', it was arranged that Byron's body should be returned to England in the *Florida*, the ship that had just delivered the Greek loan.

After the funeral Byron's embalmed corpse lay in its coffin in his former house, where Trelawny had visited it and where Pietro took a last look at the man he had revered as his heroic elder brother, recording with his sweet naivety that 'the expression, at least to my eyes, was truly sublime'. On 2 May the Ionian boats reluctantly provided by Sir Frederick Stoven, British Resident at Zante, arrived in Missolonghi. To preserve Byron's body for the voyage, holes had been bored through the layers of wood and tin and the coffin set in a large outer cask containing 180 gallons of spirits. Four officers of Byron's artillery corps carried the load to the boat which was to take it to the small harbour of Vasiladi where a larger vessel would take it on to Zante. The whole of the Byron Brigade was drawn up outside the house, stretching along the seashore. Once the corpse of their dead leader and paymaster was in place in the bark there were discharges of musketry and artillery. The Byron Brigade cannon, installed beside the coast, provided a mourning salute of twenty-five guns, one fired every minute; nine more were discharged from the Missolonghi battery and three from the fortress of Vasiladi: once again making the total of the mystic thirty-seven, sum of Byron's years on earth.

Byron's sailing was witnessed by Prince Mavrocordatos in company with local political and military leaders. The crowds who had grieved in the streets at Byron's funeral had reassembled by the shore; the *Telegrafo Greco* reported 'an immense concourse of people, whose countenances and manner bore testimony to their sorrow at taking this last farewell of their benefactor and fellow citizen'. The mass of post-funeral bills and correspondence now in the Byron archives in England and in Greece, much of it directed to the helpless Pietro, provides evidence of general dismay at the financial and political uncertainties unleashed by Byron's death.

This was to be another stormy crossing. At one point the bark was forced to anchor for the night near the same rocky cove where, on the outward journey, Byron had taken refuge from the Turkish frigate and had felt such anxiety for Lukas Chalandritsanos. The body and its attendants finally reached Zante on 4 May. Here Leicester Stanhope met them and, after the statutory period of quarantine, Byron's coffin was reloaded on to the *Florida* and the ship set sail for England on 25 May 1824. Colonel Stanhope took charge of the ship described by Blaquière, a satisfied customer on its outward journey, as 'a remarkably fine vessel' which 'sails like the winds'.

The *Florida* carried a strangely assorted cargo, as itemised by Gamba. As well as the coffin there was the trunk containing the four urns with the heart, brain and part of the intestines of Lord Byron. There were two trunks of books, two trunks of weapons, Byron's bed and campaign bed, five trunks of clothes and a canteen of champagne. There were sealed packages of correspondence, some political, some private, and a total of 7,000 Spanish dollars, the remains of Byron's widely distributed largesse. Five members of Byron's personal staff were on the *Florida*: Fletcher, Lega Zambelli the steward, Dr Bruno, Tita Falcieri and the Negro groom Benjamin Lewis. Their bewilderment was patent. Both Fletcher and Falcieri, on different occasions, compared their grief at Byron's death to the loss of a father. Only Fletcher, of the five of them, had ever been to England and he had been away since 1816. On the voyage Francesco Bruno was seen trying to learn English from a *Johnson's Dictionary*.

Pietro did not accompany the body back to England. He had intended to, but once he got to Zante he was overcome by the sense of his own invidious position as the brother of Byron's late mistress. He explained to Hobhouse that 'many reasons' prevented him from escorting the body in person: 'if you can not guess them, Fletcher and the Colonel will explain them.' Gamba made his own way to England on a different ship, sailing from Zante to Liverpool then travelling overland to London, a city where he too would be a stranger. He had not had the courage to break the news of Byron's death directly to Teresa but sent it in a letter to their father. It appears she took it bravely: perhaps she was not totally surprised.

What would have happened if Byron had survived to receive Blaquière and administer the loan? In Gamba's loyally optimistic view the boost to his authority given by the loan would have allowed Byron to fix the independence of Greece on solid foundations. 'The organisation, of which he had already formed a sort of nucleus, would have spread itself into all quarters of the confederacy.' With the input of the new funds, Lepanto and Negroponte (now Euboea) could have been taken and Greece could have moved into the offensive on land as well as sea. Whether this could really have come about, given the entrenched political and tribal rivalries in Greece, rivalries of which Byron himself was acutely aware, seems highly questionable. In the year of Byron's death almost the whole of free Greece had entered a state of civil war.

Byron's posthumous impact is more certain. Soon after he had joined the London Greek Committee, John Bowring had written to him: 'You would be a Star to guide & to gladden Greece & England alike.' Byron's image became very much more starry in death than it had been in life. The self-sacrificing death of the poet was to have a profound effect on the European imagination, focusing attention on the cause that he had died for. Byron's death helped define Greece as a country with its own recognisable character and political validity. For the rest of Europe, Byron brought Greece closer to home. If he had not died it is unlikely that Delacroix would have painted *Greece on the Ruins of Missolonghi*. Some foreign volunteers for the Greek war turned back when they heard of Byron's death in 1824, but many more set out.

*

The news of the death of 'the most remarkable Englishman of his generation', as *The Times* described him, did not reach England until over three weeks after it occurred. The despatches from Corfu, sent express via Ancona, reached London on the night of 13 May 1824. Reactions in England, as in Missolonghi, were of a peculiarly personal devastation: the news 'falls on the public ear like a shock of deep private misfortune', according to one contemporary press report. Lord John Manners, a child at the time, remembered the effect of the announcement on a ceremonial dinner being given at Belvoir Castle to the gentlemen of the Belvoir Hunt. A letter was handed to the host, the Duke of Rutland, who rose and announced: 'Gentlemen, grave news has just been brought to me. Lord Byron has died in Greece.' There was stunned silence, after which the hunting squires, recovering themselves, began exchanging their favourite passages from Byron's poetry.

If the loss of Byron affected so dramatically those who hardly knew him, how much worse it was to bear for the protective inner circle of his English friends. Since no will had been found superseding the one Byron had made at the time of his marriage in 1815, John Cam Hobhouse and John Hanson were now his official executors. The despatches reached Douglas Kinnaird first at his office and he sent them on to Hobhouse with a scribbled letter, saying: 'I can scarcely write to you, yet delay is absurd & I know not how to soften what your own fortitude alone can make you bear like a man – Byron is no more – I send herewith three letters for you. Pray come here as soon as you can.' The usually impervious Kinnaird told Hobhouse he had taken medicine and could not himself stir out. He also warned Hobhouse to destroy no letters until they had had a chance for discussion. The process of whitewashing Byron's posthumous reputation was already under way.

Hobhouse was in bed in his rooms in Albany when the package of letters was brought to him at eight in the morning on 14 May. He was woken by the messenger's loud tapping at his door. On reading Kinnaird's note he was seized with an agony of grief only comparable with that he had felt on hearing the news of the death of his Cambridge friend Charles Skinner Matthews and of his own brother on the field of Waterloo. The package contained letters to Hobhouse from Lord Sydney Osborne and from Pietro Gamba, and a letter from the valet William Fletcher to Augusta Leigh: 'Madam, I am sorry to be under the painful obligation of writing you the most disagreeable *letter*, that I *ever* to this *unfortunate moment* had ever to *write*, not only for *me* or *you*, but for all the World in general.' Fletcher's painstaking account bears a remarkable resemblance to the spoof letter written by Byron in Venice purporting to be Fletcher announcing his master's death.

Sir Francis Burdett undertook the unenviable task of breaking the news to Augusta. Hobhouse went to see her later in the day, finding her in a dreadful 'afflicting condition'. She handed him Fletcher's letter. He confessed in his diary: 'The reading this letter tore my heart to pieces – It showed the boundless & tender attachment of all about him to my dear dear friend!' He could not help bursting out in 'uncontrollable lamentation', but recovered himself enough to warn Augusta that she must be discreet about one passage in the letter in which Fletcher maintains that after Byron's fit on 15 February he asked for his Bible, the Bible that had been given him by Augusta, to be placed every morning on his breakfast table. Hobhouse explained: 'This circumstance which pleased his valet Fletcher I was afraid might be mistaken for cowardice or hypocrisy – and I was anxious that no idle stories to his discredit should get abroad.'

It was arranged that the former Captain George Byron, now the 7th Lord Byron, should travel down that same evening to Beckenham in Kent to break the news to Lady Byron; she took it badly, saying bitterly 'she had no right to be considered by Lord Byron's friends – but she had her feelings.' Hobhouse and Kinnaird spent a night of desolate nostalgia 'recalling to mind the various excellencies of our dear friend'. Two days later, in response to the *Times* obituary, Hobhouse in his diary, in the retrospect of grief, brings us as close as we can get to the reasons why Byron's friends forgave him for so much:

'The Times of yesterday announced his death in a manner which is I think a fair sample of the general opinion in this event – the writer is however mistaken in saying that others may have been *more tenderly beloved than Lord Byron* – for no man lived who had such devoted friends his power of attaching those about him was such as no one I ever knew possessed – no human being could approach him without being sensible of this magical influence – there was something commanding but not overawing in his manner – He was neither grave nor gay out of place and he seemed always made for that company in which he found himself – there was a mildness and yet a decision in his mode of conversing which are seldom united in the same person – He appeared exceedingly free open and unreserved with every body – yet he continued at all times to retain just as much self restraint as to preserve the respect of even his most intimate friends.'

Part of Byron's magic lay in his detachment, the powerful sense of mysteries undisclosed. Years later Hobhouse could recollect exactly his distinct sardonic laugh.

The *Florida* with 'the Remains', as Augusta always called them, reached the

Downs in the Thames estuary on 29 June 1824, a fortnight earlier than Hobhouse had expected. On 1 July, as soon as Hobhouse heard of the arrival, he took a post-chaise down to Rochester, stayed the night at the Crown Hotel and set off early in the morning to Standgate Creek, about fifteen miles away, where the *Florida* was anchored. He was greeted by Colonel Stanhope who was still on board with Fletcher, Dr Bruno, who had ready his sad defensive narrative of Byron's final illness, Tita, Lega Zambelli and Benjamin the groom. Fletcher sobbed to see him. Hobhouse recorded in his diary: 'Three dogs belonging to Lord Byron were playing about – I could not bring myself to look at them.' One of these dogs was Lyon, another was the bulldog Moretto. 'The remains were below – I could not bring myself to see where they were placed.'

Hobhouse remained on the *Florida* while it sailed up river for five or six hours towards Gravesend. He could not help remembering that he was the last person to shake Byron's hand when he left England from Dover in 1816: 'I recollect him waving his cap as the packet bounded off on a swelling sea from the pier head – and here I was coming back to England with him.' At about five in the evening the *Florida* reached Gravesend. Hobhouse disembarked with Stanhope and they took the Rochester coach back to London, Stanhope giving him 'some most interesting particulars of the struggle in Greece'. Hobhouse was in bed early, feeling unwell.

On 5 July Hobhouse returned to the *Florida*, now in London Dock. On board he met the undertaker Woodeson. He and his men were occupied with the task of emptying the spirit out of the large cask in which Byron's coffin had been transported. The rough-hewn Missolonghi coffin was broken open and the body transferred to a new lead coffin. Seeing them break open the coffin, Hobhouse had to retreat to the ship's cabin: the whole operation had reduced him to a state of feeling 'like a person intoxicated or in a state of feverish excitement without the power to think distinctly – and still preserving a sort of capacity for action which sometimes belongs to that condition of mind'. He started to look through the papers that had arrived sealed from Cephalonia, satisfying himself that there was no sign of a new will. Once the remains were transferred, Hobhouse kept a piece of the cotton shroud that had been around the body, but he could not view the corpse. 'I believe I should have dropt down dead if I had ventured to look at it,' he wrote. Later he came back on deck and leant against the coffin which was now covered with its lid and the ship's flag. Byron's large Newfoundland Lyon settled at his feet.

Stanhope had envisaged a triumphant public burial for Byron in Westminster Abbey or St Paul's Cathedral. He wanted Byron's executors to arrange 'that the state Barges be sent down to receive the corpse' bearing the principal mourners and bands for the performance of sacred music. Stanhope saw in his imagination that 'Britons who cherish genius and who love liberty will I doubt not crowd to the banks of the Thames'. At the beginning of July, *The Times* and other London newspapers announced that Lord Byron's remains would be deposited in Poets' Corner in the Abbey. This was not to happen. Although the general tone of the newspaper announcements of his death had been guardedly forgiving, acrimony and suspicion still lingered, *John Bull* for example reminding its readers that Lord Byron had 'quitted the world at the most unfortunate period of his career, and in the most unsatisfactory manner – in voluntary exile, where his mind, debased by evil associations, and the malignant brooding over imaginary ills, has been devoted to the construction of elaborate lampoons'.

The large question mark remaining over Byron's morality prompted Dr Ireland, Dean of Westminster, to reject the proposal of the executors, conveyed to him by the ever-energetic John Murray, for an Abbey burial for Byron. He regretted the newspapers' premature announcement and advised Hobhouse that the best thing to be done by the executors and relations was 'to carry away the body, & say as little about it as possible'. The executors had no alternative but to settle for interment in the family vault at Hucknall Torkard.

The coffin was transported up the Thames in the undertaker's barge late in the afternoon of 5 July. Byron's return was already attracting enormous curiosity and the river banks were crowded with spectators. The body was landed at Palace Yard steps in Westminster and for the next week it lay on view at 20 Great George Street, Sir Edward Knatchbull's house, which Hobhouse, as executor, had hired for the purpose. The room in which the coffin lay was hung with black, with the Byron coat of arms roughly daubed on a deal board. The following day, 6 July, with Kinnaird and Hanson, Hobhouse braced himself to view the corpse: 'Kinnaird went into the room to look at him – I followed – & drawn by an irresistible inclination – though I expected to be overcome by it – approached the coffin – I drew nearer by degrees – till I caught a view of the face.'

To Hobhouse's dismay the corpse of Byron did not bear the slightest resemblance to his friend: 'The mouth was distorted & half open – showing those teeth in which poor fellow he once so prided himself – quite discoloured by the spirits – his upper lip was shaded with red moustachios which gave a totally new colour to his face.' John Hanson too claimed he would not have recognised him had it not been for Byron's distinctive ears, the small lobeless ears once admired by Ali Pasha, and his deformed foot. Thomas Phillips' request to make a final sketch of Byron was deflected by Hobhouse, so great was the change from the resplendent nobleman in Albanian dress.

For two days, 10 and 11 July, the public was admitted by ticket to Byron's lying-in-state. In contrast to the mood of official disapproval there were displays of near-hysterical emotion among the large crowds which gathered. The scene in Westminster became almost one of riot: according to the *Sunday Monitor*, 'the uproar and confusion that prevailed beggar description.' London police sergeants were called in and a wooden frame had to be erected around the coffin to keep the spectators at bay. It was reported that 'Of the crowding visitors the number of ladies was exceedingly great.'

According to Hobhouse, of the numerous applicants for tickets of admission were 'very few persons of any name or note'. On 12 July, when the body set out on its final journey from Westminster to Hucknall Torkard, a similar contrast prevailed. There was 'a vast concourse' of people in the streets. But of the forty-seven empty mourning carriages sent by their owners to follow Byron's hearse in the first stage of the funeral procession, according to the conventions of the day, the vast majority were those of people from the pro-Greek Radical and Radical Whig opposition parties. Of the very few conservatives who sent their carriages the Earl of Carlisle and Lord Morpeth were family connections and Lord Aberdeen a Philhellene and Old Harrovian. There were still many circles in which even the dead Byron was unacceptable.

The funeral procession left Westminster at eleven o'clock on a fine summer day. Hobhouse and John Hanson, George Leigh and Captain Richard Byron were in the first coach. Augusta did not attend, although she had viewed the body. The new Lord Byron was absent, claiming to be ill. In the second coach was Kinnaird, with Edward Ellice and Henry Trevanion, both family connections. The literary trio of Moore, Rogers and Campbell shared the third coach with Colonel Stanhope and the Greek deputy Ioannis Orlandos. As it travelled through London the procession was seen by a multitude of people crowded into the streets and craning out of windows. Tom Moore noted rather disapprovingly that there were 'few respectable persons' among them. How were these ordinary people mourning Byron? As the hero of Greece? The author of *Don Juan*? Or as some less clearly defined celebrity whose life, impinging on their own lives, had given it more meaning? In mourning Byron surely people were regretting the loss of a fearless and a sympathetic voice.

One of the people in the crowd who caught a glimpse of Byron passing through Oxford Street was the ruralist poet John Clare, on a rare visit to London. Byron's near contemporary, though from a very different milieu, he was already a passionate admirer. A young girl standing beside him in the crowd 'gave a deep sigh and utterd poor Lord Byron'. Clare's later account invests the episode with an incandescent significance:

'I lookd up in the young girls face it was dark and beautiful and I coud almost feel in love with her for the sigh she had utterd for the poet . . . the Reverend the Moral and fastidious may say what they please about Lord Byrons fame and damn it as they list – he has gaind the path of its eterni[t]y without them and lives above the blight of their mildewing censure to do him damage – the common people felt his merits and his power and the common people of a country are the best feelings of a prophecy of futurity.'

Another writer and traveller, the twenty-one-year-old George Borrow, saw the procession in Tottenham Court Road. He used the strange spectacle of Byron's funeral in his gypsy novel *Lavengro*.

At the point where the London cobblestones finished, near St Pancras Church, the mourning carriages turned back. A cortège now reduced to the hearse and its accompanying undertakers went on north. As it passed through Kentish Town, Mary Shelley watched from her window with Jane Williams as the last remains of Albe went by. Mary had already been to see his corpse laid out in Westminster. 'You will not wonder', she wrote to Trelawny, 'that the late loss of L[ord] B[yron] makes me cling with greater zeal [to] those dear friends who remain to me.'

In the Hertfordshire country beyond London the cortège passed close to the Melbourne estates of Brocket Hall. Caroline Lamb gave a dramatic account to Thomas Medwin of how, on her first outing after a long illness, she was driving up the hill in her open carriage as the hearse was approaching the gates to the estate. William Lamb, riding on ahead, met the cortège at the turnpike and asked innocently whose funeral it was. It could have been a scene from *Glenarvon*. The next day, ill and distraught, Lady Caroline wrote to her old confidant John Murray: 'Lord Byron's death has made an impression on me which I cannot express. I am very sorry I ever said one unkind word against him.' She was in a panic on the subject of her letters: 'only you know that they were the most imprudent possible, & for other's sakes it were best to have them destroyed.' But Murray hoarded them.

The cortège took three days to reach Nottingham, stopping at Welwyn, Higham Ferrers and Oakham. All along the route the interest and curiosity remained phenomenal. Hobhouse organised another lying-in-state for Byron at the Blackmoor's Head Inn in Pelham Street in Nottingham. Here another immense crowd, barely controlled by 'a very large body' of Nottingham constabulary, pressed into the room to view the remains of their controversial local lord. Black-edged placards were on display throughout the town inviting people to attend the funeral of the '*great & distinguished nobleman and*

Patriot'. These notices made clear that mourners joining the procession need not feel compelled to wear full mourning dress 'as the mourning consisted more in a feeling of the heart than in external appearances'. The further Byron's body travelled from London the less was the weight of official opprobrium.

Byron's funeral procession formed up again next morning, Friday 16 July. In the first coach were Hobhouse, John Hanson, George Leigh, once again representing Augusta, and Colonel Wildman, whose purchase of Newstead had earned him a prominent position as mourner. Byron's ponderously faithful clergyman friend Francis Hodgson, the translator of Juvenal, had also now arrived. The hearse, with its twelve large sable plumes, was drawn by six black horses. Byron's coffin was preceded by his coronet, carried on its gold tasselled cushion by a rider on an ornately caparisoned state horse.

The procession took a long slow route through the then picturesque Nottinghamshire villages, passing Papplewick and Linby, gathering up additional mourners as it went. It was now in Byron country, skirting Newstead, nearing the hill of Annesley which, as Colonel Wildman unctuously reminded Hobhouse, had been immortalised by Byron in 'The Dream'. After five hours on the road the procession arrived at the church at Hucknall Torkard. The little church and churchyard were so thick with people the chief mourners had trouble pushing their way through in order to follow the coffin up the aisle. Hobhouse saw 'something striking in the contrast between the gorgeous approach of the Coffin & urn & the Coronet and the appearance of this humble church'. The coffin remained in the aisle for the first part of the service then was lowered into the vault of Byron's ancestors. Hobhouse had wanted Byron's coffin to be placed on that of his mother but this proved impractical since Mrs Byron's coffin was already so decayed. So Byron's coffin was balanced on top of the coffin containing the 'Wicked' 5th Lord.

As *The Times* reported, there were few important people present, no great poets or great statesmen. But there was an 'unaffected and overpowering display of feelings' from the ordinary people who attended Byron's funeral. Amongst them was his bewildered personal entourage. The 'poor black servant', presumably Benjamin Lewis, never took his eyes off the coffin as it was lowered into the vault. The Italian servant, Tita, 'seemed as if he were a stranger and friendless'. Fletcher, who had been with Byron for so long, had to withdraw from the front ranks of the chief mourners, with whom in the commotion the servants were intermingled, to support himself against a pew in a paralysis of grief.

A few months later Pietro Gamba paid what must have been a desolating visit to the church at Hucknall. His comment that it reminded him of

Missolonghi earned the sharp rejoinder from Hobhouse: 'not the slightest.' But in the sense that Byron was once again among a people who loved him with primitive directness Gamba was quite right.

Long before Byron's body was returned for burial the battle for possession of his memory was under way. In the same diary entry for 14 May 1824 in which Hobhouse recorded his dismay at the news of Byron's death he announces his intentions as keeper of the flame: 'after the first access of grief was over I then determined to lose no time in doing my duty by preserving all that was left to me of my dear friend – his fame – my thoughts were turned to the Memoirs of his life given to Thomas Moore & deposited by him in Mr Murray's hands for certain considerations.'

The same thought had occurred to Tom Moore on the same day. He had called at Colburn's Library to be told by the shopman that Lord Byron was dead. 'Recollected then', Moore wrote in his own journal, 'the unfinished state in which my agreement for the redemption of the "Memoirs" lay.' Since he had sold Byron's memoirs to John Murray for 2,000 guineas in 1821 Moore had had second thoughts about the wisdom of this transaction and had renegotiated the contract in the form of a redeemable loan. He was in the process of trying to raise the money to extract the manuscript from John Murray when Byron died.

Hobhouse now became obsessed with the idea that Byron's memoirs had to be destroyed. His friends rallied round and offered to buy them back from Murray, Kinnaird and Burdett each offering to repay the £2,000 while Hobhouse thought he could find £1,000 himself. Why was Hobhouse, who had never read the memoirs, so desperate to put them out of circulation? No doubt he was nervous about their sexual content. He was aware, both from Moore and from the rumours circulating amongst those who had already read the manuscript, that the second part contained accounts of Byron's erotic adventures with a multiplicity of women in Italy.

Did it include references more potentially dangerous? Hobhouse's caution arose from his long habit of policing Byron's references to unorthodox loves. This went back to his destruction of Byron's early journal, covering the Cambridge years, when they were in Albania. He suspected that his friend's predilection for mischievously veiled comments might have escaped the notice of Tom Moore. He was conscious that any posthumous recurrence of the scandals relating to sodomy and incest, rife at the time of the separation crisis, could devolve on the now reputable public figure of John Cam Hobhouse, MP for Westminster, well known to have been Byron's friend. But perhaps the strongest motive was the simple one of jealousy: a desire that the image of

Byron descending to posterity should be filtered not through Moore but by Hobhouse himself.

On 17 May 1824, after three days of agonised discussions, Byron's memoirs were burnt in the grate of John Murray's Albemarle Street drawing room, in the most famous sacrificial scene of literary history. Of the six men assembled in the room – Moore and his supporter the sociable Irish poet Henry Luttrell, Hobhouse, John Murray, Augusta Leigh's ally Wilmot Horton and Lady Byron's representative Colonel Doyle – only Moore and Luttrell had actually read the memoirs, if Murray had indeed resisted the temptation to do so in the years that the manuscript had lain in his possession. Moore was there under protest. He and Henry Luttrell had pressed the case for 'the injustice we thought it would be to Byron's memory to condemn the work wholly, and without even opening it, as if it were a pest bag'. Moore pleaded that at least the manuscript should be carefully perused and if necessary censored but that 'what was innoxious and creditable to Lord Byron' should be preserved.

Moore was argued down by Hobhouse, who urged respect for the feelings of Augusta Leigh whose fears he had aroused over the contents of the memoirs and whose anxiety for their destruction he now claimed. John Murray had also come out strongly for the burning on grounds of preservation of 'Lord Byron's honor & fame': any prospect of short-term advantage from the publication of so hot a property was outweighed by ancient loyalties to his deceased author and care for his company's future reputation. Doyle and Horton, from Augusta and Lady Byron's camp, welcomed the destruction of memoirs which purportedly told the story of the separation from Byron's own perspective, and were unlikely to portray Lady Byron in a favourable light. Once the memoirs had gone up in flames, together with a copy Moore had earlier had made of them, a laugh of nervous relief went round the room. It was Moore who repaid Murray the two thousand guineas, pulling the money out of his pocket and putting it down on the table. Hobhouse had decided not to deny him this final sacrifice.

An additional witness to the burning, brought in at the last minute to view the historic event, was John Murray's sixteen-year-old son, who eventually succeeded his father as John Murray III. In 1864 this same John issued a warning to the Comtesse d'Haussonville, Madame de Staël's granddaughter, in sending her what was probably a copy of a manuscript notebook containing Byron's journals: 'There are certain passages in Byron's Paper Book which neither Moore nor my Father would allow to be published for Byron's Sake. These ought not to see the light of day even now.' The Comtesse d'Haussonville's innocuous *La Jeunesse de Lord Byron* was published in Paris eight years later. In 1892 John Murray III gave instructions for the burning of some manuscript sheets of poetry he had recently acquired from a London dealer, Frank T. Sabin of Garrick Street. Amongst the poems, written out in Augusta Leigh's script, was 'The Fallen One', singled out by Sabin as 'a very remarkable production and one that ought not to be published'. Murray noted that he had gladly paid the £50 that Sabin asked to save these poems from publication. The family tendency for protective destructiveness died hard.

What did posterity lose with the destruction of the memoirs? Over the years at least twenty people had read them – Moore had taken at face value Byron's permission to distribute them among '*the Elect*'. The memoirs had been shown to, among others, Lady Jersey, Lady Davy, Lady Burghersh, Lord and Lady Holland, Douglas Kinnaird and his brother Lord Kinnaird. Lady Caroline Lamb appears to have extracted a copy from an indulgent John Murray. Extracts had been made and copies of the memoirs had been taken by both amateur and professional copyists.

A minority of readers expressed themselves outraged. William Gifford, who had read the memoirs at Murray's request, reported that 'the whole Memoirs were fit only for a brothel and would damn Lord B to certain infamy if published'. Lord John Russell found three or four pages 'too gross and indelicate for publication'. But the consensus of opinion was that Byron's memoirs were a bit of a damp squib. Two weeks after the destruction Mary Shelley wrote to Trelawny: 'There was not much in them I know, for I read them some years ago at Venice, but the world fancied that it was to have a confession of the hidden feelings of one, concerning whom they are always passionately anxious.' By this time the wild rumours were escalating. One was that conspirators had broken by force into Tom Moore's lodgings and carried off the manuscript; another that Hobhouse had forcibly held Moore down while the memoirs were being burned.

What of Leicester Stanhope's relieved comment that the burning of the memoirs had 'saved the country from pollution'? It was Stanhope who had been spreading innuendoes about Byron's behaviour over Lukas in Greece. The comments of those who read the memoirs do not lead one to suppose that the memoirs were explicit about homosexual sex. Byron himself, after all, maintained regretfully that he had left out all his loves 'except in a general way'. If Hobhouse could have brought himself to borrow the manuscript from Moore and read it he might not have acted with such an excess of zeal.

In the course of the wranglings over the memoirs Moore had proposed himself as author of any forthcoming biography of Byron. This was of course what Byron had originally promised him. He now demanded the commission as a kind of consolation prize following the destruction of the manuscript, expecting the gratified co-operation of Byron's family and friends. Though Kinnaird was sympathetic, Hobhouse was further outraged, exploding in his journal: 'Here was a specimen of a poet's friendship!! it was like Rousseau consoling Claude Anet's loss by thinking he should get his old coat.'

It took almost another four years, until February 1828, for Moore to reach an agreement with John Murray for the life of Byron. In the intervening period Moore had taken the biography to Longmans, had been reconciled with Murray and then rowed with him again, and endured further determined obstructiveness from Hobhouse who failed to see the need for a biography of Byron and certainly not one written by Tom Moore. Between 1824 and 1828 a mass of biographical material relating to Byron, some flimsy, some important, had appeared, beginning with Sir Cosmo Gordon's rapid potboiler *The Life and Genius of Lord Byron*, published only a few weeks after the news of Byron's death reached England. Byron's early enthusiast Robert Charles Dallas had hurriedly assembled a volume of his private correspondence, against which Hobhouse issued an injunction. Thomas Medwin had produced his *Journal of the Conversations of Lord Byron at Pisa*, much resented by those who felt that they knew Byron better than Medwin did. The flow appeared unstoppable. Stanhope, Gamba, Parry and even Edward Blaquière published their reminiscences of Byron in Greece.

It was yet another memoir, Leigh Hunt's ill-natured though astute *Lord Byron and Some of his Contemporaries*, that finally acted in Moore's favour. After this was published in 1828 Murray, realising that only Moore would be able to supply the necessary counterweight, wrote to him again to reopen the discussion. 'The late infamous book of Leigh Hunt has induced him to change his mind with respect to the publication of Lord Bs papers': there is a note of triumph in Moore's journal entry. For the second time he managed to withdraw from Longmans. His plans for the Murray biography were now resumed.

In preparing his life of Byron, Thomas Moore went through the processes most modern biographers would recognise. He travelled conscientiously around the sites: to Newstead, to Southwell, to Byron's house at Harrow, a visit recorded in his journal rather gloomily: 'doomed to the cold repast at Drurys, surrounded with chicken tongues & ugly women'. Being Byron's biographer was at times no sinecure.

He interviewed the people who had once known Byron well, making notes of the ground he hoped they might cover. He had breakfast with the now aged Lord and Lady Holland: 'Lord H. wheeled in in his gouty chair, but with his face as gay and shining as that of a school-boy'. He took a walk with Lady Jersey through the grounds of Middleton Hall, carefully steering clear of politics, after which she handed over two letters from Lord Byron. In his journal Moore registers his pleasure at receiving promises of co-operation: for example, the news from Teresa Guiccioli that she has sent him the first part of the 'Storia' of her connection with Byron with the promise of a second instalment to follow; the banker Charles Hancock's agreement to supply all he can from Cephalonia. Mary Shelley was one of Tom Moore's most productive contacts: 'Went to Kentish Town', he writes, 'to breakfast with Mrs S. Mrs S. disposed to give me every assistance in my life of Byron.' He had the impression she had known Byron thoroughly. She gave him a valuably frank account, concluding her catalogue of his bad traits with the proviso, 'but still he was very nice'.

But Thomas Moore's successes in pursuing Byron were balanced by disappointments and frustrations: an absent Dr Glennie; a suspicious Francis Hodgson. The diminutive Moore's visit to the Duke of Devonshire, Byron's Harrow contemporary 'Hart', was sabotaged by 'his tallness and my deafness combined'. He could get nothing out of Rogers except self-centred gossip. Questioned about his master, William Fletcher subsided into gulping tears. An interview, once postponed then finally rearranged, with Mrs Musters, Byron's Mary Chaworth, proved a struggle: the biographer records, 'evening rather heavy', followed by an emotional conversation the next morning. Byron's past male intimates were particularly wary. Lord Delawarr 'had nothing to communicate'. The Earl of Clare 'had been so unlucky as to have destroyed all Byron's letters to him, except one or two of very little consequence'. William Bankes said, when Moore called on him, 'he had but few letters of Bs he thought free enough from personal matters to suit my purpose, but those that were fit to be published should be at my disposal'.

In gathering the materials for Byron's life, Moore was labouring under serious difficulties. Though he now had all the material that Murray could provide, Augusta Leigh would not co-operate; her dislike of Moore outdid even that of Hobhouse. Nor, unsurprisingly, would Lady Byron assist. Hobhouse himself was still behaving inconsistently, sometimes seeming to support the project then withdrawing his help. Moore had his own personal problems to contend with. While he was working on the biography his daughter Anastasia was dying, having become mysteriously lame in one leg, a coincidence Byron would have seized on as new proof of his malignant influence.

Considering the hazards, Moore's *Letters and Journals of Lord Byron with Notices of His Life*, published in 1830, is a remarkable production. Even Hobhouse when he read it was reluctantly impressed. Moore's *Life* gives a warm and sympathetic account of Byron the writer: this is a fellow poet's portrait. Another of his triumphs is to put Byron's opposition politics into convincing context, presenting Byron as the disappointed and disaffected child of the Revolution.

At moments Moore suggests he might be on the edge of a revealing assessment of the masculine-feminine in Byron, as when he mentions Byron's 'caprices, fits of weeping, sudden affections and dislikes' as examples of a feminine cast of character. But sensitive as Moore is to nuances of Byron's behaviour his biography is on the whole conventionally guarded. It does not – how could it at that period? – bring out Byron's mobile and mischievous personality, his tricks and stratagems, his fascinating sexual variousness. Moore defines as 'romantic friendships' the liaisons with Edleston and Giraud, the poor lad in the cottage, the younger Harrow boys. The origins of Byron's Thyrza poems are glossed over. Lukas Chalandritsanos is ignored, apart from Moore's delicate commendation of the poem 'On this day I complete my thirty sixth year' for 'the last tender aspirations of a loving spirit which they breathe'. Moore's concentration on Byron's heterosexual relationships, especially his mistresses in Venice, makes this an inevitably unbalanced book.

Moore's *Life* quickly became the standard work, starting point for the many future biographies of Byron and basis of the Byron legend as it entered mainstream British culture in the nineteenth and twentieth centuries. When Dennis Price plays the ladykiller Byron in the British film *The Bad Lord Byron* in 1948 it is still fundamentally Moore's Byron that we see.

29

The European Byronists

In 1826, two years after Byron's funeral, the Belgian artist Joseph-Denis von Odevaere painted the spectacular memorial canvas *The Death of Byron* now in the Museum Groeninge in Bruges. This haunting neo-classical composition shows the flawless corpse outstretched on the deathbed that bears a strong resemblance to an altar. Byron's head is crowned with laurel leaves; his lifeless fingers hover over the poet's broken lyre and abandoned scroll of parchment. The self-conscious public idol of Byron's early portraits has now become the martyr in the cause of liberty. Odevaere had worked in Paris in the studio of Jacques-Louis David; his painting of Byron on the bier brings clear reminders of David's *Death of Marat* and, by association, of Byron's own connection with revolutionary movements.

This idea of Byron's bodily sacrifice, his youth laid waste, recurs in the many popular prints and mourning medals distributed widely in the years following his death. In some of these portrayals he is an almost Christ-like figure, the sanctified corpse in the midst of a *pietà* scene, surrounded by wailing women and welcoming angelic bands. Byron's visual impact during his lifetime had been considerable. It became even more marked after his death. The image of his corpse stirred the consciousness of the Western world in a way not seen again until 1967 when the photographs of Che Guevara's body on its ramshackle stretcher in the laundry house of the Vallegrande hospital in Bolivia came across the wires.

In France, where the moral view of him was not so tortuous, Byron was more easily acclaimed as a hero than in England. 'Who has distinguished himself like Lord Byron,' wrote Charles Dupin, a pro-Greek member of the French Institute, in an obituary accolade:

'Who has equalled him – I will not say in his poetry, in his prose, or in his oratory; but in his sacrifices? Who, like him, in the full sway of his passions, in the flower of his age, in the bosom of luxury, of pleasure, and of a dignified retirement, could at once tear himself from the delights of life, from a voluptuous country, and proceed to a soil impoverished by despotism, and desolated by intestine war? He lands in Greece, to encourage the timid – to animate the brave – to consecrate his fortune to noble purposes – and his genius to painful efforts; above all, to appease already rising dissensions, and to double, by union, the power of a people whose very existence is in danger. This is what has been done by Lord Byron. Such greatness of mind had no example; and hitherto it has had no imitators.'

From 1826 reverence for Byron's sacrifice was at the centre of a new wave of Philhellenism in France. After the siege and 'Exodos' of Missolonghi, ending with the final destruction of the town as the remaining Missolonghians blew themselves up in the powder magazine, there was an outpouring of sympathy for Greece among the French of all generations. The episode was dramatised. Missolonghi was the subject of numerous paintings and popular prints. Odevaere painted a statuesque group of *The Last Defenders of Missolonghi*. Delacroix's *Greece on the Ruins of Missolonghi* is the most powerful of all these Missolonghi paintings, an allegorical female figure of Greece standing on the rocky ruins of the town, her hands outstretched in supplication for European support against the Turks.

Byron's own earlier connections were exploited as Missolonghi became a name to conjure with. When Sgricci's play *Missolonghi* was performed in 1826, Byron's grave was *in situ* as part of the stage set. Public feeling was galvanised. Chateaubriand put the feelings of Europe into eloquent words: 'Will our century watch hordes of savages extinguish civilisation at its rebirth on the tomb of a people who civilised the world? Will Christendom calmly allow Turks to strangle Christians? And will the Legitimate Monarchs of Europe shamelessly permit their sacred name to be given to a tyranny which could have reddened the Tiber?' The fall of Missolonghi was influential in drawing the great powers into the Greek war. By 20 October 1827 the naval units of France, Russia and England had joined together to defeat the Ottoman fleet in the bay of Navarino in the Peloponnese, a decisive if chaotic victory that made Greek independence a reality at last. Harold Nicolson's claim that without Byron there would have been no Navarino is an overstatement. But Byron's shadowy presence had certainly been a major factor in the propaganda war.

In Panayiotis Kanellopoulos's recent ten-volume *History of the European Spirit*, Byron, allotted his own large chapter, is singled out as a unique phenomenon. 'There is no other poet who meant in his time what Byron meant throughout Europe.' His richly energetic life opened up the possibility for writers and artists to play a more significant role in politics. This was recognised by the Italian revolutionary leader Giuseppe Mazzini who wrote in his essay on 'Byron and Goethe': 'I know no more beautiful symbol of the future destiny and mission of art than the death of Byron in Greece. The holy alliance of poetry with the cause of the peoples; the union – still so rare – of thought and action which alone completes the human Word.' As well as challenging the conventional division between the creative artist and the political activist he had overcome the ordinary barriers of nationality: Byron became a national hero in a country not his own. And in interpreting Europe to the English and explaining England to the Continent, Byron initiated a two-way process which, it might be claimed, is not completed yet.

For Victor Hugo, Byron's death had been a 'domestic calamity'. He had lost a member of the close circle of his poetic family. In France as much as in England Byron's death came as a private, personal blow to his admirers. Hugo lamented the fellow writer in a moving obituary entitled 'Sur George Gordon, Lord Byron' published in *La Muse Française*, contrasting Byron's liberal and sceptical attitudes with Chateaubriand's monarchical and traditionally religious views. In 1830 Hugo, under fire from the establishment over his controversial drama *Hernani*, wrote a defiant poem 'Le Dédain', dedicated 'A Lord Byron, en 1811', in which he identified himself with the heroic young Byron who survived the criticisms of his early poems in the *Edinburgh Review*.

In mourning Byron, Alfred de Vigny showed the same peculiar posthumous intimacy, beginning a poem for *La Muse Française* which was announced but never published. This is a fragment:

> 'Poète-conquérant, adieu pour cette vie!
> Je regarde ta mort et je te porte envie;
> Car tu meurs à cet âge où le cœur, jeune encor,
> De ces illusions conserve le trésor.
> Tel, aux yeux du marin, le soleil des tropiques
> Se plonge tout ardent sous les flots pacifiques,
> Et, sans pâlir, descend à son nouveau séjour
> Aussi fort qu'il était dans le milieu du jour.'

It is as if these French Byronists had absorbed Byron's own capacity for empathy.

Of French writers, Alphonse de Lamartine, an exact contemporary, is Byron's closest parallel. His affinity for Byron had developed several years before Byron's death. When he visited England in 1819, an old friend had introduced him to Byron's poetry. In Geneva he read *The Corsair*, *Lara* and *Manfred* in translation and became, as he expresses it, drunk on Byron's poetry, which answered to his own interior voices. In the *Premières Méditations poétiques* published in 1820, the work that established Lamartine's reputation as one of Europe's great Romantic poets, he addresses a long section to the dark ambivalent Byron, 'Toi, dont le monde entier ignore le vrai nom'. In 1825 he published his own sequel to *Childe Harold*: *Dernier Chant du pèlerinage d'Harold*. Whether he and Byron ever met seems doubtful, though Lamartine had later half-fantastic memories of having once glimpsed Byron in a tempest near Geneva, a strange and pallid figure dressed in bizarre clothes standing on the deck of a small boat, as if inviting shipwreck. Lamartine embraced him as a spiritual brother, linked by their reciprocal commotion of the soul.

There were other retrospective bonds between the two of them. In 1827, at a ball on New Year's Eve in Rome, the imposing and immaculate Lamartine met Teresa Guiccioli. Sexual rapport between the ex-mistress and the Byronist became a pattern. Lamartine entered the pursuit. He and Teresa wandered together in the gardens of the Doria-Pamphili palace, where she gave him an edited version of her Byron story which Lamartine drew on for his *Vie de Byron*, eventually published in *Le Constitutionnel*. The Lamartine connection extends to Lady Blessington whom he met in Florence in 1828. In her judgement he was 'very good-looking and distinguished in his appearance, and dresses so perfectly like a gentleman, that one never would suspect him to be a poet'. He lacked the element of romantic disarray that made Byron so authentic. But Lady Blessington was eager to share her reminiscences of Byron too.

Byron's example in showing that a poet could also be a man of action had an extraordinary influence on the writers of his generation. His strange compelling personality and sexual charisma made him a role model for writers of many nationalities. Heinrich Heine, born a decade after Byron, in 1797, was first named 'the German Byron' by Elise von Hohenhausen, herself a translator of Byron, when he was in his early twenties. Goethe's championing of Byron made an impression on him. Heine's early tragedies *Almansor* (1820) and *Ratcliff* (1822) show an obvious Byronic influence. Heine's own translations of Byron's poems, including 'Fare Thee Well!' in the guise of 'Lebe Wohl', were published in 1821 and he went on to translate Act One, Scene One of *Manfred*. His own writings, his letters and reported observations are littered with references to Byron, whom he sometimes refers to as his cousin. 'I am deeply affected by Byron's death. He was the one person with whom I felt a real affinity,' he wrote in 1824.

Heine, like Byron, was a misfit and an exile. Jewish by birth, he was a radical cosmopolitan by nature and in 1830 he left Germany for Paris, taking on the trappings of Romanticism. In several of his portraits he wears what became almost the uniform of the European Romantics, the flung cape and the Byronic open-necked shirt. But, again like Byron, Heine was a Romantic who stood outside Romanticism, viewing it with mockery. His own fame emanated from his lyric poetry, but Heine's critical commentary *Die Romantische Schule* of 1833 is as cutting as anything of Byron's. He understood Byron's propensity for mocking to destruction the very things he loved, comparing him in a ghoulish flight of fancy to an insane harlequin who plunges a dagger into his heart in order to bespatter the spectators with his own black blood. 'If we are to grieve over Byron's soul being torn asunder, we'd better grieve about the world being torn right in the middle: as the heart of the poet is the centre of the world, it cannot help being most pitifully torn these days.' For Heine, Byron's contradictions were the essence of him, validating Heine's own call to poetic martyrdom.

Byron's Polish blood brother was Adam Mickiewicz, born in the Grand Duchy of Lithuania in 1798. Historical accident resulted in Mickiewicz being born (technically speaking) a Lithuanian Russian, shortly after the Polish commonwealth had been divided between Russia, Austria and Prussia. But his loyalties and energies were directed to the re-emergence of Poland as a separate political entity, and he was to become the great poet of Polish nationalism. His identification with Byron began as a young man when he began reading Romantic poetry, first in German, then in English. It was sharpened by an unhappy love affair and his first two volumes of verses, published in 1822 and 1823, are Byronic in their lyrical melancholy.

In the years immediately after Byron's death, Mickiewicz was exiled to Russia. In 1828 he published *Konrad Wallenrod*, a war cry for Polish nationalism in which his infatuation with Byron as poetic man of action, revolutionary catalyst, was evident to his Russian contemporaries. The next year Mickiewicz left Russia, travelling in Germany, where he visited Goethe, and living for a year in Rome. By the end of 1830, when the Polish-Russian war broke out, in which the Polish patriots resisted Russian occupation, Mickiewicz was regarded as spiritual leader of the insurgents, seen in quasi-Byronic terms as inspirational poet and political force. During 1832 and 1833, after the collapse of the revolt, he worked with painful ardour on his translation of Byron's *The Giaour*. His great Polish epic *Pan Tadeusz* was published in 1834.

Mickiewicz is the most striking of all Byron lookalikes. His physical admiration showed itself in his adoption of Byron's dandy style of dress. He wore his glossy hair like Byron, in carelessly descending curls. If Pushkin's drawing of Mickiewicz is to be believed, he even adopted Byron's facial expression of half charm and half hauteur. The famous Wankowicz portrait *Mickiewicz on the Rock of Ayudah*, now in the National Gallery in Warsaw, showing the poet staring raptly into the far distance, bears a surely not accidental resemblance to Adam Friedel's widely circulated lithograph of Byron on a rocky Grecian promontory, head in hand, Homeric helmet at his feet.

The two best known portraits of Alexander Pushkin, by V.A. Tropinin and Orest Kiprensky, both painted in 1827, show him too in distinctly Byronic mode. Byronism percolated far beyond the continental European centres. Pushkin, born in Moscow in 1799, is the most interesting if the most ambivalent of Byronists. His upbringing in a family of ancient Russian gentry; his indoctrination into subversiveness; his dismissal from imperial service and banishment; his death in a duel in 1837 – Pushkin's life, like that of Byron, had a built-in melodrama: as Vladimir Nabokov later commented, the story of Pushkin's own existence might have emanated from his own pen.

His admiration of Byron's early poetry was manifest. 'Read *Parisina*' was the advice he gave a friend who asked him to recommend a good poetic model. In 1820–1 he wrote *The Prisoner of the Caucasus* and in 1822 *The Fountain of Bakhchisarai*, the story of a khan who falls in love with a Polish girl captured by the Tartars: both these poems are clearly influenced by Byron's Eastern tales. Pushkin's *Poltava* of 1829 is a retelling of the story of *Mazeppa*. There are numerous echoes of Byron, even an epigraph based on 'Fare thee well!', in *Eugeny Onegin*, the verse narrative of contemporary life which was published in 1831. Although Pushkin denied it, friends immediately saw the resemblance between *Eugeny Onegin* and Byron's *Don Juan*.

Personal parallels between the two writers are numerous. Pushkin, like Byron, was addicted to swimming, plunging into the river even in midwinter, disporting himself in the grandiose marble public swimming pool in Moscow. He made a similar game of the erotic. In his gently boastful 'Don Juan's List', written into the album of the younger sister of a current love, he strings out the names of his former lovers much as Byron itemised his Venetian conquests. He had a streak of the same vulgarity. Taking over a Greek woman, Kalypso Polychroni, a fortune-teller's daughter who claimed to have been Byron's mistress on his visit to Constantinople in 1810, Pushkin imagined himself caught up in a Byronic chain of exchanged kisses. 'I feel as though I was communing with the English poet by reverently caressing her flesh,' he told a Russian friend.

Soon after the news of Byron's death reached Pushkin he was living under surveillance on the neglected family estates at Mikhailovskoe, near Pskov in southern Russia. He gave instructions for the village priest to hold a service in memory of 'the great man Georgios'. He wrote to his friend Prince Pyotr Vyazemsky: 'You are sad about Byron, but I am very glad of his death, as a sublime theme for poetry.' Had he still been in St Petersburg, Pushkin would almost certainly have been implicated in the Decembrist revolt against the Tsarist regime in December 1825. One of the young leaders, the poet Kondratii Theodorovich Ryleev, was condemned to death for his part in the uprising. On his way to be executed he carried a volume of Byron's poems.

The cult of Byron went far beyond the literary to encompass musicians and artists. It influenced nineteenth-century portraiture and dress, attitudes to nature, scenery and travel, views of morality and human relations, becoming in itself almost a way of life. The extent of Byron worship can be glimpsed in Josef Danhauser's painting of 1840 *Liszt at the Piano* showing seven European Romantics at the shrine of Beethoven and Byron, who is represented by the exquisite portrait drawing made by George Harlow in the year of his engagement to Annabella Milbanke. In the group of Byronists, besides the writers Alexandre Dumas and George Sand, are the celebrated violinist Paganini and composers Rossini, Berlioz and Liszt himself with his mistress Marie d'Agoult sitting at his feet.

All three composers had particular connections with Byron. Rossini, the only one of the three whom Byron had actually seen, when he was fêted in Venice in 1819, composed *The Muses' Lament* after Byron's death. When his opera *Maometto II*, originally performed in Naples in 1820, was revived for performance at the Paris Opera six years later, the title had been changed to *Le Siège de Corinthe* and the background of historical events altered from the wars between the Turks and Venetians leading up to the fall of Negroponte to the wars between the Turks and Greeks. This was partly an act of homage to Byron and his own poetic treatment *The Siege of Corinth*. It was also a stroke of commercial acumen in Philhellenic Paris of 1826.

Hector Berlioz had felt temperamentally attuned to Byron since, as a young man, he fell into the grip of what he describes in his autobiography as '*the bane of isolation*', an agony of feeling linked inextricably with the impulse to create. Travelling in Italy in the early 1830s he seems to have consciously followed in Byron's footsteps, as many of his Romantic contemporaries did. He conversed with a Venetian who claimed to have been the captain of the ship which had taken Byron on his early voyage to the Adriatic and the Greek islands. In the summer heat of Rome he would retreat into St Peter's with a volume of Byron and sit himself comfortably in the confessional 'absorbed in that burning verse'. Berlioz 'adored the extraordinary nature of the man, at once ruthless and of extreme tenderness, generous-hearted and without pity'. He found in Byron the reflection of his own life of stormy passions and the stimulus for two of his most successful works. In 1831, after the traumatic end of his affair with the young pianist Camille Marie Moke, which resulted in his failed – and totally Byronic – suicide attempt in Genoa, Berlioz made preliminary sketches for an orchestral composition, *The Tower of Nice*, which he later developed into his overture *The Corsair*.

In 1834 Berlioz drew more directly on Byron's poem *Childe Harold* for his own *Harold*, subsequently renamed *Harold in Italy*. This originated in Paganini's request for an orchestral composition which would show off the capabilities of his new Stradivarius viola. Berlioz contrarily provided a symphonic work based on 'poetic impressions recollected from my wanderings in the Abruzzi mountains'. The solo viola takes on the role of poetic commentator on the passing scene, 'a kind of melancholy dreamer in the style of Byron's Childe Harold'. The Harold theme recurs in each of the four symphonic episodes: Harold in the mountains; the March of the Pilgrims; Serenade of an Abruzzian mountain-dweller to his mistress; and the final Brigands' Orgy in which Berlioz builds on Byron's own predilection for the colours and rhythms of the primitive.

It was Byron the wanderer who most appealed to the aficionados in Danhauser's group portrait. They saw him as someone who had valued the impulses of the heart above social conventions, who had scorned the stay-at-home. For them Byron was the glorification of rootlessness. George Sand, the pseudonym taken by Aurore Dupin, Baronne Dudevant, had left her husband in 1831 to start an independent life in Paris as a novelist. Her liaisons with Alfred de Musset and with Chopin, her European travels, her emotional journeys, are all drawn on in her writing. In 1835 the Comtesse Marie d'Agoult, another married woman, left her family to join the twenty-four-year-old Franz Liszt in Switzerland. Liszt's most Byronic composition, the first two books of his piano music *Années de Pèlerinage*, are the record of their travels together in Switzerland and Italy over the next four years.

They stayed for some time by the Swiss lake of Wallenstadt. Here Liszt wrote for Marie the melancholy music echoing the sigh of the waves and the rhythm of the oars on the water which, so she tells us in her memoirs, reduced her to tears every time she heard it. In the published *Années de Pèlerinage* Liszt prefaces this piece, 'Au lac de Wallenstadt', with a quotation from *Childe Harold*:

'thy contrasted lake,
With the wild world I dwelt in, is a thing
Which warns me, with its stillness, to forsake
Earth's troubled waters for a purer spring.'

The seventh piece, 'Eglogue', and the ninth and final piece, 'Les Cloches de Genève', are also linked directly to *Childe Harold*. In the tolling of the bells from the city on the water it is Byron's Geneva as well as Liszt's we hear.

First among visual artists influenced by Byron was Eugène Delacroix. The critic Charles Blanc refers to him as the Byron of painting. Delacroix as a young man read Byron avidly. In 1824 he was listing Byron with Dante and Lamartine as authors of the books most capable of giving him inspiration, 'certain books that should never fail'. Delacroix drew on Byron's *Corsair*, on *Lara*, *Mazeppa*, *The Prisoner of Chillon*; he returned several times to *The Bride of Abydos*, extracting his own visual drama from Byron's already explicit narrative descriptions. He wrote in his journal:

'Poetry is full of riches; always remember certain passages from Byron, they are an unfailing spur to your imagination; they are right for you. The end of the *Bride of Abydos; The Death of Selim*, his body tossed about by the waves and that hand – especially that hand – held up by the waves as they spend themselves upon the shore. This is sublime, and it is his alone.'

As a painter Delacroix was attracted to lurid, violent themes and turgid confrontations. He was affected by Byron's Orientalism, his delight in the foreign and exotic. Delacroix's interest in dramatising evil found a stimulus in Byron's. He painted three large canvases based on Byron's historical dramas: *The Execution of the Doge Marino Faliero* in 1826; *The Death of Sardanapalus* in 1827; and *The Two Foscari* as late as 1855. Delacroix's interpretation of the last scene of *Sardanapalus* goes beyond Byron in its pandemonium of harem women, naked slaves and rearing horseflesh surrounding the last king of Nineveh who watches the scene dispassionately from his couch. The painting was received with considerable horror when it was exhibited at the Paris Salon in 1828.

What stirred Delacroix in Byron was his quality of daring: 'Without daring, without extreme daring even, there is no beauty.' Like other European Byronists, Delacroix was fascinated with the person of Byron, his appearance and his habits, attributing some of Byron's courage to his recourse to drinking gin. Delacroix in his self-portraits gives himself a look of Byron. In the early

Self-Portrait in Travelling Costume a jaunty Delacroix wears a peaked cap resembling the foraging cap of the portraits made of Byron in Genoa and Greece, while in the famous 1837 self-portrait in the Louvre Delacroix stares out at his spectators with a Byronic expression of disdain.

For the Italian Risorgimento leader Giuseppe Mazzini, sixteen years his junior, Byron's poetry was a part of his everyday existence. 'I have, throughout life, scattered Byrons of mine wherever I have been sojourning.' Of all the European Byronists it is Mazzini who expresses most persuasively the impact of Byron on that political generation. Quoting Byron's own *Prisoner of Chillon*, he writes:

'Never did "the eternal spirit of the chainless mind" make a brighter apparition amongst us. He seems at times a transformation of that immortal Prometheus, of whom he had written so nobly; whose cry of agony, yet of futurity, sounded above the cradle of the European world; and whose grand and mysterious form, transfigured by time, reappears from age to age, between the entombment of one epoch and the accession of another; to wail forth the lament of genius, tortured by the presentiment of things it will not see realized in its time. Byron, too, had the "firm will" and the "deep sense"; he, too, made of his "death a victory".'

Mazzini recognised Byron as the great creative individualist who had nevertheless opened the way to collective action for the libertarian cause. This was indeed the spirit in which Verdi composed his opera *I due Foscari* based on Byron's Venetian tragedy, first performed in 1844 in Rome. The memory of Byron was still alive on the barricades and in the prisons of 'the Year of the Revolutions', 1848.

The Byron worshipped in Europe was of course a different creature, more intense, more spectral, than the quipping English peer of the London coffee houses, the young sportsman who bought his pistols at Manton's and sparred with 'Gentleman' Jackson, spent marathon evenings exchanging fantastical stories with Scrope Davies, haunted the Green Room at Drury Lane. His European admirers did not comprehend the English dandy side of Byron. They had no access to his letters. His poetry most often reached them in translation and they felt most easily attuned to the stern grandeur of *Manfred*, the extended agonies of *The Prisoner of Chillon*. They had little or no appreciation of his English sharpness of wit.

When Lamartine, in his poem 'L'Hommage à Lord Byron', published in

1820, had referred to Byron as 'chantre des enfers', poet of the underworld, Byron had been indignant. Lady Blessington quoted him as saying: 'I dislike French verse so much that I have not read more than a few lines of the one in which I am dragged into public view. He calls me "Esprit mystérieux, mortel, ange ou démon"; which I call very uncivil, for a well-bred Frenchman.' Thomas Moore, in his 1830 biography, was cutting on the 'disposition so prevalent throughout Europe, to picture Byron as a man of marvels and mysteries, as well in his life as in poetry'. He was anxious that his continental readers might be disillusioned by the 'real "flesh and blood" hero' of his pages: the 'social, practical-minded and, with all his faults and eccentricities, *English* Lord Byron' whom Tom Moore, with his day-to-day understanding of his subject, had portrayed.

Moore's biography had very little impact in a Europe determined to see Byron in terms of his own Childe Harold. It was Byron the *flâneur*, the epitome of melancholy, who excited Dumas and de Musset, Gautier and Baudelaire. Gustave Flaubert made his own pilgrimage to Chillon in 1845. On this sacred visit he was conscious all the time of

'the pale man who once came there, paced to and fro, wrote his name on the stone, and went away again . . . Byron's name is written slantwise, and it is already black, as if they had been putting ink on it to make it stand out; indeed, it shines out of the grey pillar, and leaps to the eye as soon as one comes in. Beneath the name the stone is slightly eaten away, as if the mighty hand that leant there had worn it away with its weight.'

The image of the 'chantre des enfers' pervaded European interpretations of Byron throughout the nineteenth and early twentieth centuries. In *The Romantic Agony*, the wide-ranging study of decadence by the Italian critic Mario Praz published in its English version in 1933, Byron is made a prime example of 'Fatal Man'. Praz writes of 'this gloomy tragedy of Byron's life, whose scene was laid in a moral torture chamber'. In his 1930 biography of the poet the French man of letters André Maurois shows Byron in familiar guise as grand amorist and glamorously tragic hero: he was not the last of literary wishful thinkers, male biographers of Byron who portrayed their subject according to the image they wished to appropriate for themselves.

30

The Byronic Englishman

Many of the people we have come to think of as the Great Victorians were addicted to Byron in their youth. In 1824 the fourteen-year-old Alfred Tennyson inscribed the words 'Byron is dead' into the soft sandstone of a rock near his father's rectory at Somersby in Lincolnshire. He remembered it as 'a day when the whole world seemed to be darkened for me'. At school he had hated Horace and loved Byron: 'Byron expressed what I felt.'

When the news reached Thomas Carlyle in Scotland he lamented to Jane Welsh, whom he was to marry in 1826: 'Poor Byron! Alas poor Byron! The news of his death came down upon my heart like a mass of lead; and yet, the thought of it sends a painful twinge through all my being, as if I had lost a Brother!' The well-read Jane was herself an admirer of Byron, stiffening herself for what was shocking in his work. Byron's had been the language of her problematic courtship; echoes of Byron run through their correspondence and in 1822 Carlyle had sent Jane *Werner*, with a letter telling her she must not give him up. Before her future husband's letter on Byron's death had reached her she had written her own letter to him:

'And Byron is dead! I was told it all at once in a roomful of people. My God, if they had said that the sun or the moon had gone out of the heavens, it could not have struck me with the idea of a more awful and dreary blank in the creation than the words "Byron is dead!" I have felt quite cold and dejected ever since: all my thoughts have been fearful and dismal. I wish you were come.'

It is interesting that she fixes on the exact place she heard the news, a common response to the sudden death of a celebrity, comparable to that of John F. Kennedy or Diana, Princess of Wales in another century.

The aspiring young poet Matthew Arnold, eldest son of the reforming headmaster of Rugby, read Byron as a pupil at Rugby and at Winchester, winning a Winchester verse-speaking prize for a speech from *Marino Faliero*. His own early verses show the influence of *Childe Harold*, especially the gloomily oriental 'Constantinople', written in 1838 when Arnold was sixteen, and 'Alaric at Rome' (1840) in which the Visigoth conqueror shows a Byronic disaffection for his victories:

> 'Perhaps his wandering heart was far away,
> Lost in dim memories of his early home.'

Though Arnold was later on technical grounds to rate other practitioners, such as the Italian poet Giacomo Leopardi, as greater than Byron, he considered him to have outclassed all his rivals in the moral stand he took against the philistinism of 'the great middle class'. Arnold's *Culture and Anarchy*, the expression of his fears of the dilution of English intellectual life, was published in 1869. In an eloquent summing up of his feelings about Byron, written as a preface to the *Poetry of Byron* in 1881, Matthew Arnold enlists the Regency aristocrat as an ally in his own appalled resistance to the Victorian age:

'As the inevitable break-up of the old order comes, as the English middle-class slowly awakens from its intellectual sleep of two centuries, as our actual present world, to which this sleep has condemned us, shows itself more clearly, – our world of an aristocracy materialised and null, a middle-class purblind and hideous, a lower class crude and brutal, – we shall turn our eyes again, and to more purpose, upon this passionate and dauntless soldier of a forlorn hope.'

In the parsonage at Haworth in the early 1830s the surviving Brontë children, Charlotte, Branwell, Anne and Emily, read Byron's poetry and absorbed the details of his life through Thomas Moore's biography. They responded to the exoticism of the Eastern tales and the influence of Byron is clear in their invented kingdoms of Angria and Gondal. In Charlotte and Branwell's mythic Angria the central characters are Alexander Percy, Earl of Northangerland and Arthur Wellesley, Marquis of Douro, later transformed into the Duke of Zamorna. In these cycles of poems, plays and stories the young Brontës created a Byronic landscape of aristocratic bad behaviour and dark erotic power.

It was Matthew Arnold who formally registered the connection between Byron and the Brontës in his poem 'Haworth Churchyard' of 1855, in which he writes of Emily:

> 'She –
> (How shall I sing her?) – whose soul
> Knew no fellow for might,
> Passion, vehemence, grief,

Daring, since Byron died,
That world-fam'd Son of Fire; She, who sank
Baffled, unknown, self-consum'd.'

In the Brontë sisters' novels the Byronic hero, the flawed angel, the man of demoniac attractiveness, emerged with a compelling imaginative power. In Emily Brontë's *Wuthering Heights*, Heathcliff is the Byron figure: the 'tall, athletic, well-formed man' who bears the distinct marks of his former degradation in the half-civilised ferocity lurking in the depressed brows and in his 'eyes full of black fire'. There are Byronic hints of incest in the love between Heathcliff and Catherine, who have been brought up as quasi-siblings. In Cathy's proud rejection of marriage to Heathcliff as degrading there are echoes of Mary Chaworth's disdainful comments about Byron – 'What! Me care for that lame boy?' – the story related by Thomas Moore in his biography.

In Charlotte Brontë's *Jane Eyre* the saturnine hero Mr Rochester is Byronic in his past sexual transgressions, his doomed marriage, the secret horror of the madwoman hidden in the attic, his arrogant attempt to inveigle Jane into an illegal wedding. Corrupt, he is also disconcertingly attractive. Is Rochester redeemable? In creating her character Charlotte draws not only on Byron's Childe Harold and the equivocal dark-browed heroes of Byron's Turkish tales; Charlotte too had evidently read Tom Moore attentively and Rochester has attributes of the real-life Byron as portrayed by Moore.

Ruskin wandered through Venice contemplating Byron. On his first visit, with his parents, in 1835 he already felt a close affinity with Byron the poet and the man. His father, John James Ruskin, 'an absolutely beautiful reader', used to read him Byron's poetry in an early evening ritual in the drawing room after tea: Ruskin's twelfth birthday had been celebrated with permission to drink wine, to be taken to the theatre and to hear the shipwreck scene from *Don Juan*. As a boy he had met the middle-aged Scots lady, now Mrs Cockburn, who had once been little Mary Duff, Byron's childhood sweetheart. Her husband was a member of the Cockburn port family; Ruskin's father dealt in sherry. Ruskin revelled in these personal connections.

In Venice, aged sixteen, Ruskin the Byron tourist wrote down his impressions in pseudo-Byronic verse:

'I've tried St Mark's by midnight moon and in Rialto walked about
A place of terror and of gloom which is very much talked about,
The gondolier has rowed me by the house where Byron took delight
The palace too of Foscari is very nearly opposite.'

In his autobiography, *Præterita*, he claimed: 'My Venice, like Turner's, had been chiefly created for us by Byron.' More than any other Victorian commentator, Ruskin appreciated, and learned from, Byron's extraordinary ability to instil in his poetry a sense of place. He absorbed Byron's method of reanimating a landscape or a city by reaching back into the histories of the people who once lived there: 'Byron taught me the meaning of Chillon and of Meillerie, and bade me seek first in Venice – the ruined homes of Foscari and Faliero.'

For a time Byron and Turner became Ruskin's twin gods, Byron for verse and Turner for colour. Ruskin adored Byron's technical proficiency in the use of words, comparing this characteristically to the expertise of the skilled craftsman who arrives at a kind of nonchalance in action: Byron wrote 'with the serene swiftness of a smith's hammerstrokes on hot iron'. Most of all Ruskin admired and defended Byron's candour, the way in which he 'spoke without exaggeration, without mystery, without enormity, and without mercy'. Ruskin, like Matthew Arnold, saw Byron's blatant honesty as a counterblast to Victorian hypocrisy, denouncing Byron's denigrators as 'these pismires, these dogs that bay the moon, these foul snails that crawl on in their despicable malice, leaving their spume and filth on the fairest flowers of literature'. Ruskin's personal admiration for Byron led him into wistful longings that they might have met in Venice. It is hard to believe that, face to face, they would have proved compatible.

Almost immediately after his death the phenomenon of 'being Byron' began to manifest itself. His closest nineteenth-century admirers could be seen imitating his dress and aristocratic languor, contacting people who had met him, making reminiscent visits to the places he had known, writing poetry in a mock-Byronic style, infiltrating his characters into novels of their own, affecting his reputation for sexual irresistibility. Byron's style was imitated both to compensate for perceived inadequacies and, in a spirit of emulation, to further the celebrity of his imitators. Prime examples of those who modelled themselves on him in the Victorian period were Benjamin Disraeli, Edward Bulwer-Lytton and Byron's relative by marriage Wilfrid Scawen Blunt.

The early years of Disraeli, the future Tory prime minister, bear a striking resemblance to those of Byron in the way that an intense, precocious ambitiousness coexisted with a personal sense of being rejected by conventional society. Disraeli's concept of himself as an outsider was better grounded than Byron's: he was the child of a family of Levantine Jews in the largely anti-Semitic culture of early nineteenth-century Britain. But there is certainly an echo of Byron's own craving for acceptance in Disraeli's partly autobiographical novel *Coningsby*: 'At school friendship is a passion. It entrances the being; it tears the soul. All loves of after-life can never bring its rapture, or its wretchedness; no bliss so absorbing, no pangs of jealousy or despair so crushing and so keen!' Disraeli shared the same nostalgia for the 'mystic passages of young emotion that makes grey-haired men mourn over the memory of their schoolboy days'.

Disraeli's father Isaac D'Israeli had first encountered the young Byron as another author published by John Murray. Byron had a high opinion of D'Israeli's compendious *Curiosities of Literature*, telling Murray in 1813 that he had never in his life read a book that entertained him so much. Isaac D'Israeli's description of Byron in his early days as a London sophisticate reveals him at his most flamboyant:

'I once met Lord Byron before he was known, before he travelled. Such a fantastic and effeminate thing I never saw. It was all rings and curls and lace. I was ashamed to speak to him; he looked more like a girl than a boy. I remember his shirt collar was all thrown over from his neck, and I observed him, while he spoke to some one, fence with a light cane in a very affected manner.'

This was an aspect of Lord Byron that Benjamin Disraeli was to reconstruct in the dandyish persona he adopted for his own successful entrée into London society.

In 1826, two years after Byron's death, Disraeli set out on a continental tour. He was in a run-down and nervy state of health. At Geneva he hired Maurice, the boatman who had once rowed Byron and Shelley on Lac Leman, now evidently making a good living out of the connection, telling taller and taller stories. On her own haunts-of-Byron visit to Geneva, Lady Blessington had patronised him too. Disraeli reported to his father:

'I take a row on the lake every night with Maurice, Lord Byron's celebrated boatman. Maurice is very handsome and very vain, but he has been made so by the English, of whom he is the regular pet. He talks of nothing but Lord Byron, particularly if you show the least interest in the subject. He told me that in the night of the famous storm described in the third canto C[hilde] H[arold], had they been out five minutes more the boat must have been wrecked.'

On Disraeli's final evening in Geneva, shortly after dinner, another tremendous storm blew up. Maurice sent for Disraeli urgently to give him the experience of just such a sublime Byronic spectacle.

This tendency to Byron-worship reached a climax when Disraeli took into his own service Tita Falcieri, a living souvenir of Byron, the servant who had held his hand while he died at Missolonghi. Disraeli's own father was to die in Tita's arms. Tita travelled with Benjamin Disraeli in Greece, Turkey and Egypt before returning to England in 1832 and becoming house steward at Bradenham House, the Disraeli family home in Buckinghamshire. Life had not been easy for Byron's ex-employees. Lega Zambelli had joined William Fletcher in opening a macaroni factory in London, an enterprise that failed. In finding his feet in Benjamin Disraeli's service Tita was relatively fortunate.

Disraeli asserted that his works were his life. His lifelong fascination with Byron pervades his novels, not only in his portrayal of the lethal interaction between high society and politics but in the recognisably Byronic characters he created: the dandy hero in *The Young Duke*; the ambivalent Plantagenet Carducis in *Venetia*, part Byron and part Shelley. His attitude to Byron was certainly entangled with Disraeli's own sexual mysteriousness.

Edward Bulwer-Lytton, originally Edward Bulwer, novelist, playwright, essayist and poet, was the most prolific of popular writers of the mid-Victorian period. A friend of Dickens and also of Disraeli, he was in a way Disraeli's dandy twin. They were portrayed together in contemporary caricatures, in their 'flash *falsetto* dress', their cravats and embroidered waistcoats, high-heeled boots and swooping capes. Tom Moore, in his journal for 1839, gives a shuddering description of accompanying Bulwer-Lytton to the opera, 'he himself looking far more like an *opera* Apollo than a regular Parnassian – so bedizened was he with rings, ringlets and thinglets in all directions. Am sorry for this, for as far as I have seen, there is much to be liked in him.'

Bulwer-Lytton and Disraeli were united by their strong emotional ties with Byron. To Bulwer-Lytton his death had been a heart-stopper: 'We could not believe that the bright race was run. So much of us died with him, that the notion of his death had something of the unnatural, of the impossible. It was as if a part of the mechanism of the very world stood still.' Soon after the death, in 1824, Bulwer-Lytton embroiled himself in a ghostly love affair with Lady Caroline Lamb. He had known, and worshipped, Caroline from boyhood but what had been calf love seems to have been deepened by Byron's death. Their affair bears a curious resemblance to that between Byron's friend Henry Fox and Teresa Guiccioli. In both there is a Gothick hint of necrophilia.

Bulwer-Lytton was now in his early twenties, Byron's 'little volcano' an intelligent, unstable woman of almost forty, more or less separated from her husband. Bulwer-Lytton viewed his relationship with Lady Caroline as a means of getting closer to Byron. 'She interested me chiefly', he wrote in a passage of autobiography, 'by her recollections and graphic descriptions of Byron, with whom her intimacy had lasted during the three most brilliant years of his life in England.' According to Bulwer-Lytton, 'there was no bitterness in her talk of him, and whatever faults she found in his character, she fired up in his defence if any one else abused him.' She had apparently now reached an age of discretion in speaking of Byron and Augusta: 'Of the hideous calumnies concerning himself and Mrs Leigh (indeed, of all calumnies involving the charge of crime) she certainly acquitted him.' The implication is that she and Bulwer-Lytton had at least discussed the crime of sodomy.

Bulwer-Lytton's adulation of Byron was in many ways an act of physical retrieval. He wore the Byron ring that Lady Caroline bestowed temporarily on later lovers. From 1835 he lived in the chambers in Albany inhabited by Byron twenty years before. Disraeli had at one time been a contender for them too. These bachelor rooms were a retreat from Bulwer-Lytton's catastrophic marriage, a marriage in some ways worse because more long drawn out than Byron's, to the beautiful, high-spirited, individualistic Rosina Wheeler, whose mother was an Irish radical feminist. The marriage had been actively encouraged by Lady Caroline Lamb. One of its culminating scenes was the arrival at Albany of the vengeful wife, accusing Bulwer-Lytton of infidelity. She was finally ejected from her husband's apartment, screaming abuse. Bulwer-Lytton's furies pursued him along Piccadilly, as Byron's had once done, and Rosina later wrote a satire, *Cheveley; or the Man of Honour*, attacking her husband in terms as vitriolic as Caroline Lamb had treated Byron in *Glenarvon*. When Bulwer-Lytton had Rosina confined in an asylum she was released after a public outcry. Her final act of revenge was her memoir *A Blighted Life*.

Bulwer-Lytton entered Parliament as a Reform MP in 1831. But he later broke with the Liberals over such issues as the introduction of democratic suffrage and the importance of the colonial empire and, most fundamentally and indeed Byronically, over the claim that popular liberty could be promoted by the destruction of the aristocracy. He eventually became Secretary of State for the Colonies in Lord Derby's administration of 1858 and was raised to the peerage as Lord Lytton of Knebworth in 1866. His career as a writer flourished alongside that in politics. As in Disraeli's novels, fictional Byrons – Reginald Glanville in *Pelham*, the repentant murderer in *Eugene Aram* – flit in and out of Bulwer-Lytton's fashionable plots. More arrestingly, Bulwer-Lytton's final novel, the futuristic fantasy *The Coming Race*, takes up some of the questions raised by Byron in *The Island* on the values by which society should live.

In 1843, after his mother died, Bulwer-Lytton inherited Knebworth House in Hertfordshire, restoring and enlarging it in the mid-nineteenth-century Gothic style that Byron's own taste for melancholy grandeur had done much to popularise. With its domes and turrets, gargoyles and stained glass,

Knebworth is a Victorian pastiche of Newstead. Bulwer-Lytton's grandson Neville, who became 3rd Earl of Lytton, married Byron's great-granddaughter Judith Blunt, later 16th Baroness Wentworth, a latter-day connection that Bulwer-Lytton would have appreciated.

Of the next generation of Byronists, Wilfrid Scawen Blunt, born in 1840, took the cult to its most remarkable extremes. Blunt was a poet, a diplomat and traveller, maverick politician and compulsive amorist whose identification with Byron was cemented by his marriage, in 1869, to Byron's granddaughter and Ada's daughter, Lady Anne Isabella Noel. At certain stages in his life the tall handsome theatrical Blunt, who claimed that his father had been Byron's fag at Harrow, seems to have seen himself as Byron reborn.

As a young diplomat, Blunt's first posting was to Athens. In 1859 Byron's presence was still a living memory. The Maid of Athens was now the highly respectable Mrs James Black, married to the British Vice-Consul in Missolonghi. In the streets of Athens Blunt was aware that he was meeting the descendants of Byron's own Suliote soldiers in their Albanian dress of fustanella and gold embroidery. He and the diplomatic contingent used to ride out beyond Athens, 'a merry party, twice a week, following a paper chase, of which I was generally the leader on an old white horse, which, in memory of Shelley's lines, I called Apocalypse'. Blunt made the Byronic expedition to Sunium. He conversed with George Finlay, encouraging a flood of reminiscences of Byron at the time of the Greek War of Independence. He visited the romantic wooded estate in Euboea, purchased in 1830 by Edward Noel, Lady Byron's relation and protégé, and fell briefly in love with the Noels' daughter Alice. Blunt was already writing sub-Byronic lyric poetry and absorbing the Byronic ideals of national freedom that became the basis of his own controversial political beliefs.

With a similar devotion Blunt followed Byron's footsteps around the sacred sites. He stayed in hotels at Cintra and later on Lac Leman where Byron had once stopped and is even recorded as demanding Byron's bedroom. On a visit to Newstead he noted in his journal that the celebrated oak sown by Byron as a child was showing signs of dying: 'I have recommended its being pollarded as the best chance of prolonging its life, but the soil is gravel and sand.' Blunt regretted that the outside walls of the Abbey had been much spoiled by Wildman's restoration, 'so that it is difficult to make out quite what is old and what is new, and the windows have been plate-glassed, and otherwise bedevilled, but it is still a splendid possession, much larger and more important than I had at all imagined.' Blunt's own view of Newstead is proprietorial.

Blunt's marriage to Lady Byron's granddaughter Lady Anne Noel plunged him into the continuing speculation and argument over Byron's sexual behaviour – what Blunt referred to as 'the great Byron controversies'. Byron's letters to Lady Melbourne, with their half-confessions of incest, had now come into the possession of Hobhouse's daughter, Mrs Dudley Carleton, later Lady Dorchester. These letters were read with fascination by Blunt and his wife. When Lady Anne's brother, the 2nd Earl of Lovelace, was preparing *Astarte*, his book making the case for Byron's incest with Augusta, Blunt did his best to persuade him to draw back. His instinct was 'to avoid bitterness or disparagement when speaking of Byron who was certainly a man of commanding genius'. His reading of the letters confirmed his sense of identification with Byron for in them he found 'views of love and women very like my own'.

Blunt saw himself as one of the great lovers of his age. He emulated Byron in his quantity and variety of lovers, from Skittles the famous courtesan to Janey, the wife of William Morris. Blunt's delight in the process of conquest, in the stealing of the wife, the mistress or the innocent, emerges from his candid and scandalously detailed secret diaries which were not released until 1972, fifty years after his death. At their best they approach the narrative aplomb with which Byron relates his near-seduction of Lady Frances Wedderburn Webster. They reveal Blunt as possessing the Byronic gift for instant intimacy. Even in the act of love Blunt was being Byron. As related by Blunt all his affairs are heterosexual. There is no evidence that Blunt either registered or imitated Byron's bisexuality.

From the 1870s Blunt and Lady Anne were intrepid voyagers who, like Byron, went beyond the limits of conventional European travel, to the Orient, North Africa, Syria and Egypt and into the deserts of Arabia. Blunt was conscious of resurrecting the Byronic spirit of natural opposition in his championing of the nationalist causes of India, Egypt and Ireland. In 1888 Blunt was imprisoned in Galway Gaol for his pro-nationalist activities. His imprisonment resulted in a thoroughly Byronic project: the sonnet sequence published as *In Vinculis*, 'In Chains'. One of these sonnets is entitled 'Liberty, Equality, Fraternity':

'Long have I searched the Earth for liberty
    In desert places and lands far abroad
Where neither Kings nor constables should be,
    Nor any law of Man, alas, or God.
    Freedom, Equality and Brotherhood,
These were my quarries which eternally
    Fled from my footsteps fast as I pursued,
Sad phantoms of desire by land and sea.

See, it is ended. Sick and overborne
By foes and fools, and my long chase, I lie.
Here, in these walls, with all life's souls forlorn
Herded I wait, – and in my ears the cry,
"Alas, poor brothers, equal in Man's scorn
And free in God's good liberty to die".'

Blunt's recklessly anti-imperialist stance, which brought him into direct conflict with the British government, made him *persona non grata* in England, in a manner comparable to the figure of obloquy Byron became after 1816.

For Blunt the Arab lands became his adopted country. He studied Arabic. He bought an estate and built a house at Sheykh Obeyd near Heliopolis in Egypt. Both Blunt and his wife took to wearing Arab dress in a gesture that was both a mark of solidarity with the Arab races and a form of enjoyable disguise. When Byron chose to be painted by Thomas Phillips in Albanian dress he was making a political statement, demonstrating his freedom from the prescribed loyalties, reinterpreting the boundaries of liberty. The echo was deliberate.

Through the nineteenth century Byron's homosexuality became a buried subject. In 1866 *Don Leon* was published, a determinedly scurrilous poem in rollicking rhyming couplets relating Byron's life as a series of sodomitical episodes culminating in anal intercourse with Lady Byron. But the circulation of this poem was limited and its authorship remains a still unresolved mystery. After the publication of Harriet Beecher Stowe's magazine article 'The True Story of Lady Byron's Life' in 1869, expanded in book form as *Lady Byron Vindicated*, which made public Lady Byron's belief that Augusta and Byron had been lovers, speculation remained focused on the issue of incest. References to Byron's homosexuality were confined to scholarly dissertations on uranism in obscure French and German scientific publications. One of these was by André Raffalovich, rich cosmopolitan member of Oscar Wilde's circle and himself homosexual. In an article 'Uranisme et unisexualité' published in the journal *Bibliothèque de Criminologie* in 1896 in Lyons, Raffalovich lists Byron among other renowned literary bisexuals.

Wilde was already a Byron devotee. As an undergraduate at Oxford he composed, and entered for the 1878 Newdigate Prize, an ambitious poem 'Ravenna' which displays his admiration for both *Childe Harold* and its author. Byron is seen as

'a second Anthony,
Who of the world another Actium made'.

Visually the young Oscar modelled himself on Byron. A series of photographs taken in New York by Napoleon Sarony during Wilde's 1882 American lecture tour depicts the poet in knee breeches and black velvet jacket reclining luxuriously on a fur rug placed on an Eastern carpet. Wilde too knew very well how to manipulate his image. With a Byronic sense of theatre he would play to an audience, writing of his American success: 'I am torn in bits by Society. Immense receptions, wonderful dinners, crowds waiting for my carriage. I wave a gloved hand and an ivory cane and they cheer ... Rooms are hung with white lilies for me everywhere.' He too had a black servant, 'who is my slave'. He saw how fame could be fuelled by exaggerated badness: 'I give sittings to artists, and generally behave as I always have behaved – *dreadfully*.' Wilde like Byron understood, and had reason to regret, that nothing succeeds like celebrity.

Wilde empathised with Byron's vanities and subterfuges. The desperate fear of the physical transformation of ageing pervades Wilde's sensationalist novel *The Picture of Dorian Gray*. After Wilde's trial and sentence for homosexual offences in 1895 and his subsequent disgrace he began to claim Byron more publicly as someone who had suffered similarly from the savage misunderstanding of society. In the long letter of reproach to Lord Alfred Douglas which was published in 1905 as *De Profundis* he portrays Byron as a fellow martyr, if in some respects a lesser one: 'I was a man who stood in symbolic relations to the art and culture of my age ... Byron was a symbolic figure, but his relations were to the passion of his age and its weariness of passion. Mine were to something more noble, more permanent, of more vital issue, of larger scope.'

Byron's ability to be all things to all men gave him an appeal right across the political and sexual spectrums. In the twentieth century Byronists were both homosexuals and blatant womanisers; they came from the political left as well as the far right. Sir Harold Nicolson was a diplomat and writer, subsequently a politician, who moved from membership of Sir Oswald Mosley's New Party to Ramsay MacDonald's National Labour Party, before joining the Labour Party. He established himself as an authority on Byron in 1924 with *Byron, the Last Journey*, a partial biography covering Byron's period in Greece.

There are always private reasons behind the choice of a biographical subject. Why did Nicolson choose Byron? Perhaps first, most simply, because 1924 was the year of Byron's centenary: in his literary work Nicolson, always short of money, had his eye on the main chance. But there were other reasons, a network of affinities. At the time he was born his father Sir Arthur Nicolson, later 1st Lord Carnock, was chargé d'affaires in the British legation in Tehran.

His peripatetic childhood in a diplomatic household had given him a feeling for the Middle East. The Byron connection continued when in 1912, by then a diplomat himself, he was posted to Constantinople. Though in some ways the most English of Englishmen, Nicolson had a similar quality of rootlessness.

Like Byron he combined the life of the writer with that of the man of the world, a balance that did not always come easily. The Byronic dismissiveness of some of his writing, for example his scintillating essays *Some People*, led to resentment in official circles. He had a weakness for the Byronic sweeping statement, as for instance in his comment that he 'hated women, especially virgins'. The strange ramifications of his marriage to Vita Sackville-West, herself predominantly lesbian in her sexual tastes, were well described by their son Nigel Nicolson in *Portrait of a Marriage*. Nicolson's own discreetly concealed homosexuality almost certainly contributed to a defensive fellow-feeling towards Byron. 'Of course I always knew of this side to Byron's character and had discounted it,' he wrote in 1923. His view was that Byron's reputation would be best served by a conspiracy of silence over his relationships with boys.

It was for this reason that Nicolson had chosen to concentrate on Byron in 1823 and 1824 rather than his earlier Greek and Turkish travels. He told Sir John Murray, the fourth John Murray in succession to head the family firm, 'as I loathe the half-truths and dissimulations of ordinary biography, I had particularly chosen this last period as being that of which, I imagined, I could tell the whole truth.' However his confidence had been shattered. The spectre of the page Lukas Chalandritsanos, and the possibility that Byron had shared his bed with him, had raised its head again.

In the course of his researches Nicolson had been examining the Dorchester papers, including the letters which had been returned from Greece to John Cam Hobhouse as Byron's executor. After a formidable quarrel with the Lovelace family over the publication of *Astarte* in 1905, Lady Dorchester, who died in 1914, had bequeathed her Byron papers to John Murray and they were now in the Murray archive at Albemarle Street. In the packet marked 'Letters from Lord S. Osborne and Gamba' Nicolson had found Gamba's anxious account of the bed episode and his admission of Byron's reputed 'weakness' for Lukas. Nicolson claimed to have been horror-struck: 'this discovery has, I admit, been rather a shock to me.'

He was afraid that, if he used this material in his book, sharp-eyed readers would connect the account given by Gamba to the narrative of shipwreck, earthquake, fit and illness contained in Byron's late Greek poem 'Love and Death'. 'Now', Nicolson told Murray in a letter dated 21 June 1923, 'neither the poem which I have first referred to, nor the letter which I have analysed above, if *taken by themselves*, are very conclusive. But if taken together they leave no doubt that the poem was addressed to this Lucca, and however platonic and imaginative the verses may have been, yet I fear the conjunction, if made, would prove deleterious.'

Murray replied by return, in a letter marked Private and Confidential: 'The conjunction of all the points you mention does unquestionably leave a most disagreeable impression and I am glad that the discovery has come through you who regard such questions as I do. Had these papers fallen into Lord Lovelace's hands no one can say what he would have made of them.' Murray was still feeling an acute resentment over the accusations of incest that Lord Lovelace had made against Byron in *Astarte*. He explained to Nicolson:

'Amidst all the aspersions which have been flung upon B[yron]'s reputation by his own descendants, my consistent policy (& my Father's) has been to keep away as much as possible from his personal characteristics and to concentrate on his powers as a poet and letter writer. I have carefully refrained from expressing any definite opinion as to the main charge in Astarte – which is at any rate not proven. But all the time I have been able to say "There can be no question that in his later years his better self was reasserting itself: he was shaking free from the Venetian toils and settling down to good & honest work".'

Now even this comforting theory was eroded. Murray said to Nicolson of Pietro Gamba's letter: 'I certainly do not think that either of us is bound to disclose this letter: it is no dishonest concealment to decide thus.'

The tone of the correspondence between Nicolson and John Murray now astonishes. But this was 1923, four decades before homosexuality was finally decriminalised under British law. Homosexuality was still a taboo subject in what Nicolson and Murray would consider respectable society. An association between Byron and criminality would have advanced neither Nicolson's professional reputation nor the reputation of the Murray firm with whom Byron was still so closely associated. A gentlemen's agreement was rapidly arrived at and Lukas is scarcely mentioned in Nicolson's account of Byron at Missolonghi. In a letter written to Murray after the book was completed Nicolson says complacently: 'The only thing my book does, I think, is to tell the truth about Byron, without any use of white-wash.' He had the grace to add as an afterthought, 'except in *one* respect'.

The other main contender for the post of Byron's keeper in the inter-war period was Peter Quennell whose popular biography *Byron, the Years of Fame* of 1935 was followed by *Byron in Italy* in 1941. In some ways he was Harold

Nicolson's direct opposite. Quennell, the son of an architect, came from a middle-class background. He was brought up in Berkhamsted in Hertfordshire, attending the local public school where Graham Greene's father was headmaster. Quennell referred to Berkhamsted as irredeemably humdrum. His latching on to Byron as a specialist subject was part of his escape route, a factor in Quennell's often frenetic literary and social upward mobility. He was to be knighted in 1992.

Though Quennell's *Years of Fame* was the first Byron biography to pay any serious attention to Byron's bisexual tendencies, it was with Byron object of female fandom that the rampantly heterosexual Quennell, five times married, compulsive acquirer of mistresses, most readily identified. The zest with which he edited the letters *To Lord Byron*, collected correspondence from thirteen of his admirers, suggests how easily he saw himself at the receiving end of all this female adoration. Those who remember London literary parties of the period describe the confident seductiveness of Byron's alter ego: he too became a master of the under-look. Byron moved him easily, and this is one reason why Quennell wrote so well about him. The 'mood of exhilaration mixed with apprehension with that "certain sense of doubt and sorrow – a fear of what is to come – a doubt of what *is*" – which Byron declared, accompanies the fulfilment of any form of mortal pleasure'. This is something Quennell understood very well from his own restless amatory life.

Quennell also gives us the first inkling of a greater mood of tolerance towards Lord Byron infiltrating the John Murray offices. He recounts in his memoirs *The Marble Foot* how, in the 1930s, he first arrived at 50 Albemarle Street to view the Byron archives. There he met the fifth John Murray, who had taken over from his father in 1928:

'The late Sir John Murray received me kindly, if a little cautiously – he was a strong upholder of the family tradition that Byron's relationship with Augusta Leigh had been altogether blameless; but his nephew and heir, the present John Murray, gave me a warm and sympathetic welcome; and after the office had closed its doors we would sit drinking vintage port and look through the extraordinary pile of manuscripts that he heaped upon the table.'

So liberated was the atmosphere that the tall, fair-haired Isabelle, Peter Quennell's second wife, flung her arms around the Thorwaldsen bust of Byron standing on the stairway and kissed it passionately, planting a heavy smudge of lipstick on its mouth and chin.

The 'nephew and heir' Quennell refers to in his memoir was the sixth John

Murray, usually known as 'Jock', the friend of Osbert Lancaster, John Betjeman, Freya Stark, the Byron scholar Doris Langley Moore, and Iris Origo, whose book about Byron and Teresa Guiccioli, *The Last Attachment*, was published in 1949. With the encouragement of the gregarious Jock, a group of Byron devotees began assembling at John Murray, a mid-twentieth-century equivalent of the friends who gathered in the drawing room after Byron's exile to hear bulletins from Venice. Harold Nicolson's diary for 15 November 1945 describes the charm and oddity of this reconnection with the past:

'I go to Albemarle Street to watch Peter Quennell and Jock Murray collate the Byron letters with the Prothero edition (of 1904). They wish to publish a compendium of the more important letters and find on examination that Prothero left out many essential passages without indicating any omissions. It was strange to find myself in that room, with port and candles, and to hear John Murray's grandson or great-grandson read aloud the very letters which old John Murray in that very room had read to Scott and the rest.'

There was a clandestine element in these meetings of Byronists. In spite of Quennell's tentative raising of the subject, Byron's homosexuality was by no means public knowledge. James Lees-Milne's description of a dinner at Rules in 1942 makes it seem like the gathering of a secret society of cognoscenti. There were three at the table: the bisexual Nicolson; Lees-Milne himself, who as he admits in *Another Self* was 'repeatedly falling in love with someone or other and it did not seem to matter whether with woman or man'; and James Pope-Hennessy, the writer and homosexual who was murdered in 1974 by a gang of rough trade youths. The topic of conversation at Rules was predictable: 'We discussed Byron's sex life of course.'

The things that were important for Byronists of this generation were, beyond the bisexual connection, the immaculate aristocracy of Byron, his clever, funny, bitchy conversational tone. These were self-consciously literate people who could still quote fluently and accurately from Byron's poetry; architectural experts and travellers who could immediately place Byron in his setting, whether in St James's or Ravenna; literary historians who shared an inner knowledge of the exact chronology of Byron's life. Still relatively isolated in an England where homosexuality was not accepted, they used Byron as a kind of code between themselves, hoarding Byronic objects like the relics of a saint. When I went to visit James Lees-Milne to talk about Byron in 1997, he brought out the little scrap of unsigned Byron letter he had bought for £45 at Sotheby's in 1972 and took me upstairs to his library to view Lady Byron's card case, containing a piece of Byron's hair in a small transparent package. The hair was a dark auburn. Could I detect a fleck or two of grey? I could.

In the twentieth century Byron's continuing physical presence was felt even by those who most disliked him. T.S. Eliot complained of Byron as sculpted by Thorwaldsen: 'that weakly sensual mouth, that restless triviality of expression, and most of all that kind of look of self-conscious beauty'. To Virginia Woolf, writing to Lytton Strachey, Byron seemed 'tawdry and melodramatic. And Claire and Trelawny and so on and so on – I conceive them like a cave at some Earl's Court exhibition – a grotto I mean lined with distorted mirrors and plastered with oyster shells.' Quite apart from his poetry Byron himself aroused an evident physical distaste.

Conversely, those who loved him could easily resummon him in all his idiosyncratic splendour. W.H. Auden for example treated Byron as if he were still alive. In June 1936 Auden booked a passage on a ship from Hull to Iceland. On the five-day voyage he read *Don Juan*. He had signed a contract with Faber & Faber for a travel book on Iceland and it dawned on him that the focus for the book should be Lord Byron:

'I suddenly thought I might write him a chatty letter in light verse about anything I could think of, Europe, literature, myself. He's the right person I think, because he was a townee, a European, and disliked Wordsworth and all that kind of approach to nature, and I find that very sympathetic. This letter in itself will have very little to do with Iceland, but will be rather a description of an effect of travelling in distant places which is to make one reflect on one's past and one's culture from the outside.'

If it seems surprising that W.H. Auden in 1936 should reach as far back as Byron for his catalyst we need to remember the parallels between them: the cosmopolitan urbanity that Auden had acknowledged; the male-male sexuality; the belief in liberty and the capacity to follow it through, in quite another country – the following year Auden would go to Spain, having volunteered to drive an ambulance for the Republican side; the propensity for self-exile from an England Byron and later Auden both felt to be outworn – there was to be an outcry when Auden and Christopher Isherwood left England for the States in 1939.

> 'Byron, thou should'st be living at this hour!
>   What would you do, I wonder, if you were?
> Britannia's lost prestige and cash and power,

> Her middle classes show some wear and tear,
>   We've learned to bomb each other from the air;
> I can't imagine what the Duke of Wellington
> Would say about the music of Duke Ellington.
>
> Suggestions have been made that the Teutonic
>   Führer-Prinzip would have appealed to you
> As being the true heir to the Byronic –
>   In keeping with your social status too
>   (It has its English converts, fit and few),
> That you would, hearing honest Oswald's call,
> Be gleichgestaltet in the Albert Hall.'

Sharp, intimate, discursive, sometimes amiably jeering, sometimes more seriously questioning, as when Auden tests Byron's temperamental affinity with fascism: nothing shows more clearly than Auden's 'Letter to Lord Byron' his uncanny capacity to live out the centuries.

Byron was always intrigued by the phenomenon of physical changes wrought by time on human bodies in their graves. In June 1819 in Bologna cemetery, he reflected on the monument surmounted by a Bernini bust of a young Roman woman who had died when she was twenty. 'She was a Princess Barberini – dead two centuries ago,' he told John Murray, adding the information given him by the custodian 'that on opening her Grave they had found her hair complete – and "as yellow as Gold"'. The following November, expressing his shock at the sudden deaths in London of Waite his dentist and Blake his barber, Byron exclaimed: 'I have seen a thousand graves opened – and always perceived that whatever was gone – the *teeth and hair* remained of those who had died with them – Is not this odd?'

On Wednesday 15 June 1938, two years after Auden's 'Letter to Lord Byron' and a hundred and fourteen after Byron's death at Missolonghi, the Byron family vault under the parish church at Hucknall Torkard was reopened and the more stalwart members of the local viewing party assembled by the vicar, Canon Thomas Gerrard Barber, took the opportunity to inspect the physical condition of Lord Byron in his coffin. The vault had been sealed up since 1852 when Byron's daughter Ada, Countess of Lovelace, had been buried, at her own request, beside her father. Ada too had died in her thirty-seventh year.

Canon Barber, who had obtained permission for his project both from the Home Office and from the 10th Lord Byron, who was Vicar of Thrumpton-on-Trent, was anxious to stress that the reopening of the vault was 'not undertaken to satisfy a morbid curiosity, but to establish some archaeological points of general interest with regard to the existence, or otherwise of a crypt' beneath the parish church. The Canon, who had first arrived in Hucknall as a curate in 1904, was collecting material for his book *Byron and Where He is Buried* which was published the following year. At the same time, as he confided to his fellow enthusiast the writer Cecil Roberts, he was anxious to establish definitely whether or not Byron was in his coffin. Local rumours had been proliferating that the corpse had been spirited away.

A small party was assembled for luncheon at the Vicarage. Canon Barber had invited a local MP, F. Seymour Cocks; a local archaeologist, J. Holland Walker; the Diocesan Surveyor, Nathaniel Lane; a doctor and a photographer. It was only during lunch that the purpose of the meeting was revealed and the guests sworn to secrecy. The Canon explained that had the news been made public that the vault was to be opened 'hundreds of pilgrims would have sought admission to the Church'.

At two o'clock a lorry drew up discreetly at the back of the Church Hall. A number of planks, crowbars and workmen's tools were unloaded, carried into the churchyard and left on the north side of the building, near the vestry door. At four o'clock all visitors were ejected and the church locked. Canon Barber's party had now been enlarged by the arrival of two churchwardens and their wives, several members of the Parish Council and the church caretaker and fireman, James Betteridge. In a hushed, expectant atmosphere the masons started work. By six-thirty they had managed to dislodge the two heavy flagstones lying to the right of the chancel steps. Beneath these were eleven steps leading down into the Byron burial chamber. The local doctor suspended a miner's lamp into the chamber to make certain the air was not polluted. Canon Barber was the first to descend, followed by the surveyor, the antiquarian and the doctor. All were dismayed by the size of the chamber. Far from being the dignified sepulchral vault the Canon had expected, the room measured only six by seven foot wide and six foot deep, an outrage to his 'sense of reverence and decency'. The diocesan surveyor judged the Byron vault in Hucknall 'a miserable little affair', the worst he had seen in his professional career.

The floor was deep with rubble and desiccated bones which had spilled out of the now decaying coffins. The photographer's powerful reflecting lamps revealed three tiers of Byron family coffins heaped one upon the other. The weight of the top coffins had pressed down on those beneath them, crushing the bottom coffins almost flat. The heavy chest containing the urn with Byron's heart and brain stood precariously on a little coffin containing the body of a baby, maybe Ernest, a child of the 3rd Lord. The only family coffins which were not badly damaged were the two most recent: Byron's own, resting on the coffins of William 4th Lord Byron and Byron's great-uncle the 'Wicked' 5th Lord, and the coffin of Byron's daughter Ada lying on top of that of Byron's mother. It was clear that the coffins had been vandalised, probably at the time the vault had last been opened for the burial of Ada or during later alterations to the church, when the chancel had been lengthened, in 1888. Byron's coronet still rested on top of his coffin, but its pearls and its silver orbs were missing. The crimson velvet Cap of Maintenance had disappeared. There was no nameplate on the coffin and one of the handles, embellished with silver cherubim, had been removed. Most of the velvet originally covering the coffin had been stripped off and presumably recycled as Byron souvenirs.

During his detailed examination of the vault, the surveyor, Nat Lane, noticed that the lid of Byron's coffin was loose. 'As I reached over the coffin to get my rod into the far corner of the vault, the lid itself moved, moved distinctly,' he recalled in a later radio interview. At half-past ten that night, after anxious discussions about whether they ought to embark on an examination of the body for which they had no specific authority, a decision was made that 'truth ought to prevail' and the current condition of the 6th Lord Byron be made public in the book which the Canon planned to write. Five or six men, including the surveyor, the photographer and the fireman, were present in the vault when the outer coffin lid was removed, followed by the cover of the inner lead shell which, it was discovered, had already been cut into, with a large gash at the head. Inside the layer of lead was the wooden coffin containing Byron's body. It was now nearly midnight. The news of the discovery was given to the Vicar who himself now descended again into the vault. 'Very, very reverently', Canon Barber later wrote, 'I raised the lid, and before my eyes there lay the embalmed body of Byron in as perfect a condition as when it was placed in the coffin one hundred and fourteen years ago.'

Other witnesses' accounts are more telling in their detail. Byron's body was still in an excellent state of preservation, showing no signs of decomposition: a report that contradicts Hobhouse's comment, in 1824, that his friend's body had been unrecognisable. According to Nat Lane, the surveyor, the corpse was that of an 'extraordinarily handsome' young man in his mid-thirties, recognisably the model for his famous portraits, although his complexion was now somewhat sallow. The church caretaker Jim Betteridge agreed that Byron's features 'with the slightly protruding lower lip and curly hair were easily recognisable . . . The head was slightly raised and the colour of the body was of dark stone.'

Byron's head, limbs and torso had remained quite solid. The only skelet-onised portions of his body were the forearms, hands and lower legs. The hair on his head, body and limbs was intact, though now completely grey. His twentieth-century visitors were aware of the holes in his chest and the back of his head, left when the heart and brains had been removed at Byron's autopsy. The bandage which bound his skull was still in place and Nat Lane noted a drop of blood on Byron's forehead. According to the People's Churchwarden, A.E. Houldsworth, Byron's sexual organ showed 'quite abnormal develop-ment'. Mysteriously, Byron's right foot had been detached from his body at the ankle and lay on its own at the bottom of the coffin. The foot may have been removed at the time of the autopsy but, if so, it is curious that neither the doctors' reports nor Hobhouse, in his diaries, make any mention of the fact.

Early the next morning, 16 June 1938, Canon Barber returned to the vault for a second viewing, having summoned the writer Cecil Roberts. Their friend-ship dated back to the days when Roberts had edited the *Nottingham Journal*. Roberts had his own family connections with Hucknall. In his memoir *Sunshine and Shadow* he describes the deep emotion he felt at standing in the presence 'of all that remained of one who had been young, handsome and the most famous man of genius of his age, a name throughout Europe'. The two Byronists stood in silence for some minutes:

'Our inspection ended, the Canon gently replaced the lid of the coffin and said a short prayer. We came up into the chancel and went out into the summer morning. The workmen were there to close the vault, perhaps never to be opened again. When I asked the holder of the title, the Rev. Lord Byron, the gentle vicar of Thrumpton-on-Trent, if he would elect to be buried in the family vault, he said, emphatically, "No! No! That's part of a legend which should rest".'

Major Published Works of Lord Byron

Hours of Idleness: a Series of Poems, Original and Translated. S. and J. Ridge of Newark, 1807

English Bards and Scotch Reviewers: a Satire. James Cawthorn, 1809

Childe Harold's Pilgrimage: a Romaunt, Cantos I and II. John Murray, 1812

The Giaour: a Fragment of a Turkish Tale. John Murray, 1813

The Bride of Abydos: a Turkish tale. John Murray, 1813

The Corsair: a Tale. John Murray, 1814

Lara: a Tale. John Murray, 1814

Hebrew Melodies. Byron's words for music by J. Braham and I. Nathan. John Murray, 1815

The Siege of Corinth: a Poem and Parisina: a Poem. John Murray, 1816

Childe Harold's Pilgrimage, Canto III. John Murray, 1816

The Prisoner of Chillon. John Murray, 1816

Manfred: a Dramatic Poem. John Murray, 1817

Beppo: a Venetian Story. John Murray, 1818

Childe Harold's Pilgrimage, Canto IV. John Murray, 1818

Mazeppa: a Poem. John Murray, 1819

Don Juan, Cantos I and II. John Murray, 1819

Don Juan, Cantos III, IV and V. John Murray, 1820

Marino Faliero, Doge of Venice: an Historical Tragedy in five acts. John Murray, 1821

Sardanapalus: a Tragedy; The Two Foscari: a Tragedy; Cain: a Mystery. John Murray, 1821

Werner: a Tragedy. John Murray, 1822

The Vision of Judgement. The Liberal, No. 1, 15 October 1822

Heaven and Earth. The Liberal, No. 2, 1 January 1823

The Blues. The Liberal, No. 3, 23–26 April 1823

The Age of Bronze. John Hunt, 1823

The Island: or Christian and his Comrades. John Hunt, 1823

Don Juan, Cantos VI, VII and VIII. John Hunt, July 1823

Don Juan, Cantos IX, X and XI. John Hunt, August 1823

Don Juan ,Cantos XII, XIII and XIV. John Hunt, December 1823

Don Juan, Cantos XV and XVI. John Hunt, March 1824

The Deformed Transformed: a Drama. John Hunt, 1824

Sources and Reference Notes

In preparing this book my chief resource has been the Byron archive at John Murray, 50 Albemarle Street, London.

I have also consulted Byron-related material in the following collections:

Aberdeen Grammar School

Aberdeen Public Library

Bodleian Library, Oxford

    Abinger Papers

    Bruce Family Papers

    Hughenden Papers

    Lovelace–Byron Archive

    Shelley Papers

    Captain Daniel Roberts Reminiscence

British Library

    Ashley Papers

    Broughton (J.C. Hobhouse) Papers

    Byron–Leigh Papers

    Claire Clairmont Journal

    Scrope Davies Papers

    Egerton Papers

    Holland House Papers

    Lady Caroline Lamb Correspondence

    Napier Family Papers

    Trelawny Correspondence

    E.E. Williams Journal

    Zambelli Papers

British School at Athens

    George Finlay Papers

    Frank Hastings Letters and Journal

Brotherton Library, University of Leeds

    Lady Caroline Lamb Correspondence

Chatsworth House, Derbyshire

    Devonshire Collections

Classensé Library, Ravenna
  Gamba Collection
Fitzwilliam Museum, Cambridge
  Blunt Papers
Greater London Record Office
  Lady Jersey diaries
Greek National Archive, Athens
  Stanhope Papers and documents relating to Greek War of Independence
Greek National Historical Museum, Athens
Greek National Library, Athens
  London Greek Committee Papers
Harrow School, Middlesex
Hertfordshire Archives, Hertford
  Cowper and Lamb Family Papers
Keats–Shelley Memorial House, Rome
  Byron Collection
  Nelson Gay Papers, including his transcripts of Italian Secret Police Archives
  Irish Origo Papers
  Captain Daniel Roberts Journal
National Art Library
  Forster Collection
National Portrait Gallery
Newstead Abbey, City of Nottingham Museums
  Roe–Byron Collection and later acquisitions
New York Public Library
  Berg Collection
Nottingham Public Libraries
Carl H. Pforzheimer Library, New York
  Shelley and His Circle MSS
Henry Ransom Humanities Research Center, University of Texas at Austin
  Byron MS and Pigot Family Collection
Scottish National Portrait Gallery, Edinburgh
Trinity College Library, Cambridge

References

Quotations from Byron's letters and his irregularly kept diaries, including his 'Detached Thoughts', are taken from Leslie A. Marchand (ed.), *Byron's Letters and Journals*, 13 vols, John Murray, 1973–94; quotations from Byron's poetry from Jerome J. McGann (ed.), *Byron: The Complete Poetical Works*, 7 vols, Oxford University Press, 1980–93; quotations from his prose from Andrew Nicholson (ed.), *Lord Byron: The Complete Miscellaneous Prose*, Oxford University Press, 1991. Unless otherwise indicated, further quotations are drawn from material in the John Murray archive. Greek letters in the John Murray archive have been newly translated by Michael Ward.

Permission for quotation from the Lovelace Papers (Lovelace–Byron Archive) on deposit at the Bodleian Library, University of Oxford, has been granted by the Earl of Lytton (through

Pollinger); for quotation from the Abinger Papers by Lord Abinger (through the Bodleian Library, Oxford); from the Hughenden Papers by the National Trust (through the Bodleian Library, Oxford); from material in Harrow School Archive by the Keepers and Governors of Harrow School; from the Carl H. Pforzheimer Collection of Shelley and His Circle and the Berg Collection of English and American Literature on behalf of the New York Public Library Astor, Lenox and Tilden Foundations.

Other frequently cited sources are abbreviated as follows in the source notes:

Blessington *Conversations*   M. Gardiner (Countess of Blessington), *Conversations of Lord Byron*, 1834

Browne 'Narrative'   James Hamilton Browne, 'Narrative of a Visit to Greece', *Blackwood's Edinburgh Magazine*, September 1834

Browne 'Voyage'   James Hamilton Browne, 'Voyage from Leghorn to Cephalonia with Lord Byron in 1823', *Blackwood's Edinburgh Magazine*, January 1834

Clairmont *Correspondence*   ed. Marion Kingston Stocking, *The Clairmont Correspondence, 1808–1879*, 2 vols, 1995

Clairmont journal   Claire Clairmont MS journal. British Library

Dallas *Recollections*   Robert Charles Dallas, *Recollections of the life of Lord Byron from the Year 1808 to the End of 1814*, 1824

Elwin   Malcolm Elwin, *Lord Byron's Wife*, 1962

Galt *Life*   John Galt, *The Life of Lord Byron*, 1830

Gamba *Narrative*   Count Pietro Gamba, *A Narrative of Lord Byron's Last Journey to Greece*, 1825

Guiccioli *Recollections*   Countess Teresa Guiccioli, *My Recollections of Lord Byron*, 2 vols, French edn 1868, English 1869

Guiccioli *Vie*   ed. Peter Cochran, trans. Michael Rees, *Lord Byron's Life in Italy*, new English translation of Countess Teresa Guiccioli's MS *Vie de Lord Byron en Italie*, University of Delaware Press, in preparation

Hanson narrative   Newton Hanson, MS record of Byron's early life as recalled by his father John Hanson, Byron's solicitor

Hobhouse diaries   John Cam Hobhouse (Lord Broughton), MS diaries. British Library, unless otherwise specified

Hobhouse *Journey*   John Cam Hobhouse, *A Journey through Albania and other Provinces of Turkey during the years 1809 and 1810*, 2 vols, 1813

Hobhouse notes   Annotations by J.C. Hobhouse in his own copy of Thomas Moore, *Letters and Journals of Lord Byron, with notices of his Life*, 1830. This copy, formerly belonging to Sir Harold Nicolson, is now in the Byron collection of the late Harry Oppenheimer, in the care of the Brenthurst Library, Johannesburg

Hobhouse *Recollections*   ed. Lady Dorchester, John Cam Hobhouse (Lord Broughton), *Recollections of a Long Life*, 6 vols, 1909–11

Hobhouse *Separation*   John Cam Hobhouse (Lord Broughton), *Contemporary account of the separation of Lord and Lady Byron, also of the destruction of Lord Byron's memoirs*, privately printed, 1870

Hobhouse *Travels*   John Cam Hobhouse, *Travels in Albania and Other Provinces of Turkey in 1809 and 1810*, 2 vols, 1855

Hodgson *Memoir*   James T. Hodgson, *Memoir of the Rev. Francis Hodgson*, 2 vols, 1878

Hunt *Lord Byron*   Leigh Hunt, *Lord Byron and Some of His Contemporaries*, 2 vols, 1828

Kennedy *Conversations*   James Kennedy, *Conversations on Religion with Lord Byron and others, held in Cephalonia a short time previous to his Lordship's death*, 1830

Lovelace *Astarte*   Ralph, Earl of Lovelace, *Astarte: a Fragment of Truth Concerning . . . Lord Byron*, privately printed, 1905, enlarged edition, ed. Mary, Countess of Lovelace, 1921

Marchand *Letters and Journals*   ed. Leslie A. Marchand, *Byron's Letters and Journals*, 13 vols, 1973–94

Medwin *Angler*   Thomas Medwin, *The Angler in Wales*, 2 vols, 1834

Medwin *Conversations*   Thomas Medwin, *Journal of the Conversations of Lord Byron at Pisa*, 1824

Millingen *Memoirs*   Julius Millingen, *Memoirs of the affairs of Greece with various anecdotes of Lord Byron, and an account of his last illness and death*, 1831

Moore *Journal*   ed. Wilfred S. Dowden, *The Journal of Thomas Moore*, 6 vols, 1983–91

Moore *Life*   Thomas Moore, *Letters and Journals of Lord Byron, with notices of his Life*, 2 vols, 1830

Moore *Prose and Verse*   ed. Richard Herne Shepherd, *Thomas Moore: Prose and Verse, Humorous, Satirical and Sentimental, with Suppressed Passages from the Memoirs of Lord Byron*, 1878

Nathan *Fugitive Pieces*   Isaac Nathan, *Fugitive Pieces and Recollections of Lord Byron*, 1829

Parry *Last Days*   William Parry, assisted Thomas Hodgkinson, *The Last Days of Lord Byron*, 1825

Polidori *Diary*   ed. William Michael Rossetti, *The Diary of Dr John William Polidori*, 1911

Prothero *Letters and Journals*   ed. Rowland E. Prothero, *The Works of Lord Byron with Letters and Journals*, 6 vols, 1904

Rogers *Table-Talk*   Alexander Dyce, *Recollections of the Table-Talk of Samuel Rogers*, 1856

Shelley *Letters*   ed. Frederick L. Jones, *The Letters of Percy Bysshe Shelley*, 2 vols, 1964

Shelley and his Circle   ed. Donald H. Reiman and Doucet Devin Fischer, *Shelley and his Circle 1773–1822*, edition of MSS in Carl H. Pforzheimer Library, New York, 8 vols to date

Smiles *Memoir*   Samuel Smiles, *Memoir and Correspondence of the late John Murray*, 2 vols, 1891

Stanhope *Greece*   Leicester Stanhope, *Greece in 1823 and 1824, to which are added Reminiscences of Lord Byron*, 1824

Trelawny *Letters*   ed. H. Buxton Foreman, *Letters of Edward John Trelawny*, 1910

Trelawny *Records*   Edward John Trelawny, *Records of Shelley, Byron and the Author*, 1878

Trelawny *Recollections*   Edward John Trelawny, *Recollections of the Last Days of Shelley and Byron*, 1858

Williams diary   Edward Ellerker Williams, MS diary. British Library

Introduction

vii 'Baxter must wait'   B to Douglas Kinnaird, 27 February 1823
    'we live in gigantic'   B to Sir Walter Scott, 4 May 1822
    'with me there is'   Blessington *Conversations*
    'as a lover does'   ibid.
viii 'rascally time-servers'   Journal, 17 November 1813
    'Oh my head'   ibid.
    'To-day I have boxed'   Journal, 10 April 1814

'memorials'   B to Lady Blessington, 2 June 1823

'because Bonaparte'   Hunt *Lord Byron*

'so beautiful'   B to Augusta Leigh, 13 October 1816

'half worn out'   B to Thomas Moore, 6 November 1816

ix 'Since that period'   ibid., 2 August 1821

'not very large'   Journal, 17 December 1823

'I perceive that'   B to John Murray, 4 December 1821

'Two men have died'   Thomas Babington Macaulay, review of Thomas Moore's *Life of Byron*, in *Edinburgh Review*, June 1831

'Your Byron publishes'   Thomas Carlyle, *Sartor Resartus* in *Fraser's Magazine*, 1833–4

x 'fat bashful boy'   Elizabeth Pigot, quoted Moore *Life*, vol. 1

'*under* look'   Moore *Journal*, 2 July 1821

'That beautiful'   Lady Caroline Lamb, extracts from journal, March 1812. British Library

'I awoke'   Moore *Life*, vol. 1

'Byron had'   Blessington *Conversations*

'the most powerful'   additional preface to *Childe Harold's Pilgrimage*, Cantos I and II, 1813

xi 'Your room'   Lady Caroline Lamb to John Murray, 1816

xii 'would not allow'   Leslie Marchand to John Murray, 26 October 1995

xiii 'letting out'   'Detached Thoughts', no. 76, 1821–2

'really *consequential*'   ibid., no. 74

'hair-breadth'   B to Thomas Moore, 29 February 1816

'of no Country'   B to Count Alfred D'Orsay, 22 April 1823

'I should like'   B to Richard Belgrave Hoppner, 29 October 1819

xiv 'all the bullies'   B to Douglas Kinnaird, 31 March 1823

'Build me'   *Childe Harold's Pilgrimage*, Canto IV, st. 105, l. 938

1   Aberdeen 1788–1798

3 'for my son'   Moore *Life*, vol. 1

Byron's lameness   Denis Browne, 'The Problem of Byron's Lameness', *Proceedings of the Royal Society of Medicine*, June 1960, and A.B. Morrison, 'Byron's Lameness', *Byron Journal*, no. 3, 1975. Browne's views are corroborated by Dr Raymond Mills, 'The Last Illness of Lord Byron', *Byron Journal*, no. 28, 2000

4 'the embalmed'   Trelawny *Recollections*

'George's foot'   Catherine Gordon Byron to Frances Leigh, 31 May 1791

'false delicacy'   Moore *Journal*, 19 February 1828

'it was vain'   Lady Byron to Henry Crabb Robinson, 5 March 1855. *Diary, Reminiscences and Correspondence of Henry Crabb Robinson*, vol. 2, 1872

5 'What a strange thing'   'Detached Thoughts', no. 102, 1821–2

6 'very much interested'   Catherine Gordon Byron to Frances Leigh, 29 November 1792. British Library

'very early'   Medwin *Conversations*

'while washing'   The Rev. A.G. L'Estrange, *The Literary Life of the Rev. William Harness*, 1871

7 'Augusta and I'   B to J.J. Coulmann, July 1823
'ever sincerely loved'   Catherine Gordon Byron to Frances Leigh, 23 August 1791
'as haughty as Lucifer'   B to John Murray, 16 October 1820
'are out of fashion'   Catherine Gordon Byron to Frances Leigh, 23 August 1791
'romping, comely'   Pryse Lockhart Gordon, *Personal Memoirs*, vol. 2, 1830
'cankered a heart'   Blessington *Conversations*
8 'even at a reduction'   B to Douglas Kinnaird, 2 February 1821
'Come and see'   Moore *Life*, vol. 1
'ill-deedie laddie'   Mr Stephen, mealmaker at Inchmarnock, quoted R.E. Prothero,
'The Childhood and School Days of Byron', *Nineteenth Century*, XLIII, 1898
'curled darling'   B to Thomas Moore, 28 October 1821
9 'through & through'   B to John Murray, 9 October 1821
'the March of events'   ibid., 16 August 1821
10 'that little'   The Rev. W. Rogerson, 'Lord Byron's connection with Aberdeen',
Bon-Accord, 19 June 1902
'My "heart warms"'   B to Sir Walter Scott, 12 January 1822
'discourse of'   Angus Calder, 'The Islands: Scotland, Greece and Romantic Savagery',
Byron and Scotland: Radical or Dandy?, 1989
'first of flames'   Journal, 17 November 1813
'all our caresses'   Journal, 26 November 1813
11 'With respect to'   Hobhouse notes
'line of cut-throat'   B to Francis Hodgson, 14 November 1810
'I like a row'   B to Sir Walter Scott, 12 January 1822
'cudgelled to Church'   B to William Gifford, 18 June 1813
'the gloomiest'   Lady Byron to Henry Crabb Robinson, 5 March 1855. *Diary,
Reminiscences and Correspondence of Henry Crabb Robinson*, vol. 2, 1872
'winter blues'   'Seasonal affective disorder among primary care attenders and a
community sample in Aberdeen', *British Journal of Psychiatry*, no. 175, 1999
'lemancholy'   B to John Cam Hobhouse, 2 November 1811
'mist, mizzle'   Ravenna Journal, 16 January 1821
'Georgius Dominus'   Anon., *Anecdotes of Lord Byron, from Authentic Sources*, 1825. For
details of Byron's schooldays, *Bon Record. Records and Reminiscences of Aberdeen
Grammar School*, ed. H.F. Morland Simpson, 1906

2   Newstead 1798–1799

13 'with ye "i"'   B to James Wedderburn Webster, 15 September 1813
'and with precisely'   B to Sir Walter Scott, 12 January 1822
14 'virtuous mermaids'   *Don Juan*, Canto XII, st. 73, l. 577
'the *old Gordons*'   B to John Murray, 16 October 1820
'It was'   Moore *Life*, vol. 1
15 'Newstead is'   undated newspaper cutting, Murray archive
'one can well'   Wilfrid Blunt diary, 3 June 1909. Wilfrid Scawen Blunt, *My Diaries*,
vol. 2, 1921
16 'and she looked'   Hanson narrative

Byron estates   for detailed history, see John Beckett, *Byron and Newstead: The Aristocrat and the Abbey*, 2002

'in confusion'   Hanson narrative

18 'Thro' thy battlements'   'On Leaving Newstead Abbey', 1803, ll. 1–2

19 'plain forefathers'   'Elegy on Newstead Abbey', 1804?, l. 130

'Proudly majestic'   ibid., ll. 7–8

'vast and venerable'   *Childe Harold's Pilgrimage*, Canto I, st. 7, l. 56

'An old, old monastery'   *Don Juan*, Canto XIII, st. 55, ll. 434–6

'Before the mansion'   ibid., st. 57, ll. 449–51

20 Mrs Radcliffe and Nottingham   Hobhouse diaries, 15 July 1824

'the poor partridge'   *Don Juan*, Canto XVI, st. 80, l. 685

3   Nottingham 1799–1800

21 Nottingham background   John Beckett, 'Byron's Nottingham', *Newstead Review*, Summer 2000, and Gwen Beaumont, 'Byron's Nottingham', *Byron Journal*, no. 12, 1984

'of all the towns'   C.P. Moritz, *Journeys of a German in England in 1782*, 1965

'a fine sharp Boy'   John Hanson to James Farquhar, 30 August 1789

'In Nottingham county'   'Epigram on an Old Lady Who Had Some Curious Notions Respecting the Soul', 1798, ll. 1–4

22 'I am astonished'   B to Catherine Gordon Byron, 13 March 1799

'It makes me'   Moore *Life*, vol. 1

'May Desires'   B to Catherine Gordon Byron, 13 March 1799

'He told me'   John Hanson to Catherine Gordon Byron, 1 September 1799

23 'at his mother's'   Hobhouse notes

'My passions were'   'Detached Thoughts', no. 80, 1821–2

'And now if'   B to John Hanson, November ? 1799

'a true voluptuary'   Journal, 13 December 1813

'a cold temperament'   The Earl of Malmesbury, *Memoirs of an ex-Minister*, vol. 1, 1884

24 'He has Ability'   John Hanson to Catherine Gordon Byron, 1 September 1799. Harrow School Archive

'I have a perfect'   Hanson narrative

25 'travelled a great deal'   John Hanson to Catherine Gordon Byron, 1 September 1799. Harrow School Archive

'this damned place'   B to George Byron, 24 February 1801

26 'my foot goes'   B to John Hanson, November ? 1799

'This instrument'   Hobhouse notes

'fell in love'   John Cam Hobhouse, 'Lord Byron', extended entry in diary for summer 1824. British Library

'your mother is'   Moore *Life*, vol. 1

27 'one of the'   'Detached Thoughts', no. 79, 1821–2

'I could love'   B to Lady Melbourne, 26 November 1812

'completely Greek'   'Detached Thoughts', no. 79, 1821–2

'Hush'd are the winds'   'On the Death of a Young Lady, Cousin to the Author and Very Dear to Him', 1802, ll. 1–4

28 'that *political Pandemonium*' B to John Pigot, 18 August 1806
   'If I had been' Journal, 10 March 1814

4 Harrow 1801–1805

29 'I will cut' B to Catherine Gordon Byron, 1–10 May 1804?
   Harrow School background Christopher Tyerman, *A History of Harrow School*, 2001
30 'only school' Percy M. Thornton, *Harrow School and its Surroundings*, 1885
   'so they at once' Hanson narrative
   'a rough, curly' Bryan Waller Procter (Barry Cornwall), *An Autobiographical Fragment and Autobiographical Notes*, 1877
   'I have as much' B to Catherine Gordon Byron, 1–10 May 1804?
   'There goes Birron' Percy M. Thornton, *Harrow School and its Surroundings*, 1885
   'I wish' B to Catherine Gordon Byron, 1 May 1803
   'I have already' ibid., June 1803
31 'the M Post' B to John Murray, 7 February 1814
   'the Shoe intirely' Dr Laurie to Catherine Gordon Byron, 7 December 1807
   'turbulent and riotous' B to William Harness, 16 February 1808
   'he accustomed' Sir Robert Peel, quoted Moore *Journal*, 20 February 1829
   'the *Blest Spot*' B to Edward Noel Long, 14 May 1807
   'a wild mountain colt' Dr Joseph Drury, quoted Moore *Life*, vol. 1
32 'I am much' Dr Joseph Drury to John Hanson, 15 May 1803
   'inattention to business' ibid., 3 February 1803
   'animal spirits' ibid., 29 December 1804
   'He has talents' Moore *Life*, vol. 1
   'the dear preceptor' 'Childish Recollections', 1806, l. 108
   'the truth is' Catherine Gordon Byron to John Hanson, 30 October 1803
   'What, Mr Hanson' Hanson narrative
33 'Boards and Sleeps' Owen Mealey to John Hanson, 5 August 1803
   'shy and singular' B to Lady Melbourne, 29 January 1814
   'beau idéal' Medwin *Conversations*
   'amongst the Wonders' *The Derbyshire Tourist's Guide and Travelling Companion*, 1837
   'with the rock' 'Detached Thoughts', no. 65, 1821–2
34 'And I must' 'Stanzas to [Mrs Musters] On Leaving England', 1809, l. 5
   'commit the whole' B to Annabella Milbanke, 29 November 1813
   'could have leaped' Nimrod, *Hunting Reminiscences*, 1843
   'if my Son was' Catherine Gordon Byron to John Hanson, 30 October 1803
   'Do you think' Moore *Life*, vol. 1
   'I do not believe' Hobhouse notes
   'I saw two' 'The Dream', 1816, st. 2, l. 27
35 'melting character' Browne 'Voyage'
   'soft voluptuous' Moore *Journal*, 7 July 1827
   'the full under-lip' D.E. Williams, *The Life of Sir Thomas Lawrence*, vol. 2, 1831
   'peculiarly agreeable' Blessington *Conversations*

'irresistible sweetness'   Browne 'Voyage'

'picked out'   John Cam Hobhouse to B, 31 July 1810

'a great deal'   Douglas Kinnaird, quoted Moore *Journal*, 7 July 1827

'any consecutive'   Moore *Life*, vol. 2

'a catalogue'   Harold Nicolson, *Byron: The Last Journey*, 1924

'It seemed'   George Finlay, *A History of Greece*, vol. 6, 1877

36 'I cannot find'   Catherine Gordon Byron to John Hanson, 10 March 1803

'they goe'   Owen Mealey to John Hanson, 29 November 1803. British Library

'I am not'   B to Augusta Byron, 26 March 1804

'whom I detest'   ibid., 21 November 1804

37 'intimacy'   Moore *Life*, vol. 1

'a circumstance'   Hobhouse notes

'My School friendships'   'Detached Thoughts', no. 91, 1821–2

'At every public'   note to verses 'To the Duke of D[orset]', 1805

38 'P. Hunter'   Moore *Life*, vol. 1

'a Friend'   B to Edward Noel Long, 30 March 1807

'the most good tempered'   B to Augusta Byron, 2 November 1804

'you were'   B to William Harness, 16 February 1808

'begun one'   'Detached Thoughts', no. 91, 1821–2

39 'men-of-the-world'   B to Mary Shelley, 16? November 1822

'the total contrast'   Moore *Journal*, 3 July 1827

homosexuality in nineteenth-century public schools   see chapter 'A Demon Hovering' in John Chandos, *Boys Together*, 1984

'lightly-bounding boy'   Translation from Anacreon, Ode 47, 1806

'You say'   John Tattersall to B, 20 August 1805

40 'NB'   Minutes of Lady Byron's interview with Lady Caroline Lamb, 27 March 1816

'Certainly B'   Hobhouse diaries, 15 January 1829

'M knows'   Hobhouse notes

'Moore said'   *The Greville Memoirs 1814–60*, ed. Lytton Strachey and Roger Fulford, vol. 1, 1938. Entry for 9 November 1829

'That *Madcap*'   B to Edward Noel Long, 23 February 1807

'a long farewell'   'To a Youthful Friend', 1808, l. 27

'Ah! sure'   'Childish Recollections', 1806, l. 213

41 'Of the Classics'   B to Robert Charles Dallas, 21 January 1808

Byron's early reading   memorandum book, 30 November 1807, cited Moore *Life*, vol. 1

'Harrow on the Hill'   Leslie Marchand, *Byron: A Biography*, vol. 1

42 'But words are'   *Don Juan*, Canto III, st. 88, l. 793

'To your tents'   Moore *Journal*, 3 July 1827

'Of narrow brain'   'On a Change of Masters, at a Great Public School', July 1805, l. 7

43 'the *nearest relation*'   B to Augusta Byron, 22 March 1804

'I *beg*'   ibid., 2 July 1805

'George Gordon'   Moore *Life*, vol. 1

44 'had a great'   'Detached Thoughts', no. 88, 1821–2

'introduced an oath'   Henry Long, MS reminiscences. Berg Collection, New York Public Library

'Oft at'   Harrow School Archive

'which was'   B to Charles David Gordon, 4 August 1805

Eton v. Harrow scorecard   *The Times*, 7 July 1952

'I had not'   Stanley Lane-Poole, *The Life of the Rt. Hon. Stratford Canning, Viscount Stratford de Redcliffe*, vol. 1, 1888

5   Southwell 1803–1805

45   'old parsons'   B to Augusta Byron, 2 April 1804

'It is a handsome'   Owen Mealey to John Hanson, 1803. British Library

'beautiful, well-kept'   Lord Torrington, *Torrington Diaries*, June 1787

46   '*Crater* of Dullness'   B to John Hanson, 2 April 1807

'amongst the Mohawks'   B to Elizabeth Pigot, 13 July 1807

'a tedious'   ibid., 30 June 1807

'I have always'   B to Lady Hardy, 1 December 1822

'My mother Gives'   B to Augusta Byron, 9 April 1804

47   'he still continued'   Moore *Life*, vol. 1

'Our cottage'   Elizabeth Pigot to B, 3 July 1807

'even more shy'   John Pigot to Elizabeth Pigot, September 1806. Moore *Life*, vol. 1

48   'but I know'   Moore *Life*, vol. 1

'I have been'   B to Lord Clare, 6 February 1807

49   'Lord Byron'   Miss Bristoe, MS account of theatricals at Southwell, 1806

'an absolute Hermit'   B to Augusta Byron, 2 April 1804

'as a young man'   B to Captain John Leacroft, 31 January 1807

'She is'   B to John Pigot, 13 January 1807

'no less than'   B to Edward Noel Long, 30 March 1807

'first lessons'   Hobhouse notes

'his Southwell recreations'   Hobhouse diaries, 15 January 1829

50   'Why, let the world'   'To My Son!', 1807, st. 4, l. 18

'it is not'   Moore *Life*, vol. 1

'buried in'   Claire Clairmont to Edward John Trelawny, *c.* 1870. Clairmont *Correspondence*, vol. 2

51   'whole *Bevy*'   B to Elizabeth Pigot, 2 August 1807

'rather too'   'Answer to Some Elegant Verses Sent by a Friend to the Author, complaining that one of his descriptions was rather too warmly drawn', 26 November 1806, l. 41

'"Tis surely'   'To Miss E P', 9 October 1806, l. 121

52   'I am at'   B to Augusta Byron, 6 August 1805

'*wise* and *Good*'   ibid., 25 April 1805

'that detestable'   ibid., 11 November 1804

'Kitty Gordon'   Moore *Life*, vol. 1

53   'the Dowager'   B to Augusta Byron, 26 December 1805

'this female Tisiphone'   ibid., 10 August 1805

'tormentor'   ibid., 18 August 1805

'Mrs Byron furiosa'   B to John Pigot, 9 August 1806

'The Wonderful History' Elizabeth Pigot, 1807. MS in Harry Ransom Research Center, University of Texas at Austin

'I wear *seven*' B to John Hanson, 2 April 1807

54 'a large village' B to Robert Charles Dallas, 11 October 1811

55 '*pigs*, *poultry*' B to Hargreaves Hanson, 15 April 1805

6 Cambridge 1805–1807

56 'Trinity background' see Anne Barton, 'Lord Byron and Trinity, a bicentenary portrait', *Trinity Review*, 1988

'that *oozy*' B to Edward Noel Long, 30 March 1807

'any reputation' Hobhouse notes

'it was one' 'Detached Thoughts', no. 72, 1821–2

'Yesterday' B to John Hanson, 26 October 1805

57 '*Super*excellent Rooms' B to Augusta Byron, 6 November 1805

'not to damage' B to John Murray, 19 November 1820

'as independent' B to Augusta Byron, 6 November 1805

'Study is' B to John Hanson, 23 November 1805

'sedate and polished' Ravenna Journal, 12 January 1821

58 'his collegiate' B to John Murray, 19 November 1820

'ruled the roast' ibid.; 'ruled the roast' refers to the caustic bantering tone of conversation between Byron and his friends

'It was constantly' The Rev. Mr Rowse, quoted Moore *Journal*, 29 June 1833

'his *voice*' B to Elizabeth Pigot, 5 July 1807

'implicit confidence' William Bankes to Mrs Arbuthnot, 13 July 1824. Francis Bamford and the Duke of Wellington, *The Journal of Mrs Arbuthnot*, vol. 1, 1950

'I took' 'Detached Thoughts', no. 72, 1821–2

59 'Ours too' 'To Thyrza', 1811, l. 29

'*musical protégé*' B to Elizabeth Pigot, 30 June 1807

'He offered' 'The Cornelian', 1806, l. 9

'like all' B to Augusta Byron, 27 December 1805

60 'to be stationed' B to Elizabeth Pigot, 30 June 1807

'I certainly' ibid., 5 July 1807

61 'I will not' B to Augusta Byron, 7 January 1806

'If I could' 'Detached Thoughts', no. 74, 1821–2

'a violent' Ravenna Journal, 12 January 1821

62 'I don't know' B to Thomas Moore, 22 June 1813

'*Cornelian*' B to Elizabeth Pigot, 5 July 1807

'having *pared*' ibid., 13 July 1807

'*fame* in *secret*' ibid., 2 August 1807

63 'It is a sort' Henry Brougham, *Edinburgh Review*, 11 January 1808

64 'I would I were' 'Stanzas', 1807 or 1808, l. 1

'my dear *Standard*' B to Edward Noel Long, 16 April 1807

'This place' B to Elizabeth Pigot, 26 October 1807

65 'of a soft' B to Augusta Byron, 2 November 1804

'A precious Mixture' B to Elizabeth Pigot, 26 October 1807

'We will yet' B to Henry Angelo, 16 May 1806

'the glass' Henry Angelo, *Angelo's Pic-Nic*, 1834

66 'He, Hobhouse' B to Robert Charles Dallas, 7 September 1811

67 'a *white hat*' B to John Murray, 19 November 1820

'I know more' Moore *Journal*, 29 May 1822

Scrope Davies background see T.A.J. Burnett, *The Rise and Fall of a Regency Dandy*, 1981, for an important reassessment of Scrope Berdmore Davies's friendship with Byron written after the 1976 discovery of Scrope Davies's abandoned trunk

'Scrope was always' 'Detached Thoughts', no. 26, 1821–2

'the poet in bed' *The Reminiscences and Recollections of Captain Gronow, 1810–1860*, vol. 1, 1900

'a very odd' B to John Murray, 9 November 1820

'guide, philosopher' B to Robert Charles Dallas, 7 September 1811

'the man of Method' 'Farewell Petition to J.C.H. Esq.', 7 June 1810

'Citoyen' B to John Cam Hobhouse, 23 August 1810

68 'the finest' B to Elizabeth Pigot, 26 October 1807

'brought a *bear*' Edward Noel Long to B, 18 November 1807

'Then would' 'Granta, A Medley', 28 October 1806, l. 5

'manners rude' 'Thoughts Suggested by a College Examination', 1806, l. 55

69 'Sad Bruin' *The Satirist*, no. 2, June 1808

'a very sad' Postscript to *English Bards and Scotch Reviewers*, 1808

'I hope' Margaret Pigot to Catherine Gordon Byron, undated

70 'I suppose' Medwin *Conversations*

7 London and Brighton 1808–1809

71 'one of the' *Don Juan*, Canto XI, st. 31, l. 241

'Scrope Davies' B to John Cam Hobhouse, February 1808?

72 'to be seen' John Cam Hobhouse to B, 12 March 1808

'I have a notion' 'Detached Thoughts', no. 33, 1821–2

'my old friend' note to *Don Juan*, Canto XI, st. 19

'large, but not' *Pugilistica*, vol. 1, quoted Prothero *Letters and Journals*, vol. 1

'many duels' Medwin *Conversations*

'I now request' Captain W. Wallace to B, 6 September 1808

'You will get' B to John Jackson, 12 December 1808

73 'I have some' B to John Cam Hobhouse, 27 February 1808

'This person' Hobhouse notes

'a little circumstance' B to John Murray, 25 March 1821, in the Bowles/Pope Controversy correspondence

'You have heard' B to John Cam Hobhouse, 14 March 1808

'I have three' B to the Rev. John Becher, 28 March 1808

'the "chere amie"' B to John Cam Hobhouse, 15 April 1808

'Unaccustomed to' Dallas *Recollections*

'the votary' B to Robert Charles Dallas, 20 January 1808

'I hold virtue'   ibid., 21 January 1808

74 'Wealth had done'   *Don Juan*, Canto V, st. 94, l. 745

'to discuss'   'Detached Thoughts', no. 78, 1821–2

'While standing'   *The Reminiscences and Recollections of Captain Gronow, 1810–1860*, vol. 1, 1900

'been lately'   B to the Rev. John Becher, 26 February 1808

75 'I am'   B to John Cam Hobhouse, 27 February 1808

'I am still'   ibid., 26 March 1808

'such a female'   Medwin *Conversations*

'very pretty horse'   Moore *Journal*, 19 February 1828

'the young gentleman'   *Blackwood's Edinburgh Magazine*, November 1824

'I have parted'   B to Elizabeth Massingberd, 20 July 1808

'parading the Lobby'   Scrope Davies to B, November 1808

76 'a young Female'   *The Diary of Joseph Farington*, ed. Kenneth Garlick and Angus MacIntyre, 1978–84. Entry for 20 June 1813

'a citizen'   B to Francis Hodgson, 17 December 1808

'faithful and gentle'   John Cowell to B, 1808

'The notice'   ibid., 25 October 1808

'Cowell is'   B to Francis Hodgson, 11 July 1814

'Cowell's imitation'   Moore *Journal*, 12 June 1828

'I am now'   B to Catherine Gordon Byron, 2 October 1808

77 'more of '   *The Mirror*, 24 January 1824

'Cameriero'   B to Lady Melbourne, 28 September 1812

'Ursine Sloth'   Journal, 14 November 1813

'with the substance'   Percy Bysshe Shelley to Mary Shelley, 7 August 1821. Bodleian Library, University of Oxford, MS Shelley, c. 1, fols. 440–2

'Joseph Murray'   B to Augusta Leigh, 14 December 1808

78 'with a cordiality'   Moore *Life*, vol. 1

'I like him'   B to Catherine Gordon Byron, 22 June 1809

'I forgot'   B to Francis Hodgson, 3 November 1808

79 'Boatswain is dead'   ibid., 18 November 1808

'To mark a Friend's'   'Inscription on the Monument of a Newfoundland Dog', 1808

'I could not'   B to Augusta Leigh, 14 December 1808

'I can't see'   'Detached Thoughts', no. 1, 15 October 1821

'probably belonged'   Medwin *Conversations*

'I lived'   'Lines inscribed upon a Cup formed from a Skull', 1808

'Lucinda is pregnant'   B to John Cam Hobhouse, 16 January 1809

80 'You will discharge'   B to John Hanson, 17 January 1809

'tremulous anxiety'   B to Sir Walter Scott, 12 January 1822

'a country girl'   *Don Juan*, Canto XVI, st. 61, l. 531

'which the housemaids'   Washington Irving, 'Newstead Abbey'. *The Works of Washington Irving*, vol. 3, 1885

'the tenants'   B to John Hanson, 10 January 1809

81 'in high spirits'   Dallas *Recollections*

'his Heart is'   Catherine Gordon Byron to John Hanson, 30 January 1809. British Library 'portion of Ambition' B to Augusta Leigh, 14 December 1808

'I have no' Catherine Gordon Byron to John Hanson, 30 January 1809. British Library

82 '*Newstead* and I' B to Catherine Gordon Byron, 6 March 1809

'in the old' Catherine Gordon Byron to John Hanson, 30 January 1809. British Library

'I suppose' B to John Hanson, 17 December 1808

'*our* house' B to John Cam Hobhouse, 17 October 1820

'When he had' Dallas *Recollections*

83 '*these* are *great*' B to John Hanson, 2 April 1807

'I have *lashed*' B to Catherine Gordon Byron, 6 March 1809

'No muse' *English Bards and Scotch Reviewers*, l. 725

'mighty Scribbler' B to Augusta Leigh, 14 December 1808

85 'not to prove' Preface to *English Bards and Scotch Reviewers*, 2nd edn., 1809

'ballad-monger' *English Bards and Scotch Reviewers*, l. 202

'On Sunday' note to *English Bards and Scotch Reviewers*, l. 686

'notwithstanding' Dallas *Recollections*

'all the fire' Margaret Pigot to Catherine Gordon Byron, 1809

'declared they were' *The Diary of a Lady-in-Waiting by Lady Charlotte Bury*, ed. A. Francis Steuart, vol. 1, 1908

86 'engaged for' B to Augusta Byron, 10 August 1805

'to peep at' B to Elizabeth Pigot, 11 August 1807

'finest frigate' ibid., 26 October 1807

'the common *Turnpike*' B to Edward Noel Long, 1 May 1807

'if nothing' B to Catherine Gordon Byron, 2 November 1808

'If the' B to John Hanson, 16 April 1809

87 'I never will' ibid., 12 November 1809

'the *collection*' Hobhouse diaries, 6 June 1810

'talking all the way' B to John Murray, 19 November 1820

'Paphian girls' *Childe Harold's Pilgrimage*, Canto I, st. 7, l. 61

88 'Lord Byron' Henry Long, MS reminiscences. Berg Collection, New York Public Library

'I am collecting' B to William Harness, 18 March 1809

'by capital' Dallas *Recollections*

'*Nelson* was' 'Detached Thoughts', no. 109, 1821–2

'the countenance' Catherine Gordon Byron to B, 26 October 1810. Lovelace–Byron Archive

'the world' B to Catherine Gordon Byron, 22 June 1809

8 Mediterranean Travels 1809

89 'a most splendid' B to John Murray, 19 November 1820

'remarkably handsome' B to Edward Ellice, 25 June 1809

'on the state' B to Henry Drury, 25 June 1809

90 'My dear' B to Charles Skinner Matthews, 22 June 1809

'L'Abbe' B to John Cam Hobhouse, 23 August 1810

'if he' Charles Skinner Matthews to John Cam Hobhouse, 25 September 1809. British Library

'If you'   Charles Skinner Matthews to B, 30 June 1809. British Library

91 'depraving the mind'   B to Catherine Gordon Byron, 19 May 1809

'that there'   B to Henry Drury, 25 June 1809

'Huzza!'   'Lines to Mr Hodgson', 1809, l. 1

'guilty henchman page'   *Childe Harold's Pilgrimage*, Canto I, cancelled l. 64

92 'wordy preparations'   B to Henry Drury, 25 June 1809; in my view a more likely reading than Marchand's 'woundy'

'I am very'   B to Francis Hodgson, 16 July 1809

93 'a battle'   B to John Hanson, 13 July 1809

'perhaps in every'   B to Catherine Gordon Byron, 11 August 1809

'The horrid crags'   *Childe Harold's Pilgrimage*, Canto I, st. 19, l. 243

94 'the great'   B to Francis Hodgson, 25 June 1809

'a person'   John W. Ward to Helen D'Arcy Stewart, June 1812. *Letters to 'Ivy' from the First Earl of Dudley*, ed. S.H. Romilly, 1905

95 'an English'   B to Catherine Gordon Byron, 11 August 1809

'At every'   *Childe Harold's Pilgrimage*, Canto I, st. 51, l. 531

'The eldest'   B to Catherine Gordon Byron, 11 August 1809

96 'gentle Gallop'   ibid., 20 July 1810

'I have sent'   B to John Hanson, 13 August 1809

'you *know*'   B to Catherine Gordon Byron, 15 August 1809

97 'while sitting'   Galt *Life*

98 'a most superb'   B to Catherine Gordon Byron, 11 August 1809

'best suit'   Hobhouse diaries, 17–27 August 1809

'on account'   Galt *Life*

'very grand'   Hobhouse diaries, 31 August 1809

'a curious fish'   ibid., 2 September 1809

99 'I set in'   'Detached Thoughts', no. 55, 1821–2

'la Celebre'   Hobhouse diaries, 4 September 1809

'her life'   B to Catherine Gordon Byron, 15 September 1809

'*everlasting* passion'   B to Lady Melbourne, 15 September 1812

'I was once'   Ravenna Journal, 13 January 1821

'Platonic'   Galt *Life*

100 'When I was'   B to Scrope Davies, 31 July 1810

'the notion'   Hobhouse notes

'spread like'   *Childe Harold's Pilgrimage*, Canto II, st. 17, l. 151

'the greenest'   Hobhouse diaries, 26 September 1809

101 'boil'd to rags'   ibid., 29 September 1809

'a most distressing'   ibid., 30 September 1809

'Had the commander'   Hobhouse *Journey*, vol. 1

102 'obliged to leave'   Hobhouse diaries, 5 October 1809

'the unmarried'   ibid., 6 October 1809

'totally unlike'   B to Catherine Gordon Byron, 12 November 1809

'It may be'   'Additional Note, on the Turks', *Childe Harold's Pilgrimage*, Canto II

'we are'   B to Catherine Gordon Byron, 12 November 1809

103 'the benevolent'   Hobhouse diaries, 12 October 1809

'The Albanians'   B to Catherine Gordon Byron, 12 November 1809

'Albanian suits'   Hobhouse diaries, 27 October 1809

104 'in a full'   B to Catherine Gordon Byron, 12 November 1809

105 'from the'   Moore *Life*, vol. 1

'Byron is'   Hobhouse diaries, 22 October 1809

'amidst the'   'Preface to the First and Second Cantos' of *Childe Harold's Pilgrimage*, February 1812

'For if'   Moore *Prose and Verse*

'Fletcher yelled'   B to Catherine Gordon Byron, 12 November 1809

106 'to see'   Hobhouse diaries, 9 December 1809

'the eye'   Journal, 20 March 1814

107 'Oh, thou Parnassus'   *Childe Harold's Pilgrimage*, Canto I, st. 60, l. 612

'to get at'   Hobhouse diaries, 5 September 1809

'my Lord Elgin'   ibid., 21 December 1809

108 'a miserable'   ibid., 24 December 1809

'tumbling as if'   ibid., 25 December 1809

'the plain of'   note to *Childe Harold's Pilgrimage*, Canto II, st. 73

'every moment'   Hobhouse diaries, 25 December 1809

9   Greece and Constantinople 1809–1810

109 'dearly beloved'   B to Francis Hodgson, 8 December 1811

'of middle stature'   H.W. Williams, *Travels in Italy, Greece, &c*, quoted Moore *Life*, vol. 1

110 'quite "nubilis"'   Hobhouse diaries, 12 January 1810

'I like'   B to Henry Drury, 3 May 1810

'jumped suddenly'   Hobhouse *Journey*, vol. 2

'Greece has'   B to Andreas Londos, 30 January 1824

111 'Sun of the morning'   *Childe Harold's Pilgrimage*, Canto II, st. 3, l. 19

'All that'   ibid., st. 7, l. 56

'renegado Spaniard'   Hobhouse diaries, 10 January 1810

'Whatever I may'   Hobhouse *Recollections*, vol. 1

'dried fish'   Hobhouse diaries, 24 January 1810

'quickness of observation'   Hobhouse *Journey*, vol. 1

112 'the actual spot'   note to *Childe Harold's Pilgrimage*, Canto II

'The mountains'   *Don Juan*, Canto III, l. 701

Elgin marbles background   see William St Clair, *Lord Elgin and the Marbles*, 1998

'a splendid dome'   Hobhouse diaries, 21 January 1810

113 'a damp, dirty'   Benjamin Robert Haydon, *Autobiography*, 1853, entry for 1808

'Let ABERDEEN'   *English Bards and Scotch Reviewers*, l. 1027

'I opposed'   B to John Murray, 1821, in the Bowles/Pope Controversy correspondence

'when they carry'   note to *Childe Harold's Pilgrimage*, Canto II, 3 January 1809

'a place'   B to Catherine Gordon Byron, 20 July 1810

114 'by which'   Hobhouse diaries, 4 February 1810

'Theresa 12'   ibid., 3 March 1810

'a respectable'   Galt *Life*

'the old woman'   B to John Cam Hobhouse, 23 August 1810

'I was near'   ibid., 15 May 1811

'Maid of Athens'   'Song', 1810

'I almost'   B to Henry Drury, 3 May 1810

115 'Turkomania'   *Morning Post*, 1814. Prothero *Letters and Journals*, vol. 2

'Masquerade Jackett'   Prothero *Letters and Journals*, vol. 1

'the exotics'   B to Charles Skinner Matthews, 22 June 1809

'I see'   B to Henry Drury, 3 May 1810

116 'tell the boy'   B to Catherine Gordon Byron, 19 March 1810

'pine again'   Journal, 14 November 1813

'some of the'   B to Madame de Staël, 30 November 1813

'turbaned tombstones'   'Augustus Darvell: A Fragment of a Ghost Story', 1816.
Brotherton Collection, Leeds University Library

117 'nor'   B to John Hanson, 3 March 1810

'pretty well'   Hobhouse diaries, 11 April 1810

'a fat'   ibid., 9 March 1810

'brought forth'   Frederick Chamier, *The Life of a Sailor*, vol. 1, 1832

118 'I have stood'   Ravenna Journal, 11 January 1821

'the foremost'   Frederick Chamier, *The Life of a Sailor*, vol. 1, 1832

'political, poetical'   B to Francis Hodgson, 4 July 1810

119 'Leander's conjugal'   B to Henry Drury, 3 May 1810

'very decent'   Hobhouse diaries, 14 May 1810

'imagine'   B to Catherine Gordon Byron, 28 June 1810

'little pieces'   Hobhouse diaries, 21 May 1810

120 'would have given'   anonymous report in *New Monthly Magazine*, XVII, 1826

'indescribably beastly'   Hobhouse diaries, 17 May 1810

'de Turk'   ibid., 19 May 1810

121 'Good God!'   Frederick Chamier, *The Life of a Sailor*, vol. 1, 1832

'Oriental twist'   B to Edward Daniel Clarke, 15 December 1813

'Oh how I wish'   B to Henry Drury, 17 June 1810

'The charming'   *Don Juan*, Canto V, st. 3, l. 24

'grandeur of desolation'   B to Annabella Milbanke, 29 November 1813

122 'Is a Turkish'   'Additional Note, on the Turks', Childe Harold's Pilgrimage, Canto II

'caprice and feline temper'   Galt *Life*

'with as much'   Moore *Journal*, 23 May 1819

'The fact is'   B to Sir Robert Adair, 4 July 1810

123 'delighting those'   Stanley Lane-Poole, *The Life of the Rt. Hon. Stratford Canning, Viscount Stratford de Redcliffe*, vol. 1, 1880

'He was dressed'   Hobhouse *Travels*, vol. 2

'Took leave'   Hobhouse *Recollections*, 17 July 1810

'Your last'   B to John Cam Hobhouse, 4 October 1810

'even the society'   Moore *Life*, vol. 1

'What authority'   Hobhouse notes

124 'Tell him'   'Farewell Petition to J.C.H. Esq', 7 June 1810
    'H. doesn't'   Journal, 10 March 1814
    'I can't empty'   B to Annabella Milbanke, 10 November 1813
    'I shall retain'   B to Francis Hodgson, 16 February 1812

10   Athens 1810–1811

125 '*You northern*'   B to Catherine Gordon Byron, 20 July 1810
    'a brig'   B to John Cam Hobhouse, 29 July 1810
126 'in *other* matters'   ibid., 16 August 1810
127 'and love him'   Eustathius Georgiou to B, 15 March 1811
    'even better'   B to John Cam Hobhouse, 16 August 1810
    'fantastical adventures'   ibid., 15 May 1811
    'I am living'   B to Francis Hodgson, 20 January 1811
128 'I am his'   B to John Cam Hobhouse, 23 August 1810
    'above two hundred'   ibid., 4 October 1810
    'about whom'   Dr C.L. Meryon, *Travels of Lady Hester Stanhope*, vol. 1, 1846
129 'a miserable'   Moore *Journal*, 24 February 1828
    'beautiful for'   B to John Cam Hobhouse, 23 August 1810
    'vomited and glystered'   B to Francis Hodgson, 3 October 1810
    'Odious! in boards'   'Epitaph from a Sickbed', 1810
    'How pale'   Moore *Life*, vol. 1
130 'I saw'   B to John Cam Hobhouse, 4 October 1810
    'a masculine'   Hobhouse *Recollections*, 27 July 1810
    'argufy'   B to John Cam Hobhouse, 4 October 1810
    'had no chance'   Moore *Journal*, 24 February 1828
    'had a great'   Dr C.L. Meryon, *Memoirs of Lady Hester Stanhope*, vol. 3, 1845
    'stupendous traveller'   B to John Cam Hobhouse, 4 August 1819
    'much upon'   John Cam Hobhouse to B, 31 July 1810
    'Seriously'   B to John Cam Hobhouse, 19 June 1811
131 'the most illustrious'   B to John Murray, 15 November 1817
    'a number'   B to John Cam Hobhouse, 15 May 1811
    'Here I see'   B to Catherine Gordon Byron, 14 January 1811
132 'to describe'   Journal, 5 December 1813
    'might have'   Moore *Journal*, 19 February 1828
    'contained merely'   B to Thomas Moore, 1 September 1813
133 'to their pristine'   note to *Childe Harold's Pilgrimage*, Canto II, 23 January 1811
    'Where'er we tread'   *Childe Harold's Pilgrimage*, Canto II, st. 88, l. 828
    'unless it'   B to John Cam Hobhouse, 5 March 1811
    'perpetual lamentations'   ibid., 14 January 1811
134 'all taken'   ibid., 19 June 1811
    'but on a sudden'   note to *Childe Harold's Pilgrimage*, Canto II
    'infernal oven'   B to John Cam Hobhouse, 15 May 1811
    'The spell is broke'   'Written at Athens', 16 January 1810
135 'I should feel'   Constance Spencer Smith to B, 3 March 1811

'the most diabolical'   B to Lady Melbourne, 15 September 1812

'My most precious'   Nicolo Giraud to B, 1 January 1815

'a teller'   B to John Cam Hobhouse, 19 June 1811

'I can'   ibid., 2 July 1811

'without a hope'   B to Francis Hodgson, 29 June 1811

11   St James's 1811–1812

139 'tight little'   B to Douglas Kinnaird, 27 November 1816. The phrase, a favourite of
Byron's, is taken from Charles Dibdin's song 'The Snug Little Island', *The British Raft*,
1797

'in monstrous'   B to Francis Hodgson, 3 October 1810

'You have written'   Robert Charles Dallas to B, 16 July 1811. Dallas *Recollections*

140 'My friend'   B to John Murray, 23 August 1811

'none female'   Hobhouse diaries, 19 July 1811

'Your Lordship's'   Charles Skinner Matthews to B, 13 January 1811

141 'the Mendeli'   John Cam Hobhouse to B, 15 July 1811

'I had known'   note to *Childe Harold's Pilgrimage*, Canto I, l. 927

'a quantity'   B to Catherine Gordon Byron, 25 June 1811

142 'I now feel'   B to John Pigot, 2 August 1811

'There is to me'   B to John Cam Hobhouse, 10 August 1811

'Some curse'   B to Scrope Berdmore Davies, 7 August 1811

'were locked'   Henry Drury to Francis Hodgson, 1811. Hodgson *Memoir*, vol. 1

'In ability'   B to Scrope Berdmore Davies, 7 August 1811

143 'a kind of '   B to John Cam Hobhouse, 10 August 1811

'now here is'   ibid., 20 September 1811

'I will have'   B to Francis Hodgson, 3 September 1811

'wealthy dowdy'   B to Augusta Leigh, 30 August 1811

144 'unluckily receiving'   B to Francis Hodgson, 10 October 1811

'Do you indeed'   Sarah Markham, *A Testimony of her Times based on Penelope Hind's
Diaries and Correspondence 1787–1838*, 1990

145 'I heard'   B to Francis Hodgson, 10 October 1811

'It seems'   B to Robert Charles Dallas, 11 October 1811

'this stanza'   ibid., 14 October 1811

'you remember'   B to John Cam Hobhouse, 13 October 1811

'Wherever I turn'   ibid., 22 October 1811

'the most selfish'   B to Margaret Pigot, 28 October 1811

146 'Sweet Thyrza'   'Stanzas', 1811, l. 25

'Te, te, care puer'   'Edleston', 1811 or 1812, l. 1

'I must not'   'Stanzas', 1811, l. 7

'He made'   B to John Cam Hobhouse, 2 November 1811

'Your Greek'   John Cam Hobhouse to B, 12 November 1811

147 'The world'   'Epistle to a Friend', 11 October 1811, MS. Huntington Library

148 'Along thy'   'To Mr Murray', verses in letter dated 11 April 1818, l. 13

'Good paper'   B to John Cam Hobhouse, 17 November 1811

'used to amuse'   Smiles *Memoir*, vol. 1

'There are'   John Murray to B, 4 September 1811

149 'the political'   B to John Murray, 5 September 1811

'From Mr G'   ibid., 4 January 1814

'I always'   B to Douglas Kinnaird, 21 February 1824

'a little man'   Sir Walter Scott, *Journal*, 18 January 1827. *The Journal of Sir Walter Scott*, ed. W.E.K. Anderson, 1972

150 'I do think'   Journal, 24 November 1813

'the best looking'   B to Thomas Moore, 27 September 1813

'Dew Drop'   Moore *Journal*, 3–4 March 1842

151 'naming them'   Rogers *Table-Talk*

'the pure'   Moore *Life*, vol. 1

'Nothing but'   Rogers *Table-Talk*

'lighter and livelier'   Dallas *Recollections*

152 'Moore, don't you'   Moore *Life*, vol. 1

'little sensual'   B to Francis Hodgson, 25 September 1811

'a very pretty'   B to John Cam Hobhouse, 17 November 1811

'on any pretext'   B to Francis Hodgson, 25 September 1811

'carry on'   B to John Cam Hobhouse, 17 November 1811

'Master William'   B to William Harness, 8 December 1811

'By Good luck'   ibid., 15 December 1811

'It was winter'   The Rev. A.G. L'Estrange, *The Literary Life of the Rev. William Harness*, 1871

153 'tolerably enamoured'   B to John Cam Hobhouse, 25 December 1811

'Don't you'   Susan Vaughan to B, 20 January 1812

'All the *pure*'   ibid., 23 January 1812

154 'I do not'   B to Francis Hodgson, 28 January 1812

'All is over'   B to Susan Vaughan, 28 January 1812

'how miserable'   Susan Vaughan to B, 22 September 1812

'My dear Lord'   ibid., 1813

155 'He was'   Moore *Journal*, 6 June 1819

'My Lady'   *English Bards and Scotch Reviewers*, l. 557

156 'Nah, Billy'   Susan Vaughan to B, 18 January 1812

'The few words'   B to Lord Holland, 25 February 1812

'The idle'   *The Curse of Minerva*, 1811, l. 267

'How will you'   Frame-work Bill Speech, 1812

157 'very violent'   B to Francis Hodgson, 5 March 1812

'glowing with success'   Dallas *Recollections*

'His speech'   Henry Richard Vassall, 3rd Lord Holland, *Further Memoirs of the Whig Party 1807–1821*, ed. Lord Stavordale, 1905

'contracted at'   Moore *Life*, vol. 1

'*con amore*'   Journal, 14 November 1813

'if you knew'   B to Leigh Hunt, 29 January 1816

158 'a poem'   Walter Scott to J.B.S. Morritt, 4 May 1812. *The Letters of Sir Walter Scott*, ed. H.J.C. Grierson, 1932–7, vol. 3

'Wordsworth allowed' Henry Crabb Robinson diary, 24 May 1812. *Diary, Reminiscences and Correspondence of Henry Crabb Robinson*, ed. Thomas Sadler, vol. 1, 1872

'as much' Moore *Life*, vol. 1

12 Melbourne House 1812

159 'The subject' Elizabeth, Duchess of Devonshire to Augustus Foster, 1812. *The Two Duchesses*, ed. Vere Foster, 1898

'a cursed' B to Francis Hodgson, 13 October 1811

Byron's readership see William St Clair, 'The Impact of Byron's Writings: An Evaluative Approach'. *Byron: Augustan and Romantic*, ed. Andrew Rutherford, 1990

'loaded with' Dallas *Recollections*

'Childe of *Harrow's*' B to Robert Charles Dallas, 11 October 1811

160 'to certain feelings' Hobhouse diaries, 28 March 1814

'If ever I' B to John Murray, 26 April 1814

'I by no means' B to Robert Charles Dallas, 31 October 1811

'vast mental' Moore *Life*, vol. 1

161 'a vessel' Journal, 6 December 1813

'for more' John Murray to Walter Scott, 27 June 1812

'with his fine' Dallas *Recollections*

'*reign*' Journal, 5 December 1813

'stark mad' Rogers *Table-Talk*

'sort of moonlight' Jane Porter, quoted Prothero *Letters and Journals*, vol. 2

'Lord Byron' Lady Morgan to Mrs Lefanu, 7 June 1812. *Lady Morgan's Memoirs*,vol. 2, 1862

162 'It is not' Lady Falkland to B, 13 July 1812

'My Lord' Horatia Somerset to B, 21 October 1814

'Sir, I have' Sarah Agnes Bamber to B, 5 December 1814

'a woman' 'MH' to B, 21 October 1813

'You must' Sophia Louisa Macdonald to B, 20 July 1814

'instantly destroy' 'MH' to B, 21 October 1813

'a feeling Heart' Mary Watkins to B, 19 September 1814

163 'I count' anon., 6 May n/d

'You will' Isabella Lanchester to B, 6 May 1812

'female adulation' Dallas *Recollections*

'Byron says' Blessington *Conversations*

'evil Genius' B to Countess Teresa Guiccioli, 1820?

164 'the new poet' Lady Caroline Lamb narrative, *Lady Morgan's Memoirs*, vol. 2, 1862

'*les agneaux*' B to Lady Melbourne, 5 February 1815

165 'Lady Holland' Lady Caroline Lamb narrative, *Lady Morgan's Memoirs*, vol. 2, 1862

'an exaggerated' B to James Wedderburn Webster, 18 September 1815

166 'dark and winding' *Letters of Harriet, Countess Granville 1810–1845*, ed. the Hon. F. Leveson-Gower, vol. 1, 1894

'Waltz – Waltz' 'Waltz: An Apostrophic Hymn', 1812, l. 113

'a *correct*'   B to Lady Melbourne, 21 June 1813

'Byron contrived'   Lady Caroline Lamb narrative, *Lady Morgan's Memoirs*, vol. 2, 1862

167 'Lady C'   Annabella Milbanke to Lady Milbanke, 26 March 1812. Lovelace–Byron Archive

'with a sort'   Lady Caroline Lamb to Thomas Medwin, November ? 1824. Forster Collection, National Art Library

'The Rose'   Lady Caroline Lamb to B, 27 March 1812

'soft low'   *Lady Morgan's Memoirs*, vol. 2, 1862

'mixture of good'   B to James Wedderburn Webster, 18 September 1815

'I have always'   B to Lady Caroline Lamb, April 1812?

'Caro is a little'   The Hon. Mrs George Lamb to Augustus Foster, 6 November 1811. *The Two Duchesses*, ed. Vere Foster, 1898

168 'He called me'   Lady Caroline Lamb to Lady Melbourne, 1810. British Library

169 'a total want'   B to Lady Caroline Lamb, April 1812?

'people talk'   ibid., 19 May 1812?

'Lord Byron'   Harriet, Countess Granville to the 6th Duke of Devonshire, 10 May 1812. *Letters of Harriet, Countess Granville 1810–1845*, ed. the Hon. F. Leveson-Gower, vol. 1, 1894

'Your little friend'   Elizabeth, Duchess of Devonshire to Augustus Foster, 4 May 1812. *The Two Duchesses*, ed. Vere Foster, 1898

'absolutely besieged'   Rogers *Table-Talk*

'had no passion'   Moore *Journal*, 10 November 1827

170 'he liked to'   Lady Caroline Lamb to Thomas Medwin, November ? 1824. Forster Collection, National Art Library

'certain testimonies'   Hobhouse diaries, 25 July 1820

171 'the little'   Lady Caroline Lamb to William Fletcher, 1812

'the lady's *page*'   Robert Charles Dallas, *Correspondence of Lord Byron with a Friend*, vol. 3, 1825

'Women who walk'   Lady Caroline Lamb to B, 1814

'it is of'   Lady Caroline Lamb to B. British Library

'Antoinette et Georgine'   Lady Caroline Lamb to B, 1812

172 'I lov'd you'   ibid., 1813

'Such a monster'   B to Augusta Leigh, 14 September 1816

'pale and exceedingly'   Lady Caroline Lamb, extracts from journal. British Library

'starting up'   Moore *Life*, vol. 1

'I have seen'   Lady Caroline Lamb, extracts from journal. British Library

'They display'   B to Lady Caroline Lamb, 1 May 1812

'Dreadful body'   Hobhouse diaries, 10 June 1812

'this whole week'   ibid., 12 June 1812

173 'Lady Blarney'   B to Lady Melbourne, August 1812?

'The hack whore'   B to John Murray, 31 August 1820

'heard bad news'   Hobhouse diaries, 30 June 1812

'a scheme'   ibid., 29 July 1812

176 'Newstead'   Lady Caroline Lamb to B, undated. Lovelace–Byron Archive

'Caroline Byron'   ibid., 9 August 1812. Lovelace–Byron Archive

'Oh G!'   Castalia, Countess Granville, *Private Correspondence of Lord Granville Leveson-Gower*, vol. 2, 1916

177 'As I am one'   B to Lady Melbourne, 12 August 1812
'My dearest Caroline'   B to Lady Caroline Lamb, August 1812?

178 'worn to the bone'   Harriet, Countess Granville to Lady Georgiana Morpeth, 12 September 1812. *Letters of Harriet, Countess Granville*, ed. the Hon. F. Leveson-Gower, vol. 1, 1894
'I presume'   B to Lady Melbourne, 6 November 1812

179 'Vieille Cour'   Lady Caroline Lamb to B, 1812?
'undertake'   B to Lady Melbourne, 13 September 1812
'the greatest'   ibid., 13 September 1812
'I never heard'   Mabell Airlie, *In Whig Society 1775–1818*, 1821

180 'but *who*'   B to Lady Melbourne, 21 September 1812
'Champaigne'   ibid., 14 May 1813
'Very extraordinary'   Hobhouse diaries, 4 March 1827
'Lady M'   Blessington *Conversations*
'that in 1813'   Lady Noel to Sir Ralph Noel, 2 February 1816. Lovelace–Byron Archive
'She was'   B to Thomas Moore, 16 March 1818

181 'extraordinary'   Lady Caroline Lamb to B, 3 June 1814?
'one to whom'   B to Lady Melbourne, 18 September 1812

13   Cheltenham and Eywood 1812–1813

182 Cheltenham background   see Oliver C. Bradbury, 'Lord Byron's 1812 visit to Cheltenham'. *Byron Journal*, no. 27, 1999
'a very pleasant'   B to William Bankes, 28 September 1812
'By the waters'   B to Lord Holland, 10 September 1812

183 'cupped on'   B to John Cam Hobhouse, 10 February 1812
'teazing maladies'   B to Dr Henry Charles Boisragon, 3 October 1812
'very medicinal'   B to William Bankes, 28 September 1812
'diluted'   B to Lord Holland, 30 September 1812
'I have'   B to John Murray, 12 October 1812
'had some'   John Murray to B, 4 November 1812

184 'they were'   Journal, 17 November 1813
'For some'   *The Giaour*, l. 801
'The Giaour'   B to John Murray, 12 October 1813
'Betty is performing'   B to Lady Melbourne, 10 September 1812
'great and unbounded'   *Memoirs of Joseph Grimaldi*, ed. Charles Dickens, vol. 2, 1838

185 'as all Grubstreet'   B to Lady Melbourne, 10 September 1812
'applauding satisfaction'   John Murray to B, 1812
'I have no'   B to Lady Caroline Lamb, 1 May 1812

186 'a clever'   B to Lady Melbourne, 18 September 1812
'little maniac'   B to John Cam Hobhouse, 17 January 1813
'*AT THIS moment*'   B to Lady Melbourne, 28 September 1812
'As to *Love*'   ibid., 18 September 1812

187 'Does Annabella?'   ibid., 28 September 1812
'Cheltenham is'   ibid., 30? September 1812
'My dear Ly. M'   ibid., 17 October 1812
'She really is'   Elizabeth, Duchess of Devonshire to Augustus Foster, 2 June 1812.
The Two Duchesses, ed. Vere Foster, 1898
'tyrannical power'   Annabella Milbanke, 'Character of Lord Byron', 8 October 1812.
Lovelace–Byron Archive
'a new Juliet'   B to Lady Melbourne, 21 September 1812
'of great riches'   ibid., 28 September 1812

188 'a great point'   ibid., 25 September 1812
'Perhaps it may'   Hobhouse *Recollections*, vol. 2
'amiable *Mathematician*'   B to Lady Melbourne, 18 October 1812
'That would'   ibid., 14 November 1812
'The world'   John Cam Hobhouse to B, 19 October 1812
'dear Machiavel'   B to Lady Melbourne, October 1812

189 'autumnal charms'   Blessington *Conversations*
'*There* is a woman'   Journal, 1 December 1813
'Have we not'   ibid., 17 November 1813

190 'Never mind'   ibid., 6 March 1813
'the most facetious'   B to Lady Melbourne, 11 January 1813

191 'I am no longer'   B to Lady Caroline Lamb, November 1812? Caroline Lamb,
Glenarvon, 1816
'filthy Dolphin'   Lady Caroline Lamb narrative, *Lady Morgan's Memoirs*, vol. 2, 1862

192 'Your tale'   Hobhouse to B, 14 January 1813
'very *qualmish*'   B to Lady Melbourne, 4 January 1813
'really was'   HRH The Princess of Wales, quoted Lady Charlotte Bury, *The Diary of a
Lady-in-Waiting*, vol. 2, 1908
'M'amie thinks'   B to Lady Melbourne, 27 December 1812

193 'Lord Byron was'   HRH The Princess of Wales, quoted Lady Charlotte Bury,
The Diary of a Lady-in-Waiting, vol. 2, 1908
'The Mind'   *The Giaour*, l. 422
'it is in'   B to Lady Caroline Lamb, 29 April 1813

194 'the irritability'   Medwin *Conversations*
'Remember thee'   'Remember Thee, Remember Thee', 1813. It has often been assumed
that Lady Caroline Lamb's invasion took place in Byron's Albany apartments in 1814.
However, dating of the poem suggests Bennet Street
'Car L'   B to John Cam Hobhouse, 17 January 1813
'it was a lucky'   B to Lady Melbourne, 7 April 1813
'scrambling and splashing'   B to Lady Melbourne, 5 April 1813

195 'like a dutiful'   ibid., 17 January 1813
'a delightful'   Hobhouse diary, 2 June 1812
'*petite cousine*'   Journal, 17 November 1813
'Oh! let that eye'   *Childe Harold's Pilgrimage*, dedication, l. 28
'the pretty little'   B to John Murray, 29 March 1813
'whom I should'   B to Lady Melbourne, 5 April 1813

196 'He told me'   Lady Byron, 'Statement U', March 1816. Lovelace–Byron Archive
'bid him adieu'   Lady Caroline Lamb to Lady Melbourne. British Library
'He asked me'   Lady Caroline Lamb to Thomas Medwin, November? 1824. Forster
Collection, National Art Library

197 '*We* are'   B to Lady Melbourne, 19 April 1813
'all which'   ibid., 14 May 1813
'plenty of fish'   Hunt *Lord Byron*
'an extraordinary'   Journal, 1 December 1813
'a couple of'   Hunt *Lord Byron*

198 'in a sort'   Moore *Life*, vol. 1
'Ly. O arrives'   B to Lady Melbourne, 26 May 1813
'The Devil'   ibid., 21 June 1813
'*Carolinish*'   ibid., 29 June 1813
'A woman'   Blessington *Conversations*

199 'soothed by success'   Galt *Life*
'this snake'   B to John Murray, 26 August 1813
'You are indeed'   James Wedderburn Webster to B, undated
'The "*Giaour*"'   B to John Murray, 25 March 1817

14   Six Mile Bottom 1813–1814

200 'This victory'   B to Lady Melbourne, 18 August 1813
'We are just'   B to Thomas Moore, 8 July 1813
'the sins'   B to Lord Holland, 25 March 1813

201 'never having'   B to Thomas Moore, 8 July 1813
'The cause'   Mrs Byron to B, 11 May 1810. Lovelace–Byron Archive

202 'Let me know'   B to Augusta Leigh, 26 June 1813
'I think'   ibid., 27 June 1813
'a *she* voucher'   B to Lady Melbourne, 1 July 1813
'a small Waltzing'   Lady Heathcote's invitation card. Clark Library, University of
California at Los Angeles
'I conclude'   Lady Caroline Lamb to Thomas Medwin, November ? 1824. Forster
Collection, National Art Library

203 'some sharp instrument'   B to Lady Melbourne, 6 July 1813
'to the consternation'   Galt *Life*
'Ly. Caroline'   annotation to B's invitation card. Clark Library, University of California
at Los Angeles

204 'that bleak common'   B to Augusta Leigh, 26 March 1813
'dowdy'   *The Diary of Frances Lady Shelley 1787–1817*, ed. Richard Edgcumbe, 1912
'baby Byron'   Hunt *Lord Byron*
'I abominate'   B to Augusta Leigh, 30 August 1811
'He was very'   *The Diary of Frances Lady Shelley 1787–1817*, ed. Richard Edgcumbe,
1912
'the fact is'   B to Thomas Moore, 22 August 1813

205 'We made'   Hobhouse diaries, 19 May 1814

'we may have been' B to Augusta Leigh, 17 May 1819

'Incest is' Percy Bysshe Shelley to Maria Gisborne, 16 November 1819. Bodleian Library, University of Oxford, MS Shelley, c. 1, fols. 318–19

206 'Augusta knew' Blessington *Conversations*

'She & two' B to Lady Byron, 28 December 1820

'it was not' B to Lady Melbourne, 13 January 1814

'was not aware' ibid., 30 April 1814

'They had' B to Thomas Moore, 13 July 1813

'her Lord's' B to Lady Melbourne, 5 August 1813

207 'it is so' ibid., 21 August 1813

'The great' B to Annabella Milbanke, 6 September 1813

'demon' B to Lady Melbourne, 28 September 1813

'Thine eyes' 'Sonnet to Genevra', 1813, l. 1

208 'adulterated' B to Thomas Moore, 27 September 1813

'Agricultural establishment' B to James Wedderburn Webster, 25 July 1813

'Blunderhead family' B to Lady Melbourne, 5 October 1813

'The place is' ibid., 21 September 1813

'a noble subject' B to John Cam Hobhouse, 17 November 1811

'concluding by' B to Lady Melbourne, 21 September 1813

'she evidently' ibid., September – 1 October 1813

'a good deal' ibid., October 1813

209 'a foolish nymph' ibid., 21 September 1813

'the melancholy' ibid., 10 October 1813

'My proselyte' ibid., 11 October 1813

210 'like Ghosts' ibid., 13 January 1814

'very handsome' ibid., 13 October 1813

'We have' ibid., 14 October 1813

'at *one draught*' ibid., 17 October 1813

'there is no' ibid., 14 October 1813

'when there is' ibid., 21 October 1813

'When we two' 'When We Two Parted', ll. 1–2

211 'when the moment' Lady Frances Webster to B, autumn 1813

'her whimsical' B to Lady Melbourne, 10 January 1814

'very pretty' ibid., 16 January 1814

'dearest Augusta' B to Augusta Leigh, 8 November 1813

'I am' B to Lady Melbourne, 25 November 1813

'He was himself' Thomas Babington Macaulay, review of Thomas Moore's *Life of Byron*, *Edinburgh Review*, June 1831

'must write' James Wedderburn Webster to B, 18 November 1813

212 'to preserve' B to Edward Daniel Clarke, 15 December 1813

'the foot' Lady Frances Webster to B, 28 December 1813

'*two centuries*' B to John Galt, 11 December 1813

'I believe' Journal, 14 November 1813

'that rendered' B to William Gifford, 12 November 1813

'it will' B to Lady Melbourne, 25 November 1813

'Partager tous'   Augusta Leigh to B, 29 November 1813. Lovelace–Byron Archive

213 'The roads'   B to John Murray, 22 January 1814
'old love'   B to Lady Melbourne, 8 January 1814
'for if'   B to J.J. Coulmann, July ? 1823

214 'the kind of'   B to Lady Melbourne, 11 January 1814
'in ye family'   B to John Hanson, 1 February 1814
'it is *not*'   B to Lady Melbourne, 25 April 1814
'I said'   Lady Byron, Narrative R, late 1816. Lovelace–Byron Archive

215 'Oh I never'   Lady Byron, 'Minutes of Conversation with Lady Caroline Lamb',
27 March 1816. Lovelace–Byron Archive
'my Georgiana'   B to Augusta Leigh, 24 June 1814
'*con amore*'   Journal, 18 February 1814
'I believe'   John Murray to B, 1814
'& devoured'   HRH Princess Charlotte to Mercer Elphinstone, 2 February 1814. *Letters
of Princess Charlotte, 1811–17*, ed. A. Aspinall, 1949
'You can not'   John Murray to B, 1814

216 'Linked with one'   *The Corsair*, Canto III, st. 24, l. 696
'Lord Byron'   Francis Jeffrey, unsigned review of *The Corsair* and *The Bride of Abydos*,
Edinburgh Review, XXIII, April 1814
'that *I* am'   Journal, 10 March 1814
Byron's portraits   see A. Peach, 'Portraits of Byron', *Walpole Society*, LXII, 2000
Errol Flynn as Byron   David Piper, *The Image of the Poet: British Poets and their
Portraits*, 1982

217 'Do you not'   Lady Caroline Lamb to John Murray, 8 November 1813
'It is put'   B to Mercer Elphinstone, 3 May 1814
'His whole'   Harriette Wilson, *Memoirs*, 1825
'Lady C. Lamb'   Hobhouse *Recollections*, vol. 1, entry for 1 July 1814
'scolded like'   B to Lady Melbourne, 2 July 1814

218 'This night'   Journal, 28 March 1814
'elegant and'   *Minutes of the General Meetings of the Proprietors of Albany*, 22 April 1803
'I am in'   B to Lady Melbourne, 30 March 1814
'witch-like'   Moore *Life*, vol. 1
'There is something'   Journal, 27 February 1814

219 'It is a good'   Journal, 28/29/30 November 1813
'the worst parts'   ibid., 6 December 1813
'calm languor'   ibid., 10 April 1814
'We clareted'   B to Thomas Moore, 9 April 1814
'a new Actor'   B to James Wedderburn Webster, 20 February 1814
'while undressing'   B to John Murray, 6 June 1822

220 'She walks'   'She Walks in Beauty', June 1814, l. 1
'Do not I'   Henrietta d'Ussières to B, 10 May 1814
'for the remainder'   ibid., June 1814
'You talked'   B to Lady Melbourne, 26 June 1814

221 'The last time'   Lady Caroline Lamb to Thomas Medwin, ? November 1824. Forster
Collection, National Art Library

'indifference'   B to Thomas Moore, 31 May 1814
'Tis said'   B to Lady Melbourne, 21 September 1813
222 'As for me'   Journal, 16 January 1814
'an "Anti-Byron"'   B to Thomas Moore, 9 April 1814
'in a county'   B to John Cam Hobhouse, 23 July 1814
'near together'   B to Francis Hodgson, 8 July 1814
'I have been'   B to Thomas Moore, 3 August 1814
223 'a *regular*'   B to Francis Hodgson, 11 July 1814
'of *im*pecuniary'   B to Thomas Moore, July 1814
'the most prudish'   B to Lady Melbourne, 10 June 1814
'Pray heaven'   B to Annabella Milbanke, 26 September 1814

15   Seaham 1814–1815

224 'Jacky and Larry'   B to Thomas Moore, 13 August 1814
'If you did it'   Lady Caroline Lamb to John Murray, 1815
'He mingled'   *Lara*, Canto I, st. 7, l. 98
'*that* must'   ibid., st. 9, l. 139
'When she'   'Opening Lines to *Lara*', l. 1, 1814
225 'too metaphysical'   B to Leigh Hunt, May–June 1815
'diving into'   Annabella Milbanke to B, 21 August 1815. Lovelace–Byron Archive
'recollections'   Augusta Leigh to Francis Hodgson, November 1816
'she wished me'   B to Lady Melbourne, 4 October 1814
'the every-day'   B to Thomas Moore, 31 May 1814
226 'Whatever she'   Journal, 22 March 1814
'You see'   Moore *Life*, vol. 1
'Are the "objections"'   B to Annabella Milbanke, 9 September 1814
'*always* thought'   Lady Milbanke to Lady Melbourne, 25 September 1814
227 'I was'   Medwin *Conversations*
'I thank you'   B to Annabella Milbanke, 3 March 1814
'She married me'   Medwin *Conversations*
'It never rains'   Lady Byron, Narrative Q, 1816. Lovelace–Byron Archive
'Lord Byron'   Hobhouse diary, 30 September 1814
'love more'   ibid., 21 March 1814
'and stand'   Lady Caroline Lamb to John Murray, *c.* 1814
228 'C I suspect'   B to Lady Melbourne, 5 October 1814
'Nobody hates'   B to Thomas Moore, 7 October 1814
'as a sister'   Lady Caroline Lamb to B, autumn 1814
'as a bond'   Lady Caroline Lamb to John Murray, 18 November 1814
229 'some business'   B to Thomas Moore, 20 September 1814
'in the course'   Lady Milbanke to Hugh Montgomery, 1 October 1814. Lovelace–Byron Archive
'Don't you think'   B to Lady Melbourne, 31 October 1814
'I confess'   B to John Cam Hobhouse, 17 October 1814
'He had been'   Lady Byron, Narrative Q, 1816. Lovelace–Byron Archive

230 'A's meeting'   B to Lady Melbourne, 4 November 1814
'it was best'   B to John Hanson, 28 September 1814
marriage settlement   see J.V. Beckett, *Byron and Newstead: the Aristocrat and the Abbey*, 2002

231 'Mr Hanson'   Hanson narrative
'never be able'   Lady Caroline Lamb to John Murray, autumn 1814
'imbibed a mortal'   B to Lady Melbourne, 21 September 1812
'Old twaddle'   Elizabeth, Duchess of Devonshire, quoted in *The Two Duchesses*, ed. Vere Foster, 1898
'ante vel'   Hanson narrative. I am grateful to Philip Howard for his elucidation of this passage
'once every'   B to Lady Melbourne, 13 November 1814
'became quite livid'   Lady Byron to Harriet Beecher Stowe, 1856, quoted Elwin

232 'her *passions*'   B to Lady Melbourne, 6 November 1814
'had recourse'   ibid., 13 November 1814
'If it will'   B to Annabella Milbanke, 16 November 1814
'this is well'   Hobhouse diaries, 23 November 1814
'Don't scold'   B to Annabella Milbanke, 22 November 1814

233 '*The* Cake'   ibid., 7 December 1814. Lovelace–Byron Archive
'as I stood'   Eliza Francis narrative. Gamba Collection, Biblioteca Classense, Ravenna
'My dear Eliza'   B to Eliza Francis, late 1814

234 'Ld. Portsmouth's'   B to Annabella Milbanke, 18 December 1814
'tho' I can't'   Hanson narrative
'Made one'   Journal, 7 March 1814
'I have'   B to Annabella Milbanke, 8 December 1814

235 'without fuss'   ibid., 16 December 1814
'Pray, sir'   Hobhouse *Recollections*, vol. 3, entry for 19 June 1824
'Dearest A'   B to Annabella Milbanke, 25 December 1814
'Never was'   Hobhouse diaries, 26 December 1814
'the bridegroom'   ibid., 27 December 1814
'indifference'   ibid., 29 December 1814
'with great'   ibid., 30 December 1814

236 'do *do* it'   B to John Murray, 31 December 1814
'that those'   Lady Byron to Dr Lushington, 19 February 1816. Lovelace–Byron Archive
'this is'   Hobhouse diaries, 1 January 1815
'which were stuffed'   B to Lady Melbourne, 7 January 1815

237 'very plain'   Hobhouse diaries, 2 January 1815

238 'I don't dislike'   B to Lady Melbourne, 7 January 1815
'He began'   Lady Byron, Statement T, March 1816. Lovelace–Byron Archive
'*had* Lady Byron'   Hobhouse diaries, 15 May 1824
'on his marriage'   Rogers *Table-Talk*
'one animal'   Lady Byron, Narrative F, March 1817. Lovelace–Byron Archive
'atrocious crimes'   Lady Byron, Statement T, March 1816. Lovelace–Byron Archive

239 'This extraordinary'   Blessington *Conversations*
'MY YOUNG'   Augusta Leigh to Lady Byron, 8 January 1815. Lovelace–Byron Archive

'it is odd'   B to Annabella Milbanke, 20 October 1814
'vile Ebrew'   B to Thomas Moore, 8 March 1815
'exhibited a peculiar'   Nathan *Fugitive Pieces*

240 'Upon this'   B to Thomas Moore, 2 February 1815
'mysterious necessity'   Lady Byron, Narrative F, March 1817. Lovelace–Byron Archive
'The Assyrian'   'The Destruction of Semnacherib', 1815, l. 1

241 'wild mirthful'   Lady Byron, reminiscences, 1818 and 1842, quoted Lovelace, 'Digest of
Lady Byron's Statements and Narratives, etc.' Lovelace–Byron Archive
'little foot'   Lady Byron, Statement L, 1816. Lovelace–Byron Archive
'a family'   Augusta Leigh to Lady Byron, 10 February 1815. Lovelace–Byron Archive
'*comical proceedings*'   ibid., 11 January 1815. Lovelace–Byron Archive
'I am glad'   ibid., 28 January 1815. Lovelace–Byron Archive

242 'You married'   Lady Byron, Narrative R, late 1816 or early 1817. Lovelace–Byron Archive

244 'the scene of'   Lady Byron, Narrative S, sequel to Narrative R above. Lovelace-Byron
Archive
'Buonaparte'   B to John Cam Hobhouse, 26 March 1815
'utterly falsifying'   B to Thomas Moore, 27 March 1815

16   Piccadilly Terrace 1815–1816

245 'A young unmarried'   *Don Juan*, Canto XII, st. 58, l. 457
'As Ld B'   Lady Melbourne to Lady Byron, 7 March 1815. Lovelace–Byron Archive
'those *essentials*'   B to John Cam Hobhouse, 3 March 1815
'my wife'   B to Augusta Leigh, 30 August 1811

246 'We mounted'   *The Diary of Frances Lady Shelley 1787–1817*, ed. Richard Edgcumbe,
1912. Entry for 16 April 1815
'I never'   Lady Caroline Lamb to Thomas Medwin, ? November 1824. Forster
Collection, National Art Library
'Could not'   Augusta Leigh to Lady Byron, 19 February 1815. Lovelace–Byron Archive
'though he has'   Hobhouse diaries, 1 April 1815

248 'You will oblige'   B to John Murray, 2 February 1815
'the best'   ibid., 24 July 1814
'Lord Byron's'   Smiles *Memoir*, vol. 1
'Coleridge is'   B to James Hogg, 24 March 1814

249 'In Kean'   B to Samuel Taylor Coleridge, 31 March 1815
'There never were'   'Detached Thoughts', no. 67, 1821–2

250 'We are old'   Journal, 5 December 1813
'It was odd'   'Detached Thoughts', no. 70, 1821–2
'two distinct'   John Keats to George and Georgiana Keats, 13 or 14 October 1818.
Letters of John Keats, ed. Sidney Colvin, 1925
'hanging over'   The Rev. A.G. L'Estrange, *The Literary Life of the Rev. William
Harness*, 1871
'His appearance'   Hunt *Lord Byron*
'kissing one's wife's'   B to Thomas Moore, 28 August 1813
'is in'   B to Francis Hodgson, 29 April 1815

'She was dressed' George Ticknor journal, 20 June 1815. *Life, Letters and Journals of George Ticknor*, ed. Anna Ticknor, vol. 1, 1876

251 'told me' Lady Byron, Statement G. Lovelace–Byron Archive

'lowering looks' Lady Byron, Statement E. Lovelace–Byron Archive

'romantic forgiveness' Lady Byron, Statement G. Lovelace–Byron Archive

252 'Lady Byron's' B to John Murray, 9 October 1821

'He said' Lady Byron, Statement H. Lovelace–Byron Archive

'They go out' Augusta Leigh to John Cam Hobhouse, 5 July 1815. Hobhouse *Recollections*, vol. 2

'the most violent' Lady Byron, Statement W, March 1816. Lovelace–Byron Archive

'The thought' Lady Byron, Statement K, late 1816. Lovelace–Byron Archive

253 'to remove' Lady Byron, Statement G. Lovelace–Byron Archive

'What a blessing' Augusta Leigh to John Cam Hobhouse, 5 July 1815. Hobhouse *Recollections*, vol. 2

'the mass' John Cam Hobhouse to B, 12 July 1815

'Farewell to' 'Napoleon's Farewell (from the French)', 25 July 1815, l. 1

254 'Then fare thee' 'When We Two Parted', deleted st. 4, 1815

'For the first' 'To Lady Caroline Lamb', 1812, st. 4, l. 13

255 'she is most' B to James Wedderburn Webster, 18 September 1815

'Byron is not' Hobhouse diaries, 31 July 1815

'all grumbled' ibid., 8 August 1815

'*two phials*' B to Lady Byron, 31 August 1815

'Darling duck' Lady Byron to B, 31 August 1815. Ethel Colburn Mayne, *The Life and Letters of Anne Isabella, Lady Noel Byron*, 1929

'All the children' B to Lady Byron, 1 September 1815

'a little *Sparring*' Lady Byron, Statement G. Lovelace–Byron Archive

256 'her style' B to Annabella Milbanke, 19 October 1814

'a very pleasant' George Ticknor journal, 26 June 1815. *Life, Letters and Journals of George Ticknor*, ed. Anna Ticknor, vol. 1, 1876

'Lady Hardwicke' Lady Byron to Sir Ralph Noel, 5 September 1815. Lovelace–Byron Archive

'the Manager' Lady Byron to Lady Noel, 6 October 1815. Lovelace–Byron Archive

'What an assemblage' Journal, 17–18 December 1813

257 'I am looking' Lady Byron, Statement U, March 1816. Lovelace–Byron Archive

'Piece' B to John Cam Hobhouse, 9 November 1811

'you are' Susan Boyce to B, winter 1815

'Miss Boyce' Rogers *Table-Talk*

'I shall be' Susan Boyce to B, winter 1815. Subsequent letters quoted from this series, late 1815–early 1816

258 'if 'twill' ibid., April 1816

'in an *Attic*' Susan Boyce to John Cam Hobhouse, 25 November 1824

'she was' B to Douglas Kinnaird, 23 August 1821

'playful as' Walter Scott journal, 21 December 1825. *The Journal of Sir Walter Scott*, ed. W.E.K. Anderson, 1972

259 'the grossest' Lady Byron, Statement B 'Additions'. Lovelace–Byron Archive

'in that quarter' Hobhouse diaries, 25 November 1815

'a sad brute' Lady Byron to Augusta Leigh, 10 November 1815. Lovelace–Byron Archive

'Your present' B to John Murray, 14 November 1815

260 'I am very' ibid., 2 January 1816

'continues in this' Mrs Clermont's Statement, 22 January 1816. Lovelace–Byron Archive

'being of' Lady Byron, Statement W, March 1816. Lovelace–Byron Archive

'with the strongest' Lady Byron, Statement to Lady Noel, 18 January 1816. Lovelace–Byron Archive

261 'of knocking' Hobhouse *Recollections*, vol. 2

'if it was' Lady Byron, Statement H. Lovelace–Byron Archive

'Oh! what' Lady Anne Barnard, quoted in letter from Lord Lindsay to *The Times*, 7 September 1869

'guilty of' Lady Byron, March 1816. Lovelace–Byron Archive

'I have reason' Lady Byron to Dr Baillie, 8 January 1816. Lovelace–Byron Archive

'to *do*' Lady Byron, Statement to Lady Noel, 18 January 1816. Lovelace–Byron Archive

'The latter' B to William Harness, 15 December 1811

262 'When you are' B to Lady Byron, 6 January 1816

'fit for' Hobhouse *Separation*

'a fallen' Lady Byron, Statement on her consultation with Dr Baillie, 8 January 1816, revised April 1824. Lovelace–Byron Archive

'he said' Lady Byron, Statement A, 14–15 February 1816. Lovelace–Byron Archive

'There was' Lady Byron quoted Ethel Colburn Mayne, *The Life and Letters of Anne Isabella, Lady Noel Byron*, 1929

17 Piccadilly Terrace 1816

263 'I hope' Lady Byron to B, 15 January 1816. Lovelace–Byron Archive

'Dearest Duck' ibid., 17 January 1816. Lovelace–Byron Archive

'a few lines' Lady Byron to Selina Doyle, 15 January 1816. Lovelace–Byron Archive

264 'so much smaller' Augusta Leigh to Lady Byron, 18 January 1816. Lovelace–Byron Archive

'*Very recently*' Sir Ralph Noel to B, 28 January 1816. Lovelace–Byron Archive

'that *final step*' Selina Doyle to Lady Byron, probably 18 January 1816. Lovelace–Byron Archive

265 'B. went' Augusta Leigh to Lady Byron, 26 January 1816. Lovelace–Byron Archive

'left the house' ibid., 18 January 1816. Lovelace–Byron Archive

'completely knocked' Hobhouse diaries, 5 February 1816. Berg Collection, New York Public Library

'I was standing' Medwin *Conversations*

266 'I have received' B to Sir Ralph Noel, 2 February 1816

'I am really' B to Lady Byron, 3 February 1816

'Were you then' ibid., 8 February 1816

'crying bitterly' Hobhouse diaries, 12 February 1816. Berg Collection, New York Public Library

'If my heart' B to Thomas Moore, 8 March 1816

267 'accused B'   Hobhouse diaries, 9 February 1816. Berg Collection, New York Public Library

'*in the streets*'   ibid., 12 February 1816

'reports abroad'   Augusta Leigh to Lady Byron, 17 February 1816. Lovelace–Byron Archive

'There are things'   Lady Byron to Dr Stephen Lushington, 15 February 1816. Lovelace–Byron Archive

'nothing more'   Moore *Life*, vol. 2

268 'Something of this'   Hobhouse note

'I fear'   Harold Nicolson, *Byron: The Last Journey*, 1924

'responsively'   Doris Langley Moore, *Lord Byron: Accounts Rendered*, 1974

'rolling on'   Hobhouse diaries, 9 February 1816. Berg Collection, New York Public Library

'you might'   Mrs Clermont to Lady Byron, 13 February 1816. Lovelace–Byron Archive

'attempts to corrupt'   Moore *Journal*, 16 October 1827

'struck at'   Hobhouse *Separation*

'I am decided'   Hobhouse diaries, 16 February 1816. Berg Collection, New York Public Library

'disavowed cruelty'   Hobhouse diaries, 7 March 1816. Ibid.

'the two reports'   Hobhouse *Separation*

269 'something horrid'   Hobhouse diaries, 8 March 1816. Berg Collection, New York Public Library

'my name'   B to Lady Byron, 25 March 1816

'think of'   Lady Caroline Lamb to Lady Byron, March 1816. Lovelace–Byron Archive

270 'strong suspicions'   Lady Byron to Dr Stephen Lushington, 27 March 1816. Lovelace–Byron Archive

'final escape'   Dr Stephen Lushington to Lady Byron, 27 March 1816. Lovelace–Byron Archive

'it is odd'   B to Thomas Moore, 8 March 1816

'the wildest'   B to Samuel Taylor Coleridge, 18 October 1815

'wonderful talent'   B to Thomas Moore, 28 October 1815

'If you had'   Samuel Taylor Coleridge letter to a friend, 10 April 1816. James Gillman, *The Life of Samuel Taylor Coleridge*, 1838

271 'wild originality'   Claire Clairmont to B, 16? April 1816

'An utter'   ibid., April 1816

'I who'   ibid., 6 May 1816

272 'many years'   ibid., April 1816

'Ld. B'   B to Claire Clairmont, April 1816

'God bless'   Claire Clairmont, note on letter from B, April 1816

'for she is'   Claire Clairmont to B, 21 April 1816

'there we'   ibid., 16? April 1816

'tomorrow will'   ibid., 21 April 1816

'that odd-headed'   B to Douglas Kinnaird, 20 January 1817

'the woman'   Moore *Journal*, 5 January 1819

'I never loved'   B to Douglas Kinnaird, 20 January 1817

273 'I am unhappily'   Claire Clairmont to Jane Williams, December 1826. Bodleian Library, University of Oxford, Abinger deposit, c. 478

'the unworthy'   Sir Walter Scott, 'The death of Lord Byron', *Edinburgh Weekly Journal*, 19 May 1824

'The world'   Prothero *Letters and Journals*, vol. 3

'They were'   Augustus Foster to Elizabeth, Duchess of Devonshire, 23 March 1816. *The Two Duchesses*, ed. Vere Foster, 1898

'Lady Byron's'   Elizabeth, Duchess of Devonshire to Augustus Foster, 22 March 1816. Ibid.

'Fare thee'   'Fare Thee Well!', 1816, l. 1

274 'like a'   HRH Princess Charlotte to Mercer Elphinstone, 19? April 1816. Lady Charlotte Bury, *The Diary of a Lady-in-Waiting*, ed. A. Francis Steuart, vol. 1, 1908

'This at such'   B to Lady Byron, 20–25? March 1816

'Born in the garret'   'A Sketch from Private Life', 30 March 1816, l. 1

'can any'   William Gifford to John Murray, internal memorandum

275 'Lord Byron's conduct'   *The Diary of Joseph Farington*, ed. Kenneth Garlick and Angus Macintyre, 1978–84. Entry for 26 April 1816

'There was not'   Hobhouse notes

'had not'   Moore *Life*, vol. 2

'You can'   B to Scrope Berdmore Davies, 7 December 1818

276 'You had'   William Hazlitt, *Conversations of James Northcote*, no. 15

'I've also seen'   *Don Juan*, Canto XIV, st. 96, l. 761

'the different'   Medwin *Conversations*

'the atrocious'   B to Scrope Berdmore Davies, 7 December 1818

'they tried'   B to John Cam Hobhouse, 17 May 1819

'I was advised'   Prothero *Letters and Journals*, vol. 4

'even Hobhouse'   B to Scrope Berdmore Davies, 7 December 1818

277 'we shall not'   B to Samuel Rogers, 14 April 1816

'I have just'   B to Lady Byron, 14 April 1816

'When all around'   'To Augusta', 1816, l. 1

278 'judge Byron'   Lady Caroline Lamb to B, April 1816?

'I wished'   B to John Murray, 15 April 1816

'I deliver'   Hobhouse diaries, 21 April 1821

'the unleavened'   B to Isaac Nathan, April 1816

'all sorts'   Hobhouse diaries, 23 April 1816

279 'a green sod'   ibid., 24 April 1816

'kept B.'   ibid., 25 April 1816

'Farewell'   'Napoleon's Farewell (from the French)', 25 July 1815, l. 1

280 'Poor Lady'   Elizabeth, Duchess of Devonshire to Augustus Foster, 6 April 1816. *The Two Duchesses*, ed. Vere Foster, 1898

'torn "here"'   Hobhouse diaries, 22 April 1816

'But it must'   Lady Byron, 'By thee Forsaken – March 1816', from notebook 'Verses 1809–1816'. Lovelace–Byron Archive

'of his late'   George Ticknor journal, 25 October 1816. *Life, Letters and Journals of George Ticknor*, ed. Anna Ticknor, vol. 1, 1876

18   Geneva 1816

283   'I recollect'   *Don Juan*, Canto II, st. 12, l. 93
'a damned'   B to John Cam Hobhouse, 26? April 1816
'Exiled from'   Blessington *Conversations*
'in stirring'   Moore *Life*, vol. 2

284   'Sorrow is'   *Manfred*, Act I, sc. 1, l. 10
'a very tolerable'   B to John Cam Hobhouse, 26? April 1816
'fell like'   Polidori *Diary*, 26 April 1816

285   'Dr Dori'   B to John Cam Hobhouse, 1 May 1816
'a degraded'   ibid., 16 May 1816
'I sometimes wish'   'Detached Thoughts', no. 84, 1821–2
'dreadful smacker'   Polidori *Diary*, 26 April 1816

286   'level roads'   B to Augusta Leigh, 1 May 1816
'he seems'   B to John Cam Hobhouse, 1 May 1816
'a beautiful'   Pryse Lockhart Gordon, *Personal Memoirs*, vol. 2, 1830
'the glitter'   Polidori *Diary*, 4 May 1816

287   'The Plain'   B to John Cam Hobhouse, 16 May 1816
'One packet'   list of 'Articles for Lord Byron', sent from Brussels to Albemarle Street, 1817
'Stop, for thy'   quoted Pryse Lockhart Gordon, *Personal Memoirs*, vol. 2, 1830
'How that red'   *Childe Harold's Pilgrimage*, Canto III, st. 17, l. 151

288   'There have'   ibid., st. 30, l. 262
'jolting, rolling'   Polidori *Diary*, 7 May 1816
'a ludicrous'   B to John Cam Hobhouse, 16 May 1816
'A whole room'   Polidori *Diary*, 9 May 1816

289   'The castled crag'   *Childe Harold's Pilgrimage*, Canto III, l. 496
'We know'   Thomas Babington Macaulay, review of Thomas Moore's *Life of Byron*, in *Edinburgh Review*, June 1831

290   'I withdrew'   'Some Observations upon an Article in *Blackwood's Edinburgh Magazine*', 1820
'envy, jealousy'   Blessington *Conversations*
'With false'   'Epistle to Augusta', 1816, st. 13, l. 97
'From Morat'   B to John Cam Hobhouse, 26 May 1816

291   'bashful, shy'   Polidori *Diary*, 27 May 1816
'the wind'   Moore *Life*, vol. 2

292   'perpetual density'   B to Samuel Rogers, 29 July 1816
'The bright'   'Darkness', 1816, l. 2
'*Have you*'   Moore *Life*, vol. 2
'Began my'   Polidori *Diary*, 18 June 1816
'Poor Polidori'   Mary Shelley, Preface to 1831 edition of *Frankenstein* in Bentley's Standard Novels

293   'the fallen'   Mary Shelley, *Frankenstein*
'the word'   B to John Murray, 15 May 1819
'vamped up'   note to Moore *Life*, vol. 2

294 'in the halo'   Polidori *Diary*, 28 May 1816
'he was exactly'   Moore *Life*, vol. 2
'Dr Pollydolly'   B to John Cam Hobhouse, 23 June 1823
'a curst'   B to Thomas Moore, 19 September 1821
295 'Lilliput republic'   Lady Charlotte Bury, *The Diary of a Lady-in-Waiting*, ed. A. Francis
Steuart, vol. 1, 1908. Entry for 12 September 1814
Geneva police reports   Geneva Archives d'Etat
'there is'   Medwin *Conversations*
'certain robes'   John Cam Hobhouse to Augusta Leigh, 9 September 1816. Prothero
Letters and Journals, vol. 3
'*chronique scandaleuse*'   *The Diary of Frances Lady Shelley 1787–1817*, ed. Richard
Edgcumbe, 1912. Entry for July 1816
'had formed'   B to John Cam Hobhouse, 11 November 1818
296 'with Percy'   *The Diary of Frances Lady Shelley 1787–1817*, ed. Richard Edgcumbe,
1912. Entry for July 1816
'shrugging & whispering'   B to Henry Brougham, 6 May 1820
'*cut*'   *The Diaries of Sylvester Douglas (Lord Glenbervie)*, ed. Francis Bickley, vol. 2,
1928. Entry for 3 July 1816
'promiscuous intercourse'   B to John Cam Hobhouse, 11 November 1818
'flashed with'   Medwin *Angler*, vol. 2
297 'let any one'   Claire Clairmont to B, 12 January 1818
'I had ten'   ibid., 6 May 1816
'I could not'   B to Augusta Leigh, 8 September 1816
'Is the brat'   B to Douglas Kinnaird, 20 January 1817
298 'Lausanne!'   *Childe Harold's Pilgrimage*, Canto III, st. 105, l. 977
'the light of'   Percy Bysshe Shelley to Thomas Moore, 16 December 1817. British
Library
'habited like'   Trelawny *Recollections*
'cracked soprano'   Medwin *Angler*
'more abstract'   Moore *Life*, vol. 2
299 'without speaking'   Percy Bysshe Shelley to Thomas Love Peacock, 12 July 1816.
Shelley *Letters*, vol. 1
'Cagliari Majesty'   B to John Cam Hobhouse, 23 June 1816
'wretched'   Percy Bysshe Shelley to Thomas Love Peacock, 12 July 1816. Shelley
Letters, vol. 1
'the self-torturing'   *Childe Harold's Pilgrimage*, Canto III, st. 77, l. 725
'I was overcome'   Percy Bysshe Shelley to Thomas Love Peacock, 12 July 1816. Shelley
Letters, vol. 1
300 'My very chains'   *The Prisoner of Chillon*, l. 389
'the superb'   B to John Cam Hobhouse, 16 May 1816
'Lord Byron is'   Percy Bysshe Shelley to Thomas Love Peacock, 17 July 1816. Shelley
Letters, vol. 1
301 'Mrs Corinne'   Moore *Life*, vol. 1
'Mrs *Stale*'   B to Thomas Moore, 2 October 1813
'a very plain'   B to Lady Melbourne, 8 January 1814

'She has made' B to John Murray, 30 September 1816

'In all' Broglie Archives, quoted Victor de Pange, *The Unpublished Correspondence of Mme de Staël and the Duke of Wellington*, 1965

'as at some' Medwin *Conversations*

'This is' B to John Murray, 15 May 1819

'marvellous & grievous' B to John Murray, 22 July 1816

302 'a little' Lady Caroline Lamb narrative, *Lady Morgan's Memoirs*, vol. 2, 1862

'C'est possible' Charles-Victor de Bonstetten, quoted Lady Morgan, *Passages from My Autobiography*, 1859

'I read' B to John Cam Hobhouse, 31 March 1817

'The separation' B to Madame de Staël, 24 August 1816

303 'all phrases' Lady Byron to Augusta Leigh, 30 July 1816. Lovelace *Astarte*

'A moral Clytemnestra' 'Lines On Hearing that Lady Byron was Ill', 1816, l. 37

19 The Swiss Alps 1816

304 'Could I' 'A Fragment', 1816, l. 1

'the pageant' Matthew Arnold, 'Stanzas from the Grand Chartreuse', 1855, l. 136

'The world' 'Darkness', 1816, l. 69

305 'Be it known' 'Monk' Lewis to B, mid-August 1816

'set him' B to Samuel Rogers, 4 April 1817

'I could hardly' Hobhouse diaries, 30 July 1816

306 'went up' ibid., 26 August 1816

'the very impertinent' Claire Clairmont to B, 6 October 1816

'My dreadful fear' ibid., 29? August 1816

'My Lord' John Murray to B, 12 September 1816

307 'immense durated' Hobhouse diaries, 30 August 1816

'atheist & philanthropist' Hobhouse *Recollections*, vol. 2

'seals – necklaces' B to Augusta Leigh, 8 September 1816

308 'He does not' Hobhouse diaries, 15 September 1816

'Whatever has passed' John Cam Hobhouse to Lady Melbourne, 4 September 1816

'very fine' Hobhouse diaries, 1 September 1816

309 'The music' Alpine Journal, 19 September 1816

'founded on' Moore *Journal*, 27 October 1820

'the district' Alpine Journal, 20 September 1816

'just the place' ibid., 22 September 1816

310 'of all colours' ibid., 23 September 1816

'suspended like' Hobhouse diaries, 24 September 1816

'they sing' Alpine Journal, 24 September 1816

'capering' Hobhouse diaries, 24 September 1816

'the English' Alpine Journal, 25 September 1816

311 'I was disposed' ibid., 29 September 1816

'a sort of' B to John Murray, 30 September 1816

'of a very wild' ibid., 15 February 1817

'half-dust' *Manfred*, Act I, sc. 2, l. 40

'extemporaneously'   George Ticknor journal, 20 October 1817. *Life, Letters and Journals of George Ticknor*, ed. Anna Ticknor, vol. 1, 1876

'naturally much'   B to John Murray, 7 June 1820

312 'Thou lovedst'   *Manfred*, Act II, sc. 4, l. 121

'magnificent'   B to John Murray, 15 October 1816

313 'the prettiest'   B to Thomas Moore, 6 November 1816

'a stranger'   Henri Beyle (Stendhal), 'Lord Byron en Italie', *Racine et Shakespeare*, 1854

'poetical friend'   Hobhouse diaries, 17 October 1816

'the most famous'   B to Augusta Leigh, 26 October 1816

'Fanny of Rimini'   B to John Murray, 20 March 1820

314 'as at a rout'   B to John Murray, 15 October 1816

'the state of'   B to Thomas Moore, 6 November 1816

'holding up'   Hobhouse diaries, 25 October 1816

'celebrated Sodomite'   B to John Cam Hobhouse, 3 March 1820

'quietly staring'   B to John Murray, 1 November 1816

315 'plain, open'   B to Thomas Moore, 6 November 1816

'ancient'   B to Augusta Leigh, 6 November 1816

20   Venice: Frezzeria and La Mira 1816–1817

316 'It glides'   *Beppo*, st, 19, l. 150

'The Rialto'   Hobhouse diaries, 10 November 1816

'a ship'   note in Moore *Life*, vol. 2

'the greenest'   B to Thomas Moore, 17 November 1816

'Everything about'   Preface to *Marino Faliero*

317 'you have'   B to John Murray, 3 March 1817

'marine melancholy'   B to John Cam Hobhouse, 19 December 1816

'I have been'   B to Thomas Moore, 17 November 1816

318 'I am going'   B to Augusta Leigh, 19 December 1816

'their Margate'   B to Thomas Moore, 11 April 1817

'sea Cybele'   *Childe Harold's Pilgrimage*, Canto III, st. 2, l. 1

'Oh Venice!'   'Venice. An Ode', 1818, l. 1

319 'are like'   B to Thomas Moore, 24 December 1816

'a very poor'   Hobhouse diaries, 16 November 1816

'In this beloved'   'On the Bust of Helen by Canova', November 1816

'Byronean'   Hobhouse diaries, 20 November 1816

'constant'   *Ritratti scritti da Isabella Teotochi Albrizzi*, 1826. Moore *Life*, vol. 2

320 'large, black'   B to Thomas Moore, 17 November 1816

'well-looking'   ibid., 28 January 1817

'Caro Giorgio'   Marianna Segati correspondence in *Shelley and his Circle*, vol. 7

'very tranquil'   B to Augusta Leigh, 18 December 1816

321 'never a twenty-four'   B to John Murray, 2 January 1817

'here is Signora'   B to Thomas Moore, 10 March 1817

Armenian background   see Charles Dowsett, '"The madman has come back again!"

Byron and Armenian', *Journal of the Society for Armenian Studies*, no. 4, 1988–9;
C.J. Walker, *Visions of Ararat*, 1997
'very learned'   B to John Murray, 4 December 1816
'wanted something'   B to Thomas Moore, 5 December 1816
'I am always'   'Detached Thoughts', no. 99, 1821–2
'a fine old'   B to John Murray, 4 December 1816

322 'all the advantages'   unpublished Preface to the Armenian Grammar, 2 January 1817
'I went'   'Detached Thoughts', no. 55, 1821–2
'enjoying inglorious'   B to John Cam Hobhouse, 16 May 1816

323 'Capital Bull Dog'   John Murray to B, 24 January 1820
'every mouth'   B to John Murray, 27 December 1816
'a sort of'   ibid., 3 March 1816
'So, we'll go'   'So, we'll go', 1817, l. 1

324 'like the cosmogony'   B to Thomas Moore, 28 February 1817
'*let it be*'   B to John Hanson, 11 November 1816
'the *Demoiselle*'   B to Augusta Leigh, 18 December 1816
'a little'   Percy Bysshe Shelley to B, 23 April 1817. Carl H. Pforzheimer Library, New York

325 'I am a little'   B to Augusta Leigh, 27 May 1817
'acknowledge & breed'   B to Douglas Kinnaird, 13 January 1818
't'other fellow'   B to Thomas Moore, 11 April 1817
'How could'   B to John Cam Hobhouse, 14 April 1817

326 'celebrated for'   B to Augusta Leigh, 3–4 June 1817
'made & moulded'   B to John Murray, 4 June 1817
'from which'   ibid., 26 April 1817

327 'the excess'   anon. Englishwoman, quoted Lady Charlotte Bury, *The Diary of a Lady-in-Waiting*, ed. A. Francis Steuart, vol. 1, 1908
'parcel of'   B to Thomas Moore, 25 March 1817
'Don't look'   Lovelace *Astarte*
'Heaven knows'   B to Augusta Leigh, 8 September 1816
Rome background   see Peter Cochran, '"Higher and More Extended Comprehension": Byron's Three Weeks in Rome', *The Keats–Shelley Review*, no. 15, 2001
'Rome – the wonderful'   B to John Murray, 5 May 1817
'excursed and skirred'   ibid., 4 June 1817
'my first'   ibid., 9 May 1817
'& by some'   ibid., 4 June 1817

328 'I won't have'   B to John Cam Hobhouse, 20 June 1817
'He posed'   original account in Hans Christian Andersen, *Das Märchen meines Lebens*, vol. 2, 1844
'determined to'   B to John Murray, 30 May 1817

329 'working up'   ibid., 1 July 1817
'a friend'   Dedication to *Childe Harold's Pilgrimage*, Canto IV, 2 January 1818
'As for poesy'   B to John Murray, 2 January 1817
'Oh Rome!'   *Childe Harold's Pilgrimage*, Canto IV, st. 78, l. 694
'I am just'   B to John Murray, 18 June 1817

330 'more space' B to John Cam Hobhouse, 20 June 1817
     'I am just' B to Thomas Moore, 10 July 1817
     'We are' B to John Murray, 14 June 1817
     'a sucking Shylock' ibid., 7 August 1817
     'he was more' George Ticknor journal, 20 October 1817. *Life, Letters and Journals of George Ticknor*, ed. Anna Ticknor, vol. 1, 1876
331 'a small row' B to Douglas Kinnaird, 3 July 1817
     'well, and merry' Hobhouse diaries, 14 October 1817
     'He does not' ibid., 14 September 1817
332 'sauntering on' B to John Murray, 1 August 1819
     'picked up' Moore *Journal*, 8 October 1819
     'Why do not' B to John Murray, 1 August 1819
333 'as the seat of' Samuel Ayscough, preface note to *Beppo*
     'I'm sure' Hobhouse diaries, 29 August 1817
     'I am convinced' B to John Murray, 15 September 1817
     'I love' *Beppo*, st. 44, l. 345
334 'has politics' B to John Murray, 27 January 1818
     'spouting some' Captain Daniel Roberts, quoted MS journal of Joseph Chichester, 13 September 1828. Bodleian Library, University of Oxford, MS Eng. misc. c. 1400, fols. 174–9
     'a spanking gallop' B to Thomas Moore, 2 February 1818
     'We were really' Hobhouse diaries, 23 November 1817
     'zeal in everything' Moore *Journal*, 9 October 1827
335 'I should be' B to Douglas Kinnaird, 13 January 1818
     'My dear' B to John Murray, 8 January 1818
     'taken again' B to John Cam Hobhouse, 28 January 1818
     'in the estrum' B to John Murray, 27 January 1818
     'Gentil Donna' B to John Cam Hobhouse, 28 February 1818
     '*standing*' B to John Murray, 27 January 1818
     'here I have' B to Samuel Rogers, 3 March 1818

21 Venice: Palazzo Mocenigo 1818–1819

336 'Good night' B to Thomas Moore, 1 June 1818
     'up a flight' Hanson narrative
337 'charming' B to John Cam Hobhouse, 6 April 1819
     'Keep clear' Moore *Life*, vol. 2
     'my ragamuffins' B to Augusta Leigh, 28 November 1819
     'a fine fellow' Percy Bysshe Shelley to Mary Shelley, 8 August 1821. Bodleian Library, University of Oxford, MS Shelley, c. 1, fols. 443–8.
     'culpably lenient' Richard Belgrave Hoppner, quoted Moore *Life*, vol. 2
     'to get drunk' B to John Cam Hobhouse, 3 March 1818
     'caused by' ibid., June 1818
338 'fine animal' B to John Murray, 1 August 1819
     'fit to breed' B to Thomas Moore, 16 March 1818

'If she'   B to John Murray, 9 August 1819

'the learned Fletcher'   B to Augusta Leigh, 21 September 1818

'place of a'   transcript of Venice Police report. Keats–Shelley Memorial House, Rome

339 'In the autumn'   B to John Murray, 1 August 1819

'She is'   B to John Cam Hobhouse, 19 May 1818

'I am not'   ibid., 22 February 1821

340 'a Venetian lady'   B to John Murray, 16 February 1821

'*Try her*'   B to Douglas Kinnaird, 31 May 1821

'the Tarruscelli'   B to Count Giuseppino Albrizzi, 5 January 1819

'pl & opt'   B to John Cam Hobhouse, 4 October 1810

'As to "pages"'   B to Augusta Leigh, 14 September 1816

341 'he associates'   Percy Bysshe Shelley to Thomas Love Peacock, 17 or 18 December 1818.
Bodleian Library, University of Oxford, MS Shelley, c. 1, fols. 257–8

'What a miserable'   Mary Shelley to Maria Gisborne, 27 April 1819. Bodleian Library,
University of Oxford, MS Shelley, c. 1, fol. 335

'Nothing could'   Moore *Life*, vol. 2

342 'I could not'   B to John Cam Hobhouse, 25 June 1818

'in the water'   Trelawny *Records*

343 'pretty eyes'   Claire Clairmont to B, 12 January 1818

'promises with Albe'   Mary Shelley to Percy Bysshe Shelley, 30 September 1817.
Bodleian Library, University of Oxford, MS Shelley, c. 1, fols. 208–9

'Ah Coquin!'   B to John Cam Hobhouse, 3 March 1818

344 'Rt. Hon.'   baptismal certificate, 9 March 1818, St-Giles-in-the-Field Register

'I think'   Percy Bysshe Shelley to B, 28 April 1818. Carl H. Pforzheimer Library,
New York

'You will have'   Claire Clairmont to B, 12 January 1818

'very pretty'   B to Augusta Leigh, 3 August 1818

345 'she is pale'   Percy Bysshe Shelley to Mary Shelley, 23 August 1818. Bodleian Library,
University of Oxford, MS Shelley, c. 1, fols. 241–4

'an Englishman'   Percy Bysshe Shelley, preface to *Julian and Maddalo*, 1818

'He is not'   Percy Bysshe Shelley to Thomas Love Peacock, 17 or 18 December, 1818.
Bodleian Library, University of Oxford, MS Shelley, c. 1, fols. 257–8

'Allegra is well'   B to Augusta Leigh, 21 September 1818

346 'silently'   Percy Bysshe Shelley to Claire Clairmont, 25 September 1818.
Carl H. Pforzheimer Library, New York

'to the horror'   Hanson narrative

'the protean talent'   John Murray to B, 16 June 1818

348 'I have'   B to Thomas Moore, 19 September 1818

'infinitely better'   Percy Bysshe Shelley to Thomas Love Peacock, 8 October 1818.
Bodleian Library, University of Oxford, MS Shelley, c. 1, fols. 247–8

'Nothing has'   Percy Bysshe Shelley to B, 21 October 1818. British Library

'I doubt'   B to Thomas Moore, 19 September 1818

'Committee'   Moore *Life*, vol. 2

'I have'   Hobhouse diaries, 27 December 1818

'I have'   Douglas Kinnaird to B, 29 December 1818

'full of talent'   Moore *Journal*, 31 January 1819

349 'This new'   Augusta Leigh to Francis Hodgson, 17 April 1819. Prothero *Life and Letters*, vol. 4

'neither witty'   Lady Caroline Lamb to John Murray, July 1819

'a whole legion'   *Morning Chronicle*, 1 August 1820

'dimity rhyming'   Moore *Journal*, 31 January 1819

'with very near'   John Murray to B, 16 July 1819

'a damned Tory'   B to Thomas Moore, 8 January 1814

'As to poor me'   John Murray to B, 16 July 1819

'Believe me'   ibid., 19 March 1819

352 'most tasteful'   ibid., 3 May 1819

'I read again'   ibid., 27 July 1819

'*garbled* or *mutilated*'   B to John Murray, 23 April 1818

'Donny Jonny'   B to John Cam Hobhouse, 30 July 1819

'an entire horse'   B to John Cam Hobhouse and Douglas Kinnaird, 19 January 1819

22 Venice and Ravenna 1819

353 'quite given up'   B to John Cam Hobhouse and Douglas Kinnaird, 19? January 1819

'a pretty fair haired'   B to John Cam Hobhouse, 6 April 1819

'as she entered'   Guiccioli *Vie*

354 'a finisher'   B to Augusta Leigh, 5 October 1821

'You know'   Guiccioli *Vie*

'fair as Sunrise'   B to Douglas Kinnaird, 24 April 1819

'uncommonly good'   B to John Murray, 13–16? March 1821

'her graces'   Galt *Life*

'Madame Guiccioli'   Hunt *Lord Byron*

'I was strong'   Elliot Papers. Keats–Shelley Memorial House, Rome

'I was not'   Henry Fox journal, 1825. *The Journal of the Hon. Henry Edward Fox*, ed. the Earl of Ilchester, 1923

'*Essential* part'   B to Lord Kinnaird, 26 May 1819

'this last'   Moore *Life*, vol. 2

355 'mistake'   Hobhouse notes

'owing to'   B to John Murray, 18 May 1819

'Sixty years'   B to Augusta Leigh, 28 November 1819

356 'although she looks'   Henry Fox journal, 30 December 1824. *The Journal of the Hon. Henry Edward Fox*, ed. the Earl of Ilchester, 1923

'Exigeante'   ibid., 1825

'a great Coquette'   B to Augusta Leigh, 26 July 1819

'odd'   ibid., 5 October 1821. Lovelace–Byron Archive

'Mio Byron'   B to John Cam Hobhouse, 6 April 1821

'She has'   B to Augusta Leigh, 5 October 1821

'Scrivimi'   B to Countess Teresa Guiccioli, 15 July 1820

357 'River! that rolls'   'To the Po. June 2nd 1819', l. 1

'to cuckold'   B to Richard Belgrave Hoppner, 2 June 1819

'like a Sausage'   ibid., 6 June 1819

358 'a coach'   ibid., 20 June 1819
'could almost'   Medwin *Conversations*
'a bore'   B to Augusta Leigh, 26 July 1819
'*Think*, my love'   B to Countess Teresa Guiccioli, 4 August 1819
'a Stiletto'   B to Richard Belgrave Hoppner, 20 June 1819
'own dear precious'   B to Augusta Leigh, 26 July 1819
'l'ultima mia'   B to Countess Teresa Guiccioli, 22 April 1819

359 'I am writing'   ibid., 11 June 1819
'I greatly'   B to Richard Belgrave Hoppner, 2 July 1819
'our amatory'   B to Alexander Scott, 7 July 1819

360 'I have read'   inscription in Countess Teresa Guiccioli's copy of Madame de Staël's *Corinne*, in Italian translation, 23 August 1819. Gamba Collection, Biblioteca Classense, Ravenna
'She was not'   Richard Belgrave Hoppner to *The Athenæum*, 22 May 1869
'tranquille et sérieuse'   Isabelle Hoppner to Mary Shelley, 6 January 1819. Bodleian Library, University of Oxford, Abinger deposit, c. 811/3

361 'for whose'   Isabelle Hoppner to B, 25 June 1819
'I wish to'   B to Alexander Scott, 22 August 1819
'it would be'   Alexander Scott to B, August 1819
'imputed peculation'   B to Richard Belgrave Hoppner, 22 October 1819
'Bon *dì*'   B to Augusta Leigh, September 1819

362 'many splendid'   B to John Murray, 12 August 1819
'a very large'   Guiccioli *Recollections*
'It was one'   Guiccioli *Vie*

363 'forgetting'   Archbishop Antonio Codronchi to Cardinal Consalvi, 5 April 1820. Iris Origo, *The Last Attachment*, 1949
'like the Dragon'   Browne 'Voyage'
'the unsavoury inhalations'   Guiccioli *Vie*

364 'the enchanted'   Fanny Silvestrini to Countess Teresa Guiccioli, autumn 1819. Keats–Shelley Memorial House, Rome
'should not'   B to John Cam Hobhouse, 23 August 1819
'a little'   ibid., 3 October 1819
'Better be'   B to John Cam Hobhouse, 3 October 1819

365 'this mad'   Smiles *Memoir*, vol. 1
'*La Sort*'   John Murray to B, 16 July 1819
'its sale'   ibid., 14 September 1819
'a sealed book'   Lord Sydney Osborne to B, 18 October 1822
'Dear *Adorable*'   Harriette Wilson to B, 1820

366 'That women'   Dr Henry Muir, *Notes on Byron's Conversations in Cephalonia*, 19 October 1823. *Notes and Queries*, vol. 7, 1883–4
'as the Archbishop'   B to John Cam Hobhouse, 20 August 1819
'scorching and'   B to John Murray, 12 August 1819
'a sort of '   ibid., 9 September 1820
'the sublime'   B to Douglas Kinnaird, 26 October 1819

367 'filthy and impious'   *Blackwood's Edinburgh Magazine*, 'Remarks on Don Juan',
August 1819
'Your Blackwood'   B to John Murray, 10 December 1819
'one of the'   *Blackwood's Edinburgh Magazine*, 'Remarks on Don Juan', August 1819
'The letter'   John Murray to B, 28 April 1820
'the lurking place'   'Some Observations upon an Article in *Blackwood's Edinburgh
Magazine*', 15 March 1820

368 'the frank'   Moore *Life*, vol. 2
'quite fresh'   B to Douglas Kinnaird, 26 October 1819
'some of that'   Moore *Life*, vol. 2
'a curious foreign'   Thomas Moore quoted in Benjamin Disraeli's diary, 27 November
1822. W.F. Moneypenny, *The Life of Benjamin Disraeli*, 1910
'intelligence and amiableness'   Moore *Life*, vol. 2
'to stick'   Moore *Journal*, 7 October 1819

369 'observing them'   Moore *Life*, vol. 2
'The Angelina'   Moore *Journal*, 8 October 1819
'sort of public'   ibid., 10 October 1819
'My Life'   Moore *Life*, vol. 2
'I won't be'   B to John Murray, 9 April 1817

370 'autobiographical Essay'   ibid., 26 August 1818
'*Memoranda*'   ibid., 29 October 1819
'considered worthy'   Moore *Life*, vol. 2
'anything mistaken'   B to John Murray, 10 December 1819
'funeral marriage'   B to Lady Byron, 31 December 1819
'the strictest'   B to Richard Belgrave Hoppner, 29 October 1819

371 'la Contessa'   B to John Murray, 8 November 1819
'quarrelled *violently*'   B to Douglas Kinnaird, 16 November 1819
'Chairs – tables'   B to Richard Belgrave Hoppner, 7 December 1819
'He was ready'   Fanny Silvestrini to Countess Teresa Guiccioli, 10 December 1819.
Guiccioli *Vie*
'La Fanni'   B to Countess Teresa Guiccioli, 10 December 1819

372 'Bankes the Nubian'   B to John Murray, 20 February 1818
'Bankes *has* done'   ibid., 7 August 1820
'It is'   B to William Bankes, 20 November 1819

373 'empty Oyster-Shell'   B to Richard Belgrave Hoppner, 28 October 1819

23   Ravenna 1819–1821

374 'To be'   Journal, 23 November 1813
375 'It is'   Ravenna Journal, 18 February 1821
'all the'   B to Augusta Leigh, 23 December 1819
'I am drilling'   B to Richard Belgrave Hoppner, 31 January 1820
'Tita's heart'   B to William Bankes, 19 February 1820
'the utmost'   Giovanni Ghinaglia, signed testament 13 September 1865. Keats–Shelley
Memorial House, Rome

376 'the best people'   Medwin *Conversations*

'it is out'   B to Lady Byron, 20 July 1819

'the *primitive*'   B to Douglas Kinnaird, 3 May 1820

'a miserable'   Percy Bysshe Shelley to Mary Shelley, 8 August 1821. Bodleian Library, University of Oxford, MS Shelley, c. 1, fols. 443–8

'among the natives'   B to John Murray, 21 February 1820

'his manners'   'Detached Thoughts', no. 85, 1821–2

'poetical ground'   Medwin *Conversations*

'I pass'   *Don Juan*, Canto IV, st. 104, l. 825

'Sweet hour'   ibid., Canto III, st. 105, l. 929

377 'one can't help'   B to John Murray, 21 February 1820

'I shall let'   B to John Cam Hobhouse, 3 March 1820

'How could I'   B to Countess Teresa Guiccioli, January–February 1820

'The mere'   Guiccioli *Vie*

'foamed into'   B to Thomas Moore, 2 January 1820

'a friend to'   B to John Murray, 21 February 1820

378 'How came you'   'New Song', 23 March 1820

'to give way'   Hobhouse diaries, 16 April 1820

'dished, diddled'   B to Francis Hodgson, 22 December 1820

'Brummell'   B to John Cam Hobhouse, 3 March 1820

'I hear'   Augustus Foster to Elizabeth, Duchess of Devonshire, 20 July 1821. *The Two Duchesses*, ed. Vere Foster, 1898

'How is'   James Wedderburn Webster to B, 11 November 1819

379 'dotardly caresses'   B to Countess Teresa Guiccioli, May 1820?

'how to'   ibid., fragment of letter June–July? 1819

'this evening'   ibid., 3 January 1820

'putello'   letter from Foreign Office detailing Bill of Lading, Venice, 26 January 1820. Trinity College Library, Cambridge

380 'I never wrote'   B to John Murray, 8 October 1820

'taken together'   ibid., 20 May 1820

'At the sound'   statement of Guiccioli servants. Elliot Papers, Keats–Shelley Memorial House, Rome

'who are numerous'   B to John Murray, 20 May 1820

381 'for vile'   Count Ruggero Gamba to Cardinal Rusconi, draft letter, 23 June 1820. Gamba Papers, Biblioteca Classense, Ravenna

'I only'   B to Thomas Moore, 31 August 1820

'might well'   The Earl of Malmesbury, *Memoirs of an ex-Minister*, vol. 1, 1884

382 'I like'   B to Countess Teresa Guiccioli, 29 July 1820

'on whom'   Guiccioli *Vie*

'Now, I have'   B to Thomas Moore, 31 August 1820

'armed with'   Guiccioli *Vie*

'*Don Juan*'   Moore *Life*, vol. 2

383 'You are not'   B to John Murray, 16 April 1820

'these Cantos'   John Murray to B, 7 March 1820

'Upon my soul'   ibid., 13 June 1820

'the trash'   B to Douglas Kinnaird, 30 April 1820

'those two impostors'   B to John Murray, 23 April 1820

'If you would'   John Murray to B, 16 October 1820

'retouching'   B to John Murray, 18 November 1820

'You must not'   ibid., 6 July 1820

384 'What is *Ivanhoe*?'   ibid., March 1820

'a temper'   B to Augusta Leigh, 2 January 1820

'We expect'   B to John Murray, 23 April 1820

'I shall'   ibid., 16 April 1820

'inoculated among'   B to Douglas Kinnaird, 14 April 1820

385 'wild about'   B to Thomas Moore, 19 September 1821

'though last'   'Detached Thoughts', no. 31, 1821–2

'some thousands'   B to John Murray, 4 September 1821

386 'they want Union'   ibid., 16 April 1820

'like the middle'   B to Douglas Kinnaird, 20 July 1820

'Italy's primed'   B to John Murray, 12 August 1820

'the Italian'   ibid., 25? August 1820

'the Huns'   ibid., 7 September 1820

'I request'   B to Lady Byron, 25 October 1820

'If she don't'   B to Douglas Kinnaird, 25 October 1820

387 'Yesterday they'   ibid., 31 August 1820

'almost'   B to Thomas Moore, 9 December 1820

'quite destitute'   B to Lady Byron, 10 December 1820

388 'The other'   *Don Juan*, Canto V, st. 33, l. 257

'I had'   Medwin *Conversations*

'with great'   B to Thomas Moore, 9 December 1820

'for a man'   ibid., 20 January 1821

389 'The truth'   Hobhouse diaries, 28 October 1821

'Rose late'   Ravenna Journal, 5 January 1821

390 'the very Ghosts'   B to Augusta Leigh, 18? October 1820

'in the most'   B to John Murray, 18 November 1820

'the Thirty-Third'   Ravenna Journal, 22 January 1821

'obstinate'   B to Richard Belgrave Hoppner, 31 March 1820

'Allegrina has'   B to Countess Teresa Guiccioli, 7 August 1820

'tendency to mockery'   ibid., 30 August 1820

'It is now'   Claire Clairmont to B, 16 March 1820

391 'About Allegra'   B to Richard Belgrave Hoppner, 22 April 1820

'I spend'   Clairmont journal, 1 May 1820

'assuredly the eldest'   B to Richard Belgrave Hoppner, 3 April 1821

'What with'   B to Thomas Moore, 8 March 1822

392 'Allegra is well'   B to Richard Belgrave Hoppner, 10 February 1821

'it was not'   ibid., 3 April 1821

'composed entirely'   Percy Bysshe Shelley to Mary Shelley, 15 August 1821. Bodleian
Library, University of Oxford, MS Shelley, c. 1, fols. 453–8

393 'I think it'   Felice Tellarini to B, 11 March 1821

'to a life' Claire Clairmont to B, 24 March 1821. British Library

'and the head' B to John Murray, 13–16? March 1821

'*Painting* the King' ibid., August? 1821

'The king-times' Ravenna Journal, 13 January 1821

394 'I certainly' B to John Cam Hobhouse, 12 October 1821

'in the seat' Ravenna Journal, 23 January 1821

'full of their' ibid., 18 February 1821

'nothing more' ibid., 24 January 1821

'The *plan*' ibid., 24 February 1821

395 Tita Falcieri dispute see Andrea Casadio, 'Two new letters from Byron's stay in Ravenna', *Byron Journal*, 2001

'from a long' B to Elizabeth, Duchess of Devonshire, 15 July 1821

'not to be' B to John Murray, 4 January 1821

396 '*mental theatre*' ibid., 23 August 1821

'outrageous ranting' ibid., 16 February 1821

'The black veil' Preface to *Marino Faliero*, July–August 1820

'It is full' B to Douglas Kinnaird, 8 October 1820

'ycleped "Sardanapalus"' B to Thomas Moore, 22 June 1821

397 'as you may' B to John Murray, 25 May 1821

'calls for' ibid., 31 May 1821

'sly, insinuated' Moore *Journal*, 30 October 1821

'the eloquence' Guiccioli *Vie*

398 'For Orford' 'To Mr Murray', 1821, l. 1

'*three thousand*' B to Douglas Kinnaird, 29 November 1821

'The booksellers' Smiles *Memoir*, vol. 1

399 'astonishingly fine' Percy Bysshe Shelley to Mary Shelley, 10 August 1821. Bodleian Library, University of Oxford, MS Shelley, c. 1, fols. 443–8

'He has' Percy Bysshe Shelley to Thomas Love Peacock, 10? August 1821. Carl H. Pforzheimer Library, New York

'he is becoming' Percy Bysshe Shelley to Mary Shelley, 10 August 1821. Bodleian Library, University of Oxford, MS Shelley, c. 1, fols. 443–8

'a fresh harvest' ibid., 7 August 1821, fols. 440–2

'as if they' Percy Bysshe Shelley to Thomas Love Peacock, 10? August 1821. Carl H. Pforzheimer Library, New York

400 'grown tall' Percy Bysshe Shelley to Mary Shelley, 15 August 1821. Bodleian Library, University of Oxford, MS Shelley, c. 1, fols. 453–8

'an incontinence' Hunt *Lord Byron*

401 'the most violent' ibid., 7 August 1821, fols. 440–2

'he gave' Mary Shelley to Isabelle Hoppner, 10 August 1821

'it is just' B to Richard Belgrave Hoppner, 1 October 1820

'a large' Percy Bysshe Shelley to Mary Shelley, 11 August 1821. Bodleian Library, University of Oxford, MS Shelley, c. 1, fols. 449–50

'Shelley was not' Guiccioli *Vie*

402 'in all' B to Percy Bysshe Shelley, 26 August 1821. Carl H. Pforzheimer Library, New York

'a little'   B to Douglas Kinnaird, 14 December 1821
'all received'   B to John Murray, 20 September 1821
'They are'   ibid., 28 September 1821
403 'Man is'   'Detached Thoughts', no. 96, 1821–2
'a *new* woman'   B to Thomas Moore, 1 October 1821
'to be sure'   ibid., 28 October 1821
'will you not'   Mother Superior Marianna Fabbri to B, 28 September 1821. Pierpont Morgan Library, New York
'Sincere enough'   MS note by B on above
'to settle'   B to Samuel Rogers, 21 October 1821
'very voluminous'   B to John Murray, 28 September 1821
404 'It was'   'Detached Thoughts', no. 115, 1821–2

24   Pisa 1821–1822

405 'Much had passed'   Samuel Rogers, lines on Bologna, *Italy*, 1834
'to *feel*'   'Detached Thoughts', no. 115, 1821–2
406 'Lord B'   Clairmont journal, 1 November 1821
'The famous'   Cavaliere Luigi Torelli, *Arcana politicae anticarbonariae*. Florence State Archive, copy Keats–Shelley Memorial House, Rome
'a large disagreeable'   Percy Bysshe Shelley to Thomas Love Peacock, 5 June 1818. Bodleian Library, University of Oxford, MS Shelley, c. 1, fols. 233–4
'a famous old'   B to John Murray, 4 December 1821
'large, gloomy'   Medwin *Angler*
'seemed built'   Medwin *Conversations*
'a Man'   Hanson narrative
407 'I have most'   B to Douglas Kinnaird, 15 November 1821
'very nice'   Mary Shelley to Maria Gisborne, 30 November 1821. Bodleian Library, University of Oxford, Abinger deposit, d. 562, fol. 42v
'nice, good natured'   Percy Bysshe Shelley to Claire Clairmont, 16 June 1821. British Library
'Shelley read'   Williams diary, 5 November 1821
408 'an Irish'   B to Thomas Moore, 16 November 1821
'sentimentally'   Guiccioli *Vie*
'He will die'   B to John Murray, 6 March 1822
'some English'   B to Douglas Kinnaird, 18 December 1821
409 'Ay! and you will'   B to William Bankes, 19 February 1820
'Lord Byron'   Percy Bysshe Shelley to Horace Smith, 25 January 1822. Shelley *Letters*, vol. 2
'the actors'   Guiccioli *Vie*
'His voice'   Medwin *Conversations*
'Othello'   Williams diary, 28 February 1822
'He keeps'   Guiccioli *Vie*
410 'extravagant'   Mary Shelley journal, 19 January 1822. Bodleian Library, University of Oxford, Abinger deposit, d. 311/3

'she is to'   Edward John Trelawny to Captain Daniel Roberts, 5 February 1822.
Keats–Shelley Memorial House, Rome

'any one'   William Fletcher to Augusta Leigh, undated. Prothero *Letters and Journals*,
vol. 6

411   'meant to print'   Henry Crabb Robinson journal, 28 September 1822. *Diary,
Reminiscences and Correspondence of Henry Crabb Robinson*, vol. 2, 1872

'That old Serpent'   B to Douglas Kinnaird, 16 August 1821

'a Seal'   B to John Hanson, 27 February 1822

'this portrait'   B to Douglas Kinnaird, 22 March 1822

'sitting for'   Williams diary, 8 January 1822

'a fine bust'   ibid., 11 January 1822

412   'peculiar arrangement'   Guiccioli *Vie*

'exactly resembles'   B to John Murray, 23 September 1822

'Bartolini is'   ibid., 16 May 1822

'The busts'   ibid., 25 December 1822

'playing the Stepmother'   ibid., 3 November 1821

'greatly disquieted'   Guiccioli *Vie*

413   'arises from'   B to John Murray, 6 July 1821

'I am only'   Countess Teresa Guiccioli to B, note enclosed with letter from B to John
Murray, 6 July 1821

'rummage out'   B to John Cam Hobhouse, 27 September? 1821

'an Italian'   *Werner*, Act II, sc. 2, l. 396

414   'humbug Row'   John Murray to B, 16 April 1822

'then they'   Walter Scott to John Murray, 4 December 1821

'I have look'd'   *Cain*, Act I, sc. 1, l. 270

'inconceivably'   Hobhouse diaries, 28 October 1821

'I dare say'   B to John Cam Hobhouse, 23 November 1821

'wonderful'   Thomas Moore to B, 30 September 1821. Prothero *Letters and Journals*,
vol. 5

'The two'   B to John Murray, 3 November 1821

'a book calculated'   Henry Crabb Robinson journal, 9 March 1822. *Diary,
Reminiscences and Correspondence of Henry Crabb Robinson*, vol. 2, 1872

415   'a denaturalised'   The Rev. John Styles, 'Lord Byron's works, viewed in connexion with
Christianity and the Obligations of Social Life', *c.* 1821. Prothero *Letters and Journals*,
vol. 5

'Even the mystery'   Bishop Heber, review of Byron's dramas in the *Quarterly Review*,
vol. 27, 1822

'who am'   B to John Murray, 8 February 1822

'I neither can'   B to Thomas Moore, 6 March 1822

'I write'   B to John Murray, 8 February 1822

416   'an officer'   B to Edward J. Dawkins, 31 March 1822

'maledetti Inglesi'   Williams diary, 24 March 1822

417   'best servant'   B to Edward J. Dawkins, 18 April 1822

'when told'   Cavaliere Luigi Torelli, *Arcana politicae anticarbonariae*. Florence State
Archive, copy Keats–Shelley Memorial House, Rome

418 'I cannot go'   Claire Clairmont to B, draft letter, 18 February 1822. British Library
'No one'   Mary Shelley to Claire Clairmont, 20 March 1822. Harry Ransom Humanities Research Center, University of Texas at Austin
'I am'   Claire Clairmont to Mary Shelley, 9 April 1822. Bodleian Library, University of Oxford, Abinger deposit, c. 478
'light and slow'   Pellegrino Ghigi to Lega Zambelli, 13 April 1822. British Library
'The blow'   B to Percy Bysshe Shelley, 23 April 1822

419 'A mortal'   Guiccioli *Vie*
'he felt the loss'   Mary Shelley to Maria Gisborne, 2 June 1822. Bodleian Library, University of Oxford, Abinger deposit, d. 566, fols. 6–7r
'I tried'   Claire Clairmont to Lady Mount Cashell (Mrs Mason), 24? September 1822. Clairmont *Correspondence*, vol. 1
'very private'   B to John Murray, 22 April 1822

420 'G.G. Lord Byron'   ibid., 26 May 1822
'constrained to say'   The Rev. J.W. Cunningham to John Murray, 20 August 1822
'a package'   *Morning Chronicle*, 21 November 1822
'God help'   B to Augusta Leigh, 12 December 1822

421 'the insults'   Henry Dunn to B, 12 May 1822
'He *naturally*'   *Don Juan*, Canto X, st. 57, l. 452
'not only'   Guiccioli *Vie*
'those butchers'   B to Thomas Moore, 8 August 1822
'decidedly the best'   Henry Dunn to B, 9 April 1822

422 'I write'   B to Isaac D'Israeli, 10 June 1822
'an avalanche'   Guiccioli *Vie*
'the greatest'   B to Douglas Kinnaird, 26 May? 1822
'his manner'   George Bancroft, 'A Day with Lord Byron', *History of the Battle of Lake Erie and Miscellaneous Papers*, 1891
'Constitution Jones'   B to John Murray, 26 May 1822

423 'he assumed'   William Edward West, 'Lord Byron's Last Portrait', *New Monthly Magazine*, XVI, 1826
'These transient'   B to John Cam Hobhouse, 2 September 1822
'a little thing'   B to Edward J. Dawkins, 26 June 1822

424 'railing at the'   Guiccioli *Vie*
'were not'   William Edward West, 'Lord Byron's Last Portrait', *New Monthly Magazine*, XVI, 1826

425 'The day'   Hunt *Lord Byron*
'Of course'   B to Edward J. Dawkins, 4 July 1822

426 'Every body'   Percy Bysshe Shelley to Mary Shelley, 4 July 1822. Bodleian Library, University of Oxford, MS Shelley, c. 1, fols. 504–5

427 '*Alone* you may'   Guiccioli *Vie*
'how long'   Percy Bysshe Shelley to Horace Smith, 29 June 1822. Keats–Shelley Memorial House, Rome
'He seems'   B to Thomas Moore, 12 July 1822
'breakfasted'   Hunt *Lord Byron*

428 'When I told'   Trelawny *Recollections*

429 'I do not'   Percy Bysshe Shelley to Horace Smith, 21? May 1822. Keats–Shelley
Memorial House, Rome
'There is'   B to Thomas Moore, 8 August 1822
'You can have'   ibid., 27 August 1822
'are we to'   'The Cremation of Edward Ellerker Williams', 13 August 1822. Trelawny
Letters
'the matter'   Guiccioli *Vie*
430 'I restore'   Edward John Trelawny to William Michael Rossetti, 18 December 1878.
Trelawny *Letters*
'should not'   Trelawny *Recollections*
'it broke'   'The Cremation of Percy Bysshe Shelley', Trelawny *Letters*
'would not'   B to Thomas Moore, 27 August 1822
'although bedded'   'The Cremation of Percy Bysshe Shelley', Trelawny *Letters*
'With regard'   Leigh Hunt to Mary Shelley, 17 August 1822. British Library
431 'his health'   Guiccioli *Vie*
'There was'   Hunt *Lord Byron*
'drone of a husband'   B to Augusta Leigh, 4 November 1821
'How could'   Benjamin Robert Haydon, MS notes to Medwin *Conversations*.
Roe–Byron Collection, City of Nottingham Museums, Newstead Abbey
'resembled a great'   Hunt *Lord Byron*
'I have'   B to Mary Shelley, 4 October 1822
432 'through thick'   B to Douglas Kinnaird, 23 February 1822
'The death'   B to John Murray, 9 October 1822
'To occupy'   B to Douglas Kinnaird, 24 July 1822
'it will'   *Don Juan*, Canto IX, st. 37, l. 289
433 'What do you'   B to Thomas Moore, 8 August 1822
'Then being'   *Don Juan*, Canto VIII, st. 76, l. 601
'a liberally'   Hobhouse diaries, 15 September 1822
434 'So Castlereagh'   'Epigrams on Lord Castlereagh', 1822
'did not'   Hobhouse diaries, 17 September 1822
'should write'   ibid., 20 September 1822
'worn out'   B to Douglas Kinnaird, 24 September 1822

25   Genoa 1822–1823

435 'Deformity is'   *The Deformed Transformed*, Part 1, sc. 1, l. 313
'lost in the'   Guiccioli *Vie*
'more than'   B to Douglas Kinnaird, 18 January 1823
436 'the only'   B to Edward John Trelawny, 15 June 1823
'thorough Liberty'   B to John Cam Hobhouse, 19 May 1823
'under-current'   Trelawny *Recollections*
'the worst'   B to John Murray, 9 October 1822
437 'a man'   anon. clergyman, 'Lord Byron', *Blackwood's Edinburgh Magazine*, June 1824
438 'six little'   B to Mary Shelley, 4 October 1822
'joking away'   Hunt *Lord Byron*

'when in company'   Mary Shelley journal, 19 October 1822. Bodleian Library, University of Oxford, Abinger deposit, d. 311/4
'You would'   B to Augusta Leigh, 20 October 1822
'I won't be'   B to Douglas Kinnaird, 10 September 1822

439 'If you'   John Murray to B, 25 September 1822
'I have'   B to John Murray, 9 October 1822
'Murray is'   Douglas Kinnaird to B, 7 September 1823
'What will'   ibid., 3 January 1823
'With regard'   John Murray to B, 25 September 1822

440 'With regard'   B to John Murray, 9 October 1822
'I entreat'   John Murray to B, 11 October 1822
'Apotheosis'   B to Thomas Moore, 1 October 1821
'the universal'   John Murray to B, 29 October 1822

442 'You seem'   B to John Murray, 6 November 1822
'I found'   B to Douglas Kinnaird, 1 December 1822
'*Knight* – aged 40'   E.J. Trelawny, MS note
'the best'   B to Douglas Kinnaird, 1 December 1822
'some Masquerade'   B to Lady Hardy, 7 November 1822

443 'Now – as *my*'   ibid., 1 December 1822
'I quite agree'   Lady Hardy to B, 9 December 1822
'I have'   B to Lady Hardy, 7 November 1822
'Chevalier'   ibid., 1 December 1822

444 'I well remember'   Isabella Harvey ('Zorina Stanley') to B, 13 March 1823
'all my *humours*'   B to Richard Belgrave Hoppner, 27 February 1823
'and you cannot'   B to Douglas Kinnaird, 16 December 1822
'early English'   B to Leigh Hunt, 20 January 1823

445 'But Christian'   *The Island*, Canto III, st. 6, l. 139
'I am'   ibid., Canto I, st. 8, l. 164
'the blue-eyed'   ibid., Canto II, st. 8, l. 163

446 'There was'   *Don Juan*, Canto XV, st. 63, l. 497
Hanson–Portsmouth trial   see Doris Langley Moore, *Lord Byron: Accounts Rendered*, 1974

447 'You recollect'   John Cam Hobhouse to B, 2 March 1823
'It struck'   B to John Cam Hobhouse, 19 March 1823

448 'the ne plus'   B to Douglas Kinnaird, 2 April 1823
'Miladi seems'   B to Thomas Moore, 2 April 1823
'the most gorgeous'   Dr Parr, quoted Prothero *Letters and Journals*, vol. 6
'I have seen'   Lady Hardy to B, 7 June 1823

449 'Milor B'   B to Thomas Moore, 2 April 1823
'And am I'   Lady Blessington diary, 31 March 1823. R.L. Madden, *The Literary Life and Correspondence of the Countess of Blessington*, vol. 1, 1855
'Beneath Blessington's'   'On the Countess of B[lessingto]n's expressing an intention to take the Genoese Villa called "Il Paradiso" "The Paradise"', 6 May 1823

450 'Parisian Paladin'   B to Lady Hardy, 10 June 1823
'a heart'   The Earl of Blessington to B, 6 April 1823

'the Phoebus'   J.A. Froude, *Thomas Carlyle: a History of his Life in London, 1834–81*, vol. 1

'*not* the *fact*'   B to the Earl of Blessington, 5 April 1823

'I have'   B to the Countess of Blessington, 6 May 1823

451   'so far'   ibid., 2 June 1823

'I saw'   B to John Cam Hobhouse, 7 April 1823

452   'to give'   William Smith to B, 8 March 1823

'as you'   John Bowring to B, 14 March 1823

'a tower'   Trelawny *Records*

'need to'   Blessington *Conversations*

453   'your presence'   Edward Blaquière to B, 28 April 1823

'I have'   B to John Bowring, 12 May 1823

454   'You must not'   John Cam Hobhouse to B, 11 June 1823

'less capable'   Blessington *Conversations*

'were I in'   Lady Hardy to B, 17 June 1823

455   'ill usage'   B to Douglas Kinnaird, 21 May 1823

'unusual abstractedness'   Guiccioli *Vie*

'burst out'   Moore *Prose and Verse*

456   'If I could'   B to the Earl of Blessington, 23 April 1823

'Have you seen'   Hunt *Lord Byron*

'My dear'   B to Edward John Trelawny, 15 June 1823

'the most unpopular'   B to John Hunt, 10 March 1823

457   'I have received'   B to Leigh Hunt, 28 June 1823

'one day'   Guiccioli *Vie*

458   'I have'   Countess Teresa Guiccioli MS notebook. Harry Ransom Humanities Research Center, University of Texas at Austin

'take the liberty'   Charles Barry to B, 23 July 1823

'nor indeed'   B to the Countess of Blessington, 3 May 1823

'warlike accoutrements'   *The Times*, 18 September 1823

460   'It was'   Guiccioli *Vie*

'a collier-built'   Trelawny *Recollections*

'Where shall'   Gamba *Narrative*

'That he had'   Moore *Life*, vol. 2

'undisputed Sovereign'   B to Johann Wolfgang von Goethe, 22 July 1823

461   'My dearest'   B to Countess Teresa Guiccioli, 22 July 1823

'a very little'   Browne 'Voyage'

462   'On great'   Edward John Trelawny to William Michael Rossetti, 14 January 1878. Trelawny *Letters*

463   'I hope'   Blessington *Conversations*

26   Cephalonia 1823

464   Greek War of Independence   for background see William St Clair, *That Greece Might Still Be Free: The Philhellenes in the War of Independence*, 1972; David Brewer, *The Flame of Freedom: The Greek War of Independence 1821–1833*, 2001

'I don't know'   Trelawny *Records*

'not very'   Journal in Cephalonia, 17 September 1823

465 'After all'   Kennedy *Conversations*

'one of Sir John'   B to John Cam Hobhouse, 14 September 1823

'From what'   Trelawny *Recollections*

466 'All came'   Moore *Life*, vol. 2

'Dear Sir'   B to Edward Blaquière, 3 August 1823

467 'somewhat divided'   B to John Bowring, 24 July 1823

'I have not'   B to John Cam Hobhouse, 27 September 1823

468 'a little Naples'   The Rev. Richard Burges of St John's College, Cambridge, 1834. Corgialenios Historical and Cultural Museum, Argostoli

'Lord Byron'   Sir William Napier, *Life and Opinions of General Sir Charles Napier*, vol. 1, 1857

'Lord Byron'   Sir Charles Napier to Major-General Sir Frederick Adam, 10 August 1823. Napier Papers, British Library

'with his high'   Moore *Prose and Verse*

469 'frequently reverted'   Browne 'Narrative'

'I like'   Kennedy *Conversations*

'You know'   Moore *Prose and Verse*

470 'so nearly'   B to Charles Barry, 29 October 1823

'a tour'   B to John Cam Hobhouse, 11 September 1823

'When we meet'   B to Countess Teresa Guiccioli, 11 September 1823

471 'rather summarily'   Browne 'Narrative'

472 'You must'   Hanson narrative

473 'he gradually'   Browne 'Narrative'

474 'He was'   B to Lady Byron, 14 September 1821

'He bounded'   Browne 'Voyage'

'the damned'   Browne 'Narrative'

'Up to battle!'   'Song of the Suliotes', 1824, l. 1

475 'Your Excellency'   Markos Botsaris to B, 18 August 1823

'with the character'   Journal in Cephalonia, 28 September 1823

'The Noble Poet'   Edward John Trelawny to Mary Shelley, 6 September 1823. Trelawny *Letters*

476 'a really *great*'   Edward John Trelawny to John Cam Hobhouse, 30 April 1824

'wonderfully became'   Browne 'Narrative'

'they have'   Edward John Trelawny to B, 14 September 1823. National Library of Greece

'Standing at'   Journal in Cephalonia, 17 December 1823

477 'under the'   ibid., 28 September 1823

'Here are arrived'   B to Countess Teresa Guiccioli, 29 November 1823

478 'in good preservation'   B to Douglas Kinnaird, 29 October 1823

'unemphatical'   Stanhope *Greece*

479 'who is a good'   Kennedy *Conversations*

'wrapt in his'   Millingen *Memoirs*

'I have been'   B to Augusta Leigh, 12 October 1823

480 'a Cephaloniot'   Millingen *Memoirs*

'*Ultima Analise*'   B to Dr Henry Muir, 2 January 1824

481   'on the whole'   B to the London Greek Committee, 15 December 1823
'this Hebrew'   B to Charles Barry, 25 October 1823
'Signor '*Ancock*'   B to Charles Hancock, 2 January 1824

482   'you may bid'   Stanhope *Greece*
'I think'   B to Lord Holland, 10 November 1823
'I must'   B to the General Government of Greece, 30 November 1823

483   'You will be'   Prince Alexander Mavrocordato to B, December 1823
'go to headquarters'   John Cam Hobhouse to B, 11 June 1823
'as long as'   Journal in Cephalonia, 17 December 1823

484   'in some commission'   B to Countess Teresa Guiccioli, 14 December 1823
'After all'   B to Douglas Kinnaird, 23 December 1823
'if anything'   B to Thomas Moore, 27 December 1823

485   'merely came'   Charles Hancock to Dr Henry Muir, 1 June 1824. H. Skey Muir,
'Byroniana', *Notes and Queries*, 2 February 1884
'They only can'   'Thoughts on Freedom', 1823, l. 1

486   'we must be'   B to John Bowring, 26 December 1823

27   Missolonghi 1824

487   'Tomorrow'   Gamba *Narrative*
'chaced from'   B to Lord Sydney Osborne, 7 January 1824

488   'safe on'   Gamba *Narrative*
'three or more'   Millingen *Memoirs*
'of a well-bred'   Gamba *Narrative*
'of a most'   Parry *Last Days*

489   'I am uneasy'   B to Colonel Leicester Stanhope, 31 December 1823
'Luke's life'   B to Dr Henry Muir, 2 January 1824
'a Greek boy'   B to Charles Hancock, 13 January 1824
'I watched'   'Love and Death', 1824, l. 1

490   'if these Gentlemen'   B to Charles Barry, 25 October 1823
'hope and content'   Gamba *Narrative*
'*electrify* the troops'   B to John Cam Hobhouse, 27 December 1823
'in the mode'   B to Colonel John Duffie, 9 October 1823

491   'Art is *not*'   B to John Murray, *Letter on the Rev. W.L. Bowles's Strictures on the Life and Writings of Pope*, 7 February 1821
'It warmly'   summary of letter from the Executive of the Greek Government to B, 17 January 1824
'There is no'   Christoforos Krateras to B, undated

492   'a mud Istmus'   Edward John Trelawny to B, 30 April 1824
'the stink'   Henry Fox journal, 12 May 1827. *The Journal of the Hon. Henry Edward Fox*, ed. the Earl of Ilchester, 1923
'the Dykes'   B to Charles Hancock, 5 February 1824
'the typographical'   George Finlay, *A History of Greece*, vol. 6, 1877
'often as little'   Kennedy *Conversations*

'We found'   James Forrester, 'Lord Byron in Greece', private letter reprinted in
The Examiner after Byron's death, 1824

493 'assailed by'   Gamba *Narrative*

494 'Of course'   B to Countess Teresa Guiccioli, 24 February 1824
'Springs of Action'   Leslie A. Marchand, *Byron: A Biography*, 1957, vol. 3
'What does'   John Cam Hobhouse, notes on 'Lord Byron' appended to diary.
British Library
'came up'   B to John Bowring, 26 December 1823

495 'affected official'   George Finlay, MS notes in his copy of Millingen's *Memoirs*.
British School at Athens
'Dr Meyer'   B to Samuel Barff, 19 March 1824
'Give me'   Stanhope *Greece*

496 'Oft did'   *Childe Harold's Pilgrimage*, Canto II, st. 40, l. 356
'they are'   Colonel Raffaele Paevi to the London Greek Committee, 11 October 1823.
National Library of Greece

497 'both dressed'   Parry *Last Days*
'I cannot'   John H. Shipman to John Bowring, January 1824. National Library of Greece
'the only'   B to Douglas Kinnaird, 30 March 1824
'unincumbered women'   Parry *Last Days*

498 'construct ships'   B to Prince Alexander Mavrocordatos, 5 February 1824
'Parry and his Men'   Colonel Leicester Stanhope to John Murdock, 7 February 1824.
National Library of Greece
'But this'   B to George Stevens, 19 January 1824
'There is'   Colonel Leicester Stanhope to John Murdock, 15 February 1824

499 'We were'   B to Douglas Kinnaird, 30 March 1824
'Having tried'   notes on Suliotes, 15 February 1824
'You were'   Gamba *Narrative*
'boomed off'   B to Douglas Kinnaird, 30 March 1824
''Tis time'   'January 22nd 1824. Messalonghi. On this day I complete my thirty-sixth
year', l. 1

501 'Stanhope told'   Hobhouse diaries, 8 July 1824
'this little'   Edward John Trelawny to John Cam Hobhouse, 6 May 1824
'that one'   Count Pietro Gamba to John Cam Hobhouse, 11 August 1824

502 'Luke'   B to Charles Hancock, 5 February 1824
'Whatever suggestion'   Count Pietro Gamba to John Cam Hobhouse, 11 August 1824
'I am not'   Gamba *Narrative*
'I had'   Journal in Cephalonia, 17 February 1824

503 'an extraordinary'   Moore *Journal*, 14 July 1824
'I have been'   Journal in Cephalonia, 17 February 1824
'I watched'   'Love and Death', 1824, l. 9

504 'A note'   John Cam Hobhouse, MS note on poem later published as 'Love and Death'.
The Brotherton Collection, Leeds University Library
'What are'   'Last Words on Greece', 1824, l. 1

505 'from motives'   Stanhope *Greece*
'He became'   Millingen *Memoirs*

506 'whom I mean'   B to Countess Teresa Guiccioli, 11 February 1824
    'with great black'   B to Augusta Leigh, 23 February 1824
    'But as Lord B.'   Kennedy *Conversations*
    'I thought'   Millingen *Memoirs*
    'whose presence'   Parry *Last Days*
507 'On Tuesday'   B to John Murray, 25 February 1824
508 'they said'   Gamba *Narrative*
    'Almost every'   B to Samuel Barff, 7 April 1824
509 'private pecuniary'   William Parry to John Bowring, 20 March 1824. National Library
    of Greece
    'Prince Mavrocordato'   B to John Murray, 25 February 1824
    'if my presence'   B to Demetrius Parucca, 11 March 1824
510 'In a few'   B to Samuel Barff, 22 March 1824
    'he would'   Hobhouse diary, 18 August 1825
    'every hundred'   B to Samuel Barff, 22 March 1824
    'You ask'   B to Georgios Sisinis, 25 March 1824
511 'it required'   Gamba *Narrative*
    'according to'   B to Samuel Barff, 3 April 1824
512 'Sir Aubrey'   George Finlay, June 1824. Stanhope *Greece*
    'pray don't'   The Earl of Clare to B, 1 August 1823
    'I hope'   B to the Earl of Clare, 31 March 1824
513 'I am'   Count Pietro Gamba to Augusta Leigh, 17 August 1824. Account in Italian
    translated by John Cam Hobhouse
    'Have you'   Gamba *Narrative*
    'produced three'   Dr Francesco Bruno MS diary
514 'good *English*'   B to Samuel Barff, 22 March 1824
    'rough burly'   Trelawny *Recollections*
    'As there'   Parry *Last Days*
515 'safe and sound'   Vezir Mukhlis Yusuf Pasha, official receipt, March 1824
    'a manner'   Millingen *Memoirs*
    'very thin'   Dr Francesco Bruno MS diary
516 'His countenance'   Gamba *Narrative*
    'if I am'   Dr Francesco Bruno MS diary
    'Recollect your promise'   Gamba *Narrative*
517 'their illustrious'   Gamba *Narrative*
    'if the unthinkable'   Prince Alexander Mavrocordato to Count Pietro Gamba, April 1824
    'The pestilent'   Parry *Last Days*
    'Oh questa'   Gamba *Narrative*
518 'My Lord'   Parry *Last Days*
    'He died'   Count Pietro Gamba to Augusta Leigh, 17 August 1824
    'We did not'   Count Pietro Gamba to John Cam Hobhouse, 11 August 1824
519 Byron's medical diagnosis   Dr Raymond Mills, 'The Last Illness of Lord Byron',
    Byron Journal, 2000
    'we could not'   Millingen *Memoirs*
520 'Caricatures for'   Clare Clairmont journal, 8 November 1820

'he was'   Parry *Last Days*

'You will'   William Fletcher, *Westminster Review*, July 1824

'There are'   Gamba *Narrative*

'Poor Greece'   Count Pietro Gamba to Augusta Leigh, 17 August 1824

521 'I must'   William Fletcher, *Westminster Review*, July 1824

'the Genius'   George Finlay, *A History of Greece*, vol. 6, 1877

'For three'   Trelawny *Records*

28   The Return of the Remains

525 'Wherever'   George Finlay, *A History of Greece*, vol. 6, 1877

'Oh dolore!'   *Telegrafo Greco*, 24 April 1824

'How is'   Gamba *Narrative*

527 'Oh Daughter'   M. Spyridon Tricoupis, Byron's funeral oration, 22 May 1824

'the most precious'   Gamba *Narrative*

'we wished'   Richard Edgcumbe, 'More Recollections of Missolonghi', *Notes and Queries*, 11 June 1881

528 'One request'   Millingen *Memoirs*

'kick the bucket'   Parry *Last Days*

'the most'   Gamba *Narrative*

'Lord S. O.'   Edward Blaquière to John Bowring, 15 May 1824. National Library of Greece

'there is'   Edward Blaquière to John Cam Hobhouse, 4 May 1824. National Library of Greece

529 'the expression'   Gamba *Narrative*

'an immense'   *Telegrafo Greco*, 2 May 1824

'a remarkably'   Edward Blaquière to John Cam Hobhouse, 4 May 1824. National Library of Greece

530 'many reasons'   Pietro Gamba to John Cam Hobhouse, 24 May 1824

'The organisation'   Gamba *Narrative*

'You would'   John Bowring to B, 2 June 1823

531 'the most'   *The Times*, 15 May 1824

'falls on'   quoted in summary of British press reports of Byron's death, *The Examiner*, May 1824

'Gentlemen'   Edmund Gosse quoted Harold Nicolson, 'Marginal Comment', *The Spectator*, 14 May 1943

'I can scarcely'   Douglas Kinnaird to John Cam Hobhouse, 13 or 14 May 1824

'Madam'   William Fletcher to Augusta Leigh, 20 April 1824

532 'afflicting condition'   Hobhouse diaries, 14 May 1824

'she had'   ibid., 15 May 1824

'recalling to mind'   ibid., 14 May 1824

'The Times'   ibid., 16 May 1824

533 'Three dogs'   ibid., 2 July 1824

'like a person'   ibid., 5 July 1824

'that the state'   Colonel Leicester Stanhope to John Bowring, 29 June 1824

534 'quitted the world'   *John Bull*, 16 May 1824
'to carry away'   Dean Ireland to John Cam Hobhouse, 8 July 1824
'Kinnaird went'   ibid., 6 July 1824

535 'the uproar'   *Sunday Monitor*, 11 July 1824
'very few'   Hobhouse diaries, 11 July 1824
'few respectable'   Moore *Journal*, 12 July 1824
'gave a deep'   John Clare, 'Autobiographical Fragments', *John Clare by Himself*,
ed. Eric Robinson and David Powell, 1996

536 'You will not'   Mary Shelley to Edward John Trelawny, 28 July 1824. Keats–Shelley
Memorial House, Rome
'Lord Byron's'   Lady Caroline Lamb to John Murray, 13 July 1824
'a very large'   *The Times*, 19 July 1824
'*great & distinguished*'   Hobhouse diaries, 15 July 1824

537 'unaffected and'   *The Times*, 19 July 1824

538 'not the slightest'   Hobhouse notes
'after the first'   Hobhouse diaries, 14 May 1824
'Recollected then'   Moore *Journal*, 14 May 1824

539 'the injustice'   ibid., 16 May 1824
'Lord Byron's honor'   Hobhouse diaries, 17 May 1824
'There are'   John Murray to the Comtesse d'Haussonville, 19 October 1864

540 'a very remarkable'   Frank T. Sabin to John Murray, 18 May 1886
'*the Elect*'   Hobhouse diaries, 15 May 1824
'too gross'   Lord John Russell, account of meeting at John Murray's, 17 May 1824.
The Journal of Thomas Moore, ed. Wilfred S. Dowden, vol. 2, 1984
'There was not'   Mary Shelley to Edward John Trelawny, 28 July 1824. Keats–Shelley
Memorial House, Rome
'saved the country'   Moore *Journal*, 20 May 1824
'except in'   B to John Murray, 29 October 1819

541 'Here was'   Hobhouse diaries, 15 May 1824
'The late infamous'   Moore *Journal*, 29 February 1828
'doomed to'   ibid., 5 June 1828
'Lord H.'   ibid., 25 May 1828

542 'Went to'   ibid., 21 June 1827
'but still'   ibid., 25 June 1827
'his tallness'   ibid., 27 January 1828
'evening rather heavy'   ibid., 3 February 1828
'had nothing'   ibid., 5 June 1828
'had been'   ibid., 7 June 1828
'he had'   ibid., 19 February 1829

543 'caprices'   Moore *Life*, vol. 2

29   The European Byronists

544 'Who has'   Charles Dupin, 1824, included in collection of French press responses to
Byron's death

545 'Will our century'   François-René, Vicomte de Chateaubriand, 'Note on Greece', 1825
'There is no'   Panayiotis Kanellopoulos, *History of the European Spirit*, trans.
C.M. Woodhouse (Lord Terrington), publication in progress

546 'I know no'   Giuseppe Mazzini, 'Byron and Goethe', *Monthly Chronicle*, 1839
'domestic calamity'   Victor Hugo, obituary of Byron for *La Muse Française*, published
in *Littérature et philosophie mêlées. Oeuvres complètes*, ed. Laffont, vol. 12, 1985–90
'Poète-conquérant'   Alfred de Vigny, 'Sur la mort de Byron', quoted catalogue *Lord
Byron, une vie romantique*, Maison Renan-Scheffer, Paris, 1988

547 'very good-looking'   Lady Blessington, *The Idler in Italy*, 1839–40
'I am deeply'   Heinrich Heine to Moses Moser, 1824. Louis Untermeyer, *Heinrich
Heine*, 1938

548 'If we are'   Nina Diakonova, 'Heine as an Interpreter of Byron', *Byron Journal*, 1994

549 'Read *Parisina*'   John Bayley, 'Pushkin and Byron: A Complex Relationship',
Byron Journal, 1988
'I feel'   Alexander Pushkin quoted Charles Sprawson, *Haunts of the Black Masseur:
The Swimmer as Hero*, 1992

550 'the great man'   Harold Nicolson, 'Marginal Comment', *The Spectator*, 14 May 1943
'You are sad'   Alexander Pushkin to Prince Pyotr Vyazemsky, June 1824. *The Letters of
Alexander Pushkin*, ed. J.T. Shaw, vol. 1, 1963

551 'the bane'   *Autobiography of Hector Berlioz*, vol. 1, 1884
Byron and Berlioz   see David Cairns, *Berlioz: The Making of an Artist*, vol. 1, 1989

552 'thy contrasted'   *Childe Harold's Pilgrimage*, Canto II, st. 85, l. 797
'certain books'   Eugène Delacroix journal, 11 April 1824. *The Journal of Eugène
Delacroix*, ed. Hubert Wellington, 1951
'Poetry is full'   ibid., 11 May 1824
'Without daring'   ibid., 21 July 1850

553 'I have'   Giuseppe Mazzini quoted Ian Buruma, *Voltaire's Coconuts or Anglomania
in Europe*, 1999
'Never did'   Giuseppe Mazzini, 'Byron and Goethe', *Monthly Chronicle*, 1839

554 'I dislike'   Blessington *Conversations*
'the pale man'   Gustave Flaubert quoted André Maurois, *Byron*, 1930
'this gloomy'   Mario Praz, *The Romantic Agony*, 1933

30   The Byronic Englishman

555 'a day'   Hallam Tennyson, *Alfred Lord Tennyson, a Memoir by his Son*, vol. 1, 1897
'Poor Byron!'   Thomas Carlyle to Jane Welsh, 19 May 1824. *The Love Letters of Thomas
Carlyle and Jane Welsh*, ed. Alexander Carlyle, 1909
'And Byron'   Jane Welsh to Thomas Carlyle, 20 May 1824. Ibid.

556 'Perhaps his wandering'   Matthew Arnold, 'Alaric at Rome', May 1840
'the great'   Matthew Arnold, Preface to *Poetry of Byron*, 1881
Byron and the Brontës   see Winifred Gérin, 'Byron's Influence on the Brontës',
Keats–Shelley Bulletin, XVII, 1966; Lucasta Miller, *The Brontë Myth*, 2001

557 'tall, athletic'   Emily Brontë, *Wuthering Heights*, 1847
'an absolutely'   John Ruskin, *Præterita*, 1885–9

'I've tried' John Ruskin quoted Robert Hewison, *Ruskin's Venice*, 1978

558 'My Venice' John Ruskin, *Præterita*, 1885–9

'these pismires' John Ruskin, 'Essay on Literature', 1836

Byron, Disraeli and Bulwer-Lytton see Andrew Elfenbein, *Byron and the Victorians*, 1995

559 'At school' Benjamin Disraeli, *Coningsby*, 1844

'I once met' C.L. Cline, 'Unpublished Notes on the Romantic Poets by Isaac D'Israeli', *Studies in English*, no. 21, University of Texas, 1941

'I take' Benjamin Disraeli to Isaac D'Israeli, 21 August 1826. Bodleian Library, University of Oxford, dep. Hughenden 12/1, fol. 79v

560 'flash *falsetto*' Charles Sumner, quoted *Memoir and Letters of Charles Sumner*, ed. Edward C. Pierce, vol. 2, 1877

'he himself ' Moore *Journal*, 11 June 1839

'We could not' Edward Bulwer-Lytton, 1833, quoted *Byron: The Critical Heritage*, ed. Andrew Rutherford, 1970

'She interested' The Earl of Lytton, *Life of Edward Bulwer, First Lord Lytton*, vol. 1, 1913

562 Byron and Blunt see James Tetreault, 'Heirs to his Virtues: Byron, Gobineau, Blunt', *Proceedings of the 14th International Byron Symposium*, Athens, July 1987

'a merry' Wilfrid Scawen Blunt journal, 20 November 1888. Wilfrid Scawen Blunt, *My Diaries*, 1919–20

'I have' ibid., 2 June 1909

563 'to avoid' Wilfrid Scawen Blunt quoted Elizabeth Longford, *A Pilgrimage of Passion: The Life of Wilfrid Scawen Blunt*, 1980

'Long have' Wilfrid Scawen Blunt, *In Vinculis: Sonnets written in an Irish Prison 1888*, 1889

565 'I am torn' Oscar Wilde to Norman Forbes-Robertson, 15 January 1882. *The Complete Letters of Oscar Wilde*, ed. Merlin Holland and Rupert Hart-Davis, 2000

'I was' Oscar Wilde, *De Profundis*, 1905

566 'hated women' Harold Nicolson quoted James Lees-Milne, *Harold Nicolson: A Biography 1886–1929*, vol. 1, 1980

'Of course' Harold Nicolson to Sir John Murray, 21 June 1923

567 'The conjunction' Sir John Murray to Harold Nicolson, 22 June 1923

'The only' Harold Nicolson to Sir John Murray, 13 November 1923

568 'mood of ' Peter Quennell, *The Marble Foot: An Autobiography 1905–1938*, 1976

569 'I go to' Harold Nicolson, *Diaries and Letters 1930–1964*, ed. Stanley Olson, 1980. Entry for 15 November 1945

'repeatedly falling' James Lees-Milne, *Another Self*, 1970

'We discussed' James Lees-Milne diary, 17 February 1942. *Ancestral Voices*, 1975

570 'that weakly' T.S. Eliot quoted Anne Barton, 'Lord Byron and Trinity, a bicentenary portrait', *Trinity Review*, 1988

'tawdry and melodramatic' Virginia Woolf to Lytton Strachey, 21 March 1924. *The Letters of Virginia Woolf*, ed. Nigel Nicolson, 1977

'I suddenly' W.H. Auden quoted Humphrey Carpenter, *W.H. Auden*, 1981

'Byron, thou should'st' W.H. Auden, 'Letter to Lord Byron', 1936

571 'She was'   B to John Murray, 7 June 1819. British Library
'I have seen'   ibid., 18 November 1820. British Library
'not undertaken'   Canon Thomas Gerrard Barber, *Byron and Where He is Buried*, 1939
572 'a miserable'   N.M. Lane, tape of broadcast interview on Byron's exhumation
573 'Very, very reverently'   Canon Thomas Gerrard Barber, *Byron and Where He is Buried*, 1939
'extraordinarily handsome'   N.M. Lane, tape of broadcast interview on Byron's exhumation
'with the slightly'   Cecil Roberts, *Sunshine and Shadow, being the fourth book of an Autobiography, 1930–1946*, 1972
574 'quite abnormal'   A.E. Houldsworth quoted Elizabeth Longford, *Byron*, 1976
'of all'   Cecil Roberts, *Sunshine and Shadow, being the fourth book of an Autobiography, 1930–1946*, 1972

Acknowledgements

My chief thanks must go to John Murray for commissioning this biography and to his wife Virginia Murray for guiding me with expertise and patience through the vast resources of the Byron archive at 50 Albemarle Street. Diana Murray provided fascinating insights into Albemarle Street in the days of her late husband, the sixth John Murray.

It was planned from the outset that Faber & Faber would publish the paperback edition of the book and I should like to thank Matthew Evans for his interest and support. Similarly Elisabeth Sifton of my American publishers Farrar, Straus & Giroux has been constantly encouraging

No biography exists in a vacuum, least of all a book on the ever-controversial 6th Lord Byron. I am conscious of a debt to my many predecessors, most of all to Professor Leslie Marchand whose three-volume biography and magnificent editions of Byron's letters have been an invaluable source. I have also been lastingly affected by my reading of previous interpretations of Byron's life and milieu, in particular André Maurois's *Byron* (1930); Iris Origo's *The Last Attachment* (1949); Richard Holmes's *Shelley, The Pursuit* (1974); Michael Foot's *The Politics of Paradise* (1988); Louis Crompton's *Byron and Greek Love* (1985); and not least Thomas Moore's *Life of Byron* (1830) which, in spite of its excisions and evasions, surely rates among the most resonant of nineteenth-century biographies.

My understanding of Byron's poetry has been assisted at all stages by Professor Jerome J. McGann's Oxford edition with its illuminating commentary. At the back of my mind throughout the writing of this book has been McGann's belief that Byron's greatness lies in the fact that he lived a great *individual* life: 'a life lived intensely from end to end – full of pettinesses, evil, amazing and persistent follies, yet complete and thorough, like a rich and complicated poem'.

I am grateful for the generosity of several Byron specialists in making available to me their own work in progress: Michael Rees for his translation of Teresa Guiccioli's *Vie de Lord Byron en Italie*, soon to be published in Peter Cochran's edition by the University of Delaware Press; Professor John Beckett for his study of the Byron family estates and finances, *Byron and Newstead: The Aristocrat and the Abbey*, published by Associated University Presses in 2002; Dr Annette Peach for giving me a preview of her 'Portraits of Byron', published by the Walpole Society in 2000; Dr Raymond Mills for sending me his paper on 'Byron's Last Illness' and Gordon C. Glegg for giving me the benefit of his detailed research on Lady Oxford. Jonathan Ray let me read extracts from his PhD thesis on Albany. Dr Peter Cochran kindly provided me with a copy of his recent transcription of the Hobhouse diaries as well as his indispensable Byron bibliography.

I have received a huge amount of interest, encouragement and practical help with my research and travels for this biography, during the early stages of which I was Research Associate in the Department of English Literature at the University of Sheffield. I am especially indebted to the following: Susan Bennett, Archivist at the Royal Society of Arts; Geoffrey C. Bond at Burgage Manor; Gerald Burdon; David Crane; Peter Day at Chatsworth House; Damon de Laszlo, the present occupier, for showing me Byron's rooms in Albany; Patrick Leigh Fermor; Dr Chris Fletcher at the British Library; Professor Christopher Frayling for alerting me to police reports in the Geneva Archives d'Etat; Anne Holmes; Philip Howard for doing some tricky translation; Peter Hunter, Librarian, the Vaughan Library, Harrow School, and Rita M. Gibbs, Archivist; Haidée Jackson at Newstead Abbey; the late James Lees-Milne; Stephen Lloyd at the Scottish National Portrait Gallery; Charles Marsden-Smedley; Arthur L. McCombie for guiding me round Byron sites in Aberdeen; Dr David McKitterick at Trinity College Library, Cambridge; Eric Miller for showing me round the Scottish Office (formerly Melbourne House); Susan Normington; the Viscount Norwich; Timothy Rogers, Dr Bruce Barker-Benfield and Colin Harris at the Bodleian Library, Oxford; William St Clair; Claire Tomalin; Christopher Walker; Commander and Mrs Wood for welcoming me at Kinsham Court.

In Athens I acknowledge with gratitude the help of David Blackman and his staff at the British School at Athens; Sir Michael Llewellyn Smith, then British Ambassador to Athens; Dr Eugenia Kefallineou at the National Library of Greece; Peter Chenery, then Director of the British Council, and his daughter Lizzie for a memorable journey to Missolonghi; and my friends Paris and Marina Tacopoulos; in Argostoli, Theo Gasparatos at the Corgialenios

Museum; in Ravenna, Dottore Donatino Domini, Director of the Biblioteca Classense; the Mother Superior, Monastero San Giovanni Battista, Bagnacavallo; Dottore Maria Grazia for arranging my visit to the Palazzo Guiccioli; in Venice, Dottore Paolo and Signora Donatella Asta for guiding me round Byron's apartments in the Palazzo Mocenigo; in Rome, Catherine Payling and Silvia Maronini at the Keats–Shelley Memorial House; Professor Andrew Wallace-Hadrill and his staff at the British School at Rome; in Italy in general, our friends Sally and Graham Greene and Patty and Michael Hopkins for their hospitality over the years.

It has been a great pleasure to work once again with Ron Costley, designer of this book, and I am grateful to Howard Davies for his careful copy-editing and to Douglas Matthews for his *tour de force* of an index. My special thanks go to my assistant Dawn Morris for her help with research and her constructive comments on the text.

Professor Leslie Marchand was enormously encouraging in the early stages, and I am sorry he did not live to see the book completed.

List of Illustrations

1 Byron and Robert Rushton, oil portrait by George Sanders. The Royal Collection, © 2002 Her Majesty Queen Elizabeth II.

2 Mrs Byron, oil portrait by Thomas Stewardson. John Murray.

3 Captain 'Mad Jack' Byron, engraving from Fanny Burney's *Madame d'Arblay*. City of Nottingham Museums: Newstead Abbey.

4 The Castle of Gight, photograph David Mellor.

5 Brig o'Balgownie, photograph David Mellor.

6 Newstead Abbey, photograph David Mellor.

7 Byron aged 7, engraving by Edward Finden after William Kay. John Murray.

8 Old Joe Murray, oil portrait by T. Barber. City of Nottingham Museums: Newstead Abbey.

9 Mary Chaworth, portrait miniature by John Hazlitt. Private Collection.

10 The Earl of Clare aged 14, Harrow School miniature. Keepers and Governors of Harrow School.

11 *The Peachey Stone, Harrow*, engraving by Edward Finden after C. Stanfield. John Murray.

12 'Edleston, Edleston, Edleston', MS of Latin elegy, 1811. John Murray.

13 Trinity College, Cambridge, photograph David Mellor.

14 Staircase in Trinity College, Cambridge, photograph David Mellor.

15 John Cam Hobhouse, portrait miniature by W. J. Newton. Sir Charles Hobhouse.

16 The Torre de Belém, Lisbon, photograph David Mellor.

17 The Monastery of the Capuchos at Cintra, photograph David Mellor.

18 *The Franciscan Convent, Athens*, engraving by Edward Finden after C. Stanfield. John Murray.

19 First page of *Childe Harold's Pilgrimage*, MS. John Murray.

20 *Childe Harold's Pilgrimage*, MS with corrections. John Murray.

21 Ali Pasha, engraving by W. Finden after F. Stone. John Murray.

22 Teresa, Maid of Athens, engraving by W. Finden after F. Stone. John Murray.

23 Byron by G.H. Harlow, pencil sketch. Private Collection.

24 *Breakfast at Samuel Rogers's Residence*, engraving and mezzotint by C. Mottram after J. Doyle. Victoria and Albert Museum.

25 *Drawing Room at Fifty Albemarle Street*, watercolour by L. Werner.

26 Melbourne House in Whitehall, photograph David Mellor.

27 Lady Melbourne, oil portrait by Thomas Lawrence. With kind permission of Lord Ralph Kerr.

28 Lady Caroline Lamb in page's costume, portrait miniature by Thomas Phillips. John Murray.

29 Lady Frances Wedderburn Webster, engraving. John Murray.

30 Byron by Thomas Phillips, oil portrait. John Murray.

31 The Countess of Oxford, oil portrait by John Hoppner. Tate Gallery.

32 'Ianthe', Charlotte Harley, engraving by W. Finden after R. Westall. John Murray.

33 Byron Screen, showing theatre scenes. John Murray.

34 The Hon. Douglas Kinnaird, anon. pastel portrait. The Hon. Mrs Caroline Best Collection.

35 John Murray, oil portrait by W.H. Pickersgill. John Murray.

36 Annabella Milbanke, portrait miniature by Charles Hayter. The Earl of Lytton.

37 The Hon. Augusta Leigh, portrait miniature by James Holmes. The Earl of Lytton.

38 Byron, hand-coloured engraving after miniature by James Holmes. Biblioteca Classense, Ravenna.

39 Seaham Hall drawing room, photograph David Mellor.

40 The shore at Seaham, photograph David Mellor.

41 *The Separation*, cartoon by I.R. Cruikshank. John Murray.

42 Claire Clairmont, oil portrait by Amelia Curran. City of Nottingham Museums: Newstead Abbey.

43 Allegra Biron, portrait miniature. John Murray.

44 The Hon. Augusta Ada Byron, portrait miniature attributed to Anthony Stewart. John Murray.

45 Percy Bysshe Shelley, oil portrait by Amelia Curran. By courtesy of the National Portrait Gallery, London.

46 J.W. Polidori, oil portrait by F.C. Gainsford. By courtesy of the National Portrait Gallery, London.

47 Villa Diodati, Geneva. John Murray.

48 Madame de Staël, oil portrait by François Gérard. Château de Coppet.

49 Byron in Venice, pencil sketch by G.H. Harlow. John Murray.

50 Palazzo Albrizzi, Venice, photograph David Mellor.

51 Palazzo Mocenigo, Venice, photograph David Mellor.

52 Marianna Segati, portrait miniature. John Murray.

53 Margherita Cogni, pencil drawing by G.H. Harlow. John Murray.

54 Tita, from a drawing by Daniel Maclise. John Murray.

55 Byron and Countess Teresa Guiccioli (with face obliterated), double portrait miniature by Girolamo Prepiani. Biblioteca Classense, Ravenna.

56 Palazzo Guiccioli, Ravenna, watercolour. John Murray.

57 Palazzo Guiccioli, internal stairway, photograph David Mellor.

58 Monastery of San Giovanni Battista, Bagnacavallo, photograph David Mellor.

59 Countess Teresa Guiccioli, marble bust by Lorenzo Bartolini. Biblioteca Classense, Ravenna.

60 Byron's handwritten message in Teresa Guiccioli's copy of Madame de Staël's *Corinne*. Biblioteca Classense, Ravenna.

61 Palazzo Lanfranchi, Pisa, photograph David Mellor.

62 Palazzo Lanfranchi, entrance hall, photograph David Mellor.

63 James Leigh Hunt, pencil drawing by Thomas Charles Wageman. By courtesy of the National Portrait Gallery, London.

64 E.J. Trelawny, pen and ink drawing by Joseph Severn. By courtesy of the National Portrait Gallery, London.

65 Watercolour illustration to *Don Juan* by Richard Westall. John Murray.

66 Byron in Genoa, pencil sketch by Count Alfred D'Orsay. John Murray.

67 Marguerite, Countess of Blessington, oil portrait by Thomas Lawrence. Wallace Collection.

68 The *Bolivar*, drawing by Captain Daniel Roberts. Keats–Shelley House, Rome.

69 Ruins of the Monastery of Theotokos Agrilion, Cephalonia, photograph David Mellor.

70 Prince Alexander Mavrocordatos, print after Augustus Jules Bouvier, published by Adam Friedel. City of Nottingham Museums: Newstead Abbey.

71 Site of Byron's house at Metaxata, Cephalonia, photograph David Mellor.

72 Byron with his dog Lyon, watercolour by Robert Seymour after William Parry. Gennadius Library, Athens.

73 Missolonghi, engraving by E. Finden after W. Purser. John Murray.

74 *The Death of Byron*, oil by Joseph-Denis von Odevaere. Groeningemuseum, Bruges.

75 *Liszt am Flügel*, oil by Joseph Danhauser. Staatsbibliothek, Berlin.

76 Lady Byron in old age, photograph by Frederick Hollyer. By courtesy of the National Portrait Gallery, London.

Illustrations in text

Frontispiece. Byron from an engraving by H. Meyer of a portrait by George Sanders. John Murray.

54 Page from *The Wonderful History of Lord Byron and his Dog*, illustration and verse by Elizabeth Pigot. Henry Ransom Humanities Research Center, The University of Texas at Austin.

66 'Ld. B. as an Amatory Writer', caricature by Scrope Berdmore Davies on verso of letter to Byron. John Murray.

84 Inscription by Byron in the front of *English Bards and Scotch Reviewers*, 1811 edition. John Murray.

168 Lady Caroline Lamb with her son Augustus, self-portrait sketch in scrapbook. John Murray.

170 'Sir Eden the least page teaching Augustus his prayers', sketch in scrapbook of Lady Caroline Lamb. John Murray

175 Lady Caroline Lamb's instructions to her tailor, MS page in *The Life of Crabbe*. Reproduced with the permission of the Brotherton Collection, Leeds University Library

201 Captain George Leigh, anon. pencil sketch. John Murray.

203 Six Mile Bottom, pencil sketch on back of letter addressed to Augusta Leigh. John Murray.

247 Lord and Lady Byron, ink drawing by Caroline Lamb. John Murray.

350 Byron's proof corrections to *Don Juan*, Cantos I & II. John Murray.

427 *Lord Byron as he appeared after his daily ride at Pisa and Genoa*, silhouette by Marianne Hunt, engraved by Samuel Freeman. John Murray.

459 *Lord Byron at Genoa*, pencil and red chalk drawing after portrait miniature by And. Isola. John Murray.

526 Official proclamation of Byron's death in Missolonghi, 19 April 1824. John Murray.

Index

Writings by Byron appear directly under title; works by others appear under author's name. 'B' indicates Byron.

Abercromby, Mary Anne, Lady, 8
Aberdeen: B and mother live in, 6–11
Aberdeen, George Gordon, 3rd Earl of, 8
Aberdeen, George Hamilton-Gordon, 4th Earl of, 107, 113, 535
Ada (B's daughter) *see* Byron, Augusta Ada
Adair, Sir Robert, 120, 122–3
Adam, General Sir Frederick, 468
Aeschylus: *Prometheus*, 41
Aga, Hatadjé ('Hato'), 505–6
Age of Bronze, The (B), 444–5
Aglietti, Dr Francesco, 362–3
Agoult, Comtesse Marie d', 550–1
Akarnania, Western Greece, 467
Albania, 101–5
Albany, Piccadilly: B moves to, 217–21, 233; Bulwer-Lytton lives in, 561
Albemarle Street, London: Murray moves to, 159; B visits, 248–9
Alborghetti, Count Giuseppe, 357, 385, 395
Albrizzi, Countess Isabella Teotochi, 319, 335, 338, 353
Alder, William, 447
Alexander, Dr James, 459
Alfieri, Count Vittorio, 205, 285, 319, 355, 396, 409
Ali Pasha, ruler of Albania, 101–6, 108, 123, 472, 509
Allan, David, 8
Allegra *see* Byron, Clara Allegra
Almack's assembly rooms, London, 202
Alphonso II, Marchese d'Este *see* Este, Alphonso II, Marchese d'

Althorp, John Charles Spencer, Viscount (*later* 3rd Earl Spencer), 218
Amphion, HMS, 135
Anatolikon, Greece, 475, 496, 501
Anderson, James, 6
Androutsos, Odysseus (Ulysses), 467, 476, 509–10
Anet, Claude, 541
Angelina (Venetian girl), 355, 369
Angelo, Henry, 65, 72, 277
Ann (ship), 476, 498
Annesley, Lady Catherine, 209, 211
Argiropoli, Prince George, 436
Argostoli *see* Cephalonia
Ariel (or *Don Juan*; boat), 428
Armenia and Armenian language: B's interest in, 321–2
Arnold, Matthew, 304, 555–6, 558
Arqua, Euganean hills, 362
Aspe, Giacomo, 456
Aston Hall, South Yorkshire, 207–9
Athens: B first visits (1809), 108, 109–14; B revisits (1810–11), 125–33
Aucher, Father Paschal, 321–2
Auckland, Lady Elisabeth, 169
Auden, W.H.: 'Letter to Lord Byron', 570–1
'Augustus Darvell' (B), 293–4
Austen, Jane, 46; *Persuasion*, 199
Austria: and Italian revolutionary movement, 386, 394

Babbage, Charles, 70
Bacinetti, Villa, 381, 390
Bad Lord Byron, The (film), 543

Bagnacavallo: Allegra sent to convent school in, 390, 394, 400, 418

Baillie, Joanna, 151

Baillie, Dr Matthew, 25, 261–2

Ball, Sir Alexander, 98, 100, 102

Bamber, Sarah Agnes, 162

Bancroft, George, 422–3

Banff, 9

Bankes, Henry, 58

Bankes, William: introduces B to homosexual practices at Cambridge, 58, 188; leaves Cambridge, 64; friendship with Matthews, 67; B admires, 130; travels, 130, 372; Annabella rejects suit, 188; visits B in Venice, 372–3; in Ravenna with B, 375; on *Don Juan*, 382; and B's diet, 409; and Moore's biography of B, 542

Barber, Revd Canon Thomas Gerrard, 571–2, 574; *Byron and Where He is Buried*, 572

Barff and Hancock (merchants and bankers), 481, 487

Barff, Samuel, 481, 508, 510, 512, 528

Barnewell (Lisbon hotel-keeper), 93

Barry, Charles (banker), 455–8, 460, 470, 481, 490, 512

Bartolini, Lorenzo, 411

Bathurst, Captain Walter, 117

Batoni, Pompeo, 7

Baudelaire, Charles, 554

Becher, Revd John Thomas, 51, 73

Beckford, William, 37, 94, 301; *Vathek*, 193–4

Bedford, John Russell, 6th Duke of, 179

Bellerophon, HMS, 253

Bellingham, John, 172

Beltram, Donna Josepha, 94

Bembo, Cardinal Pietro, 313

Bentham, Jeremy, 452; *A Table of Springs of Action*, 494

Bentinck, Lord William, 465

Benzoni, Countess Marina Querini, 338, 353–4, 356, 362–3

Beppo (B): on sexual behaviour, 51; Italian influence on, 314, 318, 333–4; Frere's influence on, 333; poetic form, 334; publication and reception, 347–8, 352

Berger (B's Swiss guide), 279, 308, 310, 312

Berkeley, Colonel, 184

Berlioz, Hector, 550–1

Bessborough, Henrietta Frances, Countess of, 164, 165, 166, 171, 173, 176–7, 179

Bessborough House, near Fiddown, Ireland, 178

Bessy (Newstead maidservant), 152–3

Betteridge, James, 572–3

Bettesworth, Captain George Edmund Byron, 86

Betty, William Henry West ('Young Roscius'), 49, 184

Black, Mrs James, 562

Blacket, Joseph, 187

Blackwood, William, 367

Blackwood's Edinburgh Magazine, 276, 367

Blake (barber), 390, 571

Blaquière, Edward, 451–3, 466, 481, 528–30, 541

Blessington, Charles John Gardiner, 1st Earl of, 448–50, 455–6

Blessington, Marguerite, Countess of: and B's attitude to Napoleon, vii–viii; and B's thirst for celebrity, x; on B's appearance and voice, 35; and B's effect on women, 163; B confesses Augusta's knowing personal weaknesses, 205–6; and B's attitude to Annabella, 239; on B's playing up to Medwin, 411; visits B in Genoa, 448–51; approves B's commitment to Greek independence, 452; B claims capacity for feeling exhausted, 454; B buys horse from on leaving Genoa, 455–6; B requests miniature of Annabella from, 458; Lamartine meets, 547; on B's dislike of French poetry, 554; *Conversations of Lord Byron*, 450

Bligh, Captain William, 445

Blues, The (B), 456

Blunt, Lady Anne Isabella (*née* Noel), 562–4

Blunt, Wilfrid Scawen, 15, 558, 562–4

Boccaccio, Giovanni: *Decameron*, 376; 'Theodore and Honoria', 376

Boisragon, Dr Henry Charles, 183

Bolívar, Simón, 364

Bolivar, The (B's schooner), 410, 423–4, 436, 444, 455

Bologna, 326, 359–60, 571

Bonivard, François, 293, 300

Bonstetten, Charles Victor de, 301

Borgia, Cesare, 313

Borgia, Lucretia, 313, 315

Borrow, George, 536

Bosset, Major Charles-Philippe de, 468

Boswell, James, Jr, 248

Botsaris, Markos, 461, 467, 475, 477, 496, 525

Botsaris, Notis, 496

Bounty, HMS, 445

Bowring, John, 452–3, 486, 494, 530

Boyce, Francis, 48, 77

Boyce, Frederick, 257–8

Boyce, Susan, 257–9

Braham, John, 239

Brazen, HMS, 3

Brême, Ludovico, Abbate di, 301, 313

Bride of Abydos, The (B), 211–12, 215, 260

Brighton, 74–6

Bristoe, Miss (of Southwell), 49

Brocket Hall, Hertfordshire, 191–2, 536

Broglie, Albertine, Duchesse de, 301

Brontë, Charlotte, Branwell, Anne and Emily, 556–7

Brougham, Henry (*later* Baron Brougham and Vaux), 63, 75, 295–6, 302, 377, 452

Browne, James Hamilton: on B's appearance, 35; joins B on expedition to Greek War of Independence, 461–2, 465; on Cephalonia with B, 469–70; travels to Ithaca with B, 471–2; witnesses B's uncontrolled rage, 473; leaves for Peloponnese, 475; on Trelawny's Suliote costume, 476; returns to Cephalonia to arrange loan from B, 481–2

Bruce, Michael, 128–31

Bruen, George H., 423

Brummell, George ('Beau'): in exile, x, 305–6, 378

Bruno, Dr Francesco: leaves Genoa for Cephalonia, 459, 470; travels to Ithaca with B, 470; and B's falling into rage at monastery, 473; in Metaxata, 478–9; leaves for Missolonghi, 485; and B's fit at Missolonghi, 502; attends B during final illness and death, 513–16, 518; performs autopsy on B's body, 519; travels to England with B's body, 530, 533

Brunton, Mary: *Self-Control*, 144

Brussels, 286–8

Bryant, Jacob: *Dissertation concerning the War of Troy*, 118

Bulwell Wood, Nottinghamshire, 16

Bulwer-Lytton, Edward *see* Lytton, Edward Bulwer-, 1st Baron

Burdett, Sir Francis, 189, 195, 255, 452, 532, 538

Burgage Manor, Southwell, 45–6, 52

Burghersh, Priscilla Anne, Lady, 540

Burton, Robert: *Anatomy of Melancholy*, 403

Burun, Ernegis and Ralph de (B's probable ancestors), 13

Bury, Lady Charlotte, 85

Butler, Lady Eleanor, 60

Butler, Revd Dr George, 42, 63

Byrne, Oscar, 250

Byron, Allegra (B's daughter) *see* Byron, Clara Allegra

Byron (*later* Noel Byron), Anne Isabella (Annabella), Lady (*née* Milbanke; B's wife): on B's religious upbringing, 11; B writes of Mary Chaworth to, 34; and B's homosexual practices, 40, 238, 261–2; B describes Turkey to, 121; B's early involvement with, 166–7; B reads poems by, 172; B confesses commitment to, 181; B considers marriage to, 185–6; character and intelligence, 186–7; rejects B's first proposal of marriage, 187; William Bankes proposes to, 188; attachment to B, 196–7; on B's supposed assault on Lady Charlotte Harley, 196; accuses Augusta of keeping silent about B's homosexuality, 205; B tells of other loves in life, 206, 238; and B's idealisation of sensation, 207; believes Elizabeth Medora Leigh to be B's daughter, 214; on B's *Lara*, 225; engagement and marriage, 225–7, 230–3, 235–7; B visits in Seaham, 229–32; marriage settlement, 230, 260; appearance, 231, 235; meets Hobhouse, 235–6; honeymoon, 237–40, 445; suspects B's unnatural relations with Augusta, 239, 242, 251–2; makes fair copies of B's poems, 240, 260; correspondence with Augusta, 241; marriage relations, 241–2, 245–6, 250–3, 255–6, 259, 261–2; with Augusta and B at Six Mile Bottom, 242–4; home in Piccadilly Terrace, 246; pregnancy, 250–1, 259–60; approves B's will favouring Augusta, 255; relations with Sarah Siddons, 256; wary of B's theatrical interests, 256–9; and birth of daughter Augusta Ada, 261; fears for B's sanity, 262; leaves Piccadilly Terrace, 262, 263; initiates separation proceedings, 264–5; charges and accusations against B, 267–9; sexual relations with B, 267–8, 564; B addresses 'Fare Thee Well' poem to, 273–4; letter from B on leaving England, 277; B signs deed of separation from, 278; granted half of mother's estate, 278; abandoned by B on departure for continent, 280; refuses reference to Ann Fletcher, 284; Madame de Staël attempts to reconcile with B, 302; B's attitude to after leaving England, 303; presses Augusta to confess, 303; plans to send Ada to continent, 324; reconciliation hopes end, 331; Hanson enquires about B's possible reconciliation with, 347; depicted in B's *Don Juan*, 349; B corresponds with while abroad, 370, 376, 411; and B's memoirs, 370; and George IV's coronation, 377; agrees to send

Byron (*later* Noel Byron), Anne Isabella
(Annabella), Lady (*cont.*)
portrait of Ada to B, 384; B warns of
financial effect of war in Italy, 386; B tells
of assassination of Dal Pinto, 388; keeps
letters from B, 403; B hangs miniature in
Pisa villa, 406; inheritance on mother's
death, 411; B requests miniature of on
departure for Greece, 458; and Ada's
upbringing and education, 479; B warns of
Ada's possible inherited illness, 503; B
suggests sending Hatadjé Aga to, 506;
informed of B's death, 532; and burning of
B's memoirs, 539; refuses to cooperate
with Moore for B biography, 542; Harriet
Beecher Stowe writes on, 564; 'By thee
Forsaken', 280
Byron, Augusta Ada (*later* Countess of
Lovelace; B's daughter): collaborates with
Charles Babbage on early computer, 70;
B's pride in, 215; birth, 261–5; Annabella
fears B's claiming custody of, 267; B's
concern at separation from, 303, 324, 420;
B corresponds with Annabella about,
370; B requests portrait of, 384; and
death of grandmother Noel, 411; B
receives new picture of, 443; B's anxiety
over ill health, 479–80; B fears heriditary
illness for, 503; B regrets not seeing, 520;
burial, 571, 573
Byron, Catherine (*née* Gordon; B's mother):
and B's deformed foot, 4, 30–1;
background and family, 5, 7, 14; in
Aberdeen, 6–7; finances, 6; political views,
6; appearance and overweight, 7;
temperament, 7; life at Newstead, 17–18;
and B's abuse by May Gray, 22–3; and B's
education, 22, 26, 29, 32; receives Civil List
pension, 25; plans to remove B to France,
26; and B's infatuation with Mary
Chaworth, 34; and Lord Grey de Ruthyn,
36, 52; at Southwell, 45–7; quarrels and
tensions with B, 51–3; ambitions for B, 81;
hopes for B to marry well, 82; praises
Sanders' portrait of B, 88; and Rushton's
return from travels with B, 96–7; letters
from B on Mediterranean travels, 102–3,
106, 116, 125; death, 141–2; burial in family
vault, 573
Byron, Clara Allegra (B/Claire Clairmont's
daughter; Alba): B supports, 80; B's
paternal pride in, 215, 298; conception and
birth, 273, 324; upbringing, 306; Shelley
reports on to B, 324–5, 342; baptised, 344;
moves to Italy, 344; cared for in Venice,
360–1; B sends for in Bologna, 361; falls ill
with malaria, 371; with B in Ravenna, 375,
379; falls ill again, 381; B sends to convent
school in Bagnacavallo, 390, 392–4; in B's
will, 391; education, 391; Shelley visits in
Bagnacavallo, 400; B leaves in convent on
moving to Pisa, 403; writes asking B to
visit, 403; final illness, death and burial,
418–20, 429, 458
Byron, Eliza (B's cousin), 195
Byron, Ernest (child of 3rd Baron), 572
Byron, Frances (George's widow), 18, 21
Byron, Revd Frederick Ernest Charles, 10th
Baron, 571, 574
Byron, George (5th Baron's brother), 18
Byron, George Anson, 7th Baron (B's cousin
and heir), 25, 263, 532, 535
Byron, George Gordon, 6th Baron
Characteristics: identifies with Napoleon,
vii–x, 221, 244, 279; emotionalism,
11–12; feminine characteristics, 35–6;
physical appearance, 35, 47, 53, 62, 104,
120, 144, 270–1, 286, 346–7, 368, 425,
435, 444, 449, 493, 559; shyness, 47;
diet and vegetarianism, 53, 141, 151–2,
363, 368, 408–9, 444, 461, 479; poetic
pessimism, 64; treatment of servants,
78, 337; facial expressions, 97, 151, 286;
mood changes, 116, 122; moustache and
beard, 116, 368, 493; personal image
('Byromania'), 139, 160–1; impact on
women, 161–3, 169; torments women,
220; emotional indifference, 221–2;
skull examined by phrenologist, 223;
notoriety amongst English abroad,
295, 326, 342, 367; temper and rages,
331, 473; parsimony, 347, 444; sense of
fate towards others, 359; spreads
scandal and gossip, 400; personality
change in Genoa, 435; suffers
paroxysm of rage on Cephalonia,
473–4; fears growing fat and going
mad, 479; practical jokes on servants,
506–7
Education: early schooling, 9, 25–6;
attends Harrow School, 29–32, 37–44;
at Cambridge (Trinity College), 56–9,
61–2, 64–70; awarded degree, 68
Finances: allowance, 57; debts, 59, 81, 89,
122, 193, 200, 235, 247, 259, 335; estates
encumbered, 82; and sale of Newstead,
182, 186, 190, 193, 209, 223, 234–5, 255,
334–6, 346, 537; marriage settlement,

230; financial improvement, 335; financial gain on mother-in-law's death, 411; helps finance Greek war, 481–2, 497

Health: deformed foot, 3–4, 8, 22, 25–6, 30–1, 248, 519; depressions, 61, 193, 259, 304, 390, 403, 444, 460, 479; contracts fever in Greece, 129, 134, 266, 323, 371; gonorrhoea, 134, 335; piles, 134; kidney stone, 183, 194; Annabella fears nearing insanity, 262; takes laudanum, 266; rheumatism, 315; convulsions in Bologna, 359–60; health decline following swim after Shelley's funeral, 431; illness at Lerici, 436; inflammation of face, 448; fit in Missolonghi, 502–3; final illness and death in Missolonghi, 512–18, 520–1; autopsy and causes of death, 518–20

Interests and Views: swimming, 9, 74, 92, 94, 118, 342–3, 431; dogs, 16, 68, 76, 78–9, 311, 459, 493, 512, 519, 533; cricket, 44; theatre and actresses, 48–9, 184–5, 219, 256–9, 396; fencing lessons, 65; scientific interests, 69–70; gambling, 71–2; shopping, 71; and duelling, 72, 100; takes boxing lessons, 72; sailing, 74; in House of Lords, 82–3, 156–7, 197–8; Whig sympathies, 82–3; shooting, 106, 408, 416; Turkomania, 115; belief in personal virtues, 117; learns Italian, 128; disbelief in after-life, 143; defends Nottingham frame-breakers, 155–7; address on reopening of Drury Lane Theatre, 185; post-Napoleonic political views, 187; disillusion with British politics, 200; on supremacy of sensation, 207; criticised for political views, 222; religious scepticism, 227; attitude to Jews, 239; on Sub-Committee of Management at Drury Lane Theatre, 249–50; drinking, 259, 264, 479; Europeanism, 283–4; sails and rows on Lac Leman with Shelley, 291, 298–300, 559; religious yearnings, 321, 391; studies Armenian, 321–2; keeps menagerie of birds and animals, 337, 399, 437; on reasons for exile, 367; political engagement in Italy, 374–5, 384–7, 394–5; renounces field sports, 382; republicanism, 394; amateur theatricals in Pisa, 409; acquires schooner (*Bolivar*), 410, 423–4;

commitment to Greek independence, 435–6, 451–3, 491; buys Lady Blessington's horse Mameluke, 455; religious discussions with Kennedy on Cephalonia, 469–70; personal concept of liberty, 486; diplomacy and administration in Missolonghi, 507–11; fails to attend Salona congress, 510; as prospective King of Greece, 510

Literary Life: reading, 41; first published books of verse, 50–1; works published professionally, 62, 139–40, 149, 215; reaction to adverse criticism of works, 63; writing routine, 83; letter-writing as performance, 92; early memoirs destroyed, 105, 238; and professional publication, 139–40, 149, 215; literary acquaintances, 150–1; poetry set to music, 239; meets Sir Walter Scott, 248; Bible reading, 304; nature poetry in Alps, 309; co-translates Pellico's *Francesca da Rimini* with Hobhouse, 313; translates Pulci, 363, 380, 383, 456; gives memoirs to Moore, 369–70; resumes journal, 389–90, 403; dramatic writings, 395–8; attempts to retrieve correspondence, 402–3; denounced for irreligious sentiments in *Cain*, 414–15; reputation in Germany, 422, 547; founds magazine (*The Liberal*) with Leigh Hunt in Pisa, 426–8, 432; breach with Murray, 439–42; posthumous reputation and cult, 521, 530–1, 544–57; memoirs burnt at Murray's, 539–40; Moore's biography of, 541–3; European view of, 544–54; dislikes French verse, 554

Personal Life: homosexual predilections, xii–xiii, 23–4, 31, 37, 40, 58–9, 61, 76, 78, 87, 126–7, 171, 190–1, 196, 205–6, 238, 261, 267, 270, 340–1, 501, 504–5, 538, 564, 566; birth and baptism, 3, 5; attitude to father, 6–7; childhood in Scotland, 7–11; portraits, 8, 78, 88, 183, 211, 216, 289, 323, 336, 423, 427, 450, 549, 550; childhood romances, 10–11, 23, 27, 32–3; inherits title and estate, 11–12, 16–18; ancestry, 13, 18; coat of arms and motto, 13–14; abused as boy by May Gray, 22–3; putative illegitimate children, 49–50, 80; youthful romances, 49; quarrels with mother, 51–3; extravagances, 60; sexual experimentations and licentiousness,

Byron, George Gordon, 6th Baron
  Personal Life (*cont.*)
    73–6, 90; resumes residence at
    Newstead (1808), 76–81; seduces and
    impregnates servants, 80, 153, 209;
    near-purchase of Teresa Macri in
    Athens, 114–15; ghost appearances, 129;
    wills and bequests, 135, 211, 255, 391,
    457, 520, 531; death of friends, 141–2,
    144–5; and mother's death, 141–2;
    discretion on homosexual liaisons,
    146–7; witnesses public hanging, 172;
    courtship of Annabella, 186–7;
    Annabella rejects first proposal, 187;
    repelled by women's eating, 188, 259;
    putative daughter by Augusta, 214, 243;
    moves to Albany, Piccadilly, 217–21;
    growing unpopularity, 222, 273, 275–6,
    290; takes house in Hastings, 222–3;
    engagement and marriage to
    Annabella, 225–7, 230–3, 235–7; visits
    Annabella in Seaham, 229–31;
    honeymoon, 237–40; marriage
    relations, 241–2, 245–6, 250–3, 255–6,
    259, 261–2; together with Annabella
    and Augusta at Six Mile Bottom,
    242–4; in Piccadilly Terrace, 245–6;
    and birth of daughter Augusta Ada,
    261; Annabella initiates separation
    proceedings against, 264–6; rumoured
    marital sodomy, 267–8; library sold,
    277; signs deed of separation from
    Annabella, 278; as subject of scurrilous
    gossip in Geneva, 295–6; and care and
    upbringing of Ada, 325; Thorwaldsen
    bust of, 327–8; conversation, 330; lists
    mistresses in Venice, 340; speculative
    homosexual liaisons in Venice, 340–1;
    takes in Allegra in Venice, 344;
    Shelley's view of in Venice, 345;
    reputation in England, 349, 352; sends
    for Allegra in Bologna, 361; accepted
    by Gamba family, 382, 384; and
    assassination of Dal Pinto, 387;
    assassination attempt on in Ravenna,
    388; places Allegra in convent school,
    390, 392–3; thirty-third birthday, 390;
    and Hoppner scandal of alleged
    Shelley/Claire baby, 391–2, 401; daily
    routine, 399, 422, 478; adopts
    additional name Noel and new seal,
    411; Bartolini bust of, 411–12; and
    Allegra's death and burial, 418–20; and
    Shelley's death, 428; attends cremation

    of Shelley and Williams, 429–30;
    sexual vulnerability in Greece, 490;
    thirty-sixth birthday, 499–501; funeral
    in Missolonghi, 525, 527–8; body
    returned to England, 528–9, 532–3;
    news of death reaches England, 531;
    funeral procession and burial in
    England, 534–8; lying-in-state, 535;
    coffin opened (1938), 573–4
  Relationships: incestuous relations with
    Augusta, 7, 204–6, 213, 252, 563–4;
    infatuation with Mary Chaworth, 32–4,
    36, 154; with Lord Grey de Ruthyn, 32,
    36–7, 52, 61, 76; with Earl of Clare, 38,
    206, 403–4, 423, 520; early relations
    with Augusta, 43; friendship with
    Elizabeth Pigot, 46–7; with John
    Edleston, 58–62, 64, 79, 87, 105, 206,
    225, 270, 501, 518, 543; with Constance
    Spencer Smith, 99–100, 134–5; with
    Eustathius Georgiou, 126–7; with
    Nicolas Giraud, 128–9, 135, 501, 543;
    with John Murray, 147–9, 247–8; with
    Moore, 150–1; affair with Lady
    Caroline Lamb, 163–7, 169–76;
    involvement with Lady Melbourne,
    166, 179–81, 186–7, 198, 208, 214, 220–1,
    449, 563; Caroline Lamb's attempted
    elopement with, 174; and Caroline
    Lamb's disappearance, 177; parting
    letter to Caroline Lamb, 177–8; with
    Lady Oxford, 186, 188–92, 194–8, 364,
    445; flirtations and affairs, 187–8;
    Caroline Lamb burns in effigy, 191–2;
    letter of rejection to Caroline Lamb,
    191–2; persecuted by Caroline Lamb,
    193–4, 200, 221; infatuation with Lady
    Charlotte Harley, 195–6; with Augusta
    in London (1813), 202; developing
    relations with Augusta, 203–4; pursuit
    of Lady Frances Webster, 207–10, 213;
    final parting from Caroline Lamb, 221;
    Claire Clairmont approaches, 271–2;
    liaison and child with Claire
    Clairmont, 272–3, 296–7; with
    Marianna Segati in Venice, 319–21, 325,
    329–30, 332–3, 336, 338–40; antipathy
    towards Annabella, 331; liaison with
    Margherita Cogni ('La Fornarina'),
    332–3, 338–9; with Arpalice Taruscelli,
    339; with Teresa Guiccioli, 353–5,
    356–60, 362–3, 370, 375, 378–81, 422,
    433, 454–5, 490; with Trelawny,
    409–10; with Hunt and family, 431–2;

with Mary Shelley, 438; attachment to Lukas Chalandritsanos, 488–9, 493, 499, 501, 505; attachment to Greek girl Hatadjé Aga, 505–6

Travels: early travel plans, 86–7; to Mediterranean (1809), 89–98; naval exploits off Greece, 100; early impressions and experience of Greece, 109–14; travels with Sligo, 125–6; returns to England (1811), 133–4, 139; in Cheltenham, 182–5, 187; departs for continent (1816), 277–9, 283–5; Napoleonic coach, 278, 285, 312, 362; journeys through continent (1816), 285–9; in Geneva with Shelleys and Claire Clairmont, 291; occupies Villa Diodati, Switzerland, 292–5, 300–1; in high Alps, 307–12; leaves Geneva for Milan, 312–14; in Venice (1816–17), 316–24; witnesses beheadings in Rome, 328; occupies Palazzo Mocenigo in Venice, 336–9; stays in Ravenna, 357–61, 374–9, 388, 399; considers emigration to Americas and Tasmania, 364, 371, 434; plans life in Venezuela, 364–5, 371; cancels departure from Italy, 371; in Pisa, 401–2, 406–11; under police surveillance in Italy, 406, 415; in 'Pisa Affray', 415–17; in Genoa, 434, 435–7, 442, 445, 448–51; departure for Greek War of Independence, 455–6, 458–62; stays on Cephalonia, 464–70, 473, 476–9, 486; leaves for Missolonghi, 483–8; arrives at Missolonghi, 490–4; strategy and resources in Greece, 495–8

Byron, Sir John, 1st Baron, 13

Byron, Captain John (B's father; 'Mad Jack'): on B's deformed foot, 3; background, 5; death, 6; in Scotland with family, 6; gambling, 201; elopement with Lady Carmarthen, 207; and B's *Werner*, 413

Byron, Admiral John (B's grandfather), 5

Byron, Captain John ('Foulweather Jack'), 88

Byron, Richard, 2nd Baron, 573

Byron, William, 4th Baron, 15

Byron, William, 5th Baron (B's great-uncle; 'the Wicked Lord'), 11, 15–16, 573

Byron, William: killed (1794), 8

Cadiz, 95–6

Cain, A Mystery (B), 398, 414, 433

Cambridge University: B attends (Trinity College), 56–9, 61–2, 64–70;

homosexuality at, 58; B visits to vote for Clark, 232

Cameron, Caroline, 74–6, 125

Campbell, Thomas: B's estimate of as poet, 85, 150, 248, 333; B meets, 150–1; at Holland House, 161; in B's funeral procession, 535; 'The Last Man', 305

Canning, Stratford (*later* 1st Viscount Stratford de Redcliffe), 44, 122–3

Canova, Antonio, 10, 319, 353

Capuccini, I (house, Este), 346

Carbonari (revolutionary society), 384–6, 388, 394–5, 436

Carlisle, Frederick Howard, 5th Earl of: as B's guardian, 16, 25–6; visits Harrow, 32; Augusta meets, 43; and B at Cambridge, 56; B insults in verse, 83; fails to introduce B in House of Lords, 83; marriage, 226; sends carriage to B's funeral procession, 535

Carlisle, Isabella, Countess of (*née* Byron), 25

Carlo Felice, King of Sardinia, 437

Carlyle, Jane Welsh, 555

Carlyle, Thomas: political views, 156; on D'Orsay, 450; on B's death, 555

Carmarthen, Amelia, Marchioness of, 207

Carnock, Sir Arthur Nicolson, 1st Baron, 565

Caroline, Princess of Wales (*later* Queen), 85, 192–3, 442

Cartwright, Major John, 197–8

Cary, Byron, 162

Casti, Giambattista: *Animali Parlanti*, 314; *Novelle Amorose*, 313–14

Castlereagh, Robert Stewart, Viscount, 433–4

Catalani, Madame, 73

Catherine II (the Great), Empress of Russia: in B's *Don Juan*, 432

Cavalli, Antonio (Teresa Guiccioli's cousin), 385

Cavalli, Marquis (Teresa Guiccioli's uncle), 375

Cavendish Bentinck, Lord William, 285

Cawthorn, James, 86, 139

Cephalonia: B stays on, 464–70, 473, 476–9, 486, 499; earthquakes, 480

Chalandritsanos, Lukas (Khalandritsanos, Loukhas): B's attachment to, xiii, 490, 499, 501, 505–6, 540, 543, 567; with B in Greece, 488, 493; B's concern for safety of, 488, 529; B supposedly shares bed with, 502, 566–7; fever, 502–3; and B's final illness, 514; suspected of stealing from B, 518; B leaves legacy to, 520

Chamier, Frederick, 117–18, 121

Chamonix, 307

Champion (newspaper), 275, 295

Chantrey, Sir Francis, 35

Charlotte, Princess, 214, 274; death, 334

Charlotte, Queen of George III, 244, 251

Chaworth, Mary (*later* Musters): B's
    infatuation with, 32–4, 36, 154; B visits after
    marriage, 78; B's reunion with, 213–14;
    mental illness, 223, 304; letters from B,
    403; Moore interviews for B biography,
    542; dismisses B, 557

Chaworth, William, 17, 31

Cheltenham, 182–5, 187

Childe Harold's Pilgrimage (B): publication
    and success, x–xi, 139–40, 147, 157, 159–60,
    183, 199, 225, 398; and Newstead Abbey,
    18; prefigured by 'Stanzas', 64; on abbey
    masquerade, 87; on Rushton's travels with
    B, 91; on Cintra landscape, 93; Beckford
    references expunged, 94; on Sierra
    Morena, 95; on Constance Spencer Smith
    ('Calypso'), 99; on Mediterranean convoy,
    100; gestation and writing of, 105, 133; lines
    to Parnassus, 107; on Athens ruins, 111;
    composition, 117; praises Ottoman Turks,
    122; on Greek identity, 133; on Wingfield's
    death, 141; stanza on death of friend, 145;
    'Thyrza' elegies published as additions to,
    146; B revises proofs, 153; cost of first
    edition, 159–60; as autobiography, 160;
    writing of Canto III, 283, 287, 289;
    Waterloo stanzas, 287–8; on Voltaire and
    Gibbon, 298; on Rousseau, 299; Canto III
    sent to Murray, 306; Hobhouse reads
    Canto III, 308; writing of Canto IV, 329,
    345; Hobhouse takes MS of Canto IV to
    Murray, 335; on Lepanto, 496; influence
    on Matthew Arnold, 556

'Childish Recollections' (B), 32, 40, 42,
    63

Chillon, Château de, 300, 308, 554

Chopin, Frédéric, 551

Christian, Fletcher, 445

Churchill, Charles, 279

Cibber, Colley, 187

Cintra, Portugal, 93, 103

Clairmont, Charles Gaulis (Claire's brother),
    418

Clairmont, Claire (Clara Mary Jane):
    background and character, 271, 296–7;
    meets B, 271–2; affair with and child by B,
    272–3, 297–8, 324–5; at Sécheron
    (Geneva), 291, 295–6; and care and
    upbringing of Clara Allegra, 306, 343;
    leaves Switzerland with Shelleys, 306;
    makes fair copies of B's writings, 306; B
    refuses to communicate with directly, 324;
    reports on Allegra to B, 343; moves to Italy
    with Shelleys, 344–6; Byron refuses to see
    in Venice, 346; musical talents, 361;
    requests visit from Allegra, 390–1; alleged
    child with Shelley, 391–2, 401; protests at
    B's placing Allegra in convent, 393;
    accidental meeting with B near Empoli,
    406; plans to kidnap Allegra, 418; and
    Allegra's death, 419; leaves for Vienna, 419;
    illness in Vienna, 457; satiric account of
    autopsy on B, 519–20

Clare, John (poet), 535

Clare, John Fitzgibbon, 2nd Earl of: B's
    attachment to, xiii, 38, 206; at Harrow with
    B, 38–40; letter from B on life at
    Southwell, 48; slights B on departure from
    England, 88, 117; and Delawarr, 152; B
    meets in Italy, 403–4; correspondence with
    B, 403; visits B in Montenero, 423;
    recommends B and party to William Noel
    Hill's protection, 434; B writes to from
    Missolonghi, 512; and B's last words, 520;
    destroys letters from B, 542

Clarens, 308

Claridge, Sir John, 38, 143

Clark, William, 232

Clarke, Hewson, 69

Claughton, Thomas, 182, 193, 209, 223,
    234

Clermont, Mary Anne: Annabella dictates
    accusations against B to, 196; at B's
    wedding, 237; attends Annabella at
    Piccadilly Terrace, 260; and Annabella's
    initiating separation proceedings, 264–5;
    and Annabella's reaction to separation,
    268; B attacks in 'A Sketch from Private
    Life', 274; and potential court case, 284;
    B's dislike of, 356

Cobbett, William, 377

Cockburn, Mary *see* Duff, Mary

Cockerell, Charles Robert, 131, 134, 315

Cocks, F. Seymour, 572

Cocoa Tree Club, London, 219

Cogni, Margherita ('La Fornarina'), 332–3,
    338–40, 344

Colburn, Henry, 450

Coleridge, Samuel Taylor: B attacks in *English
    Bards*, 85; B attends lectures, 150; B's view
    of, 248–9; published by Murray, 249; B
    meets and sends money to, 270; describes

B, 270-1, 354; *Christabel*, 270, 292; 'Kubla Khan', 270; *Osorio* (*Remorse*; play), 248

Cologne, 288

Consalvi, Cardinal Ercole, 395

Constantinople, 119-23

Constitution, USS, 422

Contarini, Madame, 338

Conyers, Amelia d'Arcy, Baroness (B's father's first wife; *earlier* Marchioness of Carmarthen): as mother of Augusta, 5, 43

Coppet, Château de, Switzerland, 301

Cordova, Admiral Don José de, 96

Corgialegno, Messrs (bankers), 481

Corneille, Pierre, 396

'Cornelian, The' (B), 59

Corsair, The (B): writing, 204; publication and success, 215-16, 347; reprints 'Lines to a Lady Weeping', 222

Corunna, battle of (1809), 465

Costa, Paolo, 470

Courtenay, William, 3rd Viscount (*later* 9th Earl of Devon), 94

Cowell, John, 76, 78, 227, 501

Crauford, General Robert, 93

Cruikshank, George, 185, 275

Cruikshank, Isaac Robert: *The Lobby Loungers* (cartoon), 257

Cumberland, William: *The Wheel of Fortune*, 48-9

Cunningham, Revd John William, 420

Curioni, Alberico, 339

Curse of Minerva, The (B), 133, 156

Curzon, George, 50

Cuvier, Georges, 432

Daily News, 450

Dallas, Robert Charles: B recommends Southwell to, 54-5; on B's shyness in female company, 73; visits B, 81; on B's lack of domesticity, 82; on B's collection of portraits of Harrow boys, 88; and publication of B's *Childe Harold*, 139-40, 145, 159; and B's reaction to death of friends, 145; and B's vegetarian diet, 151; and B's speech in Lords, 157; and B's social life, 161; and B's effect on women, 163; sees Caroline Lamb as page, 171; B reads *The Giaour* to, 193; B passes on payment for *The Corsair* to, 215; compiles volume of correspondence with B, 541

Dal Pinto, Luigi: assassinated, 387-8

Dalrymple, General Sir Hew Whiteford, 94

Dalrymple-Hamilton, Sir Hew, and Jane, Lady, 300

Danhauser, Josef: *Liszt at the Piano* (painting), 550-1

Dante Alighieri: tomb at Ravenna, 376; Taaffe translates, 408; *Inferno*, 276, 313, 406

Dardanelles, Treaty of (1809), 120

'Darkness' (B), 283, 292, 304-5

Darwin, Erasmus, 293; *The Botanic Garden*, 70, 115

Darwin, Francis, 115

Dashwood, Sir Francis, 87

David, Jacques-Louis: *Death of Marat* (painting), 544

Davies, Scrope Berdmore: friendship with B, 65-7, 553; background and character, 67; encourages B's gambling, 71-2; and Caroline Cameron's attack on Hobhouse, 75; pledges £6,000 against B's debts, 89; B tells of near-duel over Constance Spencer Smith, 100; visits Thomas White in Newgate, 140-1; B visits in Cambridge, 145; B unable to pay off debts to, 193; B dedicates *Parisina* to, 267; accompanies B on departure for continent, 275, 278-9; visits B in Geneva, 305-7; preserves second MS copy of B's *Childe Harold*, 307; discusses B's *Don Juan*, 348; flees from England, 378

Davy, Sir Humphry, 376

Davy, Jane, Lady, 202, 540

Dearden, James, 481

De Bathe, Sir James Wynne, 40, 146

Decembrist rising (Russia, 1825), 550

Deformed Transformed, The (B), 435

Dejean, Jacques, 295, 346

Delacroix, Eugène, 552; *The Death of Sardanapalus*, 552; *The Execution of the Doge Marino Faliero*, 552; *Greece on the Ruins of Missolonghi*, 530, 545; *Self-Portrait in Travelling Costume*, 553; *The Two Foscari*, 552

Delawarr, George John Sackville, 5th Earl, 38, 40, 152, 542

Delladecima, Count Demetrius, 480, 483

De Morgan, Sophia, 252

Desart, John Otway Cuffe, 2nd Earl of, 218

'Destruction of Semnacherib, The' (B), 240-1

'Detached Thoughts' (B journal notebook), 424

Devonshire, Elizabeth, Duchess of: on B's celebrity, 159; and B's relations with Caroline Lamb, 169; on Annabella, 187; on Sir Ralph Milbanke, 231; owns Piccadilly Terrace house, 245, 296; and B's marriage breakdown, 273; B's debts to, 279; and B's

Devonshire, Elizabeth, Duchess of (*cont.*)
abandonment of Annabella, 280; son
Augustus writes to from Copenhagen, 378;
B asks to intervene over exile of Gambas,
395
Devonshire, Georgiana, Duchess of, 164, 179
Devonshire, William George Spencer
Cavendish, 6th Duke of (*earlier* Marquis
of Hartington; 'Hart'), 18, 65, 169, 542
Diana, Princess of Wales, 555
Diodati, Charles, 292
Diodati, Villa (Cologny, Switzerland): ghost
stories in, 116, 292–4, 305; B occupies, 292,
295, 297; rumours of excesses at, 295, 367;
visitors to, 305–6, 308
Diodorus Siculus: *Bibliothecae Historicae*,
396–7
Disraeli, Benjamin, 558–61
D'Israeli, Isaac, 340, 421, 559–60; *Curiosities
of Literature*, 559; *The Literary Character*,
421
Dollman (London hatter), 173–4
Don Juan (B): publication and reception, xiv,
160, 365–7, 382, 398; mermaid in, 13; on
Newstead Abbey, 19–20; on Drury, 32; on
power of language, 42; on sexual
behaviour, 51; St James's Hotel in, 71; John
Jackson, on, 72; mocks Brighton Pavilion,
74; on pregnant maidservant, 80; on
Marathon, 112; on Constantinople
entertainers, 120; social observations in,
166; cynicism in, 234; on married life in
London, 245; on female loyalty, 276; Italian
influence on, 314; poetic style, 334; B's
friends' reaction to, 348–9; Shelley
admires, 348, 399; writing, 348, 364, 432;
dedicated to Southey, 349; proof
inscriptions, 350–1; B's disagreement with
Murray over, 352, 412; on women's sexual
forwardness, 366, 413; B reads to Moore,
369; on Dante's tomb, 376; B splits Cantos
III and IV, 382; on assassination of Dal
Pinto, 388; payment for, 397–8; reference
to Allegra in, 421; Bishop of Clogher
mentioned in, 433; later cantos published
by John Hunt, 441; Murray condemns later
cantos, 441; English scenes in, 445–6;
remains unfinished, 446, 521; Pushkin's
Eugeny Onegin compared with, 549; W.H.
Auden reads, 570
Don Juan (boat) *see Ariel*
Don Leon (anonymous poem), 564
Dorchester, Charlotte, Lady (*née* Hobhouse),
328, 563, 566

D'Orsay *see* Orsay
Dorset, George John Frederick Sackville, 4th
Duke of, 29, 38
Dorville, Henry, 361
Douglas, Lord Alfred, 565
Dover, 279
Dowton, William, 256
Doyle, Colonel Francis Hastings, 265, 539
Doyle, Selina, 264, 268
'Dream, The' (B), 34, 283, 537
Drury Lane Theatre, 185, 249–50, 256–9
Drury, Anne Caroline (*née* Tayler), 87
Drury, Henry: tutors B at Harrow, 30, 32; on B
and Lord Clare, 39; helps Cowell gain
place at Eton, 76; friendship with B, 87,
89; marriage, 87; and B's favourable view
of Greeks and Turks, 110, 115; B sends
translation of Euripides lines to, 121; at
Allegra's burial service, 419–20
Drury, Revd Dr Joseph, 30–2, 42, 44
Drury, Mark, 42
Dryden, John, 85, 376; *Don Sebastian*, 239
Dudley and Ward, John William Ward, 1st Earl
of, 94
duelling, 72
Duff, Mary (*later* Cockburn), 10–11, 23, 27, 34,
557
Duff, Colonel Robert, 5
Duffie, Lieut.-Colonel John, 364, 469, 480,
490
Dulwich, 25–6
Dumas, Alexandre, 554
Dunn, Henry (Leghorn merchant), 408, 421,
461
Dupin, Charles, 544
Dupuy, Francesco, 424
Dupuy, Villa, Montenero *see* Rossa, Villa
Durville, Mrs (London bawd), 74, 125
Duvillard, Elise *see* Foggi, Elise

Eden, George, 187
Edgecombe, Richard, 361
Edinburgh Review: unfavourably reviews
Hours of Idleness, 63; reviews *The Corsair*,
216; Macaulay writes in, 290
Edleston, Ann, 144
Edleston, John: B's relations with, 58–62, 64,
79, 87, 105, 206, 225, 270, 501, 518, 543;
death, 144–5, 152, 504; in B elegies, 145–6
Egremont, George O'Brien Wyndham, 3rd
Earl of, 179
Egville, James d', 73
Ekenhead, William, 118
Eldon, John Scott, 1st Earl of, 82, 414

'Elegy on Newstead Abbey' (B), 18

Elgin, Thomas Bruce, 7th Earl of, 107, 112–13, 134

Eliot, T.S., 570

Ellice, Edward, 535

Elliston, Robert, 185

Elphinstone, Margaret Mercer: B writes to on Napoleon's paper, viii; B's friendship with, 46, 182; B gives Albanian costume to, 217; supports B against public unpopularity, 275–6

English Bards and Scotch Reviewers (B), 63, 69, 83–7, 107, 113, 149, 155, 161, 215, 248–9

Epidaurus, Constitution of (1822), 436

'Epistle to Augusta' (B), 290

'Epistle to a Friend' (B), 147

Este, Alphonso II, Marchese d', 326

Euripides: *Medea*, 41

Evans, R.H. (auction house), 277

Evian, 299

Examiner (journal), 197, 254, 426

Eywood (estate), Herefordshire, 188–92, 194, 196, 445

Falcieri, Giovanni Battista ('Tita'): joins B's household staff, 337; attachment to Bankes, 375; at shooting of Dal Pinto, 387; political activities, 394; arrested and freed, 395; at 'Pisa Affray', 416–17; rejoins B in Genoa, 437; accompanies B to Greek War of Independence, 459; visits Ithaca with B, 472; in Metaxata, 478; in Missolonghi, 493, 497; attends to B during fit, 502; and B's indulgence of Hatadjé Aga, 505; at B's final illness and death, 514, 517–18; travels to England with B's body, 530, 533; at B's funeral in Hucknall Torkard, 537; Disraeli engages, 559–60

Falconer, William: *The Shipwreck*, 112

Falier, Marin, 396

Falkland, Charles John Cary, 9th Viscount, 85

Falkland, Christine, Viscountess, 162

'Fallen One, The' (B), 540

Falmouth, 89–91

Fantasmagoriana (collection of ghost stories), 292

'Fare Thee Well' (B), 273–5, 280, 295; Pushkin quotes, 549; Heine translates, 547

Farmer, Captain Maurice St Leger, 448

Farquhar, James, 25

Fauvel, Louis-François-Sébastien, 111, 114

Fazakerley, John Nicholas, 131

Fellowes, Newton, 234, 446

Ferdinand, King of Naples, 374, 386

Ferney, 305

Ferrara, 325–6

Ferrara, Duke of *see* Niccolò III d'Este, Duke of Ferrara

Filetto, 381–2, 386

Finlay, George: on B's duality, 35; visits B on Cephalonia, 478; witnesses B's loan to Greeks, 482; on Stanhope's *Hellenica Chronica*, 495; visits B in Missolonghi, 510–12; on B's future, 521; on B's death, 525; Blunt meets, 562

Fitzgerald, Lord Edward, 28

Flaubert, Gustave, 554

Fletcher, Ann (*née* Rood; 'Roody'): marriage to William, 255, 284; at Kirkby Mallory with Annabella, 268; bailiffs seize possessions, 279; refuses to testify to B's ill-treatment of Annabella, 284; remains in London during husband's absence abroad, 284–5

Fletcher, George, 153

Fletcher, Sally, 91

Fletcher, William: as B's personal servant, 77; accompanies B on first travels (1809), 91, 105–6, 111, 113, 115, 126, 128; B gives notice to, 122; returns to England, 133–4; Caroline Lamb conspires with, 171; and Caroline Lamb's attempted elopement with B, 174; suggests partner for B, 187; on B's facial scar, 190; and B's overdrinking at Newstead, 210; with B in Albany, 218–20; marriage to Ann Rood, 255, 286; and B's potential violence to Annabella, 260; on B's leaving house doors open, 265; attempts to water down B's laudanum, 266; with B on 1816 travels, 278, 284, 289; possessions seized by bailiffs, 279; at Villa Diodati, 308; at Palazzo Mocenigo in Venice, 337; keeps mistress (Marietta) in Venice, 337–8; intimidated by La Fornarina, 338; on B's parsimony, 347; on managing B, 356; attends B during bout of fever, 371; affected by George III's death, 377; political sympathies, 394; improved appearance, 399; fears ghosts in Pisa, 406; criticises Medwin's journal, 410; and Papi's violence, 424; accompanies B to Greek War of Independence, 459, 485, 487, 502; attends B during rage on Cephalonia, 473; in Metaxata, 478; in Missolonghi, 493; deceived by cross-dressed Suliote, 506; and B's final illness, 514, 517–18, 521; B promises legacy to, 520; returns to England with B's body, 530, 533;

Fletcher, William (*cont.*)
    writes to Augusta Leigh on B's death,
    531–2; at B's funeral, 537; Moore
    interviews for B biography, 542; fails with
    macaroni factory in London, 560
Fletcher, William (son), 153
Florence: B visits, 326, 405
Florida (ship), 528–30, 532–3
Foggi, Elise (*earlier* Duvillard): attends Claire
    Clairmont, 324; moves to Italy with
    Shelleys, 344; takes care of Allegra, 360;
    replaced as Allegra's nurse, 381; tells
    Hoppners of Shelley's alleged child with
    Claire Clairmont, 391–2, 401
Foggi, Paolo, 401
Forbes, Lady Adelaide, 225
Ford, John: *'Tis Pity She's a Whore*, 212
'Fornarina, La' *see* Cogni, Margherita
Forrester, James, 492–3
Foscarini, Villa, La Mira, 330–4, 363–4, 368–9
Foscolo, Ugo, 301, 319, 353
Foster, Augustus, 159, 273, 378
Foster, John, 131, 134
Fournier, Louis-Edouard: *The Cremation of
    Shelley's Body* (painting), 430
Fox, Charles James, 83, 179
Fox, Henry: as Teresa Guiccioli's lover, 354,
    560; visits B in Genoa, 448; on
    Missolonghi, 492
'Fragment, A' (B), 18
France: B's reputation in, 544–7
'Francesca of Rimini' (B), 380
Francis, Eliza, 233
Freeman, Samuel, 427
French Revolution (1789), 6
Frere, John Hookham ('Whistlecraft'):
    discusses B's *Don Juan*, 348; *Prospectus
    and Specimen of an Intended National
    Work*, 333
Friedel, Adam, 549
Friese (German servant), 91, 97
Fugitive Pieces (B), 27, 49–51, 62
Fuseli, Henry, 107, 305

Galignani, Giovanni (publisher), 413
Galliani, Angelica (Count Guiccioli's previous
    wife), 355
Galt, John: with B on travels, 97–9, 116, 122; on
    B's near-purchase of Teresa Macri in
    Athens, 114; on B's mood changes, 116;
    and B's hunger for celebrity, 199; *Annals of
    the Parish*, 97; *Life of Lord Byron*, 97
Galvani, Alfonso, 69
Gamba family, 382, 407, 454

Gamba, Count Pietro (Teresa Guiccioli's
    brother): wariness of B's relations with
    Teresa, 364; B meets, 382; political
    activism, 385; arrested and exiled, 395;
    and B's plan to settle in Pisa, 401; in 'Pisa
    Affray', 416–17, 424; banished from
    Tuscany, 424–5; wounded by Papi, 424–5;
    in Genoa with B, 434, 437; encourages
    B's involvement in Greek independence
    movement, 436; meets returning
    Germans from Greek War of
    Independence, 454; informs Teresa
    Guiccioli of B's decision to leave for
    Greece, 455; B gives helmet to, 456;
    accompanies B to Greece, 458, 460–1;
    B fences with, 461; writes to Teresa on
    voyage to Greece, 461; at religious
    discussions on Cephalonia, 469; on
    Cephalonia with B, 470, 478–9; visits
    Ithaca with B, 471; memoirs, 478; sails to
    Missolonghi, 484–5, 487; captured by
    Turks and released, 487–8; and B's arrival
    at Missolonghi, 490; on B's life at
    Missolonghi, 493; co-edits *Telegrafo
    Greca*, 495; as B's aide in Greece, 497–8,
    502, 512; denies B's sharing bed with
    Chalandritsanos, 502, 566–7; and B's fit
    in Missolonghi, 503; on B at Missolonghi,
    508, 511; diary, 508–9; and B's final illness
    and death, 513–18, 520, 531; laments B's
    death, 525; at B's funeral, 527; and return
    of B's body to England, 528, 530; travels
    to England after B's death, 530; visits B's
    grave at Hucknall, 537; publishes
    reminiscences, 541
Gamba (Ghiselli), Count Ruggero (Teresa
    Guiccioli's father): disapproves of B's
    relations with Teresa, 364, 371; petitions
    Pope for separation for Teresa, 381;
    relations with B, 381–2; revolutionary
    political activities, 384, 394; exiled, 395;
    and B's plan to settle in Pisa, 401; banished
    from Tuscany, 424–5; in Genoa with B,
    434, 437; return to Ravenna, 455; Teresa
    accompanies to Ravenna on B's departure
    for Greece, 458; confined in Ferrara, 470
Gardner, Daniel: *Witches Round the Cauldron*
    (painting), 179
Garrick, David: *The Country Girl*, 196
Gautier, Théophile, 554
Geneva, 290, 294–5, 298, 300–1
Genoa: B in, 434, 435–7, 442, 445, 448–51; B
    leaves for expedition to Greek War of
    Independence, 458

George III, King: madness, 200; death, 377; defamed in B's *Vision of Judgement*, 402, 440; Southey's eulogy to, 402

George IV, King (*earlier* Prince of Wales and Prince Regent): in Brighton, 74; B meets, 161; Lady Melbourne's affair with, 179; and wife Caroline, 192; Leigh Hunt jailed for libelling, 197; celebrates Wellington's Peninsular victories, 200; rift with George Leigh, 201; B suggests parallel with Niccolò II of Ferrara, 260; coronation, 377–8; B disparages, 393; B writes satirical poems on, 402, 441

George V, King, 328

Georgiou, Eustathius, 126–8, 501

Germany, 288–9; supporters from in Greek War of Independence, 451, 497–8, 511

Ghigi, Pellegrino, 418

Ghinaglia, Giovanni, 375

Giaour, The: and drowning of young woman, 132, 183; writing of, 183–4, 193; pronunciation of title, 199; publication and success, 199; Lady Frances Webster reads, 211; structure, 212; Mickiewicz translates into Polish, 548

Gibbon, Edward, 298, 300

Gibraltar, 96–7

Gifford, William: praises B's *English Bards*, 86; works at Murray's, 149, 248; B explains *The Bride of Abydos* to, 212; on B's satiric poem against Mary Anne Clermont, 274; reads and praises Canto III of *Childe Harold*, 306; on B's memoirs, 540

Gight, Castle of, 5, 7, 18

Gight, Margaret Duff Gordon, Lady, 9

Gill, Mr (of Nottingham), 22

Gillray, James, 85

Giraud, Nicolas (Nicolo), 128–9, 135, 501, 543

Gisborne, Maria, 407

Glenbervie, Sylvester Douglas, 1st Baron, 296

Glennie, Dr (schoolmaster), 25–6, 31, 542

Godfrey, Mary, 273

Godwin, Fanny Imlay: suicide, 324

Godwin, Mary Jane (*formerly* Clairmont; Claire's mother), 271–2

Godwin, William: B attempts to send money to, 271; marriage to Mary Jane, 271

Goethe, Johann Wolfgang von: on B's separation from Annabella, 280; in Alps, 310; and B's *Manfred*, 312; B dedicates *Werner* to, 423; champions B, 547; *Faust*, 311; *Italian Journey*, 329

Goetz, Count (Governor of Venice), 318

Goldoni, Carlo: *La Vedova Scaltra*, 330

Gordon, Lord Alexander, 62

Gordon, Alexander Gordon, 4th Duke of, 5

Gordon, Charles David, 44

Gordon, Sir Cosmo: *The Life and Genius of Lord Byron*, 541

Gordon, Jane, Duchess of, 62

Gordon, Pryse Lockhart, 286, 314

Gordon, Mrs Pryse Lockhart, 287

Gordon, Thomas, 466

Granville, Granville Leveson-Gower, 1st Earl, 176

Granville, Harriet, Countess (*née* Cavendish), 176, 178

Gray, Agnes, 6, 14

Gray, May, 14, 18, 22–3, 26, 366

Gray, Thomas, 301

Great Marlow, Buckinghamshire, 325, 343

Greece: B first visits (1809), 100–1, 106–8, 109–12; sculptures removed to Britain, 107, 112–13; B's concern for liberty of, 112, 125, 131–2, 444, 451–3, 491; B revisits (1810–11), 125–9, 132–3; English support for, 451–2; B's understanding of character of, 477; B's plans for, 494–5; effect of B's death on, 530; French sympathy and support for, 545

Greek War of Independence: begins (1821), 434; B's commitment to, 435–6, 453–4; foreign supporters, 451, 453–4, 497–8, 508, 511; conduct of, 466–7, 480–1, 496, 530; financing of, 481–2, 496–7, 509, 517, 528–9; Great Powers intervene in, 545

Greville, Charles Fulke, 40

Grey de Ruthyn, Henry Edward Gould, 19th Baron, 32, 36–7, 52, 61, 76

Grimaldi, Joseph, 184

Gritti, Count, 336

Guevara, Che, 544

Guiccioli, Count Alessandro: and B's affair with Teresa, 353–5, 357–60; and care of Allegra, 361; makes demands on B, 361–2; confronts B over Teresa, 371; and B's move into Palazzo, 379; complex character and relationships, 379; finds evidence of Teresa's adultery, 380; petitions for separation, 381; remarries Teresa after B's death, 381; threatens to have Teresa incarcerated in convent, 387; and assassination attempt on B, 388; has Teresa's allowance suspended, 425–6; influences Gamba's return to Ravenna, 455

Guiccioli, Contessa Teresa (*née* Gamba): on B's cold temperament, 23; keeps letters from B's female admirers, 163; intelligence,

Guiccioli, Contessa Teresa (*cont.*)
186; B meets, 353–4; appearance, 354;
Henry Fox's affair with, 354, 560; love
affair with B, 354–60, 362–3, 370–1, 375,
378–80, 422, 433, 490; character and
behaviour, 356; illnesses, 357–8, 371;
suffers piles, 364; Moore meets, 368;
opposes B's return to London, 377;
husband continues relations with, 379, 381;
reconciled with husband after B's death,
381; separation order against, 381; under
threat from political authorities, 387;
attitude to Allegra, 390; B commissions
portrait of, 393; joins father and brother in
exile in France, 395; influence on B's
Sardanapalus, 397; meets and describes
Shelley, 401–2; advises B to leave Allegra in
convent, 403; Mary Shelley describes, 407;
friendship with Mary Shelley in Pisa, 408;
on John Taaffe, 408; amateur theatricals,
409; Bartolini bust of, 412; and *Don Juan*,
412–13, 421; depicted in B's *Werner*, 413;
and 'Pisa Affray', 416–17; tells B of
Allegra's death, 418; present at West's
painting of B, 423; allowance from
husband suspended, 426; Hobhouse
meets, 433; and B's illness on journey to
Genoa, 437; and B's relationship with
Lady Hardy, 443; and B's weight loss, 444;
delays B's departure for Greece, 454–5;
reaction to B's departure for Greece,
457–8; B writes to on voyage to Greece,
460–1; leaves Genoa on B's departure, 460;
letters from B on Cephalonia, 470, 477,
484; letters from B at Missolonghi, 494,
506; and B's last words, 520; learns of B's
death, 530; sends account of B to Moore,
542; Lamartine meets, 547

Haller von Hallerstein, Baron Karl, 131, 134
Halnaby Hall, Croft, near Darlington, 237–9,
256
Hampden Club, 189, 197
Hancock, Charles, 481, 485, 489, 502, 542
Hanson, Hargreaves (John's son), 24, 141
Hanson, Captain James, 3
Hanson, John: wife recommends midwife for
B's birth, 3; as B's guardian, 15–16, 26;
meets B at Newstead, 15; and Newstead
estate, 17; describes B as boy, 21; and May
Gray's abuse of B, 22–3; encourages B's
talents, 24; B's fondness for, 25; and B's
absence from Harrow, 32; and B at
Newstead, 33; B complains of excessive

clothing to, 53; and B at Cambridge, 56–7;
B sends away to Mansfield, 76; manages
B's affairs, 79–81; and sale of Newstead, 82,
133, 223, 234; and B's travel plans, 86;
letters from B on travels, 93, 96, 116; and
B's financial difficulties, 117, 259; and sale
of B's Norfolk and Lancashire properties,
133, 143; B visits before travelling to
Seaham, 229; and B's marriage to
Annabella, 230–1, 235, 237; daughter's
marriage to Earl of Portsmouth, 234;
Annabella confesses fears of B's insanity
to, 262; witnesses B's deed of separation,
278; visits Annabella after B's departure
abroad, 280; and care and upbringing of
B's daughter Ada, 324; visits B in Venice,
346–7; B requests new seal on death of
mother-in-law, 411; as B's executor, 531;
views B's body, 534; in B's funeral
procession, 535, 537
Hanson, Mrs John, 3, 141, 234
Hanson, Laura (John's daughter), 447
Hanson, Mary Ann (*sometime* Countess of
Portsmouth; John's daughter): marriage to
Earl, 234, 446–7; marriage annulled, 447–8
Hanson, Newton (John's son): on B as boy,
24; and sister's marriage to Earl of
Portsmouth, 234; visits B in Venice, 336,
346; visits Villa Lanfranchi, Pisa, 406; on
sister Mary Ann's destitution, 448
Harcourt, General William, 3rd Earl, 43
Hardstaff, Mrs (of Newstead Abbey), 17
Hardwicke, Elizabeth, Countess of, 256
Hardy, Anne Louise Emily, Lady (*née*
Berkeley): friendship with B, 46; visits B in
Genoa, 442–3; on Lady Blessington, 448;
proposes Teresa Guiccioli accompany B to
Greece, 454
Hardy, Sir Thomas Masterman, 442
Harley, Lady Charlotte, 195–6
Harley, Lady Jane, 195, 250
Harlow, George Henry, 332, 431, 550
Harness, Revd William: at Harrow with B, 38;
on B's mother, 52–3; and B's collection of
portraits of Harrow boys, 88; visits
Newstead, 152, 154; and B's reforming
homosexual practices, 261
Harrow School: B attends, 29–32, 37–44; sex
life at, 39; B revisits, 87–8, 173
Hart, Thomas, 142
Hartington, Marquis of ('Hart') *see*
Devonshire, 6th Duke of
Harvey, Isabella ('Zorina Stanley'), 444
Hastings, Frank Abney, 480–1

Hastings, Sussex, 222–3

Hatadjé *see* Aga, Hatadjé

Hatchard's (booksellers), 85

Haussonville, Louise de Broglie, Comtesse d', 539

Hay, Captain John, 409, 416

Haydon, Benjamin Robert, 431

Hazlitt, William, 426

Head, Guy: *Nelson Receiving the French Colours at the Battle of the Nile* (painting), 88

Heathcote, Katherine Sophie, Lady, 202–3

Heaven and Earth, A Mystery (B), 402, 439, 456

Heber, Reginald, Bishop of Calcutta, 415

Hebrew Melodies (B), 239–40

Heine, Heinrich, 547–8

Hellenica Chronica, 495, 502, 526

Hellespont: B swims, 118, 212

Hentsch, Charles, 481

Hepburn, Lieutenant (of Vere Street affair), 140

Hercules (brig), 456, 458, 460–4, 467–8, 474–5

Hero and Leander, 119

Herschel, Sir William, 69

Hervey, Elizabeth, 301

Heywood, Samuel, 265

Hill, William Noel, 98, 434, 437, 448

Hints from Horace (B), 133

Hoar, William, 236

Hobhouse, Sir Benjamin, 67, 73, 253

Hobhouse, John Cam (*later* Baron Broughton de Gyfford): on B's childhood loves, 10, 34; and B's abuse as boy by May Gray, 23; on B's foot brace, 26; on B's homosexual relationships, 40, 78; scepticism over B's reading, 41; on B's sexual initiation with women at Southwell, 49; visits Augusta after B's death, 53; on B at Cambridge, 56, 68; and B's reaction to hostile review of *Hours of Idleness*, 63; friendship with B at Cambridge, 65–6; background, 67; discourages B's gambling, 71–2; and B's attachment to Caroline Cameron, 75; visits Newstead, 78–9, 87, 172; admires Napoleon, 81; founds Whig Club in Cambridge, 83; manuscript diary, 87, 105; sexual restraint, 89–90; travels with B, 89–96, 98, 100–8, 109–11, 114, 116, 119–21, 123–4, 126; literary endeavours, 92; on B's swimming of Tagus, 94; on B's quickly falling in love, 96; in Albania, 101–3, 105; advises B to burn early reminiscences, 105; approves of removal of Greek sculptures to

Britain, 113; illness in Turkey, 116; and dispute over site of Troy, 118; tooth extracted in Constantinople, 119; returns to England, 123; letters from B in Greece, 128, 130–1; on Lady Hester Stanhope, 130; B brings back Greek marbles for, 134; militia career, 140; B meets on return to England, 140; urges discretion on B for homosexual exploits, 140–1, 146; B informs of mother's death, 142; and Matthews' death, 143; and publication of *Childe Harold*, 148; resents Moore, 151; and B's Newstead servants, 152; on qualities of *Childe Harold*, 160; Lady Bessborough confides in, 173; and B's difficulties with Lady Caroline Lamb, 174–5; and B's correspondence with Lady Melbourne, 180; on Annabella's rejection of B's proposal, 188; hostility to Lady Oxford, 189; on Lady Jane Harley, 195; on B's relations with Augusta, 204; annotates Moore's *Life*, 205; European travels (1813), 206; wears Albanian dress at Wellington's celebration masquerade, 217; on B's engagement to Annabella, 227, 229; votes for Clark at Cambridge, 232; as best man at B's wedding, 235–7; inspects Piccadilly Terrace house for B, 245; and B's marriage relations, 246, 252–3, 266; at bachelor dinner with B, 255; Susan Boyce appeals to, 258; knows of B's early homosexual relationships, 261, 267; and B's shock at Annabella's separation proceedings, 265; and B's marriage breakdown, 266–7; B dedicates *The Siege of Corinth* to, 267; defends B against sexual charges, 268; and reasons for B's marriage breakdown, 268; denies need for B to leave country, 275; and B's unpopularity in England, 276; buys books from B's library sale, 277; accompanies B on 1816 departure, 278–9; witnesses B's deed of separation, 278; and Annabella at B's departure abroad, 280; letters from B on continental travels (1816), 284, 290; hears Polidori read tragedy, 285; visits and travels with B in Switzerland, 305–11; on Polidori, 308; leaves for Milan with B, 312; co-translates Pellico's *Francesca da Rimini* with B, 313; and homosexuality in Italy, 314; in Italy with B, 314–16; on Countess Albrizzi, 319; on B's religious yearnings, 321; leaves Venice, 325, 341; commissions Thorwaldsen bust of B, 327–8; travels to Naples, 328; B dedicates

Hobhouse, John Cam (*later* Baron Broughton de Gyfford) (*cont.*)
Canto IV of *Childe Harold* to, 329; plans visit to USA with B, 330–1; visits B at Villa Foscarini, 330, 332; and Marianna Segati, 333; on death of Princess Charlotte, 334; takes MS of Canto IV of B's *Childe Harold* from Italy to Murray, 335; and care and upbringing of Allegra, 343; view of B's *Don Juan*, 348–9, 383; and B's relations with Teresa Guiccioli, 355, 364; on B's plan to emigrate to Venezuela, 365; and B's relations with Moore, 369; on George III's death, 377; imprisoned, 377–8, 433; political reformism, 377; deteriorating relations with B, 378, 433–4; and B's view of Carbonari ceremonial, 385; and Murray's agreement to publish B's memoirs, 388–9; B confesses republican views to, 394; keeps collection of B's letters, 402; B asks to send draft of *Werner*, 413; on blasphemy dangers of *Cain*, 414, 433; as MP for Westminster, 433; in Pisa, 433–4; counsels caution on B's satire on Castlereagh's suicide, 434; on Laura Hanson, 447; membership of London Greek Committee, 452–4, 493; denounces Karvellas' reports, 453; and B's departure for Greek War of Independence, 460; letters from B on Greek expedition, 467, 470; Stanhope confides in about B's last period in Greece, 501, 505; and B's relations with Chalandritsanos, 502; excuses B's 'Love and Death', 504; destroys B's late poem, 505; believes B destined to be prospective King of Greece, 510; and theft from B's deathbed, 518; B mentions in last days, 520; political appointments and peerage, 521; and question of B's remains, 528; and Pietro Gamba's not accompanying B's body to England, 530; as B's executor, 531, 534, 566; learns of B's death, 531, 538; meets B's body on return to England, 533–4; on public viewing of B's body, 535; with B's funeral procession, 536–7; concern for B's posthumous reputation, 538–9; and Pietro Gamba at B's grave, 538; at burning of B's memoirs, 539; protests at Moore's proposed biography of B, 541; *A Journey through Albania*, 92; *Miscellany* (*Imitations and Translations*), 87

Hoche, General Louis-Lazare, 289

Hodgson, Revd Francis: marriage, 87; B sends verses to, 91; letters from B on travels, 92, 94, 127; writes to B on travels, 117; religious beliefs, 143, 153; and B's reaction to death of friends, 145; and Webster's offer of sale of boy, 146; B sends poem to, 147; visits Newstead, 152; B complains to of servants' infidelity, 154; and B's speech in Lords, 157; B lends money to, 193; in Hastings, 222; Augusta writes to on B's marriage forebodings, 225; B informs of birth of child, 250; writes to B in Venice, 324; and Augusta's reservations over B's *Don Juan*, 349; attends B's funeral, 537; suspicion of Moore's biography of B, 542

Hogg, James ('the Ettrick Shepherd'), 248

Hohenhausen, Elise von, 547

Holdernesse, Mary, Countess of (Augusta's grandmother), 43

Holland, Elizabeth, Lady (*née* Vassall), 155, 179, 182, 318, 540–1

Holland, Henry (architect), 164, 218

Holland, Henry Richard Vassall Fox, 3rd Baron: entertains at Holland House, 154, 161; influences B's political ideas, 155–6; on B's speech in Lords, 157; and B's social success, 161; in Cheltenham, 182; asks B to write address for opening of Drury Lane Theatre, 185; and B's debts, 200; and B's impending visit to Paris, 254; on reasons for B's marriage breakdown, 268; advises B against court appearance over separation charges, 269; B recommends Greek deputies to, 482; reads B's memoirs, 540; Moore interviews, 541

Holland House, London, 150, 154–5, 161

Holmes, James, 211, 393, 423

Holmes, Miss (of Southwell), 49

homosexuality: B's predilection for, xii–xiii, 23–4, 31, 37, 40, 58–9, 61, 76, 78, 87, 90, 126, 140–1, 146, 171, 205–6, 238, 261, 267, 270, 340–1, 501, 504–5, 538, 564, 566; public attitudes to, 37, 61, 140, 567–9; at Cambridge, 58, 61; in Greece and Turkey, 86, 102, 116; in Italy, 314

Hook, Theodore, 65

Hope, Henry Philip, 107

Hope, Thomas, 307

Hoppner, Isabelle (Richard's wife): takes care of Allegra, 344–5, 360; Mary Shelley writes to protesting about alleged Percy/Claire baby, 401

Hoppner, John, 341

Hoppner, Richard Belgrave: B's friendship with in Venice, 341–2; Allegra stays with in Venice, 344, 360; B rents house from, 346; B writes to about Teresa Guiccioli, 359, 371, 375; B writes to about Allegra, 391; and scandal of Shelley's alleged child with Claire Clairmont, 391–2, 400–1; letter from B on emotional instability, 444

Hopwood, Robert and Cecilia, 144

Horton, Wilmot, 539

Houldsworth, A.E., 574

Hours of Idleness (B), 18, 42, 50, 62–4, 68, 85, 284

Houson, Anne, 49, 51

Howard, Frederick, 288

Howard, Henry Charles (*later* 13th Duke of Norfolk), 226

Hucknall Torkard, Nottinghamshire, 16, 460, 534–5, 537; Byron family vault reopened (1938), 571–4

Hugo, Victor, 546

Humboldt, Alexander, Baron von, 372

Hunt, Sir Aubrey de Vere, 512

Hunt, Henry ('Orator'), 365, 377

Hunt, James Henry Leigh: on B's lame leg, 4; and B's displaying coat of arms, 14; and B's view of House of Lords, 157; B visits in prison, 197; on B's apparent contentment in marriage, 250; overhears Coleridge's reading of 'Kubla Khan', 270; view of Teresa Guiccioli, 354; on B's spreading scandal, 400; invited to join B and Shelley in Pisa, 401; arrives at Montenero, 424–6; and B's fatness, 425, 443; publishes *The Liberal* magazine, 426, 432–3; and death and cremation of Shelley, 428–30; children, 431; deteriorating relations with B, 431; follows B to Genoa with family, 434, 438; B offers to pay fare back to England, 456; and B's helmets, 456; tells Mary Shelley of B's dislike, 457; *Lord Byron and Some of his Contemporaries*, 427, 541

Hunt, John: publishes B's later works, xiv, 440–1, 444, 456; publishes *The Liberal* with brother Leigh, 426; offends Murray, 439–40

Hunt, Leigh *see* Hunt, James Henry Leigh

Hunt, Marianne: silhouette of B, 427; B's antipathy to, 431

Hunt, Vincent Leigh (son of JHLH): born, 438

Hunter, John, 3, 24

Huntly, George Gordon, 2nd Earl of, 7

Hussein Bey, 102

Hutchinson, Dr Benjamin, 53

Hydra (ship), 134

Hypsilantes, Prince Alexander, 467

Ibrahim Pasha, 102

Ignatios, Bishop of Arta, 461, 517

Imlay, Gilbert, 324

Ionian Islands *see* Cephalonia

Ireland: Fitzgerald's rebellion in, 28

Ireland, John, Dean of Westminster, 534

Irish Avatar or Messiah, The (B), 402

Irving, Washington, 238

Isherwood, Christopher, 570

Island, The (B), 445, 561

Italy: B's reaction to, 313–14, 329; in *Childe Harold*, 329; revolutionary liberation movement in, 374, 384–6, 394–5; *see also* Genoa; Pisa; Ravenna; Rome; Venice

Ithaca, 101, 470–3

Jackson, John ('Gentleman'; 'Bruiser'), 72, 323, 364, 553

James, Henry, 318

Janina, Albania, 101–2, 472

Jeffrey, Francis: B attacks, 63; abortive duel with Moore, 150; praises *The Giaour*, 199; reviews *The Corsair*, 216

Jenkins, Captain Thomas, 448

Jersey, Sarah, Countess of, 160, 190, 275, 540, 541

Jocelyn, Percy, Bishop of Clogher, 433

John Bull (newspaper), 534

Johnson, Miss (London hostess), 161

Jones, Revd Thomas, 57

Junot, General Jean-Andoche, 94

Kanellopoulos, Panayiotis: *History of the European Spirit*, 545

Kapsalis, Apostolis, 514

Kapsalis, Petros, 527

Karaïskakis, Georgios, 511

Karpenisi, Greece, 475

Karteria (steamboat; earlier *Perseverance*), 481

Karvellas, Nikolaos, 453

Kay, William: portrait of B as boy, 8

Kean, Edmund, 205, 219, 229, 249, 256, 409

Keats, John, 250, 366, 426

Kemble, John, 152, 184

Kennedy, James, 469–70, 478–9, 506; *Conversations on Religion with Lord Byron*, 469

Kennedy, Mrs James, 506

Kennedy, John F., 555
Kennedy, Captain John Pitt, 468
Keppel, Maria, 257–8
Khios, massacre of (1822), 451
Kidd, Captain (of *Princess Elizabeth*), 91
King, Rufus, 30
Kinnaird, Charles, 8th Baron, 540
Kinnaird, Douglas: on B's appearance, 35;
    Hobhouse confides in, 204; persuades B to
    provide words for Nathan's holy songs,
    239; recruits B to Sub-Committee of
    Management at Drury Lane, 249; plays in
    pantomime, 250; at bachelor dinner with
    B, 255; lives with Maria Keppel, 257–8;
    and B's relations with Susan Boyce, 258;
    and B's lack of interest in Claire
    Clairmont, 272; and B's departure for
    continent, 278; and B's child with Claire
    Clairmont, 297; and B's acknowledgment
    of daughter Ada, 325; B urges to sell
    Rochdale property, 335; B recommends
    Taruscelli to, 340; discusses B's *Don Juan*,
    348, 383; B defends *Don Juan* to, 366; B
    instructs to persuade Annabella to
    reinvest, 386; and B's involvement in
    Italian revolutionary politics, 387; and
    Murray's agreement to publish B's
    memoirs, 388; B complains to of Murray's
    inadequate payments, 398; letter from B in
    Pisa, 407; B reports to on visit to USS
    Constitution, 422; B reports on writing of
    Don Juan to, 432; and B's wish to leave
    worthy inheritance, 435; carries part of
    Don Juan to Murray, 438; and B's breach
    with Murray, 439; and publication of later
    cantos of *Don Juan*, 441; B reports on
    Webster to, 442; and B's economising, 444;
    supports London Greek Committee, 452;
    sends money to B for Greek expedition,
    455; and B's loan to Greeks, 482; and B's
    decision to take active part in Greek war,
    484; and B's disenchantment with
    Suliotes, 499; B mentions in last days, 520;
    informs Hobhouse of B's death, 531;
    mourns B's death, 532; views B's body,
    534; in B's funeral procession, 535; offers
    to purchase B's memoirs from Murray,
    538; reads B's memoirs, 540; favours
    Moore writing B's biography, 541
Kinsham Court, Herefordshire, 190–1
Kiprensky, Orest, 549
Kirkby Mallory, 263–5, 278
Knatchbull, Sir Edward, 534
Knebworth House, Hertfordshire, 561–2

Knight, Henry Gally, 131, 255
Knox, Captain Wright, 471–2, 477
Knox, Mrs Wright (*née* Gordon), 472
Koloktronis, Theodoros, 467, 473, 476–7, 499

Lamartine, Alphonse de, 546–7; 'L'Hommage
    à Lord Byron', 553; *Vie de Byron*, 547
Lamb, Augustus (Caroline's son), 165, 168–9
Lamb, Caroline (Mrs George Lamb; 'Caro
    George'): name, 169; and negotiations over
    Annabella's settlement, 269; snubs B, 275
Lamb, Lady Caroline (*née* Ponsonby; 'Caro
    William'): on B's appeal, x–xi; misuses B's
    motto, 14; B confesses homosexual
    practices to, 40, 193, 196, 221; B's erotic
    games with, 75; spreads rumours of B's
    homosexuality, 132, 267; attachment to and
    affair with B, 163–7, 169–76; family and
    background, 164–5; marriage to William,
    164, 168; character and behaviour, 167, 356;
    devotion to son Augustus, 169; sexual
    propensities, 170–2; plans elopement with
    B, 174; disappears, 176–7; B's parting letter
    to, 177–8; leaves for Bessborough House,
    Ireland, 178–9; and B's involvement with
    Lady Melbourne, 179–81; intelligence, 186;
    letters to B from Ireland, 186, 191; burns B
    in effigy, 191–2; health reaction to B's letter
    of rebuffal, 191; persecutes and pesters B,
    193–4, 200, 221; B gives rings to Lady
    Charlotte Harley, 195; interview with B in
    London, 196; and B's relations with
    Augusta, 202, 221; supposed attempted
    suicide, 202–3; B requests return of
    miniature from, 211; and B's supposed
    fathering child on Augusta, 215;
    misbehaviour at Wellington's celebration
    masquerade, 217; Phillips portrait of, 217;
    parting from B, 221; criticises Murray for
    joint publication of *Lara* and Rogers's
    Jacqueline, 224; reaction to B's marriage,
    227–8; disparages Annabella, 231; final visit
    to B and Annabella at Piccadilly Terrace,
    246; in Paris, 254; James Wedderburn
    Webster pursues, 255; supports Annabella
    in separation negotiations with B, 269–70;
    tells Annabella of B's incest and
    homosexuality, 270; opposes publication of
    B's satiric poems, 275; Murray shows B's
    'To Augusta' poem to, 277–8; comments
    on B's *Don Juan*, 349; B attempts to
    recover letters from, 402; encounters B's
    hearse, 536; writes to Murray about letters,
    536; reads B's memoirs, 540; Bulwer-

Lytton's affair with, 560–1; *Glenarvon*, 191, 294, 301–2, 306, 536, 561

Lamb, Charles, 426

Lamb, William *see* Melbourne, 2nd Viscount

Lambros (Suliote officer), 514

Lament of Tasso, The (B), 326

Lanchester, Isabella, 163

Lane, Nathaniel, 572–4

Lanfranchi, Villa, Pisa, 406, 409–10, 416, 425–6, 431, 433

Laon, battle of (1814), 217

Lara (B), 219, 224

Las Cases, Emmanuel, Comte de, 461

'Last Words on Greece' (B), 504

Laurie, Dr Maurice, 26, 31

Lavalette, Antoine-Marie, Count, 130

Lavater, Johann Kaspar, 69

Lavender, 'Dr' (of Nottingham), 22, 26

Lawrence, Sir Thomas, 35

Leacroft, Julia, 49, 51

Leake, William, 101–2, 104–5

Leander (swimmer), 119

Lee, Harriet: *The German's Tale*, 251–2

Lees-Milne, James, 569

Leigh, Augusta Charlotte (Augusta Mary's daughter), 204

Leigh, Augusta Mary (*née* Byron; B's half-sister): on B's lame leg, 4; B's incestuous relations with, 7, 204–7, 213, 242, 252, 270, 563–4; marriage to George Leigh, 7, 77, 201, 235; B meets, 43; letter from B on relations with mother, 52; B writes to from Cambridge, 57; B requests help in raising loan, 59–60; and B's depressions, 61; B admits ambitions to, 81; with B in London (1813), 200–2; character and appearance, 203–4; B visits at Six Mile Bottom, 204–6, 213, 222, 229, 232, 235, 242–4, 251, 255; presumed knowledge of B's homosexual practices, 205–6; in B's will, 211, 255; depicted in *The Bride of Abydos*, 212; sends lock of hair to B, 212–13; putative daughter by B, 213; visits Newstead, 213; in Hastings, 222; and B's *Lara*, 224; and B's marriage, 225–6; B visits on way to marriage in Seaham, 235; correspondence with Annabella, 241, 265, 276; entertains B and Annabella at Six Mile Bottom, 242–4; appointed Woman of Bedchamber to Queen Charlotte, 244, 251; stays at Piccadilly Terrace, 246, 251–2, 263; as Annabella's supporter, 252–3; B turns against, 255–6; pregnancy and fifth child, 259, 277; and Annabella's pregnancy, 260;

intercepts Noel's letter to B requesting separation from Annabella, 264; tells Hobhouse of B's marriage relations, 266; and charges against B in separation order, 269; at B's departure from England, 277; and B's relations with Claire Clairmont, 297; Annabella presses to confess, 303; proposed to bring up Allegra, 306; B sends gifts to from Switzerland, 307; B writes Alpine journal for, 308, 310–11; B tells of liaison with Marianna Segati, 320; B disparages Claire Clairmont to, 345; reservations over B's *Don Juan*, 348–9; B describes Count Guiccioli to, 355; and B's relations with Teresa Guiccioli, 356, 358; and B's taking care of Allegra, 361; B sends hair to from Italy, 375; B sends account of character to, 384; prospective inheritance following death of Lady Noel, 386; and B's self-pity over Allegra's burial, 420; B invites to Pisa, 431; B invites to live at Nice, 438; Murray warns B about imperilling position at Court, 441; letter from B in Cephalonia on Ada, 479–80; and B's fit in Missolonghi, 503; B writes to on Hatadjé Aga, 506; illness, 512; Pietro Gamba tells of B's death, 518; Fletcher writes to on death of B, 531–2; Burdett informs B's death, 532; non-attendance at B's funeral procession, 535; and burning of B's memoirs, 539; copies B poem, 540; non-cooperation with Moore for B biography, 542

Leigh, Elizabeth Medora (Augusta's daughter): birth and B's supposed paternity, 214–15; at Six Mile Bottom, 243

Leigh, Frances (*née* Byron; B's aunt), 4, 6–7

Leigh, Frederick (Augusta's son), 277

Leigh, Colonel George: marriage to and children by Augusta, 7, 77, 201, 259; rift with Prince Regent, 201; at Six Mile Bottom, 204, 235; and B's incestuous relations with Augusta, 206, 225; B offers to settle debts, 213; on B's marriage relations, 266; in B's funeral procession, 535, 537

Leigh, George Henry (Augusta's son), 204, 207

Leigh, Georgiana (Augusta's daughter), 204, 215, 251, 253

Leipzig, battle of (Battle of the Nations, 1813), 217

Leman, Lac: B and Shelley row and sail on, 291, 298–300, 559

Le Mann, Dr Francis, 262, 263–5
Le Mesurier, Edward, 459
Lennox, Lady Sarah, 465
Leonidas (brig), 484
Leopardi, Giacomo, 556
Lepanto, 495–7, 530
Leveson-Gower, Lady Charlotte, 226
Leveson-Gower, Lord Granville *see* Granville, 1st Earl
Lewis, Benjamin, 459, 471, 478, 497, 506–7, 514, 530, 533, 537
Lewis, Matthew ('Monk'), 219, 256, 305, 311, 330, 372
Liberal, The (journal): founded, 426–8, 432–3; publishes B's works, 439–40, 456; B withdraws from, 456
Liddell, Maria Susannah, Lady (*later* Lady Ravensworth), 327
Linckh, Jacob, 131, 134
'Lines on Hearing that Lady Byron was Ill' (B), 303
'Lines inscribed upon a Cup formed from a Skull' (B), 79
'Lines to a Lady Weeping' (B), 31, 161, 222, 334
Lisbon, 92–3
Liszt, Franz, 550–2
Liverpool, Robert Banks Jenkinson, 2nd Earl of, 200
Llangollen, Ladies of, 60–1
Lockhart, John Gibson, 367
Lomellina, Villa, near Genoa, 460
London Greek Committee: formed and composition, 451–2; B reports to, 454, 486, 493; Blaquière represents in Greece, 466; B serves as envoy for, 467–8, 476, 481; sends representatives and helpers to Greece, 478; and B's active service in war, 483; sends supplies and arms to Greece, 485, 509; Stanhope represents and reports to, 492, 494, 498; strategy and organisation in Greece, 494, 496; and B's death, 528, 530
Londos, Andreas, 110, 467, 510
Long, Edward Noel: and B at Harrow, 38, 43–4, 49; at Cambridge with B, 57–8, 64; serves in Coldstream Guards, 64; and B's tame bear, 68; B visits at Littlehampton, 74; drowned, 81
Long, Henry, 87–8
Longman (publisher), 352, 541
Lords, House of: B attends and speaks in, 82–3, 156–7, 197–8, 454
Louis XVIII, King of France, 244, 253
Louriotis, Andreas, 451, 481–2, 509, 517

'Love and Death' (B), 489, 503–4, 566
Loveday, Mary, 144
Lovelace, Ada, Countess of *see* Byron, Augusta Ada
Lovelace, Ralph Gordon Noel Milbanke, 2nd Earl of, 242, 563, 567; *Astarte*, 563, 566–7
Lucy (Newstead maidservant), 79–80, 152–4
Luddites, 155
Lukas family, 473
Lushington, Stephen, 264–5, 267, 269–70
Lusieri, Giovanni Battista, 112–13, 128, 134
Luttrell, Henry, 539
Lytton, Edward Bulwer-, 1st Baron, 558, 560–1
Lytton, Neville, 3rd Earl of, 562
Lytton, Rosina Bulwer-, Lady (*née* Wheeler), 561

Macaulay, Thomas Babington, Baron, 211, 289
Magnarotto, Andrea, 332, 338
Mahmoud II, Sultan, 119–20, 123
Mahmout Pasha, 102
Maitland, Sir Thomas, 464
Makri, Katinka and Mariana (Tasia's daughters), 109, 115
Makri, Tasia, 109, 114–15
Makri, Teresa (Tasia's youngest daughter), 109, 114
Malmesbury, James Edward Harris, 2nd Earl of, 381
Malta, 98–100, 134–5
Maltby, Harriet, 49
Maluchielli, Antonio, 416–17
Mameluke (B's charger), 455, 459
Manfred (B): grandiloquence in, 284; inspired by Alpine journey, 311–12; Heine translates beginning, 547; European response to, 553
Manners, Lord John, 531
Mansel, William Lort, Bishop of Bristol, 232
Marceau-Desgraviers, General François-Séverin, 289
Marchand, Leslie, xi–xii
Mardyn, Charlotte, 257, 275–6
Marietta (Fletcher's mistress; 'the Countess'), 337–8
Marino Faliero, Doge of Venice (B), 317–18, 380, 395–6, 552
Marlow, Buckinghamshire *see* Great Marlow
Marmaratouris, Ioannis, 131, 499
Martens, Mrs (Danish consul's wife in Venice), 361
Martin, John (meteorologist and traveller), 445
Martin, John (painter), 305
Masi, Stefani, 416–18, 421, 424

Massingberd, Elizabeth, 60, 75

Matthews, Charles Skinner: occupies B's rooms at Cambridge, 57; friendship with B, 65–7, 87; background and character, 67; sees B and Hobhouse off on travels, 89; correspondence with B on travels, 90, 124, 126–8; and B's visit to Turkey, 115; and Vere Street affair, 140–1; drowned, 142–3, 433, 531

Maturin, Charles Robert: *Bertram*, 249

Maurice (Swiss boatman), 298, 559

Maurois, André, 554

Mavrocordatos, Prince Alexandros: exile, 436, 475, 477; B given letter of introduction to, 461; aims in Greek War of Independence, 467; Trelawny disparages, 476; writes to B for support, 477; sails with Greek fleet to Missolonghi, 483; and Byron's taking active part in Greek war, 484; welcomes B at Missolonghi, 490–1, 525; approves attack on Lepanto, 496; Coloctrones' rivalry with, 499; B's view of, 508–9; at Salona congress, 510; and B's final illness, 517; on B's death, 525; witnesses departure to England of B's remains, 529

Mazeppa (B), 293, 341

Mazzini, Giuseppe, 553; 'Byron and Goethe', 546

Mealey, Owen, 33, 36, 45

Medwin, Thomas: B speaks of married life to, 265; praises Claire Clairmont, 296; on Villa Lanfranchi, Pisa, 406; joins Shelleys in Pisa, 408; on B's acting, 409; as B's memorialist, 410; on B's *Werner*, 413; Caroline Lamb writes to on meeting B's hearse, 536; *Journal of the Conversations of Lord Byron at Pisa*, 410, 450, 541

Melbourne House, London, 165–7, 176, 178–9, 218

Melbourne, Elizabeth, Viscountess (*née* Milbanke): B confesses susceptibility to love to, 27; and B's passion for Constance Spencer Smith, 99; and B's sexual prowess while ill, 129; marriage, 164–5; B's involvement and confidences with, 166, 179–81, 186–7, 198, 208, 214, 220–1, 449, 563; and William Lamb's sexual relations with Caroline, 168; and Caroline Lamb's supposed female page, 171; and Caroline Lamb's disappearance, 177; background and character, 179; and B's courtship of and engagement to Annabella, 181, 186–7, 230, 232–3; and B's distaste for women's eating, 188; recovers stolen miniature of B

from Caroline Lamb, 194; and B's infatuation with Lady Charlotte Harley, 195; and B's relations with Lady Oxford, 197–8; B laments Napoleon's defeats to, 200; and B's relations with Augusta, 202, 204, 206–7, 211; and Caroline Lamb's supposed suicide attempt, 203; and B's advances to Lady Frances Webster, 208–11; and B's *The Bride of Abydos*, 212; and B's move to Albany, 218; urges B to marry, 225; letter from B on honeymoon, 238; finds Piccadilly Terrace house for B and Annabella, 245; accompanies Annabella to theatre, 256; and breakdown of B's marriage, 266–7; and B's departure for continent, 278; Hobhouse writes to from Switzerland, 308; and care and upbringing of Ada, 324; death, 372; B's anxiety to recover letters to, 402

Melbourne, Peniston Lamb, 1st Viscount, 164–5

Melbourne, William Lamb, 2nd Viscount: marriage to Caroline, 164, 168; as complaisant husband, 170; takes back Caroline after running away, 177; in Paris with Caroline, 254; separation from Caroline, 302; meets B's funeral cortège, 536

Melvin, George Gordon, 14

Mendelssohn, Felix, 239

Mengaldo, Cavalier Angelo, 342

Merryweather, Francis, 344

Meryon, Charles Lewis, 128

Metaxas, Count Konstantinos, 467, 477

Metaxata, Cephalonia, 476–80, 483, 485

Metternich, Klemens Wenzel Lothar, Prince, 374

Meyer, Henry (engraver), 183

Meyer, Johann Jakob, 495, 519

Mickiewicz, Adam, 548–9

Middleton Park, 190

Milan, 312–14, 316

Milan Gazette, 412

Milbanke, Lady (Annabella's mother) *see* Noel, Judith, Lady

Milbanke, Sir Ralph (Annabella's father) *see* Noel, Sir Ralph

Mildmay, Sir Henry, 229

Miller, William, 139, 159

Millingen, Dr Julius: at Metaxata, 478; on B's tensions, 479, 508; on Delladecima, 480; at Missolonghi, 483; on Greek paedophilia, 488; and B's convulsive fit, 502; and B's attachment to Hatadjé Aga, 505–6; and B's

Millingen, Dr Julius (*cont.*)
final illness and death, 513–18; performs autopsy on B's body, 519; and disposal of B's body, 528

Mills, Dr Raymond, 519

Milton, John, 292; *Paradise Lost*, 414

Mira, La (village) *see* Foscarini, Villa

Missolonghi: B first sees, 101; B visits (1809), 106; Greek forces at, 461; English supporters at, 478; Garden of the Heroes, 480; under siege by Turks, 483, 492, 512; B sails for, 485–8; B arrives at, 490–1; site and description, 491–2; B's strategy and resources in, 495–8; earthquake in, 503, 507; massacre (1821), 505; B's diplomacy and administration in, 507–11; tensions and disputes at, 508; B granted freedom of city, 511; B's death and funeral in, 518, 525, 527; fall and destruction, 545

Mitchell, Julian: *Another Country* (play), 39

Mitford, William: *History of Greece*, 397, 478

Mocenigo, Palazzo, Venice, 336–9, 344–5, 363, 369–71

Moke, Camille Marie, 551

Moldavia: Greek War of Independence begins in, 434

Molinella: Guiccioli estate at, 360

Moncrieff, Dr (of Malta), 98

Mont Blanc, 307

Montagu, Lady Mary Wortley, 121, 336

Montenero *see* Rossa, Villa

Monti, Vicenzo, 313

Montserrate, Cintra, 93–4

Moore, Anastasia, 542

Moore, Doris Langley, 267–8, 569; *Lord Byron: Accounts Rendered*, xii

Moore, General Sir John, 465

Moore, Thomas: on B's lame leg, 4; gathers material for life of B, 10; on B's inheriting title, 11; on pronunciation of B's name, 13; on B's arrival at Newstead, 14; on B's feminine characteristics, 35; on B's relations with Lord Grey, 36–7; denies B's homosexual practices, 40; on B's early sexual exploits, 49–50; B confesses difficulties of friendship to, 62; describes John Cowell, 76; bowdlerises B's letters, 92; and B's burned early reminiscences, 105; on Hobhouse's travels with B, 123; and B's *The Giaour* episode, 132; relations with B, 150–1; challenges B to duel, 151; meat-eating, 152; compares B with Napoleon, 158; on 'Byromania', 160;

friendship with Lady Caroline Lamb, 165; and B at Melbourne House, 166; and B's relations with Caroline Lamb, 169; and Leigh Hunt's imprisonment, 197; and B's speech in Lords on Cartwright Petition, 198; and B's dismay at Napoleon's defeats, 200; on B's relations with Augusta, 204; and B's wish to leave England, 206; theatre-going with B, 219; and B's emotional indifference, 221; and B's growing unpopularity, 222, 273; and B's marriage, 228; reports on B's honeymoon, 238; and B's anti-Semitic comments, 239; B complains of Seaham to, 240; B's estimate of as poet, 248; and breakdown of B's marriage, 266; B tells of emotional resilience, 270; and B's leaving England, 275; sees writings of B's exile poems as defiant, 284; Mary Shelley tells of B rowing on Lac Leman, 291; on Polidori's *Vampyre*, 293; on B's conversations with Shelley, 298; Wordsworth complains of B's imitating nature poetry, 309; and B in Italy, 314, 330; and B's view of Venice, 317, 319; and B's liaison with Marianna Segati, 320; on Margherita Cogni, 332; on Wildman, 334; Margherita Cogni offered to, 339; reaction to B's *Don Juan*, 348–9; on Teresa Guiccioli as B's lover, 354–5; on B's fatness, 368, 449; visits B at La Mira, 368–9; B reads part of third canto of *Don Juan* to, 369; and B's memoirs, 369–70, 388–9, 402, 441, 538–40; B tells of assassination of Dal Pinto, 387; praises B's *Sardanapalus*, 397; B discusses proposed new review with, 401; B sends *Werner* to, 413, 415; praises B's *Cain*, 414; scepticism over B's joint venture with Leigh Hunt, 427; on cremation of Shelley and Williams, 429; and Bishop Jocelyn scandal, 433; B reports on Lady Blessington to, 448; Barry tells of B's departure from Genoa, 460; and B's leaving for active service in Greek war, 484; in B's funeral procession, 535; preserves B's memory, 538; at burning of B's memoirs at Murray's, 539; proposes and prepares B biography, 540–2; on European representation of B, 554; on Bulwer-Lytton, 560; *Epistles, Odes and other Poems*, 58; *Lalla Rookh*, 333; *Letters and Journals of Lord Byron with Notices of His Life*, 34, 96, 123, 205, 267, 275, 368, 542–3, 554, 556; *The Poetical Works of the late Thomas Little*, 51

Morgan, Sydney Owenson, Lady, 164, 167

Morghen, Raphael, 412

Moritz, Carl, 21

Morning Chronicle, 161, 228, 283

Morning Herald, 420

Morning Post, 166, 378

Morpeth, George Howard, Viscount (*later* 6th Earl of Carlisle), 535

Morris, Janey, 563

Mortlock (Mayor of Cambridge), 65

Mosta, Elena da, 335

Mouchtar Pasha, 102

Moverley, Guardsman, 433, 436

Muir, Dr Henry, 469–70, 485

Mule, Mrs (servant), 218, 248

Murray, Joe: greets B at Newstead, 15; as B's chief servant, 77–8; singing, 77; accompanies B on travels, 91; returns to England, 96; drinks health to absent B, 153; B's dependence on, 218; death, 390

Murray, John II: B's breach with, xiv, 439–42; and B's identification with Napoleon, ix; collects B archive, xi; encourages B's celebrity, xi; on Scottish tour for Moore's *Life*, 10; B brings hemlock from Greece, 134; publishes *Childe Harold*, 139–40, 147–9, 157, 159, 183; B's relationship with, 147–9, 247–8, 439; publication list, 147–8; moves to Albemarle Street, 159; on B's meeting with Prince Regent, 161; offers advance to B for new poem, 183; Caroline deceives into giving B miniature to, 194; B sends gift of cheese to, 208; as B's confidant, 213; and success of *The Corsair*, 215; and B's *Lara*, 219; publishes B's *Lara* and Rogers's *Jacqueline* together, 224; Caroline Lamb writes to, 228; B cancels illustrations to collected edition of poetry, 236; publishes Coleridge, 249; sends money to B, 259; receives and publishes B's *Parisina*, 260, 267; publishes B's *The Siege of Corinth*, 267; publishes B's satiric poems against Annabella and Mrs Clermont, 273, 275; buys books from B's library sale, 277; shows B's poem 'To Augusta' to Caroline Lamb, 278; deal with Polidori for travel diary, 287; letters from B abroad, 300–1, 311, 317, 322–3, 326–7, 329–30, 332, 372, 406, 571; B sends Canto III of *Childe Harold* to, 306; and writing of B's *Manfred*, 311; and B's interest in Armenian, 321–2; and Thorwaldsen bust of B, 328; Hobhouse brings Canto IV of B's *Childe Harold* to, 335; payments to B,

335, 397–8; B introduces Taruscelli to, 340; and sales of *Beppo*, 347; sends packet to B in Venice via Hanson, 347; and controversy over B's *Don Juan*, 349, 352, 412, 438, 441; and B's request for Guiccioli's appointment as Consul in Ravenna, 361–2; and publication of *Don Juan*, 365, 382–3; disagreements with B, 367, 383; and B's memoirs, 369–70, 388–9, 402, 441; letter from B on George III's death, 377; B sends satirical poem on Hobhouse to, 378; and B's writing of *Marino Faliero*, 380; B tells of involvement in Carbonari, 385; B tells of assassination of Dal Pinto, 388; B asks to send Holmes to Italy to paint Allegra's portrait, 393; and B's new dramatic form and plays, 396–7; B satirises in poem, 398; and B's correspondence, 402–3; B urges to publish Taaffe's *Comment on the Divine Comedy of Dante*, 408; and Bartolini busts of B and Teresa Guiccioli, 412; publishes B's *Cain* with *Sardanapalus* and *The Two Foscari*, 413–14, 438; attacked over publication of *Cain*, 415; arranges Allegra's burial for B, 419–20, 438; Clare brings B journal notebook to, 423; B complains of censorship by, 438–9; publishes B's *Werner*, 441; B writes to on art and image, 491; B writes to from Missolonghi, 507–9; proposes Westminster Abbey burial for B, 534; Caroline Lamb writes to on B's death, 536; Moore attempts to purchase B's memoirs from, 538; burns B's memoirs, 539; agreement with Moore for life of B, 541; publishes D'Israeli, 559

Murray, John III, 248, 504, 539

Murray, Sir John IV, 566–7

Murray, Sir John V, xii, 568

Murray, John VI ('Jock'), 568–9

Murray's Magazine, 504

Musset, Alfred de, 551, 554

Musters, Jack, 34, 213

Musters, Mary *see* Chaworth, Mary

Nabokov, Vladimir, 549

Napier, Lieut.-Colonel (Sir) Charles James, 465–6, 468–9, 477, 483, 486, 495, 509

Naples: revolution (1820), 374

Napoleon I (Bonaparte), Emperor: B identifies with, vii–x, 221, 244, 279; threatens invasion of England, 61; B defends, 81, 222; military successes, 81; admired at Holland House, 155; retreat from Moscow, 188, 200;

Napoleon I (Bonaparte), Emperor (*cont.*)
defeat and abdication (1814), 217, 241;
escapes from Elba and enters Paris, 244,
253; Keats sees as theatrical, 250; Waterloo
defeat and exile to St Helena, 253, 279,
287, 378; B follows route in Italy, 312–13;
rules Venice, 317; B discusses on voyage to
Greek War of Independence, 461

'Napoleon's Farewell' (B), 253

Nathan, Isaac, 239, 278

Navarino, battle of (1827), 545

Necker, Jacques, 301

Nelson, Admiral Horatio, 1st Viscount, 88, 92

Neroto, Casa, Genoa, 438

New Monthly Magazine, 119, 450

Newstead Abbey: Byron family acquires, 13; B
inherits and moves to, 14–16, 20;
dilapidated condition, 16–17; B neglects,
18; B's poems on, 18–19; described, 19–20;
B revisits, 26, 33; let to Lord Grey de
Ruthyn, 32, 36; B returns to live at (1808),
76–81; Hanson urges sale of, 82; B's
household changes in, 152; B plans
auctioning of, 176; attempted sale of, 182,
186, 190, 193, 209, 223, 234–5, 255; Lady
Frances Webster visits, 209; Augusta visits,
213; suffers slight earthquake, 270; finally
sold (to Wildman), 334–5, 336, 346, 537;
Finlay reminisces with B about, 511–12;
Wilfrid Scawen Blunt visits, 562

Niccolò III d'Este, Duke of Ferrara, 260

Nicolson, Sir Harold, 35, 268, 545, 565–7, 569;
Byron: the Last Journey, 565, 567

Nicolson, Nigel: *Portrait of a Marriage*, 566

Noel, Alice, 562

Noel, Edward, 52

Noel, Judith, Lady (*earlier* Milbanke;
Annabella's mother): and Annabella's
engagement, 226; home and life at Seaham,
228–9, 240; B's antipathy to, 231, 411; and
B's wedding, 235–7; inherits from brother
and changes name, 246; B declines to visit
in London, 252; urges separation on
Annabella, 264–5, 267; hopes for private
separation settlement for Annabella, 269;
property inheritance at death, 278, 386,
411, 457

Noel, Sir Ralph (*earlier* Milbanke; Annabella's
father): and B's attachment to Annabella,
181; financial difficulties, 186; home and
life at Seaham, 228, 240; and Annabella's
marriage, 230, 237; B's relations with, 231;
changes name, 246; B declines to visit in
London, 252; and Annabella's marriage

portion, 260; writes to B requesting
separation from Annabella, 264, 266;
hopes for private separation settlement for
Annabella, 269; B contests bill in
Chancery, 331; response to revelations of
Annabella's treatment by B, 381

Noel, Revd Thomas, 236

Norfolk *see* Wymondham

North, Frederic (*later* 5th Earl of Guilford),
131

Nottingham: Byron taken to, 18, 21–2, 26;
weavers' riots in, 27–8, 155–6; B's lying-in-
state in, 536; *see also* Hucknall Torkard;
Newstead Abbey

Odevaere, Joseph-Denis von: *The Death of
Byron* (painting), 544; *The Last Defenders
of Missolonghi* (painting), 545

Oliver, Captain (of *Spider*), 100

'On the Bust of Helen by Canova' (B), 319

'On a Change of Masters, at a Great Public
School' (B), 42

'On a Cornelian Heart Which Was Broken'
(B), 145–6

'On Leaving England', 33

'On Leaving Newstead Abbey' (B), 18

'On this day I Complete my thirty sixth year'
(B), 499, 543

Ontario (frigate), 422

Oporto, battle of (1809), 93

Origo, Iris: *The Last Attachment*, 569

Orlandos, Ioannis, 481–2, 509, 535

Orsay, Count Albert d', 449

Orsay, Count Alfred d', 449–51, 455

Orsay, Countess Harriet d' (*née* Lady Harriet
Gardiner), 450

Osborne, Lord Sydney, 477, 487, 528, 531

Ostend, 283–5

Otho I, King of Greece, 510

Oxford, Edward Harley, 5th Earl of, 189–90,
198

Oxford, Elizabeth Jane, Countess of (*née*
Scott): B's affair with, 186, 188–92, 194–8,
364, 445; background and character,
188–9; relations with Caroline Lamb, 191;
champions Princess Caroline, 192; B sends
lock of hair to Caroline Lamb, 194;
children, 195, 204; leaves for continent,
198, 200; correspondence with B, 402

Oxford, Robert Harley, 1st Earl of, 190

Paganini, Nicolo, 550–1

Page, Henry, 44

Palgrave, Francis, 366

Palladio, Andrea, 315

Palmerston, Henry John Temple, 3rd
    Viscount: at Harrow, 30

Papi, Vincenzo, 416–17, 424–5, 459

Paris: British visitors to, 254

Parisina (B), 260, 267, 271

Parker, Charlotte Augusta, 27

Parker, Margaret, 27, 34

Parkyns, Ann, 18, 21–2

Parry, William: sails for Greece as fire-master,
    476; on Chalandritsanos, 488; arrives in
    Missolonghi with supplies, 497–8; cider-
    drinking with B, 502; and B's practical
    jokes on servants, 506–7; on B's
    demoralised state after fit, 508; with B
    during final illness and death, 514, 517–20;
    and B's wish for body to be returned to
    England, 528; publishes reminiscences,
    541

Parthenon marbles ('Elgin marbles'), 113

Pasta, Giuditta, 30

Patras, Greece, 100–1, 127, 129; siege of (1824),
    510

Peacock, Thomas Love, 345, 399; *Nightmare
    Abbey*, 20

Peak Cavern, Derbyshire, 33

Pearson, Dr, 75

Peel, Sir Robert: at Harrow, 30; sees B's
    'ghost' in London, 129

Pellico, Silvio: *Francesca da Rimini*, 313

Pelzet, Maddalena, 359

Peninsular War, 81, 92–3, 96, 200

Perceval, Lady, 75

Perceval, Spencer: assassinated, 172

Perry, James, 228

Perseverance (steamboat) *see Kateria*

Peta, battle of (1822), 491

Peterloo massacre (Manchester, 1819), 365

Petrarch, 362

Petronius: *Satyricon*, 90

Phillips, Thomas: portraits of Byron, 216–17,
    323, 411, 440, 564; portrait of Caroline
    Lamb, 217; asks to sketch dead B, 534

Piccadilly Terrace: B and Annabella occupy
    (No.13), 245–6, 248, 259; Augusta stays at,
    251–3; bailiffs in, 259–60, 279

Pigot, Elizabeth: on B's lame leg, 4; friendship
    with B, 46–7; transcribes poems for B, 51;
    watercolour illustrations, 53; B confides in
    by letter from Cambridge, 59–60, 62, 64; B
    requests return of ring from, 145;
    correspondence with B, 403; *The
    Wonderful History of Lord Byron and His
    Dog*, 54

Pigot, John, 47–9, 51, 53, 69–70, 142

Pigot, Margaret, 85, 145

Pinto, Luigi Dal *see* Dal Pinto, Luigi

Piper, David, 216

Pisa: B stays in, 401–2, 406–13, 425–6; 'Affray'
    (Masi affair), 415–18, 421, 424; Luminara
    (festival), 422; Leigh Hunt in, 426;
    Hobhouse visits B in, 433

Pitt, William, the younger: statue, 60

Pius VII, Pope, 381

Poems on Various Occasions (B), 40, 50, 62

Polidori, Gaetano, 285

Polidori, Dr John William: at Villa Diodati,
    116, 292–3, 298, 307; accompanies B on
    1816 travel to continent, 278, 285–9;
    literary ambitions, 285; in Geneva, 290–1;
    relations with B, 294; arrested in Geneva,
    295; social life in Switzerland, 300;
    witnesses codicil to 'Monk' Lewis's will,
    305; B parts from, 308; joins B in Milan,
    314; death, 314; *The Vampyre*, 293–4

Polykhroni, Kalypso, 549

Ponsonby, Frederick, 246

Ponsonby, Sarah, 60, 170

Pope, Alexander, 41, 85

Pope-Hennessy, James, 569

Porson, Richard, 68

Portsmouth, Countess of *see* Hanson, Mary
    Ann

Portsmouth, John Charles Wallop, 3rd Earl of,
    24, 234, 446–7

Portugal: B travels to (1809), 91–5

Praz, Mario: *The Romantic Agony*, 554

Price, Dennis, 543

Price, W.L.: *Byron in Palazzo Mocenigo*
    (watercolour), 336

Princess Elizabeth (ship), 91

Prisoner of Chillon, The (B): Bonivard in, 293,
    300; writing, 300, 383; B sends to Murray,
    306; European response to, 553; Mazzini
    quotes, 553

Prophecy of Dante, The (B), 358, 383

'Pulcella, La', 188

Pulci, Luigi, 333; *Morgante Maggiore*, 363,
    380, 383, 456

Purvis, Admiral, 96

Pushkin, Alexander, 549–50

Pylades, HMS, 115

Quarterly Review, 349, 365, 415

Quennell, Isabella, 568

Quennell, (Sir) Peter, 567–9; *Byron: the Years
    of Fame*, 567; *The Marble Foot*, 568; (ed.)
    To Lord Byron (correspondence), 568

Querini Benzoni, Countess Marina *see* Benzoni, Countess Marina Querini

Racine, Jean, 396
Radcliffe, Ann: *The Mysteries of Udolpho*, 318; *The Romance of the Forest*, 20
Raffalovich, André, 564
Rangone, Count Giuseppe, 362-3
Rasi, Dr, 418
Ravenna: B in, 357-61, 374-9, 388, 399-400; political unrest in, 384-6, 394-5; B leaves for Pisa, 403
Raymond, George, 250
Reeve, Clara: *The Old English Baron*, 26
Regny, Artemisia Castellini, 408, 409
Remonstrance to Mr. John Murray, Respecting a Recent Publication, A (by 'Oxoniensis'), 415
Retrieval of the Corpse of Shelley from the Sea at Viareggio (print), 430
Revelation, Book of, 304
Reynolds, Frederick: *Life*, 47
Reynolds, Sir Joshua, 179
Ridge, Samuel and John, 51, 62
Rigas, Velestinlis, 110
Roberts, Cecil, 572, 574
Roberts, Captain Daniel, 410, 428
Robinson, Henry Crabb, 158, 394
Rochdale, Lancashire: B inherits estate at, 17; B hopes to sell estates, 82, 143-4, 255, 335, 364, 444; estates sold to Dearden, 481
Rogers, Jeremiah ('Dummer'), 22
Rogers, Samuel: on B's childhood love, 10; sees B's putative illegitimate child, 50; B defends, 85; entertains B, 150-1; on B's appeal to women, 161; and B's relations with Caroline Lamb, 163-4, 169; friendship with Caroline Lamb, 165; B dedicates *The Giaour* to, 199; and B's honeymoon, 238; sees B with Susan Boyce, 257; and B's departure from England, 277; and B's proposal to settle in Venice, 335; reunion with B in Italy, 405; visits B in Pisa, 408, 418; in B's funeral procession, 535; non-cooperation with Moore in writing biography of B, 542; *Italy*, 405; *Jacqueline*, 224; *The Pleasures of Memory*, 150
Romagna *see* Ravenna
Rome: B visits, 325, 327-8; in *Childe Harold*, 329
Romilly, Anne, Lady, 302, 347
Romilly, Sir Samuel, 265, 347
Rood, Ann *see* Fletcher, Ann

Rosebery, Harriet, Countess of, 229
Rossa, Villa (Villa Dupuy), Montenero, 421-4
Rossetti, Christina, 285
Rossetti, Dante Gabriel, 285
Rossini, Gioachino, 550
Rousseau, Jean-Jacques, 79, 190, 308, 541; *Julie, ou la Nouvelle Héloïse*, 298-9
Rubens, Peter Paul, 286
Rundell, Maria Eliza: *Domestic Cookery*, 148
Rusconi, Cardinal Antonio, 381, 387
Rushton, Robert: as B's page, 78-9, 88, 270; accompanies B on travels, 91, 278, 284; return to England and death, 96-7, 307; letter from B in Turkey, 116; informs B of mother's death, 141-2; infidelity with Newstead servants, 154; at Aston Hall, 208; rejoins B's service, 278
Ruskin, John, 156, 557-8
Ruskin, John James, 557
Russell, Lord John, 540
Rutland, Elizabeth, Duchess of, 214
Rutland, John Henry Manners, 5th Duke of, 531
Ryleev, Kondratii Theodorovich, 550

Sabin, Frank T., 540
Sackville-West, Vita (Lady Nicolson), 566
Sade, Donatien Alphonse, marquis de: *Justine*, 262
St Clair, William, 159
St Louis, M., 26
Salona, near Delphi, 509-10
Salsette, HMS, 117-20, 122-3
Saluzzo, Casa, Genoa, 434, 437, 458, 460
Salvo, Marquis de, 99
San Lazzaro monastery, Venice, 321-2
Sand, George, 551
Sanders, George: portrait of B and Rushton, 78, 88, 183
Sarakis, Spyridon (Spiro), 134
Sardanapalus (B), 395-7, 414, 552
Sardinia, 97-8
Sarony, Napoleon, 565
Sass, Lieutenant (Swedish officer), 508
Satirist, The (magazine), 69
Schilizzi, Prince, 459, 462
Schiller, Friedrich von, 205
Schlegel, August Wilhelm von, 301
Scotland: B's attachment to, 10-11
Scott, Alexander: with B in Venice, 339, 342, 353-4; and B's affair with Teresa Guiccioli, 359; and B's taking care of Allegra, 361; entertains Moore in Venice, 369

Scott, Captain John (of *Hercules*), 462, 474–5

Scott, Mrs (actress), 258

Scott, Sir Walter: B admits to liking a row, 11; coat of arms, 13; on B's superficial knowledge, 41; B writes of seducing servants to, 80; on William Gifford, 149; B's estimate of, 151; on B's *Childe Harold*, 157–8; Prince Regent esteems, 161; reconciliation with B, 161; B meets, 248; B dines with, 258; on B's falling into unpopularity, 273; writes stanzas at Waterloo, 287; B criticises as poet, 333; B reads extensively, 389; B dedicates *Cain* to, 414; B discusses novels in Ionian Islands, 473; *Ivanhoe*, 384; *The Lady of the Lake*, 160; *Quentin Durward*, 485; *Waverley*, 248, 423

Seaham, Co. Durham: Annabella's home in, 228; B visits, 228–32; B married in, 235–7; B and Annabella return to, 240–1

Sécheron, near Geneva, 290–2, 294

Segati, Marianna, 319–21, 325, 329–30, 332–3, 336, 338–40

Segati, Pietro, 319–20, 330, 333

Selim III, Sultan, 121

Seville, 95

Sgricci, Tommaso, 314; *Missolonghi* (play), 545

Shakespeare, William: *Othello*, 409

'She walks in beauty, like the night' (B), 220

Sheldrake (surgical appliance maker), 26, 30–1

Shelley, Clara (Percy/Mary's daughter): baptised, 344; death, 346

Shelley, Elena Adelaide (Percy's alleged child with Claire Clairmont), 391

Shelley, Frances, Lady, 204, 246, 329

Shelley, Harriet (*née* Westbrook; Percy's first wife), 296, 324

Shelley, Sir John, 204

Shelley, Mary (*née* Godwin): on B's lame leg, 4; and composition of *Frankenstein*, 116, 293; elopes with Percy, 271; at Sécheron (Geneva), 291; B's relations with, 295; leaves Switzerland, 306; on Venice, 317; marriage to Percy, 324; and care and upbringing of Allegra, 343; moves to Italy, 344; letter from Mrs Hoppner on Allegra, 360; death of son William, 391; and Allegra's despatch to convent, 392; Percy praises B's *Don Juan* to, 399; and Hoppner scandal of Claire's alleged child by Percy, 401; in Pisa, 401, 407; friendship with Teresa Guiccioli in Pisa, 408; on Trelawny, 410; copies out B's *Werner*, 413;

and 'Pisa Affray', 416–17; and B's reaction to Allegra's death, 419; persuades Teresa Guiccioli to lift ban on *Don Juan*, 421; and Percy's drowning, 428; keeps Percy's heart, 430–1; and B's dislike of Hunt family, 431; takes lessons in Greek, 436; relations with B, 438; shares house with Hunts in Genoa, 438; and B's departure for Greece, 457; disagreement with B over promised money, 457; with Teresa Guiccioli on B's departure for Greece, 458; letter from Trelawny on B's indecision, 475; watches B's hearse pass, 536; on B's memoirs, 540; cooperates with Moore on B biography, 542

Shelley, Percy Bysshe: on incest, 205; elopes with Mary, 271; at Sécheron (Geneva), 291–2, 294; B spreads scandal about, 297; relations with Claire Clairmont, 297–8; sailing on Lac Leman with B, 298–300; witnesses codicil to 'Monk' Lewis's will, 305; leaves Villa Diodati, 306; Hobhouse on, 308; relations with B, 308, 429; marriage to Mary, 324; reports to B on birth and care of Allegra, 324–5; quotes *Beppo* to B, 334; on B's promiscuity in Venice, 341; and Allegra in Great Marlow, 343; health deterioration, 343; moves to Italy, 344; visits B in Venice, 345; praises B's *Don Juan*, 348, 399; dislikes Ravenna, 376; Claire Clairmont stays with in Pisa, 390–1; alleged child with Claire Clairmont, 391–2, 401; death of son William, 391; and Allegra's despatch to convent, 392; remarks on B's improvement in health and outlook, 399; visits Allegra in Bagnacavallo convent, 400; Teresa Guiccioli describes, 401–2; on Pisa, 406; life in Pisa, 407–9; builds boat, 410; in 'Pisa Affray', 416; accompanies Leigh Hunt to Pisa, 426; and publication of *The Liberal* magazine, 427–8; drowned, 428; cremated, 429–30; B named as executor, 438; ashes reburied in Rome, 456; B discontinues as executor and refuses legacy from, 457; *Hellas*, 436; 'Hymn to Intellectual Beauty', 300; *Julian and Maddalo: A Conversation*, 345; 'Lines written among the Euganean Hills', 346; *Prometheus Unbound*, 346; *Queen Mab*, 272; *The Revolt of Islam*, 205

Shelley, (Sir) Percy Florence (son of Percy and Mary), 438

Shelley, Sir Timothy (Percy's father), 291, 411, 438

Shelley, William (Percy-Mary's son), 291, 344; death, 391
Shepherd, Sir Samuel, 278
Sheridan, Richard Brinsley, 83, 165, 277, 372
Siddons, Sarah, 256
Siege of Corinth, The (B), 119, 267, 271, 550
Silvestrini, Fanny, 355-7, 364, 371
Simplon Pass, 312
Sisinis, Georgios, 510
Sitwell, Sarah Caroline, Lady, 220
Six Mile Bottom, near Cambridge: Augusta's home in, 201, 203-6, 213, 222, 229, 232, 235, 251, 255; Annabella with B and Augusta at, 242-4
'Sketch from Private Life, A' (B), 274-5
Skittles (courtesan) *see* Walters, Catherine
Sligo, Howe Peter Browne, 2nd Marquis of (*earlier* Lord Altamont): expedition to Peloponnese with B, 125-6; Moore questions about B's relations with Giraud, 129; and B's rescue of condemned Muslim woman, 132
Smiles, Samuel, 148
Smith, Constance Spencer (*née* Herbert), 99-100, 134-5, 162
Smith, John Spencer, 99
Smith, Miss (dancer), 250, 258
Smith, William, 452
Smyrna (Izmir), 115-17
'So, we'll go no more a roving' (B), 323
Society of United Irishmen, 28
'Some Observations upon an Article in Blackwood's Magazine' (B), 367
Somerset, Horatia, 162
Sotheby, William, 248
Southcott, Joanna, 291
Southey, Robert: B's feud with, 85, 327, 377, 402, 426; B meets, 150; B's low estimate of as poet, 248; on B in Switzerland, 296, 367; B criticises as poet, 333; B dedicates *Don Juan* to, 349; *The Vision of Judgement*, 402
Southwell, Nottinghamshire, 45-55
Spain: in Napoleonic Wars, 92; B travels in, 95-6
Spencer Smith *see* Smith
Spider, HMS, 100
Springhetti, Angelo, 312
Spurzheim, Johann Christoph, 223
Stackelberg, Otto Magnus, Freiherr von, 131
Staël-Holstein, Germaine, Baronne de, 202, 301-2, 305, 308, 360; *Corinne*, 301, 329, 360
Stanhope, Charles, 3rd Earl, 198
Stanhope, Lady Hester, 128-31

Stanhope, Colonel Leicester (*later* 5th Earl of Harrington): arrives in Cephalonia, 478; writes to B from Missolonghi, 483-5; B requests escort from, 489; and B's arrival in Missolonghi, 491; as official representative of London Greek Committee, 492, 494; differences with B, 494-5; publishes *Hellenica Chronica*, 495; helps finance 'Byron Brigade', 497; and Parry's view of Missolonghi, 498; on hidden significance of B's 36th birthday poems, 501, 505; and B's fit, 502-3; on B's demoralised state, 508; and loan to Ulysses, 509; and return of B's body to England, 528-9, 533; in B's funeral procession, 535; on burning of B's memoirs, 540; publishes reminiscences, 541
Stanhope, Lincoln, 74
'Stanzas' (B), 64
Stendhal (Marie-Henri Beyle), 313
Stevens (cook), 337
Stewart, Princess Annabella, 7
Stietz, Colonel, 455
Stith, Catherine P., 422
Stoker, Bram: *Dracula*, 294
Stoven, Sir Frederick, 529
Stowe, Harriet Beecher: 'The True Story of Lady Byron's Life' (*Lady Byron Vindicated*), 564
Strachey, Lytton, 570
Strané, Samuel, 126-7, 129
Strauss, Giuseppe, 416, 425
Styles, Revd John, 414
Suliotes (Albanian warriors), 468, 474-7, 483, 486, 492, 496-9, 503, 506-8
Sunday Monitor, 535
Sutton, Charles Manners, Archbishop of Canterbury, 235
Switzerland, 290-9, 305, 307-11

Taaffe, John, 407-8, 416-18
Tahiri, Dervise, 105, 134
Tartar, HMS, 86
Taruscelli, Arpalice, 339-40
Tasmania: B considers emigrating to, 434
Tasso, Torquato, 189, 326
Tattersall, John, 39-40
Tavistock, John Russell, Marquis of, 65
Telegrafo Greco (newspaper), 495, 525, 527, 529
Tennyson, Alfred, 1st Baron, 555
Theotokos Agrilion monastery, 473
Thomas, Dr (of Zante), 514, 516

Thorwaldsen, Bertel, 327–8, 412, 423, 527, 570

'Thoughts suggested by a College Examination' (B), 68

Thyrza (B's early lover), 50, 490, 504; B's elegy cycle on, 145–6, 162, 543

Ticknor, George, 250, 256, 330–1

Tilsit, Treaty of (1807), 117, 120

Times, The, 458, 531, 532, 534, 537

'Tita' *see* Falcieri, Giovanni Battista

'To an Oak in the Garden of Newstead Abbey' (B), 17

'To Augusta' (B), 277

'To Ianthe' (B), 195

'To My Son' (B), 49

'To the Po' (B), 357

Tooke, John Horne, 189

Torelli, Cavaliere Luigi, 406, 417

Townsend (Wildman's representative), 346

Townshend (ship), 97–8

Treiber, Dr Enrico, 516

Trelawny, Edward John: claims both B's feet deformed, 4; in Pisa, 409–10; relations with B, 409–10; qualities, 410; in 'Pisa Affray', 416–17; and cremation of Shelley and Williams, 429–30; on B's involvement in Greek independence, 436, 452; accompanies B to Greece, 456, 458, 460–2, 464–5; B orders helmet for, 456; removes books from B's library, 458; B boxes with, 461; on Cephalonia with B, 469–70; visits Ithaca with B, 472; in Greek War of Independence, 475–6; marriage to Androutses' half-sister, 476; describes Missolonghi, 492; forwards B's 36th birthday poem to Hobhouse, 501; and Ulysses (Androutses), 509; sees B after death, 521, 528; Mary Shelley writes to on B's death, 536; letter from Mary Shelley on B's memoirs, 540

Trevanion, Henry, 535

Tricoupis, Spyridon, 527

Trinity College *see* Cambridge University

Tropinin, V.A., 549

Troy, 117–18.

Tucker, Dr, 134

Turkey: B visits (1810), 115–24, 132; Greeks claim independence from, 434, 436, 452; and massacre at Chios, 451; in Greek War of Independence, 461, 466, 481, 492, 495–6, 507; naval defeat at Navarino (1827), 545

Turner, John Mallord William, 558

Two Foscari, The (B), 318, 395, 397, 414, 552

Ulysses *see* Androutsos, Odysseus

United States of America: B plans visit to, 330–1, 426; B's admiration for, 422–3

Ussières, Henrietta d', 220

Vaccà, Dr Andre, 417, 421, 431

Valentia, Arthur Annesley, Viscount, 146

Vassily or Vasili (Albanian bodyguard), 105, 128

Vaughan, Susan, 152–5, 257

Vavassour, Mrs: offers to adopt Allegra, 360

Vayas, Dr Loukas, 516

Veli Pasha, 101–2, 127

Venezuela, 364, 371

Venice: B visits with Hobhouse (1816–17), 314, 316–24; Carnival, 323, 325, 335; in B's *Beppo*, 333; B returns to from Villa Foscarini (November 1817), 334, 336; B proposes to settle in, 335; mentioned in *Blackwood's Magazine* attack on B, 367–8; Moore visits B in, 368–9; Bankes visits, 372–3; Ruskin in, 557–8; *see also* Mocenigo, Palazzo

'Venice. An Ode' (B), 318

Verdi, Giuseppe: *I Due Foscari*, 553

Vere Street affair, 140

Verona, Congress of (1822), 444

Vestris, Madame (Lucia Elizabeth Mathews), 170

Vicari, Geltrude, 358, 380

Vicenza, 315

Victor, Marshal Claude-Victor Perrin (*called* Victor), 93

Vienna, Congress of (1815), 437

Vigny, Alfred de, 546

Villiers, Theresa, 303

Vision of Judgement, The (B), 402, 426, 440–1, 456

Vitalis, Captain Giorgios, 461–2

Vitoria, battle of (1813), 200

Vittorio Emanuele I, King of Sardinia, 98

Vivian, Charles, 428

Volage, HMS, 135, 139

Voltaire, François Marie Arouet de, 298, 305; *Histoire de Charles XII*, 341

Vryzakis, Theodoros: *Byron's Arrival at Missolonghi* (painting), ix, 490

Vyazemsky, Prince Pyotr, 550

Waite (dentist), 390, 571

Waldegrave, James, 2nd Earl: *Memoirs*, 397

Walker, J. Holland, 572

Wallace, Captain, 72

Walpole, Horace, 15, 179; *Memoirs of the reign of George the Second*, 397

Walters, Catherine ('Skittles'), 563
'Waltz, The: An Apostrophic Hymn' (B), 166
Wankowic, Walenty, 549
Ward, John William *see* Dudley and Ward, 1st Earl of
Washington, George, 331, 483
Waterloo, battle of (1815), 246, 253–4; B visits site, 286–7
Watier, Jean-Baptiste, 150
Watier's Club, London, 150, 305, 385
Webster, Lady Frances Wedderburn, 207–13, 238, 254, 265, 272, 402, 442, 563
Webster, Sir Godfrey, 155, 165
Webster, Sir Godfrey Vassall, 165
Webster, Sir James Wedderburn ('Bold'), 74, 87, 146, 199, 207–11, 220, 255, 378, 442–3
Wellesley, Richard Colley Wellesley, Marquis of, 96
Wellington, Arthur Wellesley, 1st Duke of: B's view of, 88, 254; Peninsular campaign, 92–3, 200; enters France, 217; masquerade in honour of, 217, 250; success with women, 254; Waterloo victory, 254
Wentworth, Judith Blunt, 16th Baroness, 562
Wentworth, Thomas, 2nd Viscount: Annabella hopes to inherit from, 186, 230; illegitimate son, 236; death, 246
Werner, or The Inheritance (B), 252, 413, 441, 555
Werry, Francis, 115–16
Werry, Mrs Francis, 117
West, William Edward: portrait of B, 423–4
Westall, Richard, 195
Westbrook, John, 296
Westmacott, Richard, 275
Westminster Abbey, 534
Westmoreland, Jane, Countess of, 164–5
Wheeler, Rosina *see* Lytton, Rosina Bulwer-, Lady
'When We Two Parted' (B), 254
Whigs: B's attachment to, 82–3
'Whistlecraft, William and Robert' *see* Frere, John Hookham
Whitbread, Samuel, 198
White, Thomas, 140
Wilberforce, William, 68, 285
Wilde, Oscar, 276, 564–5; *De Profundis*, 367, 565

Wildman, Colonel Thomas, 43, 75, 334–5, 346, 537, 562
Wilkes, John, 279
Williams, Edward: B meets in Pisa, 407–9; builds boat, 410; and Bartolini bust of B, 411; on 'Pisa Affray', 416; Claire Clairmont travels with, 419; drowning and cremation, 428–30
Williams, Jane: in Pisa, 407, 419; and Claire Clairmont, 419; and Edward's drowning, 428; watches Byron's hearse pass, 536
Wilmot, Anne, 220
Wilmot, Robert John, 220, 269
Wilson, Harriette, 217, 365
Wilson, John, 367
Winckelmann, Johann Joachim, 107
Wingfield, John, 38, 40, 141
Wollstonecraft, Mary, 271, 324
Woodeson (undertaker), 533
Woolf, Virginia, 570
Wordsworth, William: B attacks in *English Bards*, 85; B meets, 150; view of B, 158; B criticises as poet, 248, 333; B's supposed imitation of, 309
Wymondham, Norfolk: B inherits estate at, 17; B hopes to sell properties, 83, 143

York and Albany, Frederick Augustus, Duke of, 218

Zambelli, Lega: relations and children with Fanny Silvestri, 356; investigates Edgecumbe's accounts, 361; background, 363; as B's household supervisor, 363; record of Carbonari activities, 385; loyalty to Carbonari, 394; and B's move to Pisa, 402–3; and 'Pisa Affray', 416; and Allegra's health at Bagnacavallo, 418; visits USS *Constitution* with B, 422; B takes over household accounts from, 444; accompanies B to Greece, 459, 478, 494; and B's final illness, 514; travels to England with B's body, 530, 533; life in England, 560
Zantakis, Andreas, 105, 115
Zante, 464–5, 514, 516, 529
Zitza, Albania, 102–3
Zograffo, Demetrius (Zografos, Demetrios), 111, 114, 134, 474